W9-CEN-241

FROM 33rd STREET
TO CAMDEN YARDS

AN ORAL HISTORY OF THE BALTIMORE ORIOLES

JOHN EISENBERG

CONTEMPORARY BOOKS

Library of Congress Cataloging-in-Publication Data

Eisenberg, John, 1956–
    From 33rd Street to Camden Yards: an oral history of the Baltimore Orioles /
John Eisenberg.
        p.   cm.
    Includes index.
    ISBN 0-8092-2486-0
    1. Baltimore Orioles (Baseball team)—History.   2. Baltimore Orioles
(Baseball team)—Anecdotes.   I. Title: From Thirty-third Street to Camden
Yards.   II. Title.
    GV875.B2 E58   2001
    796.357'64'097526—dc21   00-45150

Contemporary Books
*A Division of The **McGraw-Hill** Companies*

1 2 3 4 5 6 7 8 9 0   AGM/AGM   0 9 8 7 6 5 4 3 2 1

ISBN 0-8092-2486-0

This book was set in Adobe Garamond
Printed and bound by Quebecor-Martinsburg

McGraw-Hill books are available at special quantity discounts to use as premiums and
sales promotions, or for use in corporate training programs. For more information, please
write to the Director of Special Sales, Professional Publishing, McGraw-Hill, Two Penn
Plaza, New York, NY 10121-2298. Or contact your local bookstore.

This book is printed on acid-free paper.

ACKNOWLEDGMENTS

Thanks to my agent, Scott Waxman, for suggesting the oral history format and helping to get the project off the ground. Thanks, also, to Matthew Carnicelli, my editor at Contemporary, for believing in the idea. Numerous others helped along the way. Bill Stetka and Kevin Behan in the Orioles' public relations department were always cooperative and interested. Olwen Price was a Hall of Fame transcriber. My mother, Jean Eisenberg, was a valued listening post. Paul McMullen and Phyllis Merhige suggested worthy interview subjects. John Steadman and Ron Shapiro helped corral unwilling interview subjects. Andy Knobel gave the manuscript a terrific "baseball" read and saved me in many ways.

Most important, the many, many people whose recollections fill this book were, almost without exception, kind and flexible and forthcoming. I hope they all feel they were treated fairly.

Writing a book while also writing four columns a week for a major newspaper can be tricky, and my editors at the *Baltimore Sun*, Molly Dunham and Sam Davis, were gracious and supportive, as always. My friend and fellow columnist, Ken Rosenthal, now of *The Sporting News*, picked up the slack with unending good cheer. Thanks, Junior.

The biggest thanks go to my family—my wife, Mary Wynne, and my children, Anna and Wick. Our life is busy, and there really isn't enough time for a book on top of everything else, but they were loving and understanding and made the best of a difficult situation. You know I can't thank you enough for everything you do, Mary Wynne, but you make it all possible. Oh, and kids, it's your turn on the computer.

CONTENTS

INTRODUCTION

The *Baltimore Sun* hired me to write sports in 1984, a year that represents an unfortunate dividing line in recent Baltimore sports history. The Colts had just left town for Indianapolis, and the Orioles were just entering a decline after years as one of baseball's best teams, winning eight division titles, six American League pennants, and three World Series between '66 and '83.

Sixteen years later, pro football is back in town with the Baltimore Ravens, but the Orioles are still trying to make it back to the World Series for the first time since '83. I have become well versed in the city's ongoing love affair with baseball, best evidenced by the crowds that continue to fill the Orioles' retro-jewel of a ballpark at Camden Yards in downtown Baltimore. But outside of a couple of years in the late '90s, I haven't experienced much Orioles glory.

In essence, this book is the outgrowth of my poorly timed arrival in Baltimore. I grew up in Texas, went to college in Pennsylvania, and covered high school football and pro basketball before coming to the *Sun*. I knew the story of the Orioles' boom years, as would any sports fan turned sportswriter. But I wasn't there. I didn't live it. I hadn't experienced the Orioles in a throbbing pennant race or playoff series, with the city's stomach rising and falling on every pitch.

What was it like? That's the single, simple question that sparked my interest in going back to the beginning and tracing the Orioles' history. Sure, I had read the baseball books, learned the statistics, even interviewed some of the principals while on various assignments for the *Sun*. But I wanted more. I wanted to know how it felt, how it smelled, how it sounded. I wanted to know how the pieces fit together—how the Orioles got from Point A, a downtrodden franchise that moved to town in '54, to Point B, one of baseball's signature franchises.

The answer lay in the memories of those who had lived it, those who helped transform the Orioles organization into the secular religion it is today. I wanted to hear their voices.

All I had to do was ask.

I interviewed almost ninety past and present Orioles players, managers, coaches, general managers, front-office executives, owners, and broadcasters, some in person and some over the phone, never forgetting that I was living out any Orioles fan's fantasy, a first-person road trip through history. I interviewed Earl Weaver in Florida, Harry Dalton and Frank Robinson in Arizona, Jim Gentile in Oklahoma, Steve Barber in Las Vegas. Almost every major figure in Orioles history was generous with his time and memory, for which I'm grateful.

As I waded into the project, I quickly realized that, in a sense, I had taken on a task too great. The Orioles' history encompasses almost fifty seasons, hundreds of players, and too many stories and perspectives to measure. The story is so rich and complex that a complete oral history would fill ten volumes. I had one to fill.

I wouldn't dare suggest that I have filtered and manipulated the history into a narrative that touches all the bases. I have included most of what I felt were the most important events, developments, and voices. To my great regret, Jerry Hoffberger and Mark Belanger passed away before I could get to them, and I simply didn't get to several others I wanted to include. The reader should understand going in that, as it says on the book's cover, this is *an* oral history of the Orioles, not *the* oral history. It's still an epic—a long and amazing journey—and I think it's pretty complete. But for whatever isn't included that you'd hoped to see, I apologize.

VOICES

These are the players, coaches, managers, general managers, broadcasters, club officials, and owners who were interviewed between May of 1999 and July of 2000:

ALTOBELLI, JOE Former major league infielder; managed in the Orioles' minor league system in the '60s and '70s; managed the Orioles to '83 World Series title.

ANDERSON, BRADY Versatile natural athlete; starred for the Orioles throughout the '90s as outfielder and leadoff hitter; hit 50 homers in '96 to set a club record.

ANGELOS, PETER Baltimore-reared attorney; became wealthy representing union workers and purchased the Orioles at a bankruptcy auction in '93.

BALLARD, JEFF Left-handed pitcher; had career year in '89, winning 18 games; injured arm and was released in '91.

BARBER, STEVE Maryland native (Takoma Park); the Orioles' first 20-game winner in '63 and won 95 games from '60 to '67; traded to Yankees.

*BAUER, HANK Yankees outfielder in '50s; managed the Orioles to World Series title in '66.

BEAMON, CHARLIE Entire major league career consisted of 27 appearances with the Orioles in late '50s.

BLAIR, PAUL Intuitive centerfielder for the Orioles from '64 to '76; won eight Gold Gloves, hit 134 career homers, and played in 53 postseason games.

BLYZKA, MIKE Pitched in relief in '54; went to Yankees as part of seventeen-player deal that winter.

BODDICKER, MIKE Clever right-hander; won 79 games for the Orioles from '82 to '88; traded to Boston for Brady Anderson and Curt Schilling.

BOYD, BOB "THE ROPE" Career .293 hitter; started at first base for the Orioles in late '50s.

BRANDT, JACKIE "FLAKEY" Colorful character and fixture in center field in early '60s.

BRECHEEN, HARRY "CAT" The Orioles' pitching coach from '54 to '67.

BREEDING, MARV Second baseman in early '60s; hit .250 over four seasons in majors.

BROWN, BOB Worked in front office for three decades, mostly in public relations and media relations.

BROWN, "SKINNY" Versatile right-handed pitcher; started, relieved, and won 69 games for the Orioles from '55 to '62.

BUFORD, DON Acquired as utility infielder in '67; moved to left field and excelled as leadoff hitter from '68 to '72; now club's farm director.

*BUNKER, WALLY Heady pitcher; won 19 games at age nineteen in '64 and tossed World Series shutout two years later; arm troubles shortened career.

CASHEN, FRANK Baltimore native; ran front office as executive vice president from '65 to '75; later built World Series winner for Mets.

CAUSEY, WAYNE Bonus baby signed in '55; was traded and became solid major league infielder in '60s; hit .252 over eleven seasons.

DALTON, HARRY Worked in farm department from '54 to '66; head of baseball operations from '66 to '71; later GM of Angels and Brewers.

DeCINCES, DOUG Endured harsh treatment from fans as Brooks Robinson's replacement at third in late '70s; traded to Angels in '82; hit 237 career homers.

DEMPSEY, RICK Gritty catcher and fan favorite from '76 to '86; feuded with Earl Weaver and won '83 World Series MVP Award.

DURHAM, JOE Outfielder; played briefly with Orioles in '50s; returned in front-office role in the '80s.

*ETCHEBARREN, ANDY Catcher; played on six division winners for the Orioles in the '60s and '70s; later coach and manager in farm system.

FLANAGAN, MIKE Dogged left-hander; won Cy Young Award in '79 and 141 games for the Orioles over fifteen seasons; later pitching coach and broadcaster.

Foss, Joe   Former banker; became club's vice chairman and chief operating officer under owner Peter Angelos.

Gardner, Billy   Started at second base for the Orioles from '56 to '59; hit .237 over ten-year career.

Gentile, "Diamond" Jim   Powerful first baseman; had career year in '61 with 46 homers and 141 RBI; traded two years later.

Gillick, Pat   Minor league pitcher in the '60s, general manager in the '90s.

Ginsberg, Joe   Reserve catcher in late '50s; hit .241 over thirteen-year major league career.

Grich, Bob   First-round draft pick in '67; became All-Star second baseman in the '70s; went to Angels as free agent in November '77; finished seventeen-year career with 224 homers.

Grimsley, Ross   Left-hander; won 124 games in eleven major league seasons and 50 for the Orioles from '74 to '77 before leaving as free agent.

Hale, Bob   Pinch-hitting specialist in the '50s; went on to become college athletic director.

Hall, Dick   Precise reliever; pitched for the Orioles from '61 to '66 and '69 to '71; has one of the all-time lowest walks-to-innings ratios.

Hamper, Joe   Johns Hopkins graduate; worked in front office from '54 to '91; started in accounting department and rose to chief financial officer.

Hansen, Ron   Shortstop; played with Brooks Robinson in minor leagues; AL Rookie of the Year in '60; later became scout for the Yankees.

Harwell, Ernie   Hall of Fame broadcaster; did Orioles radio play-by-play from '54 to '59 before becoming a legend in Detroit.

Hemond, Roland   Longtime baseball executive; worked for Bill Veeck and ran White Sox in the '70s and '80s; Orioles general manager from '87 to '95.

Hendricks, Elrod   "Quintessential Oriole," says Frank Cashen; joined team in '68 as catcher; career as player and coach lasted three-plus decades.

Hitchcock, Billy   Former major leaguer; managed Orioles in '62 and '63; fired by Lee MacPhail.

HUNTER, BILLY Shortstop in '54; went to Yankees in seventeen-player trade; coach from '64 to '77; later managed Texas Rangers.

JOHNSON, CONNIE Former Negro leaguer; pitched three years for the Orioles near the end of his career; won 14 games in '57.

JOHNSON, DAVE Baltimore native; pitched heroic game as twenty-nine-year-old rookie late in '89 season; led club with 13 wins in '90.

JOHNSON, DAVEY Gold Glove second baseman in '60s and early '70s; managed the Orioles to playoffs in '96 and '97.

KELL, GEORGE Hall of Fame third baseman; ended career with Orioles in '56 and '57, making All-Star team and helping break in Brooks Robinson.

KENNEDY, BOB Sixteen-year major leaguer; played for Orioles in '54 and '55; hit club's first grand slam.

KRETLOW, LOU Ten-year major leaguer; had busiest year of career with the Orioles, throwing 166⅔ innings in '54.

KUBSKI, AL Baltimore native and former minor leaguer; scouted California for the Orioles in '60s and early '70s before going to Angels with Harry Dalton.

LOWENSTEIN, JOHN Wacky veteran; part of successful left-field platoon with Gary Roenicke starting in '79; later a TV analyst.

LUCCHINO, LARRY Lawyer in Edward Bennett Williams's firm; joined the front office and rose to team president and minority owner; resigned in '93.

LYNN, FRED Centerfielder; starred for Red Sox in the '70s; signed with the Orioles as free agent in '85 and hit 87 homers before being traded in '88.

MACPHAIL, LEE The Orioles' general manager from '58 to '65; later became the Yankees' GM and American League president; Hall of Famer.

MARR, TOM Baltimore radio personality; worked on the Orioles' radio broadcasts for eight years starting in '79.

MARSH, FRED Infielder; ended seven-year career in Baltimore, hitting .211 in '55 and '56.

MARTINEZ, DENNIS Pitcher from Nicaragua; went 108–93 from '76 to '86; alcoholism ended Orioles career; recovered and threw a perfect game for Expos.

McGregor, Scott Off-speed pitching specialist; won 138 games from '76 to '88; threw shutout to win World Series clincher in '83.

McNally, Dave Tough left-hander from Billings, Montana; had 181 wins and four 20-win seasons pitching for the Orioles from '62 to '74.

Murray, Eddie All-Star first baseman; the Orioles' cleanup hitter from '77 to '88; traded to Dodgers; returned to Orioles late in career; hit 504 career homers.

Mussina, Mike Right-hander; the Orioles' top pitcher in the '90s; started 2000 season with 136–66 career record.

Oates, Johnny The Orioles' reserve catcher briefly in the '70s; managed the Orioles from '91 to '94; later managed the Rangers to playoffs.

O'Dell, Billy Left-hander signed as bonus baby in '54; earned All-Star Game MVP Award in '58; traded in November '59; won 105 games in thirteen years overall.

Olson, Gregg First-round draft pick in '88; had devastating curveball and was fixture at closer from '89 to '93.

Palmeiro, Rafael First baseman; averaged 36 homers and 111 RBI as the Orioles' top hitter for five years in the '90s.

Palmer, Jim Hall of Fame right-hander; won 268 games and three Cy Young Awards pitching for the Orioles from '65 to '84.

Pappas, Milt "Kiddie Corps" pitcher; won 110 games for the Orioles from '57 to '65; traded to Cincinnati in deal that brought Frank Robinson to Baltimore.

Peters, Hank The Orioles' general manager from '75 to '87; began long front-office career with St. Louis Browns.

Philley, Dave Outfielder and career .270 hitter; made two stops in Baltimore ('55–'56 and '60–'61) during eighteen-year major league career.

Pillette, Duane Right-handed pitcher; came with franchise from St. Louis; won 10 games in '54.

Poitevint, Ray Scouted California for the Orioles in '60s and early '70s; signed Eddie Murray and Dennis Martinez.

POWELL, BOOG Genial slugger; hit 303 homers from '61 to '74; played left field early in career, then switched to first base; AL MVP in '70; traded to Indians late in career.

PRIES, DON Orioles scout and front-office executive in '60s and '70s; became head of Major League Scouting Bureau.

PYBURN, JIM College football and baseball star; one of the Orioles' first bonus baby signings in '55; hit .190 over three years.

RIPKEN, BILL Second baseman; younger brother of Cal; played a decade in major leagues, mostly with the Orioles.

RIPKEN, CAL, JR. Baseball's all-time Iron Man; played in 2,632 consecutive games from '82 to '98; just seventh major leaguer to have 400 homers and 3,000 hits.

ROBINSON, BROOKS Hall of Fame third baseman; won sixteen Gold Gloves and hit .267 with 268 homers for the Orioles from '55 to '77; AL MVP in '64.

ROBINSON, FRANK Hall of Fame outfielder; player, coach, manager, and front-office executive during nineteen years with club; AL MVP in '66.

SHETRONE, BARRY Baltimore native; played in the Orioles' system as an outfielder for six years in late '50s and early '60s, more in high minors than majors.

SINGLETON, KEN Right-field fixture from '75 to '84; led club in walks, runs, batting average, home runs, and RBI in different seasons; became broadcaster.

SPRINGSTEAD, MARTY Longtime American League umpire; retired in the '80s; became league's supervisor of umpires.

STARRETTE, HERM Minor league pitcher in the '60s; pitched in 27 games for the Orioles; went on to career as pitching coach and instructor for several teams; the Orioles' pitching coach in '88.

STONE, STEVE Pitcher; joined the Orioles in '79 as free agent; won club-record 25 games in '80; retired after '81 season.

THURMOND, MARK Starter/reliever; experienced low of '88 and high of '89.

TRIANDOS, GUS Burly starting catcher in '50s and early '60s; club's first premier home-run hitter.

WALKER, JERRY Phenom pitcher; won 11 games in '59; traded in '61; had long career as scout, minor league manager, and major league coach and GM.

WEAVER, EARL Combative Hall of Fame manager; won six division titles, four AL pennants, and one World Series from '68 to '82; comeback in '85 and '86 flopped.

WIGHT, BILL Left-hander; pitched twelve years in majors and won 21 games for the Orioles from '55 to '57.

WILLIAMS, DICK Utility player; had three stints with the Orioles between '56 and '62; became top manager and won pennants with three different teams.

WREN, FRANK Former assistant GM with Florida Marlins; lasted one year as the Orioles' GM under Peter Angelos; immediately hired by Atlanta Braves after being fired in Baltimore.

YOUSE, WALTER Longtime Baltimore-area amateur coach and major league scout; worked for the Orioles from '55 to the early '70s as a scout and supervisor.

ZUVERINK, GEORGE Made 197 appearances for the Orioles as relief ace in the '50s.

---

*Interviewed by author in 1986 for stories that appeared in the *Baltimore Sun*.

Growing Up
1954–59

1

Back in the Game

They packed for an overnight trip. Tommy D'Alesandro and Clarence Miles expected no more than that as their train left Baltimore for New York on September 27, 1953. D'Alesandro, the popular second-term mayor of Baltimore, and Miles, a prominent attorney with roots on Maryland's Eastern Shore, anticipated spending the day in New York and returning the next morning with a precious jewel: an American League franchise.

Baltimore had been without major league baseball for more than a half-century, since the departure of the turn-of-the-century Orioles in 1902, but the owners of the eight American League clubs were meeting later that Sunday at the Commodore Hotel in Manhattan, on the eve of the '53 World Series, with a vote scheduled on the possible move of the beleaguered St. Louis Browns to Baltimore. D'Alesandro and Miles, who had headed the city's dogged pursuit of the Browns, believed the vote would go favorably.

The Browns were owned by Bill Veeck, a renowned promoter and baseball maverick who had turned around the Cleveland Indians in the late '40s and used the money from the sale of that franchise to buy the Browns, winners of one pennant in fifty-two years. Attempting to draw more fans, Veeck resorted to such stunts as giving away free beer and ladies' stockings, signing Negro leagues' pitching legend Satchel Paige, and sending a midget, Eddie Gaedel, up to bat. But the National League's St. Louis Cardinals were far more successful and popular, and the Browns drew just 300,000 fans for 77 home games in '53. Not coincidentally, they performed almost as poorly on the field, losing 100 of 154 games to finish last.

Veeck had thought he would be spending the '53 season in Baltimore after agreeing to the terms of a move with D'Alesandro on March 14, 1953, during a meeting at Baltimore's Emerson Hotel. A front-page headline in the next day's *Baltimore Sun* read, "Baltimore's Return to Big Leagues Is All but Signed." American League president Will Harridge said the move had been unanimously approved and that an owners' vote two days later in Clearwater, Florida, was "a mere formality." Veeck and D'Alesandro boarded a train to Florida wearing broad smiles, but the owners' vote on March 16 was a stunner: 5–3 against the move. "Disappointed? That's the understatement of the year," Veeck said.

It turned out the owners were opposed to moving a club so close to the start of the season, especially a club $300,000 in debt. The owners also were uncomfortable with Veeck's plan to raise money by selling shares of the club to the public, and they were upset that Veeck had not conferred with officials from the International League, formerly the Eastern League, of which Baltimore had been a member for fifty years. "When the club owners began looking more closely into the situation, they found more complications than were apparent at first glance," Harridge said.

Veeck was furious. He was an iconoclast, preferring sports shirts to suits and ties, and bleacher seats to boardrooms. He unleashed a vicious verbal assault on the other owners. "I am the victim of duplicity of conduct by a lot of lying so-and-sos," he said. "Every reason they gave for turning me down was either silly or malicious, and I prefer to think they were malicious." What about the chances of moving the Browns to Baltimore in '54? "You'll have to ask the other gentlemen of the league," Veeck said, "and I use the term 'gentlemen' advisedly."

Two days later, the National League approved the shift of the Boston Braves to Milwaukee. Baltimore fans were bitter, but D'Alesandro was not about to give up. The son of an immigrant laborer, he had risen from the streets of Baltimore's Little Italy neighborhood to the city's highest elected office despite having just an eighth-grade education. He was a can-do politician who had overseen the opening of Baltimore's Friendship Airport and the expansion of Memorial Stadium, and although he still lived in a row house in Little Italy, he counted presidents and congressmen among his friends and was accustomed to getting his way.

His reading of the owners' vote was perceptive. Veeck's poor finances probably had killed the deal, he thought, so he set out to find Baltimore investors willing to buy some of Veeck's stock and ease his burden while allowing him to remain the club's majority owner. That was an arrangement the AL owners probably would settle for, D'Alesandro figured.

Miles, one of the original partners in a prominent downtown law firm, agreed to help the mayor recruit investors, not because he loved baseball, as the mayor did—D'Alesandro had rooted for the Yankees for years—but because he wanted what was best for Baltimore. He was from the opposite end of the social spectrum, having counted the future Duchess of Windsor, Wallis Warfield, among his schoolmates, but he shared with the mayor an aggressive sense of civic obligation. His own political career had ended early, but he had served on commissions and boards overseeing traffic, smoking, and legal reform, and he was the first chairman of the Greater Baltimore Committee, a group charged with revitalizing the city. A major league baseball club certainly would help that cause.

D'Alesandro and Miles were an odd couple—the mayor was emotional and streetwise, the lawyer reserved and aristocratic—but they worked well together. They put together a group of investors willing to pay Veeck one million dollars for 40 percent of the stock in the Missouri corporation that owned the Browns. The group included such prominent local businessmen as Zanvyl Krieger, president of the Gunther Brewing Company; Jerry Hoffberger, president of the National Brewing Company; Joseph Iglehart, an investment specialist; and James Keelty, a real estate executive. Their money, combined with the expansion of Memorial Stadium, which had already helped lure a National Football League team, made Baltimore easily the best option for the struggling Browns.

When D'Alesandro and Miles arrived at the owners' meeting in late September of '53, however, they realized their bid still wasn't assured of acceptance. Six other cities made presentations, including Los Angeles and San Francisco. The owners suddenly were contemplating the idea of putting a team in California, a booming baseball frontier with seemingly limitless possibilities. Del Webb, one of the owners of the Yankees, was not only a Californian himself, but his contracting firm was building a Los Angeles hotel for Conrad Hilton, the famous hotel tycoon and a major financial backer of Los Angeles's bid.

Webb filibustered on behalf of moving the Browns to Los Angeles before the owners voted on moving to Baltimore. When the Baltimore vote took place around ten P.M., the result was a 4–4 split. Baltimore had received one more yea vote than it had in March, but it still needed two more to get the Browns. Earl Hilligan, secretary of the American League, announced the news to reporters with a terse, one-sentence statement: "The American League did not approve the transfer of the St. Louis club to Baltimore."

D'Alesandro was stunned. "This is a shattering blow to all Baltimoreans," he said. "We have guaranteed the American League the use of one of the finest and most modern stadiums in the country. Local financial interests stood ready to provide the necessary backing. Two million fans were ready to support a big-league franchise. Yet all of this was not enough. We think Baltimore has been treated unfairly, but we will fight on."

Webb emerged from the meeting and spoke to reporters. "I still believe Baltimore stands a good chance of getting the franchise this year," he said, but there was reason to wonder. At the All-Star Game several months earlier, Webb had said, "Too much baseball is concentrated in the East. I am opposed to transferring the Browns eastward. We should go west."

For the second time in six months, D'Alesandro had to regroup—in a hurry this time. The owners were meeting for two more days, before the start of the World Series. There was still time to sway them. The mayor and Miles bought new clothes Monday morning and spent the day making their case to anyone who would listen. They finagled a meeting with baseball commissioner Ford Frick, at which they complained about Webb's control of the American League meetings, and also about competing with a Los Angeles group that had not even formally submitted a bid. Frick was sympathetic. D'Alesandro later referred to the meeting with the commissioner as "a turning point."

Back at the Commodore Hotel, D'Alesandro vented his anger at the representatives of several clubs that had voted nay. He accused Cleveland's Hank Greenberg of double-crossing him and made veiled threats to others, explaining that he was a former U.S. congressman with friends in high places such as the White House—D'Alesandro was on a first-name basis with President Eisenhower—and wouldn't hesitate to use his connections to challenge baseball's antitrust exemption if Baltimore failed to get a team.

More important, the mayor realized the owners were not against Baltimore so much as against Veeck, the indefatigable individualist who had heaped scorn on them after the March vote. Quite simply, the owners wanted Veeck, his debt, and his wild ideas out of their coalition. Webb's interest in expanding to California was genuine, but it was primarily a way of manufacturing leverage against Veeck and his plans to move to Baltimore.

D'Alesandro, Miles, and their investors spent the day raising the additional cash needed to buy out Veeck, who owned 80 percent of the Browns' stock, valued at $2.45 million. Krieger, Keelty, and Iglehart upped their contributions, and Hoffberger, in a critical move, agreed to have his brewery sponsor the Washington Senators' radio and television broadcasts, gaining the support of Washington owner Clark Griffith, who had previously opposed moving a club so close to his own. Hoffberger also compensated Griffith for his loss of air rights in Baltimore. That night, Miles was confident enough to barge uninvited into the owners' meeting and present a new offer to buy out Veeck entirely. The owners listened and adjourned until the next afternoon.

When the owners reconvened, they closed the door to a meeting room and spent two hours debating in private while D'Alesandro, Miles, and the rest of the Baltimore delegation paced in the hallway. D'Alesandro tried to see through the keyhole in the door at one point as a newspaper photographer snapped a picture of him that spoke of the city's anxiety. If this offer failed, it seemed Baltimore might never get back into the major leagues. Having the best financial package and the most suitable stadium might not matter if the owners really were intent on expanding to California.

Shortly before six P.M., the door opened and D'Alesandro, Miles, and Thomas Biddison, Baltimore's city solicitor, were called into the meeting room. Five minutes later, the door opened again and Hilligan, the league secretary, emerged holding a piece of paper. He began to read. The Baltimoreans gathered outside the meeting room were quiet until they heard the word "approved," at which point they began to shout. Moments later, D'Alesandro emerged from the room jumping up and down with joy. After fifty-one years, Baltimore finally was back in the major leagues. The Browns were moving to Baltimore. They would become known as the Baltimore Orioles.

"This is a great day for Baltimore and the big leagues," an emotional D'Alesandro told reporters. "We have been fighting for a long time, and it was worth it. We fought hard, but we fought fair. Right has prevailed."

Webb made the motion to accept the transfer of the Browns with the provision that the league expand to a ten-team league "in the near future," adding new clubs in Los Angeles and San Francisco. (The National League would beat the AL to both cities.) The Los Angeles group had failed to deliver on financial promises this time. Their challenge was empty. Baltimore's bid was the best by far. Miles and his group had agreed to buy all of Veeck's stock. The other owners were thrilled. Their nemesis was out.

Looking pale as he emerged from the meeting wearing one of his trademark sports shirts, Veeck said, "This is the best solution. The Browns obviously were in bad shape. Baltimore, on the other hand, is in fine financial shape." He credited D'Alesandro, Miles, and particularly Hoffberger for making the deal go. Asked if he would remain in the organization, Veeck said, "I'm out of it entirely. I am no longer in baseball. But like a bad penny, I keep turning up, and I am hopeful."

Across the room, reporters began pressing Miles, the new club's president. Would Marty Marion, the Browns' manager in '53, come to Baltimore as the Orioles' skipper? "I don't know," Miles said. "I'm not a technical baseball man. A baseball man will make that decision and all others of a similar nature. I will not be a grandstand manager, and neither will my associates."

Miles and D'Alesandro took a train back to Baltimore the next day, having stayed two days longer than expected but having returned with the grail they had sought. Hundreds of cheering fans met the train at Mount Royal Station, waving copies of newspapers with big, bold headlines. D'Alesandro disembarked and waved to the crowd, a conquering hero returning home. No one noticed that he was wearing the same gray suit he had worn when he left for New York three days earlier.

HANK PETERS: "I was the Browns' assistant farm director in '53. Veeck and a group had bought the club from Bill and Charley DeWitt in '51. Bill and Charley DeWitt had no money, but they bought the club on a shoestring and made some money when they sold it. But it turned out Veeck and his group didn't have any money, either. They wanted to make some money off of the team. Veeck came in and worked his butt off. He was a great PR guy. I didn't think he was a great baseball man, but he was a good PR guy. He was tireless, working to promote the team. He had all these different promotions, many of which were unique. Bat day originated with Veeck in St. Louis. And Eddie Gaedel, of course. But despite all his efforts we were second fiddle to the Cardinals, and, of course, we didn't have a good club. Most of the talent Bill DeWitt had traded or sold in order to get a little money and keep the team functioning. There was not a lot of talent left. Bob Turley and Don Larsen, two exceptional young arms. But that was it.

"It was kind of a tragic thing, actually, because the Browns originally owned Sportsman's Park in St. Louis, where both they and the Cardinals played. And at one point Fred Saigh, who owned the Cardinals, got in trouble over his income taxes and was talking about moving the Cardinals. Then he got indicted and had to sell the club, and Gussie Busch, who was not a baseball man, but a great civic leader in St. Louis, came forward at the last minute when it looked like the club was going to be bought and moved. He bought the club and kept it in St. Louis, and then he bought Sportsman's Park from the Browns because the Browns needed money. That was the beginning of the end. There was no way the Browns were going to be able to stay there after that. Something had to break because things weren't ever going to be successful in St. Louis.

"Veeck's original intent after a couple of years of trying to make a go of it in St. Louis was to move the team to Milwaukee. And he got turned down. The league turned him down. He came back and ultimately got the club moved to Baltimore. He wanted very much to own the team and move it to Baltimore, but pressures were brought to bear, and he had to sell."

BILLY HUNTER: "My first year [in the major leagues] was in '53 with the Browns. I came out of the Dodgers organization, and everyone in Triple A for the Dodgers knew more about fundamentals than the Browns. I couldn't believe this was the major leagues. In May I was in the top ten in the league in hitting, and our players just went through the motions, and Veeck called me in one day and said, 'Bill, don't pay any attention to the rest of the people around you; just do your thing.' We just didn't have the team to compete."

DUANE PILLETTE: "They weren't trying to build the club up in St. Louis. They always sold players at the end of the season to make sure they made money. You knew they weren't trying to win. But I loved Veeck. I don't care what anyone says; he was probably the greatest owner ever to play for. He was just a normal human being, one of the guys. He wanted to win so badly that he started a midget. But we weren't good. And it was tough to play. The weather was brutal. It gets hot everywhere, but St. Louis, my gosh. And the ground was hard, and we just got beat. The last game there [in '53] they ran out of balls. I was pitching. Had to use dirty batting-practice balls. The ump said, 'Just go out there and pitch.' We lost in 11 innings."

The franchise moved from St. Louis in November '53, with the new owners allowing only one member of the front office—farm director Jim Mc-Laughlin—to come to Baltimore. Otherwise, the front office started from scratch with Miles as president. The first hires included Dick Armstrong in public relations, Joe Hamper in accounting, and Harry Dalton in the farm department.

On the baseball side, Arthur Ehlers, a Baltimore native who had been the general manager of the Philadelphia Athletics, was named the general manager. Ehlers's assistant was Jack Dunn, who had served as the owner, president, manager, and general manager of Baltimore's International League franchise at various times. (His grandfather had managed the International League Orioles to seven straight pennants from 1919 to 1925.) Ehlers and Dunn brought in Jimmy Dykes as the Orioles' first manager. Dykes, fifty-seven, had played, coached, and managed in the major leagues since the end of World War I, and the Athletics had just fired him after a 95-loss season in '53.

HANK PETERS: "They let the whole [St. Louis] front office go other than Jim. Harry Dalton always told me, 'Thank God you didn't come, or I would never have gotten into baseball.'"

HARRY DALTON: "I was hired as the assistant farm director in December of '53, right before Christmas. Jim [McLaughlin] was looking for an assistant after Hank Peters didn't get to come East. I had come out of the Air Force in October and came to Baltimore because my parents had moved there. While I'd been in the service I'd decided when I got out that instead of going back to sportswriting in Springfield, Massachusetts, I would see if I could hook up with a major league team somewhere in public relations. And here were the Orioles, right there. So I wrote letters and made phone calls and finally got an interview. I got a double interview one day, with Dick Armstrong in public relations first, and while I was there, Dick said, 'You might want to talk to Jim McLaughlin. He's looking for somebody in his department.' So he set it up with Jim, and I went over and talked to Jim, and two days later Jim called and hired me on December 23.

"We had offices on Eager Street, right at the corner of Eager and Charles, by the Chanticleer Restaurant, in an old radio station. Ehlers had his office out at the stadium. We were having to run back and forth all the time for meetings. It was not convenient, but for a guy who just wanted to get into baseball, hell, I'd have gone fifty miles. We were downtown just for that first year, and then they built offices in the stadium, and we moved out there.

"I was young. I was driving a cab at night to pay off college loans and everything else. I didn't even have a car. I'd take the trolley to work, get a trolley back, and go out to College Cabs in Towson, right by the fire station on York Road. I'd moonlight at night for four or five hours, trying to get myself out from under. I was a cab driver/assistant farm director."

JOE HAMPER: "I had worked for the accounting firm that did the audit [when the club moved], and then I left them and saw in the newspaper that the club wanted someone to work for them, and that's how I got started. I started on the fifth of February in '54. Harry was one of the first guys I met, just walking in the hallway. Somebody introduced me to him. People were just working there. I mean, nobody had any titles except Clarence Miles as the president and Clyde Morris as the secretary/treasurer. And Art Ehlers as the general manager. But basically titles didn't exist, and I was just in the accounting department."

HARRY DALTON: "On the tenth of February we went to Thomasville, Georgia, to set up the minor league camp, which the Browns had established there at a veterans' home. If you want to call that the place where the Orioles really debuted, that was it. We had 360 players in the camp. The Browns were so ragtag that they didn't have uniform numbers on all the uniforms, so we would just take pieces of canvas and cut them into squares and grease-pencil a number on there and then safety-pin it to the backs of the uniforms. Didn't look very professional. It was a humble beginning."

2

100 Losses (and Who Cares?)

The Orioles' first season in Baltimore was sweet and clumsy, like a young boy's first kiss. The team formerly known as the St. Louis Browns went 54–100, finished 57 games behind the pennant-winning Cleveland Indians, and established several benchmarks for ineptitude, leaving fans without any illusions about possibly contending for an American League pennant anytime soon. On the other hand, some 350,000 people attended a parade before the home opener at Memorial Stadium, the season attendance of 1,060,910 set a major league record for a seventh-place team, and players were treated royally at restaurants and businesses around town. What they did—or didn't do—on the field was unimportant. The city was excited just to have major league baseball again after more than a half-century. For one year, at least, just being in the game was all that mattered.

The ball club that manager Jimmy Dykes fielded was an amalgam of fading veterans who had played for the Browns, journeymen acquired in waiver trades, and a sprinkling of young talent. There was no use trying to mislead the public. "A lot of these guys ought to be down on their knees, thanking the Lord they still have a chance to play major league baseball," general manager Arthur Ehlers said.

There were exceptions. Third baseman Vern Stephens had led the American League in RBI three times. Opening Day rightfielder Vic Wertz had averaged 23 homers per season since '51. Second baseman Bobby Young, a Baltimorean and the first of the Orioles to sign a contract, was solid in the field, as was shortstop Billy Hunter. Clint Courtney, the catcher, was a battler. The starting rotation included Don Larsen and Bob Turley, a pair of valued prospects just beginning their careers; Joe Coleman, a solid veteran acquired from the Athletics; and a pair of former Browns, Duane Pillette and Lou Kretlow. Satchel Paige, the Negro league legend, had pitched for the Browns in '53, but the Orioles elected not to sign him.

In spring training the club traded for first baseman Eddie Waitkus, who had been an All-Star in the late '40s before getting shot in the chest by a woman he didn't know—the real-life inspiration for Bernard Malamud's book *The Natural*. Other additions included veteran outfielders Cal Abrams, Gil Coan, and Chuck Diering. Early in the season, outfielder Jim Dyck was traded for Bob Kennedy, a third baseman/outfielder. Wertz was traded to Cleveland for Bob Chakales, a pitcher.

The pitching was better than the hitting, and moving into Memorial Stadium intensified the glaring disparity. The outfield was a vast prairie of near-comical dimensions—445 feet to a hedge, not a fence, in center field. "You could use five outfielders out there," Coan joked. The pitchers benefited while the hitters suffered. The pitchers allowed just 78 home runs all season, the fewest in the league, and compiled a commendable 3.88 ERA. The hitters totaled just 17 home runs in 77 home games and 52 for the season. Stephens, thirty-three, led the team with 8 homers—yes, 8—and 46 RBI.

The joke around town was that Baltimore had wanted a major league team in the worst way, and that's what it had gotten. But even though the club lost 14 games in a row at one point and only once won more than three in a row, it was competitive in many games because of its pitching. Turley, in a breakthrough performance, went 14–15 and led the league in strikeouts. Coleman threw 15 complete games and had a 13–17 record. Larsen was 3–21 (still a club record for losses) but pitched well enough to win a dozen.

The highlight of the season was the home opener. Businesses and schools closed, City Hall declared a half-day holiday, and a massive crowd turned out in drizzly, fifty-eight-degree weather for a morning parade. The players arrived on an overnight train after opening the season in Detroit and fronted a fifty-six-block parade that included twenty-two marching bands. Arriving at Memorial Stadium, which was still under construction, the players learned that gifts would be given to those collecting the first hit and first home run.

After Vice President Richard Nixon threw out the ceremonial first pitch in a packed stadium, Turley allowed a single to the game's leadoff hitter, Chico Carrasquel of the White Sox, then retired the side. The Orioles took the lead in the third on Courtney's homer off Chicago's Virgil Trucks and added to the lead when Stephens hit another homer in the fourth. Turley took over from there, striking out nine and finishing the 3–1 win with a seven-hitter.

Turley took a no-hitter into the ninth inning of his next start against Cleveland at Memorial Stadium, and even though the Indians rallied to beat him, his status as a fan favorite was cemented. His starts became the most popular ticket, with fans delighting in his strikeout totals.

The club was in fifth place after a month, just three games under .500, but a 10-game losing streak represented a tumble back to reality. The Orioles and Senators spent the second half of the season trading the bottom two spots in the standings, and although the Orioles passed the Senators with two weeks to go and held on to finish seventh, Dykes was fired late in the season.

ERNIE HARWELL: "Spring training in '54 was in Yuma, Arizona, which was a long way away, but Veeck had signed the contract. There wasn't much in Yuma except a drive-in marriage bureau. You could get married without leaving your car. People would drive over from California and drive right up to the justice of the peace. It was like getting a hamburger. You reached out of the window and got a marriage certificate. Otherwise [Yuma] was small and isolated. Veeck's idea had been to fly to Tucson and Phoenix, which were the only two places to play out there at the time. The Giants were in Phoenix and the Indians were in Tucson. Veeck wanted to fly back and forth every day. But the Orioles didn't want to fly, so we rode buses. It was a long trip back and forth every day. We'd stop in Gila Bend for a hamburger and a beer and move on."

BILLY HUNTER: "We'd have a team going out on the bus and a team coming back on the bus, and we'd meet at Gila Bend. Players transferred from one bus to another depending on our needs for that day. Sometimes we spent the night in Phoenix, sometimes not. We spent hours and hours and hours on buses."

ERNIE HARWELL: "They had kids in the clubhouse and all. It was a very relaxed atmosphere. We played a lot of golf. Dykes would take the end of one cigar and light another. He was the only guy I ever saw that chain-smoked cigars. He was very laid-back, a pixie kind of a little guy with a wry sense of humor. Pretty good with the needle in a nice, soft kind of a way. He'd gotten a lot of managing jobs because he was low-key and people liked him—his personality. He wasn't going to rock the boat.

"Once camp broke we barnstormed on the trains all the way back east to Detroit for the season opener. That was a long haul, really tiring. You needed spring training again after the trip ended. We'd play a day game in, say,

Alpine, Texas, or El Paso, or somewhere, and after the game we'd get back on the train at four or five o'clock and have dinner, and then there'd be some card playing, and then you went to bed. When you got up the next day, sometimes you could go to a hotel and they'd have a room where you could wash up and change and then go to the park. Sometimes you went straight to the park. We were barnstorming with the Cubs, who fired their manager on the trip, in Dallas. The way it worked, each team had a couple of Pullman cars, and each team had its own dining car. There was a lot of camaraderie between the teams. They had friends on the other team. I don't think we spent a night in a hotel for ten days or two weeks.

"I remember we stopped in New Orleans, and we had about fifty-five guys on the squad at that point. They'd send one team out to play in Mississippi and another to Alabama, and they'd all bus back to New Orleans at night. It was a mess. We stayed in the Roosevelt Hotel for a week. That was fun. That's where the gin fizz was invented, and there was an orchestra. We had a good time eating that New Orleans food. Then we finished up with a couple of exhibition games in St. Louis, where the team had just come from, which was strange, and then we went to Detroit. A lot of guys from Baltimore came out for the opener. Sid Friedman, who owned the Chesapeake Restaurant, he was there. Nate from Nate's Deli. I think the mayor was there. We had a banquet the night before the first game. It was a great time."

DUANE PILLETTE: "We lost the opener, and then I pitched the second game and won. I hit a double, and it had snowed previously and the infield was as hard as a rock. I didn't have pads on, and I slid into second and wound up with a seven-inch strawberry. I had that all year. We scored three runs and it held up. I gave up a homer in the ninth, but the lead stood up. I got the Browns' last loss in St. Louis and the Orioles' first win in Baltimore. That's my glory."

BILLY HUNTER: "After we won in Detroit we got on a train back to Baltimore. They came around and gave us our uniforms and told us to get dressed. We had no idea why we were doing that, or what was happening. Then they advised us that there was going to be a parade. It had to be the first time they had a tickertape parade before the season started. When we got to Camden Station, we got into convertibles and made the trip from downtown out to the park. It was unbelievable. There were people everywhere. I was in a car with Vern Stephens and Vinicio Garcia, the three of us sitting in back, up on the top, throwing balls or something out to the crowd. People were hanging out of the windows. It was a big deal, like we won the war or something. We were thinking, 'What a difference from St. Louis.' A big night there was 3,500 people in the stands."

ERNIE HARWELL: "We were riding in the cars and it was sort of a cloudy sky, a dreary day. We were worried about the game getting rained out, not that they would have let it happen. People were throwing plastic baseballs. We got to the park and went inside, and it was funny, they were still working on it; there was still scaffolding up, and workmen were banging around and putting in seats and cleaning stuff. It was a great thrill for all of us, that parade. Then the club went out and beat the White Sox. Turley pitched a great game."

DUANE PILLETTE: "I had never been in a parade except for my first year when we played in the World Series in Brooklyn in '49. This was so different. You sat in the back of that convertible and went, 'What in the world am I doing in this car with all these people I don't even know screaming and hollering and carrying on? How can they be so happy about getting the St. Louis Browns? Don't they know we lost 100 games last year?' It looked like the whole United States was out there. Then we went out and won the ball game, which pleased everyone and their brother. They could pick up the paper and see us with a 2–1 record, on top of the league. God, they couldn't hardly believe it. Of course, it didn't last long."

ERNIE HARWELL: "The reality was that they didn't have much of a team. When I tell people the leading home-run hitter that year had eight, they blink in disbelief. Turley and Larsen were the backbone. Joe Coleman was a pretty good pitcher. They had some guys who had pretty good records, but most of them were past their peaks. Waitkus had been shot, and he was very weak. Most of the old Browns just couldn't compete with the rest of the league. The dimensions of the park were huge. It was before they put up the fences. Not many people could hit it out there. Plus the lights were bad. That's why our pitching dominated and the hitting was so weak. The lights were so weak. But what that year was about was the newness of being back in the major leagues. Everyone was happy regardless of the record."

BILLY HUNTER: "Turley almost threw a no-hitter right off the bat, against Cleveland, which had a real good ball club that year. Al Rosen broke it up in the ninth with a line drive to left. If anyone but Turley had been pitching I would have been standing right where the line drive was hit. But Turley was throwing so hard that night that I shaded toward second base a little bit and still almost caught the ball, which was hit between third and short. He was throwing so hard that you figured they'd be late on anything if they hit it. That's why I moved. On the very next pitch Rosen hit it where I'd been. Then Larry Doby hit a ball out of the park on the next pitch. It was just a high fly, and it barely made it out. We got beat 2–1."

BOB KENNEDY: "Turley was an outstanding pitcher even then. You could see that he was going to be outstanding. He was still just a young pitcher then and throwing the ball more than pitching, as most young pitchers do. But he was strong, and he fired that ball. And he was no dummy on the mound. He had come out of the army, and he knew what to do, and he did it. Larsen probably should have been a better pitcher than he was. He was a good guy, probably too easygoing."

ERNIE HARWELL: "Turley was a phenom. He was sort of wild, which made him even more effective. He and Larsen were both pretty good pitchers. Larsen was a nice guy, but he liked to stay out all night. He was out all the time."

DUANE PILLETTE: "Larsen was just a big overgrown kid having a lot of fun. It wasn't that he wasn't competitive. He just could have won a lot more. I roomed with him in St. Louis and I called him 'Big Stupe,' which was the name of a cartoon character back then. The guy had a lot of talent, but he just didn't use it. That year in Baltimore he pitched a hell of a lot better than 3–21. We weren't scoring much. Turley was the commodity. He threw the hell out of the ball and competed hard. And we also had a guy named Lou Kretlow who could throw a ball through a brick wall."

BILLY HUNTER: "There was a lot of enthusiasm. We'd played an exhibition in Baltimore during the summer of '53, the first game played in Memorial Stadium. They had temporary seats in the outfield. I hit a home run, and Wertz hit a home run. I remember going out across 39th Street and coming out at

St. Paul, and how beautiful it was in Guilford. And we went across to WJZ to do an interview. Once it was set that we were moving, everyone was looking forward to it."

DUANE PILLETTE: "It was different in Baltimore. It was great to play for a crowd. The people were behind you all the time. It wasn't that St. Louis wasn't. The people in St. Louis were good fans. But Baltimore was enthusiastic. The restaurant guys wanted us to come in and eat on the house. We got good deals on cars and clothes. The people took to the players, and the players took to the people. I felt pretty bad because we didn't win more.

"One time we went on a 19-game road trip, and we won three games. It wasn't easy. We were still riding the trains at that point. The sleeper cars were OK. Most of them were the little roomettes. They were good if you were six feet or smaller. Me, I had to curl up. What you did, you folded the bed down on the toilet. If you had to go, you had to get up, push the bed up, go to the john, and pull the bed back down. It wasn't a big room. It was like being buried alive, that's what it was like."

BOB KENNEDY: "I got traded over from Cleveland. I'd gotten back from Korea, and I wasn't playing much. I asked to be traded someplace where I could play. They sent me over very early in the season. I was happy. I hit the first grand slam in Orioles history, against the Yankees and Allie Reynolds one day at Memorial Stadium. It was Casey Stengel's birthday. The bases were loaded, and I hit one out. It went into left-center, and in those days there was a place where they took equipment in through a gate, and I hit it just over the top of that—a pretty good belt, even for me. The next day I hit a three-run dinger. The reason it all happened, I was talking to [New York coach] Bill Dickey before the series, and he gave me a tip, told me to cock my hip and put more weight on my right side. Then I hit the two homers, and Dickey said, 'I'm never talking to you again.'"

BILLY HUNTER: "There was a promotion called Interfaith Night, which was a big deal with a lot of the churches and temples involved. They sold a lot of tickets, and we had a good crowd. As it turned out we played 18 innings against Boston. It had rained before the game, and we had no infield practice, and the stands were full, and Patti Page, the singer, was there, and she gave me a kiss on the cheek before the game. The article in the paper the next day said 'Hunter was inspired by a pregame kiss from Patti Page and had a four-hit game, the last being a bunt double in the 18th inning.' What happened, the leadoff guy got on, and I was sacrificing. On the first pitch their second baseman breaks behind the runner on first. They pitched out and were going to try to get him. Ball one. On the next pitch I see him breaking again, and I pushed the ball to second base, and it went out onto the grass. There was no one there. Jimmy Piersall had to come in from right field, and I ended up on second. I got to third, and Ray Murray hit a sacrifice fly to win the ball game. There were still a lot of people in the stands, but both teams had used all their players.

"That first year our infield was as hard as a rock. It wasn't like the field was later on. I remember one night we were playing the Senators and someone hit me a ball up the middle; it took a bad hop and hit me right on the side of the head and bounced right to Bobby Young at second base for a double play. I never touched the ball with either one of my hands, and it was a 6-4-3 double play. The infield was hard at St. Louis, too, but that first year here was very difficult."

Bob Kennedy: "There was some talent. We didn't have enough, but there was some. Basically we had a lot of guys who had been around. But the people around the park were great. The ownership was great. It was a good year. We drew over a million fans, which was a lot in those days. We just didn't have enough talent. We had some but not enough. It was tough. Wertz hit nine balls that should have gone out and weren't even hits, balls that were home runs any place but in Memorial Stadium. Even in Yankee Stadium, I'm talking about. They were caught here. Vic was so elated that he was traded to Cleveland before the trading deadline. There was no fence. There was a hedge out there. The ball was in play. No one could hit it out there. It was just terrible."

Duane Pillette: "I had my best year in Baltimore in '54. I was in the All-Star Game that year as a batting practice pitcher. Casey liked me, and I had a pretty good ERA, like 2.70, which was good for a losing record. Turley made the team, but Casey told me I could come and pitch batting practice. 'You got All-Star Game stuff,' he said. I almost got into the game. I warmed up in the ninth. That year I was making $22,500, which was pretty good. I felt good. I felt confident. We had a little better infield than we'd had in

St. Louis. The grass was nice. A little better defense in the infield. I was a sinkerball pitcher. Winning 10 with a tail-end club was like winning 17 or 18 with a good team. We just didn't score any runs. A guy showed me some statistics that we allowed a half-run less per game than we'd allowed in '53, but we scored three-quarters of a run less per game. So we lost 100 games again."

Lou Kretlow: "We had a real nice year even though we didn't win many games. We had some big crowds and played a lot of close games. The people were terrific. They were so excited to have a team. They wouldn't let you buy dinner when you went out to eat. The fans were just real enthusiastic and real nice. You hardly heard any booing at the ballpark even though we were losing. Not that we had such a bad team. We had some nice pitchers on that team, but it's tough to win when every game is 2–1 and 1–0."

Billy Hunter: "A million fans was good in those days, and in that year it was very good. It was fun. They were all for you. They were with you—win, lose, or draw. There wasn't a lot of booing even though we lost a lot. Both my wife and I are from Western Pennsylvania, and we ended up making our home here after I was traded. We never moved. I bought the house with the losers' World Series share in 1955 after the Dodgers won; that got me the down payment. The house was in Lutherville. Turley bought a house right down the street. I was in 104, and he was in 114. We'd take our sons out and go sled-riding together."

Bob Kennedy: "Dykes had been my first manager [in the majors]. He was a good man—handled people. He was glib. He was quick. One time he sent me up to pinch hit with the bases loaded, and the fans were booing. Jim said to me, 'If you don't get a hit we're both catching the next bus out of town.'"

Mike Blyzka: "Dykes didn't hardly say a word to me all year except, 'You're going to Kansas City.' I called my wife and went home and got ready to leave. They'd sent me down. But then the White Sox claimed me, so [the Orioles] kept me. Dykes called me back at home and said, 'Never mind; you're staying.' That was about all he ever said to me. I was a young ballplayer just trying to make a go of it. I guess managers have their favorites."

Ernie Harwell: "When he got fired, we were in the old Kenmore Hotel in Boston and they called a press conference. Clarence Miles was up there with his wife. Mrs. Miles let some of us scrungy media guys in the room they'd set up there, and she said, 'Did you boys motor up from Baltimore?' They were Eastern Shore socialites. Then Jimmy was coming down the hall and someone said to him, 'What goes, Jimmy?' And he said, 'Dykes does.' Shortest interview of all time. He was used to it; he'd been fired so many times. He made a speech at one of the banquets later on, and he said something like, 'I don't want to tell you how I feel about this, but when I leave I'm going to have mistletoe hanging from my belt in the back.' Jimmy was quite a guy. But when he left, that was the beginning of the Paul Richards era."

3

The Wizard of Waxahachie

The Orioles didn't just hire Paul Richards and put him on the payroll. They put their future in his hands, making him the first manager/general manager in the major leagues since the New York Giants' John McGraw a half-century earlier. Other than having to answer to ownership about budgets, Richards was given unchecked authority over all aspects of the baseball operation, from which prospects to sign to which veterans to trade to when to lay down a sacrifice bunt.

A former major league catcher from Waxahachie, Texas, nicknamed the "Wizard of Waxahachie," Richards, forty-five, was considered one of the game's most astute thinkers, teachers, and strategists. For the rest of the '50s and into the early '60s, he helped build the Orioles from scratch into a top organization. Few figures in the franchise's history would leave a larger or more indelible footprint.

Intelligent, imperious, and imaginative, able to quote literature and curse umpires with shocking language, Richards was known for emphasizing fundamentals and helping pitchers. He would retire in the late '70s without winning a pennant as a manager or general manager, but he built teams that later succeeded in Chicago, Baltimore, and Houston, and he commanded rare respect in the industry because of his intellect and insight.

His creative mind was in evidence in his high school days in Waxahachie, where he once won the first game of a doubleheader pitching right-handed and the second game pitching left-handed. He began his pro career in '26 as a lanky seventeen-year-old infielder on an Eastern Shore League team in Crisfield, Maryland. Four years later, on a Southern League team in Macon, Georgia, the manager asked for a volunteer with experience as a catcher to serve as a backup. Richards raised his hand even though he had never caught. His fabrication led to a full-time position change when he proved adept behind the plate utilizing an unusual stance in which he crouched on one leg and extended the other in front of him. He reached the major leagues two years later.

"I was extremely fortunate to be a catcher," he said in an interview in '54. "A catcher has a tremendous advantage over players at other positions. He has a better insight into the game and is forced into observing. The picture is right there in front of him."

After four years as a light-hitting backup with the Dodgers, Giants, and Athletics, he started his managerial career in '38 as a player/manager for the Atlanta Crackers of the Southern Association. He had success. One year the Crackers won the league and swept the Texas League winners in the Dixie Series. When World War II broke out and teams needed players, he returned to the major leagues and spent four years as a catcher for the Tigers. His biggest contribution was his influence on Hal Newhouser, a left-handed pitcher with great potential. Newhouser went on to four 20-win seasons, and Richards's reputation as a shrewd pitching coach was cemented.

After World War II he resumed managing, first for Seattle of the Pacific Coast League and then for Buffalo of the International League. He became renowned for using innovative tactics. The IL's top base stealer was Montreal's Sam Jethroe, a fleet leadoff hitter. Richards's plan for slowing him down? Walk the pitcher batting before Jethroe. With the base in front of him occupied, Jethroe couldn't steal.

It was only a matter of time until a major league club gave him a shot, and when the White Sox did in '51, Richards and general manager Frank Lane embarked on a rebuilding plan emphasizing speed and defense. The results were impressive. The Sox had finished 34 games under .500 in '50, but they were 74 games over .500 over the next four years, culminating with a 94-win season in '54. Richards's flair for forward-thinking strategy continued. Twice he brought in a relief pitcher, moved the starter to an infield position, then put the starter back on the mound after the reliever had retired a batter.

Richards was the visiting manager when the Orioles played their first game at Memorial Stadium in '54, but within months there was speculation he would come to the Orioles as the GM, replacing Arthur Ehlers. The Orioles needed to rebuild from scratch, as Richards had done in Chicago. Richards, having managed for close to two decades, wanted to try running a front office, but Lane was entrenched in Chicago.

Clarence Miles received permission to interview Richards in August, and they struck a deal, announced in mid-September, with a surprising twist:

Richards would also become the manager, replacing Dykes. Lane said the Orioles had tampered, negotiating with Richards to be a manager while he was still under contract for the job in Chicago. But Lane also said he would not pursue the matter. He and Richards had recently feuded over personnel moves, and while Lane respected Richards, he was not opposed to seeing Richards go.

From the moment he signed until the day he left in '61, the "Wizard" was the undisputed king of the Orioles. His tenure was marked by distinctive trends. With help from a coaching staff that included pitching coach Harry Brecheen and loyal lieutenants Luman Harris and Al Vincent, he installed the pitching-and-defense philosophy that would become the Orioles' signature. He also revived the careers of many veteran pitchers, teaching them his favored "slip pitch"—a variation of the change-up—and emphasizing changing speeds and locations.

In the early years he traded players as if they were cards in a deck and spent wildly on "bonus baby" prospects, infuriating ownership. When he saw his catchers losing the war with Hoyt Wilhelm's knuckleball in '59 and '60, he invented the oversized catcher's mitt, starting with a model so huge it resembled a pizza plate before ultimately settling on a more functional model.

When he resigned to become GM of a National League expansion team in Houston—enabling him to live closer to his beloved pecan farm in Waxahachie—a Baltimore columnist described him as "mysterious, controversial, articulate, intelligent, cold, calculating, charming, withdrawn—a paradox." That was Paul Rapier Richards.

BROOKS ROBINSON: "I thought he was the best. In all my years in baseball, I don't know anyone who knew more about the game. Richards not only knew how to run the game, but he knew every position and what made that position tick. I respect him more than any manager I ever played for. Earl [Weaver] always gave me more laughs than anyone in the game, and Earl certainly deserves to be in the Hall of Fame. He had a lot of wonderful traits. But he learned a lot from Richards.

"There's a few guys that really didn't like [Richards] because of his way and certain theories he had, and you could get on an elevator in the morning and he wouldn't even acknowledge you. But I thought he was God, really. I just think he knew more about the game. The rap against him was that he never won anywhere, but he put together the Chicago team that went to the World

Series in the late '50s, and he basically put together the Orioles. He believed in playing the game like it was supposed to be played. He believed in defense and pitching and hoped we'd score some runs."

ERNIE HARWELL: "I'd been the Atlanta correspondent for *The Sporting News*, so I knew Richards when he managed in Atlanta. I was a great admirer of his. I thought Paul was a fantastic baseball man. I think he probably felt that sooner or later they were going to have a winner in Baltimore, but it was going to take time. Richards used to say, 'Someday, when the Orioles win the World Series, they'll stand at home plate and people will remember that I started this franchise, started building it, and that I was responsible for some of these guys that are here.' And that's what happened."

DAVE PHILLEY: "I played eighteen years in the major leagues, played under a lot of managers, and he was probably the smartest. He was strictly baseball. There wasn't too much friendship involved. I guess he liked me. He traded for me twice. One time I made him look like a genius. We were playing Cleveland, and Al Rosen was the hitter, and the tying run was on third. Richards brought me in from the outfield and put me at third, and Rosen hit a dart right at me. I caught it and threw from there to second base for a double play. Then he came out and moved me right back out to the outfield. I made him look like a genius. Rosen was going to pull the ball, and Richards knew that. Freddie Marsh was playing third for us, and he wasn't sure Marsh would get in front of it, but he knew I would."

"SKINNY" BROWN: "Paul was a hard person to know. He didn't say much. He liked my work ethic and determination to win. He was a great field manager. He was way ahead of a lot of the other managers—one of the first I knew to anticipate moves, what the other guy was going to do. You know, 'If I do this, what will the other guy do?' He used what players he had to their best ability. Got the most out of them. Always seemed to be able to take old players and get more out of them. A great teacher. A stern taskmaster. It was his way and no other way. In spring training one year I was working with younger pitchers, and we were teaching them how to get over to second base if they were being bunted over. Paul had a certain way he wanted them to take a lead, take two steps. He said, 'Brownie, go show 'em.' I said, 'Your way, Paul?' He said, 'You know it's my way or no way at all.' "

GEORGE ZUVERINK: "Harry Dorish once said, 'I say two things to Paul Richards every year: hello in spring training and good-bye in the fall.' He wasn't antisocial, just quiet. But I loved him. I learned a ton. In the spring we'd go over the same things over and over—backing up, covering first base. Basics. When I was with Detroit and Cleveland we didn't do nearly as much of that stuff. He worked you hard. You got a sunburned tongue from the way it was sticking out all the time."

ERNIE HARWELL: "The players were scared to death of him. He was stand-offish with them. He usually didn't have too much truck with them. At Buffalo, they were playing a doubleheader, and a shortstop made three or four errors in the first game, and Richards got him out between games of a doubleheader to take grounders. And then if the guys weren't hustling, he'd have the whole team run up and down the steps of the grandstand after a game. They couldn't do that now. But he was a good teacher, and they did respect his strategy and knowledge."

HARRY DALTON: "He was so quiet, you never knew what he was thinking. He would walk in the [farm] office, say hi, sit down at a desk and pull out a clipboard with stats from one of the farm clubs on it, sit there for ten minutes looking at those, put it back on the wall, and walk out. That'd be our conversation for the day. You'd sit there saying to yourself, 'Did I say something wrong?' "

JERRY WALKER: "He was my first manager, and looking back and seeing the way most managers are, he was different. I didn't know that. I just thought that was the way all managers were—the way he communicated with players, or didn't communicate. He'd be sitting on the bench right next to you, get up and walk over to a coach, and tell the coach to go tell you to go to the bullpen. Some of the players who had been around, they didn't care for that. But he was in charge. I remember him telling one player he'd better straighten up or he'd send him so far out it would take ten dollars to send a postcard to him."

BILLY GARDNER: "One night I made an error, and the Yankees beat us, and they left the lights on, and I went back into the clubhouse, and Luman Harris said, 'Come on, we're going back out to hit some ground balls to you.' You knew where that had come from."

BOB HALE: "One night I was down at the far end of the bench, bottom of the ninth, we're losing 2–1, and the first two men got on base. He gave [Orioles shortstop] Willy Miranda the bunt sign, and Miranda missed. Strike one. Then he gave the bunt sign again, and Miranda missed again. Strike two. All of a sudden I hear faintly, 'Hale, go hit.' I said, 'Right now?' He said, 'Right now.' I went up; the first pitch was a high fastball; I swung and hit the ball down the left-field line. Both runners scored, and we won 3–2."

GEORGE ZUVERINK: "When I was the main relief pitcher I threw a heavy ball, and when Richards wanted someone hit, really drilled, he'd bring me in. One time he brought me in and said, 'I want you to hit this guy right between the eyes.' I was kind of pale. I threw the first pitch high and inside, and the ump called it a strike. I thought, 'I don't want a strike now.' The next pitch I drilled him in the arm.

"Another time we were in Chicago and Bill Fischer was pitching against us, and Paul wanted me to hit him. We're still in the game, like 2–1. I got him out, and Paul screamed at me, 'When are we going to get a pitcher with some guts?' I said, 'I got all the guts you want.' I didn't pitch for ten days. I said to Harry Brecheen, 'I think I made a mistake.' He said, 'You did.' "

JOE GINSBERG: "Richards was a very religious man, but he'd come up to the umpire and say, 'Sir, do you know who I am?' The guy'd say, 'Come on, Paul.' And Paul would say, 'I am the manager of this club. And not only am I the manager, I'm the general manager.' Then he'd use unbelievable language, just incredible. His first couple of words would get him tossed, and then he'd get his money's worth. He was a very soft-spoken man, but once he got mad, look out. He'd start slow and soft and get louder and worse. Then after he got thrown out, he'd call me in from the bullpen and say, 'You stand there,' and he'd go stand in the runway and give me the bunt sign and the hit sign and take sign. I'd turn around and give them to Luman [Harris], who would turn around and give them to the guys on the field."

MARV BREEDING: "I've never met anyone like him, before or since. He was one of the nicest guys, but when he went after the umpire he said words I'd never heard before. He didn't just run out there, either. He'd wait an inning after something made him mad, and then he'd come out, and you could pretty well bet he'd be gone. Maybe he waited to get his vocabulary straight. You never heard him say a cussword otherwise. He saved it for the umps. But he was smart. He'd put in defensive replacements in the sixth inning, and they'd win the game in the ninth."

Bill Wight: "He added to the length of my career. He helped me with changing speeds and that slip-pitch thing. He emphasized changing speeds and varying pitches and concentrating and getting ahead of the hitter. Even though I'd pitched a long time, he gave you a system you could use. If you missed a pitch, what can you come back with? My best pitch was a hard sinker. He'd have me throw that and come back with a cross-seam fastball. He got me thinking. If he liked you, you were in good shape. He had definite likes and dislikes. He wasn't universally liked. I got on with him good. I learned from him."

Billy O'Dell: "He taught me a lot about pitching. He was always talking to me about changing speeds, which I did a poor job of at that time. He was always after me. I didn't do it well until after I left Baltimore (in a trade in November of '59)."

"Skinny" Brown: "If you go back and look at his career, the White Sox weren't a contender when he got there, and he built them into a contender and left. Then he went to Baltimore and built them into a contender and left. Then he went to Houston and built them into a contender and left. He did it in three places. He was a better teacher and learner than a winning manager. His specialty was building a team more than winning. He really loved to teach."

Joe Ginsberg: "He liked to teach rather than win the pennant. He liked to develop players. Naturally everyone liked to win, but he was more of a teacher, a manager who would get you ready to play. I'd played four or five years in the major leagues before I got there, and I learned more from him about catching than anyone else."

George Kell: "I played with him in Detroit. He was the catcher there. He left in '47 and went to Buffalo to manage, and then when he got the job with the White Sox, he traded for me right away. Then he traded for me again in Baltimore. He was a very intelligent baseball man—one of the best managers I ever played for. But he never managed a real good ball club. He just never had a club like the Yankees. He could never prove himself that way. He was always rebuilding. I think he got tired of it. In Baltimore it was all kids and veterans. Most of them were older than I was even, and on the way out."

FRED MARSH: "Paul was a good manager, and I played for some terrible ones. It looked like he had a headache about half the time by the end of the game, he was thinking so much and trying to be ahead and figure out what the other team had on the bench. And he could take players that others couldn't get anything out of, and get a lot. He was tough on you. There was a look that fathers used to give their kids, where you just backed off when you saw it. Richards had it. Guys who were kind of happy-go-lucky, when Paul looked at them, they got down to business. If you didn't get the job done, you got that look. I was a good bunter, and one time he put me up to sacrifice, and I popped up. I came back to the bench, and he said, 'I thought you could bunt.' That was all. You didn't dare not do your best. But when it came to winning a pennant, he'd be so demanding everyone was too tight to win."

ERNIE HARWELL: "The first time I really met him I went up to his hotel room, and he was complaining about his constipation. First time I met him! Jack Dunn ate breakfast with him every morning, and he'd say, 'If Paul could just have a beer at breakfast instead of prune juice, he'd be a lot better guy to be around.' But I liked him. He had a nice wife and a daughter, an apartment out near the park. And he loved to eat. We'd go into Detroit and get off the train and he'd go straight to Mario's, a big Italian place. A lot of times he'd get the media together for meals. He said, 'Let's get everybody and go over to Mario's,' and when we were through he'd say, 'Well, Dunny, take care of the check. I've got to go to the park.' And he probably put everybody on his expense account when Dunny paid.

"One time at the All-Star break he said, 'Why don't you get my golf clubs and bring 'em out,' meaning to where we were going after the break. He wanted you to do things for him. He would take advantage of you that way, sort of trample on you if you let him. He built this big thing we called the coffin, this thing he put his golf clubs in, a heavy trunk that looked like a coffin for a midget. And he said to me, 'Do you mind if I put your name on it so people will think it's your clubs?' I said, 'You're not going to fool anybody, but go ahead if you want.' Everyone knew he played.

"He was a good golfer, took his clubs on the road and played almost every day. I played with him a lot. We'd go to Chicago, get off the train, and Paul'd say, 'Dunny, we'll have breakfast while you go get a car, and then we'll go out to Medinah [Country Club] and play.' So we'd get a car and meet after breakfast, go out to the suburbs, play eighteen holes, have lunch, then come back and go to the ballpark about two. That was the routine. And usually Richards would win some money, so he had a free lunch. The foursome would vary, but it was always Richards and somebody. We might even have two or three foursomes if we were home, and Paul would have bets with everybody, and he'd know where he stood on each bet at all times. He had an amazing mind.

"He'd lean on guys he knew who were members of certain clubs. He'd get out and play for free. One time in Cleveland, Paul knew a guy who was a member of a club, and Paul worked a deal where we got to play there. We came up to a par-three, and Richards was very impatient because some guys were on the green and wouldn't get off. They were putting. Paul said, 'Let's go ahead and hit.' He hits one, and it bounces up right at the green, and a guy is almost hit who's putting, and he looks back and gives Paul an angry look, and it turned out to be the father of the guy Paul knew who got him on the course. Paul would do things like that. Some clubs wouldn't let him play. I don't know whether anybody actually barred him or not, but at some places he was sort of persona non grata."

JOE GINSBERG: "He could do things and get away with it because he was smart. One time Billy Pierce was pitching, and he moved Billy to first for one batter, brought in a guy to get someone out, and then put Billy back on the mound to pitch. And then in spring training he'd have eight guys in the order. Just wouldn't use the pitcher's place. Trying to get his guys more at-bats, of course. And the other team wouldn't realize it for five or six innings and then they'd go, 'Hey, the pitcher never batted.' Paul'd say, 'What are they going to do to me? It's just an exhibition game.' He did all kinds of things like that."

GUS TRIANDOS: "Richards was great with pitching and certain areas of the game. The areas he had shortcomings in, he didn't get a guy to fill in for him. He fell a little short in evaluating talent. Casey Stengel was just outstanding at that, evaluating players. He was terrible on pitching but smart enough to let [pitching coach] Jim Turner handle pitching. Stengel could look at you one time and tell if you could run bases or throw or whatever. Richards was so absorbed in pitching. He was kind of an egomaniac. Not to the extent that he was a nutty professor. But he didn't really like to talk to people. After it was all over, you didn't understand it at the time, but you recognized he knew what he was doing."

WALTER YOUSE: "Richards was the one who put the Orioles in contention. He wasted some money on bonus babies, but he got the Orioles from the bottom to the top. Like Roosevelt and World War II—he wasted a lot of money, too, but he won the war. Richards was the same way. He wasted a lot of money, but he found some good ballplayers. And he knew all the angles in baseball. Every position. And he could teach them. I have to say, he was the best baseball man I ever saw. Earl Weaver was the best manager, but Richards was the best baseball man."

4

Any Warm Body

Paul Richards wasn't the "Wizard of Waxahachie" so much as "Hurricane Paul" early in his tenure in Baltimore, blowing constant change through the Orioles. In his first year he made the largest trade in baseball history and used fifty-six players in the '55 season, ten at third base alone. By the middle of the '56 season, all remnants of the St. Louis Browns were gone. The roster changed so constantly that it was difficult to remember who was on the team. Asked to assess his pitching staff at one point in '55, Richards said, "Do you mean the one coming or the one going?"

It all started with a trade that stunned baseball. The original deal between the Orioles and Yankees involved a dozen players and triggered several side deals in the coming months. Seventeen players ultimately changed teams. The Orioles sent Bob Turley, Don Larsen, Billy Hunter, and several others to the Yankees, in return receiving a slew of players including outfielder Gene Woodling, shortstop Willy Miranda, catcher/first baseman Gus Triandos, catcher Hal Smith, and pitchers Harry Byrd and Jim McDonald.

It wasn't Richards's best trade. Turley became a 20-game winner for the Yankees, and Larsen made baseball history by throwing a perfect game in the '56 World Series. They would go on to win a combined 156 games after the trade, providing the kind of quality pitching the Orioles spent the rest of the '50s trying to develop.

But the deal had a positive side. Miranda, a light-hitting, slick-fielding, lighthearted Cuban, became an everyday player and a fan favorite. Triandos emerged as the Orioles' first slugger after moving to catcher in '56. Woodling stayed only briefly in '55, but he returned in '58 as a clutch-hitting rightfielder. Regardless of its merits, the trade opened up the roster for a necessary overhaul.

BILLY HUNTER: "I was watching boxing on TV in December of '54, living on Anneslie Road, and I got a call from New York. It was Milton Richman, the writer. He called to tell me, before it was announced, that I was involved in some big trade Richards and [Yankees GM George] Weiss had pulled off at Pimlico or someplace. I don't know if that was the case, but all sorts of guys went in both directions. What it was, really, was the Yankees wanted Turley. And they got him."

MIKE BLYZKA: "I went from Baltimore to New York in the deal. The way I found out, I was working in a clothing store in Baltimore, and I read about it in the paper."

GUS TRIANDOS: "I wasn't sorry to get traded. I wasn't going to play in New York with Yogi Berra there. And Casey [Stengel] wasn't crazy about me because he didn't think I could hit to the opposite field. I think the only thing he liked about me in the end was that I helped him get Turley."

JOE GINSBERG: "Miranda was a fun guy and a great shortstop. I'm afraid he didn't hit as well as he should. I called him a switch swinger, not a switch hitter. He didn't hit much. But what fun he was. Richards would get on him about something and turn around and go back to his office, and Willy would stand up and imitate Paul. He was a good mimic. Only, of course, he didn't speak the language too well. You can imagine this little guy from Cuba imitating a tall guy from Texas. Gosh, he made us laugh. Willy taught me how to count in Spanish, and he also taught me how to swear. I knew all the swearwords. I liked to tease the Latin guys. They'd be talking and I'd go, 'Hey, I heard that.'"

ERNIE HARWELL: "They said Willy hit left, right, and seldom. He was a good kid, though. Our family was going to have a barbecue one time, and we invited Willy, and he asked if he could bring his wife. And then he brought his wife and three or four kids and his father-in-law and everybody else. But I really liked him; he had personality. He told me he'd learned English by going to the movies. He'd see four or five movies a day. A great shortstop, he was. But no power at all."

DICK WILLIAMS: "Miranda was a hell of a nice guy, funny guy, had a great arm and covered a lot of ground. But you never could take him out on a double play because he was always going somewhere. He didn't like the pitter-patter. He was out of there. Same way at the plate. He'd bail out on both sides."

Many players Richards acquired had played for him in Chicago or the minors. Hal "Skinny" Brown had pitched for him in Seattle and Chicago, Jim Wilson in Seattle, Harry "Fritz" Dorish in Chicago. Richards also had a coterie of favored position players he tapped, bringing in utility man Fred Marsh and All-Star third baseman George Kell, who came to Baltimore in '56, near the end of his career.

Richards also developed new favorites in Baltimore. He acquired outfielder Dick Williams three times, in '56, '58, and '61. He traded away Woodling and catcher Clint Courtney but later brought them back. Outfielder Dave Philley came from Cleveland in '55, was traded to the White Sox in '56, and came back in '60.

Despite all the changes, the Orioles were no better in '55. They opened the season with six straight losses as twenty-one pitchers allowed 57 runs, and they went on to lose 97 games, finishing seventh again. Their home-run total (54) was still the league's lowest, and they hit just .240 as a team. Richards tried nineteen starting pitchers and never settled on a rotation. Jim Wilson, a curveball specialist, went 12–18 and made the All-Star team. Ray Moore, Erv Palica, Bill Wight, and reliever George Zuverink also pitched well at times.

ERNIE HARWELL: "There was terrible turnover. A lot of the guys who came in were over-the-hill—Dizzy Trout, Billy Cox—a lot of guys who just couldn't play anymore. Anyone who could breathe, Paul was bringing them in. They were just passing through on their way to retirement. Trout, I believe, had already quit pitching with the Tigers and had gone to the radio booth, and he came out of retirement, signed with the Orioles, and actually pitched several games, then went back to the booth."

GEORGE ZUVERINK: "We had to start from scratch. Paul picked this and that guy off the waiver wire. Actually, he had good success at that. He'd take Harry Brecheen and go down to the bullpen and try to teach 'em that slip pitch. He tried to get me to throw what they call a 'slurve' now. You'd get the ball between two fingers and jam it in there. Some guys started throwing real well.

"But it was a situation where someone would be there one day and gone the next. You'd come in and they'd say, 'Well, Joe was let go.' Richards would trade for some guys, keep them for a couple days, and send them somewhere else. We had Cal Abrams, who had played in Brooklyn, and a ball was hit off the right-field wall, and he didn't chase it, and Paul called time and took him out, and that was the end of Cal Abrams. If you didn't hustle, you were gone. But if you hustled and gave 100 percent, he'd stick with you even if you screwed up."

FRED MARSH: "They brought in a lot of guys who would be there a while and then disappear. Gosh, he used a lot of players. I remember one day we had five different first basemen."

DAVE PHILLEY: "We had a bunch of guys who were just hanging on in the major leagues. We were trying to win. But there were a bunch of guys who weren't really big-league ballplayers."

BOB KENNEDY: "Paul got rid of the older guys from '54. We were struggling. I couldn't do anything right. I'd hit a ball hard, and it'd start a double play. I got traded to Chicago. When I came back [to Baltimore] the fans booed me like crazy. I played left field in the first game of a doubleheader, and they were giving it to me. Minnie Minoso started in left in the second game, and he got hurt, and Marty Marion was managing [Chicago], and I knew what he was going to do. I hid in the dugout, back where he couldn't see me. He looked all over the place and finally shouted, 'Kennedy, I know you're here some-where!' I had to go out and play left again. They just started booing again."

DAVE PHILLEY: "I roomed with Jim Wilson. He was a real curveball pitcher. He could throw it all day long and not hurt himself. Had two or three dif-ferent kinds of curveballs. We went to Chicago when the Orioles traded us for Kell and won about eight in a row. He threw curveballs that looked like they were out there [and hittable], and it was like he yanked the string."

BILL WIGHT: "Jim Wilson had been with Paul in Seattle and picked up that slip pitch. He didn't have a good fastball, but he had great control and a good curveball. Then he'd throw that slip pitch. We didn't have a bad pitching staff, actually, with him and George Zuverink, who threw a really good hard sinker."

BOB HALE: "In '55 I was hitting .355 at [Class B] York, and the Orioles came and played us in an exhibition game in June. I had a good night, and we won 13–1. Brooks [Robinson] was on that team with me, Brooks and Willie Tasby and a couple of other guys. A good team. A week later I was still at York, and the business manager came out to my house on July 4 and said Paul Richards wanted me to come to Baltimore and take batting practice. We had a doubleheader that day. They said I might miss the afternoon game, but I might be back for the night game.

"I drove down to Baltimore, and they gave me a uniform. Luman Harris told me to take batting practice with the pitchers. Then he told me to take batting practice with the bench. Still hadn't met Paul Richards. Then I took batting practice with the starters, and Luman walked up and said, 'Paul wants to see you in his office.' I went in, and he had a contract in his hand. He was going to start me in a half-hour against the Washington Senators. The contract was for a minimum salary, six thousand dollars. I was making four-hundred dollars a month at York. I signed immediately, played in the game, and went one for four. After the game I drove back to York and told my wife, 'Pack up, we're going to Baltimore.'"

The team took its first steps forward in '56—a sixth-place finish and 69 wins. By the end of that season the outline of an everyday lineup that would last several years was evident. The first baseman was Bob Boyd, a .293 career hitter. The second baseman, Billy Gardner, was a heady veteran who in '57 would lead the American League in doubles and earn the Orioles' Most Valuable Player award. Miranda was the shortstop. Kell, a former AL batting champion and future Hall of Famer, played third. Bob Nieman hit .322, with Dick Williams and Tito Francona, among those rotating around him in the outfield. Triandos had 21 homers and 88 RBI.

GEORGE ZUVERINK: "It was fun, although you never knew who was coming or going, and it seemed you were destined to stay in the second division. You had to grit your teeth. There weren't any free agents. You couldn't buy any good players. And you figured the Yankees were going to win every year. It was discouraging to compete against that. But you couldn't do anything about it."

ERNIE HARWELL: "Bobby Boyd was a fine line-drive hitter. They called him 'the Rope' because he hit so many liners, and he'd have a rope in his back pocket and pull it out and wave it when he got to the first base. Hit another rope, you know. One day he broke his arm—I think it was in Cleveland. Playing left field, he picked up a ball, just threw it back into the infield and broke his arm."

BILL WIGHT: "We did have some talent. Triandos was good. Nieman could really hit. Kell was solid. But there wasn't a lot of premier talent. Boyd was a good example. He was a good hitter, but first base is a power spot, and he didn't have enough. Overall we just didn't have enough power. And we were really short of speed. It was just a slow ball club. They used Skinny Brown as a pinch runner because he could run a little.

"It was a second-division club all the way. Paul picked up what he could. It wasn't a money club, either. They didn't buy players like [Boston's] Tom Yawkey did. So it was a slow process. We had a lot of guys on the way down rather than the way up. To build up a second-division club you needed young guys. We had too many veterans who weren't going to get any better. The fans were great. They accepted the fact that it was going to take a while to build the club up. They just wanted to see a good ball game."

Early in the '57 season Richards called the team "a bunch of clowns" after back-to-back losses in Washington. Insulted, the players responded with a surprisingly strong season—a 76–76 finish, good for fifth place, 21 games behind the pennant-winning Yankees. The offensive leaders were Boyd (.318), Gardner (79 runs), and Triandos and Nieman, the latter pair combining for 142 RBI. Richards, ever the tinkerer, brought in yet another wave of veteran pitchers, including Connie Johnson, a former Negro leaguer who won 14 games in '57, and Billy Loes, who had come from Brooklyn in '56.

DICK HALL: "Someone told me that Richards's theory early on was to try to get good pitching, which you can do, and then put a bunch of good outfielders out there. Every game would be close and you'd lose 4–2, but if you had a bad club the game would be close and it wouldn't look bad. If you started trying to outslug them, you'd lose 12–3."

BILL WIGHT: "The ballpark probably kept the scores down some. [Memorial Stadium] was just huge. It was a nice place and all, and if you kept it away from the foul lines you could pitch pretty good. But it was almost too far to center. The centerfielder had to play too deep. Pitchers like a good-sized park, but that was too far. [Jim] Busby looked like he was going to come back with the morning paper sometimes, he went so far out there. A lot of bloops dropped in front of him."

GUS TRIANDOS: "Richards was trying to rebuild the thing. He had a lot of ideas, and he made a few mistakes, and personally, I didn't like it. The park was big. Kept homers in. Richards signed some young kids, and some worked out and some didn't. He was in the process of building a team. It was a hell of an undertaking. You couldn't open your mouth. We signed year-to-year. In '55 I played first base then switched off at catcher [and first base] my second year. I hit .277 and .279 those first two years, then went strictly to catcher, and I don't think I hit over .250 after that."

GEORGE KELL: "Paul told me when he went to Baltimore, 'I'm going to trade for you and make you the manager, and I'm going to move into the front office as the GM.' When he traded for me, I assumed that was the way it would be. At that time I was really interested in managing. Then in '57, about midseason, he told me the owners had told him they wanted him to manage, that they'd hired him for that and no change would be made. I said that was OK. I was ready to retire anyway."

BILL WIGHT: "Kell helped us. He was a good fielder. That was when they were just bringing out batting helmets. They were optional at first. You had a choice of whether to wear them. Kell never used one, and he'd dive into the ball—a great fastball hitter; he could pull anyone foul. Then one day he said, 'You know, I think I'll wear a helmet tomorrow.' The next day he got hit in the head. Popped right in the head. That started other guys using the helmets."

DICK WILLIAMS: "Paul kept me in the major leagues, traded for me three times in all. The first time, I played four different positions for him during a doubleheader and went six for nine. That first time was short-lived. I got there in '56 and got traded in '57—traded to Cleveland even-up for Busby. We were in Cleveland at the time, and I just switched locker rooms. I roomed with Billy Gardner, and I just stayed with him the whole series, even after I'd been traded."

JOE GINSBERG: "When I got traded to Baltimore I hit two line drives that were caught, and then I went oh for 22. The people said, 'Hey, what a trade. The guy hasn't gotten one hit.' So we were playing Boston, and I finally got a hit, and they stopped the game and gave me the ball. That was the kind of atmosphere there was. I played against right-handed pitching, Gus against left-handed pitching. We didn't contend with the Yankees, but we didn't finish last, either. I played with seven clubs in my career, and Baltimore was my favorite.

I loved the food, the atmosphere, the town, the people. A couple of [off-seasons] I stayed and worked for the Mary Sue Candy Company. Johnny Unitas did the commercials, and I did the work. I sold for them."

BOB HALE: "I was twenty-one and just married. We lived on York Road right by 33rd Street. I could walk to the park. Richards had let a pitcher go, and I took his apartment. A lot of the young guys lived in a rooming house by the stadium. I loved it. The people were real good because it was a new club. They wanted to keep us there. They treated us well. They understood that Richards was trying to rebuild, and they were good enough fans that they could wait. It was a nice situation. If we won one of three from the Yankees in New York, Richards would buy us steak dinner on the train back to Baltimore. As the years went on we had to win two of three to get the steak because we got better."

GEORGE ZUVERINK: "I lived right in the neighborhood, beyond the center-field fence a couple of blocks. The big thing that happened was when the club would send you out for an autograph session and you'd get fifty dollars. You thought that was pretty neat: 'Wow, fifty dollars!' "

FRED MARSH: "I lived a half-mile from the park, and all around the stadium the people had azalea shrubs, and those things were blossoming, and that was beautiful. It smelled up the whole neighborhood. I always remember that. It was just beautiful. The odor was all over the place. You could smell it when you were coming up to bat. That didn't happen in any other parks."

GEORGE KELL: "That was the only place in my career where I walked to the park. I don't remember anyone stopping me. They probably didn't know who I was. But I enjoyed Baltimore. The fans were great."

ERNIE HARWELL: "Baltimore was a nice place for baseball in the '50s. The people were so happy to have a major league franchise that almost anything was acceptable for the first several years. In the time I was there [through '59], they had one year where they were .500 and every other year they were under .500. And they drew fairly well. They'd draw a million or close, fall below a little bit. But a million was pretty much a standard at that time. The fans were satisfied they were in the big leagues, and they saw the other teams come in.

"The guys stayed around a lot longer than they do now. You didn't have as much movement with free agents as you do now, and the fans got to know the players like Miranda and Triandos and Brooks and people like that. They established themselves, and a lot of guys made their homes there and became part of the community, and I think all of that led to the positive feeling that [the fans] had about the team."

Billy Loes was a right-hander who had made a name as a humorous character with the Dodgers; one time he had picked the Yankees to beat his team in the World Series. His career was in jeopardy because of arm problems when the Orioles obtained him, but he pitched so well in '57 that he made the All-Star team and threw three scoreless innings. Overall he made 121 appearances for the Orioles, mostly out of the bullpen, before being traded to San Francisco in November of '59.

Off the field, Loes was one of the Orioles' first eccentrics—a shrewd, slightly mysterious character who believed in the power of mediocrity; any player who had too much success, he said, was setting himself up to fail. He also was one of the few Orioles who challenged Richards. After being suspended for an incident in '58 in which he bumped an umpire, Loes nodded toward Richards and said, "I've been suspended for making God look bad."

GEORGE ZUVERINK: "Billy was a strange guy. He was content winning 8 or 9 games a season. He said, 'If you win 10, they'll want you to win 12. If you win 15, they'll want you to win 20. But if you do an average job, they'll leave you alone.' He didn't want to put pressure on himself. That was just the way he was. He had good stuff. He could have had a much better record."

CONNIE JOHNSON: "Billy could pitch better than anyone. When he wanted to win, he won. He threw everything—a big curve, a fastball, slider, change-up. But he was never going to win more than 12 or 13 games. He told me, 'If I win more than that they'll cut my salary when I don't win that many.' When I was winning 15 games [for the Orioles in '57] he told me, 'Johnson, you're winning too many. They're going to cut you. They do things like that.' And you know what? He was right. I did get [a salary] cut after the next year.

"He wasn't crazy. But one time the sportswriters asked him about an umpire, and he said, 'Oh, that guy's blind.'

"And he kept all his paychecks. I remember that. He wouldn't take his checks to the bank. Won his eating money playing cards. He knew how to play cards. Didn't wear expensive clothes. Told all the young guys getting the bonus money to put it in the stock market. He wasn't wrong about that."

GUS TRIANDOS: "Billy didn't like to talk to some people. If he didn't want to talk to someone, he'd just stare off out in left field. The guys thought he was a little flaky. But he was a smart guy. He just didn't like to show it. He had a great arm when he first came up, then ended up just getting by on his smarts."

BILLY GARDNER: "We were in Boston, bases loaded, Ted Williams up. Loes comes halfway down to the plate and says to Ted, 'You've been my idol all my life. Please don't beat me.' Ted just started laughing. The first pitch, boom, strike. Ted's still laughing. Next pitch, boom, ball. The count comes to three and two, and Loes throws one right down the middle. The ump calls it ball four. We come out of the dugout, and Gus is bitching, and the ump says, 'The man didn't swing, did he?' That was the kind of respect Ted had. The ball was right down the middle of the plate."

HARRY BRECHEEN: "One time [Loes] told me, 'I could throw really hard before I hurt my arm.' I said, 'You could?' He picked up a ball and threw it one hundred miles per hour and said, 'That's the way I used to throw.' So he could still do it. I guess he just didn't want to."

5

Bonus Babies

Before baseball's amateur draft was established in 1965, any team could sign any player. In an effort to limit expenditures and keep the wealthier teams from signing all the top players, the major leagues employed a "bonus baby" rule that took different shapes during the '50s. When the Orioles joined the American League in '54, any player who signed for a bonus of more than four thousand dollars had to stay on the major league roster for two seasons.

The rule was a well-intentioned early version of a salary cap, but it was flawed. Teams devised nefarious ways to get around it, paying players under the table or giving extra bonus money to their relatives, etc. The rule also was devastating to the careers of many young players, forcing them to spend key developmental years on a major league bench.

That didn't prevent the Orioles from diving deep into the bonus baby pool. Free agency was still two decades away, and it was impossible to build a winner from scratch with fringe players acquired on waivers or in trades. The Orioles' only hope for escaping the second division was to grow some young talent of their own.

Billy O'Dell, a pitcher from South Carolina, was the club's first bonus baby. He signed in June of '54 and spent the rest of the season in the major leagues, then he went on military leave for most of two years and rejoined the club in '57. He never played a day in the minor leagues and went on to pitch for thirteen years in the majors. (The Orioles traded him before the '60 season.)

BILLY O'DELL: "I signed for twelve thousand five hundred dollars, plus they paid me sixty-five hundred for the remainder of the '54 season. I reported in June, when the club was in Boston. I was twenty-one years old and scared to death. Weighed about 152 pounds. [Orioles manager Jimmy] Dykes was an old-school thinker. He thought you had to weigh 200 and have five years of experience. I sat around until August until I got into a game in a doubleheader with the Senators. The crowd went wild when I came in. I walk Jim Busby on four pitches, then the next guy hit into a double play, and I struck the next guy out."

After Richards took over in '54, the Orioles signed a whole flock of bonus babies. The club's board of directors had allotted him a sizable budget of two hundred fifty thousand dollars for bonuses and contracts in '55, but it didn't take him long to exceed that. Richards signed five bonus babies in '55 and added them all to the Orioles' major league roster. Assistant GM Jack Dunn joked about Richards, "He's the only guy I know who was given an unlimited budget and exceeded it."

Most of the initial scouting was done by Claude "Dutch" Dietrich, one of Richards's trusted aides. When Dietrich found a prospect, he called in Richards to make the final decision. Richards left the major league club to go on several scouting missions during the '55 season, juggling his roles as manager and GM.

His first signing was Jim Pyburn, an infielder from Auburn University. Envisioning a star third baseman, Richards gave him a thirty-thousand-dollar signing bonus and a three-year contract worth eighteen thousand dollars, for a total package of forty-eight thousand dollars—double the contract size of many of the Orioles' veterans. Pyburn, who also had played football at Auburn, jumped right to the major leagues, making his debut in the fourth game of the '55 season. Within weeks Richards switched him to the outfield, admitting Pyburn couldn't "go to his left, come in on a groundball, or throw underhanded."

Richards then reeled in Bruce Swango, an eighteen-year-old pitcher from Welch, Oklahoma, who had averaged 17 strikeouts a game and, according to Richards, was "far enough along that he has a chance to make the big jump directly to the major leagues with very little coaching." Six other teams had pursued Swango before the Orioles signed him in May of '55. Swango had an easy smile and an infectious twang, but he was so wild his teammates were reluctant to take batting practice against him, and it turned out he couldn't throw a curveball or pitch in front of crowds. The Orioles abruptly released him after nine weeks, despite owing him thirty-six thousand dollars. He never reached the major leagues.

Meanwhile, three more bonus babies signed: Wayne Causey, an eighteen-year-old infielder from Monroe, Louisiana; Tex Nelson, a power hitter nicknamed "the Babe Ruth of Texas"; and Tom Gastall, a catcher from Boston

University. The addition of so many young players to the roster compromised the Orioles' chances of winning; no team, let alone a second-division mainstay, could overcome giving up one-fifth of the roster to player development. But "our future is the kids," Richards told reporters, so the club set up a training regimen for the bonus babies involving extra morning workouts focusing on fundamentals.

After the '55 season came a supreme embarrassment: Richards was fined twenty-five hundred dollars and the club was fined two thousand dollars for subverting the bonus baby rules. Tom Borland, a left-handed pitcher from Oklahoma A&M, had pitched for the club under an assumed name in a June exhibition game in York, Pennsylvania. Baseball commissioner Ford Frick told Richards that one more stunt such as that would get him suspended.

That symbolized the Orioles' luck with their first crop of bonus babies. Nelson couldn't hit a curveball and never hit a home run in three years with the Orioles. Causey collected only 51 hits in three years and was traded. (He later blossomed into a solid major leaguer, hitting .252 during an eleven-year career.) Gastall died near the end of the '56 season when a plane he was piloting crashed in the Chesapeake Bay. Pyburn hit .190 over three seasons, returned to the minor leagues, retired, and became a football coach.

The Orioles would soon become renowned for their ability to scout, sign, and develop young talent, but their first attempt was an expensive debacle.

WAYNE CAUSEY: "The day after my high school graduation, Detroit flew me and my dad in, and I worked out for a couple of days. When I got home Dietrich came over to my house and was really interested. He seemed to think Detroit had offered me a big contract, which they hadn't. He wouldn't accept that from me. He called Richards and said he needed a bonus to sign me. Richards called back that afternoon and told him how much to sign me for—a thirty-two-thousand-dollar bonus, plus eighteen thousand dollars for three years. My dad and I decided we couldn't turn that kind of money down."

JIM PYBURN: "I was scouted by several Orioles coaches, and they finally made the offer. I talked it over with [Auburn football coach] Shug Jordan, and he said, 'That sounds like a lot of money. I wouldn't want you to stay around if you're getting that much.' The [signing bonus] rule had its good and bad aspects. The good was you realized your dream of making the major leagues right away. I roomed with Skinny Brown, who'd roomed with Ted Williams in Boston, and he introduced me to Ted. I was just goggly-eyed. But [the rule] penalized the players. I never did understand it. They were worried about what the teams were doing, but the players suffered. I should have started out at A ball. I did OK, but I wasn't ready for the major leagues."

ERNIE HARWELL: "Paul was wheeling and dealing with a lot of phenoms that never became really good ballplayers. It was a bad rule for everybody, I think. It caused a lot of problems. There was a lot of resentment from the older guys because of the money, and because the young guys were taking away jobs from veterans. It was crazy. These kids should have been in the minors instead of sitting on the bench doing nothing."

BILLY GARDNER: "Those bonus babies made more money than I was making. But you couldn't say anything. There were only sixteen major league clubs, and jobs were hard to come by. We just wanted to stay in the majors. You were scared about that. I was the MVP on the Orioles in '57, played with a broken finger, and they sent me a contract for the next season for nineteen thousand dollars—a two-thousand-dollar raise. The bonus babies were signing bigger deals. I sent a letter back to Richards asking for a bigger raise. He sent me a letter back saying 'You can live very well on this in Triple A.' I signed. You didn't have a choice."

BILL WIGHT: "The Bruce Swango signing was when Paul decided he wasn't a very good scout. I think he decided on his own to give the kid the money. And the kid did throw hard. I saw him work out in Baltimore, and he looked good. Paul gave him what it took to get him. But he got burned. The kid couldn't get the ball over. Later on, when I was scouting for [Richards] he never went to a game by himself. He always went with three or four scouts and never gave an opinion until they gave their opinions. He was a brilliant baseball man, but he didn't have a knack for scouting. Either you can do it or you can't. It's a judgment thing. He found that out in Baltimore. He signed Nelson, whose bat was a little slow, and Pyburn, who had a bad back."

ERNIE HARWELL: "Dietrich signed Swango because he saw him pitch in a gym. The other scouts didn't like him at all, but the only time Dietrich saw him, Swango was pitching indoors, and his fastball sounded a lot faster than it was. You know, it would pop in the mitt, and the sound would echo in the gym. He could throw hard. But he didn't like crowds. He was allergic to crowds. If they had over five thousand people he couldn't pitch."

WAYNE CAUSEY: "Nelson and Swango and I were renting a place three blocks from the ballpark, an upstairs apartment. I felt bad for Bruce. He could throw hard, but he wasn't comfortable in front of a crowd, which isn't a good thing. After the Orioles released him, the Yankees picked him up and tried to make an infielder/outfielder out of him. He knocked around with them for a while. Nelson had a beautiful swing, and he was strong, but he just never could put it together. He'd hit a four hundred fifty footer every once in a while, but not too often.

"On most days we'd all work out in the mornings before night games. They'd announce it the night before—'all bonus babies on the field tomorrow at ten-thirty.' It'd be a full training session—hitting, running, throwing, and fundamentals. Like spring training, basically. All the coaches were there. I know they wished they'd never heard of a bonus baby. They put in an awful lot of extra time. The club was just trying to get its money's worth out of us.

"We were all in awe of Paul. We were playing the Yankees one night in New York, and Yogi Berra hit a high pop. I was at third, Miranda was at short, and I called it. But it was foggy, and when the ball came down I was fifteen feet away from it. Richards got hot. He said, 'When you call a ball, you catch it. If that happens again, I'm going to get some of that bonus money back.'"

GEORGE ZUVERINK: "As into fundamentals as Richards was, those bonus babies drove him crazy throwing behind runners and to wrong bases and such. They were out there all the time, working out. It seemed like they always had their uniforms on."

JIM PYBURN: "Richards had a brilliant baseball brain, but I don't think he knew how to work with young players quite as well. He was used to being around veterans. And he wanted to win right away. He was trying to build the club, bring in veterans. He was a very volatile guy. I know I wasn't used to the language involved. He was well respected and all, but when you try to mix a young club with older guys, there's going to be a problem."

Joe Hamper: "When the club came to Baltimore in '54 it was waffling around without any leadership, just these local investors who didn't know anything. We didn't spend money and didn't think big. We thought small. Then they figured they had to do something, so they brought in Richards. He was a very bright guy and he opened the cash box. They started spending money when he came here. A lot of it was spent foolishly, but it changed the whole thrust of the operation. The thinking wasn't major league before he got here, and he made it major league. He had the stature and the prestige in the industry. And the personal will."

Harry Dalton: "Paul helped us tremendously because the Browns' mystique, if you want to call it that, was a problem. They were losers in St. Louis—perennially at the bottom of the league—and when they came to Baltimore, there wasn't any spirit. Richards changed that. He shocked everybody when he started spending money. He would just get a call from Dutch Dietrich or one of his cronies saying, 'This kid, boy, you've got to sign him.' And we'd give him fifty thousand, seventy thousand, whatever it took. The Lairmore twins got a lot of money. Jim Pyburn. Paul spent so much so quickly that he shocked ownership into realizing that if you wanted to be competitive, this was what you had to do. They didn't like it, but it paid off because it got us off dead center."

Joe Hamper: "In '55, we spent money we wouldn't have dreamed of spending the year before. It was like a steamroller that got going. For someone in the financial end, like me, [Richards] was a nightmare. He wouldn't do anything the way it was supposed to be done, even if it was easier. He liked to create turmoil. He was intrigued by anything that was not in accordance with the rules.

"[Tom] Borland was a highly-regarded college pitcher, and Richards signed him to a major league contract for eighteen thousand dollars a year for two or three years. And we played in York, and Richards had him pitch for the Orioles under the name of Moreland. York pounded him. Clarence Miles was there and said to Paul, 'Boy, I hope you don't sign that kid.' Well, Richards got to thinking, 'Maybe this contract isn't such a good idea.' I think he talked to them and said, 'We'll get you the money, but we'll keep you in the minors.' But other clubs recognized him pitching for us and filed a protest. Frick sent the secretary of baseball down, and the guy found the original contract in Richards's office. Frick was going to throw Richards out of baseball, but Clarence Miles pleaded and got him off with a fine.

"We had some cases taken in front of the Internal Revenue Service. One guy we signed for ten thousand dollars, and somebody told him he didn't have to pay taxes on it. There was always something going on. In the office there was a safe-deposit box in the accounting department, and I don't know that Richards had a key, but he always indicated where the money should go. He just loved that kind of stuff."

The failure of the Orioles' first bonus babies didn't stop Richards from signing more prospects. Soon, he started getting better results. In '56 the Orioles signed shortstop Ron Hansen, pitcher Chuck Estrada, and outfielders Chuck Hinton and Fred Valentine—all future major leaguers whose contracts enabled them to start in the minor leagues. The '57 crop was even better, including four pitchers who would lead the Orioles' transformation into contenders—Milt Pappas, Jerry Walker, Jack Fisher, and Steve Barber.

WALTER YOUSE: "The Orioles weren't afraid to keep spending. Richards would spend it real easy. One time he asked me to bring a pitcher to Memorial Stadium, and work him out, and I did, and they offered him thirty thousand dollars right there. A boy out of Washington. That was a lot of money for a workout. But Dizzy Dean was out there, and he said to Richards, 'This boy can pitch here tonight.' Had a real good curveball. He turned the Orioles down, went to school, and later on signed with Detroit for five thousand dollars."

Jerry Walker was from Ada, Oklahoma, the home of Harry Brecheen. Milt Pappas, from Detroit, jumped straight to the major league starting rotation in '58. Steve Barber, from Takoma Park, Maryland, was signed in obscurity for a five-hundred-dollar bonus plus fifty dollars out of the petty-cash drawer at the Orioles' minor league spring training camp in Thomasville, Georgia. Six years later, he would become the Orioles' first 20-game winner.

WALTER YOUSE: "I was scouting for the Orioles part-time and coaching an American Legion team and a high school team. And Barber had pitched against my legion team a couple of times and then decided to go to the University of Maryland instead of signing with the pros. So I called over to Maryland and talked to Elton Jackson, who was coaching there, and I said, 'You ought to have a real good pitching staff over there this year.' And he said, 'Well, Barber just dropped out of school yesterday.' So I said, 'OK.' I got in touch with Barber real quick—called him on a Friday night and he pitched for my amateur team on Sunday, and I put him on a train that night for Thomasville, Georgia. They signed him down there. Sometimes you have to get lucky."

STEVE BARBER: "The deal at Maryland was if I got through the first semester I'd get a full scholarship, because so many guys on the baseball team were getting their scholarships and then fucking up and losing their scholarships. I was studying electrical engineering, and I didn't like it and it didn't like me, and I decided maybe I'd be in Air Force ROTC and be a fighter pilot. But I just dropped out and was going to work as an electrician. About twelve of sixteen teams had been after me out of high school, and I'd told them we'd talk after school, and I guess Walter Youse heard through the grapevine that I'd dropped out of school, and he called and asked if I'd like to go to spring training. I said, 'Why not? I can always jerk [electrical] wire.'

"He offered me a one-thousand-dollar bonus, a Class A contract, and five hundred dollars a month, but he also said, 'Maybe you can do better on your own.' I said, 'I can't do any worse.' So I went to spring training in Thomasville. They had nine minor league teams there. I was like number 285 on the roster. I was there for about three weeks as a free agent, and I ended up getting a five-hundred-dollar bonus, fifty dollars on the spot, and a Class-D contract and two hundred and twenty-five dollars a month. The fifty dollars, which sealed the deal, was because they were going to send me to Paris, Texas, and I said I wanted to go home before I went there. But I was out of money. The fifty dollars got me the bus ticket home. Harry Dalton reached into the petty-cash drawer and pulled it out. And I signed."

JERRY WALKER: "When I signed, the four-thousand-dollar rule was in effect—if they gave me more, I had to stay with the major league club for two years. Baltimore was the only club willing to do that, so I signed and came to Baltimore and spent that year ['57] there. There was a lot of talk that other clubs in prior years had given players money under the table to get around the four-thousand-dollar rule. Or gave the parents a job or whatever. I just went to Baltimore, worked out, came home, and signed.

"We started working. I threw a lot of batting practice and pitched when games got out of hand. I started a game in August and didn't get through the first inning. Finally I started throwing the ball around the plate. In September I got to start another game, and I got my first win. If there was resentment [from veterans] I didn't perceive it. They were very helpful, Connie Johnson and Skinny Brown, Billy Loes, Billy O'Dell. All those guys were extremely helpful. I'd heard about older guys, but to me they were very open.

"Then they did away with the four-thousand-dollar rule in '58, and I went to Knoxville, Class A, and had a real good year. I was 18–4. My time in the big leagues helped. Had I signed and gone to the minors, I don't think I would have had that kind of a year. Ron Hansen was with me in Knoxville. Chuck Estrada was there. I came up to Baltimore and pitched at the end of the year, and then I made the club in '59."

MILT PAPPAS: "The Tigers were courting me when I was in high school. They left me tickets, and I got to use their facility and clubhouse and everything. But I liked Paul Richards. Every time Baltimore came to Detroit, I worked out with the Orioles at Tiger Stadium. I liked the fact that he looked like he knew what he was doing with pitchers, and that he had a lot of patience.

"When I signed [with Baltimore] the Tigers were very upset. They thought that I'd gotten money under the table from Baltimore and that my dad had gotten a car. All kinds of innuendos were going around about what Baltimore did for me, all of which were totally false. The Tigers even asked to see a copy of my income tax statement. They were just very upset. And they offered me the worst deal of anybody, my hometown team.

"I went right to the major leagues, and none of my [Orioles] teammates would talk to me. I wore white socks one day—I was a kid; what did I know? All the veterans gave me hell. I fought with them more than anyone on the other team. They resented an eighteen-year-old being in the major leagues and taking a veteran's job. The only teammate really talking to me was Willy Miranda, who was quite a nice man.

"Paul Richards was very sharp. Three or four days after I got there, he asked me if my arm was sore, and I said no. Then he repeatedly asked me the question, and finally he said, 'You know, isn't your arm sore?' I was eighteen; what the hell did I know? I finally said, 'Oh, yeah, my arm's sore.' He put me on the disabled list and brought somebody else up to take my place. A couple of days later Detroit came in town to play us, and I was throwing batting practice, and I'm out there throwing ninety miles per hour, and Detroit called the commissioner's office and said, 'Why is this kid on the disabled list? He's out there throwing beebees.' They started a stink there, too.

"Baltimore had to take me off the disabled list and put me on the active roster, and that's when all this stuff started about getting money under the table. Just a lot of stuff was going on. I had no idea what the hell was going on. I was eighteen years old, and I didn't know anything about the inner workings of baseball. I was getting a very fast lesson from a very shrewd man by the name of Paul Richards."

6

Brooks Begins

In the midst of their bonus-baby shopping spree in the spring of '55, the Orioles signed a less-heralded prospect, Brooks Robinson, an infielder from Little Rock, Arkansas. The story was buried in the *Baltimore Sun*, played at the bottom of an inside page of the sports section.

The son of a fireman who played semipro baseball, Robinson was an unassuming Southerner who had dreamed of becoming a major leaguer. As a boy he shagged flies at his father's games, cut out newspaper articles featuring major leaguers, and wrote an essay in eighth grade about playing baseball for a living when he grew up. He was all-state in basketball at Little Rock's Central High School before it was integrated, playing well enough to draw a scholarship offer from the University of Arkansas. But baseball was his love.

Central didn't field a team, so Robinson played on the same American Legion team his father had played on years earlier. It was a top legion team that attracted many pro scouts. The Orioles heard about him from Lindsay Deal, who played for Paul Richards on the Atlanta Crackers in the late '30s and now lived in Little Rock. Dutch Dietrich was assigned to scout Robinson and came back with a thumbs-up. Fred "Bootnose" Hofmann, another Orioles scout who had come with the franchise from St. Louis, also recommended him.

The Orioles beat out a half-dozen other teams making a play for Robinson, with Arthur Ehlers, the deposed general manager now working as Richards's assistant, overseeing the signing.

BROOKS ROBINSON: "I was a second baseman in legion ball. I'd played midget league, junior league, intermediate league, and then I played four years of legion ball. The first three years it was the Little Rock Doughboys, and then the fourth year they had more kids so they split us up into a variety of teams. I was a pitcher, actually. I pitched and caught my whole life, and then

I was a second baseman for the last three years. We won the [legion] state championship in Arkansas, and Monroe won the state championship of Louisiana, so they had a regional tournament in Louisiana, and Wayne Causey was on the Monroe team. We got to the finals, and they had to beat us twice, and they did and went on to the sectionals.

"Causey and I both signed with Baltimore, but it was different. Causey signed for thirty thousand dollars. They were giving everyone a lot of money, the Orioles were. But that probably hurt Wayne more than it helped him in the end. I mean, who can play [in the majors] when they're eighteen years old? Those are pretty vital years, and you're just stuck [in the majors] not doing much. He was overmatched and didn't get the chance to play with kids or men his own speed.

"I signed for the minimum, four thousand dollars, and I got a major league contract. My dad and I had talked about the money, and for some reason thirty thousand dollars seemed to be the number. You know, if you got thirty thousand dollars then you should take it and go for the two years and sit on the [major league] bench. And if no one offered a lot of money, I mean like fifteen thousand dollars, then we'd take the four thousand dollars and play in the minors. Then, when we were talking to teams [about signing], no one was going to give me a lot of money. And only two teams offered me a major league contract—the Orioles and Cincinnati.

"Cincinnati had a wonderful gentleman by the name of Paul Florence who was the head scout and a terrific gentleman, with Cincinnati for his whole life. But Baltimore seemed like the place. Lindsay Deal went to church with my family and had written Paul and said, 'Hey, we've got a pretty good prospect here.' Freddie Hofmann and Claude Dietrich came in and watched me play. Legion ball. Also a couple of semipro teams I was playing for. They watched me play a couple of games, and Paul called my dad. In fact, my dad ended up scouting some for Houston after Richards got there. I don't know if that was part of the deal or not. But Richards said, 'Look, we're just starting. I mean, we got no players, not much ability, and we'll give you a chance to play here early.' I thought about that. They told me they'd bring me up at the end of the year and give me a chance to play. That made the difference.

"When I signed, Cincinnati protested, and I had to go to the commissioner's office. Ford Frick took me in there, and I'm eighteen years old, and they're saying, 'Do you swear to tell the truth, the whole truth, and nothing but the truth, so help you God?' You want to talk about scared. Someone from the Orioles went up there with me. Frick said, 'They say you got more than four thousand dollars,' and they read the riot act to me in there, and it scared me to death. I said, 'Well, I got four thousand dollars, that's my salary.' I also got a letter from the IRS asking about my salary and bonus. Cincinnati had alerted them, I guess. They were mad because they didn't get me. But nothing ever came of it. I mean, Richards was doing it by hook or crook, you know, money under the table and things like that. I heard all these rumors. I'm sure it probably happened. But he never got in trouble over me.

"They sent me to York, and I hit .331 that year right out of high school. I thought it was easy. I started out, played 50 games at second and then [York manager] George Staller and Richards decided I should move over to third base. That was my best position without a great deal of speed. Third base is a reflex position more than anything else, so they said, 'Well, move him over to third base.' So I played the last 50 games at third, and that's when I became a third baseman. They saw I could catch the ball. That wasn't any problem.

"They brought me to Baltimore with about two weeks to play, like they said, and that's when I found out real quick I wasn't ready. Actually they took me with them on a trip to Cleveland first. We went to Cleveland; they let me work out. That was the first big-league town I ever went to. I roomed with Hoot Evers. What a wonderful guy he was. We took a cab down to the ballpark in the morning, and it was just a short ride, and when he got in he said, 'Don't worry kid, I'll take care of the cab.'

"They put me in the lineup when we got back to Baltimore. Played a game against the Senators. I went 2 for 4. I went back that night to the Southern Hotel, called my parents, and said, 'Mom, Dad, 2 for 4, knocked in a run, this is my cup of tea. I don't know why I was down in York all year.' Then I went oh for 18 the rest of the year. And struck out 10 of those 18. I went to Boston and faced Frank Sullivan, a big, lanky guy, and he made me look terrible. I just remember thinking, 'This is unbelievable, what he's throwing.' But that was a good lesson to learn. I probably realized right then, 'Hey, you're lucky you took the four thousand dollars and went to play in the minors instead of taking the bonus and going to the major leagues.'"

ERNIE HARWELL: "The first time I ever saw him was when they brought him into Cleveland before they let him play. They put him out at second base for a workout or something, and he was sort of a skinny kid, didn't have much weight to him, and he was pretty easy prey for the pitchers. They'd just blow him down at the bat. He didn't have much power. He couldn't hit very well. But what a terrific kid. He was about eighteen, and he'd come out to our house and play catch with my kids. One of the nicest ballplayers I ever met. Just a nice young guy."

GUS TRIANDOS: "Brooks was a nice kid with a nice twang, but he was over-matched when he first got there. It scared the hell out of him. I kind of felt bad for him. You're eighteen, you grew up reading about the major leagues, and suddenly you're right there on the field. It scared the hell out of him, is what it did. I can't think of anyone who would have command of himself at that age."

JOE GINSBERG: "Brooks had this high speaking voice when he got here. He couldn't have a beer with us. He was too young. We'd take him with us and he'd drink a Coke. And he had that high voice. I said to him, 'How in the world are you going to be a big-leaguer with a voice like that? You better catch a cold or something.'"

BROOKS ROBINSON: "That winter I played winter ball in Colombia, South America. We had thirteen guys from the Orioles organization, and we all lived in a big house, and we had a couple of maids that took care of everything. Fred Hofmann was our manager, and we drove him crazy. It was fun. What an experience. I was eighteen. Tito Francona was there, and Causey was there for a while. Earl Wilson hit me in the head [with a pitch] one night. I was lucky. That year [in the minors] all we'd worn was a little plastic liner we put in our hats. When we got to South America, that's when batting helmets came out, so we wore 'em. I had one on when Earl hit me. It scared the hell out of me and put a little knot on my head. I think the ball bounced over the roof."

Robinson spent '56 in the Texas League, playing for the Orioles' Double-A affiliate in San Antonio. It was his first full pro season, and he hit .272 in 154 games, with nine home runs and 74 RBI. For the second straight year, he came to Baltimore at the end of the season and didn't hit much (.227 in 44 at-bats). The next year he was on the Orioles coming out of spring training and played in the early part of the season, but then he injured his knee, underwent surgery, and went back to San Antonio.

The Orioles' third baseman in '56 and '57 was George Kell, a future Hall of Famer, also from Arkansas, who took Robinson under his wing, introducing the teenager to good restaurants and Broadway shows. They talked for hours, with Kell relating his experiences from many years in the major leagues and Robinson soaking up every word.

George Kell: "Brooks and I were raised ninety miles apart, same background, same family life, same church, same values. I didn't know about him when I came to the Orioles. I was gone from Arkansas when he was playing American Legion ball in Little Rock. When I got traded to the Orioles after the season started in '56, Hoot Evers said, 'Do you know Brooks Robinson?' I said no. He said, 'He's just like you, one of the finest fellas you'd ever want to meet. He was with us in the spring.' I said, 'Where is he now?' Hoot said he was in San Antonio. He came up later in '56 and opened with us in '57. He played third and I played first against left-handers. Against righties I'd play third. We spent a lot of time together. I think I helped show him how a major leaguer was supposed to live. That might have helped his adjustment.

"I retired after the '57 season. Richards wanted me to play another year or two because he said Brooks wasn't ready. I thought he looked ready, but Paul said he wasn't, and Paul was right, it turned out. Brooks was a major leaguer in the field from the first time I saw him, but he needed to work on his hitting. Pitchers were throwing him higher and higher [fastballs], and he'd keep swinging. I never thought he'd be a great hitter, but I didn't know what was inside him."

Billy Gardner: "Brooks didn't say anything when he first got there. You could see the talent. He couldn't run, couldn't throw that good, but he was quick as a cat, got a great jump on the ball, and had a quick release. We were playing the Yankees one time, bases loaded in the ninth, tie game, one out, and a hard ground ball came toward him. He dove, stopped the ball, turned around, and threw out Yogi at home. Just a hell of a play. We won the game. His reflexes were great."

Joe Ginsberg: "He had this old glove he'd used in high school, and he could use it better than anyone I'd ever seen. He was like one of those big, quick basketball players. He wasn't fast, but he was quick. He was so good even as a young player that when he missed one we couldn't believe it. We'd say, 'Must have hit a stone.'"

BILL WIGHT: "In the spring of '57 Richards told Kell, 'I'd like you to talk to Brooks about when he backhands the ball, he brings the glove over his eyes and loses sight of the ball.' Kell said, 'I'm not going to do it. I'm not going to embarrass myself. We've been here a month and the guy hasn't missed a ball yet.' That was the end of that conversation.

"He was just gifted. He'd short-hop a lot of balls, which most guys try to avoid, but he checked them against his body and made it look easy. And he was very quick to get rid of the ball. Had an average arm at best. A little below average, probably. But he was really quick. He'd throw from the grass, anywhere. He was extremely quick from the glove to the air. It was just an easy thing for him. Others had to work and work and work."

BROOKS ROBINSON: "I think it's a God-given talent more than anything else. I think that's what separates the great infielders from the average infielders, a certain instinct that you had to be born with. But I remember, I mean, I threw a million golf balls playing games by myself, up against the steps, or tennis balls, just all the time, and never stopped. But even in high school I always felt like I had that little instinct, like in basketball, just being where the ball was all the time. That's something I don't think you can acquire. You can make yourself better, but that little instinct, almost to be able to get after the ball or be where it is, you're born with that.

"The only thing I ever remember the Orioles telling me is, 'Look, we know you can catch the ball. What we'd like you to do is get that glove down just a little quicker. Just get it down and don't wait to the last second, because you can come up on a tough hop a lot quicker than you can go down. Most of the balls that anyone misses, they go under their glove, not over.' Al Vincent was the one who told me that. He had been around baseball a thousand years, and he did a lot of yelling. He said, 'Just get your rear end down a little and get that glove on the ground.' Once you got in the habit, it was easy."

7

The Color Line

Jackie Robinson had integrated the major leagues just seven years before the Orioles came to Baltimore, and although many clubs had followed Brooklyn's lead and begun using black players, it was still an issue in front offices, particularly those in the American League. The Yankees, Red Sox, Phillies, and Tigers still had all-white rosters at the start of the '54 season.

That hard stand would have drawn some support in Baltimore, where Jackie Robinson was jeered as a minor leaguer in '46 and Memorial Stadium was segregated until '51. But times and attitudes were changing, however slowly. The Colts had come to town in '53 with several black players, including popular halfback Claude "Buddy" Young. The Orioles wasted little time crossing the color line themselves.

In the seventh inning of the ninth game of the '54 season, a 14–4 loss in Chicago, then-manager Jimmy Dykes called on Jehosie Heard, a small, left-handed relief pitcher who had spent six years in the Negro leagues. Heard retired all four batters he faced and was lifted for a pinch hitter. The moment went quickly, without ceremony. The *Baltimore Sun* didn't even report the news until the tenth paragraph of its game story the next day, explaining that "the tiny Negro left-hander" had become "the first member of his race ever to appear in an Oriole uniform in a regular-season game."

The five-foot, seven-inch, 147-pound Heard had pitched effectively for the Birmingham Black Barons of the Negro leagues in the late '40s, using a slider and a screwball to make up for a lack of power. When the Negro leagues broke up, he passed himself off as a twenty-seven-year-old when he was thirty-two, signed with the St. Louis Browns, and set his sights on the major leagues. He got there after winning 36 games in the minors in '52 and '53. When the '54 season opened, he was the Orioles' only black player.

After pitching in Chicago, he sat in the bullpen for five weeks before making another appearance, again in relief against the White Sox, this time at Memorial Stadium. He was not nearly as successful, allowing five runs and five hits, including a grand slam. A week later, the Orioles sent him to the Pacific Coast League. He never pitched in the majors again, although he did bounce around the minors for four more years. He made history of a sort, but his career with the Orioles—his entire major league career—consisted of three and one-third innings pitched. Heard returned to Birmingham after his playing days, worked in a cotton mill, and signed on with the postal service.

CONNIE JOHNSON: "Heard was a little left-hander. He'd stay up all night. I don't think he ever went to sleep. He'd walk the streets at night. Then he'd go out and pitch up a storm."

Although they had integrated quickly, the Orioles were hardly progressive in their early years. They used only a sprinkling of black players in the '50s and early '60s. Bob Boyd was their regular first baseman from '56 to '59. Connie Johnson, a veteran pitcher from the Negro leagues, made 72 starts over three seasons and led the Orioles with 14 wins in '57. Joe Durham was a fleet outfielder, the first black member of the Orioles to hit a home run (in '54). Willie Tasby played center field in '59. Charlie Beamon, a promising young pitcher, shut out the Yankees in New York on the last day of the '56 season.

But other than Boyd and Johnson, few blacks had substantial careers with the Orioles in the first decade. Durham and Lenny Green were traded in '59 (Durham later returned to the organization as a minor leaguer, and Green, an outfielder, played for another decade in the majors after being dealt), and Tasby was traded in '60. Beamon's career was brief, and he was soon out of baseball.

Earl Robinson, an outfielder, was the Orioles' only black player in '61 and '62. When he was demoted in '62, leaving the Orioles with an all-white club at the outset of the Civil Rights movement, groups considered picketing Memorial Stadium. Paul Richards was the general manager in Houston by then, and when a reporter insinuated he might be prejudiced, Richards said, "If you want to think that, OK, but go ask Connie Johnson and Bob Boyd if they think I'm prejudiced."

By '63 the Orioles had other black players—outfielders Joe Gaines, Fred Valentine, and Sam Bowens; Paul Blair, a future star, was in the minor league system. Times were changing. The team traded for Frank Robinson, a black superstar, in December of '65, and other black players such as Elrod Hendricks and Don Buford became stalwarts. The color line disappeared.

But in the early years, as was the case throughout baseball, the few blacks on the Orioles often had to stay in separate hotels during spring training and on road trips, while their teammates stayed in white-only hotels. The blacks received few endorsements and generally lived the double life common to black athletes before the Civil Rights movement took off—cheered on the field, shunned off it.

CONNIE JOHNSON: "I was traded to Baltimore in '56 with Kell. Richards was all right at times. He was kind of smart in the way he'd do things. He'd get a pitcher and do something with him. He knew a lot about baseball. I don't think he liked blacks too much. He'd hide it in ways you wouldn't notice if you didn't come looking for it. But I noticed. One time he wouldn't let me pitch and told everyone my arm was sore. My arm wasn't sore. I don't think they wanted me to win too many games. One sportswriter asked me, 'When are you going to pitch again?' I said, 'My arm ain't sore.' Richards read that and said, 'Don't talk to sportswriters; they make stuff up.'

"I wasn't picked on like the others. The Baltimore fans were great. I got along great with them. I lived off Reisterstown Road. There weren't any blacks up there, but the people were nice. They took care of my kids. After I'd won 14 in '57 they wanted to give me a new contract about a month before the season was over. There was a little raise. I was making ten thousand dollars, and they offered fifteen thousand dollars. That was a pretty good raise at that time. But they were trying to sign me before I won any more games. After that, I didn't try to lose no games, but I didn't try that hard, either. We couldn't win the pennant, and I had my money."

BOB BOYD: "I was a pretty good hitter, a spray hitter. Not a long-ball man, but I could hit it in the gap in that big outfield and run. Richards brought me over. I really liked him. He really knew baseball. One time I overran a base, and he had a fit. We were in Washington. He shouted, 'How could you miss a bag, as big as it is?' But I enjoyed it there. They gave me all sorts of stuff for my wife, everything but a car. The fans treated me great. They were the best fans I ever played for. I had no problems there, none at all."

JOE DURHAM: "Boyd could hit, and he was a nice guy, but he was afraid of everything—the coaches and especially Richards. He was very scared of Paul. I used to call him 'Mr. Richards's son.'"

CHARLIE BEAMON: "When I shut out the Yankees in '56 at Yankee Stadium, I was a little wild, but I had a lot going for me. I was throwing a change-up, a curveball, and a live sinker—just getting started. The next spring I pitched a little, but not that much, not like someone who hadn't allowed a run in 13 or 14 innings the year before. They sent me back to [Triple-A] Vancouver without the right to be recalled. It wasn't what I expected. And the Orioles needed pitching in '57. They had some older guys.

"In '58 I was with the club all year, but I didn't pitch much. I'd go a month without an appearance. I think I started three games. By '60 I was out of baseball. I don't know if it was the Orioles or Paul Richards. He didn't respect me enough to talk to me. He had his coaches come over and talk to me when I was sitting right next to him. There were black pitchers in baseball then, but they were older—Connie Johnson, Don Newcombe, Joe Black. I was just twenty-one. I think it was like the black quarterback thing later in pro football. Teams didn't trust young black pitchers.

"I saw enough to know that, ability-wise, I had no problems. I saw people who were better than me who didn't make it or get as far as I did. Something bigger was in control. There wasn't anything I could do. But to not even be considered or not even respected, that hurt more than anything. In the long run I would have respected myself more if I'd spoken up, said my piece, and gone on home. When I left baseball my self-esteem was destroyed. I believed in the American Dream, that anything was possible. It took me years to get back up. As I got older I understood what had happened, and I got myself together and into a career. But I couldn't for a long time. To be honest, I'd rather forget about my time in baseball.

"Some wonderful things did happen. The camaraderie and friendships I had with Connie, Boyd, and Durham, those guys. And Lenny Moore with the Colts. He was a superstar, but he talked to me and helped me, and he was so down-to-earth. He made you understand that we were all in the same boat.

The friendships and inspirations and togetherness I felt from those guys, I wouldn't trade that for anything. You can have all that money they're making now. One day I was sitting in the dugout with Connie, and I asked him, 'Do you think I could have pitched in the Negro leagues?' And he said, 'Oh, yes, you could have done well.' That meant more to me than beating the Yankees, knowing he thought I could do well. I almost started crying right there in the dugout."

FRANK ROBINSON: "Charlie Beamon was ahead of me coming through school in Oakland, and when he came out of high school the Oakland club in the Pacific Coast League signed him. He had good stuff, really good stuff. I don't know about him off the field in those days, as far as the kind of citizen he was. But he had a good arm and had good stuff. He should have been a real good major league pitcher."

JOE DURHAM: "I came up [to Baltimore] at the end of the '54 season, went in the army right after the season, and spent all of '55 and '56 in the service. When I came back, God was the manager. Richards. The man was a hypocritical, racial son of a bitch. But at that time, you couldn't say nothing. You couldn't do anything.

"When I came back in '57 he tied a rope around me in the batting cage. Today, a manager wouldn't dare try anything like that. But you had to go along with the program in those days, with everybody saying Richards was a genius. So he says, 'Son, you're lunging, we're going to try something.' We had played the White Sox, and I hit two balls to the [center-field] hedge, which was four hundred forty feet. And I'm lunging? Jeez. So Richards came out after the game on a Sunday afternoon, and he was standing on the other side of the cage and got a harness around my waist. They threw pitches, and when I went to swing, they grabbed the rope and pulled so I couldn't move too much. The ball was coming and they're pulling the rope. That was an experience. It happened one time. They never tried it again. And they called the guy a genius?"

BROOKS ROBINSON: "Joe didn't like Richards one bit. I mean, Paul did have him tied up in the cage. I think Joe thinks he probably screwed him up more than he helped. It was different, for sure."

JOE DURHAM: "I was raised in Newport News, Virginia, and everything was segregated—schools, churches, everything. When I started playing ball I was put in [segregated] situations. Played in Hagerstown, Richmond, Norfolk. You wouldn't stay with the team. Somebody asked me, 'Was it hard to play?' It made it harder. Baseball is a team game, a family game, and when the family is split, like I don't see my teammates until it's time to go to the ballpark, that's tough.

"When I played for [the Orioles' affiliate in] San Antonio, we'd be on the road in Houston, and everyone else is at a hotel downtown, and you're out in a tourist home. Two stories with one bathtub. We'd go into Shreveport, worst place in the world. The bleacher seats had a line with 'white only' on one side, and way down in the corner was the colored section. The [whites] would stand there and call me all kinds of names. I was there for one reason, to have a decent year and get promoted. So you're doing that, and going through that, and then you run into a guy like Richards. That was tough."

BROOKS ROBINSON: "When we went to Florida [for spring training] all those guys had to stay at different hotels. We'd go by and pick 'em up in the morning and go to wherever we were going to play. You never really thought too much about it. Looking back on it now, it was really terrible that they had to do that. It was sad, really, when you think about it. But that's just the way those guys had to do it."

FRANK ROBINSON: "If you were good enough [and black] did you play? I don't know about back then. Baltimore didn't have any frontline black players. A few role players—Connie Johnson, Bobby Boyd, older guys—but that was it. I was the first black player to come in as a frontline starter, and that wasn't until '66."

MILT PAPPAS: "Whites were number one, blacks were number two. In the late '50s and early '60s, blacks dominated the National League, and whites dominated the American League. The top hitters in the AL were white, and the top hitters in the NL were black. Mays, McCovey, Clemente, Frank Robinson. The AL hadn't caught up to the NL as far as blacks were concerned, and they finally made an effort in the early '60s to start signing more black players. In Baltimore in the late '50s, the whole infield was white, and so were the catchers and outfielders. Bobby Boyd and Connie Johnson were about it. The AL started to turn itself around, but it took the AL a long time to catch up."

PAUL BLAIR: "The first year I got there [spring training in '63] it was only me and Sam Bowens. We were the only two blacks on the team. I never thought of that. I never did. Because things were changing as I came on. When they drafted me and put me on the major league roster and I went to spring training in Miami, that was the first year the black players could stay downtown in the same hotel with the white players. That was in '63. Before that the blacks just stayed in the black section and the whites were downtown in the hotel. So I didn't have that problem. When I came here in Baltimore, blacks were already here. Times were changing and things were fine. It was just baseball, the same game for everyone."

8

A Barely Civil War

There was steady change at the top of the organization in the Orioles' early years. After Paul Richards replaced Jimmy Dykes and Arthur Ehlers late in the '54 season, Clarence Miles, the attorney who had helped lure the franchise from St. Louis, resigned as club president after the '55 season. Four principal investors remained—Zanvyl Krieger, Joseph Iglehart, Jerry Hoffberger, and James Keelty, a real estate developer. Keelty became club president.

JOE HAMPER: "Clarence Miles was never around the ball club much. He was a lawyer, and he really didn't know anything about baseball. He was the leading force in getting the team here. A lot of other people participated, but he's the one who got the attention and publicity. Then he and Clyde Morris as secretary-treasurer ran the club for two years. But neither had much money invested in the team, and after two years, the people who had the money invested felt they had not been brought in on the decision-making process as much as they would like, so they sort of pushed Clarence Miles out."

After the '56 season, with ownership grumbling about the exorbitant sums Richards was spending on bonus babies, there was speculation that he would be replaced as general manager. "We have the best manager in baseball, but he has not functioned in the business end," one member of the club's board of directors said. In the end, a vice president for business, William Walsingham, was hired.

Walsingham lasted two years, during which Richards signed another crop of bonus babies, including Dave Nicholson, a powerful outfielder from St. Louis who "could hit a ball farther than any man alive," Richards said. Nicholson received a one-hundred-thousand-dollar signing bonus, the largest ever given a player. That was the last straw for the owners. After the '58 season, they took away Richards's control of the front office and hired a general manager, Lee MacPhail, the Yankees' genial, well-respected farm director. Richards remained the manager.

JOE HAMPER: "You had a mixed bag with Richards. Without him, we wouldn't have gotten Brooks Robinson. And he did a lot of other good things. But he wasn't an organization man, and pro-Richards and anti-Richards factions developed. The people who were close to Richards just worshipped him. His theory was you lined up ownership and you lined up the press, and nothing else mattered. He did that to perfection. The press thought he was the greatest. Ownership did, too. He knew how to do that. The anti-Richards people didn't like him because he was very secretive and did his own thing, and that was frustrating for people like Krieger and Keelty, not to be able to communicate. They felt they had to do something, so they brought in Bill Walsingham, and that didn't work. Then they brought in MacPhail, and he was a perfect mediator between the factions. Lee is one of the nicest guys anywhere. Nobody could get angry with him. He kind of kept everything calm."

LEE MACPHAIL: "I had worked for the Yankees for a long time. I ran their Triple-A team in Kansas City, and then I was the farm director in their New York office, working for [GM] George Weiss. We had some great years. We won five consecutive world championships. Then the Orioles decided they wanted Paul just to spend his time on the field. He wasn't really that interested in the off-field part of his job. Also, he wasn't that business-oriented, and I think ownership felt he was wasting a little money. What they really wanted was someone to say no to him on budget things.

"Joe Iglehart was on the board of CBS [television], and he got to know my brother, who was the sports director of CBS. Joe suggested to Richards that they hire my brother as GM. Richards said, 'If you're going to hire a MacPhail, hire Lee.' So late in the '57 season the Orioles were in New York, and Paul sent word that he wanted me to come down after the game and talk in the clubhouse. I went down, and he said, 'How about coming to the Orioles as GM and I'll just be the manager?' Then Iglehart called [Yankee co-owners] Dan Topping and Del Webb, talking about how they would like me to come. I really wasn't too anxious to go. My wife didn't want to leave New York. Weiss and I were very close. Then Topping said, 'Lee, George is going to be here for a long time. If you have a chance to be a GM, you should take it.'

"I stepped into a good organization. Jack Dunn, Harry Dalton, and Bob Brown were all good young guys who worked hard. Player-wise, things were very good. The Orioles had excellent scouts, and they paid bonuses. The owners were very good that way. I dealt more with Iglehart and Krieger. Hoffberger wasn't too involved at the time. Nor was Keelty, even though he was president. I don't know how Paul really felt about me coming, but he couldn't have been nicer. When I went down to interview I said I would only consider coming if I was sure it was OK with Paul. We arranged to meet, and where we met was sort of indicative of whether we could work together. He was in Texas and I was in New York, and we met halfway, in Memphis. Once I was aboard, Paul and I had no problems."

BOB BROWN: "Bringing in MacPhail was the best decision the owners ever had. Lee built morale. It hadn't been very high. Paul was never around in the winter. Prior to Lee's arrival there was a big Ping-Pong table set up in a back room, and in the winter we'd go back and play a few hours a day. When we heard Lee was coming in, we took it down and never put it up again. We worked harder than we ever had before. Lee really made it fun. He was always entertaining us, always playing games. He didn't come across that way to the public, but he was a very bright, warm guy, and the [front] office just kind of lit up."

The only constant through the '50s was farm director Jim McLaughlin, the only member of the front office who had come from St. Louis. Loyal and meticulous, he had started with the Browns in '37, risen through the ranks, and had a hand in the honing of such top players as Roy Sievers, Vern Stephens, Bob Turley, and Don Larsen. An essential if largely unknown figure in the early years of the Orioles, McLaughlin was fiercely devoted to the art of scouting and developing young players.

EARL WEAVER: "McLaughlin did a tremendous job of running the farm system. That was his life. He had no ambitions to go higher. He surrounded himself with good scouts, as many as he could find and break in to do things his way. And his minor league managers were the same. He was a shrewd baseball person. Never played, but he started at the bottom and worked his way up to the top."

HARRY DALTON: "Jim was a good guy, stubborn as a mule, a good thinker, a good organizer, and very proud of the organization. He wanted fiercely to have the major league club consist of players that we had signed and developed. And he was insistent on having things the way he wanted them. He would take the whole day, if necessary, to talk with a scout and try and brainwash him into thinking his way.

"He came up with a diagram for scouts, a circle. The upper half had the words, 'running, throwing, fielding, hitting,' et cetera. And the bottom half was 'attitude, determination,' and so forth. Jim said we had to stress the bottom half, because it was just as important as the physical tools. Some clubs didn't care that much about that in those days. Jim did.

"As much as anyone, he helped get the Orioles off the ground. His legacy was organizing the scouting and farm department, and helping establish a strong pride in the organization. The Orioles became well respected, not only because of their success on the field, but a lot of baseball people thought the organization was run very well. Jim was a part of that, as a lot of people were, but he started building a farm system and kept right on going, and then we had a decent season on the field in '60, and people started feeling proud about the talent."

HANK PETERS: "Jim hired me into baseball [with the Browns], and this might sound strange, but he didn't have a great love for baseball. He wasn't a guy who liked to go and sit at ball games, but he loved the organizational work, and he was very good at it, and he loved to try to motivate people to do things, and he was good at that, too. He did an awful lot for the [Orioles] franchise. His contribution was underrated because he never was able to project himself too well, and he sometimes had a difficult time getting along with some people. He didn't know a lot about public relations and how to promote himself, but he knew a lot about what it took to build an organization."

When MacPhail arrived, he inherited a troubling behind-the-scenes situation—a civil war simmering between McLaughlin and Richards. As a long-time employee of the franchise, McLaughlin resented the authority Richards had been given, and he loathed Richards's habit of relying on his cronies instead of McLaughlin's staff for scouting information.

The dispute grew so heated that MacPhail finally fired McLaughlin early in the '61 season, even though he was pleased with McLaughlin's work. MacPhail found McLaughlin a job with the Senators, but McLaughlin went to work in Cincinnati. Harry Dalton, who had assisted McLaughlin for eight years, replaced McLaughlin as farm director. A former sportswriter, Dalton was an Amherst College graduate who had developed a knack for working with scouts and was just as adamant as McLaughlin about the importance of player development.

After Richards left the Orioles late in the '61 season, McLaughlin returned later in the decade as the Orioles' director of scouting, working under Dalton. Although they had feuded, Richards and McLaughlin both were major contributors to the Orioles' success. Richards helped lay a winning foundation, and the minor league system McLaughlin helped build in the '50s emerged as one of baseball's best, spitting out waves of top players.

JOE HAMPER: "We had a hard-driving, hard-working minor league department. Those people worked harder than anybody I ever saw. Jim had a definite program and plan for what he wanted to do. And Harry was an exceptionally bright, hard-working guy. Everybody worked together except Richards, who would go his own way and sign guys that the other people never even knew anything about. You can't look back and say we had this well-knit, cohesive organization that was working to become successful and win the World Series. People were working like the devil, but they weren't necessarily working together."

EARL WEAVER: "The problem was Richards wanted 100 percent power on the field and in the front offices, and Jim had been the farm director for years. Now here Paul comes with very little experience to run the front office. Paul became a very good general manager in time, but Jim believed the minor league [office] should supply the major leagues with ballplayers, and it wasn't up to the major league department to go find players when you've got scouts and everybody else. But Paul had the final say as to where the money was going. There was a lot of friction."

WALTER YOUSE: "Every year Richards would send a representative down to the minor league camp in Thomasville, Georgia, and have him teach the players to do things Richards's way. But over on another field, McLaughlin would be teaching them a different way. Richards had his men, and McLaughlin had his men. It was a conflict, plain and simple. Richards had hired me as a part-time scout, and at first I didn't get along with McLaughlin because Richards had given me the job. But after a while he got to know me. McLaughlin was a very serious, no-nonsense guy. Some of the [scouts] didn't like him. I always got along with him. He did a good job. He and Richards were just different breeds. Richards was all baseball, and McLaughlin was a front-office man."

HANK PETERS: "Paul was an 'I' guy, and we were all brought up on a 'we' basis, you know, 'we will do this,' not 'I will do this.' And Jim was the opposite."

HARRY DALTON: "Paul wasn't really a developmental guy. He was in the sense that he'd work with young players, especially pitchers. But as far as signing them and waiting five years for them to be ready to help in the big leagues, that was too far off as far as he was concerned. But he had the owners bamboozled. He came in with an imperial stroke, and it became Paul's organization, Paul's headlines, and Jim couldn't quite kowtow to all that. Jim resented being bypassed on [bonus-baby] signings and things. Jim just felt he was being left out of the loop. And Paul had no experience in administration at all. Didn't want to do it. He just wanted to say, 'We're going to trade you for him,' and so forth, and build a ball club that way. And he and Jim, instead of working out their problems and getting close together, they got farther and farther apart."

LEE MACPHAIL: "It got to the point where you were either a 'McLaughlin player' or a 'Richards player' in the organization, and there were decisions made on that basis. Paul and Jim just never could get along. They were always after each other. I finally told Jim we were going to have to do something. I hated to do it."

HARRY DALTON: "MacPhail realized it just wasn't going to heal, so he called Jim in and said he was going to make a change, and then he called me in and told me he was going to move me into the job. I was thrilled, but I was upset about Jim, because without Jim I'd be back at the *Springfield Daily News* writing sports. I think Jim's pride was hurt as much as anything. He went to Cincinnati, where Bill DeWitt was, and I ended up hiring him back as scouting director. He stayed for a long time and had a great impact."

9

Thomasville

The Orioles moved their major league spring training camp from Yuma, Arizona, in '54, to Miami in '55, to Scottsdale, Arizona, for four years beginning in '56. They finally settled in Miami in '60 and stayed for almost three decades. Meanwhile, their minor league spring camp never budged. Bill Veeck's Browns had found a site in '52 in the piney woods of Thomasville, Georgia, on the grounds of a Veterans Administration home for war veterans down on their luck. The Orioles inherited the arrangement, liked it, and kept it.

They had working agreements with about a dozen minor league teams in the '50s, and as many as five hundred players at all levels from Class D on up assembled in Thomasville every spring for an eight-week, military-style baseball boot camp. They lived in barracks, ate in a mess hall, adhered to curfews, awoke to reveille, and spent their days working on fundamentals. The Triple-A and Double-A affiliates were the only ones excused, having camps of their own, usually in Florida. Every other player in the system spent the spring in Thomasville. Some spent many springs there before the Orioles moved the camp to Fernandina Beach, Florida, in '67.

Thomasville was a long way from the bright lights of the major leagues, but in some ways, the Orioles' winning foundation was established there. Paul Richards wanted his brand of fundamentals taught the same way at every level, so players moving through the system wouldn't have to learn a different system every time they were reassigned. That teaching took place in Thomasville. Earl Weaver, Cal Ripken Sr., and others who would advocate Richards's philosophy for years began appearing in the late '50s.

In the early '60s farm director Harry Dalton and several young coaches hunkered down in Thomasville and collaborated on a handbook detailing the Orioles' philosophy on all phases of the game, from pitching to stealing bases.

The book was a dissertation for a style that later became known as "the Oriole Way," although there was no such wording in the original book and no one used the phrase at the time. Having a distinct organizational playing style wasn't revolutionary—several other teams did—but the Orioles were unbending in their convictions, and their later success helped generate the "Oriole Way" nickname. It all started in Thomasville.

HARRY DALTON: "It was a huge complex, actually just south of Thomasville. We had our own administrative building with two offices and a big meeting room. A kitchen and a dining room. Barracks-style serving. Then about eight typical military barracks buildings where you put up thirty cots. It was perfect, really perfect. Pines, beautiful grounds. There was a ballpark with a small grandstand, the main field. Then they built an adjacent field next to the ballpark, just off the grounds on city property, and then on the grounds they built two more diamonds for us, so we had four to work with."

BOOG POWELL: "When I got there [in '59] they gave me uniform number 570 or something like that. Thomasville was something else. Whenever somebody would fart in the middle of the night, it was just like a regular army barracks—you'd laugh and throw pillows at them. There'd be reveille at daybreak, and you'd get up and eat breakfast, put your stuff on, and run to the field, which was about a mile away on a dirt road. Then you'd work your ass off until noon and run back to the barracks. Then you'd have lunch for an hour and run back out to the fields for an afternoon session or a game."

BARRY SHETRONE: "The barracks got me ready for when I went in the army. We had a cot with the springs and a little mattress about two inches thick. I can't remember if we had footlockers, but there was a rack behind the bed where we hung our clothes. There wasn't much to do when you were done [playing]. You'd go into town, and I think they had a pool hall, and we'd just hang out. I was lucky. I only had to go down there once compared to some guys who went down there every spring for three or four years."

EARL WEAVER: "When I signed a professional contract in 1948, the Cardinals had seven fields at their camp in Albany, Georgia, and there were over five hundred players there. Everyone vying for jobs. So every team had a camp like this. That's when there was something like fifty-six minor leagues and

God knows how many teams, and there wasn't much television. You know what the people in Thomasville did at night? They came out to the ball game, that's what they did."

HERM STARRETTE: "Spring training lasted a heck of a long time back then, and there were like one hundred pitchers in camp. You spent hours just waiting around for your turn to pitch, just doing nothing, shagging flies in the outfield or getting in trouble and giving the manager something to yell at. You played ball, worked all day, and it was just a way of life."

JIM PALMER: "I was shagging flies for [coach] Jimmy Frey one day, and the sun was going down, and Vern Hoscheit was running the camp, and I was supposed to throw that day, and I said, 'Mr. Frey, do you think Mr. Hoscheit forgot about me?' He said 'Why don't you go ask?' So I go all the way around the outfield. They had one real park and then a place called 'the Hole.' So we're down there in the Hole, and I get around to Hoscheit and say, 'Mr. Hoscheit, I asked Mr. Frey and he said to come ask you if you forgot about me throwing today?' And he said, 'Son, I don't get paid to forget about kids. Get your ass back in left field.' A half-hour later the sun was going down and they called me."

HERM STARRETTE: "You could go quacky after a couple of weeks. They had a drive-in restaurant, and I got curb service from a pretty little girl one day, and I wanted to date her. She was going to pick me up in the barracks that night. We were having bed checks, and Weaver came through, and I was in my bed in my clothes. As soon as he left, I got up and popped out the side door. And I ran right into Earl. He said, 'Weren't you just in bed?' I said, 'Aw, I got a little date set up.' He said, 'Why didn't you just ask me? Be gone for an hour and come back.' He let me get away with it. I think the thinking was, if you didn't do a little something extra, you'd go crazy."

STEVE BARBER: "My first year, I walked in and I was number 285 on the roster. It wasn't bad. I'm from a nothing background. I was used to it. It was a lot of fun in some respects. The food was decent. We had curfews. It was reasonable. There wasn't a lot to do, but there wasn't a whole lot [to do] where I'd grown up. I did get a lot of attention from the local girls because [actress] Joanne Woodward is from there, and at the time there was a likeness between

Paul Newman and myself. They did make me aware of that. But there wasn't much to do. Go out to the drive-in and get something to eat."

JIM PALMER: "Tallahassee was forty-five miles away. It was the perfect environment to focus on baseball, which was what you're trying to do, because the more you could do that, the sooner you got to the big leagues. Thomasville was nothing. I had no money, no nothing, nothing to do. The facilities were horrible. Two Ping-Pong tables. If you lost, you waited two hours. It was a perfect environment to focus on the game. I don't even think they had a TV. I just sat around the barracks and listened to George Bamberger tell stories about pitching. It was probably one of the better things that ever happened to me."

WALTER YOUSE: "They'd bring all the scouts down every year, and we'd watch the practices and games in the day and then have meetings every night and talk about various boys. We'd go around the room, and if one scout wanted to keep him, we did. We'd cut maybe ten boys a night. Spent maybe two or three weeks down there and made most of the cuts, and after we'd leave the managers would cut the rest.

"We stayed in the barracks, too. There was a place called the "Bird's Nest" where we'd go every night after we were through. We'd sit in there and talk and tell stories. Freddie Hofmann was there. Quite a character. He'd been Babe Ruth's roommate for five years. "Bootnose," they called him. I could listen to him all night telling stories about Babe Ruth. One year Richards came up with the idea of giving all the scouts cameras, so he brought six little cameras, and you were supposed to go out and take pictures of the boys. Bootnose ran his for a couple of weeks and sent it in, and there was nothing on the film. Turned out he'd never taken the lens cap off."

HARRY DALTON: "The social aspect of that camp was as good for the organization as the baseball aspect. We had long days, and then you'd go have a beer in the Bird's Nest. It was in the staff barracks at the end of the building. We'd have cold cuts, cheese, beer, and soft drinks, and people would start to unwind. Then you'd go to dinner at six-thirty, and we'd have a meeting at seven, and those meetings usually would go to ten o'clock because we kept talking about players.

"After that was over, the hardy ones would go back to the Bird's Nest, and sometimes at two o'clock in the morning they'd still be in there arguing about ballplayers or arguing about instruction, but talking about our business all the time. And they got to know each other better. And it created a tremendous sense of organization. Some of the Thomasville days were the best days of my baseball life."

BOOG POWELL: "I think we had twelve teams there. And you'd go from one team to the next and all the cutoff plays were exactly the same. All the rundowns were exactly the same. All the bunt plays were exactly the same. So there wasn't any learning to do. You just spent more time learning your trade, learning how to hit and look for pitches in certain counts and how to actually play the game. Later on in your career, when you only had one workout a day, two wasn't very inviting. But at the time, it didn't sound bad. What the hell, you were going out there and playing ball."

EARL WEAVER: "I was the camp director for a couple of years. Richards wanted everything done his way. He'd bring us to [major league] spring training to show us how he wanted things taught, and we started teaching the way Richards wanted it done. I guess each minor league manager had a few variations, but they stuck to the principles, and it was a good idea. The Dodgers had their way, the Cardinals had their way, and now the Orioles were going to have our way. Half of it was Richards. Just a mixture of stuff. My name got attached to it, but in reality there were a bunch of people contributing."

JIM PALMER: "We talked all the time about things that happened. One morning with two outs I hit a fly ball to right field and I got about halfway down the [first base] line [before stopping], and at lunch I was the guy they talked about. Saying 'I don't care if you're a pitcher, you run balls out. If you put on an Orioles uniform, you run balls out.' Every day was that way. Some guy screws up a ball in the outfield and he's screaming at himself, and they talked about him that day at lunch. 'Don't wear emotions on your sleeve.'"

HARRY DALTON: "The so-called Oriole Way really got started because we wanted to set up a manual so everybody knew what page they were supposed to be on and how we were going to do things. It was partly my idea. Just for the sake of simplicity. It wasn't like we sat back and said, 'OK, let's establish the Oriole Way.' It was just Ray Scarborough on pitching and Billy Hunter on field play and baserunning, and various other people contributing because of the position they had played or the experience they had.

"It was my idea to put it on paper so everybody would be responsible for knowing. And then it became a manual instead of a leaflet. A lot of people wrote. I asked them to commit it to paper and give it to me, and then we'd go over things together. People like Cal Ripken Sr., Billy Hunter and Scarborough, Vern Hoscheit with the catchers, all had input. Weaver. It wasn't where one person was going to put this whole thing together; it was just a case of a group effort. It just grew over the course of several years in Thomasville."

10

Knucklers

By the late '50s the Orioles were on the verge of a seismic transformation, with the franchise ending more than a half-century of losing and entering a winning era that would span seven American presidencies. There were hints of this coming metamorphosis. Talented young players such as Brooks Robinson, Milt Pappas, and Jerry Walker were appearing on the major league roster, and another wave of prospects was percolating in the minor league system.

Yet until the Orioles officially changed from pretenders to contenders in '60, it was hard to envision the pieces coming together. The club remained rooted in the American League's second division, with a roster dominated by veterans and journeymen. The city's excitement at being back in the major leagues wore off, and attendance at Memorial Stadium flattened at less than a million fans a year. Pro football's Colts ruled Baltimore, winning back-to-back championships in '58 and '59. "The Orioles were the poor relatives when I got there [in '58]," Lee MacPhail said. "The Colts were all anyone wanted to talk about."

The Orioles did little to change that in '58, finishing sixth with a 74–79 record as attendance fell to a new low, down 20 percent from '57. They began the season with hope, coming off a .500 season in '57, and an 11–9 start landed them in second place and persuaded one sportswriter to label them "The Wonder Birds." But a seven-game losing streak in late May dropped them to last place and doused the excitement. A four-game series with the Indians in early June drew a pitiful total of thirty-two thousand fans to Memorial Stadium. Another hot streak pushed them back over .500 and briefly into a tie for second in July, but a ten-game losing streak dropped them back into the second division for good.

The top pitcher was right-hander Arnie Portocarrero, a classic Richards reclamation project. Winner of four games in '56 and '57 combined, he was obtained in a trade and won 15. Billy O'Dell, the club's first bonus baby, finally bloomed and went 14–11. The fourth starter was Pappas, nineteen, who went 10–10 using just a fastball and a slider. Cocky and feisty, he feuded with teammates and umpires and was carefully nurtured, with Richards limiting him to eighty pitches per start.

The cast of everyday players was more familiar, with Bob Nieman hitting .325, Bob Boyd hitting .309, and Gus Triandos's 30 home runs tying the league record for a catcher. Brooks Robinson played third base all season, his first full year in the majors. Hitting help came from rightfielder Gene Woodling, reacquired three years after Richards had traded him away due to a slow start in '55 ("a mistake," Richards admitted). Playing every day, Woodling hit .276 with 15 homers.

GEORGE ZUVERINK: "You could see everything starting to come around. We picked up Brooks and a few others. Every time Paul got a new pitcher, he went down to the bullpen and taught 'em that slip pitch. For some guys it really worked, at least for a year or so. I was one of the constants, the Orioles' first good relief pitcher. I had a natural sinker and some good years. In '57 I went 10–6 with a 2.47 ERA, and I held out for two weeks [in '58] to get a thousand-dollar raise because they were paying these guys right out of high school one hundred thousand dollars. That was ridiculous. I was leading the league in appearances. I didn't think that was fair at all."

MILT PAPPAS: "Paul gave me the chance at that age, which was really a risk, and he put me on that pitch count, which probably saved my career. No matter what count it was, what inning it was, what the score was, or what was going on, when I got to eighty pitches, he pulled me. And that helped me because there was such a vast difference in pitching from high school to the majors.

"I was eighteen, couldn't drink, and I had a tough time with my teammates. They were my worst enemies. They were so jealous that I was straight out of high school and they had to play years in the minors to get to the majors. They were quite taken aback, and I had a rough time. I kept saying, 'Why are you fighting me? I'm here just trying to help the team. If you've got a bone to pick, talk to Paul.'"

ERNIE HARWELL: "The pitch count was pretty revolutionary. Everyone does it now, but back then [with Pappas] was the first time I'd heard of it. A lot of people thought Paul was babying Pappas, but [the pitch count] was probably a good idea. Pappas did a nice job. He pitched like a guy older than he was."

DICK WILLIAMS: "Pappas was a guy Paul really babied. The pitch limit hurt him later on, although he had a good career. Later on in his career, no matter who was the manager, when he got to that eighty-pitch limit, it was like he hit a brick wall. He did a fine job, but with that limit, he started looking toward the dugout. We used to get on him about it in a lighthearted way. Triandos got on him about it."

MILT PAPPAS: "I was extremely brash. The first time I faced Ted Williams, in my second or third start in '58, I had a three-and-two count and threw a fastball right down the middle. The catcher caught it, didn't move. Williams didn't move. The umpire didn't say anything. I didn't say anything. An eternity passed. Then Williams drops the bat, walks back toward the dugout, and the ump says, 'Strike three!' That was the third out, so I came walking in and went by the umpire and said, 'What would have happened if he'd have gone to first base?' And he said, 'Oh, that'd be ball four. He's got better eyes than me.' Here I am, eighteen, and I said, 'No wonder he hits .380 every year, with guys like you.'

"In that same start I faced Jimmy Piersall, who they'd made a movie about because he went nuts on the field. And he comes up to bat singing, 'I Got the Whole World in My Arms.' And I said, 'Holy mackerel, this guy really is nuts.' He proceeds to hit a home run, which really irritated me. And he's singing as he's going around the bases. It was a day game in Boston, cold and dreary, maybe fourteen hundred or fifteen hundred people in the ballpark, and everyone could hear him singing.

"He comes up the next time, and I said, 'Mr. Piersall better not be singing or he's going to be singing on the ground.' He wasn't singing, but I had a score to settle and threw a fastball inside as hard as I could, and he swung and broke his bat in half. Easy groundball to me. I grabbed it and yelled at him, 'Why don't you sing now, you SOB?' The Red Sox dugout jumped all over me. I could hear Williams, 'Who do you think you are, rookie?' They're all over my case, yelling and screaming, how could I talk to a veteran like that? I didn't give a shit. This guy hits a home run off me and he's singing. I should have put one in his ribs."

The big event in '58 was the All-Star Game, played before a full house at Memorial Stadium on July 8. Triandos made the team as the starting catcher, and the fans booed loudly when Yankees manager Casey Stengel, directing the American Leaguers, pinch hit his catcher, Yogi Berra, for Triandos in the bottom of the sixth. Triandos had singled in two at-bats, and Berra popped out amid a cascade of boos.

But the boos turned to cheers when Stengel inserted another member of the Orioles, pitcher Billy O'Dell, in the top of the seventh. Stengel had intended to use Chicago's Billy Pierce, but Pierce's arm tightened up in the bullpen, and O'Dell took his place. Stengel didn't have to use another pitcher. O'Dell retired nine straight batters on just twenty-seven pitches, preserving the AL's 4–3 win and earning a standing ovation.

BILLY O'DELL: "The fans went crazy when I walked in along the first-base line to start the seventh. With each pitch I threw, the roars got louder and louder. I didn't throw anything but curves and sliders, and my control was good. The guy who worried me the most was Stan Musial, and I got him out on a slider. Four years later I was with the Giants, and Casey was managing the Mets, and he came over to me before a game while I was warming up. I was wondering why he was coming over, and he said, 'Mr. O'Dell, I never had a chance to thank you for that job you did for me in the '58 All-Star Game.' "

In '59 the Orioles finished sixth for the third time in the past four years. A win on June 9 lifted them into a first-place tie, but the Indians' Rocky Cola-vito hit four homers at Memorial Stadium the next night, and the Orioles never sniffed first place again. Lacking hitting, particularly after Triandos injured his hand in July, they were in third or fourth for most of the season before fading to sixth at the end.

Pappas and knuckleballer Hoyt Wilhelm, acquired late in the '58 season, carried the pitching load, winning 15 games apiece. (Portocarrero fell apart, winning only two.) Woodling was the top run producer with 77 RBI, and out-fielder Willie Tasby batted leadoff, scored a team high 69 runs, and, on one memorable, stormy night, played center field in his socks because he feared his metal spikes would attract lightning.

GUS TRIANDOS: "I hit 30 homers in '58 and was going for an even better year in '59 when I got hurt. If I'd been hitting in Camden Yards or in Memorial Stadium after they shortened the fences [in the '60s], I would have hit a lot more. They pitched you differently in a big park like that. It probably cost me five to ten homers a year, playing in Memorial Stadium. But then I took a foul tip right on the back of my hand, and I came back too fast, couldn't hold the bat tight and ended up getting some calcium deposits. Still hit 25 homers [in '59]. And then your contract comes in the mail [after the '59 season], and they're offering you a fifteen-hundred-dollar cut. They just waited you out. The way we were going, who was going to miss me?"

BROOKS ROBINSON: "The big question with me [in the '50s] was whether I'd be able to hit major league pitching. I was up and down [to and from the minors] like a bouncing ball. I hurt my knee in '56, a partial tear sliding into second. Then I made the big club in '57, and I hit a ground ball, and [Washington's] Mickey Vernon came off the bag to tag me, and I tried to zigzag around him, and my knee locked on me. I had it operated on. I was out two months, went to San Antonio and played for a month, and they brought me back. Then in '58 I was in Baltimore all year. Didn't distinguish myself offensively. Hit .238 with three home runs.

"I had an army obligation after the '58 season. I was going to get drafted for two years, so I joined the Arkansas National Guard and went six months' active duty. Got out right when the ['59] season started. I came to Baltimore without any spring training. They had two or three third basemen, and I thought I'd get to play sporadically, but Paul called me down one morning in Chicago and told me he was sending me to Vancouver. That just took the wind out of my sails. From an ego point, man, I mean, you spend the whole '58 season in Baltimore and get a whole season under your belt and figure ['59] is my year. Then all of a sudden I'm back in the minor leagues.

"It turned out to be the best thing that ever happened to me. I went out there and got hurt at first. It was wet and I went after a pop over by the dugout, and the dugout had some bars on it to keep you from falling in, and I slipped and grabbed hold of the bar, and it had little hooks on it. I got hung up on a hook and really hurt my forearm. They told me I was really lucky that I didn't injure myself real bad."

ERNIE HARWELL: "Brooks could have ruined his career with that injury. Cedric Tallis was the GM out there, and he said, 'If the number-one prospect in the organization almost ruins his career, I figure my career was ruined, too.' But it turned out it wasn't that serious."

BROOKS ROBINSON: "I got well and played well and hit well, and Richards said, 'We're calling you back.' I came back [after the All-Star break in '59] and seemed to be an entirely different player than when I'd left. More confidence, everything. What I thought had been the worst thing that could happen turned out to be the best thing that could happen to me. I hit well the rest of that year, and then the next year [in '60] I ended up having my first real good year."

Jerry Walker had just turned twenty when he made the rotation at the start of the '59 season. A soft-spoken Oklahoman, he didn't throw as hard as Pappas, but he had control and maturity, won 11 games, and became the youngest pitcher to start or win an All-Star Game. Another twenty-year-old, Jack Fisher, pitched in relief for most of '59 before joining the rotation late in the season.

On September 11 at Memorial Stadium, Fisher and Walker started for the Orioles in a doubleheader against a Chicago team headed for the World Series. Fisher pitched a shutout to win the first game, and Walker took the mound and threw a 16-inning shutout to win the nightcap, setting a club record for longest pitching performance. (Ray Moore had thrown the first 15 innings of a 16-inning game two years earlier.)

Walker was the Opening Day starter in '60 and seemed on his way to a long and fine career, but he never had another winning season and was out of the majors by '65. (The Orioles dealt him to Kansas City in '61.) Some believe he was never the same after his 16-inning performance.

JERRY WALKER: "I wasn't throwing a lot of pitches that night. Gave up six hits, walked a couple of guys, wasn't in trouble much. They started checking with me every inning after the 10th. 'Are you all right?' they'd ask. I said fine. In the 13th or 14th they let me hit, so I kept going. When I came in from the top of the 16th Richards said, 'That's it, no more.' Then Brooks drove in a run to win the game in the bottom of the inning. I think I threw 178 pitches. That's not that many for 16 innings. Guys today throw 130 over six or seven innings. I won't say that it didn't make me sore more than I was used to, but I felt fine. I didn't have any problems. I was very sore the next day. But it was normal soreness. I got an extra day's rest.

"I think they were conscious of my well-being. A lot of people made a big to-do and said I hurt my arm then and was never the same. After I got traded Paul came over before a game and said to me, 'I don't think I'll ever let a pitcher go that many innings again,' but he said, 'I thought you were throwing good.' The thing was, I didn't want to come out, and I don't think I would now.

"In and of itself, I don't think it hurt me. I came back the next year [in '60], had some allergy problems, and was never strong. But it wasn't my arm. My arm didn't hurt until the next year. Plus, we had a bunch of other pitchers going well, and I just didn't pitch as much. My arm was fine. I don't think you can tie that game to my arm problems at all. That came only after I was traded to Kansas City in '61. I started out 7–2, but then I had elbow problems and later shoulder problems."

Hoyt Wilhelm's career spanned four decades, beginning in the minor leagues before World War II and ending just before the designated hitter was introduced in the early '70s. He pitched for the Orioles for four-plus seasons, arriving on waivers from Cleveland near the end of the '58 season and leaving for the White Sox in a trade after the '62 season. But although his time in Baltimore was relatively short, it was unforgettable.

He was thirty-five when he arrived, a relief specialist throwing a pitch that hitters couldn't hit and catchers couldn't catch. Richards converted him into a starter, and dividends came instantly. On September 20, 1958, in just his ninth major league start, Wilhelm threw the Orioles' first no-hitter on a drizzly afternoon at Memorial Stadium, beating the Yankees 1–0. He walked two and struck out eight, and Triandos gave him all the support he needed with a 425-foot home run. The toughest play was made by second baseman Billy Gardner, who ranged deep to his left to field a high bouncer and throw out Norm Siebern in the eighth. Gardner also grabbed the last out, a high pop-up.

DICK WILLIAMS: "I played third base for the first seven innings. Then they took Bob Nieman out of left, put me there, and brought in a kid to play third.

I hadn't had a play all day. Neither had Nieman. So they bring in Brooks to play third, and he makes two plays on topped balls that I wouldn't have made. And I made two plays on line drives to left that Nieman probably wouldn't have made. So there wouldn't have been a no-hitter. That was pretty good managing."

BILLY GARDNER: "With two outs in the bottom of the ninth, Hank Bauer hit a foul ball, and I ran over, got under it, and dropped it. The next pitch was another pop-up to me. I caught that one."

As a starter in '59, Wilhelm won his first nine decisions and made the All-Star team, then he went on to win the league ERA title and finish with a 15–11 record. But what fans remembered most was a muggy June night when Wilhelm was attacked by gnats in the first inning at Chicago's Comiskey Park. The game was delayed for sixteen minutes as coaches, bat boys, and trainers tried to shoo away the bugs with towels, sprays, and ointments, before Sox owner Bill Veeck finally ordered fireworks set off on the mound. The gnats disappeared, and Wilhelm returned to the mound and pitched a seven-hitter to win.

Wilhelm's knuckleball confounded hitters all season, but it confounded his catchers even more. Triandos and backup catcher Joe Ginsberg had fits trying to keep balls in front of them. Each was charged with four passed balls in a game on two different occasions in '59, and their combined season total of 49 set a major league record. When the passed balls continued to stack up early in the '60 season, Richards introduced a massive mitt resembling a pizza plate, thinking his catchers could use it to snag the dancing pitches. Richards ultimately had to cut down the mitt to a more reasonable size, but the oversized catcher's mitt was born.

Wilhelm returned to the bullpen in '60 and became a mainstay, finishing 87 games in '61 and '62 before being included in the package that brought shortstop Luis Aparicio to the Orioles. Even though he was almost forty when he was traded, Wilhelm pitched almost another decade before finally closing out his remarkable career.

HARRY BRECHEEN: "Wilhelm had had some arm problems, and when he came over to us [in '58] we didn't change anything. We just gave him the ball and let him go. He was strictly a knuckleball pitcher. Threw a fastball every once in a while. Had the best knuckler I ever saw. The ball did a lot of things. When he threw it overhand, it broke straight down. When he threw from the side, it broke to the side."

DICK WILLIAMS: "They talk about Phil Niekro and a few others, but Hoyt's was the best. He threw it harder than Niekro or anyone. He claimed he knew which way it was going to break, but I don't know how he did. And I never did see him throw a bad knuckleball, where it didn't roll over and become lunch meat for someone."

GUS TRIANDOS: "Hoyt's knuckler was consistent. It was good all the time. Skinny Brown threw one that would come in and kick down, but Hoyt's would stay alive, stay up, and you're waiting for it to break down, and boom, all of a sudden, you're boxing it. He had control of it, too, great control. It was pretty amazing."

JACKIE BRANDT: "Hoyt's nickname was 'Tilt.' One of his eyes wasn't straight or something, so he tilted his head when he pitched. I'd played with him in New York and San Francisco, and then we were together in Baltimore. He was terrific in New York [in the early '50s], but no one could catch him. Guys today throw 50-mile-per-hour knucklers. Hoyt threw it pretty hard. That's why it moved. We'd play catch in the outfield. I'd say, 'This is easy; this is nothing,' so he'd put more steam on it. It'd hit me in the chest, in the knee. I'd go in and get the chest protector and the mask."

DICK WILLIAMS: "He'd gotten released a couple of times when he got to the Orioles because no one could catch him. Richards came up with the big glove. That helped. But when there was going to be a play at the plate, the pitcher was supposed to change gloves with Gus as he ran by to back up the play—give Gus a smaller glove so he could handle the ball better. That was fine, but [pitcher] Bill Wight ran by one time and threw him the glove and he was left-handed! It was the wrong hand for Gus."

JOE GINSBERG: "Gus would catch one day and have three or four passed balls; then I'd catch and have three or four passed balls. Paul designed the big glove. We called it the elephant glove. The Wilson Company designed it. It worked in the sense that we could catch the ball with it. It got in there. But when guys would steal, the ball was in there and you couldn't grab it and get it out of there. It worked one way and didn't work another way.

"Wilhelm was hard for every catcher. Guys in New York had passed balls when he was there. It didn't bother me so much. It really bothered Gus. He didn't like it. Didn't want to do it. Paul would come to me and say, 'Gus doesn't like it; you handle it better'—that con job. I had to go out there. He hit me everywhere with that thing."

BILL WIGHT: "Gus never got much better at [catching Wilhelm] with that big glove. He thought the big glove was going to solve the problem, and he didn't work at catching it. You had to learn how to catch a knuckler, and Gus didn't apply himself in that direction. He just put on a glove and knocked 'em down."

DICK WILLIAMS: "Gus used to get madder than hell. You had to use the Paul Richards–model glove. And when you were through with it, you had to give the glove back to Paul, and he'd give you another one to break in. That big one that Wilson designed, that was a Paul Richards–model glove, too; at least it kept the ball in front of you. I think catching Wilhelm hurt Gus. I really do. He was as negative as you could find. Having to catch Wilhelm and use Richards's glove, it bothered the hell out of Gus."

GUS TRIANDOS: "It was very tiring, very hot, and a long way back to the backstop to get passed balls. You caught 98 percent of the knuckleballs, and then two or three would get by you in clutch situations, and they'd boo the piss out of you. When I first started catching, I could do the job. The more I caught [Wilhelm], the worse I got. Everything gets to you, you know? If I dropped one they'd boo, so I tensed up and worried about a ball getting by me. We tried a bunch of things to help. The big glove helped, but the only trouble was you didn't know where the ball was and guys started running on you because you couldn't get the ball out of your glove.

"Then I hurt my hand [in '59], and I just sort of tailed away after that. I had to have an operation, and the injury took away from what I could do well. I was just never the same. When they got [Jim] Gentile, Brooks, and Boog [Powell, starting in '60], they started doing well. I was glad they didn't win as soon as I got out of there [in '62], so no one could say, 'Look, they got that jerk out of there and started winning.'"

MILT PAPPAS: "Gus was a good catcher, real big, with good hands. But that knuckleball just destroyed him. He came up with a sore back and went to the Tigers [in '62], and he was never the same. Hoyt killed him. It seemed he was running to the backstop on every other pitch. I don't know if there was anybody who could catch Hoyt consistently. The big glove did make a difference, but [in '59] Gus still had the small glove, and he had a hell of a time. They'd say, 'Gus, how come you got so much trouble?' He'd say, 'For Christ's sake, if the hitter can't hit 'em, how do you expect me to catch 'em?' "

Coming Close
1960–65

11

Young Guns

The real evidence that the Orioles were about to emerge as a contender could be found not in Baltimore, but in Vancouver, British Columbia, and elsewhere in their minor league system. The chain was brimming with prospects in the late '50s, thanks to several years of shrewd scouting and a lot of money thrown at bonus babies.

The '59 Triple-A team in Vancouver featured a half-dozen players who would soon make a difference in Baltimore, including Brooks Robinson, shortstop Ron Hansen, second baseman Marv Breeding, and pitchers Chuck Estrada and Wes Stock. A handful of veterans and former major leaguers also were on the team, helping the youngsters along.

BARRY SHETRONE: "I think maybe two guys on that Vancouver team never made it to the major leagues, which is something. Causey was out there, a nice player who would do well in the major leagues, but he couldn't break into the lineup on that team. There was just a lot of talent in the organization at that time. It was tough. You had to prove your mettle to move along in the system because there was a lot of talent. You could get left behind. A lot of people did."

JOE DURHAM: "We had a guy named Joe Taylor who was one of the greatest wasted talents I ever saw. He could hit the ball a long way, stood out even on that Vancouver club with all that talent. He had bounced around at that point and got a cup of coffee with the Orioles in '59. In Vancouver he'd come to the park so hung over it was amazing he could stand up at the plate."

RON HANSEN: "I was a third baseman coming out of high school, and then a [Class-C] shortstop, an All-American from Southern Cal, broke his leg. That was a lucky break for me, because they switched me to shortstop. They'd switched Brooks from second to third, and if they hadn't switched me [from third] I would have played behind Brooks and never reached the major leagues.

"As it was, Brooks and I started out in Baltimore in '59 and then got sent to Vancouver. There were a bunch of us out there. Brooks got recalled in the middle of the season. I spent the whole year there. That [Vancouver] club was really the kind you want to have in the minor leagues, a mixture of real old players and real young guys who had never played much before."

Lower in the system, on the same Class-D pitching staff in '59, were Steve Barber, Bo Belinsky, and Steve Dalkowski—three left-handers with jaw-dropping potential, as yet untapped. Belinsky would go to the Los Angeles Angels in the '61 expansion draft, throw a no-hitter against the Orioles in '62, and become renowned for a playboy lifestyle. Barber would jump straight to the Orioles' staff in '60 and become a fixture in the starting rotation. Dalkowski had a fastball unlike any seen before.

STEVE BARBER: "By '59 I'd been screwed around for three years. No one would work with me or teach me anything to give me any control. I was really wild. One time a manager told me, 'I don't care if you walk five hundred guys, you're pitching nine innings tonight.' I walked the bases loaded in the first inning, and he walked out there and said, 'Well, you got four hundred ninety-seven to go.' But I threw hard, and some other clubs had told me, 'If you get your release, we'll sign you in a minute.' So I was trying to get my release, and the Orioles wouldn't give it to me.

"I'd go in and ask every day. I was in Pensacola, in the Alabama-Florida League. Harry Dalton came down and said, 'I hear you have an attitude problem.' I said, 'I do. They'd told me they were going to have a minor league pitching coach work with me all spring, but they did it for two days and sent the guy out on a scouting assignment. It seems to me that if I make it, it's all well and good for you, but if I don't it's no big deal because you don't have any money invested in me.' He said, 'Well, that's pretty much it.' I said, 'Why penalize me? Why not give me my release and let me take a shot?' He said, 'We can't give you your release. You have too much potential.'

"So I finished out the ['59] season. Cal Ripken was my catcher for most of the year. Then someone got hurt in Double-A, and they sent him up. They sent me up there, too. To Amarillo. I was there two weeks, started once, went seven good innings. And Eddie Robinson, who was Paul Richards's super scout, happened to be there and saw me. He recommended that I come up after the season and work out for them in Baltimore. So I went up there, and I was bad-mouthing everyone in the organization, talking to [scout Walter] Youse, and MacPhail walked by, and I said, 'And that goes for that SOB, too.' Lee was dumbfounded. He didn't know who I was.

"So I go out and start throwing, and Richards comes over and says, 'What's your name, son?' I said, 'Steve Barber.' He said, 'Where you been?' I said, 'I've been in D ball for three years.' He said, 'How come I've never heard of you?' I said, 'Probably because I'm not one of your fucking bonus babies.' He said, 'You're probably right.'

"After a few days he said they wanted to send me to the instructional league in Clearwater and get things squared away. I said that was great, that was just what I'd been looking for, but I also needed a two-hundred-dollar advance for living expenses until I went down. Richards said, 'Well, take that up with MacPhail,' who I'd just cursed. So I went in to see Lee, and he says, 'How much good do you think this trip will do you?' I said, 'If I get the instruction I need, I'll pitch right here in Baltimore next year.' He said, 'That's a pretty big jump, from Class D to the majors.' I said, 'If anyone can do it, I can.'

"So I went down, and Harry Brecheen worked with me every day at the instructional league. Ripken had helped me a lot during the season, too. I hadn't had a release point. I improved a whole lot in that instructional league. And sure enough, the next year I was in the major leagues."

BOOG POWELL: "One of the greatest things I ever saw was in a game in Bradenton in the instructional league that year. We went over to play the Braves. Joe Torre was catching. There were a bunch of guys who were really good Braves prospects. And it was cold, in the 30s, with the wind blowing. Well, Paul Richards came to the game, and it was so cold he pulled his car right up in even with the dugout and sat in the car with the heater on, watching Barber pitch. And Steve had to be throwing 120 [mph]. The ball was just singing. He's breaking bat after bat after bat. I was playing first. That was probably as good of a pitching performance as I ever saw."

In '58 and '59 the Orioles signed a spectacular crop of prospects including Pete Ward, a future standout for the White Sox; Jerry Adair, a future second baseman for the Orioles; Dean Chance, a future Cy Young Award winner for the Angels; Dave Nicholson, an outfielder who signed for a one-hundred-thousand-dollar bonus but never panned out; and John "Boog" Powell, a massive three-sport star from Key West, Florida, who became one of the Orioles' greatest hitters.

ERNIE HARWELL: "Dave Nicholson was a big right-handed hitter, sort of a country-looking kid, very strong. He had a lot of power and hit some tremendous drives, but they began to tinker with his swing, and everybody had an idea about how he should approach hitting, and he got so screwed up he couldn't do anything.

"The guys were kidding him one time in spring training, the veterans getting on him and all, and he got a little pissed. They were all taking a shower, and he turned the showers off. He went around turning the knobs on the showers, and he turned 'em so far that the guys didn't have strength enough to open them. They were out there bare-assed with soap all over themselves and nowhere to go."

STEVE BARBER: "Dave Nicholson was probably the greatest single talent I've ever seen. People asked me what I thought of him, and I said, 'I'd give him the money in a minute.' His potential was unreal. He was six [feet], two [inches], 220 [pounds], with a rifle for an arm. A real nice guy, very sincere person. He just couldn't hit the breaking ball."

BARRY SHETRONE: "He had a lot of talent, but they screwed him up. Maybe he'd have got screwed up anyway, but at least let him do it on his own. They brought him to spring training, and he was scared to death. You could just look at him and know. Who wouldn't be? You're nineteen; you're the biggest bonus baby; your father got a scouting job and two cars. Now you're in a major league camp with ballplayers you've heard of, and they start messing with your batting stance because you aren't making contact. The very first day, they had guys working with him. I felt sorry for him. It didn't make sense. They had to see something special in the guy to give him one hundred thousand dollars. Why change it right away?

"Later on, we used to sit in amazement and watch him swing. I couldn't believe it. Everything was perfect—except he never made contact. You'd be sitting in the dugout where you had a side view of the hitter, and you'd say, 'How did he miss the ball?' I used to say it looked like the bat would open up, the ball would go through, and then [the bat would] close. I couldn't figure out how he was missing the ball because his head was right on it and everything. When he hit 'em, he hit 'em hard. But not enough."

HARRY DALTON: "Dean Chance was a big signing, a tough signing. We finally got him for twenty-seven thousand dollars. A good pitcher. But Richards liked a kid named Arnie Thorsland more, a real good pitcher, too. When the expansion draft came up [in '61], Jim McLaughlin wanted Chance protected, and I did, too. Richards wanted Thorsland, so we protected him. The Angels took Chance, and then Thorsland hurt his arm that spring and was never the same."

BOOG POWELL: "My senior year in high school, in '59, I was being touted as the next Dave Nicholson. The next one-hundred-thousand-dollar bonus baby. I was all-state in football, basketball, and baseball. By the spring I'd already signed a football scholarship with Florida. I was almost more coveted in football than baseball. I had an appointment to the Naval Academy. I could have gone just about anywhere I wanted. I was a lineman, big offensive and defensive tackle. Just take the whole left side of the line and say, 'Come on guys, let's go this way.' That was fun. I liked basketball, too. Ole Miss wanted me for that.

"My dad just said, 'Do whatever you want. If you want to play football, I'm behind you. If you want to play baseball, I'm also behind you.' I wanted to play baseball. I was better at it. Football was just something to do. I just went through the motions. Baseball, I loved. My senior year I hit .570, 14 home runs, unbelievable numbers, and we won the state tournament for the second year in a row.

"At the start of the tournament, every team had a scout there. I mean, I had an offer before the tournament. Milwaukee offered me eighty thousand dollars to not go to the tournament. I said, 'No, I'm not going to do that.' I wanted to go to the tournament; plus, if I had a good tournament it could have gone to a hundred fifty thousand dollars. But I had a terrible tournament. There were a lot of scouts, and I wasn't relaxed at all. I went 2 for 17. I was striking out and pressing too hard.

"The scouts started leaving. At the end there were only two teams left— St. Louis and Baltimore. St. Louis offered me twenty thousand dollars. Baltimore came right behind and offered twenty-two thousand. Then St. Louis offered twenty-four thousand. I said, 'This can't be right. There's something wrong here.' I mean, Milwaukee was gone. They never came back to me after the eighty thousand. They just pulled it. That's how bad I looked.

"At about four o'clock that morning, we'd won the title, and we were about to go back to Key West, and the Orioles called and said they'd give me twenty-five thousand dollars. And I never heard anything from St. Louis. I said, 'Bring the contract down here, and we'll sign it right now'—my dad and I. So I signed. Freddie "Bootnose" Hofmann was the guy for the Orioles. Jim Russo takes a lot of credit, but Freddie Hofmann was the guy. I mean, he used to talk to me about catching Babe Ruth, blowing smoke, and he'd say, 'You could hit a lot of home runs. I've seen a lot of young guys, and you're one of the best I've seen.' When he thought I wasn't going to sign with the Orioles, he was crying. I mean, they were real tears. When we signed he was jumping up and down.

"I went straight to [rookie league] Bluefield, and six guys off that team wound up making the major leagues. Dean Chance. Bobby Saverine. Buster Narum. Arnie Thorsland was absolutely unbelievable. Had one of the best arms I ever saw. I faced him in batting practice the first day and went, 'What have I gotten myself into?' This guy was blowing the ball by me, and I didn't even see it. He was so good they lost Chance to keep him. Then he hurt his arm.

"I was making four hundred dollars a month, so I had beer money. And little by little, I started getting more accustomed to what I was doing. I would get just a little better day by day, and then all of a sudden I was fine. I hit like .355. Through my whole career it was like that with me. I'd start a little slow, and once I realized what people were trying to do to me and what was happening to me, I'd catch up with the rest of the league.

"After that season I went to the instructional league with Barber and a bunch of guys. Four of us rented a house on Clearwater Beach for two hundred fifty dollars a month—four bedrooms and three baths right on the beach. It was great. Ralph Salvon was the team trainer. He was still in the minors, and he came and lived on our screened-in porch. He'd come in after the bars closed, and I could hear him scuffling around in the kitchen. I'd go out there and say, 'Ralphie, what are you doing?' He'd say, 'Hey, want a hot dog?' He had the water boiling, and he'd drop a whole pack of hot dogs in there. I'd sit there and I'd say, 'Yeah, I'll eat one with you.' We're eating hot dogs at two in the morning, and we had to be at the ballpark at ten. Life couldn't get any better."

12

Kiddie Corps

With four starting pitchers aged twenty-two or younger and rookies playing first base, second base, and shortstop, the Orioles were unlikely contenders in '60. But they had their first winning season and contended for a pennant until the season's final weeks. The franchise would experience many championship seasons in the coming years, but few were as surprising or enjoyable as the '60 season.

The stable of young pitchers, nicknamed "the Kiddie Corps," was the talk of the major leagues. Chuck Estrada, a rookie, won 18 games, a club record. Milt Pappas won 15; Jack Fisher won 12. Steve Barber, jumping all the way from Class-D ball, won 10. Veterans Skinny Brown and Hoyt Wilhelm backed them up with spot starts and solid relief work, combining for 23 wins. Overall, Orioles pitchers led the AL in complete games and tied for the lowest ERA.

LEE MACPHAIL: "It was after the All-Star Game in '59 that we decided we were going to go with younger players. It was a joint decision between myself and Paul. We were going with the kids. It was time. We had all those guys in Vancouver, and others, too. In '60 we had seven rookies and practically everyone on the team was younger than thirty. And so many fine, young pitchers. If they had an arm, Paul was all for bringing them up in a hurry."

JERRY WALKER: "I was the Opening Day starter, but I think I went about eight or ten starts before I got a decision. I wasn't pitching that well. Fisher and Pappas and Barber and Estrada were. Barber had come out of D ball, and he threw a heavy, sinking fastball and was just wild enough to be effective. He was around the plate enough to get hitters out. Estrada threw a high fastball. Pappas threw sinkers. Fisher threw more conventionally, with a big curveball. I was somewhere in between. We had an interesting group of young arms."

JACKIE BRANDT: "Barber threw a shot put. Estrada threw the hardest. Pappas was slider, slider, slider. Fisher's fastball wasn't too much, but he had a grinding curveball. Walker tricked you."

RON HANSEN: "Barber threw awfully hard and never straight. I mean, he had great movement. Guys hated to hit against him because he was a little bit wild. Guys wouldn't really want to stand in there because he would throw so hard."

MARV BREEDING: "All the young guys threw well. Pappas probably was the number-one guy. Estrada threw harder, but he was young and wild in '60. Pappas had more stuff. And he was Richards's little bobo."

GUS TRIANDOS: "The young guys didn't spot pitches; they just wound up and threw good stuff. They didn't work on things. They just called a fastball and zinged it. You knew they'd be somewhere around the plate. They had good stuff, had good control. And then when Wilhelm relieved with the knuckler, it was tough on the hitters."

STEVE BARBER: "That spring I got timed as the fastest pitcher in the major leagues. I hadn't even thrown a pitch yet. This [newspaper] Sunday supplement set up the thing for an article. They used a high-speed camera and got a panoramic view and computed it mathematically. They'd already timed Bob Turley, and someone said, 'You better go time that new left-hander with the Orioles.' That's how I got included. They did six of us. Turned out I was the fastest at 95.5 miles per hour. Don Drysdale was just behind me, and Sandy Koufax was right after him."

BOOG POWELL: "Barber was incredible when he was young. He had probably the best stuff of all of them. Very intimidating. No one wanted to stand in there on him. And Pappas was no slouch. When he wanted to pitch, he was one of the best you ever saw. Fastball, slider, bang, bang, inside, outside."

MILT PAPPAS: "Our four [starters] felt that as young as we were and as good as we thought we were, we would never have any kind of a losing streak. To lose seven or eight in a row was just unthinkable. We quickly became a very respected starting staff."

The everyday lineup was overhauled almost completely from '59. Jim Gentile, a slugger who had languished in the Dodgers' minor league system for seven years, unable to supplant Gil Hodges, took over for Bob Boyd at first base. Marv Breeding and Ron Hansen, products of the Orioles' minor league system, replaced Billy Gardner, Chico Carrasquel, and Willy Miranda in the middle infield. The new centerfielder was Jackie Brandt, a fleet, natural talent acquired from the Giants after he won a Gold Glove in right field in '59. He would become a popular, eccentric fixture; teammates called him "Flakey," for the way things seemed to flake off his mind and disappear.

JIM GENTILE: "The Orioles traded for me, and I came to spring training [in '60] on a look-see basis. They paid fifty thousand dollars for me and gave up Willy Miranda, and I went to them on a thirty-day look-see. If I didn't make it, I went back to the Dodgers and the Dodgers got twenty-five thousand dollars back. So what it amounted to was the Orioles paid for my spring training if I didn't make it.

"I'd run out of options with the Dodgers. It wasn't a good situation, and I wasn't happy about it. I'd been in the minors forever, to the point that I'd started thinking about going to Japan or giving it up. My [minor league] numbers were huge, but the Dodgers had Hodges at first and a lot of people in the system, and I couldn't even get a cup of coffee [in the majors].

"My first year in pro ball, I led the league in home runs with 34, and I drove in 103 runs and hit .270, and I thought it was a pretty good year for an eighteen-year-old in Class A. But I went back to Class A the next year. Then two years in Double A, the Texas League. Huge numbers. I hit 40 homers, drove in 115, and toured Japan with the Dodgers after the season and led them in everything. That was in '56. Then they told me the next year I had to go to Triple A and learn how to hit the change-up. Then they optioned me back there the next year, and then again the next year after that.

"I was playing winter ball in Panama in '59, and Joe Altobelli came up to me and said he heard I'd been traded. I said, 'Holy cow, you're kidding. Baltimore?' He said yeah. I had no idea how big Memorial Stadium was. Joe goes, 'That's terrible; that stadium is an airport. It's a tough place for a home-run hitter.'

"When I got there, I talked to Luman Harris, and he said, 'What we need is a power-hitting first baseman. Bobby Boyd is a great hitter, but maybe we can move him to the outfield because he doesn't drive in runs.' They had a ton of first basemen in camp. Myself, Boyd, Walt Dropo. John Powers. Boog was there. And I couldn't hit a beach ball. I don't think I hit .100 that spring. The writers would say, 'What's wrong?' All I could say was, 'Wait 'til the bell rings.'"

BOOG POWELL: "I hit .350 that spring, and Gentile didn't do much. I said, 'Well, maybe they're going to take me.' I was down there working my ass off. I mean, I was the first one to get there and the last one to leave. I'd catch ground balls till whoever was hitting 'em just said they couldn't hit any more.

"One day Richards had the great idea of taking the pitching machine out to the outfield corner and aiming the throws in the dirt and having the first basemen scoop the balls out. He got us out there against the concrete wall, and it was dry and dusty, and they racked that thing up with seventy balls and fired 'em at us at, like, eighty-five miles per hour. And the ones you missed would hit the wall and come back and hit you in the ass or upside the head. Richards never showed a lot of emotion, but he was smiling that day. We never did that again, thank God.

"Near the end of camp Paul called me in and said, 'Son, I'd really like to take you with us, but you're too young. You're eighteen and you're doing good, but I'm just afraid you'd be in over your head up here on a day-to-day basis.' There wasn't much I could say. It just wasn't quite time yet."

JIM GENTILE: "On the last day Richards called me in and sat me down and said, 'Son, you can't be as bad as you look. Your stats in the minors are tremendous. You only got 36 at-bats in three years with the Dodgers. I'm going to give you 150 to 200. I'm going to bat you against right-handers every chance I get. If you hit for me in the first thirty days, you're my first baseman. If not, we're sending you back.' And I said, 'That's all I've ever asked for in seven years. Let me have a few times at bat to see what I can do.'

"We went to the team luncheon the day before Opening Day, and everyone was asking what the lineup was, and Richards had me hitting fifth. I think everybody was stunned, even the other players. And then on Opening Day I went one for four against Washington and some guy wrote, 'Gentile surprised forty-five thousand people by getting a hit.' Then we had a day off and went to Washington, and I hit two homers and drove in five runs. Then we came back over to our place, and I got two hits and drove in four. Richards was real good to me all year. He played me only against right-handers."

RON HANSEN: "The shortstop job was pretty much mine from the beginning. My job to lose. I'd been up a bit in the prior two years, and Willy Miranda had really helped me a lot. Willy was really good. He showed me some little things. I was there to take his job, but I guess he felt he was at the latter part of his career. He was very good to me. Then, fortunately, I started out the ['60] season real good, hit real well for the first month, and played very well for the whole first half. Made the All-Star team and everything. I kind of slumped in the second half but still played every day."

Holdovers in the lineup included rightfielder Gene Woodling, catcher Gus Triandos, and Brooks Robinson, finally ready at third after five years of seasoning. Joe Ginsberg was the backup catcher early in the season, but with Triandos and Ginsberg struggling to handle Wilhelm's knuckleball, the club traded for Clint "Scrap Iron" Courtney, the Orioles' original catcher in '54, now thirty-three and near the end of his career. Courtney, another eccentric who used a Cadillac instead of a pick-up truck to tend to his Louisiana farm, was an old-school character who lightened up the mood in the young clubhouse.

JIM GENTILE: "Triandos took me under his wing. He was from San Francisco, like I was. I'd wait for him to ask me to go to dinner. He'd take me to Eddie Condon's and the Copa, different places, show me around. A hell of a guy. We didn't go out all the time because Gus was more of a loner. I didn't know anything, and I didn't want to run around that much until I learned how. Then I ran around too much. But Wilhelm was driving Gus nuts. It was tough. He tried like hell, but nobody had a knuckleball like that. So they went and got Clint Courtney. Clint was lower to the ground. Ol' Scrap Iron, he'd get back there with that big glove on, and he'd just pounce on it."

STEVE BARBER: "Richards loved Courtney. One of Clint's duties was to shag Paul's golf balls. They'd go out wherever the team was, and Paul would hit golf balls, and Clint would shag them. Courtney and Hoyt roomed together. Hoyt liked to go out and have dinner and then come back to the room and go to bed. Courtney stayed out later. So early in the season, Hoyt would come back, turn off the heat, open all the windows, and take all the blankets off Courtney's bed and put them on his. Then Courtney would come in a few hours later and pass out. He'd wake up in the morning and he was freezing. So he'd get on the phone to Louisiana, 'Pa, this fuckin' guy Wilhelm is trying to freeze me to death, Pa.' Hoyt loved it."

JACKIE BRANDT: "Now, Courtney was a goofy guy. They thought I was goofy. Him and Jack Fisher bought a bunch of chickens in Louisiana. Thousands of them. Never did too good with it. I think a lot of the chickens died. But [Courtney] was great to have on the team. He and Billy Martin were getting in fights in every game.

"One time we were in New York, bases loaded, last inning, and Courtney goes to Richards and says, 'Give me a bat and get me in there, Skip; I can get that run in.' Richards says, 'That's a left-handed pitcher out there, and you're left-handed.' Courtney goes, 'I don't care; I can get that run in for you, Skip.' So Richards goes, 'OK, get a bat.' First pitch comes in, and he just sticks his head over the plate and gets whopped. Right on the head. Guy comes in and scores. Clint comes back and says, 'I told you I'd get that run in.'"

STEVE BARBER: "My first trip into Boston in '60, Clint was catching and it was the ninth. I'm ahead 2–1, two outs, no one on, two strikes, no balls. I'd thrown fastballs and sliders the whole game, but as bad as my curve was, I thought I could throw one in the dirt and get a swing. Clint called fastball and I shook it [off]. Then he called slider and I shook it. Then fastball again and I shook it; then slider again and I shook it. So he comes trotting out and says, 'Now lookee here, I done got you this far with that shit, now let's go the rest of the way with it.' I just bust out laughing. Then I got a ground ball to end the game."

RON HANSEN: "[Courtney] loved cattle and horses, and when we went to Kansas City he'd go to the stockyards and look at horses and cattle, and when we'd go to Chicago or Detroit he always went to the racetrack. Well, one day in Detroit he came in the clubhouse ranting and raving about how he could beat a quarter horse in a race. All the guys jumped on that and put up a lot of money. So at six in the morning he and a couple of the players went to the Detroit raceway. They had a trainer friend there that had a quarter horse, and they got the people to put a starting gate out, and Scrap Iron was going to race this quarter horse for 100 yards. He stripped down to his shorts and got in the starting gate, and they rang the bell, and he came back to the clubhouse that afternoon, and he was paying guys money he owed 'em. He said, 'Don't let anybody ever tell you that they can beat a quarter horse, because when that gate opened all I saw was this horse's ass.'

"Then he ordered a Cadillac from Johnnie's Used Cars—a new Cadillac. Went over and picked it up one hot day in July when it was 100 degrees. Brought the car to the ballpark, and when he came in the clubhouse he was soaking wet and water was running off him. Somebody asked him what was the matter. He said, 'Well, I went over to pick up my car, and those dummies forgot to put the handles on the windows.' He had electric windows and he didn't know it. Had air-conditioning and didn't know it. He was driving around with the windows up."

MILT PAPPAS: "One time we were playing the Yankees, and they had a runner on second, and when that happened it was routine to change the signs the catcher gave the pitcher. You know, so the guy on second couldn't steal the sign and relay it to the hitter. So Clint comes out to the mound and says, 'There's a guy on second, we need to change signs.' I said 'I'm aware of that, Clint. What kind of change do you want to make?' He said, 'The first sign after I put down two [fingers] will be the sign.' I said fine, great. The first sign after two would be the pitch.

"So I look in and Clint puts down a string of signs, two, two, two, two. I called time-out, and Clint came out, and I said, 'That doesn't fool anyone if all you're putting down is two.' He said, 'Oh, hell, you're right. OK, let's make it the first sign after one.' Fine. Great. So he goes back to the plate and gets down and starts giving the signs, one, one, one, one. I just threw up my hands and said the hell with it, I don't care what the sign is, I'm just throwing a fastball.

"I walked up to him one time and said, 'Man, Scrap Iron, Richards really loves you.' He said, 'Yeah, if he told me to clean the floor, I'd put the broom up my ass and catch and sweep the floor at the same time.' He was a guy with hardly any ability, but he had guts. I mean, he just made himself into a ballplayer. He wasn't gifted as far as being a good hitter, but he just made himself into a good ballplayer with dedication, heart, and guts. That's a lot more than I can say for a lot of other guys I played with and against."

JIM GENTILE: "He drove around in that Cadillac, and he'd have a beer and just throw it in the back like you would in a truck. One time Clint got dressed real quick after a game, and it turns out he's got three hunting dogs in the back of his Cadillac, he's left them in the back of the car all during the game. He was one of a kind, a lot of fun. That's why Richards got him. We had a lot of red asses on our club—guys who took the game too seriously— and once in a while they'd hit a chair or break something. You needed someone to loosen it up. And Clint was that thing we had."

Although the club hit only .253 overall, there was enough production to keep the Orioles in contention. Gentile was a surprise, delivering 21 homers and 98 RBI in only 384 at-bats, with Richards using him strictly against right-handers. Hansen also delivered more than expected, his 22 homers and 86 RBI serving as a revelation for a team accustomed to minimal production at shortstop. Brandt had 15 homers and 65 RBI, and Woodling hit .283 with 11 homers and 62 RBI. Triandos, fighting a hand injury and Wilhelm's knuckler, produced less than fans were accustomed to seeing, and he drew boos.

The biggest offensive surprise was Robinson, previously overmatched against major league pitching. Playing every day, he hit .294 with 14 homers and 88 RBI, and despite a lack of speed, he was on base enough to lead the club with 74 runs scored. With that production added to his flawless defense, he was "discovered" as one of the game's top young players.

JACKIE BRANDT: "I had come over from the Giants, and we had Jim Davenport at third, and he was a hawk; he could suck up anything. I got over here, and I was talking to Richards before spring training, and he said, 'We got a kid over here who can really play third.' I was telling him about Davenport. And Richards said, 'Watch this kid play before you make any comparisons.' Then we got started, and shoot, Brooks didn't miss nothing. Left, right, in, one-handed. Had a poor arm and always beat the runner by a step. Dove either way."

JIM GENTILE: "First game I ever played with him at third, the ball was hit a little to his right. I ran to first base, turned around and there [the ball] was. He just fired it. I got in the dugout and said, 'Gimme a minute, Brooks; let me get there.' He wasn't fast, but three feet to the right, three feet to the left, there was nobody faster. His reactions were like a cat. I mean, if anything was hit you'd better be there on first base because it was coming."

JACKIE BRANDT: "It was just a knack he had, natural reactions to the ball coming off the bat. He was always moving left. That's why he dove so much to his right. If you hit it in the hole, you were dead. But if you hit it down the line, he had to dive. Most players did it opposite, dove for the ones in the hole. But he just had a natural way of moving the other way."

RON HANSEN: "Brooks and I had kind of grown up together in the system. We were roommates for a couple of years and became really close, and playing next to him was even better in that respect. We were very compatible; we liked the same kind of things. It was just great, being able to play with him. He didn't have a very good arm. I used to yell 'tag up,' because it looked like a sacrifice fly when he threw to first base. He'd laugh. We'd always kid about this or that.

"But he just had that instinct, those great, quick, soft hands. Nothing ever popped out of his glove. His initial movements were good. Laterally he was good. Below average speed. If I were scouting him today, I'd say, 'below average arm, below average speed, not a great body, really a soft-body guy. But great hands and great instincts.' Nowadays a lot of people wouldn't sign a kid like that. But it was different then. Teams signed guys more on ability than tools. Today, we get out the radar gun and you have to throw ninety miles per hour or you don't get signed. Or you have to run to first in under four seconds. But how many Brooks Robinsons would you miss if you just signed guys with speed?"

JIM GENTILE: "It wasn't complicated. Day in and day out, he'd come in, get dressed, smile, say hello to everybody. Go out and play his game. If he went oh for four he still smiled, took his shower, said 'see you later.' Always even. And he never missed a game. In Detroit one time he took a hit and chipped his front teeth during batting practice. Goes in, stuffs cotton in there, and plays nine."

RON HANSEN: "As a hitter, he was overmatched for a little while. I don't think he became Brooks Robinson until he started hitting a little better. People didn't realize how great he was until he started to hit. He was always a great fielder, but he did struggle at the plate in the beginning. Once he started to pick that up and started to hit, people realized just how good he was.

"Brooks and myself and Chuck Estrada and Skinny Brown lived together that year. We stayed at a place, a family's house over near the stadium. The four of us lived there with a family that took us in. Skinny was kind of our mentor. Chuck and Brooks and myself were younger, and Chuck and I were new to the major leagues, so this was a new experience. Skinny looked out for us, kept us out of trouble.

"We'd walk to the park. There was a little place down on Greenmount Avenue called the Run In, just a little hole in the wall, but we'd go down there every morning and eat. Most of the time it was the four of us. We'd eat breakfast or a late lunch, and we'd go to the ballpark. We'd walk. Then after the game we'd walk back."

Fans began to realize something special was happening in early June, when the Orioles swept three games from the Yankees at Memorial Stadium to complete a run of 11 wins in 13 games. A Sunday crowd of 42,755 loosed a roar when Woodling hit an eighth-inning homer to give the Orioles the sweep. It was their thirteenth come-from-behind win of the season, and their eighth winning rally in the last three innings. They were in first place, two games ahead of a pack of contenders.

The euphoria quickly faded with four straight losses to the Tigers, and a later slump of 11 losses in 15 games dropped them to fourth at the All-Star break. But instead of their usual slow fade, they got hot again. Robinson hit for the cycle against the White Sox on July 15, and a spell of exceptional pitching, including a one-hitter from Barber, sparked a run of 13 wins in 14 games. By mid-August the Orioles were tied for first with the White Sox, although the pennant-race pack was bunched so tightly that a pair of losses to the Yankees over the next two days dropped them to third.

The Kiddie Corps took over after that with a remarkable run of eight complete-game wins in eleven days. The streak culminated with a three-game sweep of the Yankees at Memorial Stadium in early September. Pappas threw a shutout to beat Orioles nemesis Whitey Ford in the opener before 44,518 fans, and then Fisher, in the middle of a run of 29 consecutive scoreless innings, pitched another shutout the next day. Estrada completed the sweep with a 6–2 win in the finale. The Orioles were in first place with 22 games to go.

MARV BREEDING: "The main thing we had going for us in '60 was all that pitching and then good defense around it. We really had it going there for a while. We won a lot of games. Long around the middle of the season we started to realize we belonged with the Yankees and maybe could beat 'em. Then some of us had trouble hitting."

RON HANSEN: "The Yankees came in to Baltimore in early September, and we beat them three in a row, and the city really went wild for the first time. Everybody was really hyped about us maybe winning the pennant. The hype was more with the people in the city than the team, although we felt good about ourselves. We felt like we had a good team and we could beat [the Yankees] and win the pennant."

A mild stagger (four wins in nine games) ensued, leaving the Orioles .001 percentage points behind the Yankees heading into a showdown in New York. The veteran Yankees, accustomed to such pressures, delivered a knockout punch, sweeping the four games by a total of eight runs. Ford beat Barber 4–2 in the opener, and the Yankees then won on Saturday and swept a Sunday doubleheader in front of fifty-three thousand fans, with Ralph Terry beating Pappas 2–0 in the finale. The Yankees wound up winning the pennant by eight games.

Softening the disappointment, manager Paul Richards was named AL Manager of the Year, Hansen was AL Rookie of the Year, and Brooks Robinson finished third in the league's MVP voting. The Orioles had arrived.

MILT PAPPAS: "We didn't have any doubt that we could go up there and win, but they got us. I pitched the last game, and if I'd pitched any of the other three games, I would have won. We scored two or more runs in all those games except that one. But losing four just destroyed us. I mean, we threw our best at their best. The Yankees were such a dominant team. They'd beat you 2–0; they'd beat you 5–3; they'd beat you 10–9. Whatever it took, they beat you."

LEE MACPHAIL: "When we went into New York for the four-game series, I decided to reward the people who'd worked in the office all year and rented a bus and took the whole staff to New York. And we lost four straight."

STEVE BARBER: "I pitched the first game. A Friday night. Hung a curveball to Hector Lopez. He inside-outed it right down the right-field line, right at the foul pole, and Jackie Brandt ran over to catch it, and someone grabbed his hands and pulled them back, and the ball went over the fence. If the guy hadn't interfered, Jackie would have caught it. It was a close game. They all were. We just lost 'em."

JIM GENTILE: "We thought we had a chance, especially after beating them three in a row in Baltimore. The team was really up. We had good heads on our shoulders. But I don't think we had the kind of leadership that the Orioles got when Frank Robinson got there in 1966. I don't think we had what you'd call a team leader. We didn't have anybody get up in the middle of the dressing room and make speeches or anything like that. Everybody knew the job they had to do, and they went out and tried to perform at their best. We just didn't have the guy to get in the middle of the clubhouse and say, 'Hey look, fellas.' And we needed it. The only guy that had a cool head all the time was Brooks.

"As it was, all the games were close. Even right to the end of the last one. Pappas was pitching, and we were right in it. Then Yogi Berra came up with a guy on second. I was playing back. Berra was tough to defend against because you didn't know if he was going to pull. If the ball was inside, he'd pull. I was playing him kind of toward the line, just not a whole lot, and he hit it in the hole, and I dove for it, and it just went off my glove. And the run scored and that beat us."

"SKINNY" BROWN: "It was disappointing. We'd had some success earlier in the season with Wilhelm and myself pitching against the Yankees. But when we went up to New York [Richards] pitched the young blood, and we lost four in a row. You've got to go with your best at the end of the year. Most of the time over the years I had always pitched good against the Yankees."

RON HANSEN: "A lot of guys had good years that year. Gentile. Estrada won 18 games. I was actually in the service, and they called me and told me that I'd been selected Rookie of the Year. That was great. I'd have to say it was my favorite year in my career, because I was young; I was a kid, and everything was exciting. I mean, I was starstruck when we went into Yankee Stadium, the monuments in center field, playing against Mickey Mantle, hitting against

Whitey Ford. I was in a world I never imagined I'd be in, so it was great. We had a lot of young guys on the team that year who probably felt the same way."

BROOKS ROBINSON: "I guess we were a little nonchalant about the whole thing, figuring, 'Well, we can do it.' And the reason I say that is because when the season was all over, we didn't think much about it—at least I didn't. We'd had a real good year, our first good year, and we felt there were more good things to come. And I mean, the Yankees were supposed to win. They were the kings at that time, and we didn't feel bad. We felt like, 'Well, you know, there's next year.' "

13

Dalkowski

The Orioles' farm system produced many All-Stars and important contributors in the early years, but the most phenomenal talent never played in a major league game. Steve Dalkowski, a left-handed pitcher from New Britain, Connecticut, was truly a legend in his own time. "He was unbelievable, that's the only word," said Ron Hansen, a shortstop who came through the system at the same time.

Dalkowski signed with the Orioles in '57 and spent eight years in the farm system. He was average-sized at best—only 5-feet-11 inches and 170 pounds—but he was one of the hardest throwers in history. There were no radar guns then, but observers believe he routinely surpassed 100 miles per hour, sometimes by quite a bit. Cal Ripken Sr., a man not given to exaggeration, caught Dalkowski in the late '50s and told a reporter years later that Dalkowski threw harder than Nolan Ryan, baseball's all-time strikeout leader.

If he'd had control of his fastball, according to Earl Weaver, who managed him in the minors, he could have become another Sandy Koufax. But he was as wild as any pitcher in the game. In his first pro season, at the Class-D level, he walked 129 and struck out 121 in 62 innings. Three years later, pitching in the California League, he walked 262 and struck out 262.

WALTER YOUSE: "Physically, he wasn't that big. But he was real strong. Had long arms. Frank McGowan was the scout who signed him up in Connecticut. They didn't give him a lot of bonus money, something like eight thousand dollars or ten thousand dollars. No one knew too much about him. Frank had seen him playing football—throwing passes left-handed—and tried to keep it quiet. They got him for a pretty reasonable price. And right away, instantly, he became a phenomenon."

BARRY SHETRONE: "You had to see it to believe it. You know those fast-pitch softball pitchers whose balls rise going toward the plate? Steve did that throwing overhand. I took batting practice against him in spring training in '58, and he threw a ball to me, and his reputation had preceded him, and I see it coming, and I'm thinking to myself, 'Well he's not so fast.' Then, before I could think, the ball, which was about belt high, just zoomed up and over my head. I stood back and said, 'I don't believe I saw what I just saw.'"

RON HANSEN: "His fastball would rise, on average, a foot to two feet between the pitcher's mound and home plate. It looked like an airplane taking off. And most of the time he never threw it anywhere close to the plate. Sometimes he missed the [batting] cage entirely."

WALTER YOUSE: "Richards said he'd never seen anyone else throw a ball that started down at the shins and moved up into the strike zone. They brought him up to Baltimore and let him throw batting practice before a game against the Red Sox, and everything just stopped. All those big-leaguers came over to watch, Ted Williams included. No one had ever seen anything like it.

"I was the manager when he won his first ball game as a pro in '57. They sent me to Kingsport to manage the team there because the manager got sick. The first night, Steve pitched for me in Pulaski, Virginia. The dugout was real close to the field. You could sit there and hear Dalkowski's pitches buzzing to the plate. They made a noise like you never heard. I told him, 'Steve, don't throw your curveball so hard. Let up a little bit, throw like maybe a half-speed curveball, and try to get it over a little bit.'

"So Pulaski had a guy who was leading the league in hitting. Batting third. And the first time up Dalkowski throws one of those easy-up curveballs, and the guy hits the hell out of it for a double. And he's out there on second base and you can hear him shouting, 'Dalkowski, you ain't so hot,' and all that. The next time up, Jesus, Dalkowski throws three fastballs like bullets, and you could sit in the dugout and hear them buzzing to the plate. The poor guy never had a chance. I think the catcher dropped the third one, and the guy ran to first, and you could hear his manager saying, 'That ought to teach you, you big-mouthed son of a bitch.'

"He won that game, and the next time out he struck out 24 of 26 outs. In the eighth, with two outs, he loaded the bases, and I took him out and put him out in right field, and brought in a right-handed pitcher to get a guy out. The pitcher got the guy out, and I brought Steve back in the ninth, and he struck out the side. Struck out 24, walked 18, gave up two hits, and won 7–4.

When we went to play in Salem, Virginia, this Latin American boy came up when we got to the park and said, 'Hey, Skip, Lefty gonna pitch tonight? If he pitch, I no play.'"

HERM STARRETTE: "I pitched with a lot of guys and worked with oodles of them as a coach, but as far as raw ability, there was no one better. He could have pitched in the big leagues for years. He could have set records. He had three quality pitches—fastball, curveball, and slider. I never saw him when he didn't have good stuff. And as hard as he threw, his ball was feathery light.

"A normal game for him was seven innings, 18 strikeouts, 15 walks. He couldn't go nine because he threw so many pitches. And he set a record with every pitch. Either a strikeout or walk record. I couldn't wait for the nights he pitched. One night he was pitching for Earl [Weaver] in Aberdeen [South Dakota] and walked 18, struck out 20, and pitched a no-hitter. He must have thrown 400 pitches. Another night he was warming up in Reno [Nevada] and told me, 'The first [warm-up] pitch I'm throwing over the press box.' He threw it clean out of the stadium. Over the press box and everything. The sportswriters were ducking. Billy DeMars was managing, and he turned to me and said, 'Did he do that on purpose?' I said, 'I don't think so; that's just Steve.'"

BOOG POWELL: "I walked into the cage one day and I said, 'OK, man, give me your best stuff. I'm taking you to the bridge, brother.' And he wound up and threw, and the next time I saw the ball, it was rolling out of the cage. It hit the back of the cage, and it was rolling out. I never saw it. You couldn't pick him up. It was totally unhittable."

STEVE BARBER: "Ripken always said, 'If the ball left his hand belt high, you just turn and run for the screen.' It was going to sail, in other words. And if it left his hand looking like it was going to hit the ground, it was going to come in as a strike. But all his balls were so light, that was the amazing thing. As hard as he threw, Cal said he could catch the ball bare-handed."

BARRY SHETRONE: "They worked so hard trying to give him control. They would get the catcher to sit on the ground, giving him a target as low as possible, figuring if he threw at that target, by the time it got to the plate it would be in the strike zone. And Paul would try to wear him down so that he would slow down and throw strikes. Steve threw every day in spring training. Can you imagine that? He'd throw in the bullpen for an hour, then go out and pitch in a game. And he'd throw fairly decently in the bullpen, but when he got on the mound he couldn't throw strikes. They'd do that day after day after day. It never wore him down."

BOOG POWELL: "They'd get him to hold the ball across the seams, you know, to keep the ball down. If you throw a cross-seamer with the seams, it'll sink. They had him doing that and everything else, but it was still taking off. It was something to see. They tried and tried to figure out ways to get him together. I think his problem was he was afraid he was going to kill somebody. I really do think he thought that. He hit a bunch of guys when he was young and tore one kid's earlobe off. That scared him."

HARRY DALTON: "He hit a kid, a first baseman named Beavers. Dalkowski nailed him in the head so hard that the ball flew back and landed on the grass between the mound and second base. Everybody froze when it happened, and the ball just dropped there very softly and innocently halfway between the mound and second. They took the kid to the hospital, and the kid only played one more season and quit.

"One night later that season in Johnson City, Tennessee, Dalkowski was pitching, fifth inning, and a hitter fouled a pitch up in the air and to the third baseman for the third out. Dalkowski came in and said, 'Skip, you'd better get somebody up. I'm starting to lose it.' That was the only ball that had gone forward in five innings, fair or foul. Everything else was either a strikeout or a walk."

MILT PAPPAS: "He was such a phenomenon that they took him outside Baltimore to the Aberdeen Proving Ground and clocked him through the facilities there. Everyone wanted to know what he was throwing. They clocked him at 104 miles per hour. If that guy could have thrown strikes, I just wonder what type of career he would have had. It was just unbelievable. Paul was just so frustrated with him."

Dalkowski's wildness, along with a parallel reputation for wildness off the field, kept his career from moving forward. The Orioles developed many fine young pitchers in his era, but Dalkowski's only appearance at Memorial

Stadium was in an exhibition game against the Reds in '59. He struck out the side.

WALTER YOUSE: "He pitched that one exhibition game [in '59] and struck out three Reds on nine pitches. My understanding was that [Reds manager] Birdie Tebbetts told everyone that they had to stand back at the far end of the batter's box and just take every pitch, strike or ball. Anyone that swung, he was going to fine 'em. He didn't want 'em in there against Steve."

STEVE BARBER: "I was on the same staff with Steve and Bo Belinsky in '59, in the Alabama-Florida League. I was fast, but he made me look slow. He just didn't have a clue where it was going. And he was a different type person. Had real bad habits. He never had his underwear clean or anything. He had his sweatshirts and stuff in the locker by mine, and they smelled so bad I told him, 'If you don't wash those things by tomorrow, I'm going to cut them up.'

"He and Bo roomed together. Bo wasn't really as bad as everyone thought. He was very conscientious about getting eight hours of sleep a night. He just didn't get the eight when they wanted him to. But I remember one night, Bo and I were together, and we went into this place, and Steve's there, and he says, 'Hey, guys, come over and look at this beautiful sight'—twenty-four scotch and waters lined up in front of him. And he was pitching the next day. Then he stopped on the way home and bought a gallon of wine and killed that, too. The next night they just carried him off the mound in the fourth inning."

HERM STARRETTE: "I played with him in Stockton, Appleton, and Elmira every year, and I always liked him and tried to keep him out of trouble. But there weren't enough eyes around to keep an eye on him. Everyone loved him. If he was in a bar, he'd buy everyone a drink. People took care of him, made sure he got back to the hotel. When payday came, he'd come up and give you the money he owed you, because he always owed you, and then before the day was over he'd borrow it back.

"When I roomed with him, I roomed with a suitcase. He was just a young guy who hadn't matured, and he came in when he got tired of being out. He was a good kid. I don't think he had a heck of a lot of home life. He couldn't help that, but the kid told me himself he'd go back home in the fall and he and his father would go out and drink a lot. He had so much ability he thought he could do all that [drinking] and still perform.

"One night in Elmira he got pretty lit after a game, and he was driving around in Ray Youngdahl's Cadillac—brand new, a real beauty with fins and everything. Then the cops stopped him right near the stadium. He'd been drinking, and they were going to take him in, and then Steve threw the thing in reverse and just slammed it into the cop's car. He really rammed that cop car. It was smoking. Tore up the Cadillac. I don't know if he did it on purpose or not. But they took him down to jail and called Earl [Weaver], who was managing, and they said, 'We got Steve down here,' and Earl said, 'God-damnit, let him stay there tonight.'"

BOOG POWELL: "We played together in Arizona one fall, in the instructional league out there. He would drink to the point of just about passing out. One night we had been out, and I brought him home. I was carrying him, and there was Earl coming in. There were two entrances into the apartments, and I've got Dalko over my shoulder, and I said, 'I can't let Earl see me.' So I throw Dalko in the bushes and get down and hide and watch Earl go up the steps to his place. And I go to get Dalko out of the bushes, and I'd thrown him in a rosebush and just tore his ass up. I mean, he was bleeding like a stuck pig. He's cut all over the place.

"Now it's getting to be two-fifteen, two-twenty in the morning, so I take him up to his place, and he's still passed out. I get him in there, and I clean him up as best I can. Now we got to be at the ballpark the next day at, like, nine o'clock. So after all that it was probably after three o'clock in the morning, and then I had to go over there the next day and wake him up. He got right up. He wasn't feeling real good. He said, 'Oh man, what did I get into last night? Was there a wildcat or something?' A wildcat! So I told him what I'd done and everything else and he said, 'Oh man, I gotta pitch today. Maybe I'll beg off.' But he went and got in the whirlpool, got a little rub, and threw the best game I ever saw him pitch, even though he felt bad. That's how much talent the guy had."

Dalkowski spent every spring in the Orioles' major league camp; Paul Richards worked with him constantly. But he didn't get his act together until he hooked up with Weaver at the Orioles' Double-A affiliate in Elmira, New

York, in the early '60s. Dalkowski finally started getting the ball over the plate, struck out 167 and walked only 88 in 144 innings in '62, and fashioned a 7–8 record with a 3.07 ERA.

The next year, he pitched well in spring training and had the club made as Opening Day neared. On the afternoon of the last game of the Orioles' spring season, he was fitted for his Orioles uniform, finally on the verge of becoming a major leaguer. That night, pitching in relief against the Yankees, he severely strained a tendon in his left elbow. Dave McNally took his place on the staff and went on to win 181 games for the Orioles. Dalkowski was never the same.

HERM STARRETTE: "It was in '62 in Elmira when he became a pitcher. Earl made a reliever out of him. His velocity was about the same, maybe down a little, but he was pitching. His control was really coming around. And Earl would take him out when he wasn't pitching good. Wouldn't let him pitch into jams. Wouldn't let him fail. And it was working."

EARL WEAVER: "I got him not to throw every pitch as hard as he could. Plus he got a slider that he could throw over the plate, and in the last 55 innings in Elmira [in '62] he gave up 11 runs and didn't walk many. Struck out 104. He finally understood that at the point of release, you couldn't just rear back and throw as hard as you could. He finally understood that. Steve's IQ was about sixty. I had him tested, and he finished in the bottom one percentile in the ability to learn facts. He was also an alcoholic. It just shows you can't be too smart to throw away that kind of ability."

BOOG POWELL: "After the '62 season we went down to Puerto Rico and played winter ball together, and he had really found himself. He had hurt his arm a little, and he wasn't throwing hard anymore. I mean he was probably throwing like Nolan Ryan, in the mid-nineties, but he wasn't throwing hard anymore. I'm serious. He was still blowing people away, but he was throwing strikes. He'd figured it out all of a sudden."

HERM STARRETTE: "In '63 he went to the big-league camp and had the team made. There was no doubt. He was throwing great. And then he threw one pitch that went way wild, and he looked over at the dugout like something funny had happened, and everyone just sat there and watched. They just thought it was one of his [wild] pitches. Then he threw another pitch that went funny, and I said to Harry Brecheen, 'Cat, you better go out there. I think he's hurt himself.' It was in his elbow. He had the club made, and he was showing off his arm, like anyone would have done, and it happened. He came back after that, but his arm was never the same. It was all downhill after that."

EARL WEAVER: "No one threw harder. Nolan Ryan or any of 'em—nobody threw harder. Steve could have had years like Koufax. He could have strung some together. Talent-wise, there's no doubt. Who knows if that stretch [when he pitched well in Elmira] was just a stretch, or the start of something? If he hadn't hurt his arm, who knows?"

Released in '65, Dalkowski was soon out of baseball. Unable to stay sober or keep money in his pocket, his life spiraled sharply in the wrong direction. For years he was a farmworker, picking grapes and apricots in California. Friends from his baseball days tried to help, but he kept drinking. When his wife died, his sister brought him back home to Connecticut in '95 and put him in a nursing home. He was suffering from dementia, the result of years of alcohol abuse.

HERM STARRETTE: "In '77 I'm at Candlestick Park, and I'm down in the bullpen warming up a pitcher before a game, and I look up and there's Steve leaning over the railing. The poor guy looked seventy. He was staying at Ray Youngdahl's place, and Ray had him in rehab, but he'd go to rehab during the day and come home and get drunk at night. He had the beer stashed somewhere."

BOOG POWELL: "Then he was picking vegetables out there in California; I guess that was what he was doing. He calls me up every now and then and says, 'Hey, brother, can you help me?' And his wife or whoever he's with says, 'Don't help that son of a bitch; he'll just drink it up.' You know, I can hear her in the background. Then all of a sudden, click, the phone hangs up."

14

The Hitchcock Debacle

Encouraged by their second-place finish in '60, the Orioles chose an optimistic marketing slogan for the next season: "It Can Be Done in '61." There was just one problem—it wasn't true. The Yankees fielded one of their best teams, winning 109 games and beating the Reds in the World Series, with Roger Maris hitting 61 homers to set a single-season record, Mickey Mantle adding 54, and the two combining for 270 RBI. "That was probably the best team I ever played against," Brooks Robinson said. "There wasn't much you could do."

The Orioles didn't exactly tail off, winning a club-record 95 games as teams in Los Angeles and Minnesota began playing and the American League moved to a 162-game regular season. But they were never in sight of the Yankees after playing .500 ball during the first two months. The Tigers finished second with 101 wins, leaving the Orioles in third.

The Orioles' young pitching was still tough, with Steve Barber, Chuck Estrada, Milt Pappas, and Jack Fisher combining for 56 wins, one more than the year before. Barber relied on his heavy, sinking fastball to go 18–12 with a 3.34 ERA and eight shutouts. Hoyt Wilhelm, splendid again in relief, made the All-Star team for the second time in three years.

But the pitchers didn't generate the biggest headlines. First baseman Jim Gentile had a colossal season, setting club records for power hitting and run production that would last, in some cases, for decades. He set the tone in a game in Minnesota in early May, becoming the first major leaguer to hit grand slams in consecutive innings. Richards began using him every day after that instead of just against right-handers, and he continued to pound the ball. By season's end, he had 46 homers, 141 RBI, 73 extra-base hits, and a .302 average. After just two full seasons in the majors, Gentile was a star.

JIM GENTILE: "When I hit the two grand slams, I don't know if I should tell how it really happened, but I was out all night the night before. I'd played in

St. Paul in the Dodgers' system, and I knew these brothers who owned six bars. They came over to Minneapolis and picked me up, and we went out and ran around. I didn't drink much, but I was out with 'em. I got back to the hotel at six in the morning. I went up to the room and jumped in the shower and shaved and called room service and got toast and coffee. The bus left for the ballpark about nine. It was a day game. When I got to the park I'm saying, 'God, I don't feel like playing.' But I went outside and it wasn't cold, just nippy where it can wake you up. So I thought, 'I feel all right; I can play.'

"The Minnesota starter was Pedro Ramos, who I hit pretty good. He used to tell me he was going to hit me in my 'big ass,' because I got a few home runs off him. Brooks, Whitey Herzog, and Jackie Brandt got on base in the first. Ramos threw me two fastballs up and had me oh and 2. I'm telling myself, 'Just meet it; just meet it. You need to drive in a run.' So he threw me the same pitch, and I hit it straight over the center-field fence. I really got up on it.

"In the next inning the same three guys loaded the bases in front of me. They brought in Paul Giel to relieve. His very first pitch he threw what was supposed to be his screwball, and it just came right down the middle, and I hit it over the right-field fence. You don't think much of it when you do it. I mean, I was happy, but we didn't do the things they do nowadays, pirouette and jump around. But I was happy. I came across the plate, and as I go in the dugout, Richards is there with his leg up on the top step, like always. He says, 'You know, son, I don't think that's ever been done before.' That's all he said.

"The next day they were throwing a left-hander, and Walt Dropo played first. I had nine RBI one day and sat the next. I pinch hit in the eighth with the bases loaded and struck out. Took a three-and-two fastball I thought was inside. The next day I batted with the bases loaded and hit a double off the top of the fence. After we got off the road trip, Richards started playing me every day, and I just kept hitting.

"I consider myself a journeyman. I had some good years, some bad years, and I'm not a superstar. But I had my year. It made me, that season. I still get all sorts of mail. Whitey [Herzog] said to me recently, 'Diamond, I don't know how you had the year you had. You're the only guy that hit. You had nobody behind you, nobody hitting at all, no protection. That's why your year was so incredible.' It was just one of those years.

"And the thing was, I fell apart in September. I had 46 [homers] once I got to September, and I really wanted 50. I started thinking about it. I was hitting home runs because I wasn't thinking, but once I started thinking and saying, 'God, I'd love to beat 50—because back then only five or six guys had hit 50, and I wanted my name in a book—I started falling apart. I swung at everything."

Gentile's season pushed several other fine performances to the background. Jackie Brandt covered center field as no member of the Orioles had—with a long stride and sure glove—and also hit .297 with 93 runs scored. Brooks Robinson batted leadoff and hit .287 in a club-record 668 at-bats; he also finished second in the league in hits. He started for the AL in the All-Star Game.

There also was bad news in '61, as second baseman Marv Breeding slipped to a .209 average and lost his starting job, shortstop Ron Hansen fell to .248, and catcher Gus Triandos continued a slow decline, hitting .244. All would be gone by the start of the '63 season.

But by far the most devastating blow was the departure of Paul Richards. A National League expansion team in Houston was set to begin play in '62, and it recruited Richards throughout the '61 season, leaning heavily on Richards's desire to return to Texas. After months of speculation, the Orioles gave Richards a Texas-style ultimatum—them or us. Annoyed, Richards responded in twenty-four hours. After seven years with the Orioles, he was leaving to become the GM in Houston.

Richards left immediately, with a month left in the season. His top coach, Luman Harris, served as an interim manager in September, leading the Orioles to a 17–10 record. Richards then hired Harris as a coach in Houston, and Orioles GM Lee MacPhail embarked on a search for Richards's successor. It didn't last long. MacPhail's choice was Billy Hitchcock, manager of the Orioles' Triple-A affiliate in Vancouver.

LEE MACPHAIL: "Things weren't going as well as they'd gone in '60. The Houston club was talking to Paul. The thing went on and on. I thought it was hurting the team. I finally told Paul, 'You have to go one way or another. We can't go on like this.' He very quickly came back and said, 'OK, fine; I'm going.' He'd been negotiating with them for a long time. I hired a wonderful man as manager, Billy Hitchcock, but he was a better guy than manager. Paul was great. An excellent manager. It was too bad when we lost him. It was a setback for the club. It wasn't until '64 that we got back into the race."

MILT PAPPAS: "Paul was instrumental in the development of the Orioles, the pitching staff, some of the younger ballplayers such as Brooks and Boog Powell and Jerry Adair and Ron Hansen. But he got a deal that he couldn't refuse with the Houston team, becoming the general manager and a vice president, too. Plus, he probably had had it as far as managing. That was a sad day for the Orioles. I guess it had been rumored that he was going to be going, but it was still tough to lose him. And we missed him."

Billy Hitchcock was a courtly Southern gentleman from Inverness, Alabama, a baseball and football star at Auburn University in the '30s. He played nine seasons in the major leagues as an infielder with the Tigers, Senators, Browns, Red Sox, and Athletics, and after retiring with a .243 career average, he managed in the minors for a year and then served as the Tigers' third-base coach for six seasons. Sensing his window of opportunity for managing in the major leagues closing, he signed on as the Orioles' Triple-A manager in '61, never thinking his chance would come so soon.

BILLY HITCHCOCK: "In '61 I drove back [to Alabama] after the end of the season from Vancouver with my family. It was a long trip, and we stopped at a couple of places along the way, so we didn't rush. I remember coming through Texas and hearing Roger Maris hit his 61st home run on the radio. When I got home, my father-in-law told me someone from Baltimore had been trying to get me. It was Lee MacPhail. We set up a meeting in Cincinnati, and I got the job. I was very excited. I didn't know what to expect. It was a great opportunity. There were a lot of nice players, and Baltimore was such a fine baseball town. To say I was excited would be putting it mildly."

Hitchcock thought he was inheriting a team ready to win a pennant, but the Orioles took a major step in the wrong direction in '62. A warning sign flashed three weeks into the season, when Bo Belinsky, a pitcher raised in the Orioles' minor league system and lost in the '61 expansion draft, pitched a no-hitter for the Angels against the Orioles, beating Barber 2–0. The game was an appropriate symbol for the entire season, as the Orioles again had the league's lowest team ERA but finished ninth in runs scored. They also took a hard fall from the high standard of fundamental play Richards had demanded, committing numerous errors in the field and on the base paths and generally exhibiting little of the baseball intelligence Richards had instilled.

There were some individual successes. Robin Roberts, thirty-five, a six-time 20-game winner acquired from the Phillies, went 10–9 with a 2.78 ERA as a starter. Brooks Robinson played in all 162 games and hit .303 with 23 homers.

Boog Powell arrived from the minors as a burly leftfielder and hit 15 homers. Jerry Adair took over at second base and hit .284. Jackie Brandt hit only .255 playing every day in center field, but his 19 homers and 75 RBI were among the highest totals on the club, and his personality was different, to say the least.

Boog Powell: "Jackie had as much ability and talent as anybody. He could fly, and he had a great arm, and he could hit with power. But he used to do things off the wall. He was a character. We used to hang around together quite a bit. He danced to his own tune. One time he told everyone he'd found this great ice-cream store with thirty-one flavors, all these choices, and he took a bunch of guys out there, all excited, and they asked him which of the thirty-one flavors he wanted, and he said, 'Vanilla.'

"Then we were walking somewhere, and he had a pair of alligator shoes on, and he said, 'I think my 'gators need a drink.' And he'd just go walk in the fountain. Up to his knees—just walk through the fountain and get out of there and not say a word, just keep right on walking and go sloshing down the street. It was funny as hell. He was always doing stuff like that. I think he heard stuff [voices] from time to time. He just never told us about it."

Jackie Brandt: "I was colorful. I wasn't a Jimmy Piersall, but I was a poor man's Jimmy Piersall. I was just having fun being kind of unpredictable. I was pretty witty, and I'd say stuff. I was quite popular. I was the host of a dugout show, a pregame show. I asked goofy questions and didn't get too involved with the game. 'What did you do over the winter? What did you do after the game?' Then they'd have a player come in to the 'Bird's Nest' room before the game and talk to the fans. Can you imagine that today? I used to get them laughing. I'd ask them where they were sitting, and I'd hit foul balls up where they were and wave to 'em. The pitcher would get all pissed off.

"Me and Boog and Adair, every night we'd go out somewhere and find the country music. We saw Buck Owens, George Jones, Faron Young, Hank Snow. We'd go out with them after the games. Buck Owens knew more baseball than we did. We walked into his dressing room one night, and he told us what we were hitting. He was a huge fan. Hank Snow and his band, we spent a whole week with him in Minneapolis once. Got arrested. We were living in a hotel and raising hell and singing and drinking. They had to get Hank [Snow] out of there before the cops came.

"Wherever the country music was, we'd find it. We went to state fairs, too. That's where we met Roy Clark. He was from Silver Spring, Maryland, and every time we'd come home, he'd come over and come in the clubhouse, and then we'd go to Boog's place and have a few drinks. We'd get wasted."

BILLY HITCHCOCK: "Jackie did some leading off for us in '62, and all year he told everyone he was going up there looking for a change-up on the first pitch of the game. The guys said, 'They ain't going to throw you a change-up on the first pitch.' And he said, 'When they do I'm going to hit it out.' Well, he went up there all year looking for a change-up on the first pitch, and they never threw him one."

JACKIE BRANDT: "My manager in the minors had said I was one of the best fastball hitters he'd ever seen, so they weren't going to throw me a first-pitch fastball. He said, 'Just stand there flat-footed—don't look for nothing—and if he throws a change-up or a slow curve, kill it.' Well, I never got it. Then one day, like twelve years later, a guy finally threw me a change-up on the first pitch. I took it. They finally threw me the change-up, and I didn't swing. I got back to the dugout and they all said, 'You been looking for that change-up for thirteen years and you didn't swing!' I said, 'I can't believe that SOB threw a change-up.'"

The Orioles were still in contention as late as July 5 in '62, only five games out of first, but they lost ground steadily over the next few weeks, playing so poorly that MacPhail flew to California in the middle of a road trip to issue threats. He was "very disappointed," he said, and contemplating "slashing" salaries. Tempers were running high. Pappas threatened not to pitch after being relegated to the bullpen. Estrada and Barber argued with Hitchcock on the mound while being pulled from games. Breeding complained about his limited playing time. Discipline lagged.

BARRY SHETRONE: "I was in the army for the Berlin crisis in '61, got out in '62, and stayed with the team. It was the end of July, beginning of August, and, as the saying goes, the inmates were running the asylum. Everyone had been afraid of Richards, and Hitchcock was very laid-back, didn't say much, and everybody went wild, like they'd gotten out of prison. It was crazy. A wild time. People playing cards right up to the game time. No discipline at all. And drinking, yeah. Quite a bit of drinking was going on. Billy was just put in a difficult situation, coming into an organization where he didn't know the players, didn't know what to expect. He was just too nice a guy for this job."

MILT PAPPAS: "Billy was a hell of a man and a hell of a nice guy. But he wasn't a very good manager. I liked the man, but I just don't think he was that good of a manager as far as dealing with people and maneuvering people— the tactical aspect of the job."

LEE MACPHAIL: "Billy was recommended by some of my closest friends— Jim Campbell, John McHale—general managers who had been around. He seemed like an ideal guy. A wonderful guy. He just didn't inspire the team. Some managers have that ability. Billy didn't. He just wasn't tough enough with them. They didn't respond."

BILLY HITCHCOCK: "I was sort of easygoing with them. You can't beat them. You can't whip them. You can fine them, but that's about it. I guess Lee felt I wasn't demanding enough. Too easygoing. But that was the way I managed. When I played I didn't need to have a manager be tough on me. I was going to give 100 percent. But my approach to that situation wasn't exactly right. It didn't work. Some guys might have taken advantage of me. I could see it. It was happening. But I couldn't be a Joe McCarthy or a Paul Richards. I had to be me. But in this case being Billy Hitchcock wasn't the right thing."

STEVE BARBER: "One time he called Milt and me in. We'd both just lost close games, like 3–2 and 2–1. And he says, 'Milt, you need to lose some weight, that's your problem. And Steve, I don't know what your problem is.' I said, 'What are you talking about?' He said, 'We're not scoring any runs, and you guys are capable of throwing shutouts. So we need that to win games.' The age-old story. When you're not hitting, blame the pitchers.

"I went to Billy and said to his face one day, 'You're playing scared baseball, and you're ruining a hell of a ball club.' I loved him as a person, but I don't think he did the job as a manager. I don't think it was the 'tough guy' thing. It was the type of ball we were playing. The guys who'd played for him in Vancouver [in '61] couldn't believe he was the same guy. He was so ultra-conservative. He didn't appreciate it when I told him he was ruining a hell of a good team. But I was never bashful about saying what I thought."

For every step forward, there were two in the other direction in '62. Barber and Hansen were called up for active military duty and able to play only on weekends. Barber dropped from 18 wins to 9, and Hansen batted .173. Estrada lost 17 games. Fisher went 7–9. Gentile produced 33 homers and 87 RBI, but his average dropped to .251, and he struggled with his temper, often clearing water coolers and bat racks after striking out.

JIM GENTILE: "After I hit 46 homers in '61, broke 11 records, MacPhail offered me a ten-thousand-dollar raise. I was making fifteen thousand dollars. We didn't have agents, so you did it yourself. I wrote back and said, 'Lee, I want a 100 percent raise, that's all I want; give me thirty thousand dollars, a 100 percent raise,' because back then that was a lot. And Lee said, 'Oh I can't do that. When I was at the Yankees, even when Mickey Mantle was a Triple Crown winner he only got ten thousand dollars.' I said, 'Yeah, but he made another ten in the World Series.' I said, 'I've waited a long time to get here.' He said, 'Then make the Dodgers pay you.' I said, 'OK, trade me back to the Dodgers; maybe they will.'

"I was living in Timonium; I'd bought a house and Jack Fisher was out there, and Triandos and Pappas and Barber—we all bought homes out there. Spring training was getting ready to start, and Lee calls and says, 'Maybe I can go twenty-six thousand five hundred.' I said, 'No, I think I deserve a 100 percent raise.' He said, 'I only have so much money. If I give you thirty thousand, then I've got to cut somebody else.' I said, 'Well I really wouldn't want you to do that; maybe ask the owners for more money.' I was trying to keep it light because I'm not a good negotiator.

"Spring training started; after about four days they know you're getting itchy. I'm in Timonium reading how Boog looks real good, and I'm going, 'Oh, Jesus.' Lee called me up and asked me to come down to the office. I went down there, and we're talking, and he hands me a contract for twenty-nine thousand dollars. I said, 'Lee, really, the extra thousand, how much am I going to see after taxes and everything? It's just the principle. I think I'm worth thirty thousand dollars.' He said, 'Jeez, Jim, I don't know.' I said, 'Well, I can't sign for twenty-nine thousand.' Then he opens the drawer and hands me a contract for thirty thousand dollars. He already had it. Just wanted to see if he could get me for twenty-nine thousand.

"Then I started listening to the radio and reading the papers, and they're telling you, 'You have to do it; there's no one else.' And not being the brightest Italian around, I'm saying to myself, 'I gotta do it.' That's when my average started dropping. It was my fault. Nobody else's. I couldn't blame it on anybody else. I wasn't doing anything different. They just told me to be more patient, and I'd get up there and be patient and take a third strike.

"I just wanted to do good, wanted the team to do good, and when everybody tells you you're the man, and you get up in a [big] situation with men on base, and you strike out on a bad pitch, it used to just eat at me. I had an uncontrollable temper. I used to get mad pretty easy. I'd get madder and madder instead of saying, 'That's enough.' It was stupid, but that's how it was when I played.

"All guys are different. Brooks was melancholy, even-keeled all the time. Me, I'm Irish and Italian, a lover and fighter. There was nothing I could do. I'd blow up. I mean I could be walking back [from the plate] and everything would be fine, and all of a sudden I'd think about it and boom, I'd break a bat. MacPhail put out a thing that anybody who breaks a bat, it cost them five bucks. Boog broke one one day, and I guess they thought I was getting everybody to break their bats. So any broken bat was five dollars.

"I look back at it and say, 'Why couldn't I control myself?' And I say, 'Well, seven years in the minors was like being in jail. You're trying to get out, and when you get there, you don't want to lose it.' And there was always someone behind you. They were always telling you that. Then a new coach would come in and say, 'I hear you're hard to handle.' Like you were a bad apple. I don't know why they said I was hard to handle. I didn't bother anybody. I didn't do that much. I broke a few bats, that's for sure. But I never tore up any clubhouses. And when I didn't want to talk to reporters I put out a little statue of a guy shooting the bird. Stupid. But you know, whatever."

DICK WILLIAMS: "Gentile had a swing totally built around seeing how far he could hit it, although he hit for a fairly decent average. He had a kind of a temper. But he'd always had that temper."

MARV BREEDING: "His biggest enemy was himself. He couldn't understand why he couldn't hit the ball out of the park every time. Of course, he was running around, too. He was a wild man. That probably didn't help."

JIM GENTILE: "They called me 'Diamond Jim,' and when I had my big year it really stuck with me. The original Diamond Jim was a gambler, and

I dressed pretty flashy, had a lot of silk suits. Maybe that hurt me, trying to live up to the name. I was a pretty good patron of the Baltimore streets."

Out of nowhere, the Orioles rose up and swept five games from the Yankees in August at Memorial Stadium, winning two doubleheaders and scoring 34 runs on 65 hits. Hitchcock called it "the best team effort I've ever seen in one series." The Yankees had flown in for the series on a red-eye flight from California.

But when three losses in a four-game series with the last-place Senators ensued, the Orioles' season was lost for good. In early September, Washington's Tom Cheney struck out twenty-one Orioles in a 16-inning performance at Memorial Stadium. The contender Richards had put together ended up with a 77–85 record, in seventh place. Two of Hitchcock's coaches, Cal Ermer and George Staller, were fired after the season.

BILLY HITCHCOCK: "We felt good about the club in '62, had the nucleus from a team that had won 95 games the year before. They worked hard, had a good spring. Things just didn't go as we'd hoped. Gentile didn't drive in as many runs. That was a little disappointing. Guys have good years and bad years. It's a manager's fault when players don't perform.

"But, gosh, we had so many possibilities. There was a lot of talent. Boog Powell was just getting started. We put six coaches on him in spring training. We thought he was overweight. Well, he wore them all out. He was meant to be 240 pounds. He would have been a great tight end with those quick feet. He was a good fielder, a very good athlete. And he was just emerging as a hitter.

"And Jackie Brandt had great ability. He could throw, run, catch, hit with power. He just never used his great ability to its fullest extent. He could have hit 30 homers every season. But he was a flake. An oddball. A good fella and all, mind you. But he had a theory—if he hit .315 one year, they'd expect him to hit .325 the next. So he always hit .290. He didn't want to have a good year because they'd expect him to have a great year."

JACKIE BRANDT: "I could run good, and I had a great arm, and I was a good outfielder. That's what they wanted. But I was the second-fastest in the league running to first, and they'd say, 'Why don't you run harder?' I'd say, 'There's only one guy who can beat me, and that's Mantle.' Everyone said I looked nonchalant, but I was cooking; I was flying. I'd get there ten feet before the next guy, but people said I looked slow. OK, whatever. All I could do was the best I had. I couldn't disguise it to make it look like I was going faster.

"And I could hit the ball a long way, but I hit the ball on a line. Richards said, 'You should hit 45 home runs a year. Just lay back and swing up.' I said, 'I don't know how to do that.' I hit shots through the infield or over the infield. I'd hit 15 or 17 a year. They were all scorchers. Killebrew hit that top-spin little fly, and Maris, too, 300 feet in Yankee Stadium. We had 410 at Memorial Stadium, and I'd hit them over that. I had a lot of balls caught."

MacPhail made numerous changes after the '62 season, trading Triandos, Herzog, Fisher, Breeding, Shetrone, and Billy Hoeft, and acquiring catchers Dick Brown and John Orsino and relief pitcher Stu Miller, among others. But the biggest acquisition was All-Star shortstop Luis Aparicio, who came from the White Sox for a package including Wilhelm and Hansen. Aparicio was a Venezuelan who had led the league in steals in each of his seven years. For the Orioles, who had never had a player steal many bases, his presence promised to add a new dimension to an offense that needed help.

JIM GENTILE: "Ronnie Hansen was a nice shortstop, but getting Aparicio stepped it up quite a bit. Aparicio was quicker. Aparicio gave us a whole other dimension. We didn't steal much until we got him. Back then the game wasn't oriented to that. It was the long ball or base hits. Aparicio changed that."

LEE MACPHAIL: "With Aparicio at shortstop and Brooks at third, I honestly believe that's the best left side of the infield that's ever existed in baseball."

There was optimism as the '63 season opened, and an early hot streak pushed the Orioles 15 games over .500 and into first place. Aparicio broke the club record for steals in a season in late May, and Barber, back from military duty, won eight games before June. But things fell apart in a hurry. Seventeen losses in 22 games dropped the club to sixth, and there was no gaining back the lost ground. The Yankees won another pennant in a romp, with 104 wins, and the Orioles finished fourth at 86–76.

BOOG POWELL: "What happened, the pitching wasn't quite as good. It just wasn't there. Estrada got hurt. Hoyt left. Fat Jack [Fisher] started to falter a little bit. And Pappas was just going to win 13, 14, 15 games. He wasn't going to win no more. That's all Milt was going to win. That's all he wanted to win. I don't know why. I can't answer to that. He was a great pitcher, I mean, not just a good pitcher, a great pitcher. And Barber was throwing great with that heavy ball. But the overall staff wasn't the same."

BILLY HITCHCOCK: "In '63 we brought in Luke Appling and Hank Bauer as coaches. Trying to get some experience. Lee and I talked a lot, and we thought maybe we needed more major league experience among the coaches. We still had a lot of talent. And in '63, we started real well; then we hit a series in Kansas City and seemed to level out. It just seemed to go the other way."

Several individual performances stood out. Barber became the club's first 20-game winner, reaching the milestone with a 3–1 win over the Angels on September 18 in Los Angeles. Pappas and Roberts also had solid years in the rotation, winning 16 and 14 games. Stu Miller, thirty-five, replaced Wilhelm as the top reliever and made seventy-one appearances.

STEVE BARBER: "When I won 20 I really didn't pitch any better than I had before. It was strictly a numbers thing. They decided they were going to start me every fourth game, no matter what. So I ended up winning 20 because I had more starts than anyone had ever had. I set a club record for wins and starts."

Offensively, Boog Powell established his bat as a force, producing 25 homers—including three in one game in Washington—and 82 RBI. But for every positive development, there was a setback. Gentile's home-run and RBI totals dropped for the second straight season, to 24 and 72. Brooks Robinson's average dropped 52 points from the year before, to .251. Brandt's .248 average was the lowest of his career at that point. The Orioles were in a rut as their first decade in Baltimore ended. They couldn't catch the Yankees. Their youth movement had stalled. Attendance in '63 dropped to a per-game average of 10,755, the lowest in club history. MacPhail surveyed the situation and fired Hitchcock, offering this withering criticism in explanation: "We need a stronger man."

LEE MACPHAIL: "We had a solid fan base, but we weren't really drawing. A crowd of fifteen thousand or sixteen thousand was a good crowd. Over twenty thousand was big. It was a football stadium first. It was a Colts town."

JIM GENTILE: "We weren't drawing, but we had fun. The team was more of a family then. We all liked each other. There was no jealousy. Now you have one guy making one million dollars and another making thirteen million dollars, and it's tough. But I wouldn't take a million dollars for when I played. I mean, we had parties. A guy would say, 'Hey, we have a day off tomorrow so I'm going to have a party over at the house,' and guys would come over with their wives and get together."

JACKIE BRANDT: "We had one life. Baseball. And you weren't making much money. I started at six thousand dollars. Albert Belle makes more in one at-bat than I did in my first three years. But that doesn't bother me. We had a ball. We had camaraderie. Eight or ten of us would go out and have a blast after the game. Now, fifteen minutes after the game they're all gone. Ain't nobody in the clubhouse. We'd be in there until two in the morning, talking the game, drinking beer or whatever. Right there in the clubhouse. Six or seven of us always did that. Aparicio, Adair, Boog, me, a couple of pitchers. Why take a shower and go home? Sit down and talk things over, 'What'd we do wrong? What'll we do tomorrow?' Then open another beer or pop or whatever. Savor the victories. We'd stay in there until they kicked us out. I lived two blocks from the ballpark. I'd just walk home. Now they walk in an enclosed area with guards. We parked out in the parking lot with the people and signed two hundred autographs before we got in the car."

BILLY HITCHCOCK: "Getting fired was a tough day. Lee did it. And we were good friends. I sort of expected it. Things hadn't gone well. It was a tough decision for him. I left on solid ground. Actually worked for the organization the next year ['64] as a minor league field coordinator. Then I went to Atlanta as a scout in '65. It just didn't work out."

15

The Dalton Gang

In the final years before baseball initiated an annual draft of high school and college players in '65, the Orioles excelled in the art of scouting, signing, and developing major league talent. These weren't bonus babies signed by one of Paul Richards's lieutenants, without the affirmation of Jim McLaughlin's scouts. They were procured in the traditional fashion, by the scouting operation McLaughlin set up in the '50s and Harry Dalton took over and sharpened after McLaughlin was fired in '61.

From '60 to '63 the Orioles acquired a dazzling collection of young players and loosed them in their minor league system. Pitchers Dave McNally and Tom Phoebus signed in '60. Catchers Andy Etchebarren and Larry Haney and pitchers Frank Bertaina, Eddie Watt, and Darold Knowles signed in '61. Infielders Davey Johnson and Mark Belanger signed in '62. The '63 bumper crop included pitchers Jim Palmer and Wally Bunker, and an outfielder, Paul Blair, drafted from the New York Mets' minor league system. All would reach the major leagues, and most would star for the Orioles or bring value in a trade. These "Baby Birds" would cement the Orioles' reputation for growing young talent that started with the "Kiddie Corps."

The scouts who located and signed the players were the lifeblood of the far-reaching, multitiered scouting network. Below Dalton were national scouts Jim Russo and Arthur Ehlers, the club's first general manager, now in a new role. They "cross-checked" the work of the Orioles' scouts around the country, studied other major league clubs and their minor league systems, and generally served as the Orioles' bottom line of baseball judgment.

Below them were regional scouting supervisors such as Frank "Beauty" McGowan in New England and Don McShane in California. Fred "Bootnose" Hofmann and Hal Newhouser, the four-time 20-game winner for the Tigers, also were supervisors until Newhouser retired in '62 and Hofmann died in '64. McGowan, a former major league outfielder and manager of the

International League Orioles, was a supervisor for nineteen years. McShane had the job for more than a decade.

Beneath the supervisors were two dozen full-time area scouts such as Walter Youse in Baltimore; Dee Phillips in Texas; Al Kubski in Southern California; former major league pitchers Jim Wilson, Ray Scarborough, and Burleigh Grimes; and Don Pries, a Northern Californian who would one day become the director of the Major League Scouting Bureau. Each had a network of part-time associate scouts, or "bird-dog" scouts, helping them locate talent.

Walter Youse: "Dalton had brain power. He was a smart boy. He was the one who really believed in the minor leagues and built up the scouting system. He was a great believer in scouts. He could handle scouts, knew how good they were—or weren't. Money-wise, we were paid about the middle, not high or low. But Harry would talk to all of them, get a consensus of opinion and make the decision."

Don Pries: "We were all 'Dalton people.' As a matter of fact, they started calling us the Dalton Gang. Anyone who knew Harry and had a chance to go to work for him [as a scout] certainly would. When you talk about being able to coordinate and orchestrate an organization, Harry excelled at that."

Al Kubski: "I had grown up in Baltimore and was living in Granada Hills, California. I'd been managing in the Pittsburgh chain for ten years, but I was starting to grow a family and needed to be home. I was managing in Kingsport [Tennessee], and they were in Bluefield playing the Orioles' rookie league club. I was riding up in the elevator and Dalton was there and said, 'Are you Kubski? [Baltimore sports columnist] John Steadman says a lot of nice things about you.'

"I knew they were looking for a scout in my area, and the [major league] winter meetings were in California that December, so I called Harry. We met for breakfast at the Biltmore Hotel. Jim Russo was there. He asked a lot of questions. Asked me to scout their Bluefield club. I picked out the three best guys, and Harry went back to Baltimore and called and offered me the job. Harry didn't pay a lot, but he was great to work for. We had a lot of meetings all the time. The scouts and minor league managers sat around and talked about players and the game. If you lived baseball, it was a great place to work."

HARRY DALTON: "We got things winnowed down to the point that the scouts who didn't fit what we wanted were gone. In almost every scouting position we had a really solid person. Good scouts just about anywhere. Youse was terrific. So was Jim Russo. McShane was a hell of a scout. Freddie Hofmann didn't sign a lot of people, but when Freddie talked about liking a ballplayer, you listened.

"And we could get good information. That was the thing about scouting in those days. There was a lot more to signing players than there is today. In those days you did a lot of good spade work and got close to the family and sold yourself. Inside information, knowing who was going to sign and who wasn't, or what clubs were strong on somebody and where your toughest competition was going to be, that was key."

WALTER YOUSE: "I started out scouting full time at forty-five hundred dollars a year, which was nothing. After five years I told them what I wanted. I had another job lined up. I went to Dalton, and he said, 'I'm not going to pay you that.' But he wound up doubling my salary. After that I started to make pretty good money and got a raise every year. I was told I was in the top one percent. I never took another job after I became a full-time scout. A lot of other scouts took jobs in the off-season. I never did that. I had twenty-five or thirty associate scouts, and I'd go around and talk to them and take them to lunch.

"As far as judgment goes, I think you're born with it. And the Orioles had a lot of guys born with it. We'd meet in Thomasville in the spring and Baltimore in the fall. Then during the season you'd scout the Orioles' minor league teams. I'd go scout Bluefield or Rochester. My scouting area was Maryland, West Virginia, Delaware. I signed Barber, Haney, Phoebus, John Miller. I got my share."

DAVE McNALLY: "Jim Wilson just did the best sales job on me. I had a lot of people after me. We had a great American Legion program in Billings [Montana], where we traveled extensively. That's where the scouts saw me. Of the three years I played legion ball, we were in the legion World Series twice. I got a lot of exposure.

"Seven or eight teams were really after me. After the [legion] Series in '60 most of them came to Billings. We weeded out a lot of them. It came down to the Orioles and Dodgers. We had an attorney that was helping us out, my mother and me and my brother. He gave each team one more shot to get in and make a pitch. The Orioles had already been in twice. Actually, the offers were very even between the Orioles and Dodgers. They sent me back to my bedroom and said, 'Take all the time you want and come out with a decision.'

"I went back to the bedroom, shut the door, sat in there, mulled it over. I really can't tell you what made me go with them. Wilson did a good job. If I'd known about the Kiddie Corps [stable of young pitchers excelling in Baltimore that year] I probably would have signed with the Dodgers. But we didn't get much information about the major leagues, and I didn't really follow it, and the Orioles certainly didn't bring it up. So I signed with them."

DAVEY JOHNSON: "I was from San Antonio [Texas], which was a real hotbed, and I was scouted a lot in high school. All the top scouts came through, and I'd talk to them. But I went to Texas A&M for two years and did good, and I kind of let everybody know I wanted to play professional baseball. I wanted to play in the big leagues. A lot of scouts were around. And Dee Phillips came around, just kind of hung around me. My [A&M] manager, Tom Chandler, was actually working for Houston, and everybody said, 'Just call, let us know if you want to sign. We want to bid on you.'

"I had a pretty good last game of my last season at A&M, and we ended up losing, and I went home to San Antonio. Dee Phillips came knocking at eleven o'clock that night. He was the only one who came. And he brought Russo. I knew every club wanted to put a bid on me. But I liked the Orioles. The Orioles liked me the most. And they came out and offered me the money right there. I said, 'Just make me an offer. If it's the right offer, I'll take it.' At three o'clock in the morning I kind of agreed to it. I said, 'OK, I'm going to call Tom Chandler and tell him I'm signing with you guys.' They said the deal was off if I did that. I said, 'Well, I'll go ahead and sign. If you guys want me the most, you've got me. I don't need to be bid on.'"

Wally Bunker's case was typical of the cunning needed to sign top players in the early '60s. Bunker lived in the San Francisco Bay Area and was a high school star who favored his hometown Giants, but the Orioles worked their way to the top of his list. An amateur coach named Sterling Hammack was one of the Orioles' bird-dog scouts, and he talked Bunker into playing for the San Mateo Orioles, an amateur team the Orioles sponsored in a summer league. Bunker then later pitched for another amateur team affiliated with the Orioles in Washington state.

In the spring of '63 the Orioles had to choose between Bunker and Dave Boswell, a Baltimore prospect graduating from Calvert Hall. They picked Bunker and signed him to a contract with a forty-thousand-dollar bonus. He won 19 games at age nineteen in '64, seemingly validating the club's decision-making apparatus. Arm problems cut his career short, but not before he pitched a World Series shutout.

HARRY DALTON: "In those days everyone wanted the last visit [into the house] before the player signed. If you were the last ones in the living room, you figured you had a chance to take him home with you. The night we got Bunker, we were sitting in his living room, Don McShane, myself, and Don Pries. We were in there for about two hours, and all the time we could see this one car circling outside, going by and coming back, going by and coming back. We knew that whoever was out there was going nuts, figuring, 'Why the hell don't they come out so we can get in?' And we signed him. We let the people in the car park and go in and find out for themselves. It was the Cardinals."

The ultimate prize was Jim Palmer, a tall, athletic, multisport star from Scottsdale, Arizona. He was offered a basketball scholarship to UCLA and had numerous other options, but the Orioles talked him into pitching on an amateur team they sponsored in a summer league for college players in South Dakota, and they used that leverage to sign the future Hall of Famer.

JIM PALMER: "I had been scouted since I was fourteen. I pitched for the varsity as a freshman and some left-hander had pitched a no-hitter, and they came out to watch him, and I pitched a no-hitter and beat him, and then they were on me. They would play golf with my parents and take us to dinner and say that if I didn't play football I could go to the major leagues. All this stuff.

"So I go 10–0 my senior year. Striking out like 17 of 21 guys. And they're offering me just fifteen thousand dollars. It was the collusion of the '60s. They didn't want to give up any more bonuses. And I have scholarships to Arizona State, all the Utah schools, the Air Force Academy, Stanford, USC, UCLA. The Dodgers want me to go to Southern Cal for a year and sign with them for a real bonus.

"I really enjoyed basketball because of the work ethic involved. You really had to work hard to be a good player. The UCLA basketball scholarship would have been interesting. I would have been there with [Lew] Alcindor. I led the state in scoring my senior year. And in football I caught sixty passes, and I could run. Baseball was more of a natural sport for me. Just pick it up and throw it ninety-seven miles per hour.

"That spring, Bobby Winkles, who was the baseball coach at Arizona State, said, 'I have four or five guys [from ASU] going up to this college league in South Dakota. Why don't you go up and try to make it? You'll probably be the only high school guy there, but with your ability, you can do it.' So I went up there with five guys from ASU. Merv Rettenmund. Jim Lonborg. I went 5–2, pitched a one-hitter. And the Orioles sponsored the team. Jim Russo was up there establishing a rapport, and Jim Wilson was back home working on my parents."

HARRY DALTON: "We furnished that club with players every year, and we sent Jim in there because we thought he was good enough to compete. Then we sent the scouts in to watch him. Near the end [of the league season] Jim Wilson called and said, '[Palmer] is leaving soon. Would you like to see him?' I said I really would. They said, 'Well, we can get the manager [Harry Wise] to pitch him a couple of innings in the final game if you want to come up.' So I flew to Minneapolis, rented a car, and drove over and got there in the seventh inning. Wise saw me in the stands and brought Palmer in to pitch to three hitters, and he struck out two. I saw about fifteen pitches, and I said, 'I don't have to see anymore; you guys were right.'"

JIM PALMER: "Paul Richards had come through earlier in the summer, and they'd moved a game up to the afternoon so he could see me pitch. He was with Houston then. After the game he tells me, 'We're going to sign you when you get back to Scottsdale. Give you fifty thousand dollars and a college scholarship and ten thousand dollars the first year and three thousand dollars under the table.' I'm seventeen years old, and I have no idea what he's talking about. There are no agents, no nothing.

"So then Harry comes up to see me. It was Game 3 of the playoffs. Russo has been there most of the summer. I pitch one inning, the last inning. I get two strikeouts and a ground ball to the shortstop. That's what Dalton sees. After the game the guys I'd been with [from Arizona] are ready to get out of there, so we jump in our cars and head back to Arizona."

HARRY DALTON: "When I got back to Baltimore, Wilson was on the phone and said, 'We think we've got a chance to sign Palmer if we can get on the case right now.' That was another thing about our scouts. They were aggressive. We gave him the green light to go ahead. [Wilson] waited for Palmer to make it home. He knew [Palmer] was driving back, and he waited and waited and waited. Palmer didn't show up. Wilson got concerned that he'd lost [Palmer]."

JIM PALMER: "I'm in my red Corvair with [Luis] Lagunas, an All-American from ASU. There are five guys in two cars, and we're taking turns driving. So at about seven-thirty in the morning we're in Four Corners, and Bobby Vinton is singing 'Blue Velvet,' and I finally doze off in the back. And I wake up and Louie is on the wrong side of the road. Luckily we didn't hit anyone. I go to grab the wheel, and he wakes up and jerks the wheel, and we go flying off the road, flip the car three times. No seat belts. I hit my head three times.

"I'm in the backseat of the Corvair, and there are bags everywhere. And I'm so dazed that there's a little triangular window and I'm trying to get out of it. I don't know where I am. Some guys think we're messing around and come running down, and some patrol guy comes up on horseback. And I'm leaning against the car, and I'm in shock. All I did was cut my knee. I was so lucky. That's it. Car was demolished. So we took our stuff to the Greyhound bus stop, got home, went to the hospital, had some x-rays, got my knee stitched up.

"When I got home from that, there's Paul Richards. He says he's going to leave two telegrams, one for forty thousand dollars, one for forty-five thousand dollars, one with a college scholarship, one without. Says, 'Send one in tomorrow when you make up your mind.' He was real casual, just grabbed my mother's putter, and he's putting and chewing peanuts, and then Russo comes in. He's been working on my parents all summer, and it's a total departure in style. It wasn't that Richards was a bad guy. He just had a certain arrogance. And my parents said, 'You know, the Orioles seem like a better organization.' So I signed with them. And the next day twelve teams called."

Once the players were signed, they were fed into a minor league system loaded with managerial talent and top instructors. The Orioles fielded seven minor league teams in '62, and four of the managers—Clyde King, Earl Weaver, Billy Hunter, and Cal Ripken Sr.—were future major league managers. Another future major league manager, Darrell Johnson, replaced King at Rochester in '63. The minor league pitching instructors included George Bamberger, soon to become Weaver's trusted pitching coach in the major leagues, and later, Herm Starrette.

HARRY DALTON: "We had people with many areas of expertise, people who knew pitching. Ray Scarborough and George Bamberger were two excellent men on pitching. Vern Hoscheit on catching. Throughout the organization there were good people who made good, sensible decisions and helped players who were leveling off. Did something to correct their performance, and they prospered."

BOOG POWELL: "It just seemed like everywhere you went, you ran into good baseball people. Excellent baseball people. I can go back to rookie ball in Bluefield in '59. Ray Scarborough came down, and he spent a lot of time working with the pitchers. Ray was like the minor league roving pitching instructor. Then my manager in '60 in Fox Cities was Earl, who was already a hell of a manager.

"In '61 I had a hard time getting going in Rochester, hitting .180 or something, and Clyde King took me out to the ballpark one day, I'll never forget it. We were in Columbus, and he said, 'You're just not adapting to the curveball at this level. You need to hit a bunch of them.' So he took me to the park, and we took a big bag of balls and went out there, and him and I were the only two people. And he threw me curveballs for as long as his arm would hold up, about two and a-half hours, and he had a good curveball back in those days.

"I think we started with seventy-five balls, and there were probably fifteen left at the end of the session. I'd hit 'em all out of the ballpark. And all of a sudden I found it. I mean, I played that night, and I got like four hits, and all of a sudden it was there. All of a sudden I started seeing everything. And I went on and had a hell of a year down there, almost won the Triple-A Triple Crown."

DAVE McNALLY: "I signed in September of '60, and the next spring I went to Thomasville and ended up with Earl in Appleton [Wisconsin]. Then I had

Earl again in the instructional league after that season, and then again in Elmira, New York. He was the same as he was later, very good, although he picked on me because I was a bonus rookie. You had to carry your own bats and helmets and bags. I was a bonus kid, so he made me carry them every day. He thought that was quite clever."

JIM PALMER: "I went to Thomasville [in '64] and pitched 27 scoreless innings. I wanted them to send me to Stockton [California], which was closer to where I lived, but they sent me to Aberdeen, South Dakota. It was the best thing that ever happened to me because Cal Ripken Sr. was the manager. We won 14 in a row in spring training, beat Weaver's Double-A team all the time. We were so good that Cal rescinded the one-dollar fine for walking the opposing pitcher, which thrilled me, because I was wild and had no clue. When he did that I just relaxed. Cal made the game fun."

PAUL BLAIR: "I got drafted by the Mets out of high school and played my first year for them in the California League. Then I went down to winter ball for the Mets, and Baltimore drafted me. Winter of '62. It was a minor league draft. All a team had to do was draft you in a higher league. If I was in C ball, they could draft me in B ball. The Mets had put me on a Triple-A roster, but Baltimore drafted me and put me on their major league roster. That's how I became an Oriole.

"In '63 they sent me back to the Cal League. I was with Stockton that year. Had a real good year. My first year with the Mets in the same league I hit .228 and struck out 147 times and 417 at-bats, but I did hit 17 home runs and drive in 60, 70 runs. I guess I showed some potential, but they didn't think that I was going to get drafted, or at least on a major league level, so they put me on Triple A. Baltimore drafted me and sent me back to the Cal League, and that year I hit .326, stole 60 bases, made the All-Star team. We won the league. You could tell it was a good organization."

16

Assembling the Cast

After firing Billy Hitchcock, Lee MacPhail turned to Hitchcock's staff for a new manager, hiring Hank Bauer, a gruff former marine who had played in nine World Series as an outfielder for the Yankees in the '40s and '50s. Bauer had already managed the Athletics for two seasons, starting as a player-manager in '61. Fired after losing 90 games in '62, he joined the Orioles as a coach for the '63 season. Now, less than a year later, he was taking over as manager.

Adding to the Yankees' influence, Gene Woodling and Billy Hunter joined Bauer's coaching staff. Both had played for the Orioles, and Hunter had recently been managing in the Orioles' minor league system, but both also had played with Bauer on the Yankees in the '50s, and MacPhail was hoping that at least a little of the Yankees' excellence would rub off on the Orioles.

Coincidentally, the Yankees' dynasty finally was nearing an end, with key players aging and the farm system running dry. Mickey Mantle and Roger Maris combined to hit 61 homers in '64, as many as Maris alone had hit in '61, and there were no 20-game winners among the pitchers. The '64 club was the last Yankees team that would even contend for a pennant for nearly a decade. The '64 Orioles were their equals in many ways, reinvigorated by Bauer's leadership and strong performances from Brooks Robinson, Boog Powell, and Wally Bunker.

LEE MACPHAIL: "At the press conference when Hank was hired, one of the writers asked, 'Do you have any rules about drinking?' Because everyone knew there had been some drinking when Hitchcock was the manager. Hank said, 'Yeah, I sure do have some rules. The players aren't allowed to drink at the hotel bar. That's where I drink.' That was typical of Bauer. I liked him. I thought he was just the type we needed."

BOOG POWELL: "Hank brought a more regimented atmosphere over. We wore coats and ties at all times on the road. Hank said, 'We might not be major league ballplayers, but we're damn sure going to look like it.' We did look good. It was a pain in the ass to go to some of these ballparks when it was hot and they didn't have any air-conditioning, and it's August, and you're in there putting your tie on, and you're soaking wet. You know, it's already coming through your shirt, and by the time you get your coat on, your coat's wet.

"But that kind of stuff, along with Woodling coming back as a coach, there was more of the Yankees' tradition of winning. They brought that with them, and there's no substitute for it. And you couldn't work too hard. Hank was out there at all times. He got a lot of flak about his managerial moves, but he always maintained, 'I'm not going to win or lose this thing; you guys are. The only thing I can do is write out the lineup.' And that's what he did. And he wrote a pretty good lineup out."

MILT PAPPAS: "Hank was this gruff-talking ex-marine, and he had a raspy voice and scared the hell out of everyone. Underneath, he was the nicest guy in the world. Had a heart of gold. He made us dress up on the road, and he didn't give us a curfew, so he treated you like a man. Billy [Hitchcock] didn't command the same kind of respect. Billy had had a curfew. Hank was different. Nobody knew him. The guys were kind of scared of him. When he spoke, everyone listened. He knew what winning ways were, and he instilled them with us. That 'Hey, you know you can win. There's no reason why you can't win.'"

Jim Gentile was traded to Kansas City before the '64 season, a controversial move. Gentile's production had fallen steadily since his huge year in '61, but he still had hit 103 homers in three seasons as the centerpiece of the batting order, and that power would be difficult to replace. MacPhail obtained Gentile's replacement, Norm Siebern, in the deal. Siebern was also a veteran who had slipped from a huge season several years earlier, but he was coming off an 83-RBI season in '63 and was expected to help.

MacPhail was gambling that Powell was ready to take over as the cleanup hitter. The gamble succeeded. Powell delivered 39 homers and 99 RBI in '64, finishing second in the league in homers behind Minnesota's Harmon Killebrew. Brooks Robinson was even better, batting .317 with 28 homers and 118 RBI. He was voted the league's Most Valuable Player, becoming the first Oriole to win the award. Luis Aparicio and Siebern also played well enough to make the All-Star team. Aparicio hit .266 with 57 steals and 93 runs scored.

Siebern didn't come close to replacing Gentile, totaling 12 homers and 56 RBI, but he led the league in walks and scored 92 runs.

JIM GENTILE: "I'll tell you when I knew I was going to be traded. It was one night in '63. We're going to Washington. I got the flu. I go to the ballpark, they take my temperature, and the doc says, 'You've got 102; you've got to go home.' So Hitchcock says, 'Go on home and go to bed.' I go home, turn the TV on, and Boog's up. Ba-boom, he hits one out. The next time up, ba-boom, he hits another. I said, 'That's enough, Boog.' Then he comes up and, ba-boom, he hits a third. I turned to my wife and said, 'Better pack, we won't be here.'

"I was joking, but I look back on it and that's the time when I said, 'He's ready to make a move.' I knew he would ultimately take my job at first. I mean, I'm no dummy. Here's a six-foot, five [inch], good-looking hitter, played left field for us in '63 and did a great job, but he wasn't going to run down balls, and he had such a great pair of hands. I knew they'd move him to first to strengthen the team. I was just hoping I could stay for another year or two.

"They traded me for another first baseman, which was a shock. But I sat down and analyzed it. Bauer and Siebern were roommates with the Yankees in the '50s. Guy takes over as manager, first thing he does is trade for his roommate, right? Sounded good to me. And they wanted to bring a more low-key personality into the clubhouse. That's why they got rid of me. But people tell me even with the year I had in Kansas City in '64, with 28 homers and 71 RBI, if I had done that with the Orioles in '64, the Orioles might have won the pennant."

BOOG POWELL: "Diamond still says, 'You know, if it wasn't for you I'd still be in Baltimore.' And I say, 'Hey, you controlled the situation. If you'd kept hitting 40 home runs every year, I'd have been the leftfielder.' I might have been lucky to be that. I would probably have gotten traded."

JIM GENTILE: "The only thing that left a bad taste in my mouth was when Bauer took over. They called me and brought me and Brooks and whoever else was living in Baltimore into Memorial Stadium for the announcement. So I take a picture with Bauer, and Bauer calls me aside and says, 'Now, we're really going to work hard this year, Jim. I think we've got a hell of a team, Jim.' And I said, 'Yessir, I'm really ready.' That winter I had said to myself,

'I'm getting in shape,' and I really was doing sit-ups and going to the YMCA. Pappas and Fisher and I were playing basketball and running on the track, really looking forward to the season.

"Well, it turned out I'd been traded in November, at the winter meetings. I found out from [A's owner] Charlie Finley when he called. He said, 'Oh, we traded for you two months ago. Just didn't announce it.' The Orioles could have told me instead of making me come to the press conference and think everything was fine. Two days after that Lee called. I thought they could have handled it better. I deserved a little better. Lee could have called me in and told me when it really happened. What was I going to do, jump up and down?"

The pitching was a curious mixture of youth and old-timers. Barber, continuing a pattern of alternating good and bad seasons, fell from 20–13 in '63 to 9–13 in '64, with his ERA jumping more than a run. But Pappas (16–7) and Robin Roberts (13–7) were solid, and Bunker, just a year removed from high school, was magical, winning 19 of 24 decisions. The bullpen stalwarts were Stu Miller, thirty-six, Harvey Haddix, thirty-eight, and Dick Hall, thirty-three.

DICK HALL: "We had a nice bullpen in '64. Haddix had been around, and he didn't have the stuff to go nine innings anymore, but he still was effective and knew what he was doing. You could use him late in the game against a team with a left-handed lineup. And Stu Miller had the best change-up ever. He held it just like a fastball, and right at the last second he was able to break his wrist backwards so he had that real good fastball arm motion, and the ball had fastball spin, but it never got there. They'd sit there waiting for the change-up, but it took so long to get there that they went on and swung anyway. Then he'd pop that fastball. He was really good.

"The young starting pitchers were good, too. Bunker came out of high school like he'd been in the big leagues for ten years. He probably was ready when he was fourteen. Just smooth. Nothing bothered him. He threw sinkers, sort of like Barber. I don't think he knew he was supposed to be nervous. I don't think he realized things could go wrong. He was a veteran from the beginning, sort of like Mike Mussina later."

HARRY BRECHEEN: "It was like Bunker was made to be a pitcher. He had the perfect temperament. So many pitchers who get close to the major leagues lack the coolness you need to take whatever happens. Bunker had it."

WALLY BUNKER: "I had great control—always had it, even when my arm hurt later in my career. What can I say? I was blessed with great talent. I was never pushed into baseball, because I always won and had great success and didn't need to be pushed. In '64 I was living in a dream world. I was nineteen, and all I had to worry about was what I was throwing Harmon Killebrew."

DAVE McNALLY: "It was amazing. He was in awe of nothing. I was scared to death when I faced some of those big names for the first time. Wally didn't know one from the other. It didn't bother him a lick."

Bauer predicted before the '64 season that the Orioles would finish third, upsetting fans who thought he should be more optimistic. In the end, he was right. But for most of the season, it appeared he had undersold his club. The Orioles jumped off to another hot start, winning 30 of their first 45 games, just as they had in '63. But instead of faltering, they kept winning this time. Robinson and Powell carried the offense, and Bunker was hot. For twenty-two straight days in late June and early July, the Orioles were in first place, just ahead of the Yankees and White Sox.

On August 20 at Fenway Park, Powell leapt to make a catch against the Green Monster and came down with a broken wrist. The prognosis: a month on the disabled list. The Orioles dressed quietly after a 2–1 loss that dropped them out of first place, and they flew to Chicago for a four-game series with the first-place White Sox. But instead of folding, they won the first three games of the series, including one on Robinson's three-run homer in the ninth. The three wins moved the Orioles back in front by two and one-half games.

But they lost the final game of the series, and a slow, steady slide ensued. Robinson slumped, the bats fell silent, and the Orioles lost 17 of their next 30 games even though Powell returned ahead of schedule. The Yankees, meanwhile, won 23 of 30 games to go from five and one-half back to four up. It was the Yankees' last hurrah, a fading powerhouse's final charge. The Orioles won seven of their last eight games, but they ended one game behind the Sox and two behind the Yankees. Aparicio said it best: "We had a hell of a 140-game season."

BROOKS ROBINSON: "The Yankees could have been had in '64. That's the year we should have beaten 'em. They got hot the last couple of weeks and ran it out. And I mean, you can always look back at injuries and things, but Boog broke his wrist with about a month to go, and we really missed him."

BOOG POWELL: "I went back and jumped up for it, and I stuck my hand in one of those holes up there where they drop the scores down in Fenway. I was just hanging up there. Sure as hell, a broken wrist. And I was out almost until the end of the season. I came back with about two weeks left. I think I had 32 home runs when I did it; I came back and hit another seven. I was still hot. And I was hot when I'd gotten hurt. I think that we possibly could have pulled it off if I'd stayed in the lineup and I'd stayed hot. Brooksie was having a hell of a year, and we were close."

JACKIE BRANDT: "We had good defense and good pitching, but we were playing the Yankees. They were tough. Tough in Yankee Stadium because of the ballpark. They were suited to it. They had good defense, probably a little more power than us, good pitching, good relief pitching. And they had the perfect ballpark for Mantle, 296 down the line. They had these little pull hitters who could hit homers."

DICK HALL: "Someone would challenge them, and then they'd go head-to-head in September and win. The Yankees had a reputation for performing well in the clutch, but what it was, they'd been through it so many times that they just continued to play the same, and the other team was so full of adrenaline that they didn't perform as well. Other clubs under pressure either wouldn't think, or try too hard, or chase bad balls, and the Yankees would just keep going. Chasing the Yankees was hard. You'd have hopes and stuff, but you always kind of half expected they'd win."

In '65 there was more frustration. The Yankees faded to sixth, leaving a vacancy at the top of the American League. The Orioles were strong candidates to fill the opening as the season started, but although they won 94 games, they didn't come close to winning the pennant. The Minnesota Twins ran away with it, winning 102 games. The Orioles finished third, a game behind Chicago.

The Twins had moved from Washington in '61 and reinvented themselves as a top team after decades of failure as the Senators, with Killebrew, shortstop Zoilo Versalles, slugger Tony Oliva, and pitchers Mudcat Grant and Jim Kaat carrying the biggest loads. At a time when pitchers were dominating the game (AL hitters batted only .242 in '65), the Twins had the most punch. They batted sixteen points higher than the Orioles, whose .238 team average tied for the lowest since the franchise's move from St. Louis.

Change was in the air. A new generation of Orioles was taking over. Bunker, Dave McNally, and a rookie named Jim Palmer combined for 26 wins in '65. Curt Blefary, a cocky outfielder plucked from the Yankees' farm system, hit 22 home runs and was named AL Rookie of the Year. Paul Blair replaced Jackie Brandt in center field. At the franchise's highest levels, co-owner Joseph Iglehart sold his share of the club to Jerry Hoffberger, owner of the National Brewing Company (after Zanvyl Kreiger waived his right to purchase the stock). Hoffberger became the Orioles' majority owner in May.

At the end of the '65 season, Hoffberger brought in Frank Cashen, an advertising executive at the brewery, to oversee the Orioles' front office as an executive vice president. MacPhail, sensing his power eroding, resigned after seven years as general manager to become a special assistant to baseball's new commissioner, Spike Eckert. Harry Dalton was promoted from farm director to MacPhail's position, with a new title—vice president for player personnel. Dalton would handle the baseball decisions, although Cashen was the CEO.

MacPhail's final act as the Orioles' GM was his most important—he went to the '65 winter meetings in the first week of December and laid the groundwork for a trade that would change the Orioles forever. On December 9, 1965, two days after Dalton had assumed his new role, the Orioles traded Milt Pappas, relief pitcher Jack Baldschun, and outfielder Dick Simpson to Cincinnati for All-Star outfielder Frank Robinson.

The deal was rooted in several smaller trades MacPhail had engineered. First, he dealt Norm Siebern to the California Angels for Simpson, a young outfielder. Then he dealt Brandt and pitcher Darold Knowles to the Philadelphia Phillies for Baldschun, a veteran who had appeared in at least 65 games for five straight seasons. In effect, the Orioles traded four players—Brandt, Siebern, Knowles, and Pappas—for Robinson.

Pappas obviously was the biggest loss. A mainstay in the rotation since '58, he had impressive career numbers—110–74 with 944 strikeouts—and was coming off the latest in a long line of solid seasons, 13–9 with a 2.61 ERA in '65. But the front office and some teammates had doubts about him, and with so many promising pitchers filtering in from the minor league system, he was deemed expendable.

MacPhail and Bauer had spent two years trying to add another big, run-producing bat, thinking that was all the club needed to win. When the Giants offered a deal involving Jesus Alou, Bauer rejected it and grumbled, "We already have enough singles hitters." Robinson, thirty, was what they needed. In ten years with the Reds he'd batted .303 and averaged 32 homers and 101 RBI. Why would they agree to deal such a productive hitter? "Robinson is not a young thirty," explained Bill DeWitt, the Reds' owner/president. "If he was twenty-six we might not have traded him at all."

LEE MacPHAIL: "At one point [in the early '60s, former Yankees GM] George Weiss had called and asked me to join him with the Mets, but I thought Krieger and Iglehart had been too good to me. Then in '65 I was on the road with the team, and I got a call from Krieger. He said, 'I just bought Iglehart's stock in the team.' They had a buy-sell agreement, Krieger and Iglehart. If they sold their third, they had to sell it to the other. So Iglehart was out, and he was the one I was closest to. Then Jerry [Hoffberger] came and took over, and he was always very nice to me, but I always felt he hadn't had anything to do with hiring me, and I wasn't really his person. And the owner ought to have a right to have his own GM. I was always a little uneasy that way.

"Then about that time baseball picked a new commissioner, Spike Eckert, but they were concerned that he really didn't know anything about baseball, so they asked me to come and be his assistant. They said I owed it to baseball. And then, as the season was ending, [the Orioles] hired Frank [Cashen]. Gave him a good title. And they didn't even tell me about it in advance, nor did they invite me to be there at the press conference when he was introduced. That helped me make up my mind. Frank is a good friend of mine, but that certainly was an indication of maybe what Jerry's feelings for me were. He urged me to stay, but I ended up accepting the job in New York.

"Jerry said, 'Would you please stay through the winter meetings?' I said fine, and I went to the winter meetings with one thought in mind—adding one more bat. Our pitching had been pretty good for a long time. But we needed hitting. Bill DeWitt was running the Reds, and we'd worked together at the Yankees. We talked. They were desperate for a relief pitcher. The guy they really liked was Baldschun. We were able to put the deal together.

"Frank [Robinson] had had a few problems. At one point, the story was that he'd had a gun in the dugout, which bothered me. You know, we were giving away half the team to get this guy. Fortunately, I had a very good friend who was a coach at Cincinnati, Jim Turner, from my Yankees days. I called Jim and asked him about Frank, and Jim gave him a hundred-percent thumbs-up. I think there was truth [to the gun rumor], but I don't know how serious it was. Maybe he just happened to have a gun. But there were never any problems with the Orioles."

HARRY DALTON: "Twenty minutes before the press conference [announcing Dalton's promotion], Lee came in and said, 'Here's your first decision,' and handed me a slip of paper with the three names on one side and Frank on the other. He said, 'I've talked to DeWitt and he would make this deal. But it's yours now; do what you think.' Bauer was with me, and we liked the deal. Then we had to go into the press conference, and after that there was a dinner for Lee. Finally, after that, I went back and had a chance to think about it. And I thought about this left-handed pitcher they had in the minor leagues, down in the Florida State League. I can't think of his name now but he got to the big leagues later for Kansas City. And we had decent reports on him as a prospect, and I thought, 'Well, if we're making this a three-for-one, maybe I can get DeWitt to give us another player, and I'll ask for this guy.'

"So I called DeWitt and said, 'We'll make it if you'd toss in that pitcher.' He said, 'No, I won't do that.' And I said, 'Well, I need another player. I just can't make it three-for-one, three big-leaguers for one. I've got to make it look a little better and [the pitcher] is way down in the minors anyway.' DeWitt said, 'No, if you need a second player I'll give you Roger Craig' (who won only two more games the rest of his career). I said, 'Thanks, I don't want any part of Craig.' Lee came in later and said, 'Did you talk to DeWitt?' And I said, 'Yeah, I'm trying to get a pitcher from them, and he won't do it.' Lee said, 'Don't blow this deal.' I know he was scared stiff that he'd given it to some young buck who didn't know how to make a trade.

"But I slept on it. I went home and went to bed and thought about it and came back. I guess all the time I knew I was going to make it if I couldn't get someone else. But I had to try. So the next day I called him and said, 'We can do it now.' Lee was very happy. We all were. Pappas was a good pitcher. A hundred wins in each league. There aren't many guys that have done that. But he had fallen out of favor a little bit with the staff, coming out of ball games earlier than we all thought he should. And with the other young arms we had, we thought we could replace him."

FRANK CASHEN: "I asked Harry, 'What do you want to do? And he said, 'I want to make the deal.' Then I talked to Bauer, and in spite of what Bauer says now, he didn't want to make the deal. And he didn't want to make the deal for these reasons: Number one, nobody wants to give up their best pitcher. That was Pappas. And second, Frank Robinson had a terrible reputation. He'd had that gun in the clubhouse and had a reputation as being a guy who disturbed everything. So here I had the manager saying no and Harry saying 'I think we ought to do it.' It was up to me to make the decision, and I finally said, 'OK, let's do it.'

"We did it with some fear and trepidation because one of my theories of managing is if you've got a bad apple in the barrel, get him the hell out before the rest of the barrel goes bad. But Frank Robinson came over here, and we never had a moment's trouble. He came over here and had learned from his mistakes, and he became the leader of the ball club. Brooks Robinson said we had a good ball club, but Frank taught us how to win."

STEVE BARBER: "If [Pappas] pitched five or six innings and had the lead, and he didn't have a shutout, he was out of there. One time in '65 Tom Tresh had hit a home run off him in the first or second inning, and we go into the bottom of the sixth with a lead, and all of a sudden he's doubled over on the mound with cramps. So they made a change, and Jerry Adair went back in and told the [clubhouse attendant], 'Tell me everything he does in here.' And when we got back the clubbie says, 'He had four sandwiches and seven bottles of pop.' He was a hell of a good pitcher, but Billy Loes got to him early. You know, don't win 20 or they'll expect you to do it every year.

"I couldn't stand the son of a bitch. Nobody could. He had two or three cars in '65, and he told a clubhouse boy he could use one of them one night, and the kid made a bunch of plans, and then Pappas didn't give him the car. So I gave him mine. Then I came in the clubhouse one night during a game, and he was chewing out one of the clubhouse guys, and I said, 'Milt, give it a rest; the guy's making two dollars a game.' And he says, 'Well, I'm the player rep now so I have to be a prick.' I said, 'You've been a prick ever since I've known you.'"

MILT PAPPAS: "I was down at the ['65] winter meetings in Florida as the player rep for the Orioles, and I called home. My wife was going to come down, and we were going to look for a place to stay during spring training.

We always stayed on Key Biscayne. So my wife said, 'There's rumors in the paper about you being traded to San Francisco.' That night I was walking out of the hotel, and Bauer and MacPhail were coming in. I said, 'Hey, guys, I just talked to my wife, and she said there's all sorts of rumors about me being traded to the Giants.' Both Bauer and MacPhail looked at me and said, 'Untrue. You're not going anywhere. You're not being traded.'

"So my wife gets down there a couple of days later, and it's a rainy afternoon, and we decide to go see a movie. And the movie we pick is *The Cincinnati Kid*, with Steve McQueen. Then we spent a couple more days in Miami, found a place, and came back to Baltimore. A couple of days later I get a call from Harry Dalton, 'Milt, we just traded you to Cincinnati.' That just blew me away. MacPhail and Bauer had both assured me I wasn't going anywhere. I'd put it out of my mind, and then I was traded. It was very upsetting."

LEE MACPHAIL: "After we got Frank I remember one of the writers talking about, 'cannons at the corners.' Blefary in left, Frank in right, Brooks at third, and Boog at first. Four pretty good bats. Looking at that and the pitching, I did feel I was leaving the Orioles in pretty good shape."

FRANK ROBINSON: "My first reaction [to the trade] was shock and disbelief. The Reds were the only organization I'd known. My mind just went blank. I'd heard some rumors about a possible trade, but when it didn't happen at the winter meetings, I thought that was over. But once I got over the shock and started thinking about it, I thought it was a good deal. I was hurt by DeWitt's statement [about being an 'old thirty']. I didn't know what he meant. And I never spoke to the man again."

MILT PAPPAS: "The next spring we were down in Florida, and a photographer came up and said, 'I want to take a picture of you and Frank, the two guys in the trade.' I said fine. So I'm waiting there for thirty minutes, and the guy finally comes back, kind of sheepish, and says, 'Well, we're not doing it. Frank doesn't want to do it.' OK, whatever.

"I never faced Frank at the plate until '72 when he got traded to the Dodgers and I was with the Cubs. I was starting, and I told my catcher, Randy Hundley, 'Something's going to happen today. I'm not going to tell you, because then you'd know, but I'm just telling you something is going to happen.' He says, 'Fine, whatever.' So Frank comes up in the first inning, and

I knock him right down, throw a fastball right at him, and he gets up cussing and screaming, 'That SOB is throwing right at me.' I strike him out.

"Next time up, same thing. I knock him down, and he gets up screaming at me and Hundley, 'What the hell is he doing?' Hundley says, 'I have no idea, Frank.' Then it happens a third time, and Frank's in the dirt again, and he gets up yelling, 'Throw that SOB out of the game; he's trying to kill me.' I strike him out again. I wound up striking him out three times, and I threw at him every time. After the game Hundley says, 'Jesus Christ, what'd that guy do to you?' I said, 'He wouldn't take a picture with me in spring training six years ago.' Hundley says, 'Boy, you sure do carry a grudge.' I said, 'Well, maybe, but that's the way it is.'"

17

Jerry

Jerry Hoffberger was a relatively minor player in the Orioles' first decade after helping complete the deal that brought the club to Baltimore in '54. His National Brewing Company owned a large block of stock and was a major sponsor, but Joseph Iglehart and Zanvyl Krieger, the Orioles' other primary stockholders, were more involved. Hoffberger was mostly out of the public eye other than a failed attempt to buy the Detroit Tigers with Bill Veeck in the late '50s.

Then came the sale of the New York Yankees to the CBS television network in '64, hastening a sequence of events that led to Hoffberger becoming the Orioles' majority owner in '65.

FRANK CASHEN: "Joe Iglehart worked for CBS. He was on the finance committee at CBS. When CBS bought the Yankees, he had a conflict of interest. Either he had to get rid of CBS or his Orioles stock, and he decided he'd get rid of the Orioles stock."

JOE HAMPER: "Jerry felt CBS taking over the Yankees was not in the best interests of baseball. He was against it, and he wanted to get on the [Orioles] board [of directors] because National had such a large stake [in the Orioles]. He and Iglehart had a falling out over that. Jerry had never gotten on the board, and when he said he wanted on, Iglehart, who was chairman of the board, bowed his neck and said he didn't think that was a good idea. Then Iglehart resigned and sold his shares, and Jerry wound up with them."

Krieger and Iglehart had a buy-sell agreement—if one sold his stock in the Orioles, he had to sell to the other. When Iglehart was ready to sell, Krieger waived his right to buy Iglehart's stock and let Hoffberger's National Brewing Company buy it. In return, Hoffberger gave Krieger the right to sell his stock at any time to National at a profitable price. In the end, National owned 65 percent of the stock in the Orioles, and Hoffberger was named president and chairman of the board. Krieger still owned 18 percent and was club treasurer.

JOE HAMPER: "When the original ownership group purchased Veeck's stock in the Browns in '54, the stock was in a Missouri corporation that was publicly held and had a large operating loss. The thought at that time was that, given the tax laws, it would be advantageous to retain the debt. So rather than create a new corporate structure, the Baltimore group just bought Veeck's block of stock in a corporation with some minority stockholders.

"The group then created a holding company that was the parent [of the Orioles], the Baltimore Baseball Club, Inc. That company is what all the stock was owned in. As of '65, National had a substantial block and Zanvyl had an agreement that he could sell his block [to National] at a predetermined price at any time. It was a no-lose proposition for Zanvyl. Then everyone identified Jerry as the owner, and he ran it."

Hoffberger was forty-six when he took over the Orioles, a scion of one of Baltimore's most influential families. His grandfather, Samuel, had been a merchant who sold ice, wood, and coal, and Samuel's seven sons later were successful in a variety of industries. Hoffberger's father, Charles, was a lawyer and philanthropist credited with building Baltimore's first low-cost housing during the Depression.

FRANK CASHEN: "Jerry's father was one of seven sons, and they each had something they ran. There was 'Cold Storage Charlie'; he ran the cold storage company. There was 'Broadway Charlie,' the playboy they kind of paid to stay away. There was 'Real Estate Charlie'; he ran all the real estate. Those seven sons started all these different businesses and built the Hoffberger empire."

After serving in Africa, Italy, and France during World War II, Hoffberger became treasurer and then president of the National Brewing Company, overseeing a period of substantial success. He was a patron of educational, cultural, and religious institutions in Baltimore and Israel, and he brought the same sense of family and obligation to the Orioles when he took over in '65.

He was in charge for the next fourteen years, through some of baseball's most turbulent times and most of the Orioles' glory years. For those fourteen years he was one of the primary faces of baseball in Baltimore, an approachable owner who sat in his season ticket seats behind the dugout and cheered and groaned along with everyone else.

FRANK CASHEN: "He was an example of what every [owner] should be. I don't want to tread on any toes, particularly of current ownership, but when he made me the brewery's director of advertising, he said, 'You're smart; you go do it. If you need me, call me.' That's how he was with the ball club. He was there for you. He was interested. He never made one of your decisions for you. If you said, 'Jerry, I'm looking for a new manager, and I've got a choice between A and B,' he'd say, 'What do you think?' You'd say, 'I like A.' And he'd say, 'Well, have you thought about the fact that B has more experience?' I mean, he posed a couple of questions and quizzed you and said, 'You do what you think; you're running the club.'"

HANK PETERS: "Jerry was great for me. He gave me a free hand, and he didn't interfere. I remember when I was making the Reggie Jackson deal [in '76], which was a hell of a big deal, and Jerry was in Israel at the time. I called him and got him over there, and I said, 'I got a chance to make this deal.' He asked me a few questions, said, 'Do you like him?' I said, 'I wouldn't make it if I didn't like it,' and he said, 'Go ahead; do whatever you think you want to do.'"

JOE HAMPER: "Jerry brought a new vigor to the marketing of the team. He had a high visibility in the community and was very outgoing, and he changed the image of the ball club. In the early years, the Colts were big, and we were second-class citizens. The Colts sold out the stadium, and everybody, including myself, was a fanatic Colts fan. The Orioles didn't have anywhere near that kind of stature, and Jerry gave the ball club stature and the marketing prowess."

FRANK CASHEN: "The toughest part about the ball club at that time was that baseball was secondary. The Colts were everything. I mean, the Colts were huge. Then [Colts owner] Carroll Rosenbloom did us a great favor. He got jealous because the guy who got all the [good] publicity was Don Kellett, who was running the team, and he demoted Kellett, and their effectiveness as a public relations venture and everything else went down. That was in '67."

JOE HAMPER: "Hoffberger's family had deep roots in Baltimore, and it was as if he was really running the club for the benefit of the city. There was a strong sense of civic responsibility. Veeck had signed a concession agreement for twenty-five years, and Hoffberger always wanted better-quality food. Things like that."

BOOG POWELL: "One of the single greatest things Jerry ever did was make Frank Robinson feel at home in Baltimore. I think Frank was a little apprehensive about what was going to happen to him when he came here. He had a pretty shaky reputation when he came from Cincinnati, and Jerry made him feel at home—welcomed his family and welcomed him into the community. That was a very big part of the year Frank had [in '66]. Not that he wouldn't have had a great year despite what Jerry did, but I think it really helped solidify the whole unit."

FRANK ROBINSON: "I was the first black player to come to Baltimore as a frontline starter. The team was ready for me, but I don't know if the city was. It was tough for me to find a place to stay. I was down in Florida in March, and my wife and kid were up in Baltimore finding a place to live. It was easy as long as people thought she was Brooks Robinson's wife. Then they'd find out she wasn't, and all of a sudden the place wasn't available.

"They'd go, 'Oh, sure, great, the Robinsons? No problem.' And then when they found out it was Frank instead of Brooks they'd go, 'Oh, sorry, we can't let that place to you.' They'd do it right to her face. I went and told Jerry Hoffberger about it. My wife had said she was leaving, going back to California. I went to Jerry and said, 'My family's up in Baltimore, and they can't find a place to stay. I've got to go take care of this.' He says, 'No, I'll take care of it.' He made sure they were put up at the Belvedere Hotel, and then they found a house for us. Jerry took control of the situation."

BOOG POWELL: "Jerry was a whole-unit kind of a guy. He was in the clubhouse all the time. He was like an owner that just bought the team to come in the clubhouse. He used to hang around the guys and stuff. I think every guy on the team had a really good relationship with Jerry. Lee MacPhail and [the prior owners] were really nice people, but they were very business oriented and businesslike. When they came into the clubhouse, they talked to you about baseball or how good or bad you were doing and what you're doing right or wrong. It wasn't about your family or how you felt other than that. Jerry would come in and ask, 'How's your family? How's your wife? How are your kids?' He knew all of my kids by their first name, and they knew him, too.

"Then [in '66] we each started getting a case of [National] beer just about every week. That was cool. Whenever we'd come back from a trip, there would always be a case of beer just sitting in our locker. That was super. So we didn't have to buy beer. There were several guys on the team that didn't drink, and we were all scuffling for their beer. We also started having great parties out at a place on York Road. Jerry was right in the middle of all that. They were part of the family, him and [his wife] Alice. They were wonderful people."

Hoffberger brought business principles to the Orioles, organizing the front office more traditionally with titles, a baseball side, and a business side. Overseeing it all was Cashen.

FRANK CASHEN: "I'd been a sportswriter and went to law school [in the '50s], but I'd reached a point where I could no longer say money didn't matter. I had four kids. I had to get a job. Jerry had been after me to go to work for him, and I ended up running Baltimore Raceway, a harness track on Philadelphia Road. I went there as director of publicity and wound up running it. Then Jerry's group bought the Bel Air racetrack, and I ran both [racetracks]. Then they sold those, and I went to the brewery as Jerry's administrative assistant.

"One day Jerry said, 'I want you to go upstairs and run the advertising department.' A wonderful, big job. I said, 'Jerry, I don't know anything about advertising.' He said, 'Well, you used to be a writer; you've got a good head on your shoulders; you go ahead on up there. If you need me, I'm down here.' In those days the advertising budget was fourteen million dollars a year, which was gigantic. That was more than the Orioles were worth, way more.

"I did that for a couple of years, and then [in '65] Jerry was taking over the ball club and asked me to write a report on the ball club—who worked there, who I thought was good, who wasn't, what I thought should be done, et cetera. I did that. Mostly it was about the personnel and what I thought they'd have to do to become a winner, because they were always kind of knocking at the door, and then they'd lose. The next thing I know, Jerry called me to his house and said, 'I want you to go help Lee MacPhail run the club.' Well, I'd been a sportswriter and that didn't hold anything for me. I mean, I was a director of advertising and going to Hollywood and making commercials and had a company car and free beer. I didn't want to give that up.

"I argued, and Jerry said, 'Do it for me as a personal favor. In a year or two you'll have that all straightened out and you can come back.' Then Lee left right as I got there, and I had to start at the bottom as chief executive of the Orioles. I ran the team. Jerry went, 'Well, how do you want to set it up?' And in those days the general manager was the chief operating officer and ran the whole McGillick, sold the tickets, did the television contracts, did the whole thing. Jerry goes, 'You be the GM.' I said, 'No, let's go easy on that. I'll run it and I'm responsible, but let's get a baseball guy.'

"So one of the first things I faced was whether to take Jack Dunn Jr. as the head baseball guy or take one of the other people. And I selected Harry Dalton as the vice president of baseball operations. We never actually had a general manager in title. It was tough because Jack Dunn had been with the ball club forever, and his family had owned [the International League Orioles], and he had all the qualifications, but I just decided to go with the younger guy, and we made Harry director of baseball operations. And it was the right move."

Glory Days
1966–71

18

Frank's Masterpiece

Frank Robinson was born in Beaumont, Texas, in 1935, the youngest of eleven children. After his parents split up when he was six, he moved with his mother to Oakland, California. Asked years later how he developed his quick hands and competitive nature, he said with typical wry humor, "Try sitting down to eat with ten brothers and sisters every night."

His childhood nickname was "Pencils," after the thin legs he inherited from his father—not that anyone teased him for long. "Pencils" was a star athlete. At McClymonds High School he played basketball with future NBA legend Bill Russell, and he also played fullback. But baseball was his best sport. A youth league coach, George Powles, schooled him in the fundamentals, and Robinson played on an American Legion team that won back-to-back national titles.

Bobby Mattick, a former major leaguer now scouting for the Cincinnati Reds, noticed Robinson while scouting another prospect, a catcher named J. W. Porter. The Reds wound up getting both, with Porter signing for a much larger bonus. Robinson, considered a lesser prospect, signed for three thousand dollars.

Seldom has a small bonus returned so much. After a quick trip through the Reds' minor league system, Robinson had 38 homers and 83 RBI as a rookie leftfielder in '56, winning the National League's Rookie of the Year honor. He went on to establish himself as one of the game's brightest stars, known for his powerful bat and fierce playing style.

In '61 he led the Reds to their first pennant in twenty-one years, batting .323 with 37 homers and 124 RBI, a performance that earned him the NL's Most Valuable Player award. He also learned a lesson off the field. When an argument in a restaurant escalated, Robinson produced a gun and was later charged with a violation. He said he had the gun only because he carried a lot of money, but that didn't stop a wave of criticism.

After four more productive seasons, Robinson was dealt to the Orioles with Cincinnati GM Bill DeWitt explaining the perennial All-Star was "not a young thirty." Angered, Robinson played with a special fury in '66. "I always want to have a good year, but I guess [the comment] gave me more of an urge," he said after the season.

It is impossible to exaggerate his impact on the Orioles in '66. He took a club accustomed to losing pennant races and injected it with a refuse-to-lose fire. He led the American League in batting average, home runs and RBI, winning a Triple Crown. He even changed the AL itself, introducing the spikes-up style more typical of the National League, where black stars had made more inroads and the game was played more aggressively.

Suddenly, after years of looking up at pennant winners, the Orioles had what the rest of the American League wanted.

FRANK ROBINSON: "I didn't have to prove myself. I was still a pretty good player, had a lot of good baseball left. I just wanted to show Baltimore I was a good player. What made it easy was the way I was accepted—by the team. The first time I walked on the field in spring training they were joking with me, making me feel at ease. I got in the cage, popped everything up, and they went, 'Is this all we got for Pappas?'"

DICK HALL: "All of a sudden, you could see it. Everyone was thinking, 'Now we got it. We got the hitter we needed, and we're going to win.' There were huge expectations. It was the only time in my life I grooved a pitch. We played an intrasquad game, and Frank came up for the first time, and I thought, 'Man, with these expectations, it'd be nice if he got off to a good start.' I put a nice batting practice pitch right down the middle, and bang, base hit."

JIM PALMER: "One day in spring training, a bonus kid for the Braves threw a fall-off-the-table curve, and Frank hit a rocket right down the line, bringing up chalk. I turned to Davey [Johnson] and said, 'We just won the pennant.' He made everyone believe they could win. You talk about teams that hope to win. That was the Orioles before Frank. After he got there, we expected to win."

PAUL BLAIR: "The team was accustomed to finishing second. Then Frank came in and hit eight or ten home runs in spring training, and you could see we were going to be something special. We were good before—had great defense, good pitching, decent hitting—but Frank was the key. Not only did he play great, he showed us how to go out there and be all business and get the job done. You could laugh and joke with the other team before the game, but once that game started, it was all business. The only concern was 'How can we beat 'em?'

"The thing that stands out in my mind is when he was saying, 'Let's go,' he was walking to the plate. There are so many guys that pretend to be leaders saying, 'Let's go,' and they're walking away from the plate. But Frank, when he said, 'All right, guys, let's go,' he was taking his bat right to the plate and getting hits and starting rallies. To me, that's what a leader does. A leader isn't the guy that goes 'rah-rah.' It's the guy who goes up there and says, 'This is how it should be done; watch me and I'll show you how.' "

BROOKS ROBINSON: "No one really knew what to think when they made the trade. I mean, Frank was coming over with a reputation—had been a little hot and cold and been picked up with a gun—but he came over and really fit. He had a strong personality, and it took a little while for everyone to get used to one another. But it all worked out."

DAVEY JOHNSON: "He kind of carried a chip on his shoulder and dared everybody to knock it off. I liked that. He was a great player, but he also always had that chip and just kind of set it up there and said, 'OK, if you're good enough, you can knock it off.' And nobody really could."

The Orioles started the '66 season on a roll, winning 12 of their first 13 games, but when they lost for the second time, they found themselves a half-game behind the Cleveland Indians. In an early season showdown between the teams in Baltimore, the Orioles won three of four games. In the finale, Frank Robinson hit a ball off Luis Tiant that went over the left-field fence and all the way out of the stadium—a feat never before accomplished and, it turned out, never repeated.

FRANK ROBINSON: "Tiant had thrown three straight shutouts to open the season, but Russ Snyder got on base, and the first pitch was a fastball down and in, and it was, 'See you later.' I didn't know it went all the way out of the park. I got back to the bench, and they said, 'It went all the way out.' I said, 'Yeah, right.' They were always joking about stuff. But I realized they were telling the truth when I went back out the next inning and the fans gave me a standing ovation, like something special had happened. It was quite a thrill. I was a new guy on the team, and the fans were giving me an ovation. That made me feel welcomed."

MOE DRABOWSKY: "Sometimes you can point to one incident in a season as the big one. To me, when Frank hit that ball out of the stadium off Tiant, it galvanized the whole team. It was like, 'We're going to be tough to beat this year.'"

The Indians stayed within sight until early June, when the Orioles jumped into first place for good and ran away from the rest of the league, building a 13-game lead by late July. Not even a run of sore pitching arms could slow their charge to the pennant clincher, which came on September 22 in Kansas City and was followed by a memorable clubhouse celebration.

Pitching had carried the Orioles for years, but hitting was the story in '66. Frank Robinson, Brooks Robinson, Boog Powell (shifting to first base), and Curt Blefary all hit at least 23 homers, and all but Blefary drove in at least 100 runs. The Orioles led the league in runs and hitting, with their team batting average rising 20 points from '65. Combined with pitching as effective as ever despite injuries in the rotation—the staff ERA was the AL's fourth-lowest—the Orioles won their first pennant easily after years of frustration.

Frank Robinson was at the center of it all, hitting home runs and making diving catches. In late June he made what manager Hank Bauer called the biggest play of the season, leaping while falling backward into the right-field seats in Yankee Stadium to make a game-winning catch. Two weeks later, with the club embarking on a decisive run of 36 wins in 47 games, he hit a pair of key home runs in a five-game sweep of Minnesota, the defending AL champ. He then hit nine homers in 10 games as the Orioles opened a lead and didn't stop until the season did. His final totals: a .316 average, 49 homers, 122 runs scored, and 122 RBI. He won the AL's MVP Award in a landslide.

FRANK ROBINSON: "Everything fell into place from the beginning. In my first at-bat of the season [in Boston] I got a broken-bat single, and the next time Earl Wilson hit me. Then I got a homer later in that game, and so did Brooks, and we won. Then we hit back-to-back homers in the next game, and I hit another the day after that. The pitching was good; the defense was great; everyone was swinging the bats."

Boog Powell: "I was scuffling early, and then in Detroit I hit a home run off Joe Sparma. I hit it off the upper deck, just a line-drive bullet. And I came back, and Frank says, 'You got it now; we're rolling. It's over.' And it was. If I didn't get 'em, Frank would or Brooks would. I would dominate for a week or two weeks, and then Brooks would. Frank was really dominating all year. Our pitching wasn't that good, but we one-two-three'd everyone."

Harry Dalton: "We won in a lot of dramatic situations, where you knew the game would be decided in the next couple of minutes. We won so many that way, with Frank hitting a home run or something. Whatever it took, we did it. Teams have years like that, when everything goes right. It's almost an intangible. There gets to be a feeling of, 'We can do it, no matter what it takes.'"

Frank Robinson: "On that game-winning catch in Yankee Stadium, it was the first game of a doubleheader, and the fence was a lot lower than it is now. The ball was going over, no question. I had to jump to catch it. So when I came down, my legs hit the fence and I jackknifed right over the fence and wound up between the seats and the wall. Just wedged down in there. I came out with the ball, and the umpire said, 'Yeah, you got it' and called the out.

"[Yankees manager] Ralph Houk kicked up a fuss. Kicked dirt and kicked his hat and everything. Swore I didn't catch it. I didn't think there was any doubt because I was facing the field when I caught the ball. Then I went out for the second game, and the people were all over me, calling me names and all sorts of awful stuff—throwing batteries and food at me. They didn't tell me until after the game that thirty fans had gone in somewhere and signed affidavits swearing that I'd lost the ball in the stands when I came down and didn't catch it.

"They also told me after the second game that I'd gotten four death threats in between games. I saw the extra police and all, but I didn't know why they were there. Something like that really brings a team together."

There were important aspects to Robinson's contribution that couldn't be measured in numbers. At the urging of the coaches, he named himself the judge of a kangaroo court, a lighthearted team meeting that convened in the clubhouse after wins and levied fines on players for making stupid comments or boneheaded plays.

Robinson wore a mop on his head as he presided over the irreverent sessions that helped build camaraderie and, in a quiet way, helped instruct the team's rookies and young players, a group that included catcher Andy Etchebarren, second baseman Davey Johnson, centerfielder Paul Blair, and pitcher Jim Palmer.

FRANK ROBINSON: "[Orioles coach] Billy Hunter came to me after the season started about getting the kangaroo court going. He thought it was a way to loosen the club up and point out mistakes at the same time. Laugh and get a point across in a light atmosphere. We had a lot of fun with it. My role was to keep order and listen. We always did it right away after games, before the press came in.

"You could bring up a case against someone if they missed a cutoff man, butchered a ball in the infield, didn't pick up a sign running the bases, threw to the wrong base—anything. Or if they said something dumb, like they weren't paying attention. When the case was brought up against you, the entire ball club was the jury, and I was the judge, and everyone gave it thumbs-up or thumbs-down. Majority rule. And either you got fined a dollar or two, or the case was thrown out and the guy who'd brought up the case got fined."

BROOKS ROBINSON: "We gave out a bad baserunning award and a weak swing award, all named for past or present Orioles. If you made a baserunning mistake, you had to take a guy's shoe and keep it. If you got the weak swing award, you got a little sawed-off bat that was named for some guy who used to have weak swings. Then they'd fine you for talking to the opposition or asking some stupid question."

DICK HALL: "If there were two outs and a man on first and you were sitting on the bench and said, 'OK, let's get two,' they'd catch you. Anyone could bring up a case. Frank was the judge, and he put a mop on his head. It was all in fun. We got Bauer one time. He was up in the tunnel smoking a cigarette, and he gave the signal for a squeeze with Boog up, only what he was really doing was smoking his cigarette.

"We did it only after wins. So that became a motivation to win. I swear, you'd have something good on someone, and you'd go, 'Man, we gotta go on and win, because we gotta nail him on this.' Because things never carried over to the next day. You'd bring it up, and they'd vote on it. But it was sort of amorphous, so we kind of made up the rules as we went along. We were winning, and the atmosphere was good."

PAUL BLAIR: "It made you pay attention, and you learned from mistakes. Guys didn't make those same mistakes again. That helped us tremendously. And it brought the club closer together, made us more of a family, to the point where we could laugh at our mistakes, but we didn't make 'em twice."

BOOG POWELL: "If you had a runner on third with less than two outs and you didn't get him in, you got the Fuck Up Award and were fined automatically. Things like that were automatic. One of the things that made it so successful was we all swallowed our pride and our egos a little bit just to make it successful. If one guy was really against it, it wouldn't work. But every single guy couldn't wait to get in the clubhouse after the game to see who brought what up. Nobody was exempt. I mean, Jerry Hoffberger was brought up. Things like that just kept everybody loose and laughing, and if you'd had a shitty night then you didn't have to think about it."

BROOKS ROBINSON: "With me being from Little Rock and having gone to Little Rock Central High School, Blair and those guys used to make comments like, 'Well, I know I'm not going through Little Rock when I'm going somewhere,' something like that. And I'd always say, 'Just tell 'em you know me; you're in good shape.' We had good rapport. Blair always talked basketball. He knew I was an all-state player and said, 'But you didn't have to play against any black guys. That's the reason you were so good.' He's probably right. We were pretty open about things. We got on one another, and everybody had a good time."

STEVE BARBER: "With some teams you have personality issues or cliques or problems that evolve from that kind of thing. We had none of that in '66. It was the closest-knit group I've ever been around. There were no cliques. Everyone could run with everyone. It was just terrific. You can't create something like that. It just happens.

"One night we had a big party, and I wound up at Boog's place later that night and stayed until five-thirty, something like that. We had a doubleheader the next night, and I pitched the first game. Probably had to be at the park around three. I think I threw a two-hit shutout. And in the bottom of the ninth of the second game, Boog hit a two-run homer to tie it, and it was his second homer and 11th RBI of the doubleheader.

"Another night we had a big party at a house with a real nice backyard and a pool. Well, a lot went on that night. Boog had to go to the hospital for stitches. And Frank almost drowned. I don't think he could swim, and he put on his trunks and got in, and we looked around and he's lying at the bottom of the pool. Etchebarren dove in and pulled him out. Frank said, 'I could already see the headline: FRANK ROBINSON DROWNS IN UNDERTAKER'S POOL.'"

BOOG POWELL: "What happened, we were going to try to throw [reliever] Moe [Drabowsky] in the pool. And I had a hold of his foot, and his foot was wet, and my hands came off, and I fell back and hit my eye on the corner of a doorjamb. Just laid it wide open. It was ugly. So Curt Blefary and I took someone else's hospital card and went to the emergency room and gave 'em the card, and everybody was sniggering because they knew it was me. The doctor put about four or five stitches in, and we went back to the party. The only person that missed me was my wife. She said, 'What's that on your eye?' I said, 'Aw, nothin'.'"

A major contributor to the lighthearted atmosphere was Drabowsky, a veteran pitcher renowned as a prankster. The Orioles acquired him before the '66 season.

Far from being a typical major leaguer, Drabowsky was born in Poland, fled the Nazis with his parents, and came to the United States as a youngster. After graduating from a New England prep school, he earned an economics degree from Trinity [Connecticut] College and turned to baseball because of a live arm and an overpowering fastball. He broke in with the Chicago Cubs in '56 and spent the next decade in the majors, working in the off-season as a stockbroker.

The Orioles drafted him off Kansas City's roster after the '65 season; he was 14–32 in three-plus seasons with the Athletics. The Orioles got a lot more than they expected, on and off the field. Drabowsky, thirty, was brilliant in relief in '66, allowing 62 hits in 96 innings on his way to a 6–0 record. Off the field, he was a Hall of Famer in the fine and subtle art of giving a "hotfoot," secretly attaching a match to someone's shoe and lighting it.

As the Orioles charged to their first pennant, they discovered that a master of the practical joke was in their midst.

PAUL BLAIR: "Moe was something. They had to tell him to tone it down a little. I mean, you couldn't take your eyes off him. The man could give a hot-foot better than anybody. He was inventive. He would use cigarette lighter fluid and make a trail up, go in the bathroom, light it in the bathroom, and you'd see a trail of flame. Then it would be right next to somebody's shoe and the match would shoot up. You could really burn a guy's pants off. It was really funny."

DICK HALL: "You'd be standing there and suddenly feel twinges of heat. It made you jumpy. You can't be tense all the time. After a while we said, 'Hey, no more players.' The poor sportswriters really paid for that. Guys would set 'em up, giving real serious, earnest answers while Moe was creeping up behind them with a match. By the time you felt it, it was too late. If you went to sleep in the bullpen, you paid for it. That didn't happen too often, but sometimes. We had benches out there, and it was hard work, but Moe would crawl around and go under the bench to stick the match in. That woke them up."

BILLY HUNTER: "Moe would do things that other people would get punched in the nose for, and he'd get away with them. You could see it in people's face, 'What's he going to do now?'"

BOOG POWELL: "Obviously, Moe's parents never let him have toys when he was little, so he had a lot of catching up to do. He sat around and dreamed up things. He'd tie string to dollar bills and leave them on the floor in the air-port, then yank them away when people reached down to pick the bill up. He was basically insane."

STEVE BARBER: "Moe was fine when he was sober. When he started drink-ing, he did some crazy stuff. We had an off-day in spring training and [backup catcher] Charlie Lau and I were going out on this big boat out in the water. Took a runabout out there. We were just getting on, and another runabout comes pulling up, and there's Moe standing bare-assed on the thing shooting at us with a target pistol. Once we got to land we spent an hour trying to get the gun away from him. I have no idea what that was about."

There were many contributors to the triumph of '66. In a controversial move, Davey Johnson took over for Jerry Adair, the popular veteran, at second base. Bauer made the decision at the end of spring training and told reporters first, infuriating Adair, who demanded to be traded and was dealt to Chicago in June. Johnson hit .257 and was solid in the field.

At the same time, Etchebarren took over at catcher when veteran Dick Brown was stricken with a brain tumor in the spring, and he played so well he made the All-Star team. Etchebarren, Johnson, and Blair in center field gave the Orioles three rookies up the middle on defense, flying in the face of baseball convention. But they were superb.

DAVEY JOHNSON: "They made me into a second baseman because Aparicio was still there at shortstop. I really looked up to Jerry Adair, an Oklahoma guy who was also a shortstop who came over to play second. But he was still turning the double play like a shortstop, dragging his right foot across the bag. With Billy Hunter's help I was learning to hit the bag with my left foot and step over it, like great second basemen should do.

"So I think my pivot work was a little better than Adair's, although he was very solid out there and had set [fielding] records and all. He hit around .250, .260. I was faster. I didn't think I was going to get a shot in '66. But Bauer made the call. Then they kept Adair on the club. Kept him and played me at second. I was hitting around .250 early on, struggling, then I went four for four in Minnesota, and the next day they shipped him off to Chicago."

FRANK ROBINSON: "People don't talk too much about the defense on that team. Brooks and Aparicio were great, of course. Davey was good; Boog doesn't get enough credit. Blair was unbelievable. He ran everything down. And I never saw the guy run into the fence. He had a knack of knowing where he was, and knowing when to jump at the fence instead of banging into the fence. I saw him one time go over the fence and catch a ball without hitting the fence with his body. That sounds almost impossible, but he did it."

DAVEY JOHNSON: "Brooks took a bunch of ground balls every day, getting his uniform dirty, and I went to him and said, 'Brooks, why do you take so many grounders when you already have five Gold Gloves?' He said, 'Because I want to get another, and the only way to do it is work at it.' Aparicio was the same way. He said, 'You gotta take a lot of ground balls and you gotta play catch.' He threw fifteen minutes every day to build up his arm. That was the greatest experience. Here's two Gold Glovers, and one of them, Aparicio, has a cannon [of an arm]. And he tells me you aren't born with it; you've got to work at it. Same way with Brooks; you've got to work at it. Best lesson I ever learned."

DICK HALL: "The pitching coach was Harry Brecheen, who was left over from Richards's days, and he was the only one on the team that talked to the grounds crew. He wanted his pitchers protected, so for years he made sure the infield was soaked down and cut long. The grounds crew went along with him because no one else paid any attention to them. Then all of a sudden in '66 we had Brooks and Aparicio and Davey, and we had good pitching and good hitting, so they started thinking, 'Hey let's leave the infield harder.' Because we were scoring more runs, and it didn't matter if we were playing on concrete, Brooks and Aparicio would catch it. We benefited from the harder infield."

Offensively, outfielder Russ Snyder hit .306, Boog Powell doubled his home-run total from '65 [17 to 34], and Brooks Robinson put up MVP-caliber numbers early, driving in 50 runs in the first 57 games before slumping down the stretch. Brooks Robinson and Powell benefited from Frank Robinson's presence at the number-three slot in the batting order. They saw better pitches and didn't have to carry the offense anymore.

Jim Palmer, twenty, led the pitching staff with 15 wins, followed by Dave McNally with 13 and Wally Bunker and Steve Barber with 10 each. But Barber missed most of the second half of the season with a sore elbow, and Bunker and Palmer also spent time on the disabled list. Into the breach stepped a deep, flexible bullpen featuring Drabowsky, Hall, Stu Miller, Eddie Fisher, Eddie Watt, and Gene Brabender—a potent combination of young and old, fast and slow.

FRANK ROBINSON: "The bullpen was the key to the season. Those guys were experienced and knew what to do. They didn't ever walk anyone. You had to earn your way on. And they had a lot of tough guys. I still don't see how Stu Miller threw the ball that soft and got it to home plate. It was unbelievable. If it wasn't the best change-up ever, it was one of the best. Because hitters knew what was coming, and they still couldn't hit it. Then he'd jam them with his seventy-five-mile-per-hour fastball."

DICK HALL: "Once we got going in June, we crushed people. We would demoralize them. Go into a place like Cleveland, score 13 runs in the first game and 10 in the second. We knew by July that we were going to win the pennant. We were just coasting. But Frank kept driving us. He had an unbelievable killer instinct."

DAVE MCNALLY: "As good as he was, it was how hard he played that really made an impact. Even when we got way ahead, he only knew one way to play. There was a game when we were ahead late in the season, and Frank went crashing into the wall going after a ball. He was fine, but Bauer almost had a heart attack. You think you're trying hard until you see someone trying as hard as he did. The intensity the man had was just incredible. That and his leadership were what we were missing when we came close in '64 and didn't win in '65."

After Palmer pitched a complete game to clinch the pennant in Kansas City, years of frustration were unchained in a raucous clubhouse scene. Champagne flowed. Owner Jerry Hoffberger was among the many tossed in the shower. Powell threw potato salad and chocolate milk, pulled off reporters' pants, and slapped a piece of pie in Eddie Fisher's face. Eight cases of champagne were downed before the party ran out of steam and the players boarded a flight for Los Angeles and a meaningless series with the Angels.

In the middle of it all, fittingly, stood Frank Robinson, champagne dripping from his chin. When Hoffberger and executive vice president Frank Cashen approached him, he shook their hands and thanked them for bringing him to Baltimore. "I haven't heard from Bill DeWitt, but I want to thank him, too," Robinson said with a smile. Bauer, the manager, told reporters, "You know who's the happiest in here? Frank. He might as well be. He's led us in everything else this year."

STEVE BARBER: "The next time we went in to Kansas City the clubhouse guy told me it took three guys twenty-four working hours to clean up the mess we made. We were supposed to have an official party once we got to Anaheim, but everyone was in such bad shape that it didn't happen. So at the hotel they had a disco up on the top floor, and we said, 'Anyone who wants anymore, just go up there and sign it.' I think Drabowsky set up a house tab and signed it to Hoffberger's name. I started later that night and, believe it or not, pitched five no-hit innings. Couldn't get the ball to home plate. I was just bouncing it up there. But they were swinging at it."

Dick Hall: "That next night in Anaheim, Moe gets a real snake, a python or something, and brings it into the clubhouse. Blair got so scared he jumped right up and ran onto the field in his underwear. Camilo Carreon started jumping around, too. That's when Bauer came out and said, 'No, this is too much. Get the snake out of here.'"

Paul Blair: "Quite a few of us didn't like snakes. Myself, Aparicio, Carreon. So they started bringing these rubber snakes around and throwing 'em on everybody. After we clinched, here comes Moe, and he's got this snake around his neck. So at first I'm thinking this is just a little rubber snake. I said, 'Moe, is that real?' He said, 'Naw, rubber.' And he comes walking over and [the snake's] head jumped up, and I went flying. I told Hank, 'I ain't going back in there till you get them snakes out of there.'"

Dick Hall: "So Moe brings the snake down to the bullpen. Charlie Lau didn't want any part of it. He was afraid. So the batting cage was in the bullpen, and Lau has been partying like the rest of us, and he needs a nap, and there's enough slack in the bottom of the cage net that he crawls in there and goes to sleep, like it's a hammock. All of a sudden Moe goes, 'Where's the snake?' He couldn't find the snake. So we look around and then we see the snake. It had crawled up in there with Lau and gone to sleep. Three inches away."

Boog Powell: "What a fun year that was, from beginning to end. We had an awesome, nasty lineup. We pounded on people. We rolled. And we had a ton of fun. You can't ask for more than that. The night we clinched, that was a hell of a party. Russ Snyder caught the last out, and there we went. If you ask me what I remember from that season, I remember the party."

19

Would You Believe Four Straight?

After clinching the American League pennant, the Orioles had to wait more than a week to find out who they would play in the World Series. The Los Angeles Dodgers and San Francisco Giants took a furious National League race down to the last out of the season before the Dodgers prevailed with ace left-hander Sandy Koufax getting his 27th win to lock up the pennant.

Even though Koufax's last-day effort meant he couldn't pitch the World Series opener, the Dodgers were heavily favored to beat the Orioles. The NL had won six of the past nine Series and eight of the past ten All-Star Games, and the Dodgers were the defending Series champs, having beaten the Twins in a seven-game series in '65. In '66 they had baseball's best pitching staff, with a rotation featuring Koufax, Don Drysdale, Claude Osteen, and Don Sutton—all but Osteen future Hall of Famers.

Although the Dodgers' bats weren't as strong—seven NL teams scored more runs in '66—shortstop Maury Wills was a top leadoff hitter, and the club's overall blend of speed, defense, and pitching was imposing. Despite stronger hitting, the Orioles were deemed inferior because of a season-long epidemic of sore pitching arms. With veteran ace Steve Barber out with an arm injury, the Series starts fell to youngsters. Dave McNally had 41 career wins. Jim Palmer was twenty. Wally Bunker was twenty-one. How could they beat Drysdale and Koufax?

The Orioles flew to Los Angeles for the first two games and checked into the Continental Hotel amid rampant skepticism. Oddsmakers put the Dodgers' chances of winning at eight to five, almost a sure thing. The press's attitude was similar, with New York columnist Jimmy Cannon writing, "the American League must be kidding when it calls itself big league." Fresco Thompson, a Dodgers vice president, revealed his organization's brimming confidence, telling reporters the Orioles wouldn't be as challenging as the Twins in the '65 Series because "they can't throw two pitchers as tough as Jim Kaat and Mudcat Grant."

As the Orioles' bus motored through Los Angeles on the way to Dodger Stadium before Game 1, it passed a billboard that said, "How About Four Straight?" Anyone who dared suggest the Orioles might win in four would have been dismissed as delusional. Even the players themselves considered it only a remote possibility.

BROOKS ROBINSON: "The only guys we had that had been in a World Series were Frank, Aparicio, and Stu Miller. But I don't think our guys thought too much about that or anything. It was just exciting going to Los Angeles—your wife went out there, and you stayed at Gene Autry's hotel. It was just exciting."

PAUL BLAIR: "I think the Dodgers respected us, but I don't think anybody else did. Everybody else in the baseball world just felt the Dodgers were the class of the National League, and that was enough. And rightfully so. When you have Drysdale and Koufax and Wills and Tommy Davis and all the guys they had, and here's the Orioles, first time coming in, and you don't even know the guys on the club other than Frank and Brooks. I could understand them being the odds-on favorite."

FRANK ROBINSON: "They were the mighty Dodgers. We didn't belong on the same field, you know. I told the guys, 'Look, don't be misled by what you read. We have a good ball club. We can score runs on their pitchers. And our pitchers are good enough to stop their hitters.'"

DICK HALL: "The reality was different than the perception. Everyone said, 'Well, Wills gets on base, steals second, and someone drives him in,' but someone on our team checked the on-base statistics, and Wills was like fifth on their club. And Aparicio was even with him. Things just weren't what they appeared before the Series started."

The Series was a stunner from the beginning. After Drysdale retired Luis Aparicio and walked Russ Snyder to open Game 1, Frank Robinson took a fastball for strike one and then blasted the next pitch into the left-field seats, silencing a festive crowd. The celebration in the Orioles' dugout hadn't stopped when Brooks Robinson slammed a one-and-one pitch into the left-field seats for a second straight homer.

Given a lead, McNally struggled with his control. The Dodger Stadium mound had a sharp dropoff in front of the rubber, he said later, causing him to release his pitches before his front foot hit the ground, sending the balls sailing. After watching his lead grow to 4–0 on Snyder's RBI single in the top of the second, McNally gave up a home run, a double, and a walk in the bottom of the inning and avoided major damage only when Snyder made a diving, one-handed catch for the third out. Then he walked the bases loaded in the bottom of the third, and manager Hank Bauer replaced him with Moe Drabowsky, the veteran best known for giving hotfoots and carrying snakes.

Throwing almost all fastballs, Drabowsky gave up a two-out walk to force in a run, then settled down and put the Dodgers' bats to sleep. Bauer didn't need another pitcher. Drabowsky gave one of the best relief performances in Series history, giving up one hit and striking out eleven Dodgers over the final six and two-thirds innings. The Orioles won 5–2. So much for four straight Dodgers wins.

DAVE McNALLY: "I was twenty-three years old, starting Game 1, and I wasn't nervous as far as being in the Series, but the mound was very steep. Not that that was any excuse for being as wild as I was. Thank God for Moe. He came in and threw all those fastballs and struck a bunch out, and the rest of the staff saw that."

PAUL BLAIR: "Moe's performance was definitely the key. In the beginning the guys might have been a little afraid of them because they were the Los Angeles Dodgers, and they had such great history behind them. Maybe McNally was trying to nibble on the corners. But then Moe came in throwing just fastballs and showed [the other pitchers] that they didn't have to be afraid."

BROOKS ROBINSON: "The first game was the key. Frank and I talked about it beforehand. We needed to win the first game to show the guys that we could play with them and not be overwhelmed. Then Moe came in. He was kind of a slinger, but the ball had a little zip on it. He had good movement on it. And he struck out a lot of guys."

STEVE BARBER: "The biggest thrill of my career was being part of that team. Also the biggest disappointment, not getting to pitch in the Series. I wasn't even dressed. I went to L.A., sat with Hoffberger in the stands. He and his wife and me and my wife were sitting in the same section out by the right-field foul pole. That was a big controversy. They gave the Orioles' owner terrible seats out by the foul pole."

Drabowsky had shown the rest of the Orioles' pitchers that a diet of fastballs was effective against the Dodgers, but the Dodgers were hardly ready to concede. "Baltimore had one good inning—the first," Maury Wills said. "Except for that it was an even game, and a very dull game at that. It was the worst World Series game I've been in. They didn't show us anything we didn't expect, and I thought we looked good—not sloppy or anything."

Fateful words, it turned out.

The Game 2 pitching matchup strongly favored the Dodgers: Koufax, the game's top pitcher, against Palmer. Even though he was making his third start in eight days, Koufax had thrown two shutouts against the Twins in the '65 Series, including one in Game 7 on the road. Palmer was an impressive twenty-year-old, but he was no match for Koufax yet.

The two matched shutouts for four innings, and then the game turned in the top of the fifth. The Orioles didn't get to Koufax, but Dodgers centerfielder Willie Davis, one of the surest gloves in the game, lost two fly balls in the sun within a couple of moments and committed a third error on a poor throw to third base. As the crowd watched in horror, the Orioles scored three unearned runs.

The Dodgers went on to commit six errors in the game, and Palmer, throwing 95 percent fastballs, made history, becoming the youngest pitcher to throw a Series shutout. Final score: Orioles, 6–0.

Sensing a monumental upset, some nine thousand fans came to Baltimore's Friendship Airport to greet the Orioles' plane as it returned from California—at 1:17 A.M.

JIM PALMER: "My goal was not to embarrass myself. I was too immature to be nervous. But I was apprehensive. I already had a sore arm—a case of tendinitis in my biceps that would cause me a lot of problems over the next two years—so in the back of my mind I was wondering, 'How's my arm going to hold up?' And of course, Koufax was intimidating. I think 23 of his first 28 pitches were strikes. I was in the on-deck circle in the third, and he struck out Etchebarren on a pitch that started out six inches over Andy's head and [Dodgers catcher John] Roseboro caught on the ground.

"I was still learning how to pitch at that point, still basically just a thrower. I didn't nearly have the command I would have later. But I had it that day.

And things happened so quickly. It was a sunny afternoon with a little bit of haze like you get in L.A., and you never figure Willie Davis is going to lose two balls in the sun and throw another away. We were stunned sitting in the dugout. So I had a lead. And I was no dope. I'd watched Moe throwing all those fastballs the day before. I got the message. I threw hard, and they couldn't hit it.

"Our plane home that night hit some turbulence over the Grand Canyon, and that was the only turbulence we felt in all five days of the Series."

STEVE BARBER: "We got back to Baltimore real late, and there was a big crowd meeting us at the airport, and I looked in the back and there was one guy with a little sign saying, 'Please Don't Sweep Them, I Have Tickets to Game 5.' I thought about that later."

A sellout crowd filled Memorial Stadium for Game 3, with one sign reading, "Thanks Willie Davis, Our 10th Oriole." Wally Bunker experienced searing pain in his right elbow while warming up, but he'd pitched with it for most of the season and made the start. Osteen started for the Dodgers, and as in Game 2, the starters matched shutouts for four innings as trainers applied hot packs and oil to Bunker's sore elbow between innings.

With two outs in the bottom of the fifth, Paul Blair worked Osteen to a two-and-two count and pounded a 430-foot homer to give the Orioles the lead. That was one of only three hits the Orioles would produce against Osteen and reliever Phil Regan, but it was enough support for Bunker. Throwing fastballs and sinkers, and benefiting from rally-killing defensive plays from Luis Aparicio and Brooks Robinson, he needed just 91 pitches to complete the Orioles' second straight shutout and move them one win away from a sweep.

ANDY ETCHEBARREN: "You could tell Wally was hurting when he warmed up. But then the last few pitches he threw, he popped them in pretty good. What he did that day was one of the greatest performances I've ever seen for a guy with a sore arm."

WALLY BUNKER: "My arm was pure red and blistered from all the stuff they were putting on it between innings. I'd sit there [in the dugout] smoking a cigarette with my arm shaking. No one knows how hard that game was."

STEVE BARBER: "The game Bunker pitched was at that point the best-pitched game I'd ever seen. The average pitcher is going to make twelve or fifteen mistakes a game. I went down to the clubhouse after the game and said, 'Great job, but you're not that fucking good, and you know it.'"

Frank Robinson put the Orioles in front in Game 4 with a home run off Drysdale in the fourth. The Dodgers tried to start several rallies off McNally, but they were foiled by three double plays and failed to advance a runner to second until the top of the ninth. Pinch hitter Al Ferrara singled with one out, and Wills followed with a walk, but McNally retired Willie Davis on a liner to right and Lou Johnson on a fly to center to end the game and start the pandemonium.

The clubhouse celebration actually was tame compared with the lights-out party that had followed the pennant-clinching win in Kansas City. Maybe the players were dazed at the scope of their accomplishment. In sweeping the defending Series champions, they had allowed just two runs—the last in the third inning of Game 1. Orioles pitchers, supposedly the club's weakness, hadn't allowed a run over the last 33 innings, a Series-record scoreless streak.

The Orioles batted .200 and scored just 10 earned runs in the four games, but when you end a Series with back-to-back-to-back shutouts, you don't need much offense.

The *Baltimore Sun*'s headline the next day echoed the billboard the Orioles had seen on their bus ride to Game 1 in Los Angeles: "Would You Believe Four Straight?"

DAVE MCNALLY: "As things went along I think the Dodgers were in shock, mainly because our starters weren't supposed to be able to shut them down like that. When Osteen gives up one run like he did in the third game, they're supposed to win. Their pitching really held up. But they couldn't hit us. I had a lot of things going for me in Game 4. The movement on my fastball was sufficient, and I had a pretty good curveball and change-up. I was throwing pretty good that day."

PAUL BLAIR: "What people failed to realize was we were a very good defensive team, and that and the pitching turned out to be the winning factors. We didn't club the Dodgers to death, but we didn't make an error, and our pitching held up. I was twenty-two years old, didn't know anything, and couldn't believe I was in a World Series playing the Dodgers, who were my idols. I grew up in Los Angeles, and they wouldn't sign me, and I just wanted to beat them. I don't think anybody thought we were going to win four in a row and keep shutting them out as it went along. It was a fantasy land, really, a fantasy world for me. My second full year in the big leagues, I'm in the World Series, we win four straight, I hit a home run to win a game. I mean, this happens in the movies, not real life."

DICK HALL: "When we went by that [four straight] sign in Los Angeles, they sure didn't think it'd be four straight the other way. But all four World Series I was in, the favorite lost. The overwhelming favorite in a World Series is a 52-48 favorite or something like that. It can turn very easily, on one well-pitched game or something."

BILLY HUNTER: "Three years later, after the Mets beat us in the '69 Series, I ran across Drysdale at a banquet, and I was telling him how ridiculous it was that we had lost because we had the better team and all. And he laughed and said, 'That's how we felt in '66.'"

HARRY DALTON: "It's impossible to put a dollars-and-cents value on what that season did to the franchise. It did many things. One, it gave us a championship feeling, a base from which we rose. Two, it gave us greater national identity. And three, it gave the organization more credibility. Whatever your role, you had more credibility because you had won a World Series. That meant you knew how to do things."

FRANK ROBINSON: "Do I think [the Dodgers] expected to win? Sure. I don't think they were overconfident. But the key for us was Koufax didn't start the first game. They went with Drysdale, and we only had to face Koufax once. And then the thing with Willie [Davis] happened. I know Willie, and you can't explain it. He didn't have another day like that in his entire career."

BROOKS ROBINSON: "Not much happened. I mean, they had probably the lowest batting average for a losing team and we had the lowest batting average for a winning team in World Series history. It was kind of a fluke. That's probably not the right word, but we had a 15-game winner, and they had Koufax and Drysdale. But they just didn't hit. What else can you say? They were certainly embarrassed, like we were embarrassed when the Mets beat us."

HARRY DALTON: "The night we won [the Series] I signed Etchebarren for the next year on the dance floor. We were at the place out on York Road where Jerry [Hoffberger] would have the victory parties, and we were both on the floor dancing with our wives, and he came by and said, 'When are you going to sign me?' I said, 'How about tonight?' He said, 'OK, what do you want to do?' And I said, 'We'll give you thirteen thousand dollars,' and he said, 'OK.' It was so much fun, those days. God, it was fun."

20

Earl Arrives

The Orioles fell quickly from the high of '66. Injuries and lesser perform-ances not only dropped them out of pennant contention in '67, but out of the American League's first division altogether. They finished at 76–85, tied for sixth place. A season that began with a World Series flag–raising ceremony at Memorial Stadium ended with home attendance dropping 21 percent from the year before.

FRANK ROBINSON: "The team was just flat in '67. The year after you have success is tough because you keep expecting to have the same kind of suc-cess that you had the year before. If you aren't going good, you keep going, 'It's going to come; it's going to come.' And the next thing you know, it's Sep-tember and you're going home. Boston had a good club, but we never should have finished as far down as we did. We were way too good for that."

HARRY DALTON: "In '67 I thought [manager] Hank [Bauer] just sort of sat back and really didn't manage as hard as he could have. Not strategy-wise, but club-wise, team-wise, players playing up to their capability."

Little went right in '67. Boog Powell dropped from 34 to 13 homers. After win-ning three of four decisions, Jim Palmer was lost for the year with tendinitis in his elbow. Wally Bunker went 3–7 and lost his spot in the rotation. Steve Barber, control waning, was traded to the Yankees. Fittingly, the second no-hitter in Orioles history came in a loss. Barber walked ten Detroit Tigers in eight and two-thirds innings on April 30 at Memorial Stadium, and after tak-ing a 1–0 lead into the ninth, he gave up two runs on a wild pitch and an error. Stu Miller relieved for the last out, and the Orioles failed to score in the bottom of the ninth.

STEVE BARBER: "The no-hitter was my third start of the year. The whole game was a struggle. I walked ten, hit two, threw a wild pitch. The only reason I still had a no-hitter was in the second inning, Jim Northrup hit a line drive right up the middle, and it hit me right in the butt. We finally scored off Earl Wilson and took a lead. They put Belanger at second for defense instead of Davey, and Larry Haney in to catch. But I was wild. Everyone said to me after the game, 'Aren't you sad about losing?' I said, 'Hell, no. After walking ten I'm lucky I didn't get beat 10–1.'

"Bauer had a habit of picking on one guy as his whipping boy, and I was it. He wasn't riding me, but it was his way of taking out his frustrations. In the past it had always rolled right off my back, but in '67 I was struggling, and I told him, 'I got enough problems of my own; I don't need your shit, too.' That's when I was traded. He'd taken me out of the rotation. I'd gotten extremely wild.

"After I got traded [Yankees manager Ralph] Houk brought the [media] game notes over to me one night when we were playing the Orioles, and he says 'look at this—"over the past 65 games between the two teams, including exhibitions, the Yankees have won 13 and lost 52."' I said, 'Holy Christ, I knew we were beating you, but not that bad.' That just blew my mind.

"My first start for the Yankees was against the Orioles in Baltimore. And I had a realization. The other teams had always complained that it was too dark in Memorial Stadium and they couldn't see. We used to think it was sour grapes, but then that night Ellie Howard was catching me for the Yankees, and he's a medium-complected black man, and between that and the gray uniforms and the lights, I couldn't see the signs. I thought to myself, 'Son of a bitch, all those guys complaining are right. You can't see in here.' The Orioles had it better because they had the white uniforms."

By far the biggest setback in '67 was an injury to Frank Robinson, the '66 Triple Crown winner. He suffered a concussion breaking up a double play in June, was out almost a month, and was subpar after returning.

FRANK ROBINSON: "When I got hurt, you have to go back to the night before. We were playing the White Sox—bases loaded in the ninth, 1–1 game, Tommy McCraw on third base. Someone hit a squibber to Boog. He caught the ball and threw home, and Etchebarren caught the ball on the plate and stepped out on the grass and was getting ready to throw to first [for a double play], and McCraw cut his legs out. The ball went sailing out to right, and that was the ball game, 2–1.

"In the clubhouse we didn't even talk about it; we just looked at each other and said, 'We know what we have to do tomorrow.' The first guy who got on first base, it was time to do a job. I happened to be the first guy on, and Brooks hit a two-hopper to third, and I went into second to send a message. Al Weis was on the bag. And to this day I don't know how I missed him with my knees or my legs or my body. He wound up hitting me over my left eye. Knocked me cold.

"When I finally got up they asked me where I was, and I said, 'It's a great day for UCLA basketball!' They drove me to the hospital and put me in a room, and the nurse came in and said 'How many fingers am I holding up?' and I said 'four,' and the next thing I knew there were seven doctors in the room. She'd held up two fingers.

"I had some swelling on the brain, and it was pressing against a nerve, and I had double vision. They said they didn't know when it would get better. Could be days, weeks, months, or never. Within a month I was back in the lineup playing every day, but with double vision. Saw two balls at the plate, one above the other. I just swung at one and hoped I had the right one. It was tough. I hit 30 homers that year, but only nine after I got hurt. I wasn't the same player, and really, I wasn't the same player for the rest of my career. My motor skills and reflexes weren't the same."

There were bursts of good news dotted in between the bad. Tom Phoebus, a Baltimore native, led the pitching staff with a 14–9 record. Curt Blefary had 22 homers and 81 RBI. Paul Blair caught everything in center field and hit .293. Mark Belanger, a young shortstop with a weak bat but a brilliant glove, arrived from the minors as Luis Aparicio's heir apparent. But the season was a disaster overall.

Harry Dalton dictated changes for '68. With Belanger ready to take over at shortstop, Aparicio was traded back to the White Sox along with Russ Snyder for pitchers Bruce Howard and Roger Nelson and infielder Don Buford. Changes also were made in the coaching staff, against Bauer's wishes. Harry Brecheen, the only pitching coach in Orioles history, was replaced by George Bamberger. And the new first-base coach was Earl Weaver, who had managed in the Orioles' minor league system for twelve years, slowly rising from Class D to Triple-A Rochester in '66 and '67.

The changes made little difference in the first half of the '68 season, which proved just as unsatisfying as '67. Although Phoebus threw the club's third no-hitter in April—a 6–0 win over Boston before 3,147 fans at Memorial Stadium—and Dave McNally, Jim Hardin, and Phoebus were on their way to a combined 55 pitching wins, the Orioles were 10 games out by early July. That led to the biggest change of all. Dalton fired Bauer at the All-Star break and replaced him with Weaver.

HARRY DALTON: "Hank was sort of a laissez-faire manager. I loved him, and I hated to have to fire him, but I didn't think the club was as poor as its performance in '67 and the first half of '68."

FRANK ROBINSON: "Bauer was a veteran's manager. If you were a veteran, you had no problems. He put your name in the lineup, didn't bother you, and you just went out and played. But he was tough on the young guys. One day Davey had some problems with his back and told the coaches he didn't think he could play, and they told Hank, and Hank said, 'You tell him if he doesn't think he can play today, it's going to cost him five hundred dollars.' He played. Hank was tough on the young guys, and there were a lot of young guys on the team, which, I think, is why they took him out of there and put Earl in. Earl had been with a lot of those young guys in the minors. Belanger, Davey, Etch, even Boog."

BROOKS ROBINSON: "I think everyone thought that sooner or later Weaver would be the manager, simply because Weaver was Dalton's guy. If you're a general manager, you usually have someone in the back of your mind where you say, 'This is the guy I want to run my club.' I think all of us realized it was a matter of time before Hank got fired. That created some tension. Earl wasn't a coach Hank wanted, but he was Harry's guy. I think Hank saw the handwriting on the wall, too."

HANK BAUER: "When they made the change, I was home in Kansas City, and Dalton called me from the airport. He asked me if I was going to be home, because he was coming out. I hung up and told my wife I was getting fired. Then he comes in a cab and tells the driver to keep the meter running. A bad sign. So he comes in, I offer him a beer, he takes a sip and says, 'We're going to make a change.' I wasn't surprised. I knew it was coming after they fired my coaches, good baseball men, and hired Weaver when I didn't want him. I knew Earl was sitting in the wings, waiting in line, but there wasn't much I could do about it. Earl did great, of course, but I always maintained that ballplayers make a manager. If they do what you say, you'll do OK."

The tension between Bauer and Weaver was personified in newcomer Elrod Hendricks, a twenty-seven-year-old catcher who joined the Orioles in '68 after eight years of playing in the minor leagues, Mexico, and winter ball. Weaver had managed Hendricks in Puerto Rico in the winters of '66 and '67 and talked the Orioles into spending twenty-five thousand dollars to draft him off a minor league roster. Hendricks came to spring training as a "Weaver guy" with Bauer still the manager and Weaver a first-base coach Bauer didn't want.

ELROD HENDRICKS: "That spring wasn't easy. Not for Earl and not for me. I was sort of the outcast because Earl had brought me in, and Hank knew that Earl was going to take over if he didn't get the job done. And all spring, even though I was having a good spring, they did everything to change me around. Earl would just cringe. They changed my batting style. And they had me trying to catch like Yogi [Berra] caught, straight up to the point where I couldn't move. Balls were getting by me, and I became flustered, and Earl knew this, and he would just say, 'Just do what they want. Don't get upset.'

"I said, 'But Earl, they're changing me. I've hit this way all along.' He said 'I know, I know. But whatever they want you to do, just do it.' And Charlie Lau, who was the hitting instructor, I felt badly for him because he'd played in Puerto Rico and saw me hit and said, 'I know you're not comfortable this way, but that's what they want.' He was good about it. He said just try it. I said, 'I don't feel too comfortable this way at all.' He said go ahead. And Earl would see it, and he'd just shake his head and cringe.

"There was tension between Earl and Hank. I sensed it. I'd been around eight years by then. And I found out some other things going on. Little things. Like, the coaches would all go out, like they always do, and the manager had an expense account and usually picked things up, but Earl would wind up having to pay for his own bill. It bothered me to the point where I said, 'I don't care if I make this club or not.' I could always go back to Mexico.

"Occasionally Hank would say, 'Well, [as a left-handed hitter] in Baltimore you're playing against that heavy wind blowing in from right field in Memorial Stadium.' Like he wasn't sure about taking me. And I'm thinking to myself, 'I'll be all right in Memorial Stadium,' and gradually, with two weeks to go, he started relaxing a little more with me, Hank did. Even though he still wanted me to change hitting. So one evening Earl sat me down in the hotel, and we talked for a while, and he said, his exact words, 'They're trying to fuck you, and me, but do whatever they want you to do.'

"And then, with two days to go, Hank said, 'You're going north with us.' With two days left. At that point I didn't care; I just said OK and left it at that. Well, when the season started, Etchebarren was the regular catcher, Larry Haney was the backup, and I was the third catcher. I pinch hit a couple of times, and I got my first start in Minnesota on probably the coldest day of the year because Etchebarren didn't want to catch. Dean Chance was pitching, and Etch didn't want any part of Chance that day. It was a miserable day, like nineteen degrees. Snow in the outfield. That was my first start.

"I played a little more and got a couple of hits, but I still didn't feel comfortable catching. Balls were getting by me that shouldn't, and I couldn't blame the pitchers for not having confidence in me. It wasn't until Earl took over in the middle of the season that he said, 'Go back to catching the way you did,' and then I started catching more relaxed, and things got better. The pitchers started relaxing a little bit more with me. I had felt the tension [under Bauer] when I was catching those guys, because they felt that they had to make their pitches right down the middle of the plate for me to catch it. But not anymore."

When Weaver took over at the All-Star break, Dave McNally was twenty-five years old with a 56–46 career record. He was a tenacious left-hander with an array of quality off-speed pitches, but he wasn't dominant. A major leaguer since '62, he had never won more than 13 games in a season, and he was 8–8 at the break in '68.

Starting with the second half of the '68 season, he was a different pitcher. He won Weaver's first game as the Orioles' manager, then reeled off 11 more wins in a row, becoming the second 20-game winner in club history, after Steve Barber in '63. He ended the '68 season with a 22–10 record and went on to win at least 20 games in each of the next three seasons.

Dave McNally: "A few things happened in '68. First, I got in much better condition. Then [coach] Vern Hoscheit worked me in the bullpen every day, worked on my control. He would sit [as a catcher] on the inside corner until I hit it; then he'd go to the outside corner until I hit it. Sometimes it took a while until I hit it, but I started getting more confidence in my control. I also developed a slider that year. Etchebarren and I were throwing in the spring, and I said, 'I'm going to throw a short curve,' and I threw one, and he said, 'Man, that's a hell of a slider.' I started throwing it.

"I wasn't even in the rotation at the start of the year. Just sort of. But I got my chances and did well. At the break [in '68] I had a 2.10 ERA. I had pitched really well, just didn't get the breaks. In the second half everything came together. Having Bamberger was great, too. He knew how to talk to you and work with you. He was just a fantastic pitching coach. Mentally, if you deviated from your routine, he could pick out what you were doing and get you back on track. And he was such a great guy that you just listened to him."

Davey Johnson: "Harry Brecheen was a really fine gentleman, but he babied his pitchers. I mean, he really babied 'em. And some of the young pitchers had come up with sore arms. Maybe it was because they were rushed. I don't know all the reasons. But our whole pitching staff had sore arms in '67. And they made a change, bringing in Bamberger. That made a big difference. Aparicio preached throwing every day for fifteen minutes, and Bamberger came in with that philosophy, too. Brecheen believed you only had so many throws in you. Bamberger believed in throwing a lot, and he made them all throw a lot in the spring—playing catch every day. That built a really good basis for preparing arms. The way he treated arms, I thought, was really outstanding."

Frank Robinson: "McNally was like a machine. No flair, no nothing, just got the ball and pitched. No matter what happened, whether you made four errors, he said, 'I got beat today, no problem.' He didn't say, 'Well, if they'd play a little better behind me' or something like that. No excuses, ever. He got the ball and threw it, the same every time. I didn't like hitting against him in batting practice because he threw so nice and easy and then, boom, the ball was on you. Jarring your hands. He wasn't superfast, but he had that easy motion, and the ball was on top of you."

BOOG POWELL: "McNally worked quick. It was, 'Let's go, boys; let's get it over with and get out of here; we've got better things to do.' He moved the ball in and out, and right on the black [corner of the plate]. He didn't have overpowering anything, but he was a magician with that stuff he had. He knew how to put a little bit on and take a little bit off, and that was all it took."

Another change occurred in '68 when Ralph Salvon took over as head trainer for Eddie Weidner. Salvon, a genial gourmand, had worked his way through the ranks, starting in the St. Louis Browns' minor league system in '53 and working in the Orioles' system for seven more years before joining Paul Richards's club in Houston for four years starting in '62. Returning as Weidner's assistant on the Orioles in '66, he was now ready to take over after thirteen years of grooming.

Suddenly, the cast of characters was set. Weaver was the manager, Bamberger was the pitching coach, and Billy Hunter was the third-base coach. Behind the scenes, Bob Brown was public relations director, Phil Itzoe was the traveling secretary, and Salvon was the trainer. They had all worked for the Orioles for years, but each would become a fixture in his current role, carrying the club through its greatest era.

In Salvon's case, he would serve as the head trainer for two decades, until his death in '88. "Ralphie" would become one of the club's most familiar and beloved figures, with his care contributing to a remarkable twenty-three 20-win pitching seasons spanning the generations from McNally to Palmer to Mike Flanagan to Mike Boddicker.

BOOG POWELL: "God, I don't know where you start with Ralphie. He came in as the assistant [in '66] because Eddie Weidner needed some help. Eddie was getting on up there [in years]. Eddie was an institution. Eddie always had something to say. You'd come into the clubhouse, and Eddie would say, 'Well, the tide comes in and the tide goes out, and what have you got left?' You'd say, 'I don't know, Eddie—sand?' I guess there was a message in there somewhere.

"Anyway, Ralphie was there for all of that, and he saw all the techniques and everything Eddie used. Ralphie was a hell of a trainer. I saw him save a guy's life in the instructional league once. Guy was swallowing his tongue, and Ralphie went in there and knocked his teeth out and pulled his tongue out and saved his life. He was a great trainer and a great listening post.

"I don't think there was a maître d' between Baltimore and Tokyo that Ralphie didn't know on a first-name basis. Joe's Stone Crabs [in Miami] or wherever you went, didn't matter, Ralphie was the man. I never saw anything like it. There was a place in Milwaukee that we used to love, a mafioso place. Ralphie would call over if the game was running late, and the chef would say, 'Don't worry, I'll stay for you.' When the game was over, we'd hustle and get there, and the chef was waiting. Ralph would hand the maître d' a little bag with a couple of balls in it and go in back and do the same with the cook.

"I have a friend that got married and was going to San Juan with his wife, and Ralph knew him, and Ralph says, 'Oh, go see the guy at the San Juan Hotel.' So they go to see this guy, and he says, 'You know Mr. Salvon?' And they say, 'Well, yes, Mr. Salvon told us to come here and see you.' And it was, 'right this way,' front-row table, tab picked up, the whole show, everything. Ralphie was a legend."

MIKE FLANAGAN: "He was like one of the old boxing trainers, part psychologist and part trainer. He was great. He was five-foot, one [inch], maybe, and 250 pounds. Always had a smile. Flowing, distinguished white hair, easy laugh. Made the time pass. An incredible judge of who he could tease and who he had to be straight with. Knew Earl as well as anybody, and a lot of times he'd be the father. We'd go in there bitching about Earl, and most times he'd agree and tell a funny story about what [Earl] did to him.

"That old trainer's room in Memorial Stadium, that's where everybody really lived. It was a ten-by-five room, and everything was solved in there, and it was Ralph in the middle orchestrating and teasing and seeing what restaurants we were going to and whatever else we were going to do on the road.

"We all liked to go get pizza in Chicago after the game, and there'd always be a line around the building, and Ralphie would say, 'Just follow me.' We'd walk in; he'd see somebody cleaning off a table and go sit down and say, 'What's this? Clean this mess up; we've been sitting here.' And we'd be in front of a hundred people. Then he'd go to McDonald's and order the apple pie that comes in the cardboard box, and he'd eat it and go 'watch this' and walk back up with the empty carton and say, 'Look, you forgot to put the apple pie in here.' They'd give him another one.

"We used to talk about him having sponsors. He'd get up at six in the morning, and whatever player came through the lobby, he'd say, 'Hey, wanna go out for breakfast?' Free breakfast there. Then another player would come down about ten o'clock and he'd say, 'Wanna have lunch?' Free lunch. Ralph would just eat three times a day, and he'd never tell if he had breakfast with somebody else. Even though you paid, you felt like you were special if he was going to go to lunch with you.

"Ralphie was what the Orioles were all about. You had Bob Brown and Phil Itzoe. They were constants. And Ralphie was a constant. He had stories going back to [Steve] Barber to entertain us. I don't know how much of that goes on anymore. I'm not sure they'd want to know the stories. But it's all connected, and those are the common denominators of everyone who came through here."

FRANK CASHEN: "In those days we were a meager organization. When Eddie Weidner retired and got the pension, he made more money from the pension than he ever made with the Orioles. Then they had Ralph, and he was also the equipment man and he trained. He and Phil Itzoe were the only two non-uniformed personnel that we traveled. Phil did the press notes on the road. That was it."

BOB BROWN: "It was a great place to work—a rare time, I think. The people were great, and everyone got along. A lot of the credit goes to Jerry [Hoffberger] and Frank [Cashen]. Jerry was different from other owners because the players liked him. The front-office staff and the players and the owner had a real sense of unity."

Earl Sidney Weaver was always a fighter. As a twelve-year-old growing up in a tough section of St. Louis, he played baseball well enough to compete with sixteen-year-olds, but he also was small enough to lose the fights that inevitably ensued. "Whenever I got into a fight, I got beat up," he told a *Baltimore Sun* reporter years later.

After high school he signed with the St. Louis Cardinals. A feisty second baseman with an average bat, he rose as high as Triple A but failed to reach the majors. After nine years in such places as Winston-Salem, Denver, Houston, Omaha, and New Orleans, he was sold in '56 to the Knoxville [Tennessee] Smokies, an unaffiliated team in the South Atlantic League.

When the Smokies' manager was fired during the season, the club asked Weaver to take over as a player-manager. As fate would have it, the next day, Harry Dalton, then the Orioles' assistant farm manager, visited Knoxville to discuss a working agreement for the '57 season. Dalton watched Weaver in action and offered him a contract to manage a Class-D team the next year. Thus began his career with the Orioles.

Weaver showed immediate promise as a manager and began moving through the minor league ranks. He was hard-headed and combative, but also shrewd and successful, managing three pennant winners, five second-place finishers, and ten straight winners in such places as Dublin, Georgia, Aberdeen, South Carolina, Elmira, New York, and, finally, Rochester. Overall he spent twenty years in the minor leagues as a player and manager before making his major league debut on July 11, 1968. McNally beat the Senators 2–0 before 6,499 fans at Memorial Stadium.

EARL WEAVER: "The Browns had tried to sign me out of St. Louis in '48. That's the first time I met [Orioles farm director] Jim McLaughlin. I went to high school right there by the stadium and, believe it or not, I was a sought-after player and had six or seven clubs make offers. The Browns were one, and Jim was assistant farm director at that time. But I signed with the Cardinals. I was on the major league roster in '52 but never did get there."

JIM GENTILE: "I played against him in Class A in the early '50s. He was just like he was as a manager later. Boy, he could get mad at umpires. But he was a good little second baseman, really scrappy. One night we were playing in Denver, and I hit a ball between first and second, and he ran over and dove for it, came up with it, and threw me out at first. As I crossed the base he jumped up and said, 'Take that, you big donkey!'"

BARRY SHETRONE: "In his first year in the organization, he was managing and still playing some second base. They were playing some team that was getting all over him. Earl hits a ground ball, and their dugout was on the first-base side, and they throw him out at first, and he makes his turn, comes by their dugout, and all of a sudden just stops and runs and dives right into the dugout to fight.

"Well, they beat the hell out of him. Before his players could get over to the fight, the other team had already thrown him back out on the field. They've got to put him on a stretcher; I mean, he's beat up pretty bad. They take him into the clubhouse, and they're waiting for the ambulance. Earl's kind of coming to, and he's lying there waiting for the ambulance, and he says, 'I don't know whether I'm going to live, but if I do, I promise you one thing. I'll never do that again.'"

BOOG POWELL: "In Appleton, Earl had a fight with a guy named Dick Hunt. He was a right-handed pitcher, and Earl came out to take him out, and Dick drilled him with the ball. Hit him right in the chest. Earl didn't do anything; and then after the game Dick Hunt had had five or six beers by the time Earl got in there, and they just went right at it right there on the food table, throwing crap everywhere. But you know what was great about Earl? The next day it was forgotten. Even a brawl like that. Dick Hunt didn't make it, but that was because he didn't have any talent. If Hunt had had some talent, I guarantee you he would have still been there, no matter what. Because Earl wanted to win that bad."

HERM STARRETTE: "I pitched for Earl in Aberdeen [South Dakota], and one time in the first inning I'd given up three runs with two outs. He comes out mad and says, 'If you don't get this guy, you're out.' I said, 'Earl, you can't take me out; you don't have anyone warming up.' He turned around and said, 'Damnit, you better get this man out.' I went on and had a good game, but he didn't speak to me for three or four days. Then he told me I was doing a good job.

"There were times when you were going good when he'd walk through the clubhouse without speaking to anyone. He didn't want you to know how he was going to be. Sometimes that's what managers need to do—keep players on edge to a point. A lot of guys hated him, and a lot of guys loved him, but at the end of the year you always said he was a good manager. When you got to the seventh inning and looked down the dugout, you said, 'He can guide us through this. He can do the right things and win.' He was hard on some players. But he wanted to win so bad, he didn't care if you liked him or not. That was secondary. All that mattered was whether we had done as much as we could to win. If you did, he was satisfied. Even if you lost."

HARRY DALTON: "Earl did it all. We still had all the classifications in those days, D ball and C ball and B ball and A ball, and he went step-by-step. And he was good right off the bat. He was so competitive. It was funny; he started giving us a lot of trouble right away with league presidents. They had a man in Georgia who was the president of the Georgia-Florida League, W. T. Anderson, one of those prim and proper Southern gentlemen, always wearing a shirt and a tie and a coat and a hat, like he was going to church. W. T. Anderson would call up, and he'd say, 'Mr. Dalton, can't you do something about your man Weaver? He gave my umpires such a bad time last night.'

"I had to fly into Springfield, Massachusetts, once, when he had the Elmira club in the Eastern League. He really got out of line one night—threw a bunch of bats on the field. Just went in the dugout and took all the bats and threw 'em on the field. And he'd had a mishap like that a couple of weeks before, and I was worried he was going to get [suspended], so I flew up, didn't tell him I was coming, just walked in the ballpark and I took him out after the game. I laid down the law. You know, 'This is it or else. You just can't keep badgering the umpires the way you are.' He said, 'They're wrong.' I said, 'Maybe they are, but I don't want to lose you, and you don't want to get sent down, so just back off.' I could always talk to him that way, and he responded. We had a good relationship."

WALTER YOUSE: "One night up in Charleston, West Virginia, I was scouting Rochester, and he was managing Rochester, and he got thrown out before the game for saying something, but then they couldn't start the game because they couldn't find third base. Turned out Earl had taken third base with him. Just pulled it up and took off."

BARRY SHETRONE: "I played for him down in Venezuela one winter, and there was an out call he didn't like. Earl comes out, and it's an American umpire, and he gets in this guy's face. They served beer in mugs in the stadium, and the fans started throwing the mugs on the field. We look up and they're throwing bottles and mugs, and they're breaking on the grass on the infield. But Earl and this umpire are so intense, they're at one another, and they don't even know it. The bottles are flying all around their heads. We finally had to grab 'em and get 'em out to second base to continue the argument."

HARRY DALTON: "I started thinking about him as a major league manager when we got him up to Class A or Double-A in the early '60s. Because now he was dealing with more experienced ballplayers and showing he could handle them—guys who, in some cases, weren't going to make the majors and weren't happy about it. Earl took those guys and won. And when he starts doing that, taking castoffs and misfits and making a championship club out of them, you had to have respect for what he's doing. Plus, he won every year. You had to say to yourself, 'He must be doing something right.'"

WALTER YOUSE: "He was a good manager. You could see it early. He was in the fourth inning when the rest of them were in the first. And he was good with pitchers—knew when to make a move with pitchers. Weaver was shrewd, just plain and simple. I went to the dog track with him down in Florida, and he knew which dogs to pick. He was a shrewd little guy. He knew baseball, he knew how to manage, and he knew how to motivate guys, with a little bit of fear. I don't believe in that, but he did. He'd get on their asses something terrible."

HARRY DALTON: "One very high-ranking baseball official, and I can't say his name because I wouldn't want it to reflect poorly on him, said to me once, 'You're crazy about Weaver, aren't you?' And I said, 'Yeah, he's going to manage in the big leagues some day.' And the guy said, 'He's got no chance to be a big-leaguer.' A lot of people didn't like his attitude. He was feisty, cocky. And he would fight you. If you were playing checkers, he'd do everything to beat your butt.

"I brought him up to the big-league level [at the start of '68] because I wanted a good coach, and I also wanted to get Earl some major league veneer. If I had to make the change, he was going to be my man. There wasn't any doubt in my mind, although I had Billy Hunter, and Billy was a candidate because of his baseball sense. But I had Earl ahead of him in my rankings. And I didn't want to fire Hank, but I felt I had to. And Earl was ready."

BOOG POWELL: "Earl was very low-key that year as a coach. He was real interested in where to go out to eat and that kind of stuff. His locker was right next to mine. We talked all the time. I kind of welcomed him into the big leagues and all that stuff—[told him] where to go to eat and stuff like that. After he took over, the whole demeanor and attitude of the club changed.

And it wasn't that Hank was doing a bad job, but we were in a rut, and we couldn't seem to get out of it. We were all having kind of iffy years. Frank was still coming back from his injury. All of a sudden [with Weaver] we started running the bases, started doing things, playing some little ball instead of just hanging around. And we started winning again."

FRANK ROBINSON: "When Earl took over in '68 he had a lot of ideas. He wanted his outfielders playing deep. They could hit balls in front of you all day, but if one got over your head, he would start screaming. Blair drove him crazy. Blair liked to play shallow. And he told me when he took over, 'You, you're not going to run anymore. I don't need you getting hurt. No more stealing bases. I need you to hit home runs and drive in runs. That's it.' He even told me not to slide into second base to break up double plays."

PAUL BLAIR: "Bauer would bark out what he wanted you to do, but you didn't really get close to Hank. He was more aloof, from a different era. Earl grew up with most of us in the minor leagues, and by the time he got there, just about the whole ball club came from the minor leagues. We had all dealt with him, and he made it fun to play. I mean, he was funny himself, with all his superstitions and things he did and his run-ins with the umpires. He was just the type of manager you appreciated. He backed you up 100 percent when you got in an argument. He always came and took over the argument, so you could stay and play. And he was fair, which is all you really ask of a manager when you're a player. Just be fair. He played the best out there. That was it. Whoever was doing the best played. That was understood."

21

Powerhouse

When Earl Weaver replaced Hank Bauer at the All-Star break in '68, the Orioles were muddling along in third place, ten and a half games behind the first-place Detroit Tigers and 119–122 since winning the '66 World Series. They took off under Weaver, winning 35 of 52 games to pull within four games of first by late August. It turned out catching the Tigers and 31-game winner Denny McLain was asking too much, especially with Frank Robinson experiencing his poorest season—15 homers, 52 RBI—but it was clear that, if anything, Weaver was going to make things more interesting.

No one could have envisioned what followed. Thanks to several deft personnel decisions, some good fortune, and a lot of baseball brilliance, the Orioles emerged as a dominant team, a powerhouse, easily the American League's best club. In '69 they won 109 games and swept Minnesota in the inaugural AL Championship Series [the league had expanded to twelve teams and two six-team divisions], then they won two more pennants in '70 and '71. Totaling 318 wins, three pennants, and one World Series title over the three seasons, the Orioles were baseball's reigning model of excellence.

HARRY DALTON: "The '69 team, and really the team that stayed together for the next three seasons, was one of the best baseball has seen in a long time. I think that club probably cemented the Baltimore reputation as a good baseball city and a good baseball organization. The response was great, the fans really took to the ballplayers, and we had a collection of good people—the Dick Halls, that type of player. We didn't have any goats on that club. And if we did, we let them go. We had a team that was no problem off the field—good citizens, good in the community. And they could play like hell."

The basic framework of the '66 World Series winner was still intact going into '69, with Frank Robinson, Boog Powell, and Brooks Robinson anchoring the lineup, Davey Johnson at second base, Paul Blair in center field, and Dave McNally fronting the pitching staff. A few changes had taken place—Weaver was managing, Mark Belanger had replaced Luis Aparicio at shortstop, and Elrod Hendricks had joined Andy Etchebarren in a catching platoon—but after finishing a combined 27½ games out in '67 and '68, the club needed help.

Help came in many ways, but most important, it came in the form of comebacks. After experiencing vision problems, illnesses, and injuries for a year and a half, Frank Robinson suddenly was healthy and able to see clearly again in '69, and he was back to his old self: .308, 32 homers, and 100 RBI. Even more magical was Jim Palmer's return. Deemed a lost cause after missing almost all of '67 and '68 with an arm ailment, he was left unprotected in the first round of the '69 expansion draft, and neither the Seattle Pilots nor the Kansas City Royals took him. But his arm strength returned in '69, and he won 16 games and pitched a no-hitter against the Oakland A's in August.

FRANK ROBINSON: "My vision cleared [before the '69 season] when I was down in Puerto Rico managing winter ball. In '68 the ball wasn't double, but it was fuzzy. It wasn't sharp, like there was a haze around it. I couldn't see the spin real clear. But in Puerto Rico it came back. I was throwing batting practice all the time, and it just got better. I also changed my stance a little bit, moved farther up in the batter's box than even I was before. I was in about the middle of the box, but I moved forward, just to make myself quick. And I got off to a great start in '69, hit something like 10 home runs in April."

JIM PALMER: "It was amazing that I was even pitching. It was a gift from God. I probably never should have pitched again. I had biceps tendinitis, which led to me favoring that area and tearing my rotator cuff. I would play catch with Billy Hunter in batting practice, and I couldn't even throw the ball back to him. One day I was combing my hair in the clubhouse, and Ralph Salvon said, 'Hey, you have a hole in your back.' I went to the hospital, and they said, 'It's damaged nerves, the rotator cuff; let's see if it regenerates.' Off I went to the instructional league [in '68], and I got massacred. My last start, I think I gave up 14 hits and 10 runs in five innings. I was throwing eighty miles per hour."

HARRY DALTON: "We were very worried about him. The expansion teams could have had him in the first round before we pulled him back. Finally I called Hiram Quevas, who ran the Santurce team in the Puerto Rican winter league, and I said, 'Ram, Jim Palmer's got a bad arm, and we've got to find out if he can pitch or not. I'd like to send him to you, but I realize he may not help you, so we'll pick up his salary.' Jim went down there and pitched and seemed to be getting stronger. Then he came to spring training, and it was Palmer again. Miracle cure, it really was."

JIM PALMER: "Before I went to Puerto Rico I came back to Baltimore to get some things, and the doctors gave me some anti-inflammatory medicine, and I took it for two days, and it cured me. Just like that, I went from throwing eighty [MPH] to ninety-five. Bamberger couldn't believe it. It was a miracle as far as I was concerned. Like getting a new toy. The chance to pitch again."

EARL WEAVER: "Palmer was a star, and then he hurt his arm, and they didn't believe him. I think Bauer thought he was a hypochondriac. He went through the expansion draft, which I wasn't too crazy about, but I was a first-year manager, and I wasn't going to say shit. Then he went to Puerto Rico and pitched well down there. I didn't see him, but he pitched for Frank [Robinson], and Frank had good things to say, so I had to keep my eye open for him. We had a young phenom pitcher—I forget the name—a kid—and a job was going to him or Palmer. And neither gave up a run all spring. Finally, the kid gave up a run, and Palmer had pitched in the '66 Series, and we took him. And he went 16–4."

JIM PALMER: "Throwing the no-hitter that year was nothing compared to what I'd been through. It was ugly. I walked 6, struck out 8. Bobby Floyd played shortstop for us, and Donnie Buford was at second. It was like a night off for the rest of the team. But I got to the last out, and it was Larry Haney, who had played for us, and I knew he couldn't hit me, so I was standing there knowing it's done. He hit a ground ball, and I had the no-hitter."

Another All-Star arm was added in a trade—one of the best Dalton made. Mike Cuellar was a Cuban-born left-hander with a nasty screwball that confounded hitters. His 8–11 record for Houston in '68 was misleading; the Astros finished last in the NL with 90 losses, and Cuellar had a 2.74 ERA, evidence of good stuff. The year before, in '67, he'd had 16 wins. But he was having off-field problems in '68, and the Astros were ready to dump him. The Orioles obtained him for a package led by Curt Blefary, the '65 Rookie of the Year who had dropped to .200 in '68. Cuellar won 23 games in '69 and 143 for the Orioles over eight seasons. Blefary played one year in Houston.

HARRY DALTON: "After '68 I felt like we needed pitching, and I talked to [Houston GM] Spec Richardson, and he let us know Cuellar would be available. Cuellar didn't have a good year with Houston, and one of our scouts found out that he was in a bad marriage and really beset with financial troubles. Apparently his wife was spending a lot of money and charging things all over Houston. And the conclusion was, 'The guy's just had so much on his mind that he can't pitch up to his ability, but he's got great stuff, and he knows how to pitch; he's a very smart pitcher, and we should get him.'

"We made the trade, and Mike came to spring training, obviously made the club, and then came home [for the season] and asked to borrow some money. And I said, 'Tell me how much you owe. Let's see if we can help you on this thing.' So we sat down together, and he brought all his bills to me, and I went through them all. And he might have owed five thousand or six thousand dollars. He had about seven or eight accounts open. And I said 'OK, we'll see what we can do.'"

EARL WEAVER: "I had been in the loan business, and I told Harry, 'You can call some of these people, and they'll settle for something on the dollar, and you can advance Mike that money and bail him out. Take it right out of his check,' which Harry did. And it made Mike a happy guy, and it made him feel that, 'Boy, this is the place to be.'"

HARRY DALTON: "I called every one of those accounts and said, 'Look, this fellow's an employee, and he's not in a position to pay you back. We can give you 10 percent if you want to take that. But he's just not going to be able to solve this debt.' And about four of them right in that phone call said, 'OK, we'd do that.' And then we worked on the others, and we finally got it down to where he owed about fifteen hundred or two thousand dollars. And he was able to pay that back. We advanced him enough so he could live and pay his current expenses. He was out of debt by the end of the year. That was one of the biggest things for him, because he felt free again. In the meantime, he got divorced and married a great gal—a schoolteacher—and straightened himself out and then just concentrated on pitching and winning."

ELROD HENDRICKS: "I had seen Cuellar throwing in Puerto Rico back in '64 and '65, and he was throwing hard then, but without a breaking ball. When he came to us, he didn't throw as hard, but he was a pitcher. He already had a screwball, and his curve was just beginning to come around, and Bamberger worked with him and developed a curve."

EARL WEAVER: "Elrod helped a lot with him. Cuellar was a wonderful person—my wife's favorite—but he didn't want to run [in practice], and I had to make him. Bamberger wanted everyone to do everything the same, and that's what I wanted, too. Even if they walked, Bamberger wanted them going across that field. Myself and Elrod finally made Cuellar understand. Elrod spoke to him in Spanish, which helped because there's a lot lost when you're interpreting."

ELROD HENDRICKS: "Cuellar and I became roommates, and we'd talk about how we wanted to pitch guys. If we knew he was going to be pitching in a series, we would go over the hitters so we were on the same page. I knew exactly what he wanted to throw. I knew if a pitch wasn't working what I could go to, and he had the confidence in me calling the game as a roommate. I caught most of his games, and we had a good thing going. It got to the point where, if we played against a club that did not have Latin players, rather than going out to the mound, I would yell to him from behind the plate in Spanish."

FRANK CASHEN: "Let me tell you something—general managers get too much credit. I know that's a sin to have other guys hear me say that. Too much credit for some of the trades we make because we trade for guys that the scouts have seen, and scouts will say, 'Hey, if you can get this guy, get him.' When we traded for Cuellar, none of us had ever seen him play. But our scout, Jim Russo, said—and I'll never forget it—he said, 'This guy is an artist.' I said, 'What do you mean, he's an artist?' Russo said, 'Well, he paints. He paints one part of the plate, and then he paints the other part of the plate.' And we went out and got him."

DICK HALL: "Blefary for Cuellar was one of the all-time great trades. Cuellar was a terrific pitcher, and Blefary could only hit fastballs. Couldn't hit curves. He had a pretty good eye for a fastball, but the scouting had gotten wise to him. If they threw him a curve, he flat-out wouldn't swing, and most curveballs aren't strikes, so if they missed with a curveball, he'd wait for them to throw a fastball and hit it. Then they got wise to him and started throwing him a mediocre fastball on the first pitch for a called strike, and then he was in a hole and had to swing at the curve. Once he was never ahead of the pitchers, he couldn't hit and never did hit."

PAUL BLAIR: "Cuellar was superstitious. He did a lot of things; he had a routine, and please don't interfere with it. It was only the games that he pitched. He would walk to the mound the same way, same steps. Step on the mound. Go to the front of the mound, and the resin couldn't be on there. Somebody had to come and kick the resin in the back of the mound or he wouldn't get on the mound. Then he'd walk off the mound the same way. He'd come in the dugout the same way, he'd make the same steps to the water cooler. Everything had to be the same every time he went out there."

Adding Cuellar and a healthy Palmer and Frank Robinson wasn't all that transformed the Orioles into a pennant winner. Weaver platooned Etchebarren, Hendricks, and Clay Dalrymple, generating 18 homers and 70 RBI from a weak spot in the batting order. Weaver also moved Buford, a career infielder, to left field, gambling that Buford could handle the position next to Blair, who covered so much ground in center. The gamble was a success. Buford was adequate at best, but Blair covered for him, and Buford was exceptional at the plate in '69, with a .400 on-base percentage and 99 runs scored as a leadoff hitter.

EARL WEAVER: "It was the same team, with two or three exceptions, that was 10 games out in July of '68. Buford and Hendricks made the difference. Hank Bauer's problem was he was so loyal to the guys who had won in '66 for him, Blefary and Etchebarren. He went a year and a half with those guys, and they were doing nothing. Blefary wasn't hitting, and he wasn't a good player. Just the insertion of Buford and Hendricks made a heck of a difference."

DON BUFORD: "When I came over in '68 I had played second and third for the White Sox, and the Orioles thought I'd be a utility player. But Belanger was in the military, so I opened up at second, and Davey opened up at short-stop until Mark came back. And I got off to a good start, and the outfield was struggling, and I talked to Earl and said, 'I played outfield in the minor leagues. I think I can play some outfield and help out until those guys get going.' He thought it was a good idea, but he was still a coach. I said, 'Why don't you bring this up to Hank?' He said, 'No, you should do it.'

"I went to Hank and discussed it with him, and he said, 'No, I'm going to stick with the guys who played real well for me in previous years.' And that's the way it was until Earl took over. Hank was resistant to it. After Earl took over I was out there every day—and batting leadoff. It was easy to play next to Blair. I knew the extremes of his coverage area, and that enabled me to cheat a little bit more toward the line and get to more balls hit down there. So the extremes of our coverage were expanded. Frank was doing the same thing on the opposite side. He took away a lot of extra-base hits down the line because he could cheat over that way, too.

"I batted first, Blair second, Boog third, Frank fourth, Brooks fifth, Elrod sixth, Davey seventh, Belanger eighth, and the pitcher ninth. With that behind me, the opposition wasn't going to walk me to get to Blair and Frank, so they threw me a lot of fastball strikes. Being a fastball hitter, I talked to Earl and said, 'You want me to take a [first-pitch] strike, but if I'm taking a strike, the pitcher is ahead of me and it's easier to get me out. If I can hit a first-pitch fastball for an extra-base hit, I'll be on base.' Once I convinced him of that, he let me swing the bat as a leadoff hitter. I got first-pitch fastballs and got base hits. They always want leadoff hitters to get on base, and having a small strike zone, they figured I should get a lot of walks. You have to show you can swing the bat, and I did. That was a turning point."

ELROD HENDRICKS: "The way the [catching] platoon worked, I started against right-handers, with the exception of when McNally pitched. Etchebarren caught him because they grew up together, came through the system together, and all that. Mac felt more comfortable with Etchebarren, and I didn't have any problem with that. I was just happy to be here. I caught the majority of Cuellar's games, and when Jimmy [Palmer] came along, I'd caught him in Puerto Rico [in '68], and I think he felt a little more comfortable with me. Jimmy didn't really care who caught him, because he had his game plan, but I became a regular catcher of his in '69 also."

Suddenly, the Orioles had it all. Frank Robinson, Powell, Brooks Robinson, and Paul Blair had power. Blair and Don Buford had speed. Frank Robinson was a leader. The defense was the best in the game, with Brooks Robinson, Davey Johnson, Mark Belanger, and Blair winning Gold Gloves in each of the next three seasons [except for Belanger in '70]. The starting pitching also was the best in the game, with 20-win seasons from Jim Palmer, Dave McNally, and Mike Cuellar becoming routine. The bullpen was as strong and versatile as ever, with Eddie Watt, Pete Richert, Dick Hall, and Dave Leonhard in featured roles.

PAUL BLAIR: "With Cuellar, McNally, and Palmer, you could almost ring up 60 wins for us when the season started because each of them was going to win 20. And with Cuellar and McNally, you never knew if they were winning 10–0 or losing 10–0. They were the same guys. They never looked out from the mound and said 'Why did you make that error?' If we made a mistake, it wasn't because we didn't try. They appreciated the effort, and we appreciated their effort, because every time they were on the mound we had a chance to win.

"They were two really great left-handers, and the reason they were so great was they didn't have the talent Palmer had. They didn't have the ninety-five-mile-per-hour fastball Palmer had. They had to learn to pitch, know the hitters, hit corners, and they did it. And they didn't complain. They never complained. Those kind of guys, you just die for. You break your neck to go out there and win for them."

ELROD HENDRICKS: "Of course, the biggest difference for any pitcher coming to Baltimore was the defense. I mean, you had Blair playing right behind the shortstop and taking away a lot of base hits. Anything that got up in the air, he caught. And it was tough to get any ball by Davey and Belanger and Brooks."

BROOKS ROBINSON: "Where were you going to hit it? Davey was a shortstop coming up and outstanding at second. I don't see how you can be any better than Belanger. I have a hard time separating him from anyone—Aparicio, Ozzie Smith. And Blair in center. How can it get any better than that? Blair probably doesn't get his due. I mean, Willie Mays because of who

Willie Mays was, but I don't know of anyone else as good as far as going after balls and getting them."

PAUL BLAIR: "It had to be one of the best defensive clubs ever. There were two Gold Gloves for sure every year, at third and in center. Then Belanger came in, and he was another. I'm not taking anything from anybody, but they say Ozzie Smith was a great shortstop, and Ozzie never won a Gold Glove until he went to St. Louis and played on artificial turf. Belanger played on grass his whole career. He didn't get nearly the acclaim Ozzie got. And in my estimation, there was no comparison. Belanger was head-over-heels better. He was sure-handed, had a great arm, covered a lot of ground, went in the hole, and he never had the advantage of throwing balls on the AstroTurf.

"Davey also was sure-handed and had a ton of range. And let me tell you, Boog should have won a couple of Gold Gloves. Boog was a real good first baseman. The only drawback was he didn't cover a whole lot of ground, but you couldn't throw a ball in the dirt that he couldn't dig out. He had great hands. Any ball that was hit to him that he could get to, he caught. He should have won some Gold Gloves. So we could have had five every year, but because Boog was big and didn't cover a whole lot of ground, he didn't get the accolades.

"We discouraged opponents with our defense. You couldn't hit the ball to center field. You couldn't bunt. And you couldn't hit a ground ball on the left side. That didn't leave a whole lot of area where you could hit, so a lot of the hitters came to the plate trying to hit home runs, and that made it easier for our pitchers. We had the advantage when we went into every ball game, because they're adjusting to us because of our defense."

EARL WEAVER: "Belanger was so good that it didn't matter what he hit. It would have mattered if we didn't have the type of team we had. But here's the deal. They got men on first and second, one out, and that ball hit to Brooks's left or Belanger's right never went through. It was up to second and on to first, three outs; we're sitting on the bench. And I'd seen the same ball against our opposition go into left field; we got one run in; there's still only one out and men on first and second. I mean, you're saving a whole lot of pitches, a lot of runs. It was just the most fantastic thing in the world."

Elrod Hendricks: "The first time that I saw Brooks put on a show was Opening Night in Oakland in '68. Catfish Hunter was a good athlete, could run, and he was on first. Bert Campaneris was the hitter, another fast guy, and he puts a bunt down, and I'm used to guys picking that ball up and going to first. Well, Brooksie came in, and, I mean, he picked it up and never even looked at second base, just threw the ball across his body out there [to second] as his momentum took him all the way across home plate. And it was bang-bang at second, bang-bang at first, double play. I'm sitting out in the bullpen, and I say, 'Whoa, you gotta be kidding me.' I was sitting out there, and I can't believe he did that. There was no instant replay yet, but I wish I could have seen it again, because it looked like a blur when it happened. I said, 'Did you guys see that?' They said, 'Oh, he does that all the time.' By the next year I knew they were right. All the time."

Paul Blair: "I had an ability to recognize where you were going to try to hit the ball, and I played accordingly. And probably the best thing I had going for me was I had no fear out there. I wish I'd had the same confidence at the plate. In the outfield, you just couldn't hit a ball I couldn't catch. That's the way I felt.

"It was nice to know players on other teams were saying, 'Well, you can't hit the ball to center because Blair's out there.' That makes you feel real good. I took pride in that. It's something I worked on all the time—my defense. I should have worked just as hard at the plate, and maybe I would have had much more success. I did get on base, and I did score a lot of runs. That was my job, to get on base. I mean, you had to score a lot of runs hitting in front of Frank.

"But my whole theory was if I was head-and-shoulders better than anybody on the team in center, I was going to play through any slumps. I never wanted to sit on the bench. Never. And I never sat on the bench in my whole life. Park leagues, high school, minor league—I couldn't stand sitting on the bench. So that was my way of trying to ensure that I was going to play every day. Center field belonged to me. You don't hit a ball out there; that's just the way I felt.

"I give a lot of the credit to Earl, because I never left spring training with a blister on my hand. We didn't hit a lot. We worked on defense all the time. We worked on our plays, cutoffs, and such. It became second nature. We didn't have to think about it. We knew where everybody was supposed to be on every play that was conceivable. Hitting was going to come, you know, it was going to be there, but defense, we had to be perfect and we just about were."

DICK HALL: "It helped Earl that his stars were team players. Frank, Brooks. When that's the case, other guys will go along with things. We had one or two who would glare at the official scorer on a tough play, or be happy with three hits in a loss, or be mad after going hitless in a win. There were some like that, but not many."

ELROD HENDRICKS: "Frank was hard on the players. If he thought you didn't hustle on a ball, he would let you know when he came in. He would come off that field and he'd be screaming, 'What, are you tired? Are you hurting? Are you sick?' Anyone, he didn't care. If a guy on a ground ball didn't go hard or didn't try to break a double play up, he would let him know. So in a lot of ways he was like a manager. He took a lot of the pressure off of Earl. He didn't care if it was Brooks or Boog, he would let them know. I'd played with a lot of guys like Roberto Clemente and others who I had great respect for. And I'd heard everything about Frank, and I was never disappointed in anything he said. Whatever he said to me was the gospel.

"Brooks led differently. Brooks would work. I made it my business to watch him take ground balls because I never knew what he was going to come up with. He'd take 150 ground balls a day and work on everything. He'd work on short hops, backhands, the slow jumpers, the things he would do in the game. Billy Hunter would hit him ground balls, and instead of coming in and making the play, he'd back up and try to get it on the in-between hop. Then he'd have a little fun. The ball would be hit over to his left, and he'd go over, go to second between his legs, flip behind his back, and just have a little fun doing it."

BROOKS ROBINSON: "We had a lot of fun with it. Went out every day. We always played little games, and I tried to take a lot of balls off the bat—go to your position during batting practice and take a lot of balls off the bat; that's even better than taking ground balls, really. If you're taking 'em off someone hitting to you, you're anticipating all the time, and you find yourself getting in a little bad habit every now and then. I worried about that. I always told Billy Hunter, 'Watch me and make sure I'm not leaning one way or the other.' "

ELROD HENDRICKS: "Guys like Frank and Brooks and Belanger, they came out to win. I'd played on winning teams in the minors and winter ball, but I didn't know how to win. When I came here, they taught me how to win— just watching those guys and the work ethic, and the things the coaches would say, just little things that let you know that you'd messed up, but also how to correct it. They never raised their voices. They never humiliated you in any which way. It was just, 'Let's try it this way.'

"The pitchers would give up rockets, and we'd go back to the dugout, and Bamberger says, 'Nice pitch.' And I'm saying, 'Nice pitch? He almost got Brooks killed—took it off his chest and threw the guy out—and he said nice pitch?' But the other pitchers listened, and they realized, 'Well, OK, I can afford to make a mistake, I don't have to be perfect with that defense.'

"As a catcher, the confidence I had [in '69] was special. I would see a guy positioned [in the field] from behind the plate, and if I wanted to make a pitch for a certain hitter, I could get up and walk in front of the plate and motion the guy to move over. And they were never offended. In '68 I would never dare do that, but in '69 I felt comfortable enough. I would look at Belanger and go 'Move over a little,' and he would do it. There was no ego. You just went out there and played. And you won."

Looming over the whole scenario was Weaver, chain-smoking cigarettes, riding the umpires, playing the odds, and pulling strings. He was the youngest manager in the American League, but he was full of ideas and sure in his beliefs. Pitching, defense, and three-run homers were the keys to winning. Bunting was overrated. ["If you play for one run, you get one run," he said.] Outfielders played deep to limit big innings. Pitchers didn't throw at opposing batters, because someone important might get hurt when the opposition retaliated. And instead of relying on overall batting averages and pitching statistics, he obtained each Orioles batter's average against individual pitchers, and also each Orioles pitcher's numbers against opposing batters. Then he made his moves accordingly.

PAUL BLAIR: "The key to it all was Earl. Earl didn't allow cliques. We won and lost as the Baltimore Orioles. And he instilled in us that we were good enough to be the best. All we had to do was go out there and play up to our capabilities and we'd be the class of the league—and we were. And if we won 15 in a row and lost the 16th, we'd better win the 17th because nobody's got no business beating us two games in a row. That's the attitude we took, and it just spilled out on the field, and we were just the class of the American League."

DICK HALL: "Earl was a good manager. He'd get upset, but the next day he'd start fresh. He never carried a grudge. And he had very defined roles for everyone—used all twenty-five guys. You had your starting lineup and your everyday pitchers and bullpen, and the rest were scrubeenies, but he had everyone on that club in a first-string role of some kind. He'd have catchers catching specific pitchers, so they'd have something to look forward to every fifth day even if they weren't playing much otherwise. Curt Motton was probably the twenty-fifth man on the club, but Weaver gave him the role of, in the ninth inning, if we need to get someone on base, you're my man. That was his first-string role. In my case, seventh inning, close game, need a pitcher, I'm in. Or extra innings, I'm in. Weaver kept all twenty-five guys happy."

BROOKS ROBINSON: "Earl just had a way of getting everyone involved. I always think that's the highest recommendation. He got everyone involved in the game. Everyone knew their job. I think he learned a lot from Paul Richards when Richards was managing. He was under Richards's tutelage somewhat.

"We tried a lot of different things as far as pickoffs and trick plays, like where the guy stumbles going to second base and draws a throw and the guy on third scores. There was one [trick play] for Vida Blue specifically. Certain situations cropped up and Earl was always on top of those situations, you know, 'This is a good time to do that; we're not scoring runs; let's try to steal one.'

"I admired the simple fact that here's a guy who was never going to do anything in his life except be a second baseman in the big leagues, and he didn't have the talent and went back and excelled [as a manager] in the minor leagues. Worked his way up and now he was the manager of a big-league club. He was determined and competitive. And he was funny. He gave us a lot of laughs."

EARL WEAVER: "One day in Minnesota, [umpire] Bill Haller saw me smoking a cigarette down in the ramp during a game, and he said, 'OK, Earl, I'm reporting you; that's going to be a two-hundred-dollar fine'—because you couldn't smoke during games. I told Haller, 'That's terrific, Bill; that's just great.' He didn't actually eject me, I don't think. When I took the lineup card out the next day, I went out there with a candy cigarette in my mouth, you know, like I was smoking it. That was better than smoking a lit one, I guess. There were four guys in the [umpiring] crew, and two laughed, and the other two just stood there with a straight face. I don't think Haller thought it was too damn funny. He ejected me later that day.

"The thing with the statistics, I went to [public relations director] Bob Brown. You could tell guys hated to see certain pitchers, so I went to Bob and said, 'How hard would it be for you to go back a year and tell me what Blair's hitting against [Mickey] Lolich?' Or what every player on the team is hitting against him. He said that wouldn't be hard at all, so he'd give me a sheet, Lolich on top and all my players, listed alphabetically, what they did against Lolich. And we went accordingly. If a guy was 1 for 25 [against Lolich] he didn't play."

BOB BROWN: "We started off modestly. I spent the winter [before the '69 season] putting together the stats from the previous year. Over the next year or two, we were able to go back through the earlier scorebooks and get more information. This was precomputer, so we wrote it all out longhand. There were no index cards. We gave each pitcher a page, and then how each hitter did against that pitcher was listed on the page. Before each series we gave Earl the appropriate sheets, and then we took them back after the series and updated them. We were continually updating them, using white-out. For a few years no one had this but us. Earl really relied on them for pinch hitting and as an excuse to get regulars out of the lineup."

FRANK CASHEN: "It was the beginning of all this situational, lefty-righty stuff they do now, and the greatest thing that came along were those little handheld calculators. Then Bob could punch in the numbers after that. He didn't have to do the math anymore."

DON BUFORD: "Earl didn't play for one run. He played for big innings. He wanted me to get on base and let the big guys do their job. We didn't steal many bases. I think I ended up with 30 or so. With the White Sox I had 51 one year. I could have had a lot more [in Baltimore]. But the guys behind me were hitting, and one pitch was a home run, and he didn't want anyone getting out on the bases. His idea was, 'Let the bats do the job.' And they did."

DAVE McNALLY: "Earl gained everyone's respect very early. In my opinion, his biggest asset was how he prepared a team to play a season. In spring training we prepared for every situation and really emphasized defense. We worked on bunts and pickoff plays, and Earl was very intense during the drills. It was serious business all the time. But you were prepared to play when you left spring training."

BOOG POWELL: "Earl was a very sound baseball man. He was an astute judge of, not only personalities, but talent. Personalities more than talent, I think. I never had a problem with him. Brooks never had a problem with him. Guys that went out and did their job every day never really had a problem with him. He couldn't stand mental mistakes. Hated that. If you screwed up mentally, he was just all over you. He was just nasty. He was mean, and he could say words you'd never heard before in your life. And never heard again. I'm serious. There are words and parts of words and stuff. It was quite an education hanging around him. But in my years we never made many mental mistakes."

The rest of the AL East never had a chance in '69. The Orioles jumped into first after nine games and never fell out. They were 30 games over .500 by mid-June, 14 games in front by mid-July. A big win over the Angels on August 19 put them a breathtaking 51 games over .500 and 17 in front. Displays of domination came almost daily. Palmer threw his no-hitter. Powell hit a ball out of Tiger Stadium. McNally took a no-hitter into the ninth against the Twins. Cuellar took a no-hitter into the ninth against the Twins.

The lack of suspense actually hurt attendance. The 14,495 per-game average at Memorial Stadium was lower than the average in '67, when the Orioles finished sixth. Only 7,115 came to the last regular-season game. But even that couldn't dull the shine on a team that won as many games as the '61 Yankees, regarded as one of the best teams ever.

ELROD HENDRICKS: "It just seemed like everything clicked. Frank was healthy again; Blair was great; Palmer was back. We went out there knowing we were going to win every game. It got to the point where, if we were down three in the seventh, guys would say, 'Hey, OK, let's get to work.' And we won a lot of one-run ball games because the defense and the pitching were so good. People talk about the "Oriole Way," but the Oriole Way was no different than anybody else's. The Oriole Way was 'never beat yourself.' And that's why we won so many close games. We let the other team make mistakes and beat themselves, and when the opportunity came we'd jump on it. After we'd win, Billy Hunter would say, 'Boy, isn't it great to be young and an Oriole?' That was the thing. Everybody felt proud of being a Baltimore Oriole."

22

Miracle Upset

Despite winning 109 games, the Orioles still needed three more wins to get to the World Series in '69. Baseball was inaugurating divisional play in the wake of another round of expansion, with the American League and National League each divided into two six-team divisions and the winners meeting in a best-of-five League Championship Series to decide the pennant.

The Orioles, champions of the AL East, still had to beat the Minnesota Twins, champions of the AL West. That was hardly assured even though the Orioles had won 12 more games than the Twins had during the season. The Twins had a fiery rookie manager, Billy Martin; the AL batting champion, Rod Carew; and the AL MVP, Harmon Killebrew, whose 49 homers and 140 RBI had earned the award ahead of the Orioles' Boog Powell.

The first game of the first AL Championship Series (ALCS) was played on October 4, 1969, before a far-less-than-sellout crowd of 43,076 at Memorial Stadium. Mike Cuellar started for the Orioles against Minnesota's Jim Perry. Homers from Frank Robinson and Mark Belanger gave the Orioles a lead, but the Twins rallied and took a 3–2 lead into the bottom of the ninth. But Powell homered off Ron Perranoski to force extra innings, favoring the Orioles and their deeper bullpen. Paul Blair won the game with a suicide squeeze in the 12th.

The second game of the series was just as tense, with Dave McNally and Minnesota's Dave Boswell—a Baltimore native the Orioles had contemplated signing in '63—matching shutouts through nine innings. After McNally put the Twins down in order in the top of the 11th, Powell singled, advanced to second, and scored on Curt Motton's game-winning single off Perranoski, who had relieved Boswell with one out. The Orioles were up 2–0 in the series.

When the series moved to Minnesota, the Twins collapsed after the tough losses in Baltimore. The Orioles completed a sweep with 18 hits and an 11–2 win. For the series, Orioles pitching limited the Twins' league-leading offense to just five runs and a .155 average, with Carew managing one hit in 14 at-bats and Killebrew failing to homer.

ELROD HENDRICKS: "There was more pressure in the [AL] playoffs than the World Series that year. It was the first time for the playoffs, and we'd won 109 games, and it wouldn't have meant anything if we lost to Minnesota. It would have been a nothing season. And we rose to the occasion—played a great series. The first two games were great games. We capitalized on their mistakes. And Blair won the opener on a bunt. How often do you see that?"

DAVE MCNALLY: "The game against the Twins was probably one of the best games I ever pitched. They were good hitters, and I just had everything working that day—as good a fastball as I could have, great control, breaking stuff very sharp. Things just worked well. Boswell threw great, too. He became my teammate [on the Orioles] later and cussed me a couple of times for that game."

The sweep of the Twins polished the Orioles' reputation as one of the decade's best teams, and they opened the World Series as clear favorites over the National League champions, the surprising New York Mets, who had swept Atlanta in the NL Championship Series (NLCS).

Until '69 the Mets had been inept since joining the NL as an expansion team in '62. They were so pitiful at first, losing 120 games in '62 and 111 in '63, that New York fans, starved for NL baseball after losing the Giants and Dodgers, embraced them as lovable misfits. The Mets began outdrawing the Yankees after moving from the Polo Grounds to Shea Stadium in '64. But they still lost, finishing last in '67 and ninth in '68 despite adding young pitchers Tom Seaver and Jerry Koosman.

The '69 season began typically, but the Mets started winning in May and kept winning until they reached second place in the NL East behind the powerful Cubs. When the Cubs began to falter in August, the Mets, with Seaver leading the way, bore down on them. In the end, the race wasn't close. The "Miracle" Mets won 10 in a row, passed the Cubs in early September, and won the division, finishing with 100 wins.

Just getting to the World Series was a triumph for the Mets and manager Gil Hodges. The Orioles were under more pressure. Not only were they expected to win, but Baltimore's fans were counting on them to avenge a pair of losses to New York teams in other sports earlier in the year. The Baltimore Colts, in a bitter defeat, had lost to the New York Jets in Super Bowl III in January, becoming the first NFL champion to lose to the AFL champion in pro football's new title game. Less than three months later, the Baltimore Bullets lost to the New York Knicks in the NBA playoffs. It was up to the Orioles to avoid strike three.

The Series opener was a step in the right direction. Cuellar held the Mets to a run, and the Orioles beat Seaver 4–1 at Memorial Stadium before a sellout crowd. The game resembled many of the 112 the Orioles had already won in '69. Don Buford led off the bottom of the first with a homer, and a three-run rally with two outs in the fourth gave Cuellar enough room.

Then things got tougher. The Orioles hit Mets starter Jerry Koosman hard in the early innings of Game 2, but the Mets made every play, and Koosman took a no-hitter and a 1–0 lead into the bottom of the seventh. Blair, having a brilliant October, led off with a single, and Brooks Robinson drove him in for a 1–1 tie. But those were the only hits the Orioles managed against Koosman and reliever Ron Taylor, and the Mets turned three two-out singles into a run in the top of the ninth. Their 2–1 win evened the series.

ELROD HENDRICKS: "We had the best club in the world. Won 109, got in the playoffs, won three in a row, beat Seaver in the first game. Things just seemed so easy. It almost seemed too easy, like we knew we were a superior team. Then I remember sitting out in the bullpen during Game 2, and Koosman is pitching, and we're hitting line drives everywhere, and it's the sixth inning, and I looked at the scoreboard and said, 'No way. All those line drives and we don't have a hit yet?' Then we got one, but they were making plays all over, and from that point on it seemed like things were changing."

A sellout crowd at Shea Stadium was roaring for Game 3, and although the pitching matchup favored the Orioles—Jim Palmer against rookie Gary Gentry—the Mets rolled. Mets centerfielder Tommie Agee led off the bottom of the first with a homer, and the Mets scored two in the second, one in the sixth, and one in the eighth. Gentry walked five and allowed three hits before leaving in the seventh, but Agee ran down line drives hit by Hendricks and Blair to kill possible rallies, and Nolan Ryan relieved Gentry and finished the 5–0 win.

FRANK ROBINSON: "The key to the Series was Gentry. We got a scouting report that he had an average fastball, but he threw the ball right by us. That was the key. That was the third game. If we'd won that game, we'd have been on our way. But he shut us down, and they got momentum going, and that was it. And they pitched great the whole Series. It was devastating. We were all shell-shocked."

EARL WEAVER: "There weren't many radar guns back then. There were none, in fact. And [Baltimore's scouts] apparently had caught Gentry on a couple of bad days, because he threw a lot harder than we expected. But that wasn't the point. They made a lot of unbelievable plays, but they were making plays in the ballpark. You can't make plays out of the ballpark. And those pitchers kept us in the ballpark."

ELROD HENDRICKS: "Gentry threw the ball better than the reports said, but we still should make that adjustment. And we didn't. They made some great plays behind him. I mean, I hit the ball in the gap to left-center, and I never hit a ball to left-center in my life. When I saw where it was and where Agee was, I said to myself, 'That's a triple.' Then [Agee] goes running it down and catching it. Then Blair hit a shot into right-center, and Agee catches that one, and I'm saying, 'Wait a minute. They're not supposed to be doing this.' With two guys on base. That really broke our back."

PAUL BLAIR: "Gentry didn't really surprise us. I mean, look how many times we had the bases loaded. Then Agee makes a catch on Elrod—catches the ball in the well of his glove—then he dives and catches my ball. That's six runs right there. So it wasn't like we weren't hitting the ball. They just made the plays."

The Mets' Donn Clendenon homered off Cuellar in the second inning of Game 4, and Weaver then became the first manager in thirty-four years to get ejected from a Series game, as home-plate umpire Shag Crawford heaved him in the top of the third. The Mets, with Seaver pitching, carried the 1–0 lead all the way to the top of the ninth, when the Orioles rallied and threatened to deal the Mets a devastating blow.

With one out, Frank Robinson singled and then went to third on Powell's single; Brooks Robinson then sent a drive into the gap in right-center. Mets rightfielder Ron Swoboda, a Baltimore native, charged, dove and backhanded the ball just inches off the ground as he tumbled—a spectacular play. Frank Robinson tagged up and scored the tying run, but any shot at a big inning was lost.

BROOKS ROBINSON: "I thought it was a hit all the way. I see him all the time, and I say, 'Swoboda, no one would ever have heard of you if I hadn't hit that ball to you in '69.' He just went after it and dove and made that spectacular catch. It would have been a two-run triple. Even with my speed, it would have been a triple. It wasn't the right [defensive] play to make. He knows that. It wasn't the right play, but he just went after it and got it."

The game went into extra innings, where the Orioles had thrived all season. This time their luck was bad. The Mets' Jerry Grote led off the bottom of the 10th with a bloop double to left off Dick Hall, and after an intentional walk, the Mets' J. C. Martin dropped a bunt in front of the mound. Reliever Pete Richert covered it quickly and threw toward first to get Martin, but the ball hit Martin on the wrist and ricocheted toward second base. Rod Gaspar, running for Grote, came around to score the winning run. The Orioles argued that Martin had been inside the base path when the ball hit him, but Crawford let the play stand.

DICK HALL: "When I came on in the bottom of the 10th, I threw Grote a three-two slider breaking right on the fist, and he hit a little bloop to left. That time of year the sun is lower, especially at Shea; the stadium is real high, and it has a black background, and the sky is brighter that time of year, so the ball went from black all of a sudden to really bright. It was hard to pick the ball up, and Buford didn't pick it up. Belanger ran way over and almost caught it, but it dropped in for a double, and Grote went to second. I walked the next guy intentionally, and Richert came in, and Martin bunted, and it ricocheted off him into right field, and oh boy, that was my run that scored."

PAUL BLAIR: "It just seemed like we lost in every key situation. Either they made the play or got the call. The Swoboda catch. I mean, come on, I could fall out of the sky and he couldn't catch me, and he dives and catches this ball. That cost us the ball game. Then J. C. Martin is out of the baseline. He's clearly out of the baseline; everybody knows it; even Shag Crawford knows he's out of the baseline, but he comes back and says he didn't do it intentionally. Who cares? The rule is you can't be in there. And that cost us the game."

Incredibly, the powerful Orioles, seemingly on the verge of a coronation just days earlier, were down 3–1 in the Series. There wasn't any great mystery involved—the Orioles had scored two runs in the last 32 innings—but that didn't make it any less stunning.

They still were capable of running off three wins, and McNally and Frank Robinson homered off Koosman in the third inning of Game 5 at Shea Stadium. Then things got weird again. Koosman appeared to hit Frank Robinson with a pitch in the top of the sixth, but plate umpire Lou DiMuro ruled the ball had hit Robinson's bat first. In the bottom of the sixth, the Mets' Cleon Jones claimed he was hit on the foot by a McNally pitch, but DiMuro again ruled no—until Hodges emerged from the dugout with a ball bearing a shoe polish stain. DiMuro reversed his call and awarded Jones first base. The next batter, Clendenon, homered to pull the Mets within a run.

PAUL BLAIR: "Every key situation we lost. I mean, a ball goes in the dugout, and granted, it was Gil Hodges, but anything could have happened to that ball before it got to Gil. So he says there's shoe polish on the ball, and they give Cleon Jones first base instead of strike two when we might have struck him out. Then the next batter hits a two-run homer, and we lose. Just crazy."

As if all that wasn't "crazy" enough, weak-hitting Mets second baseman Al Weis then homered off McNally to tie the score in the bottom of the seventh. A .215 hitter in '69, Weis had clouted six homers in a seven-year major league career—none at Shea. As his hit cleared the left-field fence, the Orioles had every reason to believe a larger force was at work.

Eddie Watt relieved McNally in the eighth, and the Mets scored twice, with Swoboda driving in the go-ahead run. Powell and Watt then committed errors to give the Mets an insurance run, and the upset was complete. After 109 wins and an AL playoff sweep, one of baseball's best teams of the '60s had crashed with a thud when it mattered most.

FRANK ROBINSON: "They got the pitching, and they made all the plays. Plain and simple. We were better, but what did that matter? They got the big hits. Al Weis hitting a home run. Swoboda making a diving catch in right-center field with two runners on. Agee making that play on Elrod, a pull hitter. Elrod could pull a bullet, OK? And Agee is playing him over in right-center, and he goes over to left-center to catch a ball off Elrod. Then he goes that far the other way to catch a ball off Blair. Cleon Jones diving in left to catch a ball. They did what they had to do."

EARL WEAVER: "The whole thing about the Series was we were going to show everybody in the world how good we were, and we didn't do some of the things that we did to get us there. Buford wouldn't walk. Everybody was going to hit the ball out of the ballpark. And those [Mets] pitchers, we didn't know how good they were, but they were getting corners on two-and-oh and three-and-one counts, and we were trying to pull the ball in place of just doing what we were capable of doing. We were overanxious, and they ate us up."

ELROD HENDRICKS: "We got down, and it seemed like we started trying to do things a little bit different. But you have a guy like Al Weis hitting homers, and Swoboda making diving catches when you know in your heart that it's a dumb play, because if the ball gets by him, they lose the game. He took a chance and made a sliding catch, and you say to yourself, 'This can't be happening.'"

PAUL BLAIR: "I still feel, and this was thirty years ago now, but I still don't believe they beat us. I still believe in my heart that if you win one of those games up there, you come back to Baltimore and win. But we didn't. Sometimes the best team doesn't win. The Dodgers, even though they were the best team, we outplayed 'em in '66. The Mets didn't outplay us; they really didn't. They just got all the breaks."

ELROD HENDRICKS: "After the last game, I was in a daze. I'm sitting out in the bullpen saying, 'I don't believe this.' Then all of a sudden it sunk in. We lost. Knowing we had the better club, I remember sitting out there and watching fans jumping around, and I left Shea Stadium. Even though I had to go to Puerto Rico and play winter ball, all I could think about was next year."

BROOKS ROBINSON: "The Mets had been so horrible since '62, but they weren't horrible anymore. You win 100 games, you're playing some good ball. They were a hot team. They caught Chicago, and I thought Chicago had a hell of a team. I always felt if the Cubs had won that year, they might have won two or three years in a row, too, they were that good. But the Mets caught 'em and beat 'em, and then they beat Atlanta three in a row. So it was a big upset but maybe not quite as big as people like to make out.

We won the first game, but then guys just started trying to do things they couldn't do. They started pressing. We lost a couple, and now instead of the leadoff guy trying to get on, the leadoff guy's trying to hit a home run. Everyone started pressing a little, and that's the only rationalization I have for it. It's too bad because the '69 team was the best team I played on, and of course, when you lose the World Series you never get the credit you think you deserve."

JIM PALMER: "The Mets won 100 games. If you do that, you have a good ball club. And they had a good ball club because they had good pitching. They had a lot of role players who really didn't have to overachieve to win because the pitching was so good. You were going to be in the game so you didn't have to bludgeon someone to death. You just had to play the game the way it was supposed to be played, which is pitch and play defense and steal a base at the appropriate time and make a play at the appropriate time.

"When they run it on ESPN Classic, I walk out of the room. Game 1, Buford hits a homer off Seaver and we win. The next game, we hit balls all over the place. We hit rockets. But they win 2–1. And that's a perfect example of how they won games. A little bit of luck, they made the plays, they pitched well enough. Game 3 was the only time in my career I gave up a lead-off home run.

"It was a very similar feeling, except in a negative sense, to what happened in '66. When I walked out of the park in '66 I never realized how easy it was to win a World Series. Because we went to L.A. and won a couple of games, and then we came home and won two 1–0 games, and it's over. We're the world champs. I don't know if the Mets felt that way, but I got in touch with how easy it was to lose a World Series—how fast it could go and how little it took—because you're in the games, and they're close, and then it's over."

23

Hoover

The stage was set for the Orioles to stumble after their loss to the Mets in the '69 World Series, but they didn't. In fact, they picked up right where they had left off before running into the Mets. They opened the season with five wins and ran away with their second straight AL East title after beating back a challenge from the Yankees in June. With an intimidating sense of purpose, they won 19 of their last 22 games to finish with a 108–54 record and a 15-game lead.

The blueprint was the same as '69. Mike Cuellar, Dave McNally, and Jim Palmer each won at least 20 games, and the veteran bullpen seldom faltered, with Moe Drabowsky returning from Kansas City in June to help. Paul Blair, Brooks Robinson, and Davey Johnson won Gold Gloves. Offensively, Don Buford and Paul Blair continued to get on base, and Frank Robinson (.306, 25 home runs), Brooks Robinson (94 RBI), and Boog Powell (35 homers, 114 RBI) continued to drive them in. It was Powell's best year, and he was named the AL's MVP after finishing second to Harmon Killebrew in '69. Elrod Hendricks continued to carry a catching platoon that produced 17 homers and 74 RBI, and outfielder Merv Rettenmund, a product of the farm system, hit .322 with 18 homers.

FRANK ROBINSON: "If we had beaten the Mets in '69, I don't know that we would have come back as strong. That was a lesson for us. The best team doesn't always win. You also have to be the best-prepared team and go out and do the job. Losing set us back on our heels, but only for the moment. We recovered over the winter and rededicated ourselves to coming back and getting in good shape and winning [the pennant] again and getting back to the Series."

BOOG POWELL: "I thought I should have won the MVP in '69. Killebrew led the league in RBI; he was right there in home runs and everything else. But

I think I hit over .300 that year and he about .270. One of the nicest things that ever happened to me was that Killebrew came up and said, 'You should have won the MVP.' That's a nice thing. Then I went and got it in '70."

There was a sobering moment early in the runaway season when Blair was beaned one night in Anaheim, California. The Angels' Ken Tatum threw a pitch that hit Blair in the face and dropped him as if he were a losing gunslinger in a western movie. Blair was on his way to a second straight strong season, having produced 26 home runs and 76 RBI in '69 and given indications that he might surpass those totals in '70. He missed three weeks after the beaning and came back to finish with 18 home runs and 65 RBI, but he seldom produced that well over the rest of his career, and some speculated he was never the same at the plate.

BROOKS ROBINSON: "He really looked like he was coming into his own, and then that terrible beaning was the worst I've ever seen. Oh, it was just unbelievable. Tatum threw sidearm and hit him flush and just crushed him. He was never the same after that as a hitter."

PAUL BLAIR: "I was out twenty-one days, and they threw me back in there and I hit .304 the rest of the season. People say, 'After you got hit you didn't hit the same,' but I did. Before I got hit I stood on top of the plate. After I got hit I stood on top of the plate. The biggest factor why I didn't hit as high was Frank Robinson getting traded after the '71 season. With him behind me, I knew at two and oh or three and one [counts] what they'd throw me. They're not going to walk Paul Blair to get to Frank Robinson, so they're going to throw me a fastball. After Frank was gone, they were throwing breaking balls, too. And the slider was a pitch I had problems with. I wasn't disciplined enough to take those pitches and walk. And that was my biggest downfall right there."

EARL WEAVER: "I don't know, getting beaned affects you. I got whacked in New Orleans when I was playing in the Southern Association, and I never did stay in against a right-hander after that. If you talk to Blair, he's going to say it didn't have an effect on him, but if you look at the stats, him hitting left-handers as opposed to right-handers, there were certain right-handers I had to pull him out against.

"He still got over 400 at-bats a year, so he was still in there hitting some right-handers. Was 26 homers [in '69] a fluke? I didn't think so. I think Blair could have continued to do that. I think the beaning had a little bit to do with the fact that he didn't. It didn't affect his defense. And it didn't bother him against certain pitchers. But it has to have an effect long-term."

One change from '69 to '70 was the return of Drabowsky, the eminent prankster who had gone to Kansas City in the expansion draft before the '69 season. Now thirty-four and near the end of his career, he was reacquired during the '70 season and won four of six decisions, helping fill out a veteran bullpen. He also returned with a new array of practical jokes, many involving telephones.

DICK HALL: "One night he ordered Chinese food from the bullpen. Just got on there and talked to the guy and ordered some egg rolls or something and had them delivered. Another time—and he got in trouble for this—he set off some M1 firecrackers. He crawled through the hedge over to the other bullpen to set off the firecrackers, and the front office saw him from the owner's box.

"But the best was when we went to Kansas City, where Moe had played and knew everyone. The bullpens were set back, so you couldn't really see them from the dugout, and it was early in the game, and we're winning 1–0 or something, and the K.C. pitcher is pitching all right. So Moe gets on the phone and dials up their bullpen and clears his voice and imitates a coach, 'Get Krausse up.' Lew Krausse was a guy in their bullpen.

"So it takes Krausse a minute or two to find his glove, and pretty soon he starts warming up. Meanwhile, their pitcher hadn't really been in trouble. There was no one on base. And you can kind of sense when you're needed. So Krausse started slowing down a little, and he'd put his hands on his hips, and we're just dying laughing.

"All of a sudden Moe gets kind of scared. Because here's a guy throwing early in a game when he isn't needed. It's kind of a no-no. What if he was needed later on? And the K.C. dugout has no idea, because they can't see the bullpen. So poor Moe realizes he needs to get back on the phone. So finally he calls the bullpen and says, 'No, this is Moe; I was the one who told Krausse to get up.' And Krausse had stopped throwing anyway, because there were two outs and a man on first, and the guy was pitching good."

Winning a division title wasn't the Orioles' goal in '70. Nor was winning the AL pennant, normally an achievement that makes a season. The Orioles' only goal in '70 was to win the World Series. It wouldn't erase the memory of '69, but it was all the Orioles could do now to ease the memory, and they took every swing and made every pitch with the thought in the back of their minds.

They faced Minnesota again in the AL Championship Series, and the outcome was the same as '69—a Baltimore sweep. Cuellar gave up a run in each of the first two innings of Game 1 in Minnesota, but he hit a windblown grand slam in the fourth as part of a seven-run rally that put the game away. Game 2 was closer, with McNally holding a 4–3 lead going into the ninth, but another seven-run inning ended the suspense. Back home for Game 3 before only 27,608 fans, the Orioles finished off the sweep with a 6–1 win as Palmer pitched a complete game. With a .330 average and six homers, the Orioles had beaten the explosive Twins at their own game.

The Orioles wanted another shot at the Mets in the World Series, but the Mets faded to third in the NL East in '70, and the Cincinnati Reds won the pennant convincingly, with a 102-win season and a sweep of Pittsburgh in the NL Championship Series. The "Big Red Machine" had an imposing lineup featuring NL MVP Johnny Bench (45 homers, 148 RBI), Tony Perez (40 homers, 129 RBI), Pete Rose (.316), Bobby Tolan (.316), and Lee May (34 homers, 94 RBI). The Orioles' pitchers would have to shine.

The Series opener at Cincinnati's new Riverfront Stadium was the first Fall Classic game played on artificial turf. The Reds scored a run in the first inning off Palmer, and then May hit a two-run homer in the third. Ghosts of '69 began haunting the Orioles, but only briefly. Powell's two-run homer in the fourth off Reds starter Gary Nolan cut the lead to one, and Hendricks hit another homer to tie the score in the fifth.

BROOKS ROBINSON: "The big question after we worked out in Cincinnati [before Game 1] was what kind of shoes do we wear. It was our first time playing on AstroTurf, and we didn't know if we should wear cleats. We finally decided just to wear our normal cleats, but be sure when you move to pick 'em up. You can't just let 'em slide because they'll catch and stop and there goes a knee."

BOOG POWELL: "With the way the Mets had kicked our asses the year before, when we got down 3–0 in the first game of the Series, we were going,

'No, this can't happen again.' I went up to the plate in the fourth inning saying, 'I have to do something.' I just made up my mind that he wasn't going to get me out. I don't think I'd faced Gary [Nolan] more than once or twice in spring training, but it didn't matter who was pitching, I was going to do something.

"He helped me out and hung me a breaking ball, and I hit it OK. It barely went out and it was barely fair, but it was a home run. A Mickey Mouse home run, but worth two runs. So their lead was down to 3–2, and that took all the pressure off. When I got back to the dugout it was like a big sigh of relief. You could feel everyone go, 'OK, we're all right now; they can't play with us.' I hit another homer the next day, a huge one to the upper deck in center field. I don't think anyone else has ever hit one up there. I mean, I crushed it. But the only one anyone remembers is the Mickey Mouse one. That was our wake-up call."

The Reds almost regained the lead in the bottom of the sixth, but strong defense and a bizarre play at the plate cut short the rally and raised hope among the Orioles that their bad Series luck in '69 was about to even out. Lee May opened the inning with a hard, bouncing shot over the third-base bag, a ball seemingly destined for the left-field corner and extra bases. Brooks Robinson leaned hard to his right, stretched and grabbed the ball, then threw blindly and across his body toward Powell at first. The ball skipped on the artificial turf and landed in Powell's glove an instant before May hit the bag.

BROOKS ROBINSON: "Of all the plays in that Series, that one stands out. I'd never made a play like that. Most of the time, any time you backhand the ball, you catch it, stop, plant, and try to get the good, long throw. This one, I just got it, and it was like I almost thought the ball was foul. You know how you just kind of go over and get a ball and throw it back to the pitcher? I think I had in my mind it might have been almost foul and I just kind of got it and then went ahead and threw it and one-bounced it to Boog."

FRANK ROBINSON: "It's one of the best plays ever. He took three steps across the foul line before he even released the ball, and he didn't even look at first base when he threw. It was a blind thing. Brooks did that a lot. He'd come up with a ball in foul ground and throw to second without even looking. Just from having done it. Knowing where he was on the field. He was the best."

The importance of the play became apparent when Palmer walked Bernie Carbo and gave up a single to Tommy Helms, sending Carbo to third. Pinch hitter Ty Cline then hit a chopper in front of the plate, and one of the wildest plays in World Series history ensued. Plate umpire Ken Burkhart moved out from behind the plate and into the baseline to make a fair/foul call as Carbo headed for home, and Hendricks grabbed the ball and dove to make a tag with his glove. Carbo and Hendricks became entangled with Burkhart, who wound up sitting down with his back to the plate. Burkhart called Carbo out because he saw Hendricks make a tag, but the ball was in Hendricks's other hand, and Carbo never touched the plate. Reds manager Sparky Anderson argued, but the call stood, and Palmer got the last out to end the inning. Given a break, the Orioles made the most of it when Brooks Robinson homered in the top of the seventh to give the Orioles a 4–3 lead that held up for the win.

ELROD HENDRICKS: "We had a meeting before the game, and we were listening to the scouting report, and just as the meeting was about ready to break up I said, 'Just one second. If Carbo gets on, he'll run the bases crazy. Don't be surprised by anything he does out there. Just be ready for anything.' So sure enough, he's on third, the ball is hit back off the plate, Palmer comes in, and I'm not even thinking about him coming home, and he throws it to me.

"When I caught the ball, I saw Carbo ten or fifteen feet up the line, so I figured I had plenty of time to get down, block the plate, and make my tag. As soon as I started down, there was Burkhart sitting under me. I never saw him. He came out to get a better look at the play, but I didn't see him at all under me because he wasn't standing straight up. He was in a crouched position, looking up, and when I came down and saw him I said, 'Uh-oh.'

"Then Carbo knocked me back, and that's when the ball goes out [of the glove]. Then we're all down. And I saw that Carbo slid right into [Burkhart's] shin guards and got pushed off the plate. So my whole thing was to hold [Carbo] off long enough to get my balance back and go tag him. I pushed Carbo with the glove. Then Burkhart called [Carbo] out. I'd had the glove on his shoulder, and that's what he saw. He was turned around, looking behind his back, and he saw the back of my glove, and he took for granted that the ball was in the glove. He just made the call. Had to make a call. There was another runner on base.

"Then Carbo got up and looked and said, 'He never tagged me.' Then he was jumping up and down on the plate, and Sparky came running out and said, 'He never tagged him.' Burkhart said, 'Yes, I saw the tag. He tagged him.' But Sparky said, 'No, he didn't have the ball in the glove.' He argued and argued. But once Sparky came out, I knew the play was dead, so I didn't worry. Sparky finally said, 'What the heck, [Carbo] never touched home plate anyway,' and he walked away.

"When he walked away Burkhart said, 'You tagged him, didn't you?' I said, 'Well, yeah.' I told him [the truth] the next day. And he saw it [pictured in the papers]. He came to me and said, 'What happened?' I got all kinds of threats and hate letters from Cincinnati. By the time we got home I had a locker full of hate mail. But what they didn't understand was it was a continuous play, another runner on the bases, so he had to make the call immediately instead of waiting.

"Years later we were in spring training one afternoon, and Burkhart said, 'Ellie, did you ever make any money off that?' I said no. He said, 'I guess we went down in history as part of the play of the century, and we didn't even get paid for it.' I told him I got my reward. I got a [World Series] ring."

The Reds jumped ahead in Game 2, scoring three unearned runs in the first. After Tolan homered in the third to make it 4–0 and Bench walked, Weaver pulled Cuellar and brought in Tom Phoebus, who immediately benefited from another brilliant defensive play by Brooks Robinson. May hit a hard smash into the hole, but Robinson sank to his knees and caught the ball, then whirled and threw to second to start a double play.

The Orioles got one run back in the fourth on Powell's second homer in two days, then scored five runs in the fifth, with Brooks Robinson providing the game-tying single and Hendricks doubling to left to score two runs and put the Orioles ahead for good. Reliever Dick Hall, pitching with a one-run lead, recorded the last seven outs to lock up the 6–5 win, with last-out help from Blair, who raced to the fence and caught a drive with his back to the plate.

ELROD HENDRICKS: "It just seemed like all the bad things that happened in the '69 Series went in our favor in '70. In the second game I hit a ball right down the third-base line for a double, and Brooks scored from first base. That shows you how far around [to the right] they were playing me. [Third baseman] Tony Perez was playing me at shortstop. I remember getting to second, and Lee May turned and said, 'You never hit the ball that way.' "

After two one-run wins, the Orioles had a much easier time in Game 3 at Memorial Stadium, as McNally pitched a complete game and became the first pitcher to hit a grand slam in the World Series. Frank Robinson and Buford also hit homers, and Brooks Robinson made yet another memorable stop—a diving grab to his left that robbed Bench of a hit. Final: Orioles, 9–3.

Dave McNally: "I hit the homer off Wayne Granger. The first pitch he threw me actually bounced before Bench caught it, and I swung at it. Then he did it again, and I swung at it and went, 'Holy cow.' Then he threw a ball, and I fouled one off, and then he threw another ball. I'm sure his philosophy was, 'I can't go to three and two and possibly walk this guy,' so he threw a fastball in about the only place I could hit it—waist-high inside. And I hit it. My lifetime average was under .150, but I had two World Series homers and nine overall. Basically, if you threw it waist-high and inside, I could hit it."

Riding a 17-game winning streak going back to the last weeks of the regular season, the Orioles went for the sweep the next day at Memorial Stadium and had a 5–3 lead in the top of the eighth when Palmer suddenly tired, walking Perez and giving up a single off the wall to Bench. Weaver put in Eddie Watt, but May hit Watt's first pitch for a three-run homer, and the Reds won 6–5. Watt was booed for the rest of his Orioles career, the fans seemingly unable to forget the sweep that almost was.

The Reds then scored three runs in the top of the first of Game 5, but those were the only runs they scored on a wet, gloomy afternoon. The Orioles pounded out 15 hits and won easily, 9–3, clinching their second Series title in five years.

After Brooks Robinson took a called third strike in the bottom of the eighth, the fans gave him an ovation as he returned to the dugout, paying tribute to the defensive brilliance he had shown throughout the Series. He then made another stop in the top of the ninth, lunging to his right to grab Bench's sharp liner in foul ground. Fittingly, he also recorded the last out of the Series, throwing out pinch hitter Pat Corrales on a routine grounder. That he would be named the Series MVP was a given. Aside from his defense, he batted .429 with two doubles, two homers, and six RBI.

PAUL BLAIR: "I was so proud of the way we came back in '70 and won 108 ball games and became the world champions. Everybody just figured the Big Red Machine was going to roll all over us. We made 'em a little toy wagon. And I led everybody in hitting. Don't nobody know that but me because Brooks had such a fantastic World Series, but I hit .474. Out-hit everybody in there."

ELROD HENDRICKS: "There was a weight on us all year. All year. There was one goal, to win it all. After we beat the Reds in Game 5, I looked around the [clubhouse] and people were so tired. I couldn't even celebrate. I was asleep that night by nine o'clock—just totally exhausted and mentally drained from having pushed all year."

FRANK ROBINSON: "The Reds weren't 'on the way up' or anything. They were there. A great team. But Brooks really deflated them. It got to the point where they didn't think they could get a ball by him. Bench was talking to himself, muttering, because Brooks made a couple of plays on him. It demoralized their whole team. That was a tough team to demoralize, but he did."

EARL WEAVER: "The most amazing thing was to have all of those chances in a five-game series to be able to display your talents at third base. Brooks was the best third baseman that ever played, defensively, and he averaged a little less than three-and-a-half chances per game. So the opportunities aren't there really at third, but the Reds just kept whacking the ball to him, and he kept catching it. One was better than the other. He did that all year, but you might go two or three days and Brooks had two chances, a couple of high bouncers. But we had two left-handers [pitching], and the ball came to him."

BROOKS ROBINSON: "I made an error on the first ball hit to me in the Series, threw a ball high, and I'm standing there thinking, 'Can you believe this? How in the hell can you make a bad throw?' I'm saying, 'Here we go again, '69 Mets.' But things got better after that. And I got a lot of chances. That was the thing. Belanger and I went into that Series knowing we were going to get a lot of chances because of [lefties] Cuellar and McNally and [righties] Bench and Perez and May. I knew we were going to be busy.

"A lot goes into making a play, like who is pitching and hitting and those things. I was always kind of thinking. Like the play I made to catch a semi–line drive Bench hit in foul territory. People say, 'How in the hell do you catch that?' Well, Cuellar was pitching, and Bench doesn't hold back. And Belanger said, 'Be alive, Brooks, a curve is coming.' A big, slow curve. And you could kind of see Bench slow his bat down and still get out in front of it. I just changed my thinking, and I was kind of leaning [right], and I just leaned right into it. That's when Sparky made the comment about me coming down from a higher league or whatever, which was funny."

ELROD HENDRICKS: "Lee May and I went out after Game 4, and all he could talk about was Brooks. He said, 'I've never seen anything like it. No matter where you hit that ball, he's there. And you have that little skinny guy over there at shortstop that nothing gets by. And you have Blair out there playing that shallow, and you can't hit it over his head, and you can't hit a line drive, so everybody's trying to uppercut it and hit it out of the ballpark.' He shook his head and said, 'I see why you don't have many .300 hitters [in the AL].'

"[Reds] at the plate would be talking to themselves, and I didn't quite understand because I'm concentrating, but it was like 'Don't hit to the left side; get a good pitch to hit; hit the ball up; got to get it in there.' They couldn't get it by Brooks and Belanger, and they were fouled up. Tolan tried to bunt one, and he fouled it off, and I said, 'That's not a good idea. Don't test him.' Tolan looked at me like, 'Who are you to be telling me that? I'll bunt it at anybody over in the National League.' But they got the message.

"The thing I tried to tell Lee and some of the writers from the National League who hadn't seen Brooks, I said, 'These are things he does on a daily basis. This didn't just happen; he does this all the time.' And they said, 'Yeah, right.' And I said, 'I'm serious. The world is seeing this now, but I watch him day in and day out, and he's amazing. You have to watch him day in and day out. He does this all the time. That's the way he plays. Seventy million people are watching now, but that's the way he plays all the time.'"

24

The Oriole Way

Not only were the Orioles baseball's best team in the late '60s and early '70s, they also were baseball's best organization. No club was better at scouting, drafting, signing, and developing players; fielding title-winning minor league teams, and honing top front-office talent. Three times between '66 and '72, the Orioles won the Topps Company's "Baseball Organization of the Year" award. It was a golden era when the club operated as smartly as a Fortune 500 company.

When Harry Dalton replaced Lee MacPhail as the top baseball operative in December of '65, he hired Walter Shannon as his director of scouting, Lou Gorman as his director of minor league clubs, and Frank "Trader" Lane as a special assistant. Gorman's new assistant was John Schuerholz, a Baltimore native who quit a better-paying job as a local schoolteacher. Jim McLaughlin, the club's first farm director, returned as a scouting coordinator in '68.

By '67 more than a dozen past, present, or future major league general managers and managers were on the payroll—Dalton, Lane, Gorman, Schuerholz, and Frank Cashen in the front office; Billy Hunter and Hank Bauer on the major league staff; Arthur Ehlers and Jim Frey as scouts; and Earl Weaver, Cal Ripken Sr., George Bamberger, Darrell Johnson, and Joe Altobelli as minor league managers. Don Pries, future director of the Major League Scouting Bureau, was a scout based in California, and future major league pitching coaches Herm Starrette and Billy DeMars were minor league coaches.

HARRY DALTON: "We had good people everywhere, all over the place, we really did. Look at what they did for the balance of their baseball years. So many went on to do so well. There was a picture taken in front of Memorial Stadium during the organizational meetings one fall, and like half of the people in it ultimately were major league managers or general managers."

WALTER YOUSE: "I think we were considered the best organization of them all at that point as far as getting good guys to the big leagues. We were the tops. Lou Gorman and John Schuerholz came through on their way up. John quit a job as a teacher making thirty thousand dollars a year and took a job making seven thousand dollars a year. He was a sharp young boy."

DON PRIES: "When you look at the people we had in our employ at that time and how they went on to other organizations in executive roles, it's remarkable. Gorman wound up running the Red Sox. Schuerholz ran the Royals and now the Braves. Frey became the manager and general manager of the Cubs. Hunter managed in Texas. Bamberger managed in Milwaukee. Weaver and Altobelli and Ripken managed the Orioles. We were all there together at one point. A group of quality men. We had the reputation of doing things right."

JOE ALTOBELLI: "In '66 I was in Rochester as a player-coach, with Earl as the manager. Dalton needed a manager at Bluefield, and he called and we talked. I decided to take the job. I could have played another year or two, but I'd decided I'd like to stay in baseball. It was a good organization. We were winning at the major league level and in the minor leagues, too. Everyone looked to us when they wanted a player or two.

"I got great training as a manager in that organization. We had scouts like Dee Phillips and Walter Youse who weren't just great at signing talent. The Orioles would bring in those guys in the spring, and they taught me a lot about managing—how to foresee how a player might develop. There were just a lot of good people around. Then McLaughlin came to spring training, and him and I went toe-to-toe. He didn't know the field [part of the game], but he knew the other part. Five years later I had to apologize to him. He was teaching me things that had to be taught. It was just an organization doing things right. Other organizations tried to do the same things, and some did, but we had the people that could do it."

EARL WEAVER: "When I took over [as the major league manager] in '68, I went back to Paul Richards and the way he wanted everything done as far as instruction throughout the minor league system. Richards, in his day, would bring the minor league managers down to spring training and show us how he wanted things taught, so the instruction was all the same at every level.

Every minor league manager had a few variations, but we stuck to the principles, and it was a good idea.

"When Richards left [in '61] they brought in Billy Hitchcock, who didn't initiate any policy. His idea was, 'Just teach kids how to play baseball in the minor leagues.' And Richards's thing went out. But it stayed with me when I was [managing] at Elmira and Rochester. Then Hitchcock lasted two years and Bauer came in, and Hank brought us all down [to spring training], too, but Hank was from the Yankees school: 'Just get the talent, put the ball and some bats on the field, and let's go get 'em.' There wasn't a hell of a lot of a program, not that Hank didn't make the players work. We worked our butts off. But as far as the instruction, it wasn't like when Richards was there and things had to be exactly right. Hank was just, 'Let's go play.'

"When I finally got there [in '68] I still had the Richards influence. So it was, 'Let's go back to that.' As well as using some of the other stuff I learned along the way in the Cardinals organization [in the '50s], from guys like George Kissell, who was a dedicated baseball man, and a guy named Andy Cohen, who wasn't quite a fundamentalist but organized. I played at Denver with Andy, and Kissell was in the Cardinals chain. Just a mixture of stuff. Half of it Richards's. The Dodgers had their way, the Cardinals had their way, and now, OK, the Orioles were going to have our way."

DON PRIES: "When I became the director of player development [in '69] I wrote a manual, *The Oriole Way to Play Baseball*. There was basic instruction for every position. In spring training each person at various positions was required to take this manual and in an evening classroom atmosphere write down what the manual said. Then they were to take their manual with them, as written by them, as a reminder of the proper way of doing things. My feeling was, if they write it, they remember it. That was something I implemented.

"And we had a philosophy, clearly stated. You have to develop the mind as well as the body. I always felt that was important, and that was an ingredient we had at the Orioles. We had young men who were not only gifted athletically, but wise in how to play the game properly. There are two ways to play. One team goes to the park to play the game. The other goes to the park to beat you. We went to the park to beat you, not just to play the game. There was a method, and it was carried out. You had to think it all through, 'How do we win today?' Earl used to talk about the three-run homer. But also what to do with the ball when you get it. Thinking. Being smart. That was the Orioles."

Getting the right players into the system was still essential, of course. The Orioles' scouting apparatus had flourished before baseball instituted an amateur draft in '65, and it continued to excel in the late '60s and early '70s with Shannon overseeing regional scouting supervisors Walter Youse, Dee Phillips, and Don McShane and a staff of area scouts such as Al Kubski and Ray Poitevint.

DON PRIES: "I was with Walter Shannon at the Cardinals, when he was the scouting and farm director there, before he came to the Orioles. Walter was brilliant. He could talk about any topic intelligently, not only baseball. He was a gifted man in the area of evaluating talent, and also able to motivate."

WALTER YOUSE: "One time at a meeting with Cashen and Dalton, someone was talking about how much money was being spent, and Walter said, 'We aren't in the banking business, we're in the business of finding ballplayers.' In other words, we had to spend money. Walter was good. He could really motivate you. I mean, he'd bullshit me, and I'd work twice as hard. Scouting is like playing the game; you have to motivate guys to do their jobs. And if a guy isn't doing what he's supposed to do, you tell him. If you're going to be a scouting director, you have to do that. Walter did."

HARRY DALTON: "Once the draft came in, things changed to some degree as far as scouting. There weren't as many secrets. Scouts weren't hiding players out. All the Machiavellian stuff was out. You still had to do your homework, but as far as getting to know the family [of a prospect] so you'd have the emotional edge, that didn't matter anymore. All you did was draft the player and negotiate. But you still had to find out about the player, find out about the 'inner half' that we talked about all the time and felt was so important. And we had scouts who just excelled at that."

DON PRIES: "Al Kubski was a grinder, a digger. He was a chance-taker. He would give the player the benefit of the doubt. And many times, the ones he gave that to, they came through. Frank McGowan, they used to call him

'Beauty.' He was immaculate, with silver-gray hair, not a hair out of place. A quality scout. Youse got to know the player being scouted. He was so thorough in evaluating talent. Dee Phillips was also very thorough, very analytical."

WALTER YOUSE: "The three supervisors all got along. Sometimes you get situations where supervisors don't respect each other's judgment, but we did. If one liked a guy and wanted him, we didn't argue. That helped make the organization. I might be blowing my own horn a little bit, but it was a good arrangement. Dee was the Mideast-Midwest guy, I was on the East Coast, and McShane had California."

RAY POITEVINT: "I had been an associate scout for the Orioles for seven years in California, and then I had a chance to go work full-time for the Cubs in the late '60s. At the time I was a sales manager making seventy-five thousand dollars a year for an institutional food company. They had a lot of plans for me. The Cubs offered me twelve thousand dollars [a year salary]. I flew to Baltimore, and they countered and started me at eighteen thousand dollars. Walter Shannon said later I was the best negotiator he ever saw. But I'd been negotiating contracts for years in the food industry, dealing with corporations such as McDonald's and hotel chains. Getting into baseball was like going on vacation.

"I was the youngest guy in the [Orioles] organization. I had the blessing of getting to rub elbows with Dalton and Pries and Walter Shannon and scouts like Bill Werle and Russo and Ray Scarborough. Really good baseball people. I don't know if they even make those kinds of baseball people anymore. They were totally unselfish, took me under their wing and gave me a foundation. Taught me to do it right. We would cross-check each other. It was all about getting the players."

FRANK CASHEN: "Jimmy Russo was probably the best scout I ever saw in my life. He handled the National League the whole time I was there. Bill Werle did the American League. And both of them, besides doing that, they did high schools and colleges for the draft. Bill Werle would get in and look at the best young pitchers in high school or college, and he'd give us a list, numbered one to ten. And that's how we drafted, right off his list. He was a crackerjack."

As one generation of players such as Jim Palmer and Davey Johnson established itself on the Orioles in the late '60s, another generation was being drafted and signed and beginning the slow climb to the majors. The Orioles' top two draft picks in '67 were Bob Grich and Don Baylor, each a future All-Star and symbolic of the Orioles' innate nose for excellence. Grich, a shortstop from California, and Baylor, an outfielder from Texas, all but forced the Orioles to dismantle a championship club when they were ready for the major leagues in the early '70s.

HARRY DALTON: "In '67 a lot of our people thought Baylor should be the first [round] pick and Grich should go second. As we got closer [to the draft] our scouts that had seen a lot of Baylor said he wouldn't go [in the first round] because he didn't have a strong throwing arm at that point. If we flip-flopped them, maybe we could get both—Grich and then Baylor. It was a big gamble when we decided to do that, because we might have lost Baylor. But we got both."

AL KUBSKI: "Grich was in my territory. He was at Wilson High School in Long Beach in '67. Great football player. A quarterback. UCLA was after him. [UCLA coach Tommy] Prothro really wanted him. Prothro told him, 'Come with us, and we'll make you a Heisman Trophy winner.' It was tough. In baseball, in the two-to-eight range scouts use [with eight the highest], he was a lot of fives. A five runner, a five fielder. Had some power. But Brooks [Robinson] was a two runner and a three thrower, and he's in the Hall of Fame. There are a lot of guys with great natural ability who can't play.

"When it came to the draft we had Baylor listed ahead of Grich, but Harry said, 'We have a lot of outfielders in the minor leagues, and we need infielders. If those two guys are up, we'll take Grich first and Baylor second.' We offered Grich thirty thousand dollars, and he was sitting on it, and then I read in the paper where Prothro had recruited three other quarterbacks, and that helped us. We upped the offer to thirty-five thousand dollars, and he signed. Baylor signed for seventy-five hundred dollars."

BOB GRICH: "There were three future major leaguers on my high school team—Jeff Burroughs, Eddie Crosby, and myself. We were scouted a lot. I didn't know who was interested. My high school coach came to me on the morning of the draft and said, 'Congratulations, the Orioles just took you in the first round.' I hadn't heard from them. The only team I'd heard from was the Yankees. They called the night before the draft and asked, 'If we pick you first, how much would you want?' Like an idiot, I told them. And they didn't draft me. They ended up drafting Ron Blomberg. He signed for seventy-five thousand dollars. I had said one hundred thousand dollars.

"I held out for about two weeks, as long as I could. I didn't know what to do. It was a tough decision. Al Kubski and Bobby Mattick were talking to me. Kubski had followed me the most, and Mattick came out to work with Al to sign me. They got Russo involved. There was going to be some stiff competition at UCLA. I was a decent high school quarterback. Prothro was telling every quarterback that they were going to win the Heisman. I made the right choice."

JOE ALTOBELLI: "I had Grich and Baylor throughout the minor leagues—at rookie level, A, Double-A, and Triple-A. They were the top of the heap. Good ballplayers, good leaders. They both probably could have been All-American football players. Both went on and got their college educations. They were just good, driving-type people and ballplayers. As a scout or even as a fan, you knew both of those guys were going to make it."

BOB GRICH: "I went to Bluefield after I signed, and Donnie came up and put his hand out and said, 'Welcome to the team.' I never forgot that. Being number two, he could have laid in the weeds and been jealous or competitive, but that wasn't his character. We had a great relationship and still do. We played together every year, four and a half years in the minors from Bluefield to Stockton to Dallas to Rochester."

JOE ALTOBELLI: "They both played on our '71 team at Rochester, which was a real good club. Baylor hit .313 with 20 homers. Grich was .336 with 32 homers. We flirted with disaster early and then jelled and really came on. Our record was 33–34 at one point, and we finished 32 games over .500. And there was a Junior World Series that year, so we played Denver [of the American Association]. Had to play all seven games in Rochester because they had a scheduling problem with the [NFL] Broncos. We won in seven."

Grich and Baylor weren't the only prospects coming through the system at the time. Future major leaguers such as Al Bumbry, Doug DeCinces, Wayne

Garland, Terry Crowley, Rich Coggins, Enos Cabell, Bob Bailor, Don Hood, Jesse Jefferson, and Mike Reinbach also were drafted between '66 and '70. Those who didn't become mainstays for the Orioles were traded and brought value in return.

AL KUBSKI: "I went to see a catcher I kind of liked, and there was a cen- terfielder playing against his club, weighed about 150 pounds, but he could run and throw above average. Coggins. I said I'd take him over the catcher, but I had no information on him. So I looked around the crowd watching the game, and there was only one black guy there, and I said, 'Excuse me, but is that your boy out there? And is he interested in playing pro ball?' And he said, 'Well, sure.' So I get all the info from the dad, and we take him in the twenty-first round.

"Well, I go to the house to sign him, and it was a big home. Coggins was an engineer from Detroit and he had a three-hundred-thousand-dollar home up on a hill. So I get there, and I have four thousand dollars to sign his boy. So we're talking, and I'm getting along with the dad. The youngster ain't say- ing a word. The dad says to his son, 'Do you want to play pro ball or go to college?' He says, 'Dad, I want to play pro ball.' The dad turns and says, 'Al, four thousand dollars ain't much.' I said, 'That's what your round gets.' He said, 'Well, the money isn't the thing. I want him to play for three years. After that I want you to tell me if my son can get to the big leagues or not.' And that little son of a gun went out and really played. Made it to Baltimore in three years. But the sad part was, his daddy died before he got to the big leagues. A blood disease.

"Then in '70 there were all sorts of prospects in California. We drafted Reinbach in the first round, [Jim] Fuller in the second round, and DeCinces in the third round. Reinbach was a tremendous prospect—an infielder. Pries loved him. He was a good athlete, could run, throw, field better than Fuller. He'd gone to UCLA on a football scholarship as a quarterback and hurt his shoulder. He signed for twelve thousand dollars and had some big years in the minors, and then he hurt his knee and went to Japan and played there.

"Fuller was an outfielder, and what power. I offered him five thousand dol- lars coming out of high school, and he said he was going to junior college because he thought he could do better than that. Then he called from junior college and said he wasn't getting many swings and wanted to sign, but could we get him more money? I got him another thousand, and he signed for six thousand dollars."

Clint "Scrap Iron" Courtney

Paul Richards (center) shows off a catcher's mitt to Gus Triandos (left) and Connie Johnson.

Reliever George Zuverink
hands Lee MacPhail a
signed contract.

Lee MacPhail, Orioles general manager, 1958-65

Jim McLaughlin, architect
of the Orioles' minor-
league system

Steve Dalkowski, the hardest thrower of all

Hoyt Wilhelm

Spring training 1960 (left to right): "Skinny" Brown, Milt Pappas, Hoyt Wilhelm, Jerry Walker, and Jack Fisher

Steve Barber

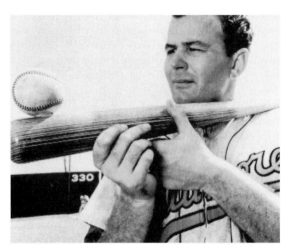

"Diamond" Jim Gentile

Brooks Robinson,
Mr. Oriole

Doug DeCinces

Joe Hamper

Bob Grich (left) and Mark Belanger

Jim Palmer,
a portrait of
elegance

Paul Blair goes over the fence to make a catch in '74.

Earl Weaver, having another "discussion"

Boog Powell takes a swing.

Frank Robinson in 1966

Elrod Hendricks

Reggie Jackson, during a brief stop in
Baltimore

Wild Bill Hagy incites
the crowd.

Frank Cashen (left) and Jerry Hoffberger

Earl Weaver greets John Lowenstein on the base paths after Lowenstein's game-winning run in Game 1 of the 1979 American League playoffs.

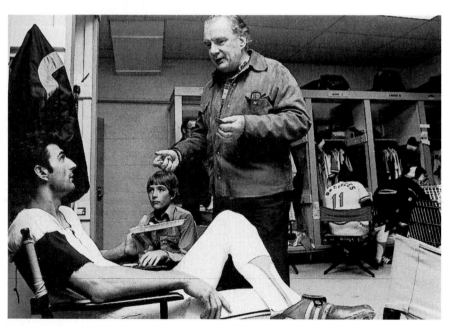

Edward Bennett William (right) in the clubhouse with Mark Belanger

The Orioles celebrate after the last out of the 1983 World Series.

Hank Peters (right) and Edward Bennett William in the clubhouse after the 1983 World Series

The three Ripkens—Cal Jr., Cal Sr., and Billy

Orioles of all ages wave to the crowd at the last game at Memorial Stadium.

The first night game at Camden Yards
(Copyright © *Baltimore Sun*)

Gregg Olson

Brady Anderson, the 50-homer man
(Copyright © *Baltimore Sun*)

Mike Mussina
(Copyright © *Baltimore Sun*)

Pat Gillick
(Copyright ©
Baltimore Sun)

Cal Ripken takes a victory lap around
Camden Yards after breaking Lou
Gehrig's consecutive-games record.
(Copyright © *Baltimore Sun*)

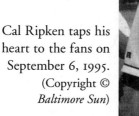

Cal Ripken taps his
heart to the fans on
September 6, 1995.
(Copyright ©
Baltimore Sun)

Rafael Palmeiro
(Copyright © *Baltimore Sun*)

Peter Angelos

RAY POITEVINT: "Fuller should have been the greatest hitter of all time. He had more power than anyone."

AL KUBSKI: "He went to the Florida State League and hit 30-something homers, which was unheard of in those big parks down there. The rest of the team didn't hit 30. The manager said he was the best ballplayer he'd ever seen. When he went to Double A he hit 20-something homers, then he went to Rochester and had a huge season, 30-something homers. Everything looked great. But Jim Frey is the hitting coach there, and he tells me the kid has some holes in his swing, and if he doesn't close them he's going to be in trouble.

"They sent him to Puerto Rico for the winter-league season, and Frank Robinson was managing and playing him in right field, and I went down to scout the league. We flew back together on the same plane for a dinner, and I asked Frank, 'Is Fuller going to play in the big leagues?' Frank says, 'I don't think so.' I said to Frank, 'You're a horseshit scout. The guy is our best prospect.'

"Frank says, 'The pitchers have better control in the majors than what he's hitting. If he doesn't close those holes [in his swing] he ain't gonna make it.' I said, 'Frank, why don't you help him?' He said he'd tried. Frank said he'd given some suggestions, but Fuller said, 'I tried that; it didn't work.' He kind of shut off Frank and Frey. He had those holes and never did correct them. And he never did much in the major leagues.

"Frank also had DeCinces playing third down in Puerto Rico, and he liked him. It's funny. DeCinces had less ability than either Reinbach or Fuller. Our organization called him a 'chance' prospect when we drafted him. But he was like Grich; he could play the game. In high school he was going with a girl who lived two houses up from me, so I knew him, knew he had some ability. We signed him for two thousand dollars. And he wound up playing fifteen years."

DOUG DECINCES: "The first time I met Kubski, he goes, 'Yeah, I know who you are.' Kubski's wife was best friends with my future wife's mother. And my dream was to play in the major leagues, of course, and Al said, 'Yeah, I've seen you play. You don't run good enough and you throw like a girl.' He really shattered my dreams. Al had a way of testing your personality. It was a very crowning success for me when he signed me later on. I said, 'Does this mean I still throw like a girl?' He kind of chuckled and said, 'Oh, you remember that?' But you don't forget things like that."

The Orioles' minor leaguers held their spring training camp in Fernandina Beach, Florida, from '67 through '71 (after finally leaving Thomasville, Georgia) and spent the season either in Bluefield (rookie), Miami (Single A), Dallas–Fort Worth (Double A), or Rochester (Triple A). The entire system played .538 ball—the game's highest winning percentage—over a twelve-year period starting in '62. Miami won four straight division titles starting in '69, and Rochester, with Altobelli managing, won four titles in six years starting in '71.

JOE ALTOBELLI: "The Triple-A club would train in Daytona Beach, and the rest in Fernandina Beach, just north of Jacksonville. You could always spot some top-quality athletes real quick in the spring, guys like Grich and Baylor. We had good teachers everywhere. Vern Hoscheit was the camp coordinator at Fernandina Beach. We went by the clock. We had limited space, so we had to do everything precisely. It was an organization, at the time; when we went to spring training, we were preparing for a championship season, not just a season."

BOB GRICH: "Orioles baseball was good, sound, fundamental baseball. Good defense. It was just a good feeling of unity throughout the organization. They certainly were not the highest-paying organization. More middle-of-the-road as pay scale. But they had the best GM in baseball in Dalton. They didn't rush their players. That's what they were known for. Other organizations would bump players along two steps at a time. The Orioles were adamant about being patient with their young players. They just about never bumped them more than one class at a time. If there was anyone who could have been bumped it was Baylor, but they held him back. Other organizations certainly would have rushed him along, but the Orioles were patient."

25

The Last Hurrah

After winning 217 regular-season games and back-to-back American League pennants in '69 and '70, and a World Series title in '70, the Orioles struggled early in '71. Seemingly bored, they trailed the first-place Boston Red Sox throughout May. Then one pitch gave them all the motivation they needed. In the second game of a doubleheader at Comiskey Park on May 31, Chicago's Bart Johnson plunked Don Buford in the back after Buford had hit two home runs, one in the first game and another in his prior at-bat. Buford charged the mound, and White Sox fans spent the rest of the day throwing debris at the Orioles.

Awakened, the Orioles won nine straight games, moved into first on June 5, and opened up a lead. Although they didn't run away with the division title as easily as in '69 and '70, they never spent another day out of first and ended with 11 straight wins and 101 overall, giving them three straight seasons with at least 100 wins.

DON BUFORD: "I hit a home run off Joel Horlen, and Bart Johnson came in, and I hit a home run off him into the upper deck, and the next time up he threw one behind my head, and I went to the mound and challenged him. There was no fight or anything. But then fans were throwing things at me on the bench, and someone threw a broken seat from the upper deck that whizzed just past my head. Then I was on the on-deck circle, and a fan hit me in the back with some rocks. So I went over to the guy and said, 'If I get hit again, you and I are going to go after it.' Another guy jumped over the dugout and came toward me, and the other players stopped him. That day got the club going. We went on a winning streak and started kicking people's fannies."

The '71 club made pitching history, becoming the first major league team in fifty-one years and only the second in modern history to have four 20-game winners. Jim Palmer, Dave McNally, Mike Cuellar, and Pat Dobson, acquired in a trade with San Diego, all won at least 20 and combined for 70 complete games. Dobson's record in July—eight starts, eight wins, eight complete games—summed up the year.

The offense also was solid, as the Orioles led the league in batting and runs. Buford excelled in the leadoff spot again, producing 99 runs, 19 homers, and a .415 on-base percentage. Frank Robinson was his usual productive self at age thirty-six, leading the club with 28 homers and 99 RBI. Brooks Robinson and Boog Powell combined for 42 homers and 184 RBI, and surprising help came from shortstop Mark Belanger, who raised his average 48 points to .266.

DON BUFORD: "I'd have to say the '71 team was our best. We had four guys win 20. A lot of guys had good years. If you go position by position, it's tough to say any club was better. We had Gold Gloves all over the infield. A bunch of guys made the All-Star team. I made the All-Star team. We had three Hall of Famers on that club. It's kind of hard to top that. The competition between the players was good. With Palmer, McNally, Cuellar, and Dobson, it got to the point where they didn't want to lose when they went out there."

FRANK ROBINSON: "It was still the '69 Series paying a dividend. After that we didn't take anything for granted. We wanted to come back and win it and win it and win it as often as we could. We'd learned a lesson. I thought the '71 team was the best I played on. Our pitching and defense were such that we didn't give away any runs, and our offense wasn't too bad. We were always in the game."

A dangerous opponent awaited the Orioles in the AL Championship Series—the Oakland A's, who also had won 101 games with a strong stable of young talent including pitchers Vida Blue, Jim "Catfish" Hunter, and Rollie Fingers, as well as Reggie Jackson, Joe Rudi, and Sal Bando. Oakland's manager was former Orioles player Dick Williams, who had guided Boston to a pennant in '67 and was established as one of the game's best managers.

The series opened in Baltimore, with the Orioles trying to preserve their undefeated ALCS record after sweeps of the Twins in '69 and '70. The A's seemed set to end the streak after scoring twice in the second inning off McNally and taking a 3–1 lead into the bottom of the seventh behind Blue, a 24-game winner. But pinch hitter Curt Motton doubled in two runs to tie the score with two outs, and Paul Blair doubled in two more to give the Orioles a 5–3 lead, which reliever Eddie Watt protected.

Stunned, the young A's lost again the next day as Cuellar pitched a six-hitter and the Orioles hit four homers off Hunter in a 5–1 win. Palmer then wrapped up the Orioles' fourth pennant in six years with a seven-hitter in Game 3. Jackson hit two homers to keep the A's close going into the seventh, but Frank Robinson hit an RBI double, and Palmer struck out the side in the ninth to lock up the 5–3 win and give the Orioles a 9–0 record in ALCS games.

DICK WILLIAMS: "We clinched way ahead of time, and I had Blue and Hunter and all the time in the world to set up our pitching. But Blair hit a fastball off Vida to drive in two runs, and that beat us after Vida had such a fabulous year. They got us. They had a hell of a team. You couldn't drive a ball through the left side of the infield. That was the best I've ever seen, Belanger and Brooks. And Davey [Johnson] was a good second baseman, and Boog was great. Three All-Star infielders, and Boog saved them all a lot of errors."

FRANK ROBINSON: "Oakland was real good, but they were young. We left them crying on the dugout steps. They just got wiped out. They were shocked. They were upset. They were out there crying."

After winning 97 games and the National League East, the Pittsburgh Pirates lost Game 1 of the NLCS to San Francisco, then won three straight to lock up their first pennant in eleven years. Their strength was hitting more than pitching, with rightfielder Roberto Clemente and left fielder Willie Stargell leading a balanced offense that led the NL in homers, hits, and runs. The starting rotation had four fewer 20-game winners than the Orioles' rotation, but Dock Ellis was a 19-game winner, and Steve Blass, a 15-game winner, had thrown five shutouts during the season. The bullpen ace was Dave Giusti.

The heart of the team was Clemente, one of the game's most complete players—able to run, hit, field, and throw as well as anyone. But he felt unappreciated at age thirty-seven after a career in the shadows of Willie Mays, Hank Aaron, and the other superstars of his generation, and as the '71 Series began, he exhibited a fierce sense of purpose. He wanted the respect he felt he deserved.

The Orioles fell behind in Game 1 at Memorial Stadium when the Pirates scored three unearned runs in the second, but McNally settled down and allowed two hits and no runs the rest of the way, and the Orioles rallied to win 5–3. Merv Rettenmund's three-run homer in the third put them ahead, and Buford added another homer in the fifth. After a rainout, the Orioles won a bizarre and ugly Game 2, turning 14 singles and seven walks into 11 runs. Palmer got the win, although he yielded seven hits and eight walks and threw 168 pitches before coming out after eight innings.

Having finished the regular season with 11 straight wins, the Orioles were working on a 16-game winning streak as the Series shifted to Pittsburgh's Three Rivers Stadium for three games. The Pirates started out just trying to hang on and ended up doing much more.

Steve Blass pitched a three-hitter to win Game 3, and then came Game 4, the first night game in Series history, drawing a television audience of sixty-two million, the largest ever to watch a Series game. The Orioles jumped on starter Luke Walker for three runs in the top of the first, bringing on reliever Bruce Kison. As the Pirates rallied against Pat Dobson, who hadn't pitched in fifteen days, Kison, twenty-one, limited the Orioles to one hit over six and one-third innings. Pittsburgh pinch hitter Milt May singled in the go-ahead run in the seventh, and Giusti saved the Series-tying win.

The Game 5 pitching matchup favored the Orioles—McNally against Nelson Briles, a spot starter who hadn't pitched in the playoffs. But Briles limited the Orioles to two hits and four baserunners, and McNally was knocked out in the fifth. The Pirates' 4–0 victory gave them a 3–2 lead in the Series.

Back in Baltimore for Game 6, a less-than-sellout crowd saw Clemente homer off Palmer to give the Pirates a 2–0 lead in the third and Pittsburgh starter Bob Moose shut out the Orioles through five, stretching the Orioles' streak of scoreless innings to 22. Then Buford homered in the sixth, and Davey Johnson singled in the tying run in the seventh, and the game went into extra innings. Weaver brought in Dobson to pitch the 10th, and with two outs and the tying run on second, on came McNally, the Game 5 starter. He walked Stargell to load the bases, then retired Al Oliver on a fly to center for the third out.

In the bottom of the 10th, Frank Robinson drew a one-out walk and embarked on a historic tour of the bases. Hobbled with injuries, he made it from first to third on Rettenmund's single up the middle, barely beating outfielder Vic Davalillo's throw. When Brooks Robinson lifted a fly to medium-center field, Frank tagged up and headed for home. Davalillo's throw bounced high off the mound, and Robinson slid under catcher Manny Sanguillen's tag with the winning run, forcing Game 7 and providing perhaps the most vivid example of the will to win Robinson exhibited in his six years in Baltimore.

FRANK ROBINSON: "Both of my Achilles tendons were hurting, really aching. My hamstring was bugging me, too. After I got to first, I knew I had to get to third [on the single]. I hit second and said, 'I'm gone.' I didn't need a coach. Had to make a headfirst slide from the outfield side to get there. If [Davalillo] had come in and made a quick stop of the ball, I would have stopped. I wasn't going to get thrown out at third base. But it was a lazy ball, and I never stopped.

"Then Brooks came up and hit a 250-foot fly ball. Billy Hunter's standing there and says 'Go!' and I said, 'What?' I took off. The good thing that happened was the throw bounced off the mound and hopped up higher than normal. The throw was good, but the bounce slowed it up, and that gave me a chance to get home. It was the typical play of making them make the play."

Incredibly, another less-than-sellout crowd came to Memorial Stadium for Game 7. Cuellar was sharp, retiring the first eleven batters he faced, but Clemente homered with two out in the fourth, and the stadium fell quiet. Orioles hitters were unable to get to Blass, who was so nervous he vomited before the game and even between innings, but he allowed just two hits through the first seven innings.

Taking a 1–0 lead into the top of the eighth, Pirates manager Danny Murtaugh called for a hit-and-run with Stargell on first. Jose Pagan doubled to left-center, and Stargell scored when Rettenmund bobbled the carom and Powell cut off the relay.

ELROD HENDRICKS: "People asked me, 'If Boog had let that ball go through [instead of cutting it off] would we have had a play [on Stargell] at the plate?' I say no, Boog made the right play. The ball was fading to the third-base side. As the play was developing I thought we'd have a play, but we needed a perfect throw, and when I saw the ball fading, I knew we didn't have a play."

The Orioles finally got to Blass in the bottom of the eighth, as Hendricks and Belanger led off with singles and Tom Shopay sacrificed the runners to second and third. Buford grounded out to first, scoring one run and advancing the tying run to third, but Blass retired Johnson on a grounder to end the inning. In the ninth, Blass retired Powell, Frank Robinson, and Merv Rettenmund in order, and his teammates mobbed him on the mound as the Orioles watched in frustration.

They had lost the World Series for the second time in three years, this time because of a lack of hitting. After leading the AL in runs and batting average, they hit just .205 against the Pirates, with Powell managing just three singles in 27 at-bats and Johnson and Merv Rettenmund also batting under .200.

Just as the '70 Series had provided Brooks Robinson with the ultimate stage to exhibit his greatness, the '71 Series was a crowning moment for Clemente, who realized his goal of proving to the public that he was among the best of the game's best players. He hit safely in every game and finished the Series with a .414 average.

DON BUFORD: "When you get into the World Series situation, whoever gets the hot hand at the right time is going to win. To this day I'm sure we're better than the New York Mets in '69. Cincinnati [in '70] was good, but we were better. Pittsburgh? Hard to say. If it wasn't for Clemente, we win. He made an outstanding play in the last game. We had a runner on second, and he went into the corner and made a one-hop throw to home to keep a runner from scoring from second. That made a big difference."

DAVE McNALLY: "The Pittsburgh series was like what we did to the Dodgers in '66 in the sense that they had these pitchers who weren't supposed to be that good, but they pitched fantastic. Blass and Kison and Briles pitched far better than the years they'd had."

ELROD HENDRICKS: "In the twenty years I played, I don't think I ever wanted to hit as badly as I did in the ninth inning [of Game 7]. I was two hitters in the hole and there were two outs when Rettenmund hit a ball up the middle. I said good, a hit. I was getting ready to root for Davey, who was hitting ahead of me. Then [Pittsburgh shortstop Jackie] Hernandez got to the ball and threw Rettenmund out from the outfield, and my heart just fell to my feet.

"I just walked back and went to my locker and sat there and cried. That's the only time in my career a game hurt me that bad that I sat in my locker and just cried. Frank Cashen came by and said something that made me feel better, 'Ellie, you played your heart out today.' Whatever it was that made Blass [ineffective] after that, he wasn't the same. He was never the same. But I saw the ball off him that day, and I felt comfortable, and that's why I wanted to hit again. All I wanted was a couple of guys on and one more shot at it. That really hurt me, not being able to get one last at-bat."

JIM PALMER: "They had Clemente, a dominant player of that era. He did so many things. But they pitched so well and defensed us so well. Rettenmund's hitting balls up the middle, and Jackie Hernandez is right there. They were pitching to their defense. They had a game plan.

"We had a great ball club. That and the '70 club were the best I played on. The '71 club had great pitching. They were all great clubs. But the litmus test for any great club is how you do in the postseason. If we'd had the success that Cincinnati had in '75 and '76 and Oakland had from '72 to '74, then we'd be considered one of the best clubs that ever played. But losing two of three Series, we didn't pass that test. I still know we were one of the best clubs that ever played. Those were all great World Series. We just didn't win."

DAVE McNALLY: "Losing two of the three World Series was disappointing. Especially when Game 7 in '71 was in Baltimore and there were probably fifteen thousand empty seats. I thought, 'Jeez, I don't know about this.' The Colts were still more popular. And baseball itself wasn't as popular. Only a few towns had good attendance."

BROOKS ROBINSON: "The Pirates were an outstanding team, but that was a crazy Series. We beat up on 'em here and then we went out there and didn't win a game. Came back here and then I hit that little short sacrifice fly that Frank scored on. I was watching it on ESPN Classic the other day, and Frank made a hell of a baserunning move when he went from first to third on a single and then the same thing on the sacrifice fly. Both were bang-bang plays.

"You like to win, especially after winning the first two games. You'd think you'd win one in Pittsburgh. We had the lead in Game 4, but they came back. And Clemente was spectacular. Here's a guy who was hitting, running, catching balls in the right-field corner, wheeling, and throwing a strike to third. It was a real showcase for him because he always felt he got the shorter end of the deal when you talked about Mays and Aaron and these guys. There was always a little animosity there. I saw him vent it a couple of times in exhibition games, talking to writers. He was always a little angry that playing in Pittsburgh held him back as far as getting acclaim. But that Series moved him to another level, and it was certainly a level he deserved."

BOOG POWELL: "We shouldn't have lost to Pittsburgh. We were so flat, we just couldn't get it together. We just stunk as a team; we really did. We beat the hell out of them for two games and then went out and lost three. And Blass was incredible, that garbage he was flipping up there. That was trash—just a little hanging breaking ball that nobody could hit. I was so frustrated. I knew everybody was counting on me, being the left-handed hitter in the lineup, to take care of this right-handed pitcher, and I just couldn't solve him.

"Losing two of three World Series, that hurt. I was in four World Series and you say, 'You won two and lost two in your career; that's not so bad when you look at it that way.' But if we had won those three World Series in a row we'd probably be considered one of the greatest dynasties of all time, because I don't think any team ever had four Gold Glovers, four 20-game winners, three guys in a row driving in a hundred runs. That's pretty awesome. We had one hell of a team. But other than in '70 we just never put it together at the end of the season. We just didn't do it."

Turbulence
1972–78

26

Storm Clouds

In the early '70s it was clear a revolution was coming in baseball, with the players wanting more money and freedom after decades under the domineering and penurious rule of the owners. Players were beginning to let agents handle their contract negotiations, and the players' union was gaining influence under executive Marvin Miller, whose organizational skills and knowledge of labor relations—honed while working for the United Steelworkers of America—overmatched the owners.

After the '69 season Cardinals outfielder Curt Flood rejected a trade to Philadelphia and sued baseball over the reserve clause in the standard contract, a stipulation that restricted player movement. The case reached the Supreme Court in '72, and although Flood lost, the case further unified the players and added to their resolve. The '72 season was the first disrupted by a work stoppage; a player strike delayed the opening of the season and shortened it by eight games.

The Orioles were not immune from this turbulence. With their low attendance and modest revenues, they weren't among the better-paying clubs, leading prominent players such as Brooks Robinson and Dave McNally to hire agents, much to the front office's dismay. And although owner Jerry Hoffberger promoted a family atmosphere, he was aligned with his fellow owners in firm opposition to the union.

BROOKS ROBINSON: "Management had the hammer for so long. Harry Dalton and Lee MacPhail and those guys, they would just shake their head when you asked for a raise. MacPhail would always say, 'We didn't pay Mickey Mantle this much.' One year I went to Dalton and held out for five hundred dollars. I said I needed five hundred more. Harry said, 'Let's talk about it.' I was in Florida, and I hadn't been to the park, and so I went over to the park, and we're in the office, and we talked, and Harry said, 'OK, tell you what I'm going to do. I'm going to leave the office, and I'll be back in about ten minutes, but you search your soul, and when I come back we'll make a decision.'

"So he left and came back, and I'm just sitting there. I said, 'Harry, I deserve the five hundred dollars. I mean, hell.' And he said, 'OK, I'm going to give you that, but just remember when we negotiate next year that you took advantage of me.' I mean, just crazy things like that. It was terrible. You'd go home to your wife, and she'd say, 'Well, did you get what you want?' She could have negotiated better than me.

"I mean, as players, we wanted to play. We wanted to get to spring training. And [management] had a budget, and they were trying to live within that budget, and that's just the way things were. We were very closemouthed and never talked about what the other guy made. That was one of the ploys that they used. No one knew what the other guy was making. Better off for them. McNally was the one who wouldn't take it. McNally did it right. He was so stubborn, he just said, 'Well, I'm not signing, see you later.' Mac fought them tooth and nail."

DAVE McNALLY: "I held out at the start of every year. The [first] year I won 20 games [in '68] I was bound and determined to get a twenty-thousand-dollar raise. That was horrendous to the ball club. That was way too much for them. And then I had an agent. In '70 I was holding out down in Miami, and I played in the Doral tournament pro-am with Bob Rosburg, who was a baseball nut, and he said, 'Hey, spring training has started; what the heck are you doing?' I explained it to him, and he said, 'If you want, I'll get you in touch with the International Management Group,' which was the Mark McCormack [agent] group.

"There was a guy named Ed Keating who happened to be coming down to negotiate [receiver] Paul Warfield's contract with the Miami Dolphins, and he said he would come over and see me. I signed with him, and the Orioles didn't like that at all. They wouldn't deal with the guy for a while. Cashen just wouldn't deal with agents. Brooks had signed with one, but I was among the first. [Keating] said, 'Don't even talk to [Cashen].' Frank's been pissed at me ever since."

FRANK CASHEN: "The toughest guys I ever negotiated with, and maybe this is why they ended up getting agents, were Bobby Grich and Dave McNally. McNally was a tough son of a bitch. *Intractable* was a good word for him. He was a special kind of an athlete. He was a guy who would go out and pitch, and if his fastball had nothing or his curve wasn't working, he'd throw up more shit than you ever saw until he found something that was working. And he hung in there. He wouldn't quit. Earl Weaver would go out to [pull] him, and you'd think he was going to get in a fistfight with Weaver. A lot of stuff you saw across the negotiating table was the reason he was a great pitcher."

BROOKS ROBINSON: "I was the first baseball player to sign with McCormack's group. [Basketball's] John Havlicek and [hockey's] Stan Mikita had signed, but I was the first baseball player. I just went for help money-wise, with appearances and whatever. But Ed Keating was the guy, and Ed had a hard time convincing Cashen that Cashen should talk to Ed and not me. Not that I was going to get a monstrous raise. I was at the end of my career. The club just said, 'Hey, we're going to talk to you, not to this other guy,' because they had the advantage. They didn't have to talk to anyone."

FRANK CASHEN: "I had to handle the first agent that was ever in the Orioles' office, a guy named Jerry Kapstein. His first two baseball clients were Grich and Baylor, before they made the major leagues. I thought it was crazy; I wanted to throw him out of the office."

DAVE McNALLY: "I was one of the first to go to salary arbitration with the club. The union had gotten that for the players, and I went to New York and met an agent, and we went to the arbitrator's place. It was Peter Seitz, the same guy the owners later hated [for granting the players free agency in a '75 ruling]. We went into this big boardroom, and it was me and the guy on one side, and the Orioles with eight or ten people on the other side. We presented our cases. A couple of days later he ruled in my favor. I think it was over about ten thousand dollars. I don't think the Orioles ever looked at me in the same light after that."

BROOKS ROBINSON: "I got along good with Hoffberger. But he had his opinions. Back in the '60s I was at a golf tournament in California and there was a guy who was going to form a new league. He met with Drysdale and myself and four or five players that were there, and he was going to give us five hundred thousand dollars up front apiece, and we were going to start with a new league. I came back and called Hoffberger and told him that I had this offer and that I was going to be going with this new league if it happened. He said, 'Well, I just want to tell you, it'll be Hoffberger vs. Robinson in court.' And that was that.

"He was very pro-owner. In '72 Belanger and I flew to Dallas for a big [union] meeting during spring training. The player reps from every team were there. We were all on the executive board of the negotiating committee. And we authorized a strike, and Belanger and I came back to town, and I saw Joe Iglehart, who had owned the club at one time, and he said, 'Well, you've done it now.'

"We had a team meeting at a hotel, and Belanger and I stood up and said, 'This is the way it is.' And we laid out what we had discussed at the meeting in Dallas. And then Hoffberger came in and gave his side. Hoffberger showed a real keen interest in all the players and their families and all that, but when it came down to nuts and bolts, he was certainly on the owners' side. He didn't want anything to change. None of the owners did. In their mind, the union was the worst thing that had ever happened. The owners' philosophy was, 'Hey, guys, it's been this way for a hundred years, so it's going to be that way.' Marvin was always one step ahead of them."

FRANK CASHEN: "The brewery was all unionized, so it was not a completely new thing to Jerry, and he was very much a liberal, anyhow. It was a disappointment to him when the union went out on strike or something, which they did. But it didn't destroy him or destroy his relationship with the ballplayers, such as it was."

BROOKS ROBINSON: "When we were on strike [in '72] the pressure was really on for me in Baltimore. This is a more conservative town than some places, and the fans and sportswriters were really against it. I was the player rep, and Marvin came to town for my benefit because I was catching a lot of flak. We had a team meeting at my house, and Marvin really came to my rescue, just to lay the facts out and tell the players to hang in there and things were going to work out. They were crazy times. I got booed after the strike. I got nasty letters. I mean, when I look back on it, it was a terrible ordeal."

┌─────┐
│ **27** │
└─────┘

Breakup

Three days after losing Game 7 of the '71 World Series, the Orioles left Baltimore for a thirty-one-day, twenty-thousand-mile tour of Japan, sponsored by Japan's largest newspaper, which also owned the Tokyo [Yomiuri] Giants, Japan's top team. The tour included eighteen games in fourteen cities, with the Orioles traveling via plane, train, bus, ferry, and hydrofoil. They went 12–2–4 on the trip and were unbeaten in eleven games with the Giants, upholding American baseball's honor.

The tour group included baseball commissioner Bowie Kuhn, American League president Joe Cronin, Orioles owner Jerry Hoffberger, and Orioles executive vice president Frank Cashen. One prominent member of the front office was missing—Harry Dalton, the club's baseball architect since '66 and a front-office figure since '54.

Feeling vaguely unmotivated after helping the Orioles become the game's most respected organization, Dalton was ready for a new challenge. He found it while the Orioles were in Japan, agreeing to take over as the general manager of the California Angels, who had played a decade in the AL without challenging for a playoff berth.

Dalton's departure initiated a breakup of the powerhouse club and elite organization that had produced back-to-back-to-back pennants since '69. The breakup continued through the early '70s, as players from the championship teams departed and several of Dalton's top scouts and front-office aides such as Walter Youse, Al Kubski, and Walter Shannon joined him in California.

HARRY DALTON: "It probably sounded arrogant to a lot of people when I said I needed a new challenge in '71. But the idea of trying to build it again really did appeal to me because I loved that process; it was more fun. And I had always had a fondness for California, and I was in love with the Anaheim ballpark. I thought that was the best baseball stadium in America. All those things made me go to California rather than decide to leave Baltimore. It wasn't a negative of Baltimore. It couldn't have been much better there. But maybe that was part of it—I couldn't do much better there, where I thought I could in California.

"I could have stayed for another couple of years, and we probably would have been good, maybe more than that, but the California thing appealed to me. And they did a good sales job. The day the club left for Japan I flew to L.A., and we spent about eight hours together—[Angels owner] Gene Autry, his lawyer, his co-owner, and myself. I had a hundred questions. In the end I decided my wife and I were young enough, the kids were young enough, we could go. And it never worked out while I was there [in California], of course, from '72 to '77."

The Orioles didn't replace Dalton; they just moved Cashen, the club's executive vice president since '66, into the baseball decision-making chair. One of Cashen's first moves in December of '71 was a stunner—he traded Frank Robinson and reliever Pete Richert to the Los Angeles Dodgers for four prospects, including Doyle Alexander, a promising pitcher.

Robinson had led the Orioles to four pennants and two World Series titles since coming from Cincinnati in late '65, and he was coming off a productive season in '71. But he was thirty-six, and the club needed to make room for Don Baylor, who had put up colossal numbers at Rochester and was ready for the major leagues.

Coincidentally or not, the Orioles didn't make it back to the World Series until eight years after Robinson was dealt.

FRANK ROBINSON: "I knew I was going after the '71 season. Baylor had to have a place to play. He and [second baseman] Bob Grich had terrific years in Rochester in '71 and couldn't crack the lineup. I knew someone had to go. I was the oldest guy, and I was making a good salary. It was no secret. Frank Cashen talked to me on the Japan tour, asking me where I would like to go. I told him since I was near the end of my career, and although I didn't want to leave Baltimore, I wanted to be close to my home in Los Angeles. He said he'd see what he could do and traded me to the Dodgers."

HARRY DALTON: "I was a little bit surprised [at the trade] because Frank [Robinson] had meant so much. I don't know what the inner thinking was, and I've never talked to Frank [Cashen] about it. But I know Frank [Robinson] helped us turn the corner back there in '66. I got him back for the Angels the next year, in '73."

EARL WEAVER: "Moving Frank was a terrible decision to have to make. If only we'd had the designated hitter [DH] a year earlier. But in '70 Grich had hit .340 at Rochester, and Baylor had been the minor league player of the year, and I had to sit in that office down there in Miami [in '71] and say, 'You guys have to go back [to Rochester] and do it again.' And they did. Then you have to make room. But wow, that hurt. Because Frank could still play. If we'd had Frank and Baylor, I think they would have started splitting time in the outfield. Donnie wouldn't have liked it, but I'd have broken Donnie in as a designated hitter, and I think we would have been pretty damn good."

PAUL BLAIR: "I was very disappointed. In my estimation, you just don't trade a Frank Robinson. Here's a guy who should have stayed and retired in Baltimore, because he did everything to turn the team from just a decent team to the class of the league. He'd been there for six years, and we'd gone to the Series four times. Why would you send this man out? He was the center of our ball club. When we needed a big hit or a run, Frank got it for us. Even at the end. There was just no reason to trade him.

"Oakland had a nice ball club, but their three-year reign never would have happened if Frank had stayed. We would have kept winning. As it was, we finished five [games] out in '72 and got to the playoffs in '73 and '74. If we'd had Frank, I think we'd have gone to the World Series all three years. The club would have stayed the same, and we would have made it to the Series six years in a row, from '69 to '74. I think the Orioles owe me three more World Series rings."

Without Frank Robinson, the Orioles faltered in the strike-shortened '72 season, falling to third in the AL East and finishing just six games over .500. Instead of four 20-game winners, there was one, Jim Palmer. The team batting average fell 32 points from '71, with Baylor and Merv Rettenmund struggling to replace Robinson.

PAUL BLAIR: "I think everybody felt, 'OK, we have to make up for Frank, and I have to add a little more to my game because Frank's not here.' Brooksie, Buford, Davey [Johnson], all of us were trying to do a little more than we were capable of doing, which threw us off. And let's face it, when you lose a guy who is going to hit 30 home runs, drive in 100 runs, and score 90 runs, and he's your leader, that's a lot to lose. When he left, they pitched me differently, so I wasn't having the same kind of year. And Frank wasn't on base as much, so Boog wasn't having the same kind of year. It affected the whole ball club."

DON BUFORD: "I had a terrible year in '72 because Frank was gone, and we all tried to do things that we normally didn't do. I tried to hit the ball with more power. Basically, they let Frank go one year too quick. Frank would have hit if he'd stayed and been the DH. And he would have made an outstanding contribution to the club. If they'd stayed with him another year, things might have been different. But they had Baylor and the other guys coming up, and Earl felt they needed to play, so that's the way it goes."

ELROD HENDRICKS: "Losing him was a setback. But Rettenmund had hit over .300 as a part-time player, and you couldn't ask Baylor to go back to Triple A, and Frank was the most logical guy to go. You could get something for Frank and open up room. Then, when Rettenmund started playing on a regular basis, the pressure was on him because now he had to hit 30 home runs and drive in 100 runs and hit .300 to replace Frank. Baylor, same thing. He was going to be the next Frank. That was a lot of pressure on those two guys. That hurt us in '72."

In the wake of the '72 season, Don Buford signed with a club in Japan, and there was a major trade with the Atlanta Braves. Pat Dobson, a 20-game winner in '71 and 18-game loser in '72, and Davey Johnson, now expendable with Grich on the scene, were dealt to the Braves with two more players for Earl Williams, a power-hitting catcher, and a prospect. Johnson hit 43 homers for the Braves in '73 after hitting five for the Orioles in '72.

DON BUFORD: "Baltimore was offering me a large cut in salary. And my contention was I didn't get large raises over those four years when I was getting on base at a .400 percent average, so why should I take a large cut when I have an off year? I was very much opposed to the cut, and I wouldn't accept it, and they sold my contract to Japan, and I went over there and doubled my salary and took my family over there. I couldn't turn that down."

DAVEY JOHNSON: "In '71 I think I had close to 16 home runs and was hitting .300 at the All-Star break, and there were certain games I think I even hit fourth. I was tearing the cover off the ball. Then I ran over a catcher in Boston and hurt my shoulder. For the last half of the year, my left shoulder would collapse. I took painkillers, did everything, tried to exercise it. But it just would collapse.

"It hurt me the whole next year in '72. I tried everything. I built a batting cage in my yard; I worked out religiously; I went to the Mayo Clinic. Weaver never believed I was hurt. He said, 'The doctor says you're OK; there's nothing wrong with you.' I said, 'Well, Earl, every time I go to extend my arm it collapses.'

"I went through a miserable year. I mean, it was awful. I hit .221 with five home runs. For a year and a half I was no good. I told Cashen, 'I'm the only one you can trade, but I'm hurting. No one knows it, but I'm hurting. I may not play next year. If I can't extend my left arm, I'm done.' Grich was ready, and I said, 'I'm the one to trade. If I was healthy, the one to trade would be Belanger, but I'm not, so you need to trade me.' And they did."

FRANK CASHEN: "If you go back and you look at what Earl Williams had done and talk to the scouts, he was going to be a superstar. The first couple of years in Atlanta he hit 33 and 28 home runs, and he could throw, and he was going to be a great player, great player."

The glory days returned in '73, with the Orioles winning 97 games and their fourth division title in five years, thanks primarily to a 14-game winning streak in August. In some ways, the blueprint for success was the same as ever. The starting pitching was strong—Jim Palmer won 22 games and the AL Cy Young Award, Mike Cuellar won 18, and Dave McNally won 17—and Brooks Robinson, Paul Blair, Mark Belanger, and Grich won Gold Gloves.

Yet offensively it was a team unlike any Weaver had managed, thanks to a pair of fleet rookies, Al Bumbry and Rich Coggins, products of the farm system. Bumbry batted first, hit .337, and was named AL Rookie of the Year. Coggins batted second and hit .319. The emphasis was on speed instead of power, with Baylor (.286) stealing 32 bases and Bumbry stealing 23.

In addition, the AL had approved the use of a designated hitter (batting for the pitcher) amid fears that pitching was too dominant, and the Orioles adapted well. Veteran Tommy Davis was brought in as the DH and hit .306

with 89 RBI. Earl Williams also had 22 homers and 83 RBI, but he hit just .237 and brooded in the clubhouse.

ELROD HENDRICKS: "We had a scrappy little ball club. Bumbry and Coggins would get on base, and Tommy Davis would drive them in. We weren't the same type club we'd had. We didn't have the same power. But we'd added speed. And we played a different game. The basic game was still defense and pitching, but we didn't have that raw power, and we had Baylor and Grich, who could run, and the rookies, who could run."

EARL WEAVER: "In '72 when we didn't win, the catching offensively had dropped from 20 home runs to three or four, and that's why we got Williams. He helped us win, but it didn't work out as well as it should have because Earl didn't want to catch. He threw away a fantastic career, just a fantastic career he threw away. He had soft hands, a great arm; what a player he could have been if he'd tried. But he wouldn't run to first base."

ELROD HENDRICKS: "I don't think [Earl Williams] wanted to be here. He would scream after a long out, 'That ball would have been out of the park in Atlanta.' And Earl [Weaver] would scream back, 'You're not in Atlanta anymore. Learn to hit in this goddamn ballpark if you want to play. And another thing, I don't like your attitude.' It got to the point where the pitchers didn't want to throw to him at all. He didn't want to warm anybody up. They'd called him 'Big Money' when he came over, and the fans started calling him 'Small Change.'

"One time he brought out a chair to sit in and warm up Palmer, and Palmer said, 'What the hell is this?' And Bamberger, who had a brilliant way of getting things across to people, says, 'Earl, it looks bad, you sitting like that on that stool.' Earl said, 'Well, they do it in Japan.' And George says, 'Well, you're not in Japan. I want my pitchers throwing to a catcher that's willing to catch.' Palmer was fuming, trying to warm up. Finally, I ran out there."

In the ALCS the Orioles played the A's, the defending world champions. The Orioles knocked out Vida Blue in the first inning of Game 1 at Memorial Stadium and went on to a 6–0 win, running their lifetime ALCS record to 10–0. Then the A's won Game 2, and the series moved to Oakland. Game 3 was a classic, with Cuellar and Ken Holtzman matching extra-inning complete games. Cuellar allowed three hits in 10 innings and struck out 11, but Oakland's Bert Campaneris led off the bottom of the 11th with a homer, giving the A's a 2–1 win and a 2–1 lead in the series.

The Orioles seemed beaten when the A's knocked Palmer out in the second inning of Game 4 and took a 4–0 lead into the seventh behind Blue. But Andy Etchebarren hit the biggest home run of his career, a game-tying three-run shot, and Grich followed with a homer off relief ace Rollie Fingers to give the Orioles a stirring win and force Game 5. But the Orioles had to pitch their number four starter, Doyle Alexander, in the deciding game, and the A's started 21-game winner Jim "Catfish" Hunter. It was no contest. Hunter allowed five hits and pitched the A's to a 3–0 win and the pennant.

BOB GRICH: "Oakland was the same kind of team the Orioles had been a couple of years earlier. That Oakland team was a great team. We were a team in transition. We weren't that far away, like one hit or one play away. It was close. We still had Palmer and Cuellar and Brooks and Blair, and Baylor and Bumbry were there. We were right there with them. But they had a great team all around, no weak spots. It was going to take a great team to beat them. The best team won."

More pieces of the pennant-winning Orioles were dealt after the '73 season. Rettenmund was traded to Cincinnati for Ross Grimsley, a young pitcher, and reliever Eddie Watt was sold to Philadelphia.

The season that followed resulted in yet another division title, the Orioles' fifth since '69, but unlike the others, it was earned in a pennant race that went down to the final days. The Orioles were two games under .500 and eight games behind the division-leading Red Sox on August 29, but they won 28 of their last 34 games to overtake the Sox, hold off the Yankees, and win the race.

Palmer had a subpar season, with injuries limiting him to 26 starts and a 7–12 record, but Cuellar won 22 games, Grimsley won 18, and McNally won 16. The offensive mix was the same as '73, just not as potent. Davis had a club-high 84 RBI, and Grich had 82, but the best run producer after that was Blair with 62 RBI. Brooks Robinson batted .288 but drove in just 59 runs, and Earl Williams had just 14 homers and 54 RBI. At the top of the order, Bumbry's average fell 104 points from '73, and Coggins's dropped 76 points.

Oakland was the ALCS opponent again, and the A's had it easier this time, eliminating the Orioles in four games.

Ross Grimsley: "The trade [to Baltimore] was kind of a shock. I was twenty-three and didn't realize what I was getting into. I was in the rotation with Palmer, McNally, and Cuellar. Brooks and Belanger and Grich and Boog were the infield. Just some great players there. What a pitching lesson I got. Cuellar, in particular, was helpful to me. We pitched similarly, and he really taught me a lot. Between he and myself and McNally, we had three soft-tossing lefties, and we all had different ways of getting people out.

"I had a great season in '74, won 18 games, pitched almost 300 innings, had a long streak of scoreless innings. Everything went right. And the defense, gracious, I'd never seen anything like that. Blair ran everything down in the air from one gap to the other. And any ball hit on the ground never got through [the infield]. Belanger was amazing. I've never seen anyone play shortstop like that, before or since. He never dove for a ball. He just anticipated what the pitcher was going to do, and he was in the right place. They all did that, really, him and Brooks and Grich. And Brooks could still pick it at third. His bat had slowed, but he was still great in the field.

"There were balls hit off me that had been base hits when I was with the Reds, and I'd turn around [to follow the ball], and Belanger and Grich were making the plays. One time one got through and I had a disgusted look on my face, and Belanger said, 'Grims, we can't get to everything.' I just laughed.

"We were way back, but when we got hot you'd go to the park and know you were going to win. It was just a matter of how. The other team knew it, too. It was like, 'How are they going to do it tonight?' Most of the wins were well-pitched games, and there was always a great defensive play or two. We weren't a great offensive team. There was a doubleheader against Boston, who we were chasing, and Cuellar and I pitched, and we both shut them out 1–0. We weren't a great offensive team, but we had guys who knew how to win, and we did."

Elrod Hendricks: "We were in Kansas City with about five or six weeks to go, and Earl called Etch and me into his office. We were eight or nine games out, and Earl said, 'I think we can still win, but we can't win with that SOB [Earl Williams] back there catching. He don't know how to win; he don't want to win; he don't want to play.' He said, 'You two are my catchers for the rest of the year. I don't care if we lose by 20 games, you guys are gonna be my catchers.'

"Etch looked at me, and I looked at Etch, and we got hot and wound up winning. Then after we lost [the ALCS] to Oakland that second time, Earl [Williams] was sitting at his locker and just sobbing. He said, 'I've never been this close to winning.' And I remember thinking we could have won here for two years if he'd wanted to play."

EARL WEAVER: "Every team gets old, but I think the organization did a hell of a job of supplying players so that we didn't really go down the drain. We were winning 90 games a year, but just not making it. You were always that one player, two players short. And Oakland had an outstanding team. You could see it coming when we beat them [in the ALCS] in '71. We beat them three straight, but boy, they had some talent. And we lost some of our talent, you know, and the fact that we went with rookies with Baylor and Grich in place of Frank and Davey."

BOOG POWELL: "No one denied Oakland was good. But they didn't get us in our prime, in '69, '70, or '71. They beat us after our prime."

ROSS GRIMSLEY: "Oakland was good, but man for man they weren't any better than us or anyone else. They just made some plays, got some hits, and knew how to win. Reggie [Jackson] was their only real star on offense. They just had real good pitching and, like the Orioles, had some guys who knew how to make plays to win."

After the '74 season, two archetypal Orioles departed. Dave McNally was traded to Montreal for Ken Singleton in a five-player deal, and Boog Powell, whose RBI total had fallen to 45 in '74, was dealt to Cleveland for Dave Duncan in a four-player deal. Only Mark Belanger, Brooks Robinson, and Paul Blair were still in the lineup off the pennant-winning teams, and only Jim Palmer and Mike Cuellar were still in the rotation. Blair went to the Yankees after the '75 season.

DAVE MCNALLY: "The breakup was inevitable. A lot of it had to do with age. You can't play forever. They made changes they thought they needed to make. You didn't have a lot to say about it. In my case, my arm was killing me my last few years [in Baltimore]. I went out to see a doctor in Los Angeles. He was a big horse racing fan and owned a bunch of thoroughbreds, and he examined me and called me back into his office and said, 'Well, the best thing I can tell you is that if you were a horse we'd shoot you.' That was after the '72 season.

"He said they'd tried an operation on a couple of football quarterbacks for the same thing I had, and they never threw again. So I just went out and pitched in pain. I was still winning some games, but I was getting away with murder. My breaking balls weren't breaking sharply, and I'd lost all the pop on my fastball. It just wasn't the same. Plus, my arm and shoulder were just dying.

"The Orioles could tell my arm was shot. I had the right to OK a trade because I was a veteran, and I had given them a list of teams I'd go to, and they called the night before the deadline and said, 'Montreal wasn't one of the teams you listed, but would you go there?' I went back and forth between wanting to go, my arm killing me and thinking new scenery might rejuvenate me. I talked to the guy representing me, and he said, 'Hell, let's give it a go.'"

Frank Cashen: "I had heard that [Montreal's] Gene Mauch was a manager who would turn on a guy and hate him, and he had something against Singleton. I went to see [Montreal GM] John McHale and made the deal because McNally was at the end of the rope. I also gave them Coggins, who was a nice young player. McNally went up there and didn't do much, and John McHale still claims I knew there was something wrong with McNally when I sent him up there."

Boog Powell: "I'd had a shoulder problem that I'd been playing with all year in '74. I had like eight cortisone shots in my right shoulder, and I couldn't raise my arm even to brush my teeth. I just kept going out there, and I was playing first, and you don't have to make too many real great throws or anything. But the problem was that hitting, I couldn't get at anything inside. And the pitchers found out and exploited that. After the season, rumors were out that I was going to be traded. Enos Cabell was coming along, and they were grooming him to be the next first baseman. I saw the handwriting on the wall. It didn't take a mental giant to figure out that they really wanted this kid to play, because he could fly. And they thought he had some power; they thought he could hit.

"I was a little disappointed that I didn't have any more value than Dave Duncan. And Don Hood went along with me for Dave Duncan. I asked Earl about it, and he said, 'It wasn't my trade.' That's all he would say. Jerry [Hoffberger] called me up, and I said, 'Thanks for all of the things you've done for us over the years.' He was kind of shaken up. It was the end of an era. His voice was quivering."

PAUL BLAIR: "Age is going to catch up to everybody. We understood that. There was no problem letting the transition happen. I'd been there thirteen years, but I had no problem moving on. I wish Frank had stayed and we all had stayed and retired in Baltimore, which would have been much better. But when you don't win, you make changes. And the biggest change was sending Frank out. If they don't, we probably would have won, and then they wouldn't make a lot of changes, and maybe we could have stayed and retired, and they could have filtered in Baylor and Grich. But that one key trade knocked everything out of whack."

28

Cakes

On Opening Day in '75, Jim Palmer pitched a three-hitter and the Orioles beat the Tigers. By the time Palmer pitched again five days later, the Orioles were in fourth place. So went their '75 season. Palmer was brilliant, winning his second Cy Young Award with a 23–11 record, a 2.09 ERA, 25 complete games, and 10 shutouts in 323 innings, but the rest of the Orioles couldn't follow his lead, and the club failed to reach the playoffs for only the second time since '69.

The problem was an unusually slow start leaving them 10 games under .500 in late May and still three games under .500 at the All-Star break. Their usual late-season rally pulled them within three and one-half games of the Boston Red Sox with a week left, but the threat was never serious, and the Sox ended up four and one-half games better. Palmer's final shutout, in the season's penultimate game, gave the Orioles 90 wins.

Palmer didn't carry the whole load. Although Brooks Robinson hit just .201 and was nearing the end of his career, he won his 16th straight and final Gold Glove. Paul Blair won his seventh straight Gold Glove and eighth overall. Mark Belanger won his third in a row and fifth overall. Bob Grich won his third in a row. Right-hander Mike Torrez, one of two players acquired from Montreal for Dave McNally, was a 20-game winner in his first year in the American League. Ken Singleton, also acquired for McNally, batted leadoff, hit .300, and set a club record with 118 walks. Lee May, acquired from Cincinnati to replace Boog Powell at first base, had 20 homers and 99 RBI.

DON PRIES: "Frank Cashen had dispatched me to go scout the Expos in 1974, and I came back with a simple report: 'Whatever it takes, go get Ken Singleton. He's an excellent young player who can do it all.' In the end that was one of the better trades the Orioles made."

DAVE MCNALLY: "As shot as my arm was, the Orioles made a fantastic trade to get Torrez and Singleton. Even if I'd been healthy and throwing good, that was a good trade."

KEN SINGLETON: "The night before the trade, Mike [Torrez] and I were out with our wives, and the Orioles had just traded for Lee May. We were talking about it during dinner, you know, 'The Orioles are going to be good; Lee May's a good hitter.' The next morning at six o'clock, my phone rings, wakes me up, and it's Torrez. He says, 'Ken, I got news; I just got traded to Baltimore.' I said, 'We were just talking about that last night.' He says, 'Yeah, I know. I'm going to Baltimore.' And I said, 'Man, you're going to a good club; you're really going to enjoy it; I'm going to miss you.' He says, 'No, you don't understand; you're going with me.' I said, 'What do you mean? Nobody's called me.' He said, 'As soon as you hang up, the phone's going to ring.'

"About two weeks into spring training, Weaver calls me in the office and asks, 'Have you ever led off before?' I said, 'No. I think the most bases I ever stole was about six.' He said, 'That's not the idea. The idea is to have somebody to get on base, and you and Grich are the only two guys on this team willing to take a walk, so you're going to bat first, and he'll bat second.' And I said, 'Well, I'm not going to steal.' I think I stole three bases that year, but that wasn't the idea. He wanted men on base in front of Lee May.

"On Opening Day, my first time up in the American League, batting leadoff in Detroit, I walked. Went to third on a base hit by Tommy Davis, and then Lee May hit a three-run homer in his first at-bat in the American League. He comes around and comes into the dugout and looks at Weaver and says, 'I think I'm going to like this fucking league.' And Palmer pitched a three-hit shutout, first of 25 complete games and 325 innings that year. Unbelievable. Talk about things that just don't happen anymore. We started off well that year, but we played poorly in May, and that's what really set us back."

Singleton and May were additions that would prove lasting and meaningful. May was a fixture in the lineup for the rest of the '70s and a commanding clubhouse presence. Singleton would spend the rest of his career with the Orioles, delivering hits and solid overall play for a decade.

DOUG DeCINCES: "Lee May and Donnie Baylor had the most authority in the clubhouse of anyone I was ever around. Lee just had infinite wisdom in so many areas."

ELROD HENDRICKS: "Lee was fantastic, like a father figure. He nurtured rookies until he felt they could be on their own and he saw they were doing things just right. Lee would go out and buy the rookies a suit. And he'd see guys doing things, and he'd say, 'Hey, hey, son, come here, we gotta talk. You just don't do that, you know.'"

KEN SINGLETON: "Lee just had a strong personality. When you look at baseball teams there are certain guys I would say who, they don't have to be the star players, but they are the ones that everybody kind of goes to and leans toward for advice. That was Lee. He was a terrific addition to the team."

In the end, the '75 season belonged to Palmer, who was at the peak of his powers at age twenty-nine, with his high leg kick, riding fastball, and peerless command confounding hitters. He struck out 193 and walked only 80—typical numbers for a pitcher who knew he had top fielders behind him. The 20-win season was already the fifth of his career and the first of another run of four straight. (He also had won 20 every year from 1970 to 1973.) At a time when the Orioles' starting rotation from their World Series years was breaking up, with McNally gone and Cuellar slowing down, James Alvin Palmer was just getting better.

He would lead the pitching staff for the rest of the decade, helping tutor a new generation that included Mike Flanagan, Scott McGregor, and Dennis Martinez. When he finally retired in '84 as the greatest pitcher in Orioles history, he had 268 wins, 53 shutouts, 211 complete games, more than 2,200 strikeouts, and almost 4,000 innings pitched. He never gave up a grand slam, he won four pennant-clinching games, and, in the end, he was only the third pitcher in American League history to win 20 games eight times. His selection to the Hall of Fame was assured.

Palmer would become a lasting symbol of the franchise itself—smart and imperious, demanding and generous, forever complaining about various ailments. He constantly feuded with manager Earl Weaver—his opposite in size, looks, and playing ability, but his twin as a baseball savant and self-appointed smartest guy in any room. Nicknamed "Cakes" in the '60s for his habit of eating pancakes for breakfast on the days he pitched, Palmer was a portrait of elegance on the mound, mixing pitches, speeds, and locations. Some teammates resented him and others accepted him as a driven, demanding talent, but they all respected him and wanted him on the mound for any games that had to be won. That was the ultimate compliment.

JIM PALMER: "I played for great teams and had great guys to emulate. I remember a game [Pat] Dobson pitched in '71, beat Oakland 1–0. He threw breaking balls and change-ups the first two times around [the order] and then blew them away [with fastballs] the last time around. He could change gears. I saw that. Then I saw the tenaciousness and intensity of McNally. In '69 he was going for his 20th win at the end of August, and Weaver takes him out for a pinch hitter, and he throws the bat and throws the helmet and the jacket. Goes into the trainer's room, and Earl follows him in there, and Dave says, 'All you care about is yourself. I'm out here busting my butt for you, trying to win 20 games, and all you care about is winning 112 and breaking the old record [for wins in a season].' Earl started to cry.

"You saw Cuellar. He was as good as any pitcher in that four-year period [from '70 through '73]. Probably should have won a couple of Cy Young Awards. You saw the ability to change speeds. And you also saw him mess around in drills and then all of a sudden, instead of winning 20, he was winning 16 or 18. Maybe not taking it quite as seriously. That was the great thing. You could decide who you wanted to be like.

"There was nothing like being on a winning team. Baltimore was a great place to play. Great place to raise your children. Memorial Stadium was one of the best-kept fields. You could pitch away and keep the ball in the ballpark. All in all, all I had to do was worry about myself. I didn't have to worry about anyone else. They were going to catch it and hit and whatever.

"Robin Roberts taught me a lot when I was a rookie. They roomed us together in '65. I was nineteen, he was thirty-eight, and they thought I might learn something. He still jokes about how I used to put him to sleep. He'd go, 'Kid, just go to sleep; stop asking so many questions.' My nickname was 'Brash' because I used to ask so many questions. But we had so many veterans you could talk to. Dick Hall and Harvey Haddix and Stu Miller. I was just there. Robin told me, 'the best pitch in baseball is the fastball, and you have a great one; I hope you're smart enough to realize that.' Also 'rock back and get your arm out in front. And don't walk many people.' Great advice.

"As I went along, the things I benefited from were more experience, better health, coming up with a change-up. And [pitching coach George] Bamberger was terrific. In [Class-A] Aberdeen [in '64] I led the league in walks, wild pitches, strikeouts, and ERA. He'd have me work on my windup without a ball. And all of a sudden I was getting the ball around the strike zone more. Then [in the '70s] McNally and Cuellar, their careers were winding down and I was able to get weaned into the position of being the number-one starter.

"The ability was there. Before the '70 Series Jim Russo was giving a scouting report, and the Reds were all high fastball hitters, and I was pitching the first game, and we got to about the sixth or seventh high fastball hitter, and I raised my hand and said, 'Earl, why am I pitching? They all pound the high fastball.' And he said, 'Not your high fastball.'"

DAVE MCNALLY: "Palmer had a very live fastball. Very good control. Very intelligent. He just knew what to do and not to do when he was pitching and did it for years. I don't know what the radar gun [speed] was, but it wasn't overwhelming; it was just how he delivered the ball—a very live fastball that got on you quicker than it looked like it would."

BOOG POWELL: "Jimmy was so smart. He took a lesson from McNally—how to add a little bit to a fastball or take a little bit off. That was one of Jimmy's strongest suits in the end, the ability to make that fastball either ninety-five or ninety-two [miles per hour]. I don't know how he did it. That's all it takes. But he was still a power pitcher, more so than Cuellar or McNally. The other two were more or less magicians. And they were great. I guess what set Jimmy apart was his fastball. That and his ability to change speeds, which was incredible."

KEN SINGLETON: "Whenever he said his shoulder hurt or his neck hurt or anything, that meant he was going to have a good game. He was going to pitch well. When Jim was quiet and didn't say anything was bothering him, I was worried that something wasn't right, that he wasn't going to pitch well. But when something was wrong, he was going to be the best, and he was the best."

PAUL BLAIR: "Palmer's ego was just as big as Reggie [Jackson's]. There's no question about that. When he was young, Frank [Robinson] kept him in line.

He was a key part of the team, but he wasn't the team. McNally and Cuellar had more success at that time. How was Palmer going to outshine them when they're doing better? Once we were all out of there, then he was more of the team, because he was the only one left.

"He loved Jim Palmer, but hey, that's OK, you can love yourself. I mean, that's quite all right. He pitched well, but I think he owes a lot to Earl. When [Hank] Bauer was the manager and [Palmer] didn't have his number-one stuff, he really didn't want to pitch. If he didn't have his number-one fastball, sometimes he might feel a twinge here and there and come out of the game. But Earl made him pitch. He'd say, 'You can hurt all you want to, you're going nine.'

"So Palmer learned to get his fastball over, his curveball over, and he learned to pitch because, under Earl, he was going nine. He was not going to go five or six and say, 'I got this twinge in my back,' which Bauer would take him out for. Earl made Palmer learn to pitch, and he became a real, real good pitcher. But he was a little baby, and Earl made him kind of grow up a little bit."

MIKE FLANAGAN: "Palmer was the leader among the pitchers. He showed us how to run, how to pitch. I was a maximum effort guy on every pitch, and that's when you don't know what you're doing and the only thing you can do is go max effort. So he'd say stuff like, 'Well, you're not using your fastball enough,' and proceed to go out and pitch a game and throw 122 pitches, of which 116 were fastballs. Well, that's pretty good. What I'd always heard [from coaches] was, 'You're not throwing your fastball enough, but I can't go out there and show you.' That's what Jim did. He would go right out there and do it, and the rest of us would see it."

BOB GRICH: "Palmer had pure, raw talent with that fastball in the high nineties with some jump on it, and that big, slow hook. Plus, he was quick off the mound. Like a big cat. Helped himself in the field. And he was very smart, had a great memory. Just a very intelligent guy. He remembered situations from three years earlier. He could recall everything. He amazed me. He'd tell you, 'Move over one step to the left,' and sure enough, the ball came right to you. Some guys didn't like it when he moved them around. Blair didn't like it. But I always felt, if Palmer wanted me to play somewhere, I was going to play there. When he got beat it was usually poor defense. Because he always kept you in the game. I don't remember him getting really beat up. When he lost it was 4–3 or 3–2, and usually someone made an error."

KEN SINGLETON: "Playing behind him, he didn't like you making mistakes. Not many pitchers do. I can remember, I made not an error, but a play he didn't like. And I didn't like what he did. He stared out at me in right field. The run scored, and I remember going up the tunnel—it was in Kansas City—and just throwing everything because I was really ticked. Then I got quiet and calmed down and sat down next to him, and I said, 'Good thing you weren't in the tunnel.' He didn't look at me like that anymore. He was a perfectionist. I mean the guy wanted everything to be perfect. If he made a good pitch [and got beat], somebody screwed up."

BOOG POWELL: "Jimmy would move Paulie [Blair] over in center, and Earl would run out on the mound and move him back. And they would have a few words, and then after Earl got back in the dugout Jimmy would move [Blair] back; Jimmy knew what he was doing. He knew how to pitch. And never one time did he make a mistake. Paulie was always at the right place. But he'd come in, and he and Earl would go down the runway, and there were some really good shots taken. Then the next day it was forgotten. They were smiling and laughing."

MIKE FLANAGAN: "From my view, the thing between Palmer and Weaver was more philosophical. It was nothing really personal. They would go at it in the dugout, you know, 'Why are we doing this? Why are we throwing this pitch in this situation?' Little things."

BOB GRICH: "Palmer would say, 'Get the guy out this way,' and Weaver would say, 'No, get him out that way.' They had many differences of opinion over certain guys. Plus, Weaver wasn't always a huge fan of small ball. He never played for one run, especially in the first six or seven innings. He wanted guys on base for the three-run homer. Palmer would say, 'Why don't we hit-and-run more? We're not hitting; let's get one run.' But Weaver was the eternal optimist. Stuff like that got between them all the time."

PAUL BLAIR: "The fights between them were father and son, that's exactly what they were, because both of 'em wanted to get the last word. I don't care what it was, Earl wanted to get the last word, and then Palmer was going to get the last word in, too. They went back and forth like that. And we would have our meetings when we would go over hitters, and they would be arguing, and Earl would say, 'We're going to pitch from this end.' And Jim would say, 'No, Earl, I think it's best that we do this and this.' And it got to the point of, 'Well this is what we're going to do, guys.' Everybody on the pitching staff pitching one way, and Palmer his way. That's the way our meetings went. But it was all in good fun and good nature. There were no ill feelings toward anybody. Just both of 'em had egos."

EARL WEAVER: "Many a time I was very aggravated, and I'm sure Jim was too at times. I don't know what he had to get aggravated about, but he certainly did get aggravated. He was Mr. Perfection; it had to be perfect, and if everything wasn't perfect, then it wasn't right. You've got to accept some little shit. Not injuries or anything like that, but when things don't go right, you've got to accept it. He didn't want to. But he was a good pitcher."

RICK DEMPSEY: "I was in the middle between Palmer and Weaver. One of the reasons Earl was such a great manager was he knew how to press some buttons on certain players. He was hard. He was not a soft manager at all. He wanted things done a certain way. He wanted to win more than anything. Palmer was one of the most knowledgeable pitchers I ever caught—and one of the most talented at the same time. He knew how to pitch. The only thing Earl could really help him with was to get his intensity level up. And Earl knew how to do that, and that was fight him. Try to tell him how to do something, and that would inspire Palmer to try to find a better way. He would try to tell Jim how to do certain things. Every player makes mistakes, I don't care who you are; and Weaver would capitalize on Palmer's mistakes, and the more he brought it up, the more Jim would go out to prove him wrong. That was Earl's approach, and it worked.

"When Earl got on Jim about pitching, he knew what kind of a reaction he was going to get. I remember Earl going to the mound one time to tell Jimmy how to pitch to the next hitter. I was standing in the background. It was always kind of embarrassing for me when they started arguing and fighting. And Palmer turned around and told Earl, 'The only thing you know about pitching was you couldn't hit it. Now get off the mound.' They would get so upset with each other that they'd start firing barbs at each other. A lot of it was just show, I think, to see which one was more clever. Because neither one could do without the other. Both benefited greatly from that relationship. Palmer made Weaver a better manager, and Weaver made Palmer a better pitcher."

JIM PALMER: "Earl couldn't even see what was going on out there most of the time. But he was a bottom-line guy, and so was I. The problems came with the gray area in that bottom line. He wanted to win; I wanted to win. But he was annoying. I'd sit there and listen to him, and he'd second-guess everybody. A guy would pop up in the second inning with a man at third and less than two outs, and he'd exhale and make a big scene, and Lee May would say, 'Hey, the little genius gave up; let's go get 'em.' I mean, guys would laugh.

"You could laugh about them because we won so much over the course of fourteen or fifteen years that it made it palatable. But there were times when we weren't playing well that it became so annoying that you just reacted to it. You'd be out there struggling—and I don't care if you're in the Hall of Fame, there are times when you struggle—and he'd be up there on the top step tapping his foot.

"He just had a level of expectation, and I guess he felt that even though it made my life difficult, I was professional enough not to let it affect what happened out there. And most of the time it didn't matter if he yelled at me or screamed or whatever. It wasn't going to affect my performance, and it might even enhance it sometimes. And he knew that. That's why I got to the Hall of Fame. Because he gave me the responsibility of winning my own ball games. He'd run out there and say, 'There's no one better out there [in the bullpen]. You can do this.' And that belief fosters a self-belief.

"We didn't always show respect for each other, but I think we had it. He would come out and ask me if I was trying. One time Belanger makes two errors, Boog loses a ball in the sun, they score a couple of runs in the first inning, and he comes out and asks me if I'm trying. I said, 'You made out the lineup. You put the shortstop out there. Why don't you go over there and ask the big boy [Powell] if he's trying? He might just step on you and squash you. If you don't have anything worthwhile to say, why don't you just get out of here?' And he looked at me kind of funny and left. But the bottom line is we were out there trying to do the same thing."

FRANK CASHEN: "Jim and I had some memorable sessions negotiating contracts. I'd sit him down and say, 'Jim, you had a great year. I can't argue with anything you did. But you know the kind of money we make, and you know what things are like here, and you had a good year, so what do you think?' And he'd say, 'Well, I think I deserve a ten-thousand-dollar raise. And I would say not that high, and he'd say, 'How about eight thousand dollars?' and I'd say, 'Jeez, I was thinking more about five.' And he would say, 'Well, you're the guy.' Then we'd pause, and I'd say, 'Hey, I don't want to disappoint you, I mean, you think you deserve that. I don't want to give you five. How about seven? We'll go to seven, and I'll give you the hammer this year. And he'd say 'No, all right, eight. Forget about the hammer.' And then the next year I would remind him that he had the hammer last year. But in all the years, I never said to him, 'You don't deserve it.' That was a phrase that never came up when you were dealing with Jim Palmer. Because he deserved everything and more. He was the best."

BOOG POWELL: "If you had to pick one guy to win a game, he was my guy. As much as I loved Mike Cuellar, and as much as I loved Dave McNally and Pat Dobson, and you can go all the way back to Milt Pappas, who was a hell of a pitcher, if I had one game to win, Palmer was on the mound for me."

29

The Last Class

With the Orioles on their way to another American League East title in '74 and a new young generation of players in the lineup, another championship team was forming in the farm system. On a Class-A team in Miami, Florida, a Double-A team in Asheville, North Carolina, and a Triple-A team in Rochester, the Orioles' last great class of prospects was beginning a journey that would end with division titles, World Series appearances, and awards.

In '74 Miami had three players who would ultimately play a combined 64 seasons in the major leagues, a majority with the Orioles—first baseman Eddie Murray and pitchers Mike Flanagan and Dennis Martinez. A level above, Asheville had Rich Dauer, who would become a fixture at second base for the Orioles. Third baseman Doug DeCinces, who would soon take on the challenge of replacing Brooks Robinson, was at Rochester. Together, they would constitute much of the heart of the Orioles' last great homegrown team, which would win two AL pennants and a World Series title and consistently contend from '77 to '83.

DeCinces signed in '70, and Murray, Flanagan, Martinez, and Dauer all signed in a twelve-month period that began with the '73 amateur draft. The Orioles selected Murray, a high school catcher from Los Angeles, in the third round and Flanagan, a pitcher from the University of Massachusetts, in the seventh round. Martinez, a waif from Nicaragua, signed as a free agent in December of '73. Six months later, Dauer, an All-American shortstop from Southern California, the nation's top college program, was picked in the first round of the '74 draft.

For more than a decade, the Orioles' farm system had produced identifiable generations of talent, starting with Milt Pappas, Steve Barber, and the "Kiddie Corps" pitchers in 1960. After that came Dave McNally, Boog Powell, Wally Bunker, and Jim Palmer in the early '60s, and then a sprawling group including Paul Blair, Andy Etchebarren, Davey Johnson, and Mark Belanger. After that came a premium class featuring Don Baylor and Bob Grich. Al Bumbry and Rich Coggins arrived together in '73.

In years to come the Orioles would continue to draft and develop major league talent such as Cal Ripken Jr., Mike Boddicker, Storm Davis, and Mike Mussina. But never again would a crop of players move through the system, reach Baltimore together, and spend almost a decade on the field, winning games and challenging for pennants. The Orioles ultimately would lose their touch after years of producing generations of players, a loss that would haunt the franchise for the rest of the century. DeCinces, Murray, Flanagan, Martinez, and Dauer were the last class. But what a class.

DOUG DECINCES: "After I got drafted I went to [rookie league] Bluefield and started off playing second, left, and first. All spot playing. Never played third, even though I'd been all-state in junior college in California. The first couple of weeks were not very positive. There were two of us on the bench, not playing. Me and Bob Bailor—the only two guys off the team that made it.

"Then [scouting director] Walter Shannon came through and said, 'Wait a minute; I saw this kid play. Give him a chance.' I got in the lineup and hit a homer, and the next day I made some plays. Shannon said, 'Get prepared; you're playing every day.' I don't know what they thought exactly. Don Pries told me, 'You're never going to hit 20 homers [in a season]. You need to spread your feet and hit the other way.' When I hit my 20th in the big leagues years later, I had the batboy get the ball and I sent it to Pries. I wrote on the ball, 'Here's my 20th home run that you said I would never hit.'

"The next year [in '71] I went to Dallas, played second, and sustained a very serious injury on the field. I was going back on a ball, and the center-fielder never called me off, and we collided. I had nineteen fractures in my face. I think the Orioles had serious doubts about whether I'd come back. I didn't play the rest of the season. I remember waking up in the hospital and watching [Detroit's Mickey] Lolich beat the Orioles on TV. I was wondering if I'd ever get a chance.

"Once I got well, Cal Ripken, who had been the manager in Dallas, came to me and said, 'Do you want to go to the instructional league?' We went down there, and he worked with me until I was ready to stick my face back in there and get a ground ball. I give Cal a lot of credit. It took me a while.

My nose and cheeks were broken, and they had to rebuild my sinus cavities. I was a mess. Every bad hop I had to regroup. But I finally got over it."

DON PRIES: "I was the assistant to Frank Cashen in '73, and he sent me out to scout the West Coast. I was to come back and give my opinion as far as who I felt we should draft. I flew out, went to Southern Cal and saw a short-stop, went to Garr High School in Los Angeles and saw a catcher, and then went to San Diego and saw an outfielder. And I told them this is the way you draft—the shortstop at USC first. That was Richie Dauer. Then the outfielder from San Diego second. His name was Don Whiting. And then you take the catcher from Garr High School third. He can't catch, but I believe he's going to hit someday, and he'll probably end up at first base. His name was Eddie Murray. Dauer went in the first round [in '74]. Don Whiting had three out-standing years in the minors and then damaged a knee and never played again. And Murray became a Hall of Famer."

AL KUBSKI: "I was scouting for the Angels by then. Still had the same area in California. I saw Murray a lot. He put me to sleep. He wasn't a high-energy player."

RAY POITEVINT: "How could you not take a guy about six [feet], three [inches] with a powerful body, and when he swung the ball went about ten miles? He could do anything he wanted. He could bring the bat through there. He could catch. He was messing around with switch-hitting. He could run. Just a good, powerful, strong guy. Maybe if he had been a little more energetic someone would have taken him higher. I talked our scouting direc-tor into it. I said, 'Get this guy for sure.'

"I probably saw him [in high school] seven or eight times, starting when he was a sophomore. I never talked to him. I talked to his older brothers, who had played some ball. Before the draft I went to the house and asked what their thoughts were. I felt I had a good rapport with the family. The mother was in charge—a really nice person. The family was good people.

"It was a really tough signing because Baltimore didn't have a lot of money. We signed first-round picks for twenty thousand dollars when the average was about fifty thousand to seventy thousand dollars. Dauer got twenty thousand dollars. That's all we had. With Eddie I took sixteen trips into his home and still had the same amount on the table. I gave them what I had—sixteen thousand. They thought I had more in my pocket, and I didn't. It took me a long time to convince them I was telling the truth. Eddie wanted to play baseball, but they just kept hammering away. We finally got him."

EDDIE MURRAY: "I went down to the instructional league, and we shared a team with the Yankees. There were maybe four Orioles coaches and four Yankees coaches. I just felt like I was in the right spot [with the Orioles] right away, meeting Cal Ripken. You know, work was something you liked. Flanny, Kiko Garcia, Dauer, and Dennis, that was my class. I never played with Baylor or Grich, but they had a feeling for me when I first came up. Even before I did anything, I had on an Orioles uniform. That made me something special. I almost felt those guys were brothers. That was the way I felt about it. Even when [Grich and Baylor] left and went to the Angels [as free agents], I felt like they still wanted to be with us. There just wasn't enough room."

AL KUBSKI: "Murray went to Miami [in '74] and hit .290 or so, and then to Double A [Asheville] in '75 and started slow, still hitting just right-handed. The manager there is a guy named Jim Schaffer, who was a catcher in the major leagues, and Eddie is hitting .210, and breaking balls are tailing away from him, and Schaffer wants to get rid of him. He's sending in reports [to the Orioles] saying, 'Get me a first baseman; I can't stand this damn Murray.'

"Then one day they had a morning workout, and Schaffer noticed him swinging from the left side, and Schaffer asked him, 'Did you ever hit left-handed?' Eddie said, 'Well, I tried in high school.' Schaffer said, 'You ought to try it. You can't hit the slider or a breaking ball the way things are going.' So Eddie tried it after practice, and he did pretty good. And he wound up going with it, and it really helped him because he didn't have to worry about the breaking ball tailing away from him anymore."

RAY POITEVINT: "Eddie could do whatever he wanted to do. It just took him a little time to wake up, that's all. He was a kid, and he didn't like practice and all that. He had a lot of skills he didn't realize he had when he was eighteen, nineteen. He was just a kid who didn't want to do stuff. But as he got older, he realized he could be good."

MIKE FLANAGAN: "I was playing at UMass [in '73], and we were playing the University of Maine, and it was the only time the Orioles really scouted me.

A scout named John Stokoe came to watch. At the time I was being visited a lot by Mets scouts, a guy who had played with my dad in the early '50s. There was a tie there, that I was Ed Flanagan's kid, so he seemed to be around a lot.

"I didn't pitch against Maine that day, but I hit three home runs. The draft wasn't too long after that, and Stokoe called at home and said I'd been picked in the seventh round. And they said, 'We'd like you to sign and go to Miami, but we're not sure if it's as a hitter or a pitcher.' I was flattered because I figured I'd be able to go the furthest as a pitcher.

"So I signed and went to Miami within a week or so. I can remember saying to myself, 'Boy, this pro ball is tough. A lot of guys here are better than anything I saw in college.' You had a lot of roommates through the course of the summer. We had tremendous changeover. I said, 'Boy, this is a rough business, and I'm four steps away [from the majors], and they just had four 20-game winners in Baltimore. I'm going to be here a while.' I went 6–4 and got my feet wet, but I really didn't see myself as better than anybody.

"The next year [in Miami] there was me and Eddie and Dennis. How many guys can say they had three guys on their A-ball team play twenty years in the major leagues? I'm proud of that. Eddie was still a straight right-handed hitter. I was really dominating the league. I was twenty-one by then, and there were a lot of kids in that league who were sixteen or seventeen. I had 120 strikeouts or so in 100 innings, starting to feel good, and got called up to Asheville in late June of '74.

"The ballpark there had a short porch in right field, and there were a lot of left-handers in the organization at the time, and there was a certain reluctance to pitch in that ballpark. Not knowing any better, I said, 'Rip, I'll be glad to pitch. Take the ball every fourth day.' I just wanted to get through that league and get to Triple A. And I had a good year for Rip, a good half-year, passed a lot of guys by, and the next spring [of '75] was with the Triple-A club. A good group. They were used to winning because the team in Baltimore was always so good and a lot of guys were stuck below that.

"That year I won 13 games. Mike Willis, who later went to Toronto in the expansion draft, won 15. Mike Reinbach, Royle Stillman, those guys all hit .330. We had a really good Triple-A team. That's where I learned the value of teamwork. We had Kiko Garcia at shortstop, Larry Harlow in center field, Reinbach, Stillman, Jim Fuller, guys who were all-around players and had had a taste of the big leagues. We were good, a really good team, and I could see where that could really help me as a pitcher, being on a team this good. They caught the ball, threw it, did things right. That's where I really started to learn my craft, what pitching was all about."

RAY POITEVINT: "A guy named Julio Blanco Herrera had a beer distributing firm Jerry Hoffberger used in Miami. Julio was pushing [beer] in Central America and went down there a lot. Julio was a real baseball buff. Beer was his business; baseball was his hobby. He told Jerry there were a lot of ballplayers down there. Julio couldn't tell a ballplayer from an elephant, but he told Jerry they played a lot of ball in Nicaragua. And there were no scouts there, so I went.

"I went to see a kid named Tony Chavez pitch, and he was pretty good, and I signed him. I started going down there four times a year. I met a Cuban manager by the name of Tony Castano. The following year we're sitting in the dugout watching the [Nicaragua] national team work out, and Tony Castano says, 'Ray, there's a kid out there with a good hook.' I'm watching him from about 250 feet away. He's in the bullpen. I see him. Tony's right; he has a good curve. It's a kid named Dennis Martinez. He's the tenth pitcher on the team. The national team had, like, thirty-four-year-old guys on it.

"The following day he had a chance to pitch three or four innings. I saw him and said, 'I want to sign him.' I got Julio to get hold of the mother, and she came to the hotel, and I signed him. Two days later there were a dozen scouts in the stands, and the pitcher gets hurt, and they bring in Dennis. He pitched the rest of the game and shut the other team down with about six strikeouts. Here come all the scouts. They're trying to get his attention. I took him through the first-base dugout and got the hell out of there. It was illegal, actually, because he had signed, and you couldn't pitch as a pro in that tournament. But in those days you had to do that stuff. Before they caught up with me, I was on a plane."

DENNIS MARTINEZ: "Tony Castano was a Cuban who was in charge of the national team. He'd played for a long time and managed in Mexico and played with a lot of people professionally. So he knew a lot of people, and he knew Julio Herrera. I was on the national team, the amateur team that participated in the Olympics and the World Series tournament. The scouts came after Chavez and saw me pitch a little bit. I was a different kind of pitcher. I was throwing more breaking balls. Chavez was throwing fast. Real hard.

After Chavez signed, I went to Castano and said, 'Hey, I'd like to sign, too.' Tony said he'd see what he could do. He talked to Ray Poitevint and Julio. I was in my first year at a university, studying to be a civil engineer. [Signing] was more like a favor thing [from the Orioles]. The money wasn't big.

"I played the first two years on the baby Orioles in Miami. Flanny was a little older than me, and I was a little older than Eddie. We had a pretty good team. The manager was a guy named George Farson. The organization was very tight. It wasn't an easy place to get to the major leagues. There was a lot of talent. But I knew I was ahead of a lot of kids, basically because of the way Tony Castano prepared me. He had all that pro experience, and he trained me well. Plus I'd played with a national team, so I'd played against older kids. That was an advantage for me. So I was able to dominate right off the bat."

MIKE FLANAGAN: "Dennis weighed maybe 135 pounds soaking wet. You could put your thumb and index finger together and go around his biceps. But what a wonderful arm. You could see he had it all. Loose, limber. I mean, his sideline [sessions between starts] were better than anybody's games. He was that good. You could see it. But he didn't speak any English, and the manager would go to the mound to talk to him, and Dennis would just nod yes to everything. 'How do you feel? Do you feel pretty good? Are you tired?' Dennis would just continue to nod and then get taken out of the game and get all upset and say, 'I didn't want to come out of the game; I was just nodding yes.'"

RAY POITEVINT: "Dennis looked like a pencil. But he had natural talent, as much as anyone. And he was hungry. He wanted to be something."

DENNIS MARTINEZ: "I had a lot of determination. Coming from another country, a small country, to a big nation where you had to compete, the chances were a million-to-one that you make it. But between my skill and my determination, I beat the odds. Most of my friends at the university, when they found out I had signed, they said, 'Well, in a week or two we'll see you back here again.' Like I was just like everyone else. So I said, 'How much you want to bet?' I think I kind of grasped that as motivation, to prove to them that they were wrong. That became my way of survival.

"Toward July [in '75] I went from Miami to Asheville and then got called up to Rochester at the end of the year. I was putting up some good numbers.

They couldn't stop me from getting to the major leagues. There's always people looking for a reason not to give you the opportunity. But I didn't give them a chance. My numbers were really good. They had to give me a chance.

"My stuff was decent. I had a good curveball. My fastball was decent. My curveball made my fastball better. Everyone was aware of my curveball, so my fastball went right by them. But mostly, I had a big heart. When you have a big heart, that hunger, that desire, you show all you got. When you do that, you go to the next level. It isn't the stuff you have, it's how you execute it. With desire, determination, that's how I did it. That made my stuff as good as anyone's."

RAY POITEVINT: "Everyone knew about Rich Dauer. He was the shortstop at USC and led the nation in hitting. But the Orioles had a rule that you couldn't draft a college kid unless he could start at Double A. [USC coach] Rod Dedeaux told all his players that playing at USC was like Double A. So we drafted him and signed him, and he went to Double A, and pitchers were throwing balls past him left and right. He had a tough adjustment. His first year was tough. But at the same time, anything he could touch he could catch, and he was a tough guy, a winner type of person. Once he got past the early stuff, he adjusted. He'd been a winner all his life. He was perfect for the Orioles."

30

Stirring the Drink

On paper, the '76 season was one of the Orioles' dullest under manager Earl Weaver. Their usual slow start and a nine-game losing streak in early June left them far behind the Yankees, and they never made up much ground despite playing almost .600 ball over the last three months. The Yankees led by ten and a half games at the start of August and ten and a half after the season's final pitch.

But beneath that bland surface, one of the Orioles' most tumultuous seasons played out. It was the year Reggie Jackson made a brief, controversial stop in Baltimore, the year Doug DeCinces replaced Brooks Robinson at third base, and the year free agency hit the Orioles like a slap in the face. There was a run of jolting news in '76.

The club entered a new era in the front office before the season when executive vice president Frank Cashen left to return to owner Jerry Hoffberger's brewery, and Hank Peters was hired as the new general manager. Peters was a veteran executive who had worked in several major league front offices and most recently run the National Association of Professional Baseball Leagues.

Peters took over the Orioles in December '75, one week after arbitrator Peter Seitz's landmark ruling that players who played for a season without a signed contract could become free agents. Suddenly, baseball was on the doorstep of a new era with free agency starting in the fall of '76. No one knew how it would play out, and in the beginning, no team was affected more than the Orioles.

Jackson, Oakland's powerful cleanup hitter, had the right to become a free agent after the '76 season, and penny-pinching owner Charles Finley sought to trade him rather than pay an inflated salary. The Orioles gave up Don Baylor and Mike Torrez in a deal consummated late in spring training. The Orioles believed they could sign Jackson to a long-term contract, and they gave up a lot. Baylor had batted .282 with 25 homers the year before. Torrez had won 20 games.

Jackson balked at reporting until late April, when the Yankees already had a lead. Upon arriving, he hit poorly and irritated some teammates with his cockiness. But he played hard, heated up after the All-Star break, and ended up having a solid season—.277 with 27 homers and 91 RBI in 498 at-bats. When the Orioles failed to offer him a contract he wanted, he entered the free-agent pool after the season and signed with the Yankees.

HANK PETERS: "Frank [Cashen] told me when I started that we really needed a left-handed hitter. He thought he had a deal set up with the Mets to get Rusty Staub. Doug DeCinces was involved in that. But Frank said he wanted a black player. This is twenty-five years ago, and there wasn't a lot of black talent around. And lo and behold, Detroit came into the picture and traded Mickey Lolich to the Mets for Staub, and we got shut out on that one.

"Things kind of quieted down because of all the turmoil with the new reserve system and whether or not we were going to have a strike, and we finally got into spring training two or three weeks late. Finley and I had been talking some, and Finley said, 'Would you like to have Reggie?' Of course. I knew Reggie very well. He wanted Torrez, who was tough to give up. And I knew Baylor was popular. But Baylor was kind of one-dimensional in that he was an offensive player, not a defensive player, and he couldn't throw. And Reggie at that point was a complete player. He could run and throw and hit, and he had outstanding power. Guys like Reggie just don't come along every day.

"We finally worked it out. Finley wanted Mike Flanagan, but I was going to hold onto him. We finally made the deal. It was an emotional deal because Baylor was quite upset, but a deal was a deal so he had to go. Then Reggie said he wasn't sure he wanted to report or even play anymore, and this is after he'd been demanding a trade."

KEN SINGLETON: "One day in spring training, right in the middle of a game, Don Baylor was playing left field and then, boom, in the third [inning] he was out of the game. It was hard to figure out why, so when we came up to hit I went to the clubhouse, and he was sitting in the trainer's room, crying. Now, Donnie wasn't liable to cry about anything, so I asked what was up, and he said he'd been traded to Oakland. I felt so bad for him because he'd been with the team for six years. I finally got up the nerve to ask him what we'd gotten in return, and he said 'Reggie.' And I went, 'Oh, man.'

"Reggie played my position, right field. And they thought they could sign him to a long-term contract. But then Reggie took the rest of spring training off and held out for a bigger contract once the season started. Once he finally showed up, he had a great desire to win and ended up having a pretty good season. Off the field was another story, because the way he was wasn't the way the Orioles had been over the years. You never knew what you were going to get when Reggie came to the park. It was either the 'kind' Reggie or the 'I'm the man' Reggie. Some guys tiptoed around him. Me, I didn't care what he said. And neither did Earl. They had it out a few times."

ELROD HENDRICKS: "Reggie came here like a whirlwind. He was a month late, and we're struggling along, and he came and did a good job, but he would talk real loud in the clubhouse, 'Hey, who's this guy, what's a decline?' Meaning DeCinces. Then he said to poor Timmy Nordbrook, 'Gee, are you the batboy or something? I've never heard of you.' That was Reggie. The guys didn't really understand his sense of humor at first. Lee May sat him down and bucked him up a little. Reggie still tried to bend all the rules.

"We had to dress in a shirt, tie, and jacket on road trips, and he came one day without a tie. Earl said, 'Reggie, where's your tie?' Reggie says, 'I don't have one.' Earl says, 'Well, you find one or get the hell off the plane.' Reggie goes, 'I'm not leaving.' Earl says, 'This plane's not going until you get the hell off it and find a tie.' Dave Duncan gave him a cowboy string tie, and he put it on. Reggie was hot. He went up to Earl and made a big show. Earl said, 'Is that a tie?' Reggie said, 'It's a western tie.' He just was determined to do things his way. Earl said, 'OK, start the plane.'"

KEN SINGLETON: "Reggie was Reggie. He was used to being 'the straw that stirs the drink,' as he mentioned in New York later. I liked him. He was a good guy. But he was a star, and he knew it. I mean, not many guys could hit a ball as far as he could. There was one he hit in Kansas City that was unforgettable. [Royals manager] Whitey Herzog made a move to bring in Larry Gura to face Reggie with the bases loaded. Well, Reggie hit the first pitch to the back of the bullpen in right field. It hit the wall back there. That's close to 500 feet, if not 500. The fans were booing, and Whitey didn't want to go back out there, so he left Gura in to face Lee May, and Lee hit the next pitch to the back of the bullpen in left field. Those were the longest back-to-back home runs I've ever seen."

ROSS GRIMSLEY: "I got along with him. With some people he'd say hello one day and walk right past them the next day like he didn't see them, but we had a thing in common when he was there. We had CB radios and customized vans. I used to drive around and talk to Reggie on the CB going home after games. We'd shoot the bull on the CB. He had his moments, but he was a good guy and very generous with people."

EARL WEAVER: "It cost us the season that Reggie came in late because he had no spring training, and he hit .160 until the All-Star break. He told me, 'Listen, I'll take this league over after the All-Star break.' And he did. But it wasn't enough. And he was the guy who stirred the drink, you know. Well, some people want to hear it and some people don't.

"Could we have locked him up [to a long contract]? Definitely. But we weren't smart enough. Well I don't want to say that. Let me put it this way: we didn't wrap Reggie up. And we lost Donnie Baylor, too. But nobody knew what was going to happen with free agency. Hank kept flying out to Arizona because Reggie's agent wouldn't fly. Reggie was having fun, knowing what was going to happen. And Hank kept coming back saying, 'The figures are mind-boggling, just mind-boggling.'"

HANK PETERS: "When he wouldn't report I flew out to Arizona early in the season because his agent wouldn't fly. I met with them and didn't get very far, and I came back. Then I went out a second time, and we finally hammered out a deal to get him in for the rest of the season. We still wanted the long-term deal.

"We were sitting in a coffee shop in Tempe, Arizona, talking about different concepts, me and Reggie and the agent. And finally I said, 'What in the hell do you want?' The agent took a heavy cloth napkin and started writing down figures. And he gave me the thing. He wanted something like three million dollars spread out over five or six years. I said, 'Are you out of your goddamn mind? Nobody's ever going to get that kind of money.' That's how naive I was in my thinking."

EARL WEAVER: "John Mayberry from Kansas City was the first guy to sign, something like one million dollars over five years. Hank went right to Reggie and offered him that, and Reggie laughed and said, 'No stats, no nothing, and that's what he got.' And that was the end of that. And from that point on, unless we'd have come up with maybe five hundred thousand dollars a year, we weren't going to get him. If Hank could have thrown five hundred thousand at him for three or four years, a two-million-dollar contract,

Reggie might have jumped on it. He signed for four hundred fifty thousand [a year] with New York. Now, whether his choice would have been New York regardless, we'll never know. But we could have wrapped him up for five hundred thousand dollars a year for four years."

JIM PALMER: "He was asking [the Orioles] for two hundred fifty, two hundred seventy-five, three hundred thousand dollars, and like a five-year deal, with fifty thousand to his dad. He got significantly more at the end of the year. The Orioles ended up offering four hundred thousand dollars. Hoffberger was a terrific guy, but he and Hank Peters didn't have a lot of foresight. That doesn't mean they aren't good owners or general managers, and hindsight is 20-20, but in this case, Reggie got here so late it cost us the pennant, and he wasn't asking for that much during the season. We could have signed him then, when the price was going higher. If he'd stayed, we would have won a bunch more World Series. And it's not just that Reggie didn't stay; it's who we gave up to get him. Baylor goes on to be American League MVP in '79. Torrez pitches well. But that's the lack of foresight. You don't trade Baylor and Torrez for Reggie Jackson, who is gone at the end of the year. You had to be able to see where that was going."

HANK PETERS: "When he became a free agent, we tried to sign him badly. As a matter of fact, the day that he finally agreed to terms with the Yankees, I had a date to meet him in Chicago. He went on a tour—I think they got a bus—he and his agent and their entourage, and they went all over. We met in Chicago at some hotel, and I walked in the lobby, and there was George Steinbrenner waiting to go up. And I thought, 'I haven't got a chance.'"

KEN SINGLETON: "Reggie told me years later that he would have stayed for two hundred fifty thousand dollars more overall. Nowadays that's a pittance, but in those days that was an awful lot to the Orioles, who just couldn't afford him. And one thing Reggie also said years later—during my ten years in Baltimore I was on teams that finished second six times—Reggie said, 'You remember all those years in Baltimore that you finished second? If I'd stayed, you'd have won.' And he's probably right. We would have won. Out of those six [second-place finishes] I'm sure we would have won at least four."

Two other Orioles also left the club as free agents after the season. Second baseman Bob Grich signed with the California Angels, the team he had rooted for as a youngster in Southern California. Pitcher Wayne Garland, a 20-game winner in '76 in his first season as a starter after three years in the bullpen, signed a deal with Cleveland that stunned baseball: ten years, 2.3 million dollars—unthinkable figures prior to free agency. Garland never had another winning season.

Ross Grimsley: "The Orioles didn't pay. Never did. When you looked at Palmer and Belanger and Brooks and the guys who'd been there, the [small] amount of money they made was amazing. Hoffberger was an excellent owner, and Frank Cashen and Hank Peters were outstanding general managers, but with those small crowds, they just didn't have a lot of money to pay guys. Other clubs just had more [money].

"When free agency came in, you were going to get more somewhere else. I left [for Montreal] a year after Grich and Garland, and I got the kind of money I never would have gotten in Baltimore. Six years, 1.75 million dollars. I never would have gotten that if I'd stayed with the Orioles. I don't think they offered anything, actually. Or nowhere near that. I had a chance to go somewhere else and get a lot more. I [would have been] an idiot not to take that."

Bob Grich: "The Orioles just didn't have the budget. The ballpark was in a rough area of town. The city itself had less than a million residents, so the market wasn't that big. People weren't going to come from [Washington] D.C. It just wasn't the market that New York or Southern California was. In 1970, we won 108 games and drew something like nine hundred thousand people.

"When I was a free agent, it was always my dream to play in California. The Angels were my club. I used to go out and watch them all the time. They were always my favorite team. Not that I disliked Baltimore. I had a good time there. It was a great organization. But my dream was to play in Southern California. The Orioles made an effort to keep me. They offered me a five-year contract. Hank Peters made every attempt to keep me. They showed me every bit of respect I could have asked for. Hank said, 'Here's a great five-year contract. It's the best contract I've ever offered anyone. It's the best we could do. I hope you stay.' I said, 'I can't.' He said, 'I really don't blame you.'

"When I came back to Baltimore [with the Angels] I was amazed. The reception was very surprising. I got booed hard, real hard. People came down and stood on top of the dugout and cursed at me and leaned over the dugout roof and yelled obscenities into the dugout and threw things at me. I was absolutely surprised. Shocked, even. I couldn't believe it. I thought I had given them five good years. But they were mad at me. They were furious.

"They said, 'Why'd you leave?' I said, 'I had a chance to go back home and play for my favorite team for more money. If you begrudge me that, you're wrong.' But it was an unprecedented situation, free agency, and the people didn't know how to react to it. All they saw was the money. I went from eighty-two to a hundred and seventy thousand dollars, and the blue-collar fan in Baltimore didn't like it one bit."

HANK PETERS: "Our crowds were small, our TV [revenue] was zilch, and we didn't have much of a revenue stream. And we were a public corporation. Hoffberger gave me a mandate when I started, said, 'Just operate it like it's your own ball club. But remember, we don't want to lose money. We do have stockholders. And all of our operations are public knowledge because we have to publish financial reports.'

"By about the middle of the '76 season, with free agency coming, I wrote a memorandum to Jerry and the board of directors. We held a meeting to discuss it. I said, 'I'm not certain the Orioles are going to be able to compete in the future because we do not have the revenue to support the type of contracts you're going to have to give to better players.' I didn't think of myself as a prophet, but it was the truth. We struggled through '76, and we tried to sign some free agents ourselves but didn't have much luck.

"As the season ended we were trying to sign Garland, who was represented by Jerry Kapstein. Garland won 20 games that year, but he and Earl had a very bad relationship. Jerry and I started negotiating, and on the last morning of the season, Jerry and Wayne came in and Wayne says, 'There's no way I can play for that little son of a bitch.' I said, 'Well, that little son of a bitch doesn't like you any better than you like him, but let me tell you something, it'll never stop him from pitching you every fourth day. He'll pitch you every fourth day even though he hates your guts. That's why you won 20.'

"But Wayne was adamant. He went out in the free-agent market and signed, and Cleveland's general manager, Phil Seghi, made the statement, 'Everybody's entitled to one trip to fantasy land, and I just took mine.' But he did us a favor because, unfortunately for Wayne, he developed arm problems, and his career never took off."

Brooks Robinson was the Orioles' Opening Day third baseman for the twentieth straight season in '76. The future Hall of Famer was thirty-nine years old and still adept in the field, but he was no longer able to produce at the plate. In '75 he had won his sixteenth and last Gold Glove, but hit just .201 with six homers in 144 games. His heir apparent, Doug DeCinces, had spent the year on the bench as a utility player.

The club's reluctance to make a change at third was understandable. Robinson was easily the most popular player in franchise history, a fixture dating back to Paul Richards's tenure as manager. Removing him from the lineup not only would be unpopular, but it would be hard on his replacement. Who wanted to go through that?

When Robinson continued to struggle early in the '76 season, the move became necessary. The moment the Orioles had dreaded finally was at hand. DeCinces began replacing Robinson more and more, fighting boos at home and scorn on the road. Predictably, the young player struggled through the season, batting .234 with 11 homers in 129 games. But he made it. The next year, he played third on Opening Day with Robinson still in uniform as a player-coach, and despite continuing boos, DeCinces established himself as an everyday player with 19 homers and 69 RBI.

His interest suddenly waning, Robinson played little in '77, managing just seven hits in 24 games. He did provide a final dramatic moment against the Indians on April 19, slugging his only home run of the season to win a game in extra innings. But he retired on September 18, with the club needing his spot on the roster in a pennant drive, and that was that. After twenty-three seasons encompassing 2,896 games, 2,848 hits, and unmatched brilliance in the field, the career of the consummate Orioles players was over.

DOUG DECINCES: "After my first spring training in the major leagues [in '73], Jim Frey and Billy Hunter sat me down and said, 'We want you to go to Rochester and play third this year.' I said, 'Whoa, that's Brooks's position. Why me?' They said, 'We think you're strong enough to do it.' They said, 'Grich is at second, Belanger at short. Where are you going?' Back then I was most comfortable at shortstop, but I was just adequate. So I went down and played third.

"I felt I definitely could be playing in the major leagues somewhere, if not Baltimore. I knew some organizations were interested in me. Danny Ozark came up to me at a golf tournament and said, 'I tried to get you.' Other guys said that. When I went back to Triple A, guys on other teams would say, 'I know our organization is trying to get you.' So you're sitting at Triple A, and you know other teams are after you. That was interesting. Then in '75 they wanted to give Brooks one more chance. When I realized they were con-templating sending me back down again, I went in and said, 'I'm not doing that again. If I'm going, I'm going somewhere else [in the major leagues].' So I made the club and sat in '75."

BROOKS ROBINSON: "When you get near the end of your career, in my case, defensively there was no difference, but you just hit the ball and it wouldn't go as far. And then it becomes a mental thing, and you make changes and try to get more bat speed, and so it just gets worse. And Earl liked to go along with veterans. Doug probably should have played before he did. No question, he probably should have played a little sooner than he did. But Earl liked to have the guys that had been around. Doug was waiting around. We had a good relationship through it all. He was a good guy, a real good guy. It just took him a while to get a chance to play, that's all."

DOUG DeCINCES: "Earl gave Brooks every opportunity, and it cost me. Cost me playing time, opportunity, experience, everything. But I understood it. It wasn't just anyone [he was replacing]. The timing was just unfortunate. When I finally started playing in '76, there were some very ugly times. It was very difficult not to take it all personally. Every town I went to, someone would come in and write about whether I could replace Brooks. The heir-apparent tag was sometimes positive and sometimes negative.

"We went to Detroit, and I played in a game and made a couple of plays and blew a routine play, and the next day the columnist just laughed at my abilities. Not only was I getting it in Baltimore, but everywhere. I got hate mail saying, 'You'll never replace Brooks. You're a California kid.' But I didn't have a choice. If this was what I was going to do, I had to do it. I made sure to give Brooks the respect, but when it was time to play, no one was going to stop me.

"At first [in '76] I played some short and second, too. If they announced me at third, the fans started booing. Opposing players would say to me at third, 'Boy, am I glad I'm not you.' Brooks would slap me on the butt and say, 'Hang in there.' On the field Belanger was a big help. He was standing next to me and he'd hear it all. He'd just say, 'Hey, come on, don't listen to that. Let's go.'

"There's one game in particular that summed it up. It was in late June, the second game of a doubleheader at Memorial Stadium. My grandmother was in town. It was the first time she'd seen me play pro baseball. I was out warming up, starting. When they announced my name, there was a smattering of boos. It was because they loved Brooks. I understood that. They didn't hate me so much as love Brooks.

"We were playing Minnesota, and in the first inning Cuellar was getting smoked. The ball was flying all over the place. In a bases-loaded situation Larry Hisle hit one down the line, and I dove and knocked it down, and the ball trickled over by the tarp, and two runs came in. The fans started chanting, 'We want Brooks!' The next hitter hit a two-hopper off my chest, and I pick it up and throw to first, and the guy is safe. Now the chant is really strong, 'We want Brooks!' And I'm there on that field, and I'm thinking, 'I'm diving all over the place, the ball is getting smoked, and I'm getting booed.'

"The next inning Hisle hits it at me again, and I air-mail it over the first baseman's head, and I'm going, 'You got to be kidding me.' The chant is loud and ongoing. I go up to the plate for my first at-bat and it's 'We want Brooks!' And I strike out. I'm coming back to the dugout, and I can feel my teammates, but no one is saying a word. And Earl comes up and says, 'Should I take you out?' I said, 'Over my dead body.' For the rest of the game I made the plays in the field, and in my next three at-bats I had a single, a three-run homer, and a triple driving in two runs with two out in the ninth.

"So I'm standing on third, I'm three for four, we're down 5–4, and the fans start giving me a standing ovation. [Billy] Hunter came over and said, 'Don't do anything rash.' He could see the anger on my face. The next guy popped up, and the game was over, and I went in and ripped my uniform off. From that point on I decided the fans weren't going to dictate my career. That was the breaking point, the one game. I could have collapsed and that could have been [the end of] my career. I felt it was that close.

"The booing didn't stop until 'Thanks Brooks Robinson Day' the next year. And the tag [of replacing Robinson] was always there. I look back at replacing Brooks as the single greatest accomplishment of my career. Throw out the home runs and everything else. The fact that I was the one who had to go in there and replace him, and did it and went on to have a career, that was pretty special. I don't know that everyone could have done that."

BROOKS ROBINSON: "I think it was definitely hard for him. Every time it was, 'Brooks would have had that.' It had to be hard for him. I didn't meet with him or talk to him or anything, but I thought he handled it well. I really did. I don't think I'd like to do that, and it probably shortened his career, not getting here sooner. But we had a lot of guys like that. Grich, Baylor, they were all chomping at the bit to get in there, but we were in the throes of a pretty good run, and they had to wait.

"But by '77 I suddenly was ready. I couldn't wait to get out. Plus, I thought I was probably going to be doing the TV [broadcasts for the Orioles], so I was just going to be nursed off it, you could say. But I really lost interest. I guess when you don't play as well and then don't play at all, you can lose interest. In '77 I just hung around hoping I'd play, but about the middle of the year I lost interest. And then on September 18 Earl said, 'We need the spot,' and I said, 'Fine.'"

BOB BROWN: "Brooksie hit his last home run on a gloomy night in April [of '77] at Memorial Stadium. Very small attendance. We were playing Cleveland, and Frank [Robinson] was managing the Indians, and they had a 5–3 lead in the bottom of the 10th. Looked like a loss. Dave LaRoche was pitching for Cleveland. Brooksie was pretty much through at that point. Didn't even want to play anymore. But he got up there as a pinch hitter, and lo and behold, he hits one out for a three-run homer to win. And everyone knew it was his last hurrah. The press box went crazy, which isn't supposed to happen, but you couldn't help it. Earl said in the clubhouse that it was the second biggest thrill of his career after winning the '70 World Series."

BROOKS ROBINSON: "It was a great career, but I remember I was on a bus one day with [Scott] McGregor when I was doing the TV years later, and we were talking. I said, 'Mac, the one thing I wish maybe I'd done was start some kind of physical program, Nautilus or something, when I got to be about thirty-four or thirty-five. I think it would have really helped me and prolonged my career.' He just busted out laughing. I said, 'What are you laughing at?' He said, 'What do you want? You're in the Hall of Fame, you almost got 3,000 hits, and here you're worried about working out.'

"But I probably should have started on some program at some point. Maybe I could have gone on a little longer. But when I started out playing, you still had to go out and get a job in the off-season. The money wasn't as big, and there was no getting around that. I guess I just played the hand I was dealt."

31

Reloading on the Run

The Orioles' last great team was not unlike a musical group's greatest hits compilation. It was the product of smart managing, smart player development, smart trades, and smart play—baseball's version of a string of number-one songs. A shortfall in any of those areas probably would have undermined the whole enterprise. To become the winners they were from 1977 to 1983 without the same talent they had from 1969 to 1974, the Orioles had to do almost everything right, large and small, on and off the field. Catcher Rick Dempsey said later, "We didn't have great talent, but we had a great team."

The heart of the team came through the minor league system together and flowered in Triple A as the '76 Rochester Red Wings, who were the class of the International League, winning 88 of 138 games, including a remarkable 30 of 31 at one point. Rich Dauer batted .336 with 78 RBI. Eddie Murray drove in 40 runs in 54 games after being promoted. Dennis Martinez led the league in wins, complete games, ERA, and strikeouts. Scott McGregor joined the club in June and was named the league's top left-hander. Mike Flanagan won six games in seven starts for manager Joe Altobelli. It didn't take much imagination to see the Orioles' next great starting rotation forming.

MIKE FLANAGAN: "The team was really loaded. When I got there [from Baltimore, in July] they were in the midst of a 16-game winning streak. Then they throw me in the rotation, and I lose. And now I've even screwed up the Triple-A team. They're giving me all kinds of grief, you know, 'We don't want this big-leaguer; we were doing well without him.' And they proceeded to win 14 more in a row. And of course, I hear about who lost the one game out of 31.

"A fan sent every player on the team sixteen dollars for the 16-game streak. Altobelli said, 'What are we going to do with the money?' The players said, 'Let's put it on a horse.' So we all put our sixteen dollars on this horse. The team had some pretty good horse players. I just threw my money in the pot. The race went off one night at seven-thirty. It was Dauer's job to listen and see what happened. So we're playing, and this team was so confident that no lead was insurmountable. I think we were losing 4–0 in the second. Then all of a sudden you look in the dugout and Dauer's going down to talk to Altobelli, and you hear this big roar. They had won the bet. We're losing 4–0, and you hear this roar from the dugout. That's the kind of team it was. They rolled the winnings over to the next night until each player had like $300 apiece. I mean, it was a very, very laid-back team, and a very good team."

JOE ALTOBELLI: "We had a great club [in Rochester] in '71 with Baylor and Grich, but it was built around offense. The '76 club was built around pitching. Just one of those things when a lot of good young pitchers came together. The offense was decent. We only had Eddie for the second half of the season. He was real quiet, wouldn't say much. He'd just started switch hitting and wasn't quite pulling the ball yet. But it was coming together."

The trade that brought McGregor to the Red Wings was one of the biggest in Orioles history and a deal that would resonate positively for a decade. On June 15, 1976, with general manager Hank Peters pulling the strings, the Orioles sent five players to the Yankees—veteran pitchers Ken Holtzman, Grant Jackson, and Doyle Alexander; catcher Elrod Hendricks; and minor leaguer Jimmy Freeman. The Yankees gave up McGregor, backup catcher Rick Dempsey, and pitchers Rudy May, Tippy Martinez, and Dave Pagan.

To say the Orioles got the best of the deal is an understatement. McGregor, Martinez, and Dempsey each played at least a decade in Baltimore; McGregor won 138 games as a starting pitcher, Martinez totaled 105 saves in relief, and Dempsey became a fixture behind the plate. The Yankees didn't get as much in return. Holtzman, Jackson, and Alexander pitched well in '76 and helped the Yankees win their first pennant in twelve years, but all three were gone within a few years. Hendricks, near the end of his career, batted 64 times for the Yankees and re-signed with the Orioles in November of '77.

HANK PETERS: "Alexander was very unhappy. I had a lot of respect for him as a pitcher, but he was a miserable human being. Miserable. And he wouldn't sign. So he was going to be a free agent at the end of the year. And Holtzman wasn't signed, and he was going to be a free agent, too. He was just as miserable as Alexander. And our catching was awful. We had [Dave] Duncan and Elrod, and both were finished. We had the worst catching in the league.

"So we're coming up on the trading deadline, and I'm trying to shop around and trade these guys. We played in Kansas City over the weekend before going to Chicago. I thought I had a deal with the Royals for Holtzman, but Holtzman said he wouldn't sign with them, so the deal was off. I said, 'That miserable bastard.'

"The trading deadline was Tuesday at midnight, and I'm in Chicago. A lot of things came together. Gabe Paul was [GM] with the Yankees, and he had purchased Vida Blue from Charlie Finley in Oakland. Finley had sold his players to different clubs and [baseball commissioner Bowie] Kuhn stepped in and wouldn't let him do it. So now Gabe was in Chicago, where Finley lived, trying to work out something for Blue. And I guess they couldn't get things going. But Gabe was staying in the same hotel I'm in. We got to talking, and we had so many names down. At one time we were going to get Graig Nettles and Ron Guidry and, oh, God, the names went back and forth.

"I had one big advantage. Clyde Kluttz, who was our director of player personnel, had been with the Yankees for five years before he came over, so he knew McGregor and Tippy, which was a big help. On Tuesday night I never made it to the [Orioles] game. Gabe and I worked the deal out, and it was a big deal for both teams. Holtzman and Alexander helped them win the pennant. And we got Scotty and Tippy, and got rid of two guys who were miserable people on our team, and got a catcher we liked very much, which we really needed."

RICK DEMPSEY: "At the time we were in first place by 12 games over the Orioles, and I was looking forward to being in the playoffs and the World Series for the first time. I really didn't think the trade was a great opportunity for me. I loved all those guys on the Yankees, even though I was a role player, a backup to Thurman Munson. I couldn't look far enough ahead to see that it was a great chance for me to become a first-string catcher. I was strictly thinking about the season we were having in New York.

"When I got traded over, Earl didn't seem too happy to have me. He said, 'I'll get you in there when I can. My catcher is doing a pretty good job and getting some hits, so he's going to play pretty much every day until I can find a spot to get you in there.' That was it, see you later. I thought it was a pretty big slap in the face. Dave Duncan was the catcher. Pretty good defensively. Not a big hitter, but he had a little power, and he was on a little streak where he was swinging the bat pretty good, so Earl was going to stick with him for a while.

"I joined the Orioles in Chicago, didn't play, went to Minnesota, didn't play. We got home, and I checked in to a Best Western out on the beltway. It was hot and humid, about three o'clock in the morning. I was tired and depressed. I got to the hotel with my two suitcases that were heavy, and I walked across the parking lot about half a mile and dragged all my luggage up to the second floor and all the way to the end of the hall, only to get there and find out they didn't give me the right key. I walked back down the hall, went outside on the balcony, and threw my luggage down into the parking lot and sat down on the top steps and just cried.

"I couldn't believe it had come to this. Not only had I been traded to a second-place team, 12 games out of first, but I hadn't even played for them in my first week there. The next day I was in the lineup, played my first game against Kansas City, and threw a couple guys out stealing, which was what they wanted me to do. And from then on I was the regular catcher for the next ten years for the Orioles."

HANK PETERS: "Duncan was a con man, and he had some of our pitchers believing they couldn't really be a successful pitcher unless he was their catcher. When we got Dempsey, Earl wasn't catching Dempsey. Finally, I sat down with Earl and told him, 'Earl, I didn't make that deal to get Dempsey to sit on the bench.' I said, 'Let me tell you something. Duncan's not going to be here next year, and Rick Dempsey will. You'd better start to catch him.' I never told Earl who to play or pitch, but I told him he'd better start to use this guy, and he did after that. Earl was a good company man."

RICK DEMPSEY: "It was a great trade for the Orioles, really set up the pitching and catching. I may have looked like the weak link in the deal at the time, but it was a pretty solid deal for them. I was a blue-collar catcher, down there in the trenches with all of the fans, fighting and scrapping just to break even. I intermingled a lot with the fans. They felt the game like I did. We had a lot of scrappy times together. I think they appreciated my approach to the game. I might dive into the grandstand or dive into the dugout to catch a ball or something. I never played it safe. A lot of the things I tried to do, climbed screens and such, you'd never see that today."

SCOTT McGREGOR: "I was great at Triple A in '74, and the Yankees didn't call me up, which freaked me out, so I was in a funk from the end of that '74 season through '75. I came to spring training in '76 and [manager] Billy Martin was there, and they were through with me. When I got traded over, it was like a catapult. I went 9–1 with six shutouts pitching for Rochester. Then I got called up at the end of the season and pitched two great games against Milwaukee and Boston."

MIKE FLANAGAN: "I had started the ['76] season in the bullpen for the Orioles. That was the way it was here. You spent a year in the bullpen and tried to learn as much as you could by osmosis. Learn your craft. Get used to big-league life. Everybody did it. It was not unique to me. Dennis Martinez learned in the 'pen. I can't think of anybody that walked up and went right in the rotation.

"But I pitched on Opening Day and did well, and then the phone didn't ring for two months. I got up [to warm up] all the time, but I was the scare tactic, you know, 'Get Flanagan up to scare Palmer and Cuellar into pitching better.' To make them go, 'Oh, God, he's warming up, they're going to bring him in.' My heart jumped every time the phone rang, but I didn't have a chance [of getting in] even though I was throwing all the time. That was very difficult.

"Then right before the [big] trade in '76, Bamberger said, 'Look, kid, we know you're worn out; take tonight off, get a good sideline in, and we're going to give you a couple of days off.' Well, the next day Holtzman was supposed to start, and I walk in the clubhouse in Kansas City, and Holtzman is scratched. I'm starting. And I'm going, 'What is going on?' Nobody would talk to me. I said, 'Well, I'm going to go out in the field like it's a normal day and shag and throw.'

"Bamberger comes running out all excited going 'Jesus, Mike, get in the clubhouse—you're pitching today.' I go, 'George, didn't you just say yesterday that I was done for a couple of days, that I'm worn out?' And he goes, 'Jesus, I can't tell you right now, but there's something going on.' So I went out there [to pitch] and had nothing. I had spent it all in the bullpen the night before. It was an embarrassing performance. Earl told me years later, 'We couldn't have Holtzman getting hit in the head with a line drive and screwing up the trade, so we had to throw you out there.'

"That was my first start in '76, and after that, I'll never forget it, because I sort of knew I was the heir apparent to Cuellar, but the Royals ran me into the ground that day, must have stolen six bases in two innings, and then Cuellar took me in the outfield and spent hours with me working on my pickoff move. I felt a little sheepish because I was there to take his spot. But he never withheld any information. If anything, he went out of his way to smooth the transition for me—volunteered his insights. Just did it. Palmer did the same thing.

"Believe me, it wasn't like that everywhere. People withheld information. They weren't going to help you. It was 'I figured it out, so you figure it out.' I saw that in other clubs. But with the Orioles it was, 'If you're going to be better and take my job, then it's going to happen and I can't control it, so I might as well help you as much as I can.' That was a product of years of winning. It was a real lesson, and it always stayed with me."

The new blood from the trade and the farm system blended together in '77 with an existing nucleus that included Jim Palmer, Lee May, Ken Singleton, Mark Belanger, Doug DeCinces, and Al Bumbry. With Earl Weaver manipulating the pieces in the prime of his career, the Orioles were formidable again despite losing Reggie Jackson, Wayne Garland, and Bobby Grich to free agency after the '76 season.

The Orioles were in first place as late as August 1 and still in contention with a week to go. In the end, they won 97 games and finished tied for second with the Boston Red Sox, two and one-half games behind the Yankees. Eddie Murray was a revelation, winning the AL's Rookie of the Year Award for hitting .283 with 27 homers and 88 RBI as a switch-hitting designated hitter. And although veterans Palmer and Rudy May led the starting rotation with 20 and 18 wins, Mike Flanagan and Dennis Martinez were almost as impressive. Flanagan went 15–10 with 15 complete games, and Martinez went 14–7 with 5 complete games.

KEN SINGLETON: "Pat Kelly and Lee May were standing in the outfield watching Eddie hit in batting practice in spring training in '77—Eddie's rookie year. And he was hitting shot after shot up near the light towers at

Miami Stadium. And Kelly and May are watching from the outfield, and Kelly goes, 'I wonder what position he plays?' So they watched him, and after he hit, he ran around the bases, and then he went over and picked up a first baseman's mitt. And Pat looked at Lee and went, 'Oh, Lee.'"

ELROD HENDRICKS: "Lee was great. He didn't mind working with Eddie at first base, even though Eddie obviously was going to take his job. But Lee took him under his wing. He would tell Eddie, 'Hey, this is the way you dress,' and then they'd go out to eat, and Lee would say, 'Kid, you don't make any money, put it away. You're going with me tonight.' He just showed Eddie the way."

EDDIE MURRAY: "Lee May had some good qualities, and he tried to show me the right way to do things—and not do things. Some were off the field. Like, always listen. If someone tells you five things, you might use two—but that's two more than you had. And he said, 'If you sit down and break bread with someone, you should be able to pick up a check.' So not just baseball things, but being a major leaguer. It was a learning thing. And then the way when Earl would scream at someone, and Lee would come along behind [Earl] and pat the guy and say, 'Way to go.' Keeping his head up. They were almost a team that way. Earl was making his point, and Lee was, too.

"Earl was entirely different to me than he was to Dauer or Garcia. The report he got was I was someone who knew how to play, and that he wouldn't see the same mistake over and over. I did see him scream at people. He screamed at me once and it had no effect. We had to wear ties on planes and trips. And we were all stuffed in a car rental place in Miami, a little small office, and it's hot, and he screamed at me, 'Where's your tie?' He didn't say it; he screamed it. I just took it out of my pocket, showed it to him without saying a word, and put it back in my pocket. You know, it was just too hot. And then we didn't really speak until July. He didn't say nothing to me, he just put me in the lineup. I was that quiet."

KEN SINGLETON: "Eddie was so quiet that Earl went to Lee and said, 'Lee, this guy hasn't said a word to me in about a month.' And Lee told him, 'Hey, rookies are just quiet.' Lee had told Eddie, 'Listen, just play ball.' You know, 'Don't say anything.' And Eddie took it to heart. That's the way it was. But you could see then that he was going to be a great player."

EARL WEAVER: "Eddie, I had to play. He didn't say boo, but he could play. Lee May had done nothing wrong, drove in his 100 runs, made three errors all year. You just don't displace a veteran like that until you find out if Eddie is going to be able to hit. But Eddie got in the lineup [in '77] and never got out.

"Lee was a great person, and he could see the writing on the wall, so. Eddie got to start playing a little more first base, a little more first base, and he had much more range than Lee. And Lee was intelligent, and he accepted it. The only bad thing was Eddie got broken in as a DH, and people got the wrong idea about his defensive ability, because he was a good first baseman."

RICK DEMPSEY: "Eddie was an impact player from the beginning. He had tremendous offensive ability, that poise and control of himself that a lot of players look for offensively. He could do things with the bat that not very many players could do. Not only was he a good power hitter, but he was a good average hitter. He could spray the ball around. He could take a pitcher's best pitch and serve it down the left-field line hitting left-handed, or even right-handed, go the opposite way with power."

JOE ALTOBELLI: "When I managed Eddie [in Rochester] in '76, he was on the quiet side, but his mind was always working. If someone were to ask me what player prepared himself best to play, he would be at the top of the list. He just wouldn't let anything bother him or sway him from doing that. A lot of times that's what got him in trouble with the media and vice versa. I don't know that people outside of baseball know how much it takes for a good ballplayer to prepare himself."

EDDIE MURRAY: "It came together for us as a club in '77. I don't think anyone played over their heads. We could play, and we knew we could play. Everyone on that club knew it. After a while guys around the league could see it in us. Those '77 and '78 teams were good. It wasn't like people were saying, 'Oh, they got lucky.' We could catch the ball and pitch it. We stayed in games and gave ourselves a chance to win."

DENNIS MARTINEZ: "We were good defensively. That was the objective of the Orioles. The mentality, the philosophy. Good pitching, good defense, do the little things, win a lot of games. We were so good on defense that as a pitcher all you had to do was get them to hit the ball. Dauer was great;

Belanger was great; Bumbry out there in center, he caught everything. We had veterans who knew how to play. Belanger was the key when I got there. He was the coach out there. He had the outfielders positioned right and throwing to the right cutoff man. He couldn't hit, but he could catch every ball. It was like, 'Hey, I don't worry about my hitting because we have eight or nine guys who can hit. My job is to do everything right. Be in the right place. Be aware of the plays. Make the cutoffs. Make the plays.' He was the man."

MIKE FLANAGAN: "I was 2–8, and Palmer went to bat for me at Fenway Park. I was reading in the paper where I was going to Rochester if I had another bad start. In the urinals of Fenway Park, Palmer was in there, Weaver was in there, and he said, 'Why don't you just give the kid a pat on the back or tell him something? Tell him you believe in him. Say something to him.' Earl never said anything to me directly, but he said it in the paper that day. I'd lost the previous day in Kansas City, and he brought up the topic and said, 'I'll bet my paycheck by the end of the year he's a winning pitcher.' That relieved all the stress that I was going to Rochester. He said, 'I'm going to give him the ball every fourth day.' It was just as simple as that. I went 13–2 in the second half and ended up 15–10."

KEN SINGLETON: "The Yankees were tough, but we were right on their heels. We were the overachievers because we didn't have as much money, and we were losing players. I mean, Reggie left us; Grich and Garland left us. All of them signed elsewhere as free agents. And everyone left us for dead in '77, and we played like hell. The Yankees had signed Reggie, and everyone felt sorry for Earl, but the Oriole Way was in effect. If we played correctly, we could win. And we did. Once those pitchers came around, every night we had somebody who was capable of throwing a good game."

The club wasn't quite as competitive in '78 despite winning 91 games, finishing a quiet fourth in the division as the Yankees and Red Sox took an epic pennant race into extra innings. The Yankees won a one-game playoff and went on to win the World Series for the second year in a row. McGregor replaced Rudy May in the rotation and was immediately effective, winning 15 games and completing 13 of 32 starts. Flanagan and Martinez were even better than the year before, combining for 35 wins and 32 complete games. Palmer won 20 games for the eighth and last time. In the field, Murray and May switched places, with Murray taking over at first base and May becoming the DH. Murray, May, Singleton, and DeCinces each had at least 20 homers and 80 RBI. After four years of sitting out the playoffs, the Orioles were ready to bust loose.

MIKE FLANAGAN: "The nucleus came together, and it stayed the same for a while. We won a lot of games—had a way to play. We were all taught the same things and the same vocabulary about those things. I know Eddie said it. He said there was an Oriole Way, and whether it was right or wrong, we believed it. I never felt like it was me against Guidry. I had Belanger and who-ever else behind me, and it was us against them.

"The importance of a single out was at a premium. We would work on plays for hours in the spring. A single pickoff play. A single defense of a dou-ble steal. Something we would do once, and it would work once and win a game. The importance of hitting a cutoff man. We were this entity that was not going to mess up.

"There were some great-hitting teams in the [AL East] division then—Mil-waukee, Boston, the Yankees. Tons of hitters from Fred Lynn to Jim Rice to Boomer Scott to Reggie to Cecil Cooper. You could catch your good stuff and give up four or five home runs. So it was pretty good baseball. But we always felt the other team was going to mess up before we did. And if they opened the door, we were going to get in it.

"We surprised a lot of people. So many guys had left, and we were kind of left with the young guys and a sprinkling of the veterans. Some things were starting to change, and it was kind of our generation from then on. In '77 and '78 we were really starting to believe in ourselves. We left with an eight-man pitching staff out of Florida in '78—four starters, four relievers. That's why Earl had this great bench all the time, all the great pinch hitters. We were car-rying three less pitchers than we should have had."

RICK DEMPSEY: "Dennis Martinez had four major league pitches, two vari-ations of each. He was flat-out one of the best young pitchers I ever saw come into the game. He was awesome. He and I never got along very well. In fact, I know he doesn't like me much at all. He didn't like how I set up his game for him. But the proof was in the pudding. We won a lot of games together. We had a 2–1 win-loss ratio. You don't do that with too many guys.

"Dennis went in and complained about me to Earl on numerous occasions, forcing him to do certain things. Earl tried other catchers, but he wasn't as successful. We were 42–20 [together] at one point, and Earl said, 'I'm sorry you have problems, but he's going to catch you.' And that was it. We had some problems, but I loved the guy as a competitor. He had a lot of energy. He was fun to call a game for."

DENNIS MARTINEZ: "I had a lot of disagreements with Dempsey. Whatever I was doing, it wasn't good enough or I wasn't doing things the right way. I wound up using the second catcher a lot. I always felt that for me to be successful I had to move [the ball] around the plate a lot, and a lot of [catchers] don't want to move.

"There were a lot of things happening early in my career that people didn't understand. They had Palmer and Flanagan and McGregor, and I had to prove I was one of them. Sometimes I feel I was set up to be a scapegoat, because I wasn't them. There were a lot of things put on me because they expected a lot out of me. But I told myself, 'I'm not going to let myself down.'"

SCOTT MCGREGOR: "Dennis was amazing. When he threw on the side [between starts], Flanagan and Palmer and I would run out and watch him. Just to watch him. We'd go, 'Please, God, let us throw like this.' He had no idea what he was doing, but he had the best arm of all of us. You could hear his curveball going to home plate, like, buzzing. You went, 'My God, what is that?' He just laughed. He didn't know how to pitch, but Palmer would program him, tell him every pitch to throw. And he would go out and win."

RICK DEMPSEY: "Scotty McGregor was just a quiet, hard worker—went about his job consistently every day. He changed his speeds, maybe only gave you 83–84 [mph], but he knew how to pitch. He was a very intelligent guy on the mound. Stuck to a game plan as good as you could do. With that slop that he threw up there, to win as many games as he did, he was very smart. Sometimes I didn't even know the difference between some of his pitches, but he had tremendous location. And he had no fear at all. Throw it up there and make them hit it. He had big heart and a lot of intestinal fortitude, and he just made himself a great pitcher."

SCOTT MCGREGOR: "In '77 I went 3–5, and I was getting spot starts. I had a fastball, change-up, and curve. Bamberger and Earl came to me [in '77] and said they wanted me to get my curveball down into the sixties. My fastball was in the high eighties, and the change-up was around seventy-one or seventy-two. They wanted the curve even slower. They wanted three pitches in three different time zones. Earl kept screaming, 'Throw that slow one!' I could hear him from the dugout.

"I was scared. You're in the major leagues, and someone is saying take a little off a pitch to Dick Allen. You'd go, 'Yeah, right; he's going to hit it over the roof.' But then you did it, and it worked. He missed the pitch. I saw that and made a bunch of adjustments at the major league level in '77 and '78. We got out there with a radar gun and worked it, and when I slowed the curve down, a hesitation appeared at the top of my delivery that proved to be very effective. Starting in '78 I was one of the winningest pitchers in baseball."

Rick Dempsey: "Flanny was just a bulldog—the toughest guy I had to catch because he threw such a heavy sinker. But he was a grinder. Every fourth day that he was on the mound, he didn't care about anything, how much he hurt or anything. He was going to find a way to beat you. On his good days he was unhittable. On the days when he didn't have good stuff, he just kept coming at you. He would change his rhythm, change his speed, drop down, throw a sidearm curveball—use every weapon in his arsenal to get you out. And then on the days when he had good stuff, you had no chance against him.

"He made adjustments year after year after year to the opposition. He studied them pretty well, knew the hitters real well. He made more adjustments than any of the other pitchers out there. He was smart. I was very fortunate to catch guys who were pretty good thinkers out there on the mound."

Dennis Martinez: "We were a four-man rotation. We threw a lot. All those complete games. And they weren't complete games for the hell of it. A lot of 2–1 games. Close games. And we went six or seven innings every time. It was competitive between pitchers. Always. We had a great relationship, and we all had one purpose—to win as many games. But if Flanny threw a shutout, I wanted to throw a shutout. If I threw a shutout, Scotty wanted to throw a shutout. If Scotty threw one, Palmer wanted to throw one. That was a situation that worked. It wasn't so much who was going to win more as 'Let's keep doing this, one after another.' Because we felt like we had the best stuff in baseball. And I think we did. And we dominated."

Magic
1979–83

32

Junior Begins

It is tempting to say Cal Ripken Sr. made his greatest contribution to the Orioles when his son Cal Jr. was selected in the second round of the '78 amateur draft. "Junior" would become one of the Orioles' greatest players, renowned for playing in 2,632 consecutive games from 1982 to 1998. But to call him Senior's greatest contribution would be downplaying all Senior accomplished and represented in decades of unsung work for the franchise.

From '55 to '92 he was at various times a minor league player, minor league coach, spring training camp coordinator, minor league manager, scout, major league coach, and, ever so briefly, a major league manager. But a simple listing of titles doesn't do justice to his career.

He was the organizational glue, the guy who knew how things worked, the one who got the things done that no one else wanted to do. Although he wasn't an All-Star player or even a well-known figure until relatively late in his tenure, he was the insider's symbol of the way the Orioles were when they were at their best, playing the game simply, intelligently, and selflessly.

Signed as a tough, spindly catcher out of Aberdeen (Maryland) High School in '55, his career was limited by size and a .253 career average mostly in the low minors. But the organization spotted his grasp of the game and his teaching ability, and he was managing by age twenty-five. From '61 to '74 he worked his way up the organizational ladder, spending his springs running the Orioles' minor league camps in Thomasville, Georgia, Fernandina Beach, Florida, and Miami and his summers managing everywhere from Fox Cities, Wisconsin, to Aberdeen, South Dakota, to Asheville, North Carolina.

A no-nonsense stickler for details and fundamentals on and off the field, he was the classic foot soldier, taking on everything from driving the team bus to pitching batting practice to building dorms and fields—whatever he was told to do, whatever had to be done. When his son was making baseball history years later, those who knew Senior would say they recognized the roots of Junior's work ethic.

WALTER YOUSE: "My first scouting assignment for the Orioles was Cal Ripken Sr. Jim McLaughlin sent me up to Aberdeen to see if I thought he could play in the Arizona State League. I came back and said, 'Yeah, I think he can.' They called him into the office and signed him. He was a pretty good player. Tough guy, good catcher. Didn't have much power as a hitter. Very good athlete, outstanding soccer player. And mentally tough, very tough. That's where his son got it. He was a hard worker and all. Great desire. Wanted to win."

HERM STARRETTE: "I worked with Cal Sr. for sixteen years. I loved that guy. He worked as hard as anyone I have ever seen for the organization. When they moved the minor league camp to Biscayne College in Miami [in '72], he and Jimmy Tyler took wheelbarrows and hauled dirt in and made the infield. Put the infield down. On three fields, no less. They'd had one there and Cal Sr. built the other two. I went up to see him one night, and he didn't have a dry stitch of clothing on."

DON PRIES: "We had to build everything ourselves at Biscayne College—pitching mounds, backstops, batting cages. Cal Sr.'s sweat was responsible for it all. I would say to him, 'I'll meet you at the park tomorrow morning at eight A.M.,' and then I'd get to the park and he'd be sitting there in a tractor, and he'd been there since seven. There was nobody that worked like Cal Ripken Sr. Nobody.

"Not only did he know baseball, but he knew all these other things—how to build things, fix things, get things done. I was lost without him. He oversaw everything as we built at Biscayne. The only mistake we made was when we put a lake in because we wanted the beauty of it. We thought it was 375 feet from home plate [to the lake], and we later measured it and found out it was 275 feet. The left-handed hitters loved it. They hit balls in the lake on purpose."

JOE ALTOBELLI: "Cal and I took turns coordinating the minor league camp in the spring. He'd do it one year; I'd do it the next. Cal was still a young man. He'd become a manager at age twenty-five. He did a lot of things for the club. He used to fix those 'iron mikes,' the pitching machines. He used to go around with all the tools in the back pocket of his uniform. Quite a guy. A very hard worker."

FRANK CASHEN: "You go to the minor league camp, and Ripken was up at six in the morning. He went out there, prepared the fields and everything, and then came in. He was a great teacher. He was best at that, taking young players and teaching them the right way to play. Probably better at that than managing, truth be told. But what an instructor. I finally brought him up to the major leagues as a coach because he deserved it after all those years, and he had a good long run as a coach."

CAL RIPKEN JR.: "These days the Orioles need a truck to get all their equipment from Baltimore down to Florida for spring training, but in those days all they had was a black station wagon with little orange lettering on the side that said "Baltimore Orioles," printed. And Dad drove it down. They hooked a little trailer up, and Dad drove that black station wagon, and that was what they took to spring training. He and [Orioles clubhouse man] Jimmy Tyler would go down there.

"Jimmy was a young kid at that time, and Dad took him down, and they worked together on that complex, spent all day long with each other. He did everything from measuring the fields, grading, to pouring concrete to actually building the dormitories. He'd have the hammer and nails in his hand after the practice was over, and he would sit out there and turn the car lights on so he could do the work at night. He'd put his uniform on at six o'clock in the morning, go in at a certain time after the workout, grab a bite to eat, and go back out and build a dorm until ten o'clock at night.

"Dad was teaching Jimmy Tyler certain things at the time, and one day he told him to wash the station wagon. He said, 'You know, it's got bugs all over it from driving down from Baltimore. Really give it a good cleaning.' And Jimmy was so conscientious and wanted to do such a good job that he cleaned everything from the inside out and actually pulled open the hood and got the hose and scrubbed inside the thing, and then the car wouldn't start. And Dad said, 'No, that's not how you clean the inside of a car.' But Dad came home and told us that story with a sense of pride, because Jimmy was such a hard worker and wanted to do things right. That was what Dad was all about."

HARRY DALTON: "Every successful organization has a guy like Cal. He did so many things over the years. Whatever needed to be done, whether it be hammer a backstop or scout a prospect or drive the bus, he was ready to do it."

EDDIE MURRAY: "When I went to the Florida instructional league at the start of my career is when I was first introduced to the so-called Oriole Way, because that's where I met Cal Ripken Sr. and saw his work ethic and how he went about doing his job. Even as a manager he did things you didn't see the other managers doing. He was on the field; he was there early; he was there late; he was always teaching."

BILL RIPKEN: "Calling him a foot soldier, that's so true. And you can sum that up when I got drafted and they gave me a contract to sign or whatever, and I said, 'Should I read it?' And he goes, 'No, I'll tell you what's in there right now. Just sign it, and then whatever they ask you to do, you do it.' That's what he'd done for years. That was his approach. You sign and then you do whatever they ask.

"He drove the bus. Threw batting practice. One year in the minor leagues they took BP out in a field in the middle of nowhere because the bus broke down. Dad went and got the equipment off the bus, and the guys piled off and went out there in street clothes and took batting practice. He said, 'We're not just going to sit around and be miserable about it, we're going to get something out of it.'"

KEN SINGLETON: "The guy was a dedicated coach and wouldn't ask you to do anything he wouldn't do himself. When we did our baserunning drills in spring training, he'd be the first one around the bases. So it's nine in the morning, and you feel kind of tired, but you say, 'Well, if he's going to do it, I can do it.' He'd run, and he'd slide, get all dirty. And he'd do all the relay plays. When I first got there [in a trade] I thought, 'This guy, number one, he really likes his job, and number two, he really wants us to win.' He could be stubborn and all that, but boy, he wanted to win games."

When Cal Ripken Jr. started his pro career in '78 with the Orioles' rookie league club in Bluefield, West Virginia, he was hardly a stranger to minor league life. Growing up, he and his sister, Ellie, and two brothers, Fred and Bill, spent their summers far from home in Aberdeen, Maryland, holed up with their parents wherever the Orioles had dispatched Senior for the summer. They literally grew up in minor league parks, cleaning out lockers and clubhouses, helping their father, and getting a firsthand education in professional baseball.

BILL RIPKEN: "The first place I went was Miami in '67. I was two. Cal cut his head open playing checkers. He was triple-jumping someone, and he was gloating—jumped back and hit his head on the windowsill. My sister got hit with a coconut that year out of a tree—all while Dad was on the road, of course. The years I remember best were '72, '73, and '74 in Asheville. We stayed at a place that had a pool. Could go to the ballpark any time we wanted. Fred worked in the visiting clubhouse. Cal worked in the visiting clubhouse one year with Fred. I was a batboy for three dollars a game, which was huge money.

"The famous sniper incident happened there. There was a big hill out in right field with some woods up there, and I was out early with Cal, Don Hickey, and Doug DeCinces, and somebody shot a gun from up there, and a bullet came down onto the field. And Doug grabbed Cal and carried him off the field. Don Hickey left me out there. Just left me. I was seven or eight, and I remember the sound, and we heard the gun, and you could hear the bullet hit the ground.

"When I was nine I went to the ballpark an awful lot, and I'd go out and shag flies. Dad was always out early, and he'd throw to me and Cal. Then we'd have to stay out. Cal probably crept into the infield that year because he was thirteen and allowed to stay in there and take ground balls. I was shunted out to the outfield. It just seemed like the normal thing to do. Go to the ballpark, put on the uniform, go out there and shag, stay there, batboy the game. And if I didn't, I'd go up in the stands and sit with Mom. Every day was filled that way."

CAL RIPKEN JR.: "My clearest memories are from Asheville. Fred ran the clubhouse. My sister swept the bases with a broom, rode around on a motorcycle with Ozzie the Oriole, and put the score up between innings. I was old enough to be in a uniform, on the field. Dad would actually ride a tractor around making the field nice. He was the pitching instructor, the batting practice pitcher, hit ground balls. I mean, it was all in one.

"I got a uniform, and I was out on the field all the time. The clubhouse job came up, and it was alluring because it was a legitimate chance to make a little money. But I wasn't willing to give up the privilege of being out in the field, so I was Fred's helper. He was the head clubhouse guy, and I was a laborer in the morning who actually did shoes and uniforms and did a lot of the physical work, but he was the head guy that stayed all day.

"I was ten when [Senior] said for the first time, 'Go out there and shag. Go out with the pitchers, stay out of the outfielders' way, and if the ball gets by them and goes to the fence, go chase it and pick it up off the fence and throw it in.' I found out quickly that the pitchers didn't like to shag; they just wanted to stand there. So they started wanting me to cover that whole area, and I did. But you had to be really careful, because the outfielders wanted to work on balls, and that could get dangerous.

"The next step was coming into the infield to take ground balls. You're starting to feel like you're good, and you start creeping in shallower in the outfield. Finally, when I was fourteen, I could take ground balls on the back of the dirt. Dad would make me stand back on the edge of the [outfield] grass and say, 'Let the ball come to you. Don't get up there and mess up that dirt for the person who has to take the field.' As a sign of respect for that guy's office, his space. The ball could use the dirt, but your feet couldn't.

"One day at Memorial Stadium when I was fourteen, I snuck in when Dad wasn't looking during batting practice. Carlos Lopez was hitting. He hit a line drive, a hook with a little spin on it, and I reached down to try to catch it, and the ball got there a lot faster than I thought it would and hit me square in the wrist. I thought it was broken. But I couldn't shake it or fall down on the ground and yell, because I shouldn't have been there. So I just slinked back to the outfield."

MIKE FLANAGAN: "The first time I saw him, he was a little energetic kid. You couldn't slow him down. He was not stoppable. He came out to Memorial Stadium, and he was very skinny—wasn't very big at all—and I saw him work out one day, and he did all the stuff right, but he clearly wasn't that far ahead of anybody else we'd seen at that age. They bring a lot of kids out. He came out and took batting practice, and I'm sure he was nervous. But you sort of make a casual assessment of what you see, and you project, and you see Cal Sr. standing next to you, and you say, 'Well, that's probably as big as Junior is going to be.'"

CAL RIPKEN JR.: "I was sixteen years old and playing in a [summer league] in Baltimore, and I drove down to the stadium all the time with Dad that summer. He was coaching the Orioles by then. That was the first year I really took a lot of batting practice. I'd drive to the stadium early, real early, and get some batting practice in. Dad would throw to me, and I would hit. And at that stage I could pull the ball down line and reach the seats. I'd been trying to do that and going, 'I can reach it, I can reach it,' and I finally did. That was big. I think I was fifteen. The next summer was when I took all the hitting, and then I'd drive to my game, come back to the stadium after that, and drive home with him after the Orioles game."

As a senior at Aberdeen High School in '78, Ripken pitched and played shortstop. He was 7–2 with a 0.70 ERA and 100 strikeouts in 60 innings, and he won the county batting title with a .492 average. The Orioles selected him in the second round of the amateur draft, after three other players—Robert Boyce, a third baseman from Cincinnati who went in the first round, and two second-round picks: Larry Sheets, an outfielder, and Edwin Hook, a pitcher. Bob Bonner, a shortstop from Texas A&M, was picked in the third round.

CAL RIPKEN JR.: "Before I got drafted I came down and took batting practice so Earl and some other people could see me. With Dad throwing the ball and almost hitting my bat every time, because he was so good at it, I could almost close my eyes and swing, and he could hit my bat. I started hitting balls in the seats. It kind of made a few people open their eyes, and Earl watched me a few times. When I was being scouted, most of the teams saw me as a pitcher. I was scouted very heavily as a pitcher. I think the Orioles were the only team that had interest in me as more than a pitcher.

"After I got drafted the decision came, 'What's he going to be?' There was a split in the organization. Some people said pitcher, some said shortstop. The scout who signed me, Dick Bowie, wanted me to be a shortstop. No question. And Tom Giordano, who was the director of scouting at the time, the way I remember it, he wanted me to pitch. There were mixed responses everywhere else. Earl said, 'I've seen him hit. And I think we should give him a chance to hit.'

"My dad's contribution wasn't to say one way or the other. But he said, 'My experience is that if you start out as a pitcher and it doesn't work out, it's very difficult to go the other way because you've been away from the developmental process of hitting. But if you start out as an everyday player and it doesn't work out, then you can revisit the idea of pitching.' I think he really just wanted me to have the choice to do whatever I wanted.

"Ultimately the choice was presented to me, and I said, 'I want to play every day. I don't want to pitch.' They let me decide. And then I went to Bluefield and made a ton of errors. I think I made 32 errors in that 60-game schedule. Threw a lot of balls in the front row. I thought I wasn't going to make it. I mean, I thought I was going to turn around and be a pitcher. I regretted having made the decision. I thought it would have been easier [to pitch]. I measured myself against the arms that were there, and then I measured myself against Bobby Bonner, who was there playing shortstop. He'd played five years at Texas A&M, and I took ground balls with him and watched him play, and I went, 'God, I'm never going to play here. This guy's great.'

"Then before the season started Bonner was sent to Double A, where he should have been to begin with. But overall, I thought my pitching was more comparable than my playing. But then I got my feet on the ground and made some strides offensively. Pushed it to .264 and hit some doubles, and at shortstop started to feel more comfortable and confident. Then I went to the instructional league after the season, and normally they take two shortstops, and the other one they invited was hurt, so I had played in all the games. It's kind of interesting how my whole career goes like that. Maybe some of it is coincidence and some was set up that way, but I played every possible game everywhere along the way. Both years I went to the instructional league, once as a shortstop and once as a third baseman, the other person was hurt. And I played every day.

"In '79 I went to Miami to play [Class-A ball], and my throwing woes repeated themselves early in the year. I would be accurate during the three o'clock workout, then, when it became about seven o'clock, it was iffy. I also struggled with my hitting in the first part of that year, but then a third baseman got hit in the hand, and I moved over to third to fill in, and at that stage I was much better at third. So I relaxed and started hitting like crazy in the second half. That was the first indication that I was going to be all right.

"The next year I had a monster year in Double A [Charlotte]. Hit over 20 home runs and drove in quite a few. I turned twenty that summer, and [Orioles pitching coach] Ray Miller was managing at Caguas [in the Puerto Rican winter league]. It wasn't normal for a Double-A guy to go there. Puerto Rico had mostly Triple-A guys. But I was invited down, played pretty well, and was one of the RBI leaders for the league, as young as I was. Then I went to the major league spring training camp right after that, so I played eleven and a half months that year, which was good. I mean, your whole life is baseball at that point. I loved it; I'd grown up with it. I wasn't married and didn't have kids yet. What else was there to do but play?"

33

Love, Hate, and Earl

By the late '70s Earl Weaver was in the prime of a career that would lead to the Hall of Fame, as established and recognizable as any baseball figure. He was tough, shrewd, intense, and successful, having led the Orioles to the playoffs in five of his first eight full seasons as their manager. He also was loud, profane, and combative, a bane to umpires as well as to his players.

He barked and brayed at the umps from the first pitch many nights, and they responded with 91 ejections—a major league record—over the course of his career. Outside of Baltimore, Weaver probably was best known for his cartoonish arguments with the baseball law, eyes bulging, cap turned backward, mouth roaring, feet stomping, dirt flying on the umpire's shoes.

There was no limit to the lengths he would go to make his point in an argument. In September '77 he got so upset one night that he pulled the Orioles off the field and forfeited a key game in a pennant race. Two years later, he brought a rule book onto the field. The umpires fought back in various ways. In '79 veteran ump Bill Haller wore a hidden microphone and gave the tape of a profane argument with Weaver to a radio station.

The perils of war.

EARL WEAVER: "When you think you're getting cheated and it's going to cost you a ball game, I wish I could have accepted it more, but I couldn't. And then, when a player would get upset, you had to get out there because you didn't want to lose a player. You had to get in between him and the umpire real quick and do his arguing for him. That happened a number of times. Then something would be said, and the umpire would say something back, and you'd lose your temper. Just stupid. The people enjoyed it. I know it. But I hated it. Those incidents, I just hated them with a passion. They just happened. You couldn't make it up. I sure don't like seeing them on TV now.

"I guess if one stands out, it's the one in Cleveland when Larry Barnett wouldn't pay attention to the rules and I ran and got the rule book and took it out and showed him. Couldn't help it. The one I really hate was when Haller wore a [microphone] wire and then called a balk on Mike Flanagan to get me out of the dugout and into a fight, and then he gave the tape to a radio station in Washington. That SOB. I'll never forgive him for that. There's no doubt he called the balk just to get me out of the dugout. He denied it, but I feel that and know that. He wanted this on tape, so he got it. Probably the dumbest conversation ever between two adult men."

KEN SINGLETON: "He was constantly at odds with the umpires, always yelling, always on the verge of getting thrown out. Even the first pitch of the game, he might go off, 'Is that the way it's gonna be all day?' Stuff like that. I just thought he was loud and profane and that sometimes we were playing against the umpires as well as the other team. I mean, any time you have a manager thrown out of ninety-odd games, the umpires don't like him. He felt we were always getting the short end of the stick. Sometimes I think his approach with the umpires worked against the club a little bit."

MARTY SPRINGSTEAD: "He was just a pain in the ass, yelling from the dugout, screaming when he didn't get a pitch. All kinds of shit. In between [cigarette] puffs. I don't know how many times I threw him out. He says eleven, I say thirteen. It wasn't even fun after awhile. I said one day, 'You know, I could throw you out.' He said, 'You've already proved that.' I said, 'It's not even fun any more.'

"Back then, if Earl and I went to church together, we'd have been in a fight by the end of the service. We'd have found something to fight about. Either my hymn book was bigger than his, or his hymn book was bigger than mine. Something like that. We'd be at each other's throats. That's just the way it was. He wanted everything his way, and you don't always get that. And sometimes he just wouldn't listen to reason. That's where we had most of our problems. Either he didn't want to hear your side, or he didn't believe it. He'd come out there with his cap turned, and he knew how to turn it so he could pop you with it."

KEN SINGLETON: "We were playing at Yankee Stadium one day, first game of a doubleheader. Dauer is at the plate, and there's a bad call on a pitch, and

Earl hollers, and the umpire behind the plate says, 'I'd like to kick his little ass.' Richie gets called out on strikes, and he's mad and goes back to the dugout and says, 'Earl, this guy wants to kick your ass.' And Earl says, 'Yeah?' So the second game comes up, and at the meeting at home plate Earl brings the lineup out and jumps right up to the umpire and says, 'You want to kick my ass?' And the umpire said, 'What are you talking about?' So Earl whistles and brings Richie out and says, 'Richie, did he say he wanted to kick my ass?' Richie says yes. Earl starts throwing stuff and gets kicked out of the game. He was always begging for a fight."

MARTY SPRINGSTEAD: "Here's typical Earl. We were in the Kingdome, and I wasn't having a good day. We have those days, contrary to what people believe. We were in the fifth inning. Chuck Cottier was managing Seattle. In between innings, here comes Earl with his hat half-crooked, pointing to left-center. I go, 'Oh, shit, what do you want?' He goes, 'I want to tell you something.' I said, 'What do you want to tell me?' He says, 'You know, you're having a horseshit game.' I thought about it and said, 'You know what, Earl? You think I'm doing any better for the guy over there [Cottier]?' He just scratched his head and walked away. That was late in his career. I wished I'd used it earlier.

"But after all those fights we get along good now, after he got out. When they gave him a day in Baltimore before he went into the Hall of Fame, no one knows this, but I drove the car around the park when he went around waving to the crowd from the back. They invited me to the ceremony. Somehow I wound up driving the car. And I had this thought, about halfway through, that I ought to slam on the brakes and send him sprawling over the back. Smack his little ass in the dirt back there. Then I'd turn around and say, 'Earl, you got that coming. I owe you that.' But it was his day, and I didn't do it. I thought about it. The rest of the way around the field, I sat up there listening to the people cheering and thought, 'I oughta slam on these brakes and send that little bastard flying.'"

On September 15, 1977, the Orioles were in second place, two and a half games out of first. They were playing Toronto at Exhibition Stadium in Toronto, and the Blue Jays, then a first-year expansion team, were winning 4–0 after four and one-half innings. Weaver's most infamous argument ensued.

EARL WEAVER: "It was raining, and we were losing, although that was beside the point. But the bullpens were in foul ground, and the grounds crew covered the mounds with tarps while the game went on, then put concrete blocks down to hold the tarps down. Well, those blocks were no more than six or eight inches away from fair territory. The outfielders could have killed themselves. But the umpires wouldn't amend the ground rules, so I pulled the team off the field. I told Marty [Springstead], 'I'm not sending my club back out there until those blocks come off.' Marty just kept saying, 'Play ball!' Finally he said, 'If your club isn't out there, we're going home.' But I wasn't going to put my players in danger, so we forfeited."

MARTY SPRINGSTEAD: "He was in a pennant race, and the pitcher for Toronto was shutting him down. I'm the crew chief. I'm working third base. So it started raining, really raining, and we had to get this game in. We're in the bottom of the fifth. The game is already legal. All of a sudden the [Orioles'] leftfielder went over and slipped on the tarp in the bullpen. Earl comes running out and starts a tirade about taking the tarp off. I said, 'I'm not taking the tarp off. What if they have to warm someone up?'

"I agreed to take it off one of the two mounds. I don't know why I said that. But he didn't like that, either, so I said, 'The hell with you; I'm not taking 'em off anything.' He said, 'OK, we ain't gonna play.' I said, 'What do you mean?' He said, 'We ain't gonna play.' So he takes his team and brings 'em in. I get Bamberger, and I say, 'Bammy, what's he doing? Protest the game, do something, but don't just walk off.' Bammy says, 'I'll go try to talk him out of it.' He comes back out and says, 'They ain't comin' out.' After fifteen minutes the rain was getting worse, and I said the hell with it. I forfeited it. That put the world in shock. It was my only forfeit in twenty-six years [of umpiring]."

KEN SINGLETON: "After he pulled us off the field, I'm in the clubhouse, my locker was next to Eddie, and he said, 'You think we're going back out there?' I said, 'Nope. I think we have forfeited this game.' I said, 'Let's get a newspaper and see what's playing at the movies.' We went downtown and went to the movies. That was it. I mean, we weren't going back out. Earl was too ticked to go back out.

"And Toronto wasn't the only time he did that. One year in spring training we went all the way from Miami to Fort Myers for a game with the Royals—about a three-hour trip. So we get there, and we're playing; it's going along fine, and there's a rookie umpire behind home plate. And in those days they were a little lax with the [rule] changes in spring training. Well, for some reason Earl wanted to get on this rookie ump, and he goes, 'I want those changes and I want 'em now.'

"The rookie umpire is kind of scared; he looks around for the other umpires, who are veterans, and they didn't do anything. So Earl didn't get his changes. And the place is packed. Three hours from Miami. And Earl turns and says, 'Batboy, pack up those bats.' Floyd Rayford says, 'Are we doing what I think we're doing?' And I said, 'Yep. We're going back to Miami,' and walked off. The people were stunned. Earl got suspended for that, but as he was getting on the bus, the last one on, he looks back at everybody and looks at his watch and says, 'Might get back in time to play nine holes.'"

Weaver's feud with the umpires was public, taking place on the field, for all the fans to see. His battles with his players were more private, taking place in the dugout and the clubhouse. He was only motivating the old-fashioned way—with fear—and trying to win games, not arguments. But his driving, humiliating brand of inspiration left an indelible mark on those who played for him.

The first generation of Orioles he managed was a veteran group that was established before he came along, policed itself, and didn't need his cajoling. But when a new, young generation arrived in the late '70s, Weaver was the master of the Orioles' domain and expert in the art of love/hate managing.

RICK DEMPSEY: "Earl was perfect for his era. Earl could not manage in today's game. His approach was too old-school. With today's players making eight and ten million a year, you couldn't have a manager come in and yell and scream at them in front of everybody. That gets a manager fired now, having too much confrontation with his players. But that was part of Earl's program. He was deliberate about it. Push the buttons. Get them going.

"He tried to humiliate me every day. When he got tired of yelling at the pitchers, he came looking for me. Every single day. I mean, he pounded on me as hard as anyone ever pounded on me. He always said things to me so that the pitchers and other players could hear him. It took me eight years to figure it out. He wasn't mad at me; he just wanted to make a point to everyone, and he knew I could take it. He wanted the ones who couldn't take it to hear what he had to say.

"Like, he would complain about guys giving up hits on certain pitches: 'Jiminy Christmas, why did you call that fastball? You can't call a fastball to that guy. I'll get somebody else in here if you can't call the right pitches.' Well, he wasn't really yelling at me; he wanted the pitchers to hear that and go, 'Hmm, maybe I should have thrown something else.'

"But he knew I would never give up. I would fight him tooth and nail to the end. We had battles. We had physical battles. One time I was giving the sports scores on the six-fifteen news from the field, and I was supposed to be in his office at six-thirty, and he got the time wrong and came out and was cursing and swearing at me right on television. I was so embarrassed I just turned around and said on TV, 'Well, ladies and gentlemen, I have to go; there's an asshole calling me.'

"Then I threw my bat at him in the dugout, and he picked the bat up and was getting ready to hit me and said, 'If you weren't in my starting lineup, I'd crack you with this thing.' We argued all the way back through the clubhouse, yelling and screaming, went back to his office, and he looked at the clock and realized I was on time, and he never apologized. He would never apologize for anything. He just never mentioned it again."

KEN SINGLETON: "He embarrassed me a couple of times. Maybe I deserved it. One time in Milwaukee I tried to steal third and got thrown out. I was mad because I got thrown out, but he walked the length of the dugout to point a finger in my face and tell me, 'Look, I'm the one that puts the steal sign on here, and you're not going to get it very often.' I was really ticked, and I took all the helmets and just knocked them all off. I don't think any of them hit him, but they came close. And he didn't yell at me all that often, but I think it was because he didn't have reason to yell at me all that often. He yelled at some guys a lot. Like Dempsey. I mean, just every day it was something.

"I remember him yelling at Lou Piniella one time when Piniella was with the Yankees. Earl was getting all over him at Yankee Stadium. I think Lou played for Earl in the minors and didn't like Earl. So Earl was yelling, and Lou's a hothead, and Earl yelled the wrong thing, and, I mean, Lou slammed his bat and started for the dugout. And I'm playing left field, and I'm watching our dugout, and not too many people are helping Earl. They wanted Piniella to get to it. So Earl ran up the tunnel. He didn't want anything to do with Lou."

MARTY SPRINGSTEAD: "Brooks and them guys didn't even listen to him. He never bothered those guys. They just looked at him and ignored him. Thank God he had a team like that, veteran guys like McNally. They'd have been lunatics otherwise, trying to put up with all his shit. Boog said to me one time 'Marty, just leave the guy alone.' I think it was tougher [on the players] later on."

DOUG DeCINCES: "When I was a rookie, Earl would show disgust for Brooks. He'd strike out, and Earl would say, 'Can't anyone hit this guy?' Finally Brooks grabbed a helmet and bat and said, 'Here, if you think it's so easy, take this and you try.' I think that got Earl. Brooks was struggling, and he didn't need to hear that. At times Earl just overstepped. He couldn't help himself. And he didn't really care. His goal was production."

SCOTT McGREGOR: "We'd get on the bus after a game when we won, and Palmer and Reggie Jackson would be screaming at him, and people would even be throwing stuff at him. If we lost he'd be screaming at us, just totally chewing our butts. When I first got there I went, 'These guys are nuts.' But it was all by design. He had an ability to make a team play like anything. Because you knew he hated to lose."

DOUG DeCINCES: "At the start of the '78 season they were experimenting with playing Eddie at third and me at second. I was struggling, playing second one day and third the next. I was all over the place, never comfortable. On an oh-and-two pitch against Cleveland with runners on second and first, a ball came up the middle. Mark [Belanger] caught it with a lunge and threw to the side of me at second, and I snagged it and lost my balance, and the runner was safe at second. When I fell over, the runner from second scored.

"Earl came running out, and I thought he was screaming at Dennis for throwing an oh-and-two pitch down the middle. Then we get out of the inning and get into the dugout and Earl starts screaming. I say, 'Who is he mad at?' Lee May says, 'You.' I guess I was his whipping boy then. I guess I wasn't making him look too good with his decision to try Eddie at third. He took out his frustrations on me.

"But I was equally frustrated and said, 'Hey, are you talking to me?' He came firing back at me and jabbed me in the chest with his finger, like I was an umpire. I grabbed his hand and said, 'Don't ever do that again.' He turned around and said, '[Billy] Smith, go play second. DeCinces is out of the game.' I said, 'You can play Smith for the rest of the season. I'm tired of this.'

"We started yelling back and forth, and Pat Kelly and Elrod grabbed me. I go down in the hallway, and Earl came down and said, 'I'm not through with you,' and I lost it and threw Kelly off and went after him. If not for a policeman who was there in the hallway, I might not have been playing baseball anymore. It took me a long time to calm down. Kelly and Elrod said, 'Get ahold of yourself.'

"This was the first game of a doubleheader, and when it ended he had a clubhouse meeting. He says, 'We're a team, and sometimes I may push people too far, but I'm here to push you. That's my job. And I hold no grudges. There are going to be times when people explode, and I understand that, and I'm the manager, and I control this team, but I don't hold grudges.' In a way he was saying, 'I pushed you too far.'

"The next game, Palmer was going for his 200th victory, and I look on the lineup [card], and I'm playing third. Belanger and some of the guys are laughing, saying, 'Hey, way to go.' Because everyone at some point wanted to do the same thing. Then Palmer is pitching a shutout, and I come up and hit a two-run double off the right-field wall, and out comes Dauer to pinch run for me. Dauer comes out with this scared look and goes, 'Don't get mad at me; it's Earl.' And I'm standing there, and the ump goes, 'Hey, Doug, you gotta leave.' I'm burning coming off the field, and when I reach the top step of the dugout, Lee May, in his infinite wisdom, grabs me and says, 'You're coming with me. And remember, Earl holds no grudges.' He made me laugh and I grabbed my stuff, and he took me by Earl."

KEN SINGLETON: "I played for Gene Mauch, who was as fiery as Earl, but he didn't have the horses to back it up. Earl had the horses. And if you talked back to Gene, he'd take it personally. Earl didn't. Earl didn't have a doghouse. I mean, you could say anything to him. But he didn't worry about yesterday's game or tomorrow's game. He worried about today's game. And through that type of leadership, we had great focus for all those years. Earl was really good in that respect. I appreciate him more now than I did then.

"He had a funny side to him. We got killed in Toronto one day. Flanagan started, and by the third inning it was 18–2, and Toronto was an expansion team. And all the regulars were in the game. He left them in. About the sixth inning, I mean, we were so far behind, so I just kind of went down and sat next to him on the bench, thinking he would see me and say, 'OK, go inside.' Well, he got up, and this was more for my benefit, and he yelled, 'For all you regulars who think you're getting out of this game, if I have to sit here and watch this crap all night long you're going to have to watch it, too.' I just got up, got my glove, and went back in the outfield."

JOHN LOWENSTEIN: "Palmer and I were always questioning his strategy. He'd come by and ask us what we thought, and if we disagreed he'd go down to the end of the dugout and mumble. Well, one day in Oakland I was sitting next to Cakes [Palmer], and Earl's down at the end of the dugout going, 'Damnit, can't anyone here make something happen?' I told Cakes, 'If I get in the game, I'm going to make something happen.' So I pinch hit, get on base, and steal second on the first pitch. Then I steal third on the next pitch. On the next pitch, I'm stealing home. Three straight pitches, I'm stealing.

"Lenn Sakata is at the plate, and he turns and stares at me [coming down the line] like I'm some foreign object. I slide across the plate and [umpire] Dale Ford has the gall to call me out. So I go back to the dugout, sit down, and Earl walks over and just stares at me for a long time with that cigarette dangling. Then he says, 'I hope the hell you got that out of your system.' Then he leaves, and Cakes comes running over and says, 'Hey, way to go! You made something happen!' "

MIKE FLANAGAN: "Earl talked out loud. Whatever was in his mind came out. One time I heard him tell the pitching coach to go tell this pitcher that if the next pitch was a ball, he was going to Rochester. And then ask [the pitching coach] when he got back, 'Did you tell him?' So when you're sitting in a dugout, which I did every four days, you're wondering what is he saying about you when you're out there. There was that sort of thing, and it made you sort of thick-skinned. But it added a certain pressure because he was the boss and could control where you went. And if you did something he didn't like, you were gone in three days.

"He just didn't tolerate anybody that didn't conform to that sort of system. Frank and Brooks and Palmer, that generation, they could handle Earl. They'd been around him and knew what to expect. Earl had his thing, but that team was good enough and the guys were empowered enough to know that if he yelled, they could yell back. Then our generation came along, and we had to learn to conform to his system.

"When I had just come up, I was working with Cuellar a lot on my pick-off move, and one day Earl came out and was watching. Just him being there made me pitch like it was the seventh game of the World Series. And so Cuellar is talking to me, and I'm coming with all my moves on, and Earl just takes off running to second. And then he got right in my face and said, 'I just stole second base on you; you're not concentrating.' And I said, 'Well, how'd you get on? I know I didn't walk you.' I had to have a comeback.

"Palmer ran the clubhouse for the pitchers, and Lee May ran it for the everyday guys. They would come in behind Earl and counteract him, 'This is how you handle him; this is what you need to focus on to fit into the system.' Because if you just walked in cold, you couldn't believe the stuff that was going on. I mean, the intensity. It was the seventh game of the World Series every day."

Elrod Hendricks: "He'd walk out to the mound with a young rookie out there, a kid. I saw him do this a million times. The poor kid is shaking, and Earl goes, 'If you can't get this guy out, you're gone.' Then he leaves, and I'm there with the kid, and I say, 'Hey, you're throwing OK; he doesn't mean what he says; just try to block him out.' Then I'd go back to the dugout [after the inning] and Earl'd say, 'What'd you tell him?' And I said, 'Same thing you told him.'

"He brought Storm Davis in for his first game when Storm was nineteen. Next Jim Palmer and all. First day in the big leagues. We're playing Oakland, and Earl calls out to the bullpen and says, 'Get the kid up.' I said, 'Who?' He says, 'That fucking kid they just brought up; get him up.' Storm threw maybe fifteen pitches [in the bullpen], and Earl calls and says, 'You ready yet?' I say, 'Not quite; he's close.' And Earl says, 'That's good enough for me.' Walks out to the mound. Calls the kid in. Bases loaded, nobody out. Fifth inning. Gives up a pop-up, a fly ball, and then strikes out Cliff Johnson. One run in. And after the game Earl says, 'The kid's going to be all right.' If he had walked anybody he'd have been back down to Rochester."

Dennis Martinez: "The way he went about his business could be intimidating to young kids. I was scared and intimidated when I got there. But then you have Palmer and Brooks and Belanger and May telling you, 'Hey, don't worry about that little guy screaming. Just do the job.' That's all I needed to hear.

"He got pretty upset with me at times. I guess they want to find out what you're made of. He played a big part in my success by letting me know that if I didn't get it right, I might not be there anymore. He touched me real deep inside. He made me feel challenged. I wanted to show him what I could do and prove him wrong. And he got what he wanted from me. It worked. I couldn't find a better teacher."

RICK DEMPSEY: "He was not soft in any way. If a guy was eight for eight and coming up against a pitcher he'd never hit, Earl didn't give a darn; he was going to pinch hit for the guy in that situation. The guy who had the best opportunity to get a hit was going to bat. He upset a lot of people with things like that. It takes a special person to be able to handle people in that cold, hard, old-fashioned way and get away with it, and he did.

"After a while you started to respect him because he was successful. When you got pinch hit for, the guy went up there and got a hit. When you got taken out for another pitcher, the other guy went out there and did the job. After a while you had to go, 'This guy knows what he's doing.' I take my hat off to him. As much as I hated him while I was playing for him, that's how much I loved him after I was finished. He drove me and drove me, and I took the blame for a lot of things that went on, but the bottom line was, he played me every day, and we won a hell of a lot of ball games."

KEN SINGLETON: "One year it was Earl's birthday, and one of the reporters went around the room asking, 'What would you give him for his birthday?' Lee May said, 'I'm not going to give him anything, because he didn't give me anything.' And Kiko Garcia said, 'I'd give him one day in the big leagues, so he'd know it's not that easy.' He'd get everybody to hate him, so we'd play harder and try and shut him up. But then after a while you realized, 'Well, he's not going to be quiet; why don't you just play hard anyway for yourselves?'

"Then there was the time he got suspended for a weekend series against the Brewers one year, and as he's leaving on Friday he tells us, 'If you guys keep winning, I won't come back.' So you know what we're thinking: 'Man, if we win six or seven in a row, we won't have him around for a week.' So we win Friday, win Saturday, but blow Sunday. And he's back in the clubhouse with a big smile on his face, and he says, 'I knew the pressure would get to you guys.'"

SCOTT McGREGOR: "Years later he's still the same way. We go down to these Dream Week [fantasy] camps now, and one year Jimmy Dwyer was there on Earl's team, and he didn't get a hit for a week, and Earl benched him. Just like when we were all playing. He put Dwyer on the bench at Dream Week. And the lesson was simple. If Earl isn't winning, everyone is in trouble."

MIKE FLANAGAN: "There were games where the pitcher would throw balls on the first two pitches of the game, and he'd be going, 'Oh, here we go; I'm going to have a rough one tonight.' I had games later on in my career, when I knew him well enough, where I'd sit down [in the dugout after warming up], and he'd look at me, and he'd talk to the rest of the team and say, 'Boys, we're going to need a bunch of runs tonight.' It was funny now. It wasn't so funny then. It was like, 'Oh, yeah, really? I'll show you.' And you'd go out and dig deeper.

"He was always pushing you that way. When I hurt my ankle in '78 and missed a start, I was throwing in the bullpen when I was coming back, and he was standing behind me with a radar gun. I'd wind up and throw as hard as I could, and he goes, 'That's not good enough.' I tried to throw it harder, but my ankle really wouldn't let me. And he'd say it again, 'That's not good enough.' It was humiliating.

"From the first day of the season to the end, he never said hello, good-bye, good game, anything, because we were supposed to win, and that was all he was about. Losing was unacceptable. You were going to lose 60 games a year, and those 60 games were not going to be pleasant. But you looked back at the end of the year and you'd say, 'Boy, I got the maximum out of my ability.' The biggest fear of any player is that you go home after a season and say, 'God, if only I'd worked a little bit harder.' And I don't think too many guys of my [Orioles] generation have that regret."

34

Oriole Magic

The '79 season represents a dividing line in Orioles history. Attendance was poor before it and terrific after it, steadily rising to unthinkable heights in the '90s in a new ballpark at Camden Yards. Also, ownership changed hands in '79, with a twelve-million-dollar sale marking the change from the familiar stability of Jerry Hoffberger's Baltimore Baseball Group to the edgy, hands-on command of Edward Bennett Williams, a powerhouse attorney from Washington with ideas about moving the club to the nation's capital.

Gone forever were the days of the Orioles as a local, family-oriented operation.

Against that backdrop of noise and tension, the club played brilliantly, winning 102 games and the American League East title for the first time in five years. The season was a return to the glory days of the late '60s and early '70s under manager Earl Weaver, but this club was different in nature and spirit. The talent wasn't as dominant, but a blend of heart, skills, and original personalities produced a team as compelling and effective as any in Orioles history.

The team had won 90 games and drawn 1.05 million fans in '78, maintaining a depressing attendance level that hadn't changed in twenty-five years. With player salaries rising and profits falling, Hoffberger was under pressure from his family to sell. He announced in '78 that he would entertain offers, and Williams's purchase was completed in August '79. The lawyer said he would move to Washington only if attendance continued to disappoint. Ironically, crowds had already begun to swell earlier in the season, before Williams laid down his challenge.

Years later, it's still hard to say what happened in the summer of '79, what caused Orioles games at Memorial Stadium to become more popular. It didn't hurt that pro football's Colts, long more popular, were coming apart under owner Robert Irsay; with the team losing and Irsay threatening to move, fans were abandoning the franchise and looking for an alternative. Another factor was a change in the Orioles' flagship radio station: after twenty-two years on WBAL, the games were now on WFBR, a smaller, hipper station with a younger audience. The change helped recruit younger fans, which led to a Woodstock atmosphere, particularly in the cheaper seats in the upper deck.

In section 34 down the right-field line, a bearded cab driver named "Wild" Bill Hagy became the symbol of the awakening. He would rise from his seat, stand in front of his section, and spell out O-R-I-O-L-E-S with his body, twisting his arms and legs into recognizable facsimiles of the letters. When other, nearby sections joined in the cheer, it grew in popularity until the entire ballpark was following Hagy's lead, sending roaring cheers into the night.

HANK PETERS: "The '79 season was the turning point for the Orioles. Even though we won [the World Series] in '83, '79 was the biggest year because it turned so many things around for us. I really think it was the thing that got the Orioles rolling, because while they had been a successful club on the field for a number of years, they hadn't enjoyed the recognition and fan support teams like that normally get. In '79 those things finally started to come into focus.

"A lot happened that year, on and off the field. We went down to Washington and bought our way onto WTOP [radio] down there. Now they pay the Orioles big money to broadcast the games, but we had a little five-watt station carrying the games, so we were nonexistent down there. I told our staff, 'We're never going to draw people here unless we tap that Washington market. And the only way you're going to get some recognition down there is to get on the air.' So we went down and cut a deal with WTOP, and I forget how much we paid them to carry our games, which is kind of unheard of, but we did.

"Then our [Baltimore] radio and TV contracts had run out. They had been owned by National Brewing Company, but National had been sold by the Hoffbergers to Carling, which had no interest in continuing, which was a break for us, because while you had the security of knowing your rights were always taken care of with National, we weren't getting any money. So we shopped around and made a TV deal with Channel 2, and a lot of this deal was made not on the basis of getting more revenue, but promotion. We had to have people that were willing to promote the ball club. We weren't getting that. Then we took a chance on the radio with WFBR, and they promoted the hell out of us. WBAL had said, 'We'll take you back.' That's all they had to say. Screw you."

TOM MARR: "WFBR was far more hip than WBAL. We had Johnny Walker in the morning, kind of a pre–Howard Stern type. I did a pregame show, which they had not done on WBAL. And we did a very extensive postgame show. People listened on the way home. The big difference was when we decided to take the home runs hit the night before and play them all day on the radio next day. We added music to them, and this really caught on fire with a lot of people, especially those in the upper deck, the younger set. It just took off, more of a rock 'n' roll thing. The team was playing well, and people would hear the highlights all day and music with it. We were the first flagship that used replays so extensively. And it was such a great year for drama and highlights. We had a lot to work with."

HANK PETERS: "Then there was fear on the part of some people about what might happen to the Orioles [possibly moving], so that built some interest. Mayor [William Donald] Schaefer got involved with his office, and that resulted in a slight increase in season ticket sales. But what really happened was we put together the Designated Hitters organization, to sell season tickets to corporations. [Royals owner] Ewing Kauffman came in from Kansas City, where they had started that type of program, and he met with community leaders. I think we ended up that winter selling something like five thousand or six thousand season tickets, whereas we'd been selling about twelve hundred or thirteen hundred a year.

"But the biggest thing of all was what was happening on the field. It was just a tremendous year. We won games that were so damn dramatic. It was one of those storybook years. But that and all of those other things were coming together. If it had happened a year earlier, I don't think Hoffberger would have entertained the thought of selling, because we finally broke the attendance barrier [in '79] and drew 1.6 million. And we made good money that year. And Ed Williams walked right in and inherited that."

The '79 Orioles didn't have a high payroll, but they won with a blend of intelligence, strong fundamentals, and guile. An amalgam of All-Stars and role players who jelled under Weaver's forceful hand, they pitched well, made key plays in the field, hit in the clutch, came from behind, and won games in unusual ways. The phenomenon was given a nickname—Oriole Magic—and it stuck.

Earl Weaver: "The talent level on that team was nowhere close to the teams with Brooks and Frank and Boog. Not anywhere close. But they won. They were good in their own right."

Doug DeCinces: "That season was the ultimate in team chemistry. We all believed in each other. We all believed we were going to win. It was the start of Oriole Magic. We started believing, and then the fans started believing, and it filtered right into the clubhouse."

Ken Singleton: "The fans learned not to leave early. Things seemed to happen from the seventh inning on. There was a game against Nolan Ryan when he had about 15 strikeouts and we were losing 3–0 in the bottom of the eighth. And we only had two guys that really hit him decently, Pat Kelly and Belanger. So Nolan walked a couple like he usually did, and somebody made an error, and we had the bases loaded with Kelly coming to the plate. I'm sitting next to Earl in the dugout, and Earl says, 'We got 'em right where we want 'em.' And I'm thinking, 'What is he thinking?' The next pitch Kelly hit for a grand slam. We won 4–3. You could almost see smoke coming out of Nolan's ears."

Rick Dempsey: "We played the game to the max. We were a great come-from-behind ball club; we played solid defense most of the time; we had a pretty good pitching staff. We fought amongst each other; we had great times together, but when it was time to play ball we were as solid as a rock. And the fans appreciated it. We played some of the most unbelievable games in history on 33rd Street. And the people who were regular fans in those days know what I'm talking about."

Those carrying the heaviest loads were outfielder Ken Singleton, who had a career-best year with 35 homers and 111 RBI and finished second in the AL MVP voting; first baseman Eddie Murray, who had 25 homers and 99 RBI;

and pitcher Mike Flanagan, whose 23–9 record, 3.08 ERA, and 16 complete games earned him the AL Cy Young Award.

MIKE FLANAGAN: "We were going with a four-man rotation with Palmer [injured], and that led me to develop a change-up around June. I felt I needed another pitch to somehow cruise and be able to get some outs without having to be max effort on every pitch. It was really wearing me down. Up to that point everything was max and everything was earned, and the new pitch changed things. I'd watched Scotty [McGregor] pitch, and he had this nice, slow change-up, and all of a sudden the lightbulb went on in my head. I could throw something slow. It went against everything I'd ever believed in, where you had to be maxed out. But the lightbulb went on, and it just made my job easier. I had a really nice run with that. I felt like I was stealing."

Numerous other players had their roles, large and small. Rich Dauer, Kiko Garcia, and Doug DeCinces filled out the infield, with Garcia, a farm-system product, taking over for aging Mark Belanger at shortstop. Al Bumbry batted leadoff, stole 37 bases, and ran down balls in center field. Rick Dempsey hit just .239, but his get-dirty style behind the plate made him a fan favorite.

Don Stanhouse, a closer acquired in a six-player deal with Montreal before the '78 season, made the AL All-Star team despite a habit of narrowly escaping jams; Weaver nicknamed Stanhouse "Full Pack," as in the full pack of cigarettes Weaver nervously smoked to help him get through Stanhouse's appearances.

Weaver's idea of platooning veteran John Lowenstein and rookie Gary Roenicke in left field succeeded beyond his wildest dreams. Roenicke, acquired in the Montreal deal, had 25 homers and 64 RBI in his first full season in the majors. Lowenstein, acquired from Texas on waivers after the '78 season, added 11 homers and 34 RBI. Their combined totals of 36 homers and 98 RBI represented one of Weaver's greatest managerial feats.

EARL WEAVER: "The platoon just kind of came about. Lowenstein didn't want to play against any left-handers. Roenicke wanted to play against a lot of right-handers, which he got to do against certain ones whenever the [favorable] stat showed up. That was a happy situation. Gary wanted to play more. He wanted to be a regular. But he accepted it, and that was good, because he was still getting close to almost 400 at-bats a year. That's almost a regular."

JOHN LOWENSTEIN: "Earl never intended to use me against left-handed pitching. I faced it once and hit a ball to the wall, and I came back in, and Earl said, 'Did you bat right-handed?' I said, 'Earl, I played the game a long time before I came to see you.' But that was a terrific platoon, no question. The benefit was you knew who you were going to play against, so you could fashion a plan. I think Gary wanted to play all the time, but it was working. If only one guy had played, we wouldn't have gotten as much production as we did. Gosh, we got a lot of mileage out of that. We were the best one-two punch in baseball, statistically, at that position."

Not only did Weaver adroitly push those buttons all season; he also found places to plug in reserve outfielder Pat Kelly, who batted .288; pinch hitter deluxe Terry Crowley, who batted .317; and Benny Ayala, a reserve outfielder with a knack for extra-base hits. Lee May still received the majority of the designated hitter at-bats, producing 19 homers and 69 RBI.

But pitching was still the heart of the club. The Orioles had the AL's lowest team ERA and limited opponents to a .241 average, the league's lowest by 12 points. After Flanagan, there was Dennis Martinez (15–16, 18 complete games), Scott McGregor (13–6), Steve Stone (11–7), and Jim Palmer (10–6), who was injured and failed to win 20 games for only the second time in the '70s. The bullpen, with Stanhouse, left-hander Tippy Martinez, and right-handers Tim Stoddard and Sammy Stewart, had 28 wins and 30 saves.

It was a group that jelled not only on the field but off the field as well.

KEN SINGLETON: "We had four guys who sat in the back of the bus. It was Lee May, myself, Stanhouse, and Pat Kelly. We used to call it 'the shitter.' We'd sit back there from the hotel to the ballpark, and the airport or whatever. We'd just sit there and listen to Lee go off. Lee May was probably the funniest player I ever knew. He had a great sense of humor. He'd sit back there and say, 'Well, we're as far away from authority as we can get back here.' I'd say, 'Yeah, that's true.' When Lee left the club he willed his seat to someone else. It was a place of great respect.

"Benny Ayala wasn't officially in the shitter, but he sat close by, and whenever he said something it was sort of like the Pope talking. He was something else, Benny. Incredibly funny guy from Puerto Rico. He could really hit, couldn't do much in the field, and he had all these sayings like, 'You can lead a horse to water, but you can't make him talk.' Somewhere in the translation from Spanish to English it would lose its meaning and become something new altogether.

"And Lowenstein was great—a well-educated man. Had these theories that were outrageous. Everybody sat in the same place on airplanes, and I sat across from John, and he'd sit there and say, 'Know what? I have this airline business figured out.' I said, 'What do you mean, John?' knowing I was in for it. He said, 'You know all these places where you really want to go? Hawaii, the vacation spots? You know how far away they make these places? And places you don't want to go, like Cleveland, they're a half-hour away.' He said, 'The earth isn't really that big. What they do is they get you up there and they fly you around accordingly and they charge you accordingly.' He said, 'I bet Hawaii isn't more than three hours away from Baltimore.' I said, 'John, I never thought about it, but they're ripping us off.'

"What a character. But he could hit a fastball. All these guys could. We had a very good fastball-hitting team. That's why guys like Nolan Ryan or Goose Gossage weren't as effective as they were against other teams. I remember Lowenstein hitting a grand slam at Yankee Stadium, first time I ever heard the Yankees really booed at that park. A pinch-hit grand slam off Gossage."

MIKE FLANAGAN: "We had stuff like 'The Son of the Week,' which was a total rub in Earl's face. Belanger and Singleton and Dempsey and them, anybody that Earl was really nice to, he was 'the son.' You'd get votes for being the son. And this was all done on the team bus, and Earl would be up in the front, laughing. He liked it. I think he saw guys pulling together in a certain way, maybe against him, but that's exactly what he wanted. We were very tight. You had a common bond in a certain way, and that was to handle this time bomb in the dugout."

After starting with eight losses in their first 11 games, the Orioles won 51 of 67 to take control of the division, sustaining a red-hot roll for as long as any time in Weaver's tenure. They took over first place on June 6 with Dennis Martinez throwing a shutout in Kansas City, then won 14 of 15 after that. It was too much for the Yankees, the defending World Series champs, who fell behind not only the Orioles, but also the Milwaukee Brewers.

The constants were well-pitched starts, timely late-inning hitting, and a flair for the dramatic. On June 22, with the Orioles playing Detroit before thirty-five thousand fans at Memorial Stadium, the Tigers took a 5–3 lead into the bottom of the ninth, seemingly set to end the Orioles' six-game winning streak. But Singleton hit a home run, and after Eddie Murray reached base, DeCinces slugged a two-run homer to win the game. It was the night Oriole Magic was born.

DOUG DeCINCES: "I had hurt my back and was just coming back, and the team was doing well, and I felt I needed to contribute. This was one of my first opportunities. Dave Tobik was pitching for Detroit. Singleton hit a homer to bring us to within one, and then Eddie got on, and I hit a low line drive. I knew it was gone as soon as I hit it. The crowd was big, and they were really excited. Everyone was cheering, and I went into the clubhouse, and someone came and got me and said, 'You better come back out.' The fans wanted more. I went out and said, 'Oh, my gosh, everyone is still here.' They pushed me back on the field, and the place was going nuts.

"After that, lo and behold, we started doing that on a regular basis. That night, that game, that home run, it triggered something. It was the game that triggered things. The emotion just multiplied from there. It was such an event, and the chemistry was there already. The radio broadcast had a lot to do with it. I heard the tape later. The announcers, Bill O'Donnell and Charley Eckman, were going wild. Their excitement really came through."

The Brewers, a coming power, were still within two games of the lead at the All-Star break, but the Orioles won 15 of 18 after the break to open an eight-game lead, and the Brewers were never closer than four games after that.

KEN SINGLETON: "We set a team record for home runs that year. The pitchers were really good. Flanny had a Cy Young season. Palmer was hurt some, but Scotty was good, Dennis was coming into his own, and no one could stay with us night after night on the mound, not even the Yankees. And they had some injuries. Gossage got hurt. The Yankees had a mystique, but it didn't matter that year. We just seemed to be able to get it done. We got ahead and continued to build a lead. Unusual things were happening a lot. I mean, just somebody would come through. Benny Ayala hit a home run with a fungo bat in Cleveland. If the umpire had actually looked at it, he wouldn't have let Benny use it, but he just felt if he hit it just right, he could hit the ball with a lot more bat speed. So he used the fungo bat with a big knob at the end; the umpire didn't notice it, and boom, home run."

TOM MARR: "There was real magic in the air that year. In the eight years I did the broadcasts, I saw it break out only a couple of times, but that year was it. The stadium just erupted. There were great crowds every night. The upper deck was very loud. It was an affordable stadium for families and working-class people, unlike [Camden Yards], and the crowds were very enthusiastic and supportive."

Edward Bennett Williams had tried to get into baseball for years. He had failed to win the new franchise that sprouted in Washington in '61 after the original Senators moved to Minnesota, leading him to buy a stake in pro football's Washington Redskins to feed the intense competitiveness that had helped him become one of the country's best trial lawyers. But he never stopped looking for a way into baseball. When the Senators moved again after the '71 season, this time to Texas, he tried and failed to buy the San Diego Padres and move them to Washington.

Throughout the '70s, Williams continued to look for struggling teams to buy and move, and he was joined in his search by baseball commissioner Bowie Kuhn, who was under increasing pressure to get Washington back in the major leagues. Kuhn identified the Orioles as a potential candidate, pointing to their poor attendance at Memorial Stadium despite a history of winning.

Knowing Hoffberger was looking to sell, Kuhn suggested in '78 that former treasury secretary William Simon try to buy the club. Simon brought Williams in as a partner, and the pair negotiated with Hoffberger, but Hoffberger rightfully felt they might move the club to Washington, and as a proud Baltimorean, he wanted no part of such infamy. Simon ultimately became frustrated and pulled out, leaving Williams and several Baltimore groups as potential buyers.

The chances that Williams would win out were slim, but the Baltimore groups failed to meet Hoffberger's demand for twelve million dollars, and Williams ultimately did. The agreement, announced in August, stunned Baltimore. Fans awoke to the possibility that their team, in the midst of a glorious season, might escape to Washington in the near future. Williams, ever sly and politically astute, told reporters he would keep the team in Baltimore as long as the fans were supportive.

FRANK CASHEN: "Every time Simon and Williams met one of Jerry's demands, Jerry came back with another. Finally Simon said, 'I don't think you really want to sell this ball club; you're wasting our time.' And he gave Jerry some date and said, 'If I don't hear back from you by that time, I'm out.' They were talking about a price of ten million or eleven million dollars, with a million or two in cash in the bank. The Orioles had that sitting there. That was part of the deal.

"So the date came and went, and Simon said, 'I'm out.' Then Ed Bennett Williams went to Simon and said, 'Are you sure you're not interested anymore? Do you care if I've got this crazy idea of going in and negotiating for myself?' Simon said, 'You're crazy; you're wasting your time, but if you want, go ahead.' And Williams was one of the great negotiators and sweet talkers of all time, and he went in and bought the club, and if you ever examine it, he put up a hotel or something that he owned. He didn't have any goddamn liquid assets, any cash money. But he dazzled baseball with his rhetoric."

The change from Hoffberger to Williams was the most seismic in the franchise's history. Hoffberger had run the club as a local, relatively low-budget enterprise, an extension of the Orioles' hometown, a city without airs. Williams took over control of many areas, broadened the marketing efforts, spread the radio network to seven states, dropped 'Baltimore' from the front of the uniforms, and advertised the Orioles as a regional franchise.

JOE HAMPER: "When Williams bought the team, everything was handled out of Washington, suddenly. There was no organization. What he wanted to do was what was done. If he consulted with people and asked them what they thought and they didn't agree, he did it anyhow. When Jerry ran the club, I felt like I was involved in any decision. He'd get you together and talk about it, and you felt like you had input. When Williams bought the club, you didn't mean anything. You never felt like what you had to say mattered."

Despite the change, attendance rose steadily under Williams, with the season total surpassing two million for the first time in '83, quashing any ideas Williams had about moving. With Washingtonians making up a quarter of the crowds, the Orioles were more popular under Williams than they ever were under Hoffberger, the local owner. And with more money coming in, Williams could put more money back into the player payroll, signing Murray, Palmer, and others to large contracts in keeping with the game's rising standards.

Even though Williams never actually said he was moving the club, he also never said he was staying. He wanted a new ballpark, and his steadfast refusal to sign a long-term lease at Memorial Stadium kept politicians on edge, especially after Irsay moved the Colts to Indianapolis in '84. Williams used the paranoia that set in after that as a wedge, continuing to sign short-term leases until the state finally agreed in '88 to build a new ballpark in downtown Baltimore.

Williams was dying from cancer when the deal was signed, but as unpopular as he was with some Baltimore fans for forcing them to share the Orioles with Washington and the rest of the Mid-Atlantic region, there's no denying he was the one with the foresight and political savvy to get the Orioles from Memorial Stadium to Camden Yards.

FRANK CASHEN: "I say this unequivocally: the guy who turned the attendance around was Ed Bennett Williams. When the Senators left, sports fans in Washington really disliked Baltimore. Ed Williams made it socially acceptable to come to Baltimore to see a ball game. And how he did it—he probably did it unwittingly—he started bringing over Supreme Court justices and judges and congressmen, and that got publicity, and then the people started coming. He's the guy that changed the whole thing around as far as drawing people. I give him all the credit for that."

JOE HAMPER: "People thought he was going to move to Washington. He never said it himself. He was brilliant in many respects. He couldn't be as successful as he was as an attorney without having some savvy. I think he kept the political people on edge all the time about whether the team was going to stay or not. And that was responsible for getting Camden Yards. Williams did that. He got Camden Yards built. If Hoffberger had kept the team and not sold it, he never would have gotten [a new ballpark] because people would have never, ever thought he would move. He was too deeply wedded to Baltimore. Of course, by the same token, as the attendance rose, the team might have made enough money to build its own stadium.

"That's the irony. Hoffberger sold the team in a year when we drew 1.6 million fans for the first time, and we had never drawn anywhere close to that many, and if we had drawn that many in '78, when Jerry put the team up for sale, he probably wouldn't have sold. It's funny. We tried all sorts of things to try to get people to support the club for all those years [in the '60s and '70s], and it didn't take. Then Williams buys the club and attracts the Washington crowd, and the attendance goes way up. We had tried to do that, court Washington, but we were Baltimore. Williams got the attention of the press and the people down there, and it took off. But then, it was already taking off in '79, before Williams bought the club. That was quite remarkable. Something happened that year. Something happened, and the ballpark started to fill up. It's been filling up ever since."

LARRY LUCCHINO: "Initial impressions are hard to change. Ed came in and talked about moving, and it was a possibility, no question. He was stretching himself so thin financially that he'd have to move if the support didn't increase. That cast him in a negative light in Baltimore. But he also had lived in Maryland for forty years, and he didn't want to do something that would leave a black mark, and he was determined to make things work in Baltimore. And in the end, he did. Someone else could have bought the club and moved it, but Ed kept it there and put a lot more money into it than Jerry Hoffberger ever did. That should be recognized. Whatever you think of him as an owner, would the Orioles still be in Baltimore without him? I doubt it. And would there be a Camden Yards without him? I doubt it."

35

Heartbreaker

For the first eight games of the 1979 postseason, the Orioles were in command, displaying the same potent blend of starting pitching, clutch hitting, and resourcefulness they had exhibited throughout the regular season. They swept through the California Angels in four games in the American League Championship Series, then beat the Pittsburgh Pirates in three of the first four games of the World Series.

Piling onto the team bus outside Pittsburgh's Three Rivers Stadium after rallying to beat the Pirates in Game 4, the Orioles felt on the verge of a triumph. Not only would they have three chances to get the one win they needed to finish off the Pirates, but they had their top three pitchers lined up and ready to go, and the final two games of the series, if needed, would be played in Baltimore. It seemed almost inevitable now that the season of Oriole Magic would deliver the ultimate prize.

MIKE FLANAGAN: "We had a lot of guys on that team that played the odds, and Earl managed by the odds, and we figured one of those three games would be won for sure. We may have counted our chickens a little prematurely. I can remember being on the bus [after Game 4], and Mark Belanger was always sort of the money guy, and he said, 'What do you think a full [World Series] share would be worth?' and, 'That's a lot of money for doing this.' That kind of thing. I think we did count our chickens a little early."

It was hard to blame them. The Angels had played tough, hard, and smart in the first three games of the ALCS, with former Orioles Don Baylor [the AL MVP in '79] and Bob Grich leading the way, but the Orioles, as always, found a way to win—in particularly dramatic fashion in Game 1 at Memorial Stadium, when John Lowenstein, batting for Mark Belanger, hit a three-run homer with two out in the bottom of the 10th. It was the first pinch-hit homer in ALCS history.

JOHN LOWENSTEIN: "I sat on my ass until the bottom of the 10th. John Montague was pitching for them. And Earl was very proud of his three-by-five [index] cards [with the statistics on them]. And what he had on his card was what I'd done against Montague in '78, when he was with the Mariners. I hit a home run, I remember. So I had a check by my name on the three-by-five card. If I had to come in against Montague, I'd be expected to do something.

"So now I'm watching Montague pitch [the 10th], and he's throwing fork-balls. And he never threw forkballs. And Earl says, 'Get ready.' I said, 'Earl, that three-by-five card is based on fastballs and sliders, not forkballs. You better look at someone else.' He looked at me with a cigarette hanging out of his mouth and said, 'Get a bat.' Then as I'm heading up [to hit] he growls, 'Hit one out.'

"I get up there, and those forkballs are diving in the dirt, and I foul a couple off and go, 'How am I going to hit this? Earl can't hit it; I can't hit it; no one can.' So I decide I'm just going to look for a forkball. If he throws me anything else, I'm a dead duck. So he throws a forkball, and I hit it way up in the air, really high. I didn't follow the flight of the ball. I was watching Larry Harlow in left, and he goes back to the fence and looks straight up, and I said, 'I'll be damned, it's out of here.'

"So the place is going crazy, and I'm rounding second, and normally you get to third and shake the coach's hand and head home, but this time, lo and behold, I get halfway to third and who is standing there? It's Earl. He's got a big smile on his face, and he never smiled. He slaps me on the ass and goes, 'Way to go.' And I'm going, 'What's this little dwarf doing between second and third?' "

In Game 2 the Orioles built a 9–1 lead in the first three innings and then held on—barely. With closer Don Stanhouse on the mound in the top of the ninth, the Angels scored twice to cut the lead to 9–8 and loaded the bases with two outs. But Brian Downing grounded to third baseman Doug DeCinces for the final out.

Two outs from a sweep in Game 3 in Anaheim, the Orioles blew a lead and gave the Angels hope. Trailing 3–2, the Angels' Rod Carew doubled with one out in the bottom of the ninth, knocking Orioles starter Dennis Martinez from the game. Stanhouse walked Downing, and Carew scored the tying run when Grich hit a soft liner to center that rolled out of Al Bumbry's glove. The Angels' Harlow, another former Orioles player, then doubled in the game winner.

But any chance of the Angels furthering a comeback evaporated in Game 4. Scott McGregor pitched a six-hitter, and the Orioles rolled to an 8–0 win to finish off the series.

KEN SINGLETON: "The boldest move I ever saw by a pitcher was from McGregor before Game 4. We should have won Game 3 and closed out the series. Bumbry catches that ball a thousand times in a row. About knee-high, no problem. I'd seen him do it. But this one hit his glove and fell out. Carew was on second and had taken off as soon as the ball was hit, thinking it was going to fall in. If Bumbry had caught the ball, he could have walked it to second base and stepped on the bag for the double play, and we go to the World Series. I mean, the series was over. Instead, the Angels tied the game and won, and our clubhouse was quiet. We knew we'd blown a chance to go to the World Series.

"Well, McGregor was scheduled to pitch the next day, and he gets up in the middle of the clubhouse, and he kind of walks over toward Bumbry and, loud enough for everybody to hear, says, 'I guarantee you we will win tomorrow.' I've never heard a pitcher do that before. Everybody said, 'Yeah, OK.' Well, he threw a shutout the next day. Backed it up."

SCOTT MCGREGOR: "I guess I was hyped up, because I never did anything like that before. After I watched us lose, I was walking to the clubhouse with Richie Dauer, and I said, 'I guarantee a win tomorrow.' He looked at me, and Dauer was the wrong guy to say that to, because he went ballistic, going through the clubhouse and telling everyone. He stood up and said, 'Mac guarantees tomorrow's game.' The press didn't know until later. And we won 8–0. I just knew I had what it took to beat them. I beat them 20 times in my career. I had their number."

The Pirates had won 98 games during the season and swept Cincinnati in the NLCS to reach the World Series. Led by slugger Willie Stargell, thirty-nine, and managed by Chuck Tanner, they were older than the Orioles and played with the patience and intelligence that come with age. Embracing a team philosophy, they had a theme song, Sister Sledge's disco hit "We Are Family." No player embodied the anthem more than Stargell. When he made a key error to lose a game late in the season, he shrugged, played cards in the clubhouse, and said, "I screwed up." The next day he hit a home run, and the Pirates won.

Weaver's plan was to blitz the Pirates and knock them out before they knew what hit them. The strategy worked in the opener, played on a frigid night at Memorial Stadium. The Orioles scored five runs in the bottom of the first, and ace Mike Flanagan made it stand up—barely—with a gritty, complete-game performance.

DOUG DECINCES: "I was freezing my butt off, first of all. You dream as a little leaguer of stepping up to the plate in the World Series, and here I was in the bottom of the first, and it was so cold. We'd gotten rained out the night before, and I opened the blinds the next morning, and there was a foot of snow on the ground. I said, 'Oh, my God.' The field was frozen, but they pushed the snow off, and away we went. The conditions were terrible.

"I walked to the plate in the bottom of the first and had to step out of the box, my stomach was so jumpy. I got to a three-and-one count, and [Pirates starter Bruce] Kison threw a fastball down the middle, and I hit the ball pretty far. I started running and got to second and said, 'Oh, my gosh, I just hit a homer in my first at-bat in a World Series.' That was childhood stuff. I don't even remember touching home plate."

MIKE FLANAGAN: "It was the culmination of your dreams, starting Game 1 in the World Series. You flash back to Little League and the people you imitated in the backyard. Then they get you five runs in the bottom of the first. I went, 'Do I change my game plan? What do I do?' They cracked away at me through the whole game, and Stargell hit a homer, and it was down to 5–4.

"They had a runner on third with two out in the eighth, and I got out of that, and then they had a runner on third with two out in the ninth and Stargell up again. I was thinking, 'You're exhausted after a long season, your best season, a snowy day, and you're still pushing. But you've played your whole life for this pitch, and it's going to be the hardest pitch you ever threw.' I wound it up, max effort. Stargell was late, whatever that means, whether it was the hardest one I had thrown that night or not. He hit a little fly to left, and Belanger ran out to the short outfield with those little, choppy steps, and he caught it, and the game was over."

The second game was tense, tight, and pivotal. With the score 2–2 in the bottom of the eighth, the Orioles put runners on first and second with no outs, hinting at another Oriole Magic ending. But Lowenstein hit into a double play, and the rally died. The Pirates then won on Manny Sanguillen's two-out, pinch-hit single off Stanhouse in the ninth.

JIM PALMER: "Of all the Series we lost, the one we should have won was '79. We could have swept it. Weaver should have bunted [with no outs and runners at first and second] in the bottom of the eighth of Game 2. You're one game up; it's just good baseball to bunt. I don't care how you got there, hitting home runs and such. There are certain times you bunt. But Lowenstein hit into a double play. I see Manny Sanguillen all the time, and he got the game-winning hit that day, and he says, 'I still don't know why you didn't bunt.' But that was Earl. That was the good news and the bad news. The good news being that he didn't bunt and a lot of times it worked out. The bad news being that it didn't work out that time. But that's the way that [situation] should have been played. And it wasn't."

HANK PETERS: "Stanhouse was going to be a free agent after the ['79] season, and there were suspicions about his arm. We got into postseason play, and he really struggled. But he didn't want to come out and say anything was physically bothering him, because to do so would have destroyed his value on the free-agent market. And the game we should have won was the one where he gave up the base hit to Sanguillen. That one killed us."

The Pirates took a 3–0 lead early in Game 3, but the Orioles came back with two in the third and five in the fourth and went on to an 8–4 win. The next game was almost an instant replay. The Pirates had a 6–3 lead until the Orioles rallied for six runs in the top of the eighth, with Weaver operating at his best. With the bases loaded, Lowenstein pinch hit for Gary Roenicke and doubled in two runs. After another pinch hitter, Billy Smith, was intentionally walked to reload the bases, a third straight pinch hitter, Terry Crowley, doubled in two more runs. Weaver then let pitcher Tim Stoddard bat, and he singled in another run.

DOUG DeCINCES: "The game started late in the afternoon for television, and no one could see at all, and then all of a sudden, we broke out in the eighth and made that comeback, and to be honest, I think we thought we had the

Series. We were looking at Flanagan, Palmer, and McGregor. We felt, 'We've got our best pitchers lined up. When was the last time we lost three in a row with them?' But the Pirates weren't there because they were bad. They were good too."

With a 3–1 lead, Weaver could have used starting pitcher Steve Stone, an 11-game winner, in Game 5 and pushed Flanagan back—the ace had thrown almost 150 pitches in Game 1—but the manager stuck with his philosophy of being aggressive and started his 23-game winner. The Pirates, meanwhile, had to start Jim Rooker, a four-game winner, in Game 5.

A team less experienced than the Pirates probably would have folded under the disheartening weight of a 3–1 deficit and unfavorable pitching matchups. The Pirates just put "We Are Family" on the stereo and kept grinding. Flanagan took a 1–0 lead into the sixth, but Pirates leadoff man Tim Foli walked, advanced to third, and scored on Stargell's sacrifice fly. Weaver then pitched to former batting champion Bill Madlock instead of walking him to get to rookie Steve Nicosia, and Madlock singled in the go-ahead run. Meanwhile, Rooker allowed just one run in five innings and gave way to reliever Bert Blyleven, who shut out the Orioles the rest of the way. Pirates, 7–1.

Mike Flanagan: "I had the lead, and I just ran out of gas. I'm guessing I threw 150, 160 pitches in Game 1, and I was max effort right down to the last pitch. There was some talk about holding me back [for Game 6] because I was 15–2 at home, and I would have loved the extra day's rest. But again, you're playing the odds, and you want three [top starters] going instead of two. And holding me back a day would have bumped Palmer or McGregor. As it was, I got to the sixth inning with the lead, and they got a couple of hits and went ahead."

The Orioles still needed just one win at home, but the momentum had turned. Jim Palmer and Pittsburgh's John Candelaria matched shutouts for six innings in Game 6, but the Pirates' Dave Parker singled in a run in the seventh, and Stargell drove in another with a sacrifice fly. Pirates reliever Kent Tekulve pitched three scoreless innings to lock up the win. Pirates, 4–0.

In Game 7, Rich Dauer hit a homer in the third to give the Orioles a 1–0 lead, and McGregor took a shutout into the top of the sixth, reviving hopes of an Orioles win. But the Pirates' Bill Robinson singled with one out, and Stargell then crushed a home run, his third of the Series, to give the Pirates the lead. The Orioles had a chance in the bottom of the eighth, down a run with Murray up and the bases loaded, but Tekulve retired Murray on a fly to the warning track, and the Pirates scored twice in the top of the ninth against five Orioles relievers. Tekulve then struck out Roenicke and DeCinces, and Pat Kelly flied out to end the Series. The Pirates had become just the fourth team in World Series history to overcome a 3–1 deficit and win a best-of-seven series.

For the third time in four World Series appearances under Weaver, the Orioles' hitters hadn't delivered, this time hitting just .232 with four homers in seven games and totaling two runs over the last 28 innings—not enough from a team that had pounded a club-record 181 homers during the season. Meanwhile, the Pirates hit .323 against Orioles pitching, compiling the second-highest team average in World Series history. As much as the Orioles felt they had given away a world title, the Pirates had earned it.

DENNIS MARTINEZ: "When we went up 3–1 we felt like, 'OK, we won it; we got it in our hands.' I think the death of Chuck Tanner's mother inspired them. She died during the Series, and we all felt badly for him. But for them it was, 'OK, let's go out and do it for Chuck's mother.' That was a motivation. But they were a good team, a real good, tight bunch of guys, and it was the last time around for them. They knew it. They were a lot older than us, and this was their last shot. We still had a long way to go. At 3–1 [down] they made it happen. For some reason everything just turned the other way. They didn't have great pitching, but Rooker threw a great game out of nowhere." Then Candelaria in Game 6. It didn't take much.''

RICK DEMPSEY: "We were up against a team that was probably more talented than we were, but we should have won it. There was an incredible amount of good fortune for them in the last three games where they just got on a roll and everything they did was right. They had quite a few lucky things happen. Dauer hit a ball up the middle with the bases loaded and no outs, and [second baseman Phil] Garner stopped it. But he had no chance to get anyone, so he just threw the ball blindly up in the air, and [shortstop Tim] Foli grabbed it by one hand, barely, and turned a double play. Garner wasn't trying to do anything spectacular. He just had no choice. But to just toss the ball up in the air and have it work, it saved the game. Otherwise we probably win the Series in Game 5.

"Then Eddie, with the bases loaded [in the bottom of the eighth of Game 7], hit a line drive to right field, and Dave Parker came in and fell down and just threw his glove up in the air and caught the darn ball. The ball should have gone over his head easily. Just things like that. We hit a lot of line drives, and they made some great plays, and it just didn't work in our favor. We didn't get the breaks the last three days. We hit the ball hard, but it was one of those things."

EARL WEAVER: "Losing that Series was terrible. Just awful. They were out of pitching, and we had everyone set up on the proper amount of rest. We just couldn't get any runs. That was just one of those slumps that Eddie had at the time. He finally whacked one in at Parker with the bases loaded, but it went right to Parker. That ball goes on either side, we win. But you can't blame the whole thing on Eddie, who hit .154. We just quit hitting. It was like when the Mets got us with four straight [in '69]. Exactly like that. We just went into a slump. You always figure you're coming out of it tomorrow, but it didn't happen."

36

Near Misses

In the years immediately after their pennant-winning performance in '79, the Orioles perfected the art of the near miss. They played .590 baseball during the next three seasons, a winning percentage equivalent to 96 wins over a 162-game season. In '80 they reached 100 wins for the second year in a row and the fifth time in club history. In '81 they had the fewest losses in the American League East. In '82 they won 32 of their last 43 games and were tied for the division lead on the final morning of the season. Incredibly, despite all that success, they didn't once qualify for the playoffs.

In '80 they stumbled in the first half of the season and fell 11 games behind the Yankees after the All-Star break. They rallied breathlessly, winning 17 of 19 games—including six of eight with the Yankees—to pull within a half-game, but the Yankees never gave up the lead and pulled away again in September. The final margin was three games, with the Orioles becoming the first AL team since the '61 Tigers to win 100 games and miss the postseason.

Despite the frustrating ending, the '80 club was among the most balanced the Orioles ever fielded. The defense committed the fewest errors in the league. Al Bumbry was superb, batting .318 and scoring 118 runs, and Eddie Murray had his first monster season after signing a contract making him the club's first million-dollar-a-year player, hitting .300 with 32 homers and 116 RBI. Ken Singleton's .304 average gave the Orioles three .300 hitters for the first time and an offense that scored 48 more runs than the pennant winners of '79.

But as usual, it was the pitching that led the way, most notably starter Steve Stone. Toting a 78–79 career record before the season, he suddenly won 25 games, a club record. He also won the Cy Young Award and pitched three scoreless innings as the All-Star Game starter. Behind him came Scott McGregor with 20 wins, Jim Palmer and Mike Flanagan with 16 each, and Tim Stoddard with 26 saves.

STEVE STONE: "Earl was planning to use four starters in '80. I was slotted for the bullpen. I asked if I could contend with Dennis Martinez for the number-four job, and he said, 'No, Dennis is number four, you're number five; that's the way it is.' But that spring Flanagan and Dennis hurt their arms, so Earl had to start me. It worked out pretty well.

"It had all started with a meeting [pitching coach] Ray Miller set up between myself and Earl in '79. I was 6–7 and struggling, and Ray said, 'I'm tired of listening to you complain about [Weaver], and I'm tired of listening to him complain about you.' Earl had one goal, the proper goal, winning games for the Orioles, and he had twenty-five guys to do that. He was much less interested in my health and welfare. A lot of players tend to believe that 'what's good for me is good for the team.' That's not always the case. When I really understood what Earl was trying to do, things came a lot easier. You get a little older and hopefully a little smarter if you live through it. He had twenty-five people to do what he needed. I had to go to the next step.

"My transformation was owed mostly to a set of mental gymnastics that I devised after reading various self-help books, because I was fairly inquisitive about how to better myself as a pitcher. I had a pretty good idea there was a good pitcher in there. I just couldn't find it consistently. So I took the best of creative visualization, imagery, self-hypnosis, and a number of positive-thinking things and boiled them down into a system that worked for me.

"It was also the product of a radical realignment of my thought process as far as concentrating. I used to spend a couple of hours meditating on the day I pitched, visualizing every hitter in the lineup. I went through a number of things, used little tricks to heighten my concentration. I told myself that when the situation was tougher, I'd concentrate better.

"I started using [the new approach] after the All-Star break in '79 and carried it through '80. I went to the mound fifty times in that time, lost 7 games and won 30. We were a really good pitching staff, really gifted. Between Dennis, Palmer, McGregor, Flanagan, and myself, I was very much the weakest. I had a great eighteen months, but those guys were great pitchers. There were only nine on the staff altogether [in '80], which is a testament to how good we were. If you only have nine, all of them obviously can pitch. Sammy Stewart was the classic guy out of the bullpen. He could go long, short, start if needed, close. He was very valuable."

Manager Earl Weaver's three-way left-field platoon of John Lowenstein, Gary Roenicke, and Benny Ayala continued to excel in '80, producing 24 homers,

88 RBI, and one of the truly unforgettable moments in Orioles history—Lowenstein raising his arms in triumph as he was carried off on a stretcher after hitting a key double one night against the Athletics at Memorial Stadium.

JOHN LOWENSTEIN: "I had hurt my Achilles [tendon], and I was out for some time. When I came back, I was not at full strength. I was sitting in the dugout, and Earl said, 'Can you hit?' He always asked guys that, like you might say no. I said, 'Sure, I can hit. I can't fucking run, but I can hit.' It's late in the game, Rick Langford on the mound [for Oakland], slider city. I walk up [to the plate] going 'This is going to be good.' The first pitch I hit into the right-field corner.

"Now, I can't run, and as I round first the [relay] is flying over my head. [Oakland first baseman] Jeff Newman sees he's got me dead, then he turns to the plate and sees he's got no play there, and he turns back and throws to second. The ball hits me in the back of the neck, and I go tumbling head over heels into second. Somehow, I'm safe. But I'm also knocked out. I'm lying there unconscious for twenty seconds.

"When I wake up, I'm aware. And [pitching coach] Ray Miller is leaning over me. I look up and wink at him. He turns around and makes a throat-slashing motion. Get me out of there. So here comes the stretcher, and they load me on it. Now, there was something I'd always wanted to do, because I saw Norm Cash do it in Detroit before thousands of fans years earlier. He was on a stretcher, and when he got to the dugout, he raised up and got a hell of an ovation.

"Now I'm on the stretcher. And the doctors and trainers are all worried, telling me not to move my head and all that. [Trainer] Ralph [Salvon] is going, 'Don't move, don't move.' I knew this was my chance. As we get to the dugout, I suddenly raised up with my fists and yelled, 'Awwwright!' And the doctor who was carrying the stretcher reared back like I was some wild mountain lion. His eyes bulged, and he said, 'My God, man, what are you doing?' I said, 'Get me off this thing!' The place just went totally crazy. You could hear a pin drop until I reared up, and the fans went nuts. God, it was worth every second of all the planning and all the years it took for me to do that."

The '80 Orioles had it all, in many ways repeating their brilliant performance in '79. But in the end, they were stuck with an unfortunate tag—the best Orioles team not to go to the playoffs.

STEVE STONE: "We were an excellent team, but we were a slow-starting team. We were so far back in July, and then we got to within a half-game, but we never took the lead or even tied the Yankees. And the Yankees were great. I don't think [closer Goose] Gossage gave up a run in September. As the years went on, we were the only team for a long time that won 100 games and didn't make the playoffs."

The '81 major league season was mangled by the first midseason work stoppage in pro sports history, a fifty-day player strike. The owners and players were at odds over how to compensate teams losing free agents, and the exasperated players finally walked out on June 12. At the time the Orioles were in second place with a 31–23 record. When play resumed on August 9, the owners said the prestrike standings were finalized as a "first half" of the season, with the winner in each division advancing to a playoff series against the team with the best record in the remaining games. When the Orioles finished second in the "second half" to the Brewers, they failed to make the playoffs even though their combined record from the two halves (59–46) was second-best in the East.

The season was bizarre from the beginning. Murray, establishing his eminence as a slugger, led the league in home runs and RBI, but Bumbry's average dropped 45 points, Singleton's dropped 26, and the team's dropped from .273 to .251. Stone, the new ace, won on Opening Day, but he soon developed elbow soreness, became ineffective, and was out of the rotation by the end of the season, having dropped from 25 wins to 4. Then he retired, abruptly. The rotation was back in the hands of Martinez, McGregor, and Flanagan, who combined for 36 of the club's 59 wins.

STEVE STONE: "When my elbow starting hurting in '81, I always felt it was the quality of the career that mattered, not the quantity. I probably could have hung on for a couple more years taking cortisone shots. But I started the All-Star Game in '80, pitched in a World Series in '79. I was the only pitcher in the '80s, it turned out, to have a 25-win season. I got to over 100 wins in my career. Most of the good things that happened to me happened in Baltimore."

As the strike ended, Cal Ripken Jr. was called up from Rochester, never to return again. He had excelled in Triple A all season, playing solidly at third base (with a few weeks at shortstop mixed in when Bob Bonner was injured) and batting .288 with 23 homers and 75 RBI. Ripken made his major league debut as a pinch runner in the Orioles' 3–2 win over the Kansas City Royals on August 10 at Memorial Stadium. The idea was just to introduce him to the major leagues the rest of the season. Ripken played in 12 games at shortstop and 6 at third base and batted .128 in 39 at-bats.

Despite that unimpressive start, Ripken was at the core of a heated internal debate. He obviously was going to play in the major leagues, but where? Manager Earl Weaver envisioned him as a shortstop despite his six-foot, four-inch, 200-pound frame, and the club needed a shortstop with Mark Belanger at the end of his career. But Ripken had come through the minor league system as a third baseman, and some wanted him to replace Doug DeCinces, who had power and a solid glove but also had a sore back and didn't hit for a high average.

The decision was made after the '81 season. DeCinces was traded to California for veteran outfielder Dan Ford. Ripken was going to play third for the Orioles.

MIKE FLANAGAN: "Having seen Cal as a kid [before he was drafted], and then seeing him again three years later in the major league camp, he was three or four inches taller and thirty pounds heavier, and you went, 'My God, how big is he going to get?'"

CAL RIPKEN JR.: "Early in the ['81] season there was an injury to somebody in Baltimore, and they took Bob Bonner up, and Earl came out in the paper and said he wanted me, but they overruled him or something and brought Bobby up, and I stayed down. And then DeCinces got hurt right before the strike, and there was some talk about bringing me up then, but they didn't want to have me locked in without playing. So I was really enthused about the possibility that I was right on the edge of getting that call-up. Then the strike went really long, and I got tremendous coverage. They started covering Triple-A games on TV, and Mel Allen came down and *This Week in Baseball* did things, so it was a good atmosphere for us.

"When I got called up, I didn't play much. It seemed like the at-bats that DeCinces didn't want, I got. After the '81 season I went back to winter ball in Puerto Rico. They wanted me to go down and play some shortstop because Earl looked at me as a shortstop, and it seemed like an opening at shortstop was kind of developing. Bonner was the heir apparent to Belanger. I played with him in Triple A, and I thought he was one of the best shortstops I'd ever seen. He had a good year [in Rochester in '81], and I thought it was his position for sure.

"But they wanted me to play some games at short in Puerto Rico. So I go back, and Ray Miller is the manager again, and I'm playing third. Hitting great, like .355. Leading the league in RBI and maybe a little ahead in home runs. But I went to Ray and said, 'You know, they kind of wanted me to come down here and play short.' He looked at me and said, 'Don't worry about that.' And then a day or two later they announced that DeCinces had been traded and his spot was wide open now, and basically, it was mine."

DOUG DECINCES: "I got traded because of my position with the union. I was the player rep, a position my teammates had voted me into. I had talked with Edward Bennett Williams all the time during the strike. He would fly me up to the [union] meetings in New York and then fly me back to talk to him. I would tell him what went on and then [owners' negotiator] Ray Grebey would talk to him and call me a liar. After the season, the word came down that I should be traded."

HANK PETERS: "No one was ever traded for his union activities. The things that entered into the DeCinces trade were, one, make room for Rip, and two, Doug had a back problem, a major back problem. So we were looking for an outfielder, and we got Danny Ford, who played well for us over the next few years. Those were the reasons. It had nothing to do with the union."

EARL WEAVER: "I got up and walked out of the organizational meeting when they traded DeCinces. I wanted Ripken to play shortstop. My last words were, "Look, if you don't let the kid play shortstop, you're going to beat him out of a chance to go to the Hall of Fame.' Those weren't really smart words, because he'd have gone to the Hall of Fame, anyway. But I had grown up watching Marty Marion, a six [foot], four [inch] shortstop with St. Louis who just seemed to take two steps and reach out and have the ball. And there was no question about Rip's arm. He had a great arm. I thought [trading DeCinces] was a mistake. Just think what we could have done in '82 with DeCinces hitting his 30 [homers] at third base and Ripken doing as much as he did at shortstop."

DOUG DECINCES: "I knew that winter that Cal was coming up, but Earl had said he had no interest in trading me. When the trade came down, Earl called and we had our best conversation. He told me, 'This is the first time in my career that I've been overruled as far as the team I want to have. That means it's time for me to leave.' He told me, 'I think they just traded away the pennant because Cal is going to end up at short. Now I don't have a third baseman.'"

HANK PETERS: "If Earl says he walked out of the [organizational] meeting, he probably walked out to get a drink or something. That's a bunch of crap."

The '82 season was a classic, even though it eventually was as frustrating as those that had preceded it. Murray had 32 homers and 110 RBI. Jim Palmer, in his last hurrah, went 15–5. Ripken slumped in the beginning, gathered himself, and ended up as the AL Rookie of the Year, hitting .264 with 28 homers and 93 RBI. After all the debate about where he should play, he started the year at third base, switched to shortstop in July, and never looked back. After sitting out the second game of a doubleheader on May 29, he played in every game for the rest of the season. His consecutive-games streak was underway.

KEN SINGLETON: "Cal was different than most rookies. You could see he was well-schooled. He knew exactly where to play. He was a good enough hitter at first. Batted down in the lineup. His personality was like his dad's—all business. We didn't have the sense that he was going to become a megastar, but an All-Star, sure."

CAL RIPKEN JR.: "On Opening Day I hit a home run in my first at-bat. Put us ahead. Singleton was on first. I chased him around the bases. He was in his normal, slow pace, and I was going three thousand miles an hour inside and outside. And then after Opening Day I got four hits in my next 55 at-bats. Earl called me into the office a few times. I think he was trying to play mind games with me saying, 'Look, we don't have anybody else. We traded DeCinces. You're not going anywhere. I'm not sending you down. You're it. All right. See you later.'

"I was working on my swing and kind of fighting with Earl about what to do, and then there was an argument on the field one night. Reggie Jackson was standing on third, and he called me over and said, 'You know, you got to the big leagues; just hit the way you want to hit.' With his presence and stature, that helped. My dad was probably saying the same things. It all just kind of clicked.

"That's where Eddie [Murray] and I became really good friends. We had similar upbringings in the game, and everybody else on the team was older and had families. When we came back from a road trip, the families and the wives were at the airport, and the two of us were always catching the bus to satellite parking to pick up our cars. When I was struggling, he tried to offer me advice and comfort. I was very grateful. He was the one person that knew what I was feeling, so we hung out and became really exceptional friends."

MIKE FLANAGAN: "Earl always tested a young player right away. Some guys responded, and other guys crumbled. One who didn't make it was Bobby Bonner. There was a game in Toronto [in '82] when he got a start, made two or three errors, lost the game, and the next thing you know, he's a missionary in Venezuela. Meanwhile, Cal was playing third, and Earl knew he could catch the ball and throw the ball, and we needed a shortstop. We'd tried everybody in the farm system, from Bonner to Lenn Sakata, trying to replace Belanger, and none of it was working, and this kid could catch the ball and throw it, and that was important to Earl. It was just a natural fit."

HANK PETERS: "Bonner was one of these reborn Christian kids and wore it on his sleeve, and Earl didn't take to him. He never did. He crumbled him. And this was one of the best-looking shortstop prospects you'll ever want to see. Earl just destroyed that kid. He never did bounce back from it, which is a shame."

MIKE BODDICKER: "Bobby Bonner was a great shortstop. But after Earl blasted him that day, he just crumbled and was never the same."

CAL RIPKEN JR.: "When Earl moved me to shortstop, it came out of the blue. One day there was a '5' by my name, the next day there was a '6.' I thought, 'Well, sometimes they make mistakes.' I started getting dressed, and Lenny Sakata came over and said, 'You know you're playing short tonight?' And I said, 'I saw that "6" by my name, but I haven't played short in a long time. There's got to be a mistake.' And he goes, 'It's not a mistake.' Then Earl brought me in and said, 'I'm putting you there to try and get more offense in the lineup. I don't want you to try to do too much.' I still thought it was temporary; I thought I was going back to third soon. And I did—fifteen years later."

HANK PETERS: "While Junior relearned shortstop, he made no double plays for a couple of months. It was a tough transition. It certainly worked out very well in the long run, needless to say, and I give Earl credit for that. But initially it was a tough transition and, of course, it left us with a problem at third base. We transferred our problem from short to third."

DOUG DeCINCES: "When I came back to Baltimore the first time after the trade, I felt like an artist whose paintings had become famous, but I was able to see it before I died. I felt like the people, all of a sudden, started appreciating me because they were running everyone out there at third and having a problem."

After starting slowly and falling eight games behind the Brewers in mid-August of '82, the Orioles rallied furiously. They won seven games in a row, lost one, won ten in a row, swept five straight from the Yankees, and won two of three in Milwaukee to pull within two games of the Brewers with a week left. In the end, they needed to sweep a season-ending four-game series with the Brewers at Memorial Stadium to complete the comeback. They won the first three before roaring crowds, pulling even, and sent Palmer out to pitch the finale against the Brewers' Don Sutton. Fans brought brooms to the stadium, anticipating the final scene of one of the Orioles' greatest comebacks. Instead, the Brewers pounded Palmer and won 10–2.

DENNIS MARTINEZ: "We played some great ball coming down the stretch. I pitched two of the games when we were coming back, one in Milwaukee and one in Baltimore. And it was tough because my dad died. I flew to Nicaragua for the funeral and came back when we were going to Milwaukee. Pitched two days later. They didn't know how I was going to react, but once I got out there it was my job, and I was doing what I had to do. I was saying to myself, 'OK, Dad, this is for you. Help me out; help us out.' I was praying, 'Let us come through.'"

HARRY DALTON: "We [the Brewers] had a doubleheader on Friday night and got whomped. Saturday, lost again. I went out that night, didn't know where

I wanted to go for dinner. I just wanted to be alone and think about things. I must have driven around town for an hour trying to decide what place I wanted to go to, and I said the heck with it and went and got a pizza and took it back to the room.

"On Sunday it was a playoff atmosphere. I watched the game from the press box. Stood there in the first inning with my foot on the railing and watched [Milwaukee's] Robin Yount hit the home run that put us in front. And I never left that spot. I'm not superstitious, but I went, 'I like it here. I'm staying for the whole ball game.'"

DENNIS MARTINEZ: "Everyone felt we were going to win the last game. People were carrying brooms, and we said, 'Oh, gosh, wait until after the game.' But Harvey Kuenn was their manager, and he did a good job of keeping them cool. They had a good team, a good bunch of guys, and they knew what to do in that situation."

MIKE FLANAGAN: "I'm not a gambling man, but I'd have bet anything I owned that we'd have won that last game."

JIM PALMER: "It was probably the most dramatic game I ever pitched—even more than any World Series game. You're nervous, extremely nervous because it means so much. We'd come from so far back. The disappointing thing was when a club plays that well—and we had beaten Milwaukee two weeks earlier throwing guys out at the plate, then swept the first three games, the way we got there was so fantastic—to not be able to deliver when needed was disappointing.

"We'd scored a bunch of runs in the first three games to get there, but Sutton was a better pitcher, and we just didn't do it that day. They had an awfully good ball club, and I gave up three solo home runs. We were still in it until the sixth or seventh. But I wasn't able to pitch the way I had the last three months."

KEN SINGLETON: "I'm still kind of ticked about it. I felt all we had to do was score first, and they would have folded. They couldn't have gone back to Milwaukee after losing four in a row like that. But they scored first, and it got out of hand. After the game I was riding home with my wife and two young sons, and the car was quiet. I guess their mother had warned them that this was a big game. But I said, 'What are you talking about, guys? I mean, we lost. We'll win next year.' And sure enough, we did."

After the final out of the loss to the Brewers, an emotional spectacle unfolded at Memorial Stadium. The disappointed sellout crowd rose and started to cheer, and kept cheering for forty-five minutes. The Orioles' players left the clubhouse and came back out onto the field to wave, and then Weaver did, too, setting off the biggest roar. The cheers were mostly for him.

Weaver had announced in March that the '82 season would be his last managing the Orioles. He was retiring after that and moving to Florida to play golf. An era was ending. The news had been in the headlines and the back of everyone's mind all season, yet it was almost forgotten as the Orioles chased the Brewers down the stretch. Now, suddenly, the moment was at hand. Weaver was pulling off his uniform for the last time. And the fans weren't going to let him go without a salute.

BOB BROWN: "After that last game [in '82], the thing that got me was we'd lost the pennant and no one left the ballpark. To me it indicated that Baltimore had really become a baseball town. It also indicated that we, as an organization, had matured to the point that we were a beloved institution in Baltimore. And it was not always thus.

"Howard Cosell was broadcasting the game [on ABC-TV], and he'd never had anything nice to say about Baltimore, and as the crowd cheered, he was going on about Baltimore and the mayor and the Inner Harbor, and the people in the stands were cheering, and Howard says, 'The story isn't out there where the Brewers are celebrating; the story is in the stands.' Weaver went in and did a thirty-minute press conference, and when that ended he had to come back out because the people were still cheering. Then Earl and Harvey Kuenn hugged, and the players came back out in various stages of undress and took bows. What a day of emotion. The people were cheering for Earl, but also, maybe even more so, for what baseball in Baltimore had become."

Few managers had ever received such a rousing send-off, and that was fitting, for few managers had compiled a record so glowing. Weaver had won six division titles, four American League pennants, and one World Series in his fourteen and a half years as the Orioles' manager. Not once had they finished under .500, and only twice had they finished lower than second. His .596

career winning percentage ranked fifth among the hundreds of managers who had worked exclusively in the twentieth century.

FRANK CASHEN: "When I left Baltimore and went to New York [to run the Mets in '80] and saw Billy Martin, there was no longer a doubt in my mind that Earl Weaver was not only a good manager, he was the best manager in baseball. He was a manager for all seasons. Some guys are good when they've got a winning ball club, but when things start to go bad, they don't know what to do. Or they're a good manager with a good ball club, but a bad manager with a bad ball club. Or they look like a pretty good manager, but they've never been in a pennant race. Earl had everything. He drank his brains out. But he was a fucking genius."

ELROD HENDRICKS: "He was good. Man, he was good. When I'd just started coaching and Tony LaRussa was the hot, new thing [managing], he'd come in and make all sorts of moves, and Earl would just sit back with his arms crossed. And LaRussa is looking over at Earl like he's getting him, you know. And then it's the eighth inning, and LaRussa is out of bullets, and here comes Earl with Jim Dwyer and Terry Crowley and that bullpen. Earl just hammers him. And you go, 'Boy, that's good. That's as good as it gets, right there.'"

EARL WEAVER: "As wonderful as the '82 season was, you're still looking forward to [retiring] the next year. It was there all the time. You worked hard, and everything was going good, and everything was wonderful, and that year flew by."

HANK PETERS: "He left at the right time because he was pretty well finished. The sparks were about dead after the '82 season. When you work with somebody for the number of years that I worked with Earl, you can tell whether or not a guy is really at the top of his game. And driving the way Earl had driven, maybe things just kind of caught up with him. He lived the fast life off the field, and I think that took its toll on him, frankly, and things just got to the point where you knew he wasn't the same Earl Weaver who had managed so successfully for so long. His personality changed in that he started to want to be loved. He really did. There were just little things you pick up on.

I was disappointed in '82. We should have won. I know it was a dramatic ending of the season. But it should have never gotten to that point. We were a better ball club than Milwaukee."

JIM PALMER: "Weaver had a meeting before that last game and stood up and said, 'Listen, thanks for your effort, it was a great season,' all that. Then Richie Dauer said, 'Whew, we thought you were going to tell us you weren't going to retire.'"

37

All the Way

For the first time since 1968, the Orioles were in the market for a new manager in the wake of Earl Weaver's retirement after the '82 season. They settled on a candidate who, like Weaver, had learned his craft in the Orioles' minor league system years earlier, but unlike Weaver—to say the least—was tight-lipped and almost simplistic in his approach to the game.

Joe Altobelli, fifty, had spent the previous three seasons working for the Yankees, first as a minor league manager in '80 and then as the major league third-base coach in '81 and '82. Before that, he had managed the San Francisco Giants from '77 to '79, never reaching the playoffs but winning the National League's Manager of the Year Award in '78. He'd remained true to the Orioles at heart throughout his travels, owing to the decade he spent as a winning manager in the minor league system in the '60s and '70s. Now, in a sense, he was coming home.

He inherited a team of sharp, unflappable veterans, hardened by years of tight pennant races, heartbreaks, and Weaver's fury. Altobelli's approach as the newcomer? Don't touch a thing.

JOE ALTOBELLI: "When Earl retired, they passed questionnaires around the office looking for candidates, and my name came up. I met with Hank Peters and Edward Bennett Williams, and bingo, I got the job. I didn't feel like a new kid on the block. I knew the coaches, and I kept them. I knew most of the players. A lot of them had played for me in Rochester. The surroundings weren't new. I'd been to Miami, where we trained in the spring. It was a club that had had a chance in '82 and was disappointed on the last day. Part of my talk [to the team at the start of spring training] was about that. I mentioned that they'd started slow [in '82], and I told them, 'All you have to do is win five or six more games early in the season, and we'll win the division.'"

JOHN LOWENSTEIN: "Everyone says Earl was the smartest manager I ever played for, but I think Altobelli was the smartest because he did nothing when he took over. He just put that lineup up in the dugout and sat down next to it and made his pitching changes. He relied on the team and let it fly, and that was smart, because we were fine-tuned to win in '83, and he recognized that and didn't screw it up."

The Orioles ran hot and cold for much of the '83 season, dodging various pitching catastrophes. Three starters had major problems. A back ailment limited Jim Palmer, thirty-seven, to five wins. After a strong start, Mike Flanagan suffered knee ligament damage when he fielded a grounder and his spikes got caught in the grass. He was out eleven and a half weeks. And Dennis Martinez, battling alcoholism, went 7–16 with a 5.53 ERA and won just once in the last two months.

Young pitching saved the season. Mike Boddicker, a twenty-five-year-old rookie, was promoted from Rochester and emerged as an ace, going 16–8 with a 2.77 ERA and five shutouts. Storm Davis, a top prospect who had pitched mostly in relief in '82, took over a spot in the rotation and won 13 games. Add 18 wins from Scott McGregor, the only veteran who was healthy and effective all year, and the Orioles were able to win 98 games and finish with the league's second-lowest team ERA despite the many injuries.

JOE ALTOBELLI: "We were a good club, but we could have had problems with all those pitching injuries. It was a constant thing. But [pitching coach] Ray Miller worked with Boddicker, and they developed this pitch they called a 'foshball,' basically a change-up, and Boddicker was really effective with it. He really pitched well and made a difference."

MIKE BODDICKER: "I had been in Rochester since '79, really. If I'd been there another year, I would have run for mayor. But there was no place for me to go. The Orioles had all these Cy Young guys and quality relief pitchers. What were they going to do, get rid of a Cy Young winner? I just bided my time. I understood. Meanwhile, teammates like Mark Wiley and Steve Luebber explained the big leagues to me, and I taught myself a curveball. I figured if Steve Stone could win a Cy Young throwing curveballs, I could, too. I went from a sinker-slider pitcher to a curveball–change-up pitcher.

"Hank Peters liked me. I never caused any trouble. I just said, 'I'll wait.' Hank would bring me up every year against Weaver's wishes. The last time I got cut in spring training, after about four years in a row, Earl said, 'Why don't you think about going home and getting a job?' He was testing me. I said, 'I can pitch somewhere and you better keep me, because if you don't I'll come back and beat you.' He just laughed.

"I came up [in '83] when Palmer had a bad back. I started out and did OK. Hank said, 'Don't give up your apartment [in Rochester] because when Palmer comes back, you're going back. I kept the apartment until Tippy Martinez had an appendectomy. Then it was too much. I knew I was staying. I was pitching pretty well. It was a veteran team, but they made me feel welcomed. The pitchers took a lot of pride in their work. They did their business correctly. I worked my tail off imitating them.

"Flanagan, McGregor, and Palmer would sit me down and explain stuff and get you thinking. Palmer'd say, 'They'll tell you someone's a great curveball hitter, but who says they can hit *your* curveball? Go find out.' Flanny told me how he was going to pitch Lou Piniella and where Piniella would hit it, and sure enough, a high fastball and Lou would pop it to center field. I said, 'That's awesome.'

"And Scotty could just embarrass people. Watching him, I figured I had a chance. Scotty would eat good hitters up and you'd go, 'How'd he do it?' He'd locate [the ball], get the hitter anxious. I learned from them and put it to work. I had guys on other teams telling me, 'I can't wait to face you because I know you can't throw your fastball by me.' They knew my change-up was coming and still couldn't hit it."

The Orioles maintained a slim lead over Milwaukee early in the season, endured two seven-game losing streaks, and bounced between first and fourth until mid-August, when they took control of the division with a run of 15 wins in 18 games and, ultimately, 32 of 40. That gave them an 8½-game lead and locked up a trip to the playoffs.

Offensively, it was a two-man show—and what a show. Eddie Murray put up MVP-caliber numbers batting cleanup, with 33 home runs, 111 RBI, and a .306 average. But he finished second in the MVP voting to Cal Ripken Jr., who played in every inning of every game, batted .318 with 27 homers and 102 RBI, and became the third Orioles player to win the award after Frank Robinson in '66 and Boog Powell in '70.

But numbers couldn't quantify the heady way the Orioles went about their business in '83. They found ways to win that at times were almost unimaginable. On August 24 at Memorial Stadium, just as the Orioles were taking over the division, they trailed Toronto by one run in the 10th inning. Tippy Martinez came on with no outs and a man on first and immediately picked off the runner, who was trying to steal off emergency catcher Lenn Sakata. Martinez then walked a batter and picked him off, too. Finally, Martinez yielded a single and picked off his third runner of the inning. Then, after Ripken tied the game with a homer in the bottom of the inning, Sakata hit a three-run shot to win it. Oriole Magic was alive.

KEN SINGLETON: "Altobelli didn't have the same fire as Earl, but I think part of winning in '83 was just to show Earl we could win without him. You ask the guys, I think that might not be the first thing they say, but they'll say part of it was we wanted to show him we could win without him. And we did. We had our share of injuries and just played right through them. Nobody could stay with us."

RICK DEMPSEY: "Did we want to win it all partly to prove to Earl that we could win without him? Absolutely."

MIKE BODDICKER: "The overall talent level wasn't super other than Cal and Eddie, but we meshed very well. And if the score was close in the seventh inning, the game was ours. Our hitters knew it; our pitchers knew it; the other team knew it. Close games were ours. And with our pitching, most of the games were close. Fundamentally, we were so sound. We threw to the right bases, positioned ourselves perfectly. Cal was fabulous at short. Eddie was fabulous at first. Al Bumbry was fabulous in center. He had no arm at all, but he ran everything down."

TOM MARR: "They won a lot of games in dramatic fashion, like in '79. The game where Tippy picked three guys off, there'll never be anything like that again. The Toronto play-by-play announcer came to me, and he actually felt the stadium was kind of possessed. He wasn't a believer in black magic or anything, but he said, 'There's something going on here that's unbelievable.' He was stunned, thinking there was some element involved that couldn't be explained."

EDDIE MURRAY: "That was the year [Detroit manager] Sparky Anderson made his club sit in the dugout and watch us practice one afternoon before a night game. And the next year they got off to a 35–5 start. Sparky wanted them to see how we would do our jobs and have fun doing it. That's what we did. We worked, but we had fun. We had little games to get through stuff. Might as well have some fun."

MIKE FLANAGAN: "After the season [sportswriter] Peter Gammons made the comment that we were 'maybe the last great, fun team to cover.' The guys had a good time, maybe because of the pressure of having Earl in the dugout for all those years. We all had to find our own buffers for that in some comic relief and other things."

HANK PETERS: "We were struggling at third base, and then we went out and picked up Todd Cruz, who did a fine job for us. We got him about the middle of the year. We just wanted somebody to make some plays. He did that. Now and then he'd jerk the ball out. Picking him up really solidified the infield defensively."

DENNIS MARTINEZ: "Earl had retired, and people were thinking we would go downhill, but because of what we did in '82, that enabled us to do what we did in '83. The team was already together and ready. Altobelli did a nice job. I didn't help much because that's when I was having a drinking problem. I wound up in relief, but then Boddicker and Storm came in, so there were more pitchers to help."

MIKE FLANAGAN: "After all we'd been through going back to losing the '79 Series after being up 3–1, it was like, 'We've had enough of this. It's not going to happen again.' It was a much more mature team, with guys in their prime, and they just knew how to win and what it took. In the spring of '83 I could have told you we were going to win it all. In that sense, it was really no surprise. Once the season started, it all came together, everything we had stood for for a few years. Great pitching and defense, timely hitting, being smart. It was just a very confident, relaxed team that knew it was good."

In the AL Championship Series the Orioles faced a formidable opponent. The Chicago White Sox had won 99 games, one more than the Orioles, and cruised to the AL West title by a 20-game margin. With young Tony LaRussa managing and veteran Roland Hemond as the general manager, the Sox had a potent lineup featuring outfielder Ron Kittle (35 homers), catcher Carlton Fisk (26 homers), designated hitter Greg Luzinski (32 homers), and outfielder Harold Baines (99 RBI). And their starting pitching was strong, too. LaMarr Hoyt was a dominant ace, having led the league in wins for two straight seasons. His 24–10 record in '83 had earned him the AL's Cy Young Award. After Hoyt came Richard Dotson, a 22-game winner, and Floyd Bannister, a 16-game winner.

Hoyt beat the Orioles in Game 1 at Memorial Stadium, taking a shutout into the ninth and beating McGregor 2–1. That put pressure on Boddicker to deliver in Game 2 or have the Orioles down 0–2 in a best-of-five series with the rest of the games scheduled for Chicago. Boddicker came through, pitching a shutout and striking out 14, a performance that would earn him the series MVP Award.

MIKE BODDICKER: "The only thing I tried to do was pitch as well as Scotty in Game 1. He lost, but he only gave up a few hits. I told the press, 'If I do as well as Scotty, I'm happy.' That was my mental approach, just keeping the team in the game. As it turned out, my curveball was really sharp. I was throwing it right where I wanted all night. And changing speeds really well. It was one of my better games. And I still almost lost. [Chicago's Julio] Cruz hit the ball down the left-field line just foul with the bases loaded, late in the game. I ended up striking him out."

In Game 3 at Comiskey Park, the Orioles scored three runs in the first and rolled to an 11–1 win in a testy game that featured several bench-emptying incidents. Then came Game 4. Chicago's Britt Burns threw nine shutout innings, as did the Orioles' Storm Davis and Tippy Martinez. The Orioles finally broke through in the top of the 10th when Tito Landrum, a late-season acquisition, hit a homer off Burns—a pennant-clinching hit. The 3–0 win put the Orioles in the World Series for the second time in five years and the sixth time in eighteen years.

MIKE FLANAGAN: "We were really apprehensive about Chicago. They were really good. We'd had our best battles during the season with them. Chicago was a very tough place for us. We'd lost a lot of games there over the year.

"In the first two games [of the series] there had been some talk that we were throwing at their hitters. LaRussa was young. When we got to Game 3 even, I pitched. We were up 3–1 in the bottom of the third, and I hit Kittle with a three-and-two breaking ball, two outs, nobody on. And their dugout was in flames, 'Here they go again; they're throwing at us.' It came out later in the paper that LaRussa went up and down the dugout and told Dotson to pick out somebody [and hit him], that they weren't going to take this.

"To me, it was the turning point in the series. Cal led off the next inning and, again, the game's still very much in jeopardy, and Dotson threw a ball behind Cal. Then Eddie was next, and Dotson threw a pitch behind Eddie, and Eddie just stood there, and both dugouts emptied. They were, we felt, sort of out of control. We're going, 'We've got the lead; why would we hit Kittle with two outs?' Then things quieted down, and Dotson, I think, was rattled. Eddie hit one in the alley, Lowenstein hit a double, and before that inning was over it was 6–1, and the game was over. That took some of the pressure off, because now we knew if we won Game 4 we wouldn't face Hoyt again. I don't know how it would have turned out if we'd had to face Hoyt."

JOE ALTOBELLI: "Before the fourth game Eddie shouted to the club as we were going out the door, 'I want to see the clubhouse in shambles after the game,' meaning we would have won and were having a party. That [Game 4] was the longest, toughest game. Chicago could have won, but we made some great plays to throw out runners on the bases. My whole life went through me during that game."

CAL RIPKEN JR.: "The biggest fear was having to play Game 5 with LaMarr Hoyt on the mound. If Burns had beaten us, I mean, we barely touched LaMarr in that first game. If the series had gone to Game 5, they would have been in the driver's seat. I still wonder why LaMarr didn't pitch again [in Game 4]. But I guess with no off days, maybe Tony didn't have any other choice."

ROLAND HEMOND: "Boddicker hit Luzinski in the elbow [in Game 2], and for the rest of the series [Luzinski] couldn't generate any power in his swing. That was a big turning point, when our big hitter got hurt. Then Flanagan hit Kittle in the knee in Game 3, and that game got ugly. Murray pounded a ball, and they demolished us. So we're down 2–1, and I get to the park the next day, and Kittle is dragging his leg. He had a stiff leg. We'd lost him, and Luzinski couldn't swing.

"The fourth game was a classic. Burns and Storm Davis both pitched great. We had many chances. Vance Law tried to score from third on a ball that got by Dempsey, but the stands were eight feet closer because of the temporary seating for the playoffs, so Rick got to the ball quicker and got back in time to make the play. Then we had runners on the bases, and Baines hit a screaming line drive to left, and Gary Roenicke went over and made a sliding catch on his rear. After he caught it, he gave a sigh of relief. Then we had Law on second and Jerry Dybzinski on first. A ball was hit sharply to left and [Sox third-base coach Jim] Leyland had to hold Law at third. Dybzinski thought the play was at the plate, and he overran second and got in a rundown and got tagged out, and that ended a rally. What a frustrating game."

MIKE FLANAGAN: "You see stuff like that happen, and that's when you believe, maybe, in some faith, and that there's a lot of other stuff going on here. Then Tito Landrum had one quality swing."

ROLAND HEMOND: "I had tried to trade [with the Cardinals] for Landrum earlier that year, when he was playing in [Triple-A] Louisville. They said no, they couldn't trade him, they had a deal with Baltimore. He was frozen in Louisville, and Floyd Rayford was frozen at Rochester. In those days, if a player was outrighted before the season, you couldn't bring them back. So Baltimore and St. Louis traded one player for another, and I wasn't able to get Landrum. Then, over the winter, they traded 'em both back. I was upset about that and let a few people know. It still gets under my craw. If we could have won that fourth game, Hoyt was ready to go. And he was really invincible that year, had great control and complete command. There's no guarantee he would have won it, but we would have liked our chances."

The young group of Philadelphia Phillies who won the National League pennant in '50 were nicknamed the "Whiz Kids." The veteran Phillies who won the National League East and eliminated the Los Angeles Dodgers in four games in the NL Championship Series in '83 were the "Wheeze Kids." Their infield included eventual career-hits leader Pete Rose and future Hall of Famers Joe Morgan, Tony Perez, and Mike Schmidt, but Rose was forty-two, Perez was forty-one, Morgan was forty, and Schmidt was thirty-four. Left-handed pitcher Steve Carlton, another future Hall of Famer, was thirty-eight.

The Series opened on a rainy night in Baltimore, and Jim Dwyer gave the Orioles a 1–0 lead with a homer in the first, but he was the last of the Orioles to get as far as third against John Denny. Morgan tied the score with a homer off McGregor in the sixth, and outfielder Garry Maddox put the Phillies ahead with a homer in the eighth. Denny retired 22 of the last 25 batters he faced, and reliever Al Holland retired four straight Orioles to save the Phillies' 2–1 win.

As in the ALCS, the pressure was on Boddicker in Game 2—and he came through again, this time pitching a three-hitter as the Orioles won 4–1. The Phillies had a 1–0 lead in the bottom of the fifth when Lowenstein homered off rookie starter Charlie Hudson, starting a three-run rally. Dempsey drove in the second run with a double, and Boddicker followed with a sacrifice fly.

The pitching matchup for Game 3 at Veterans Stadium was Flanagan against Carlton, each a former Cy Young Award winner. The Phillies took a 2–1 lead into the bottom of the sixth, and Phillies manager Paul Owens let Carlton bat with runners in scoring position. Carlton struck out to end the threat, and the Orioles took the lead off Carlton in the seventh. Dempsey doubled and scored on Benny Ayala's single. John Shelby also singled, and Ayala scored the go-ahead run when Phillies shortstop Ivan DeJesus booted a grounder. Relievers Sammy Stewart and Tippy Martinez secured the Orioles' 3–2 win.

In the sixth inning of Game 4, with the Phillies leading 3–2, Altobelli sent four straight pinch hitters to the plate with two out. Lowenstein was on third and Dauer on second when pinch hitter Joe Nolan drew a walk to load the bases and pinch hitter Ken Singleton drew another walk to force in the tying run. Shelby then broke the tie with a sacrifice fly before Dan Ford, the fourth straight pinch hitter, struck out to end the inning. The Orioles won 5–4 to take a 3–1 lead in the Series, having come from behind in each of their wins.

HANK PETERS: "A lot of people said Joe sat back and let the team run that year, but that's not giving enough credit to the guy who had to make a lot of decisions. He did an especially good job in the World Series with matchups and pinch-hitting moves."

KEN SINGLETON: "When we got to the same position against Philly that we had been against Pittsburgh in '79, up 3–1, there was no celebrating. I think we had fifteen players from that ['79] team, and we all had the memory of '79. We were a lot more serious in '83."

SCOTT MCGREGOR: "I always remember Richie Dauer after Game 4 in '79; we're on the bus and he's going, 'Sixty thousand bucks!' There was no way we were going to let that happen again when we got in the same position. You could hear a pin drop after Game 4 against the Phillies. I felt sorry for the Phillies, because for us it was, 'Been here, done that, and we aren't making the same mistake twice.' They had Charlie Hudson pitching [Game 5], and I knew we were going to kill them."

MIKE FLANAGAN: "The memory of the Pittsburgh Series flashed in after the fourth game, for sure. There was no talk of 'What do you think a [winning] World Series share would be?' There was no talk like that in '83, not until it was done."

The Series clincher was a breeze. McGregor pitched a five-hitter and won 5–0, with Ripken catching the last out on a soft liner. Eddie Murray emerged from a slump to hit two homers, and Dempsey added a third homer to finish the Series with a .385 average and five extra-base hits. He was named MVP, although the difference clearly was the Orioles' pitching, which limited Schmidt to one hit in 20 at-bats and the Phillies to a .195 overall average.

The Orioles had lost the first game of the regular season, the first game of the American League Championship Series, and the first game of the World Series, all at Memorial Stadium, all in front of large crowds. But they lost little else in a season that started slowly and kept gaining momentum until it ended up providing the crowning achievement for a generation of Orioles and a front office that had sought the right mix of talent for a decade.

KEN SINGLETON: "Scotty came in from warming up [before Game 5] and said, 'The Series is over.' Just like against the Angels in the fourth game [of the ALCS] in '79. It wasn't boasting. He was just convinced it would happen. And each time he threw a shutout. I couldn't see Palmer doing it, although Palmer could go out and pitch the game and win. But he wouldn't say something like that ahead of time. McGregor was just a big-game pitcher. To say that with the stuff he had, I mean, he probably threw two curveballs that day. The rest was just his change-up, take a little off, add a little, mix it up. But he was right. The Phillies couldn't hit him.'"

EDDIE MURRAY: "I was hurt. Everyone on the club knew it, but I didn't want anyone to know. My wrist was hurting. I got a hit the night before [during Game 4], and Dauer came over to me [before Game 5] and said, 'Kid, can you guarantee it?' I said I could, so he went around telling everyone in the clubhouse, 'The kid's guaranteed it.' You know, everyone was going to jump on my back. So I came out and hit the two home runs, and after the second one I sat on the bench and told Dauer, 'That might not be it.' And my wrist was hurting, so I knew I only had one swing left. And I pulled a ball out of the ballpark, just foul."

JOE ALTOBELLI: "After we beat Chicago, Eddie had come to me and said, 'Thanks a lot. You're one of the best managers I ever played for.' Then, when he hit two homers to win Game 5, I walked into the shower with my uniform on and said, 'Thanks a lot. You're one of the best players I ever managed.' That was about the total of our conversation all year."

MIKE FLANAGAN: "When Eddie's second home run went off his name on the scoreboard, I knew it was over. Scotty could have pitched underhanded the rest of the way. They just weren't going to score. They had a chance in the ninth, and Morgan was on third, and he was going to tag up and walk home with a meaningless run, and he tripped coming off third and had to hold. I'm going, 'Well, we've got all kinds of gremlins out there on our side.' It was a done deal."

JOE ALTOBELLI: "We didn't know Philadelphia. We had to rely on the scouts. We knew about their greatness, Rose and Morgan and Schmidt. But our pitching staff did a great job. Our pitching was outstanding. We only lost two games in the whole postseason, each by 2–1. Schmidt got one broken-bat single in five games. Morgan hit a couple of homers. Rose got benched for a game. He didn't do anything. We didn't score a lot of runs, but we were pitching so well it didn't matter."

MIKE FLANAGAN: "To be honest, once we got by Chicago, as tough as they were, we thought it was a done deal. The Phillies were an older group, and we kind of felt that they had had their day, and we were in our prime. And they had some stuff going about who should play, should it be [Tony] Perez or Rose at first. They just seemed to have some undercurrents."

CAL RIPKEN JR.: "The difference was our pitching and experience. I think everyone benefited from '79, those that were there. And those that weren't benefited from '82 and coming so close. We had come together as a team. We had a good depth and some stable heads on the mound. The game McGregor pitched at the end was typical. We had a solid defense, didn't beat ourselves, got timely hitting. And the pitching controlled the pressure. Those guys could handle it. Those guys always put you in a position to win."

KEN SINGLETON: "We rode back to Baltimore on a bus, which was kind of humorous. When we all got on to ride home, you kind of went, like, 'What is this?' I mean, you'd ridden buses in the minor leagues thirteen or fourteen years ago, and here we were, having just won the World Series, and we're riding a bus back to Baltimore. So it kind of put it in perspective. But it was very satisfying. At least now I was going to get a World Series ring. I could go out having the feeling that I'd accomplished what you go on the field every year to do. At least I got it done once."

MIKE FLANAGAN: "On the bus ride home there were cars all the way down both sides of the road saluting us, and big signs from the state police, 'Welcome Back to Maryland.' Then we had a big parade. And I know I kept thinking about all the frustration we'd experienced from '79 until '83. We'd had that huge parade after '79, and we couldn't believe how the people turned out, and we felt very disappointed. I remember dragging myself to the parade; we'd just lost the World Series, and I think that really stuck with that club until that game in Philadelphia. And then that feeling just went away."

SCOTT McGREGOR: "One day in '84 we were in Detroit, and I was sitting in the clubhouse across from Lowenstein, and I said, 'Look around, Lo, these are the world champions.' And we both started laughing. Because no one knew who we were. Still. We'd won the World Series, but we were Ayala and Lowenstein and Dauer and McGregor. We were no one. Just a group of characters. But we played great together.

"For six or seven years we had a great ride. No one ever had more fun playing baseball than we did over that time. When we got to the ninth inning we looked over at the other dugout, and they looked at us and went, 'How are they going to beat us tonight?' We were good. I'm glad we finally won in '83 because it cast the whole thing in a better light. We won as many World Series as the great Orioles team from '69 to '71. That's still by far the most popular [Orioles] team. And that was a great generation. But as time goes by, as far as history, I think people have started to respect us, too."

Grounded
1984–91

38

Hitting a Brick Wall

The run was over. No one knew as the Orioles celebrated their '83 World Series triumph, but their time as one of baseball's elites was up. After almost a quarter-century as a stable, highly successful organization, they were about to enter an era marked by failure and instability. It would take them thirteen years to get back to the playoffs and fourteen years to win another division title. The century would end without them winning another American League pennant.

The fall started gently, with another winning season, the club's seventeenth straight, in '84. But although the Orioles won 85 games, they finished a distant fifth behind the World Series–winning Detroit Tigers, and major changes were made. Jim Palmer was released in May after refusing to retire, and Al Bumbry was released after the season. Ken Singleton retired.

Another generation groomed in the minor leagues was ready to step in— outfielders Mike Young, John Shelby, and Larry Sheets; and pitcher John Habyan, among many—but owner Edward Bennett Williams chose to sign free agents to fill the holes. Closer Don Aase and outfielders Fred Lynn and Lee Lacy, all veteran major leaguers, signed long-term deals.

The new mix of talent fared no better in '85. With starters Scott McGregor, Dennis Martinez, Mike Flanagan, Mike Boddicker, and Storm Davis finishing a combined two games under .500, the Orioles finished fourth with an 83–78 record.

JOE ALTOBELLI: "Detroit started 35–5 [in '84]. It was just unbelievable that any team could do that. It wrecked our season. No one was going to catch them. Then after that season we made a lot of changes. I think a problem with Earl [Weaver] was he'd been there for so long that he hated to release guys like Palmer, even though I think Earl probably thought Palmer had had enough. So they left good enough alone for a long time, and then we had a lot of guys to release. That was tough. They were all great guys and had done a tremendous job. But there comes a time, and I think they all felt it.

"When they went into the free-agent market, they thought they needed a centerfielder because Bumbry had played there. Lynn had been a good player for Boston and the Angels, but he was almost in the same boat as the guys who left us. Father Time catches up to you."

KEN SINGLETON: "Winning in '83 really affected our team in '84. We were getting to be older and had that feeling of accomplishment, that we'd gotten it done. It was like they blamed us in a way, me and Bumbry and Benny Ayala, because they got rid of us all together. Palmer was already gone. Four guys. I don't know. Maybe it was time. There was a chance for them to save some money—get rid of our hefty contracts. I didn't blame 'em.

"They released me on the road. They don't do that to veterans at home. I talked to Hank Peters in September of '84, and he goes, 'What are your thoughts about the team?' I said, 'Hank, there aren't many players to replace us in the minor leagues. The team's going to go down. There's only a couple of ways you can do this. You can take the hit, or you can go out and buy some free agents who have no respect for what Orioles baseball means.'

"That's what they did. They brought in guys with no real feel for Orioles baseball. They were more mercenary. Orioles baseball was a warm summer night at Memorial Stadium, packed house, section 34 going nuts. Players with feelings for each other. There was a bond. And that just went away. You could see it on the field. Things changed very quickly, and they didn't change for the better."

HANK PETERS: "When you're having success, [owners] don't bother you too much. Then when things start to change a little bit, they start to get more involved. As each year went by, Williams would become more and more of an authority on the game. But it's one thing to be able to use the language of baseball and another thing to really understand baseball. Some people think because you learn all these little nuances and things that you are now a baseball authority and you can sit down with the guys and talk baseball. That's a load of crap. Because they knew nothing about talent. They knew nothing about how you put ball clubs together. But they own the ball club, so they can do what they want.

"The big turning point with the Orioles and my relationship with Ed Williams took place in Japan at the end of the '84 season. We took the team over there as a result of having won the '83 World Series. The whole club was invited to Japan after the '84 season for a tour. We were there for three weeks, and Ed went over for the first few days, and then he left and came back. And while we were over there we had time on our hands, so we had meetings. And in this one meeting Ed says to me, 'I can't let you run things any longer the way we've been doing. I've got to have the final word. I have all my money tied up in this team, and I can't let somebody control my fortunes.' I said, 'Well, it's your ball club. I don't think you can run a team with the owner making the final decisions. But if that's what you want, so be it.'

"We also went over the free-agent list, guys who were available and what we needed. Some of our talent had gotten old. We had guys in our system, I don't know how good they might have become had we gone with 'em, Shelby and Sheets, but we had quite a number of young, talented people. I told Ed, 'We're getting old. You're going to have to go through a transitional period where maybe we don't win. We have to rebuild.' And he said, 'Bullshit.'

"Now you have to appreciate the fact that this man was ill [with cancer], and he knows more about his health than I do. And I guess he knows his years are numbered, and he didn't want to go through a transitional period. He wanted to win now because he might not be here to enjoy the stardom of a Shelby, a Sheets, or a Young.

"Anyway, so he leaves after telling me he's calling the shots, goes back to the States, and I'm still in Japan for another two and a half weeks. And the day before I got back, he called and wanted me to be in his office at nine o'clock. It turns out he's got Lee Lacy and his agent coming in for a session. Then he's got us going to the West Coast to meet with Fred Lynn and his agent. He's got us doing this and that. He set it all up, and that was the beginning. That was the beginning."

FRANK CASHEN: "Ed Williams wasn't like Jerry as an owner. To say he was more 'hands-on,' I wouldn't even call it that nice. But he thought because he'd appeared before the Supreme Court that he knew how to run a ball club, and he was wrapped up in his own importance. And Hank was spoiled. I mean, Jerry was about the best owner there ever was as far as staying out of the way. There were others like him, but they were dwindling fast."

LARRY LUCCHINO: "What happened in Japan, because I was there, too, Ed got everyone together, the manager and coaches, and said, 'What do you guys need? What can we do?' And they got out the free-agent list and made some choices. You can say Ed went out and got them, but it was the group making the decisions. Ed empowered them, and then Hank and everyone went out and did it. When it didn't work out, he certainly lost faith in the judgment of some of his baseball people, and as much as he liked Hank, he began to have doubts."

FRED LYNN: "After the '84 season the owners were colluding, and I was getting the same offer from everyone, and then Edward Bennett Williams stepped in and said, 'We need this kid,' and I got a better offer and signed. If there was any animosity about me coming in as a free agent, I didn't feel it. In fact, the players saw me as a vital part of their chance to win. They welcomed me with open arms. They were bringing me in to play center, which they needed, and also I was a left-handed hitter to hit behind Eddie and give him a break, because otherwise he'd walk thirty-two hundred times. So I fit right in.

"In '85 they brought in myself and Lacy and Aase, and we had a pretty solid club. But the pitching staff started to get old. They all seemed to tire out at the same time. For years I had gone in [to Baltimore] and known I was going to have tough pitching to hit, which was part of the reason I signed there, but almost as soon as I got there it was like we turned into another Red Sox team. We just out-clubbed people. We had some bats and good defense, but the pitching wasn't the same as in the past. For years the strategy [of the Orioles] was to stay close, hit a three-run homer in the eighth, and win in the ninth. But we couldn't stay close enough."

DENNIS MARTINEZ: "When they brought in all the free agents in one year, that was something that had never been done. They might bring in one guy, but never five or six from different teams. And there was no way it was going to work. Free agency can work when you put in one or two guys to a team that's already good. But you can't build a team that way. Because when you bring in guys from other teams, they bring in a different way of playing and a different mentality, and it's really hard to get them to play together. Because they all play the way they were trained, with the attitude they had. And when the [old] Orioles saw that, they didn't like it. And there were disagreements."

FRANK ROBINSON: "When they started dismantling the '83 team, the wheels came off. Those late '70s early '80s teams were good in the Orioles tradition—the Orioles way of playing. Good, sound, fundamental baseball. Don't beat yourself. Good pitching, good defense. Make them beat you. They started getting away from it when they started bringing in the marginal free agents. Lynn. Aase. Lacy. All those guys had had their better days. And there were questions about injuries and attitude and things, and all of a sudden they were getting away from the way they'd always done it—started going for the quick fixes."

SCOTT MCGREGOR: "Free agency wiped us out. The whole atmosphere was different. Everyone went, 'We won, now we have to get our money.' We were in the hunt every year from '77 to '83, but once it was over it all fell apart. Guys started playing out their options, and the front office brought in guys who weren't Orioles baseball. We had guys I'd admired, who I thought were great players, but if anything was wrong with 'em and they were in the lineup, they ripped it off the wall and threw it at the manager and said, 'Change it.' I said, 'Man, things have changed.'"

MIKE FLANAGAN: "I thought we were going to win forever. But age started to show up. In '85 I still had visions that we weren't that far away. Probably an unrealistic view. It had just run its course. The team basically had been together for a decade. And bringing in the free agents changed the dynamics. They had their own way—the Pittsburgh way or the Red Sox way—and they were different. And maybe we even started questioning who's right. Like, 'Are they right? Are we right? Wait a minute.' The thinking was, 'This guy had great numbers for them, so he'll have great numbers for us.' But what was missing was the team dynamic. The new guys were nonbelievers, basically. They really didn't want to hear about the Oriole Way or Oriole Magic. Now there were different stories being told on the bus. All of a sudden, there were Pittsburgh stories and Boston stories. It wasn't the same. I still believed we had enough to win, but there was a change going on."

In June of '85, with the club three games over .500, Williams fired Altobelli and lured Earl Weaver out of retirement to come back and manage. Fans were stunned and thrilled, but Weaver fared no better than Altobelli in '85, winning 53 and losing 52.

JOE ALTOBELLI: "I got fired when we were over .500. It wasn't that disaster had set in. But things happen. I got called into a meeting with EBW and Hank, and they did most of the talking. I wasn't in a talkative mood. Just get it over with. Just say good-bye. When they got finished and said, 'Do you have anything to say?' I said, 'No. Good-bye.' That was it. I wasn't frustrated, just mad. And I wasn't surprised Earl came back. When you quit, it's hard to stay away."

Hopes were high in '86 with another acquisition added to the mix—second baseman Alan Wiggins, replacing Rich Dauer—and Weaver starting a season as the manager for the first time in four years. After winning on August 5, the Orioles were 12 games over .500 and in second place, two and a half games out of first. Their pitching was mediocre, but they were pounding home runs almost every night with Ripken (25 in '86) and Lynn (23) leading the way.

Then, suddenly, the club's gentle slide from the high of '83 accelerated rapidly. The Orioles fell apart. They lost five games in a row, then four in a row, then seven in a row. By season's end, they had lost 42 of their last 56 games and finished 16 games under .500, in last place for the first time since divisional play began in '69. It was Weaver's first losing season in the majors, and he retired again.

EARL WEAVER: "I had my [same] coaches back, and we went back to doing the same things again, but it didn't work out for me, and I didn't enjoy it. I wouldn't have retired in the first place if I wanted to be there, but I promised [Williams] that if anything happened I'd come back for a while. Those were the words when I left, and he got all excited and talked me into coming back. It wasn't that anything was different. Joe had continued everything that went on before. There was just less talent there now. Mr. Williams went out and got some free agents, and some worked out, but not all of them.

"Financially, it turned out very well for me because the salaries had escalated really high, but if I had it to do over again, I don't think I would have come back. It was a different situation. You just don't get into it sometimes, not that you didn't want to get into it. We worked just as hard, went over the stats, went over everything. But I wasn't enjoying it. It wasn't the same as it had been in the '70s. Things couldn't be the same anymore because of free agency. You have to buy the right free agents, those who adjust to wherever they go and don't do things the way they'd done them elsewhere."

HANK PETERS: "Earl should never have come back. The only reason he came back was for the money. I'll never forget when [Williams] told me what he was going to do. I said, 'You're out of your mind.' And the salary was like five hundred thousand dollars, which was a lot more than Earl ever made with us and probably made him the highest-paid manager in baseball."

DENNIS MARTINEZ: "When Earl came back, he didn't have it anymore. Most of us thought he just came back for the money. We had that doubt. We didn't know if he came back for the money or because he loved the game. Because that's when the big bucks were coming in. So he tried to project the way he was before, but he didn't have the same control as before. Because he made us the way we were before. And he didn't make the new guys coming in. So he didn't feel comfortable. He tried to fashion them to his way, but they didn't respond."

FRED LYNN: "When Earl came back, he was a little more tame. As an opposing player I'd loved watching him. When he came back he was pretty much under control as far as his emotions. I don't know that he had that same fire. If you retire and come back, I don't know if you have the same energy. I don't know if anyone can do that. Plus he was used to having Palmer and McNally and Brooks and Boog. He wasn't used to having to struggle. He'd had some serious horses and could just let them go. When the horses weren't there, well, that's different.

"We still had it going for awhile in '86. But we had to win with our bats. And we went on a streak there where we hit a million homers. It was just ridiculous. We were hitting five a game out of the park. That's how we had to win. Then we lost a game to Texas when we hit two grand slams. Both teams hit a couple of grand slams, in fact. We lost a couple of games like that, and it really hurt us. It just drove home the point that if we weren't getting hits, the other team sure was hitting us pretty good.

"And Baltimore is similar to St. Louis in that if you're down on the field a long time, with all that heat and humidity, you're going to get tired. I was on the field a lot. I ran down a lot of balls, and with our pitching, I was on the field thirty to forty minutes longer than our opponents. And it took its toll. On everyone. All those twenty-minute innings weren't conducive to [the team] hanging in there in September. We just couldn't keep up that pace."

CAL RIPKEN JR.: "In '84 we still had a pretty good year, but our talent started to go down. In '85 our offense came up, but our pitching wasn't very good. At that point I thought we had some potential to be competitive, in '84 and '85. Then Joe gets fired, and they bring Earl back, and the magic of Earl was going to take this team back to it. But in '86 we were still short on talent, and I think Earl knew it. It seemed like Earl was the first to recognize that he didn't have the horses to be able to do it, and that all the magic in the world and all the moves in the world and all the setting up you can do, if you don't have the horses to ride, you can't do it."

HANK PETERS: "We fell off a cliff starting in August [of '86], and in the first part of September Earl comes to me and says, 'We're not going anywhere, and I'm not coming back next year. I'd like to go home now if it's all right with you.' I said, 'It's fine with me, Earl, but I'll have to check with Williams.' So I called Williams and told him Earl wants to go home, and he says, 'Tell that little son of a bitch'—now he's a little son of a bitch—'he can go home, but he won't get paid.' So I got hold of Earl, and I said, 'Earl, quoting Mr. Williams, tell that little son of a bitch he can go home, but he won't get paid.' Then I said, 'It's up to you, whatever you want to do.' Earl stayed, because money is like a religion to Earl. And he just sat in that dugout. And what was a bad situation became almost intolerable. Talk about going through the motions. And that was the end of that. The honeymoon between Earl and Ed Williams was over."

As Williams's relationship with Weaver deteriorated, so did his relationship with his best player, first baseman Eddie Murray, a fixture as the Orioles' cleanup hitter since the late '70s. He experienced some injuries and his first down season, falling from 31 homers and 124 RBI in '85 to 17 homers and 84 RBI in '86.

HANK PETERS: "Williams was a very good speaker, and he knew it, and he liked to address the ball club from time to time. The first time he did it, it was kind of spellbinding. After the second time it was kind of over with. One night in '86 it was raining before a game, and Williams decides this will be a night he's going to give another address to the troops. So down to the clubhouse we go, and he gives his talk. And part of the theme was, 'We're all family; we're all in this together; we've got to support each other.'

"Then he goes up to his box next to the press box, and it's still raining, and he's all by himself. I'm not up there. His henchmen are not with him. And the media guys that are up there in the press box kind of drift over into his box. And Williams starts to ramble. He did that. He would hold his court. Well, this time he decided to analyze the ball club and why things weren't going better. And in doing so he ripped Murray pretty good.

"So eventually we had to call the game because of the rain, so there's no game story to write, and the press writes about the interview with Williams. And Williams said later, 'I didn't think they were going to write all this stuff.' What did he expect? He didn't say it was off the record. So the rip of Murray is in print, and the very next day Murray is going through the roof and wants to be traded. I talked to Eddie, and he was pissed but good. And from then on things got bad."

EDDIE MURRAY: "That's when I said it was time to go. The only thing that mattered to me was what my teammates thought, what the other side thought, and what ownership thought. When he said what he said, it was time to go. It was that simple. That was just something I didn't have to deal with. If that was the way he felt, it was time for him to get rid of me. If you stop and think about what he said, in one week I went from being the best thing that ever happened to the worst thing. It didn't make sense, but you don't fight a battle you can't win."

HANK PETERS: "I'd always had a great relationship with Eddie, but then I started having problems, too, and over the stupidest things. We had a club rule in effect for years: every Sunday morning was weigh-in day, and a coach was on hand, and the players would come in and get on the scale. Eventually they'd send the listings up to me, and sometimes I'd look at them right away, sometimes it might be a week or two. So I started to check, and Murray hadn't been on the scale for about a month. He'd just refused to weigh in.

"I talked to him, and he still didn't change, so I was with the team, and I called Eddie up to my suite, and I said, 'Eddie, this is the stupidest meeting I think I've ever had with a player. But it's a club rule, and there are no exceptions, and if you don't weigh in, we're going to have to take disciplinary action, which would be crazy.' He didn't have anything to hide [on the scale]. It was just 'screw you guys.' I don't know what he thought he was accomplishing. He started to weigh in again, but from that time on he didn't like me, either. But he didn't like anybody by that time, and, let's face it, he didn't play the game the way he had played it, unfortunately. His heart wasn't in it."

The new manager for the '87 season was Cal Ripken Sr., finally getting to manage the Orioles after thirty years of service to the organization in many roles. His timing was awful. The deep well of pitching that had carried the Orioles for years was dry. Mike Flanagan's career seemingly was winding down, the league had caught up to Scott McGregor's change-up, and Dennis Martinez was gone, traded to Montreal in '86. Boddicker and rookie Eric Bell were the heart of the rotation, which included youngsters Ken Dixon, John Habyan, and Jeff Ballard, all of whom were hit hard. The resulting 5.01 team ERA was the highest in franchise history.

With Ripken Jr. and Murray around, things held together long enough for the Orioles to reach six games over .500 in late May; they were in third, four games out of first. Then came a frightful collapse similar to the one the year before, a run of 30 losses in 35 games. That effectively ended the season, and the Orioles spent the second half playing for the future. Flanagan was traded to Toronto, and second baseman Bill Ripken was promoted from Rochester and installed next to his older brother. Never in major league history had a father managed two of his sons on the same team. The Ripkens played well together, but there were few other high points in a 95-loss season.

DENNIS MARTINEZ: "Before I left you could just see the organization on a down cycle. Hank Peters was on his way out; I don't think he was happy with some things there. Then Eddie had some problems. You just looked at it and you knew the team wasn't the same. The guys weren't the same as before. It was a new era. The guys that were coming in [from the farm system] were guys who got to the big leagues and thought they knew everything, when in fact they knew nothing. They didn't need the help of the older players. I knew the Orioles were in trouble then."

MIKE FLANAGAN: "Before I got traded, I was fully intent on going home [and retiring] because I'd had a wonderful run. I had just come off an elbow

injury, and I think the club at the time envisioned the Flanagan-Cuellar scenario playing out, but now it was [Jeff] Ballard-Flanagan, and I was in the
Cuellar [teaching] role. And I tried to help him, but in some ways he was
reluctant. Things were definitely different."

FRANK ROBINSON: "The clubhouse chemistry, which was always so strong,
it went south. For the first time since I'd been in the Orioles clubhouse,
going back twenty years, you avoided a player. Alan Wiggins. Walked around
him to get to the shower. You didn't even say hello to the guy because he'd
make some kind of an argument. It wasn't good. He was a poor man's Albert
Belle, I guess. Lee Lacy wasn't real good in the clubhouse, either. He was one
of those 'I, me' players."

HANK PETERS: "I couldn't believe we signed Wiggins. The guy had been in
drug rehab. I told Williams, 'We've never had a player like this.'"

DICK WILLIAMS: "Wiggins had played on a World Series team for me in San
Diego in '84. Played his tail off. I moved him in from left field to second base.
He never gave me a bit of trouble. He was his own worst enemy because he
got into the stuff [drugs], and in the locker room no one would have too
much to do with him. The next year, '85, we're in first place, and he doesn't
show up for a Dodgers series. He was suspended. This was the second time
it happened. He was gone. And Baltimore went and got him. They told us
he was causing problems over there. He was really withdrawn."

FRED LYNN: "Everything stems from the mound, and by '87 we just didn't
have enough. When the other team is putting up a four-spot in the first
inning with regularity, it wears you down. Then you start pressing and struggle. I loved Cal Sr. as a manager. If you loved baseball, you loved him. He
was just a baseball man through and through. He knew the game. He appreciated hard-nosed play and doing the right things. I enjoyed being around
him."

HANK PETERS: "The feeling was maybe we owed Cal the opportunity. And
it was a tough season. No pitching. One night we gave up 10 home runs in a
game in Toronto. Someone made a video of all the home runs swings, one

after the other, bam-bam-bam. It was funny, but at the time [of the game] it wasn't too funny."

CAL RIPKEN JR.: "Dad inherited a team that was short on talent. It was obvious. If they'd said they were going to rebuild, that was a workable situation. But it was kind of half and half. They wanted to bring some young kids up and still keep the veteran team together. I think the expectation was still that we were going to get back to the World Series like the '83 team, and it was very obvious that we didn't have the horses to do that.

"I felt extremely bad for my dad. What really bothered me about the whole situation is that he could have been the next one in line [in '83 when Altobelli replaced Weaver], and he could have stepped in and inherited a team that was already there, and who knows what would have happened after that? He certainly seemed to be the next person [in line] among the people there, but they got Joe. Then Earl came back. By the time my dad got the chance, the team wasn't as talented."

BILL RIPKEN: "It was special to look around the locker room and know that if you needed somebody to talk to, there's your family. And being on the field with Cal, that was fun. We didn't do it growing up. He's four and a half years older, so we may have played some pickup games and things like that, but I didn't play an organized baseball game with him until spring training of '87. Then, suddenly, there we were. He made it real easy. We got a double play out of the way in the first game. That was fun. There was a comfort zone dealing with him out there. He's not a dictator, but he can give advice, and if you don't listen, you're foolish.

"The good part was that stuff, and the bad part was losing. You still have to have the horses to pull the wagon. And our wagon was stationary. But you never heard my dad bitch. It was, 'Here's the hand you're dealt; play it.' He never complained and said, 'Well, I didn't get this or that,' and when he got fired [in '88], you didn't hear him say anything about the players. It just didn't happen."

CAL RIPKEN JR.: "As the talent started to deteriorate and we weren't getting talent from the minor leagues any more, no one admitted it. No one ever said, 'We're going into a little bit of a rebuilding situation.' If they had, some stability could have been established and you could have had that point to build on. But instead it just continued to be negative and spiral down and caused all kinds of issues. They always said, 'Hey, we're competitive; we're just one or two players away,' and you'd look around and see that when you matched up your team against somebody else's team, you were short.

"As things deteriorated, sometimes I tried to do more and Eddie tried to do more; we all tried to do more to make up for what we were missing. The tendency was for people to look around, some of us who contributed heavily, and try to bear too much of the burden. Mike Boddicker became the number-one pitcher and said, 'OK, I can't give up any runs if I want to win.' I told him, 'Bod, you're trying to do it all yourself. Just limit it to one run every three innings, and you'll be fine.' He said he could do that, and from that point on he got back to doing things he could do. All that got him was a trade out of here [in '88]. But that was indicative of a lot of people who were left over from the good teams and saw something special slipping away."

After the '87 season Williams not only fired Hank Peters, the Orioles' general manager since '75; he blistered Peters in a press conference, saying the Orioles had just five minority players out of one hundred in their minor league system. The new general manager was Roland Hemond, a veteran executive who had worked for Bill Veeck, among others, and built the division-winning Chicago White Sox in '83.

ROLAND HEMOND: "The club I took over wasn't the same Baltimore club I had admired. It was always a model organization. But no matter how good you are for how long, there can be a drought for various reasons. Sometimes some of your young personnel doesn't materialize, or veterans go the other way quickly. It can happen to an organization. The Yankees hit a downslide after '64. With the Orioles, I don't think they'd had the best of luck with some of their free agents."

HANK PETERS: "I had the job twelve years, which is a pretty long tenure for a major league general manager. And up until August of '86, we were pretty good. We had a bad season in '87 and a bad season overall in '86 because of the last two months. Other than that I'm pretty proud of what went on for ten years prior to that. And I don't put all the blame on Ed Williams because we all share in these things. We share in the glory of winning; we have to share in whatever you want to call it for losing. But he took over in '85; it was his show from then on. It was all up to him. The front office didn't do all that much. Whatever happened was his doing.

"One thing I really resented when I left was the stuff about not giving blacks fair opportunities. When Al Bumbry quit playing, we wanted to hire him as kind of a coach, to do PR work and things like that. We wanted him as an instructor, but I didn't have enough money in our minor league budget to give him what he needed, so I tried to carve something out of the PR budget, but we still didn't have enough. I went to Williams, and he turned me down. Said no more money. And then at the end of the year they blast me for not hiring Bumbry. Things like that stick in your craw, but, you know, time goes by."

39

0–21

During spring training in '88, the Orioles didn't think of themselves as serious contenders for a division title, having lost 95 games the year before. But they didn't expect the horror show that unfolded once the season began. Their lineup included Cal Ripken Jr., Eddie Murray, and Fred Lynn, and their starting rotation had Mike Boddicker, Mike Morgan, and Scott McGregor—all players with track records. New general manager Roland Hemond had overhauled the rest of the club since taking over in November, making six trades involving nineteen players. More than half of the Opening Day roster was new, including leftfielder Jeff Stone, a speedster the Philadelphia Phillies had once regarded as a future star.

"Damn right, we're contenders," manager Cal Ripken Sr. said optimistically near the end of spring training.

But that assessment was wrong, brutally wrong. And the Orioles found out immediately.

They opened the season before a packed house at Memorial Stadium on a warm, cloudless afternoon. Milwaukee beat them 12–0. "You can't judge us off one game," Boddicker said. But you could. After another loss to the Brewers, the Orioles went to Cleveland and lost four more games in a hurry. The series finale was tied in the fifth inning before the Orioles' Joe Orsulak dropped a fly ball, leading to a Cleveland rally. In six games the Orioles had been outscored 43–7.

Ever the optimist, Ripken Sr. told catcher Terry Kennedy on the flight back to Baltimore, "We might be 12–12 soon." The next day, after a morning court appearance to face a drunk-driving charge, the manager went to Memorial Stadium, sat down in his office to make out a lineup, . . . and was fired. It was the earliest in-season managerial firing in major league history, six games into the season.

BILL RIPKEN: "I heard it on the radio. I was driving to the park, maybe two o'clock. That's kind of unsettling when you hear that on the radio. I'm glad no police were on Cold Spring Lane. I sped up pretty quickly to get to the stadium. Dad had told [trainer] Ralph [Salvon] to talk to me. Ralph said, 'This has nothing to do with you. Don't let it affect you. You have a job to do. Go out and do your job.' I mean here's a man [Senior] whose dreams had just been shattered, and he still thought enough to tell Ralph to tell me that.

"I changed my uniform and wore his number the next night. Nothing was easy. I mean, it was all very unfair. We'd been around the game a long time, and you know when something isn't right, one guy gets fired instead of twenty-five. And that happens, and you know that. But in that situation, just six games, that didn't seem like much of an opportunity—certainly not what other people seemed to get. I don't know if they did it because he was the company man and everybody knew he would just go ahead and step down and say, 'You're right; it's me.' I don't know. But it wasn't the easiest thing to deal with. Looking back, there's a lot of bitterness."

CAL RIPKEN, JR.: "I had a chance to win some of those [six] games, and I didn't come through. One in particular: Doug Jones came in in a game in Cleveland, and I ended up hitting into a double play, but it was a situation where we could have done some damage and won a game. If you look at the scores, we could have gone 4–2 in those six games with certain luck. We only got blown out of a couple."

MARK THURMOND: "Firing the manager after six games, frankly, I didn't think that was appropriate. But it wasn't my call. I mean, maybe spring training hadn't gone that well, but we weren't very good."

ROLAND HEMOND: "Senior was up against it, no question. There was a lack of talent. Mr. Williams asked me in the spring, 'What do you think?' I said, 'I'm really worried. This is the slowest club I've seen in some time.' There wasn't much a manager could do, because it wasn't a good defensive club in the outfield. A slow club. [Firing Senior] was a very difficult day. I know it was difficult for him because he'd meant so much to the organization for so long. I brought him back the next year as a coach. If we didn't have someone like Frank Robinson aboard already, maybe we wouldn't have made the move as early as we did. But we had a capable and logical choice to try to get things going."

The new manager was a familiar face—Frank Robinson, who had moved into the Orioles' front office as a special assistant after a long career in uniform as a player, coach, and manager. Now fifty-two, he laughed when asked about taking over a winless team playing so poorly. "My family thinks I'm crazy," he said.

After the season-opening losing streak reached eight games, it almost ended against Kansas City at Memorial Stadium. Boddicker threw a five-hitter with 10 strikeouts and had retired eighteen Royals in a row when Jim Eisenreich singled with two out in the top of the ninth and the score tied. The next batter, Frank White, hit a routine line drive that Stone, in left, charged and then lost in the lights. Eisenreich came around to score the winning run.

The next two losses also were by one run. McGregor took a 2–1 lead into the eighth, but the Indians scored twice and won. Then Morgan and Cleveland's Greg Swindell matched shutouts for nine innings. After the Indians finally scored a run in the top of the 11th, Murray crashed a one-out, one-on double off the top of the right-field wall, missing a game-winning homer by six inches. But the runner, Jim Traber, advanced only from first to third before having to stop, preventing the tying run from scoring. Kennedy then struck out with the bases loaded to end the game. He never took the bat off his shoulders.

BILL RIPKEN: "We lost in every way. We scored runs and gave up more, and then sometimes when we didn't score, we gave up just a little, but it was enough. The one with Stone [and the lights], the poor guy. He did everything in his power. He gave up his body. He tried to get hit in his face if he couldn't catch it."

CAL RIPKEN JR.: "Sometimes you just start the season and things don't bounce right. That's happened many times. One year we were experimenting with Eddie at third and DeCinces at second [in '78], and Milwaukee scored 100 runs in a three-game series out there. Those kind of things happen, losing streaks and slumps. But then Dad got fired, and that just threw the whole thing into a state of shock. Whatever could happen bad after that seemed to happen. It was the worst streak of crazy circumstances I can recall. So many things you would just shake your head at and say, 'I thought it couldn't get any worse.' But it just kept getting worse."

EDDIE MURRAY: "It had started before that season. We hadn't played well for a couple of years. But that was hard to take. When Traber was on first and I hit a ball off the top of the wall, and Traber didn't score, you went, 'How can this happen?' But we had a team having on-the-job training, basically."

FRED LYNN: "The ways we lost were amazing. On the play where the runner [Traber] didn't score on [Murray's] ball off the wall, I mean, we couldn't even run the bases. I wouldn't want to go through it again, not in any line of work. You couldn't get away from it. No matter what we did or where we went or what time it was, people were reminding us. Like we didn't know. They'd go, 'You know, you've lost 10 in a row.' And you'd go, 'Oh, jeez, thanks for reminding me.' And you couldn't even turn on the TV. It was all over the TV."

With Ripken and Murray each batting under .200 and the team average at .186, the club stopped posting averages on the scoreboard—too embarrassing. Leaving on a 12-game road trip never sounded so good. But the trip opened with an epic show of ineptitude in Milwaukee, a 9–5 fiasco featuring four errors, two passed balls, two missed signs, a baserunning blunder, a misjudged fly ball, and another blown lead. The Orioles' record was now 0–13.

BILL RIPKEN: "[Reserve catcher] Carl Nichols came in to pinch hit in the ninth that night in Milwaukee, and it was freezing. Carl came all the way in from the dungeon out there in the bullpen, running across the field to pinch hit. He came in, and he had three parkas on, and he'd been sitting out in the 'pen for nine innings, and he looked like he was frozen solid. He actually hit a ball out to right-center. But they caught it, and that was the game."

EDDIE MURRAY: "Somehow all the blame got put on me. I didn't have a whole lot of protection behind me and not a whole lot of people getting on in front of me, but I still put up some decent numbers—even though the other teams knew there weren't many people in the lineup who could beat them. The guys on the other side were going, 'How can you be doing what you're doing, and we're not even supposed to be pitching to you?' My thing was, it had to be done early in games. I remember Sparky [Anderson] walking me intentionally with a man on third in the first inning."

With the national media converging on the spectacle, the Orioles yielded nine runs to the Royals in the bottom of the first of loss number 16. "That was not a professional ball game as far as the Baltimore Orioles were concerned," Frank Robinson said. The next day, the Royals scored the winning run in the bottom of the ninth after a wind gust blew Bo Jackson's routine fly ball off the wall for a triple. A 3–1 loss after that pushed the streak to 18 and dropped starting pitcher Mark Thurmond's record to 0–4.

MARK THURMOND: "You can laugh about it now, but at the time, going through it, that was miserable. Absolute torture. I remember waking up and thinking, 'Hey, we're already out of it.' That was pretty depressing. We were not a very good team. That was obvious. There were some players who could play and had put up some good numbers at other places, but anything that could go wrong did. Add that to the fact that we weren't very good to begin with, and you have a streak."

BILL RIPKEN: "You can't fathom it. The press was all over us. I mean, I saw cameras with CNN in the clubhouse, and they weren't even covering sports yet. It's not good to start getting national coverage for something like that. But I mean, you still go out and compete. Nobody on that team quit or blamed anybody else. That's a tribute to the guys. We never said a word one way or another. No, 'you stink.' There was none of that."

The players tried everything to change their luck. They wore their caps sideways and backward. They turned their uniforms inside out. They watched home-run videos. Outfielder Ken Gerhart showed up with a dozen roses one day and placed them around the clubhouse, trying to make the place "smell like victory." Nothing worked. The losses continued to pile up. As inept as the Orioles had been in '54, when they lost 100 games, they were even worse now. Their fall from the high of '83 was complete. They weren't the O's anymore, they were the Zer-O's, an industry laughingstock.

Robinson used gallows humor to deflect attention from the players. He opened one postloss press conference, "To answer your first question—I don't know." Before another game he told reporters, "To hell with the Gipper; we're going to win one for me." When the streak reached 19, President Ronald Reagan phoned Robinson to offer encouragement, saying, "I know what you're going through." Replied the manager, "No, you don't."

Increasingly desperate, Hemond operated a shuttle between Rochester and Baltimore, trying to inject life into the club. After Stone injured a finger making yet another blunder on the base paths, reporters asked Robinson if the error-prone leftfielder was the next to go. "I hope so," Robinson said. A new closer, Bill Scherrer, arrived from Triple A and entered a tied game in Minnesota in the eighth inning. Boom, the Twins' Tim Laudner launched a home run. Boom, teammate Kent Hrbek launched one even farther. So much for the new closer. The streak was at 20.

CAL RIPKEN JR.: "People can laugh about it now, but it was pretty awful. It was the worst thing you could go through because you were getting national attention, worldwide attention, for things that you don't want attention for. I mean, for the worst possible reason. You were looked at as a laughingstock. You were looked at as the worst. It was just bad. Terrible."

In the eighth inning the next afternoon, Hemond received a package containing the champagne-soaked suit he had worn when his White Sox clinched a division title in '83. He put on the "lucky" suit, but it didn't stop the streak from reaching 21 with a 4–2 loss.

Beginning a weekend series with the White Sox in Chicago the next night, the Orioles were already 16 games out of first place. They had set a major league record for the longest losing streak at the start of a season, and they were within three losses of the longest losing streak in major league history. With their starting rotation in tatters, they started Mark Williamson, a reliever, on a cool Friday night at Comiskey Park.

Finally, the end.

Ripken hit a homer to give the Orioles the lead, and Murray followed with another homer. The Orioles jumped in front 7–0, and Williamson, unlike the starters before him, didn't give back the lead. Final score: 9–0. The streak was over. "Maybe we won't be household names anymore," Williamson said. But despite the relief in the clubhouse, there was little joy. Several cases of unopened champagne remained corked. The message? A 1–21 team doesn't celebrate.

BILL RIPKEN: "The night we won, I got beaned right in the doink [head]. I was down, and Cal came out and said I had one eye looking at left field and one eye looking at right field. That didn't feel very good. Sort of summed it all up. But at least we finally won."

ROLAND HEMOND: "When we clinched the pennant in Chicago in '83, I'd brought an extra suit to the park in case we clinched. I got drenched in champagne, and they took the suit and put it in a glass case [in Comiskey Park]. When we had lost 20 straight, and we were playing in Minnesota, [Sox president] Eddie Einhorn called me and said, 'Hey, Roland, I'd like to mail you the suit. Put it on.' He wanted us to win before we got to Chicago that weekend.

"They took it out of the glass case and rushed it to me, and it didn't get there until the seventh inning of loss 21. I quickly changed into it, and it still had the scent of champagne and beer. Carl Nichols was leading off the ninth, and he got a hit, and I thought the suit was working. Then we hit into a double play and lost. We went to Chicago, and the next day I wore it again. It didn't smell too good, but it worked. After the last out [of the win] a friend sitting behind me said, 'What about it, Roland?' He poured beer all over me."

After losing the last two games in Chicago, the Orioles returned from the road trip with a 1–23 record. Incredibly, a sellout crowd showed up at Memorial Stadium on a Monday night to show their faith in their hometown team. The stunned Orioles responded with a 9–4 win over the Texas Rangers.

ROLAND HEMOND: "I forever cherish the day we returned from the trip [at 1–23]. I was hearing that there would be a large crowd for our return, but little did I realize what would happen. To have a complete sellout and a standing ovation when we took the field, that was amazing. A fan said, 'Hey, Roland, you're doing a great job.' I laughed and thought, 'What a great place. We're 1–23 and they think I'm doing a great job.'

"It was an emotional day. We released Scott McGregor and rushed Jay Tibbs in from Rochester to pitch. Edward Bennett Williams had said he wanted [Tibbs]. We were on the field to acknowledge the fans, and Williams got up and announced he'd signed an agreement for a long-term lease and the building of a new ballpark at Camden Yards. That was [Williams's] last game at Memorial Stadium. After that he wasn't well enough to come back. He died [of cancer] later that summer."

SCOTT McGREGOR: "I was supposed to pitch that night, and Roland called me in that morning and released me. He started crying, but it was the right move. I was done. And I went into the clubhouse after that, and Terry Kennedy came up and said, 'You lucky SOB; you don't have to play here anymore.'"

After that high, a season already drained of suspense lapsed into a long drumbeat of lows. The Orioles kept losing and losing until they finished with their worst record ever, 54–108, good for last place in the AL East by 34½ games. In the wake of a defining moment of ineptitude, an 0–21 start, they were at a low ebb.

FRANK ROBINSON: "I'll tell you what about that team. It wasn't that they didn't try. They just didn't have the talent. It wasn't there. Sometimes we didn't play good baseball, like in the Kingdome when we had three or four guys come over for a ball, and it dropped, and we lost 5–4. But we didn't get blown out but about one or two times in that streak. We just didn't have the talent to win. We tried."

BILL RIPKEN: "A few years later when some team lost 12 or 13 in a row, they asked me if I wanted to see the [21] record fall. I said no. I wouldn't want to see anyone lose 22 or 23 games in a row. Because that's the all-time worst thing, going through something like that. Any way you could possibly lose a game, you did. It's not a good feeling. And I don't wish that on anyone."

FRED LYNN: "We had Eddie, Cal, and myself batting three, four, five, and that's pretty good. But we can't win one game? You couldn't make that bet, that any major league team could lose 21 in a row, especially to start the season. It was beyond amazing. The season was over. It was absolutely over in three weeks. I'd never experienced that. We were 15 out. We were gone, done."

40

Why Not?

Before the '89 season started, there were major changes on and off the field. Edward Bennett Williams's estate sold the Orioles for seventy million dollars to Eli Jacobs, a New York investment specialist who was the chairman of Memorex Telex, a computer equipment company, and also reportedly owned a controlling interest in other companies with annual revenues exceeding five billion dollars. Jacobs, who pledged not to meddle in the baseball operation, had two minority investors: team president Larry Lucchino and former U.S. ambassador Sargent Shriver.

In December of '88, Eddie Murray was traded. The Orioles' All-Star first baseman had been feuding with the media, the front office, and even the fans for several years, and the club finally dealt him to the Los Angeles Dodgers for a shortstop prospect, Juan Bell, and pitchers Ken Howell and Brian Holton. Howell then was traded to Philadelphia for veteran outfielder Phil Bradley.

ROLAND HEMOND: "When I first got there [in '88] Eddie asked me to trade him. I said, 'Eddie, one of the reasons I came to Baltimore was you. You wore me out in Chicago.' But at the end of the ['88] season he was still hopeful we'd trade him. He said he wanted to go to the West Coast, but [Will] Clark was [playing first base] in San Francisco, [Mark] McGwire was in Oakland, and San Diego had Wally Joyner. There was only one place for him to go."

EDDIE MURRAY: "It was time to leave. It was the only organization I'd played with, but it got to where the best thing was to leave. [The press] had done a job on me. It was time to split. I had teammates out in the parking lot almost fighting [reporters]. And the talk shows had started to get out of hand. That was the closest thing to a lynching mob I had seen. The media wasn't the same. It had gotten to the point where negative stuff sells, and I know our city and our club wasn't used to that. That started to separate the guys and the way they felt about playing here. So I left, and I got to go home to Los Angeles and play in front of my dad every day."

When *The Sporting News* asked 186 baseball writers around the country for predictions before the '89 season, 170 picked the Orioles to finish last in the American League East. They had lost 107 games in '88 and then traded Murray, their best hitter, and now they were starting over with Cal Ripken Jr. and some rookies, fringe major leaguers, and journeymen.

Frank Robinson: "In spring training I said, 'I don't even want to hear about '88. This is a fresh start, a fresh year, and we're going to go back to fundamentals. We're going to teach the kids how to slide, hit behind the runner, advance a runner, score a man from third. We'll work with the outfielders on how to field ground balls.' We went back to all that. I told them, 'If we can have some fun and execute some fundamentals, we have a chance to win some games.' It was a bunch of guys who hadn't done a whole lot. But they came together."

On Opening Day the Orioles rallied to beat Roger Clemens and the Boston Red Sox, the defending AL East champs, at Memorial Stadium. With the 0–21 debacle on everyone's mind, the Orioles trailed until Cal Ripken hit a three-run homer off Clemens in the sixth and then delivered an extra-inning win emphasizing that '88 was over.

Jeff Ballard: "It was one of those storied games, especially after 0–21. To come out and beat the division champs and a great pitcher in the first game of '89, the fans were going nuts. It was like winning the World Series. It was close to the best game of my whole career, as far as memorable games, and I didn't even play. Just a great day for the fans who had supported the team through '88. The players were into it, and the game was close and tight, and to win on a homer by our best player, there was electricity in the locker room."

Later in April there was another key moment in the late innings of an afternoon game at Oakland. The Orioles were trying to protect a 2–1 lead, and rookie reliever Gregg Olson, the club's first-round draft pick in '88, pitched a scoreless eighth. Robinson sent him back out for the bottom of the ninth, and a closer was born.

GREGG OLSON: "Until then I was kind of setting up for Mark Williamson. I threw the ball well in the eighth, and I kind of figured I was done. But no one said anything, and I went, 'OK, I guess they're sending me back out there [for the ninth].' I just followed everything [catcher] Mickey Tettleton put down. It was like, 'Whatever you say.' I faced Dave Henderson, Dave Parker, and Mark McGwire. Mickey [called] a fastball inside, and I thought, 'Dave Parker?' I threw it, and Parker was standing there eyeballing me, and I was like, '[Tettleton] told me to do it.'

"But I got him, and then I got McGwire to end the game on a curveball, and Billy [Ripken] came running in, and he was screaming. I was kind of cool about it. I didn't think of the ramifications, that I might take over the [closer] role. But then I started getting some saves in the middle of May, and I had a good month."

BILL RIPKEN: "He just abused those guys. McGwire is a good breaking-ball hitter, and he doesn't flinch [at a curve]. Olie threw him one, and Mac kind of buckled, and then he got a little wider with his stance, and you could see him like, 'Nope, I'm not going to move on this one.' Next pitch, he did it again. Then got wider, and he said, 'I'm never going to move on this one,' and he got his hands out, and Olie buckled him again, three straight times."

FRANK ROBINSON: "Three up, three down. I said, 'Well, there's my closer.' I kind of knew it. It had been a long time since I saw a pitcher who could lock hitters like that with his curveball. The last one before Olson was 'Sad Sam' Jones back in the '50s."

After a modest start, the Orioles ran off 13 wins in 14 games, ending with a 16–3 win in Yankee Stadium. That pushed them into first place in early June—with a five-game lead, no less. When they not only held the lead, but expanded it, ultimately sitting in first for 98 straight days, signs appeared at Memorial Stadium asking a simple question—"Why Not?" As in, why can't the Orioles win a division just a year after 0–21? It became the Orioles' rallying cry.

ROLAND HEMOND: "As bad as '88 was, that's as good as '89 was. It's one of the greatest comebacks in baseball history. We had traded Murray, Lynn, and Boddicker, so we had a much younger club. Our entire payroll was eight million dollars. I had difficulty at times believing we could actually be in the race with such an inexperienced club. Frank Robinson did one of the most remarkable managing jobs of all time."

FRANK ROBINSON: "That was a fun, fun, fun year. Everyone contributed. Everyone did the little things. And we had fun. We enjoyed playing the game. Once Billy Ripken bunted a guy into scoring position and the fans gave him a standing ovation. That's how excited the fans were to see the little things."

Surprise performances fed what was ultimately a thirty-two-and-a-half-game improvement from '88, the second-largest improvement in AL history. Olson racked up 14 saves in a row at one point and 22 overall. Left-hander Jeff Ballard led the rotation with an 18–8 record after starting the season with 10 career wins. Left-handed reliever Kevin Hickey, who had been released four times in a career that started in a fast-pitch softball league in Chicago, limited left-handed hitters to a .206 average. Mark Williamson was terrific in relief with 65 appearances, 10 wins, nine saves, and a 2.93 ERA. Rookie starter Bob Milacki went 14–12. In all, eight rookie pitchers combined for 32 wins, 28 saves, and a 3.95 ERA.

MARK THURMOND: "Like everything went wrong in '88, everything went right in '89. Ballard wasn't an overpowering pitcher, but he knew how to pitch and compete, and he won a bunch of games. And Olson was tremendous. He had that curveball that dropped off a table, and a ninety-mile-an-hour fastball to go with it, and getting thrown into the fire like that as a rookie closer, he did a great job."

CAL RIPKEN JR.: "Ballard was a control lefty. He had a good change-up, and he knew how to work it, and sometimes, just the sheer nature of lefties in the rotation has an effect. It's hard to imagine another year being the same way for him as that was, because I think he could have won 21 or 22 games. As well as he did, there were a couple of games that were lost that he was leading in."

BILL RIPKEN: "We turned a million double plays for Ballard. He was around the plate, threw a lot of strikes, didn't walk anyone, gave up like 230 hits in 190 innings. But he had enough in that little sinker and change-up that every hit he gave up, he could get a ground ball and a double play."

JEFF BALLARD: "I started out as the number-five starter, and things just snowballed. The defense was great, running down everything in the gaps and making double plays. I went 5–0 and didn't look back. When I needed to throw a ground ball, I'd throw a sinker on the outside corner and get a ground ball. I was just in a zone."

BILL RIPKEN: "Olson made it interesting at times. But I don't think there was ever a time we doubted he was going to get things done. When I went to Texas in '93, John Russell was the backup catcher, and he told me Olie struck him out on a hook, but that the hook hit his arm and was still a strike. It was coming down and breaking so sharply that it nipped his arm and wound up in the strike zone. Russ said, 'I can't tell the umpire it hit me, because it's a strike.' When you hear other people talk about it, you see how nasty it was."

JEFF BALLARD: "Olson was really vital. He was just phenomenal that year. We really needed that because we didn't have a lot of horses. We needed someone to shut doors. The setup guys did a good job to get to him. Hickey pitched well. Williamson pitched great. That staff, for a bunch of no-name guys, everyone had a role, and it worked."

GREGG OLSON: "At the time, blown saves weren't really a stat, so I didn't think about it. I just went, 'I have a lead to protect, that's the bottom line.' I always seemed to get myself in trouble, walk the first guy or something, get myself in a jam. But I got out of it. It was pretty basic. I had one inning to get through. I didn't think about anything. I wasn't scared of who I was facing. It was just, 'OK, this is fun.' I was just mixing the curveballs with fastballs that were up, and everything was [thrown] as hard as I could."

With Murray gone and Ripken experiencing an average season by his standards—.257, 21 homers, 93 RBI—the offense should have been a problem, and it was in the end. The Orioles led the major leagues in runs scored through July 18, but they batted just .238 in their last 71 games, one of the main reasons they gave up the division lead and spent the last month of the season trying to catch the Toronto Blue Jays. Still, the offense was resourceful, featuring 63 sacrifice bunts, their most since '75; 118 stolen bases, their most since '76; and 593 walks, second-most in the majors.

Individually, the biggest offensive surprise was Mickey Tettleton, who had a breakthrough season with 26 homers, almost doubling his career output to that point. After a Home Team Sports interview in which his wife credited his success to his habit of eating Froot Loops, Tettleton was nicknamed "The Cereal Killer." Another surprise was first baseman Randy Milligan, getting his first extended shot in the majors after eight years in the minors. He hit 12 homers and led the club with 74 walks and a .394 on-base percentage.

Other rookies playing every day also were major contributors. Craig Worthington played 145 games at third base, drove in 70 runs, and was named The Sporting News AL Rookie of the Year. Mike Devereaux hit .266, stole 22 bases, and made just one error in center field. The whole outfield defense went from awful in '88 to magnificent in '89, with the fleet Devereaux, Steve Finley, Brady Anderson, and Joe Orsulak splitting time in right and center next to Phil Bradley in left.

MARK THURMOND: "The big difference in '89 was the outfield defense. We picked up a bunch of guys who could really go get the ball. Balls that would have blooped in before or gone into the gap, they ran them down. That makes all the difference in the world. The infield defense actually had been solid the year before with Cal and Billy and Eddie. But the outfield really picked up."

FRANK ROBINSON: "They caught everything. Nothing got between them. If they dove for a ball, they caught it. If they went for it, they caught it."

CAL RIPKEN JR.: "We had some real gazelles out there. It became really contagious in that they were trying to outdo each other, which is a great thing. You had four or five guys kind of interchanging. Frank was trying to find out where they could play. It was weird that center field was kind of being switched around and right and left was switching around. That's not easy to do, and those guys were turning some bloopers into outs and turning some rockets into outs, and they were doing a lot of great things."

The season reached an emotional high point on a Saturday night in July at Memorial Stadium, shortly after the All-Star break, with the California Angels in town and more than forty-seven thousand fans in the stands. The Orioles trailed 9–7 in the bottom of the ninth, but the Orioles scored two runs to tie and then won on a Devereaux home run down the left-field line—a homer the Angels and more than a few fans thought was foul. When the Orioles won in extra innings the next day on another ball that was arguably foul—a Tettleton dribbler that went over the first-base bag—it was hard not to conclude they were destined for glory.

JEFF BALLARD: "We didn't even think about '88. So many of the players were new, and we were so young. Everyone was caught up in the games themselves. There were a lot of guys who didn't experience the o–21 thing and the real bad '88. We just had a lot of youthful energy. The only thing we strove to do was win. There was no contract stuff. No free-agency stuff. It was just guys trying to establish themselves in the big leagues and perform. It was real loose. What did we have to lose? That team had its focus just right."

CAL RIPKEN JR.: "You could just see the level of talent starting to pick up. Before Eddie got traded, other teams would tell me, 'If you or Eddie don't beat us, we'll win.' But then we started to get people who had nothing to do with o–21. I mean, there were a few of us left with a lingering effect, but we just wanted to forget about it, anyway. And there were enough people that didn't know anything about it. There was a freshness to the '89 team that was different from '88—a certain magic. I know Earl always said that momentum is tomorrow's pitcher. But there's a certain feeling as a team that can take hold, and that particular team is an argument for momentum, because there was a lot of confidence that came on in the first half of the season on an individual basis, and that impacted the team collectively."

GREGG OLSON: "We were a bunch of young guys. We didn't know any better. We didn't know we were supposed to be brutal. No one told me I wasn't supposed to close. Nobody told us we weren't supposed to be doing what we were doing. We just went out and played hard. Didn't play real well at the beginning, hung around .500, but then we started playing better, and it wasn't a real strong division at the time, and we took over first place.

"Then whenever someone challenged us, we responded. The Brewers cut the lead down and came in, and we swept them. Then Boston came in, and we beat them, too. Kept ourselves in first place. It was a lot of fun. No one had any expectations. Just a bunch of young guys who hadn't been around long enough to know what their limitations were."

BILL RIPKEN: "There was one point where we won every series for, like, a stretch of ten or fifteen in a row. We were real good at that, just winning two out of three. It wasn't like we were sweeping everybody, but everyone was going, 'Damn, this is a lot of fun. This is good.' I mean, I thought we couldn't be caught."

After pushing their lead to seven and a half games in late July, the Orioles suddenly lost their magic. They lost eight games in a row, won one, then lost five more in a row. Coming home from a twelve-game trip with their lead in jeopardy, they found new life, unexpectedly, in the right arm of pitcher Dave Johnson, the most heartwarming of their many longshot stories.

Johnson, twenty-nine, was from Middle River, one of Baltimore's working-class communities. After seven years in the minor leagues with the Pirates and Astros, he was obtained in a trade in the spring, sent to Rochester, and called up in early August. Commuting to Memorial Stadium from his home in Middle River, he pitched a pair of complete games in front of cheering friends and family members.

DAVE JOHNSON: "I'd been asked not to pitch about three different times in Rochester because they were going to call up someone. Then they told me, 'You're going to Boston, and it's supposed to rain, and if it does, you won't pitch, and you'll come back.' I got there and ended up pitching into the seventh because the bullpen was wasted. Then we came home, and I sat in the bullpen for a week. When I finally pitched against the Twins, I gave up a run in the first, pitched out of a jam in the fourth, and we won 6–1. I pitched a complete game. Five days later against Boston I gave up a run in the first and pitched eight shutout innings. They named me American League Player of the Week. The week before I wasn't even going to be activated if it rains, and then I'm AL Player of the Week."

ROLAND HEMOND: "Dave Johnson sort of summed up what the season was all about. In that game against Minnesota he just missed giving up a grand slam to a guy who had never hit a home run in the majors. I watched the ball going and said, 'Oh, Johnson's going back to Rochester.' But then he struck the guy out and kept going. It was a year like that. We got heroics from so many unlikely people."

BILL RIPKEN: "DJ threw those eighty-four [mph] fastballs and said, 'Here it comes; here's my stuff; let's see what you can do with it.' And it worked. He might give up a solo homer, but he worked to keep the [big] innings down. He certainly shook off the catcher more than any human alive. They'd say, 'You know, you can't throw that stuff to some of these guys up here.' And they'd put down two [fingers, the sign for a curveball], and DJ would shake it off and step up and throw the ball under the catcher's glove for a strike. He was accused of doing everything to a baseball. I don't know what he was doing. He touched his head more times than Gaylord Perry. I'm not saying he put anything on it, but he sure touched his head an awful lot."

When Johnson and the starters other than Ballard and Milacki struggled down the stretch, the veteran Blue Jays finally passed the Orioles as Robinson resorted to a four-man rotation. Somehow, the Orioles scraped together enough wins to reach a season-ending three-game series in Toronto just one game out.

The series opener was a classic. Phil Bradley hit Toronto starter Todd Stottlemyre's first pitch for a home run, and Ballard made that stand up until Robinson pulled him in favor of Olson with one out and a runner on first in the bottom of the eighth. The runner, Tom Lawless, stole second and advanced to third on a groundout, and then Olson threw a curveball that bounced away from backup catcher Jamie Quirk, allowing Lawless to score. Olson struck out the batter, Kelly Gruber, on the next pitch—one pitch too late. The Blue Jays scored the winning run in the 11th off reliever Mark Williamson.

JEFF BALLARD: "It had to be as close to the playoffs or World Series as you could get without being there. I got out there with a 1–0 lead, and they talk about Canadian fans being kind of docile, but they were hardly that. Lloyd Moseby was the leadoff hitter, and Bob Melvin called a fastball, and the crowd was roaring so loud I was thinking, 'They're vibrating me.' I distinctly remember thinking, 'I can't feel the ball. I'm numb. I might throw this in the press box.' But it went right to the glove for strike one, and I went, 'Whoa, cool.' Moseby got a hit, but I got out of the inning.

"I felt in command throughout the game. Frank made the decision to take me out, which I don't disagree with. I had pitched pretty effortlessly, but we needed to win this game, and Olson had been phenomenal, and it was

[Robinson saying], 'I'm going to try to stretch [Olson] to five outs.' That's a decision a manager has to make. I can't say it would have turned out any differently if he'd left me in.

"Gregg came in, and he was as sharp as anything. They didn't touch him. But they could steal off him, and they got [Lawless] to third with two out, and he threw a curveball as nasty as he'd ever thrown, and it bounced over Quirk's head. Quirk was phenomenal taking the blame. He said, 'I should make that stop.' I went, 'Jamie, you had no chance.' There was nothing he could do. Gregg struck out the batter on the next pitch—gave up a run without giving up a hit. And they went on to win in extra innings."

Gregg Olson: "They got a guy on in the eighth, and I came in. Lawless stole second, I got an out, then there was a ground ball to short, and he was stealing third, so he got to third. Two out. Kelly Gruber was up, and he was having a good season. I went, 'I'm going to throw a good breaking ball here.' If you're looking at a clock, my normal one was probably one o'clock to seven, going down. I said, 'I'm going to come down a little bit and throw him something different.' About one-thirty to seven-thirty. A little more tilt. And I just flew open and came across it, and it was gone.

"Quirk said after the game he should have blocked it. But that ball was so far in the left-handed batter's box. It airmailed everything. I caught abuse in the off-season, but I looked at it and said, 'I kept us in the game in the eighth, kept us in the game in the ninth, kept us in the game in the tenth. I gave us a chance to win.' No one got a hit off me. I failed in the situation, and I was upset at blowing the win, but I did my best."

Frank Robinson: "Earlier in the game we had a man at second with no outs and hit the ball to the shortstop. It was about the sixth. We were up 1–0. We didn't get that man to third. We might not have gotten him in, but we would have had a better chance. Then the guy died at second base, so it was still 1–0 in the eighth.

"They could steal on Olson. He was slow to the plate. Lawless was at second, and he starts to take off to third, and the ball is hit right to Rip. Ordinarily Lawless wouldn't advance, but he was already going, so we had to take the out at first. So he was on third, and then he scored on the wild pitch. He would have been at second if he hadn't been breaking. But Olson threw a ball over in the left-handed batter's box. No one was going to get that ball."

With the Orioles now two games out with two to play, Robinson penciled in rookie Pete Harnisch as his starter for the next game, but Harnisch stepped on a nail walking home from SkyDome on Friday night and had to scratch. Robinson gave the ball to Dave Johnson, who hadn't won in a month. Johnson responded with a performance that summed up the Orioles' season. He limited the Blue Jays to two hits through seven innings and took a 3–1 lead into the bottom of the eighth.

DAVE JOHNSON: "Pete and I had pitched in Milwaukee, and Frank said the one who pitched better would get the Saturday start in Toronto. Pete won, and I didn't pitch well. I was planning on sitting in the bullpen [Saturday]. Elrod always takes two balls and puts them in the shoes of the starting pitcher, and when I got to the park, the balls were in my shoes. I thought Elrod had just messed up. I gave the balls to [pitching coach] Al Jackson. Al said, 'What are you doing? Didn't you hear? Pete stepped on a nail. You're starting.'

"The magnitude hit me. Fifty thousand fans. I'm a ground ball pitcher, pitching on a rug. The whole season on the line. National TV. It was kind of crazy and real challenging. But it was neat to be in that position. I'd never shunned it before. I thought, 'What the heck? I didn't pitch well in September. Here's a chance to redeem myself.'

"I gave up a run in the first inning, and I came off the mound ticked off. Frank just tore into me. He basically said, 'Get your head out of your ass. There's a long way to go.' After the third inning I relaxed, and the dome was open, and the wind was swirling, and it was impossible to hit a ball out. I just kept throwing fastballs up there, saying, 'Here, whack it.' Devereaux and Finley and Bradley kept running 'em down."

Robinson finally removed Johnson after he walked the leadoff hitter in the eighth. On came Hickey, then Williamson, mainstays out of the bullpen. But Toronto scored three runs to win 4–3 and nail down the division title.

DAVE JOHNSON: "I got to the eighth with a 3–1 lead and went, 'What in the hell am I doing here? I'm basically just throwing the ball down the middle of the plate.' I walked Nelson Liriano to start the eighth, and Frank brought in Hickey. I wasn't tired, but I was mentally drained. I thought for sure he was going to bring in Olson. I don't know if he was sore. But it didn't matter if he'd thrown nine innings the day before. He was our guy, and we needed him to win the game.

"Hickey walked the next guy and went two and oh on the guy after that, and then Frank brought in Williamson. The moves were right. Throw Hickey against the left-hander, as he had all year. Kevin threw strikes. The guy fouled off a bunch of pitches. And Williamson had had a huge year. But then Mookie Wilson hit a seeing-eye single in the hole that got through on the turf and scored the tying run. And then they scored the winning run on a sacrifice fly."

FRANK ROBINSON: "Dave Johnson gave me seven-plus fantastic innings. The only thing I second-guess myself on was maybe I shouldn't have let him go back out there for the eighth. Because he was out of gas. I didn't realize it until he went out and couldn't get the ball over the plate. But the problem was the bullpen was just gassed. Williamson was just worn out. He was a real unsung hero that year—took the ball night after night, two, three innings, whatever. He was all used up by the time we got to Toronto."

JEFF BALLARD: "Frank got us there to have a chance to win. We just didn't. The disappointment wasn't real long-lived. A lot of the guys on that team had had no idea what it was like to be in a pennant race. I'm not saying we weren't disappointed. I just don't think we had an understanding of what disappointment was all about. I understand it now. At the time I thought I'd have other chances to get back there."

FRANK ROBINSON: "After the [final loss] I told them to hold their head high. It was hard to feel too bad, but I sure would love to have won that year. We were just a bunch of misfits, a bunch of guys who came together as a team, and that would have been very exciting if we'd actually won a division. A fair number of those guys had been on the '88 team. To go from that ['88] season to winning a division would have been amazing."

GREGG OLSON: "If I don't throw that wild pitch [Friday night], and I save the game in the ninth—and I did go through the ninth—then Williamson wouldn't have come in that night, and neither of us would be dead. So both of us would have been fresher [Saturday]. He would have been fresher when he came in, and I could have pitched instead of being unable to get things going when they got me up to get ready. So we win that game, too [on Saturday]. That's two wins. So we win the series. Who knows what would have happened on Sunday, but at the least there would have been a playoff, which we could have won. Basically, if I don't throw that wild pitch, we win the pennant. That's the conclusion I've come to over the years. My wild pitch cost us the pennant."

41

Good-Bye, 33rd Street

The Orioles' final years at Memorial Stadium were a forgettable end to an unforgettable era. The "Why Not?" high of '89 proved illusory, a mere pause in the decline that started after the World Series triumph of '83. The Orioles spent just three days over .500 in '90, finishing fifth in the American League East, nine games under .500. They were even worse in '91, the final season at Memorial Stadium, winning just 67 of 162 games.

What caused the collapse? It wasn't the pitching. Orioles opponents hit for a lower average in '90 than in '89, even though '89 ace Jeff Ballard fell to 2–11 and out of the rotation in '90 after undergoing surgery to remove bone chips from his left elbow. That was a setback, but the staff survived. Dave Johnson won 13 games, Pete Harnisch won 11, and rookie Ben McDonald, the number-one pick in the '90 draft, went 8–5 with a 2.43 ERA. Out of the bullpen, Gregg Olson had 37 saves, and Mark Williamson had eight wins and a 2.21 ERA.

The hitting, or lack of it, sent the Orioles back into a dive. Many players who had hit well in '89 had major problems in '90. Mickey Tettleton fell to 15 homers and a .223 average and set a club record with 160 strikeouts. Craig Worthington hit just .226 with eight homers. Cal Ripken's .250 average was a career low. Overall, the Orioles finished next-to-last in the league with a .245 team average.

Meanwhile, Eddie Murray hit .330 with 26 homers and 95 RBI in his second year as the cleanup hitter for the Dodgers, underlining how badly the Orioles missed his bat. Recognizing the problem, general manager Roland Hemond swung a deal to try to replace Murray. Three young players—Harnisch, pitcher Curt Schilling, and outfielder Steve Finley—were dealt to the Houston Astros for first baseman Glenn Davis, who had averaged 29 homers over the past five years.

BILL RIPKEN: "In '89 we played over our heads. I don't think there's any question about that. And that caught up with us after that season. I mean, if you compared our talent to the opposition, we just didn't measure up in enough places. We also lost some key talent. Ballard had real problems after that surgery, and he'd won 18 games. That's huge. Then we traded Tettleton and lost Harnisch and Schilling and Finley. So we lost a lot there."

The Glenn Davis trade was initially praised by the media and fans who envisioned Davis, thirty, leading the club back into playoff contention. But the trade was a disaster still resonating a decade later. Davis was never the player the Orioles expected. Shortly after signing the largest one-year contract in club history, worth $3.275 million, he suffered a mysterious and serious injury in spring training in '91, damaging the spinal accessory nerve in his neck, a condition that weakened his right shoulder. He missed a majority of the '91 season, hitting just .227 with 10 homers, then strained a rib cage muscle early in '92. In all, he was on the disabled list for 128 of his first 168 games in Baltimore. He wound up hitting .276 with 13 homers and 48 RBI as a DH in '92, but he was injured again in '93, sent to the minors, and finally released.

Meanwhile, the Orioles lost so much in dealing for Davis that it boggled the mind. Tettleton was traded to the Detroit Tigers several days after the deal in what was obviously a cost-cutting move; rather than give Tettleton a raise after his poor season in '90, the club unloaded him and used the money to help pay for Davis. That backfired when Tettleton reemerged as a potent power hitter in Detroit and also later for the Texas Rangers.

Far worse was the loss of Harnisch, Schilling, and Finley, all of whom went on to have long, productive major league careers. Harnisch and Schilling combined for more than 200 wins after the deal, with Schilling emerging as one of the game's best pitchers. Finley, a three-time Gold Glove winner, was still playing every day a decade later.

ROLAND HEMOND: "Maybe the '89 season gave us a false impression of how close we were [to being a serious contender], although we recognized that it was an overachieving year. But then in '90 we had problems with run production that led to us making the trade that came back to haunt us. The sad part about Glenn Davis's injury was that the doctors told me that usually only jackhammer operators or wrestlers come down with that injury. I think we got the only baseball player who injured his spinal accessory nerve. But it atrophied, and he couldn't build it up or get his strength back. That set us back.

"I was a little concerned about the trade after we made it because we were lauded excessively. That scared me. It's usually better if the media doesn't like it. We'll never know what would have happened if Davis hadn't come up injured, because we thought he'd be a 40-plus home run hitter [per year] in Camden Yards. But that injury destroyed his career. He left us and played in [Triple-A] Omaha and [Independent League] St. Paul, and then he hung it up.

"As far as what we gave up, at the time Finley was the same type player as Brady Anderson, so we had two of the same type. They hadn't learned to hit with power, and we needed some punch. Schilling became one of the best pitchers in the National League, but he was just a prospect at the time. And we saw the promise in [Mike] Mussina and [Ben] McDonald, so we felt we had the [pitching] depth to do the deal.

"I've seen [Schilling] since then, and he said, 'Hey, Roland, you made the right move at the time because I hadn't matured yet.' He wasn't into it. One time in Toronto the pitchers had been discussing how to pitch Kelly Gruber, and Schilling got called in from the bullpen, and as he was heading to the field he turned around and said, 'Hey, how do you pitch to Gruber?' [Reliever] Joe Price went nuts. He said, 'We've been talking about that!' And Gruber cleared the bases."

Davis's injury ruined the Orioles' chances of making the last season at Memorial Stadium even remotely interesting. Frank Robinson was fired as manager after winning just 13 of the first 37 games in '91. The new manager was Johnny Oates, a former Orioles catcher who had served his apprenticeship as a minor league manager and coached first base for the Orioles since '89. Oates was bright and organized, but he couldn't compensate for a lack of starting pitching.

ROLAND HEMOND: "Frank [Robinson] was a victim of the lack of run production. I'm not throwing all the blame at Glenn Davis, but that injury created additional problems that might not have occurred otherwise. Managers pay the price when the club isn't winning. Frank was a great team man. I know it was disheartening for him to take off the uniform. It wasn't easy for him to accept. But he came and played a role in the front office [as assistant GM] and was helpful to Johnny Oates. He showed a great deal of class."

Johnny Oates: "Getting the job was a total surprise. I had no idea. I mean, I didn't have any inkling. What's odd, Frank usually liked to get together with a coach every once in a while, and that morning he came by for me to have breakfast in Detroit at the Ritz-Carlton. We had brunch together that morning. And then we played that night and came home. When I got to my apartment about three o'clock in the morning, there was a phone call from Roland."

There was little for the fans to cheer for in '91 other than Ripken, who batted .323 with 34 homers and 114 RBI and became the first American Leaguer to win the league's Most Valuable Player Award while playing for a losing team. The other positive developments in '91 were the arrival of another highly promising rookie pitcher, Mike Mussina, and the triumphant return of Mike Flanagan, who fashioned a 2.38 ERA in 64 games in relief at age thirty-nine. But overall, the Orioles were floundering as their time at Memorial Stadium drew to a close.

Cal Ripken Jr.: "We had made some nice strides toward rebuilding, brought in some nice players for future development. Then the success in the '89 season changed that mind-set. After '89 the rallying cry still should have been 'We're rebuilding' and 'We need to keep developing players continually.' But then, all of a sudden, we went to the last week of the season [in '89] and were so close to the playoffs that the expectations came back—similar to the expectations in '82 and '83, only they were legitimate [expectations] then.

"You had to recognize [after '89] that we had young talent, and we were overachieving, and things kind of went our way—that we had a chance to be good, but that we were still rebuilding. But that's not how we responded as an organization after '89. The mind-set changed. It was like we felt we were close enough to make the deals that would get us there [back to the playoffs], and we lost some good players. The expectations were unrealistic. The patience level changed. You don't trade [Harnisch, Schilling, and Finley] if you're still in a developmental mode. And to think about those pitchers with what developed [Mussina and McDonald], I mean, you can go crazy."

The Orioles had one of baseball's lowest payrolls in the early '90s despite drawing 2.5 million fans per season, an increase of some 150 percent from Jerry Hoffberger's era. Owner Eli Jacobs didn't interfere with the baseball operation on a daily basis, but he was criticized for not reinvesting more of the profits in the payroll.

Joe Hamper: "Jacobs didn't pay a penny for the ball club. He never put in a penny. The baseball rules required you to put in 60 percent equity. Well, he went to, I think it was Citicorp, and he borrowed the 60 percent from them personally. And then the other 40 percent he borrowed as a company loan.

"Then you had Sargent Shriver and Larry Lucchino as minority stockholders, and every month the club would declare a dividend large enough to pay the interest and the principal on that [Citicorp] loan. Larry and Shriver would get their [dividend] shares, which was a small amount. The ball club was generating enough money to pay that plus the interest on the loan. [Jacobs] didn't have to put in a penny. He also was drawing a big salary.

"My eyes really popped when I saw the way they operated. As far as the [low player payroll], he didn't care anything about that stuff. I can't tell you firsthand, because I never had a conversation with him. It was the operatives [handling the club]. But it was unbelievable. I mean, you forgot they even had a team because there was so much emphasis and so much done regarding the finances and meeting these various financial commitments. You have to maintain a certain level of cash in expenditures and meet all these covenants when you borrow money. And you had to make monthly statements. I mean, if somebody said, 'Well, how about the team?' You'd go, 'Jesus, is there a team here?' "

Peter Angelos: "They were paying twenty-eight million dollars in payroll, and they were packing the house, especially starting in '92 at Camden Yards. They were making twenty million dollars a year."

Larry Lucchino: "Remember, these were the go-go '80s, and Eli was a classic of the times. He was LBO [leveraged buyout] all the way—borrow the money and pump the revenues up to pay down the debt. Sure, we ran the team that way. It was a time when many other corporations around the country were being run the same way as a result of LBOs. To make the statement that it was hard at times to remember it was a baseball team, that's fair.

"I didn't know Eli from the man in the moon before he bought the Orioles. Sargent Shriver and his son brought him to me [as a potential buyer from the Williams's estate]. The night the sale was announced, Agnes Williams [Edward Bennett Williams's wife] sent Sarge a bottle of champagne and a note saying, 'I hope you have as much fun with the Orioles as we did.' It looked like Sarge was going to be active and Eli was going to be a passive investor, or so he described himself. That didn't prove to be the case. I was the president and CEO, but the budgets had to be determined with Eli and Sarge. And then Eli and Sarge had a falling out after the deal closed and essentially communicated through me. It was a hard and anxious time for all of us."

ROLAND HEMOND: "Jacobs was very kind, very helpful, very supportive. Larry had more of the direct, daily contact with him. We were under some [financial] constraints. But we made it work in '89. I was accustomed to it. It was no different [working for] Bill Veeck in Chicago. Veeck used to say, 'Roland, don't bother preparing a budget; we don't have any money. We'll think of something.' So [Jacobs's constraints] didn't bother me. Oh, there were times. Toronto acquired David Cone for the stretch run in '92, and we got Craig Lefferts. But you try. You just do the most you can do."

Even though the Orioles were out of contention early in '91, the season still built to a memorable climax—the final game at Memorial Stadium, played before a sellout crowd on a Sunday afternoon in early October. With little else to sell, the club focused on marketing the final three-game series against the Detroit Tigers as the end of a glorious era. The fans responded, filling the stadium for all three games and turning the weekend into a warm, noisy celebration of memories.

The Tigers won the opener Friday night, and the Orioles won 7–3 the next day, setting up the main event—the final game on Sunday afternoon. The game itself, like the whole '91 season, was forgettable. Bob Milacki started for the Orioles, and the Tigers pounded him. It was 7–1 by the top of the ninth with Olson on the mound for the Orioles.

With one out, Oates summoned Mike Flanagan, the former ace concluding a fine comeback season in relief. The move was anticipated and highly symbolic. As Flanagan slowly walked in from the bullpen to a standing ovation, he represented a one-man summary of the franchise's glory days, the many years of success the Orioles had experienced on 33rd Street. With the crowd roaring and history bearing down on him, he recorded the Orioles' final two outs at the park.

GREGG OLSON: "We really wanted Flanny to throw the last out. The only thing that would have been fun, if the last out was a save situation, then I was going to do it. But I started the ninth, and I was supposed to go to two outs, and Flanny was going to come in for the last one, but I got the first one, and I felt so bad that I motioned to Johnny, like, 'Come on. I got my one out; get me out of here.' So Johnny came running out, and Flanny came running in."

MIKE FLANAGAN: "I didn't get in Friday night, didn't get in Saturday, and I go, 'Something's up. There's a plan here.' There were rumors that they were saving me for the last inning. And I got up that morning, and I remember saying to myself, 'This is really going to happen.' Then in the fourth inning [Sunday] I went into that little bathroom under the left-field wall, and I looked in the mirror and said, 'This is not happening.'

"Over my whole career I had been able to deflect the idea of 'me against them.' I was always able to convince myself that I was part of a team. But this was me. We were in sixth place at the end of a bad season, and it was all on me. I had a great fear that I was going to fall on my face and give up ten runs and people would be groaning. I really did feel I had the weight of all the years on my shoulders to finish this up. It was the seventh game in the World Series. It was a totally selfish moment.

"I walked in from the bullpen. Only time I ever did that. I always ran in, but if I'd tried to run that time I would have fallen. And I get out there, and Olson's comment to Oates was, 'What took you so long? These people are going to run me out of town. Get him in here.' And Bob Melvin looks at me and says, 'How about a piece of gum?' Then he said, 'Let's do this right.' I don't know what was going on for the Tigers. I'm sure they just wanted to go home. But I threw two curveballs to Dave Bergman, struck him out. They missed a pitch at two-two, but I got him. Then Travis Fryman was the last up, and I threw him a three-two breaking ball, and he struck out. I was an emotional mess."

After the Orioles were retired in the bottom of the ninth and the field was cleared, a poignant ceremony surpassing all expectations unfolded on the field. With just music playing, no announcements, Brooks Robinson, the consummate Oriole, emerged from the dugout—in uniform—and took his place at third base, as if a game were getting ready to begin. Then Jim Palmer, tears in his eyes, trotted from the dugout to the mound. One by one, a procession of legends took the field in uniform—Frank Robinson, Boog Powell, Mark Belanger, Rick Dempsey, then some sixty players in all, the club's entire history gathering. Fans cheered and cried. Memorial Stadium had closed magnificently.

BRADY ANDERSON: "I didn't have the memories there, so it wasn't a meaningful day for me. But seeing how emotional Flanagan was, it made me think that it wasn't emotion over the loss of the stadium, but over realizing that your life has gone by and how quickly it goes and that maybe some of the best times of your life had passed. That, I could relate to. And I think that's what people mourned for at the loss of Memorial Stadium. It wasn't specifically that stadium, but just the passing of time that makes people sentimental."

MIKE FLANAGAN: "After the game, it was like going back in time, walking through a time line. We came back through the tunnel to the clubhouse, and there was Brooks and Boog and Frank, and they didn't know what had happened on the field. They were all lined up for the ceremony, and they said, 'We heard the cheering; what happened?' There were guys everywhere, and I quickly changed my shirt and got back into line, and then the emotional stuff just carried over. There was Brooksie running out to third, and Palmer going out with tears in his eyes, and Belanger with those same, choppy steps, all of them just like they'd been, only older. It was something. It was really the weight of all the years coming down. It all culminated on that day."

JOHNNY OATES: "That's one of those days that really made an impression on me. I still get chill bumps. We all had to come in the clubhouse after the game, and you see Brooks trot to third and the music's being played, and I cried. I didn't want anybody to see it, but it just showed what that group of players had. To see them going out there together, it was still special. These were the guys who put the Orioles on the map. Then Frank went out, and there were tears in Palmer's eyes. Then Boog and Davey Johnson and Belanger and the pitchers came out, and Earl. I said, 'That's what it means to be an Oriole right there.' You have a half-dozen special days in your life that are a little better than the rest, and that was one of 'em."

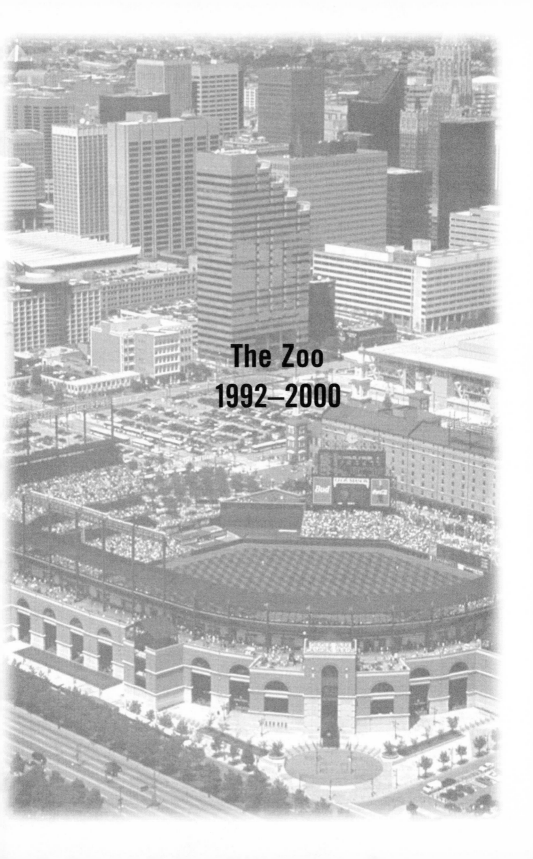

The Zoo
1992–2000

42

Camden Yards

Discussions about a new ballpark for the Orioles had bounced around Baltimore since the early '70s, with the issue always centered on preventing the club from moving to Washington or elsewhere. When Edward Bennett Williams and Maryland governor William Donald Schaefer announced in April of '88 that a new ballpark would become a reality at Camden Yards, the Orioles' future in town finally was secure, and the frame of Baltimore's ballpark conversation changed to architecture and amenities.

The questions were many and varied. Would the facade of the Orioles' new home be made of brick or concrete? What about the outfield dimensions? Would the upper deck be pitched as steeply as the upper deck at Memorial Stadium? Would the scoreboard have video? What about the name? The answers to all questions were important, even vital, in a city with a losing team drawing 2.5 million fans a season.

The answers came at a slow, steady pace over the four years between Williams's announcement and the first pitch at Oriole Park at Camden Yards on Opening Day in '92. But even as the pieces of the puzzle began to fit and the concept of the ballpark evolved from fuzzy to vivid, it was impossible to calculate the sheer magnificence of the Orioles' new home until it opened.

"This is a building capable of wiping out in a single gesture fifty years of wretched stadium designs, and of restoring the joyous possibility that a ballpark might actually enhance the experience of watching the game of baseball," wrote Paul Goldberger, architecture critic for the *New York Times*.

The architects, planners, and decision makers—a broad collective including many in the Orioles' front office—knew the ballpark would alter the Orioles as no prior force had, quadrupling revenues and turning a team from a midsized market into a financial powerhouse capable of handling player payrolls as high as any in the game. That was Williams's original motivation, after all.

But no one from the Orioles, the Maryland Stadium Authority, or their architects—a team headed by the Hellmuth, Obata & Kassabaum (HOK) Sports Facilities Group of Kansas City—could have known they were effectively reinventing baseball as they raised the ballpark from the ground to a glistening finished product on the grounds of an old railroad yard.

The impact of Camden Yards would surpass all expectations, spreading throughout the industry in the coming years as teams sought to re-create the distinctive ambiance and eye-popping revenue stream, and a generation of knockoffs sprouted across the major leagues.

The allure of Camden Yards lay in a simple, brilliant irony—a new stadium with an old feel. The prior wave of American stadiums, built in the '60s and '70s, had looked to the future, incorporating twenty-first-century elements such as domes, artificial turf, baseball-football designs, "exploding" scoreboards, and luxury suites. Camden Yards went in the opposite direction, looking to the past and baseball's unmatched tradition, yet with the best of the twenty-first-century amenities included.

There was no dome or artificial turf; the "summer game" would be played where it belonged—on grass, under the sky, and downtown, in a baseball-only park with a relatively small capacity (forty-eight thousand). The outfield configuration was asymmetrical, with a tall wall and hand-operated scoreboard in right field—a salute to Brooklyn's Ebbets Field and Fenway Park's Green Monster. Instead of using bright, modern coloring, all seats were painted dark green, as at Chicago's Wrigley Field. Other long-gone but venerated ballparks such as New York's Polo Grounds and Pittsburgh's Forbes Field also were used as influences.

The B&O Railroad warehouse—rising behind right field—as well as the red brick walls, high arches, cast-iron gates, and 1890s Baltimore Baseball Club logos emblazoned at the end of every row spoke of the past, yet there also were video scoreboards, luxury suites, clubhouses as posh as a country club's, and a state-of-the-art drainage system that kept the field immaculate. The park was truly a marriage of the old-fashioned and the newfangled—a marriage as successful as any in the history of sports architecture.

Camden Yards was an instant attraction, with the Orioles drawing 3.5 million fans in '92 and selling out a major league–record 65 straight games from May of '92 to April of '93. In their first eight years in the park, they drew an average of 44,865 fans per game and a total of 27.3 million—the same amount they drew in their first twenty-seven years in Memorial Stadium.

ROLAND HEMOND: "The club had such a rich history in Memorial Stadium that people would say, 'Oh, we love Memorial Stadium; we don't need a new park.' Then after Opening Day in '92 they said, 'Hey, Roland, forget it. This is beautiful.' I give a great deal of credit to Eli Jacobs and Larry Lucchino. Their approach was, 'Let's build a park with the modern amenities, but with the nostalgia from the past and memories of the old parks.' That hadn't been done, and it was rendered magnificently. [Orioles vice president of planning and development] Janet Marie Smith did a wonderful job with the project.

"The decision to restore the warehouse [instead of knocking it down] was a major positive decision. The warehouse gives so much character to the park. And there was a lot of input from the baseball people. Frank Robinson and Johnny Oates helped with the clubhouse, batting cages, and conditioning rooms. It's rare when you have a new park and you say immediately that it's one of the best of all time, but that was the case with Camden Yards."

BRADY ANDERSON: "I know there was a lot of sentiment with Memorial Stadium, but I felt the park was dark and hard to see, and I wasn't crazy about it. I like being in the city, I like ballparks in the city and the excitement and the atmosphere. Our park changed the way parks are made. It's become the prototype for what you want in a stadium, and people have just taken our model and tried to tweak it. It's about having a great view of the game and also modern technology and amenities. You can't beat it."

JOE HAMPER: "Larry Lucchino was responsible for the appearance of the stadium. A lot of people were in on it, but Larry is the one I certainly give the credit to."

LARRY LUCCHINO: "I was the one who first suggested a baseball-only park to Ed Williams. It was after the Colts left in '84 or '85. I took a simple rationale. Look at the game's most storied, stable franchises like the Dodgers, Red Sox, Cubs, and Yankees. What do they have? They play in baseball-only facilities. Ed said, 'You want to float that idea, go ahead. Keep my name out of it. I'd get crucified.' But we mentioned it, and the response was surprisingly good. The Colts were gone, and the attitude was, 'Let's take care of the team we've got.' Plus a multisport facility would have cost millions more.

"Ed and the governor [William Donald Schaefer] did the heavy lifting as far as the politics and financial packaging. The governor deserves an enormous amount of credit, as much of a curmudgeon as he was. He was fanatically committed to keeping the Orioles. Then they let me run with the design. It started as just a concept, and we ran into a little initial opposition from [baseball commissioner] Peter Ueberroth because he had a prototype of a generic park that could be done cheaply. He said, 'Just go do this.' We gave that out at a Maryland Stadium Authority meeting. Then at the next meeting I put a Yugo brochure at each place [around the table]. And I said, 'We don't drive [cheap] Yugos, and we don't plan 'em, either. Let's talk about a distinctly Baltimore facility that isn't vanilla.'

"As the principal tenant, we felt we had the right to design it, and we brought in HOK. They were working at the time on the new Comiskey Park [in Chicago], and they brought in a model that we actually tore up. We said, 'We don't want another carbon copy. We want something different. And it's got to be intimate and old-fashioned.' We knew we kind of liked the concept of a traditional, old-fashioned ballpark. We just didn't know the whole world would love it.

"In the end, Ed was less interested in the design and details than upholding his word [to build a new ballpark]. The simple truth is, the vision for an old-fashioned park was mine. Not all the ideas were mine, and a ton of people were involved along the way. And Janet Marie did a wonderful job of implementing it. But I am proud of the fact that I had one good idea sometime in my life, and that was probably it."

As splendid and successful as Camden Yards was, and as much as it represented great leaps of progress from Memorial Stadium, there were still a few drawbacks. The busy blend of music, mascots, scoreboards, and interesting food drew attention from the game, offending purists. Higher ticket prices kept some fans from the Memorial Stadium days from attending, frustrating them and ultimately turning some off. A wealthier, quieter crowd including more tourists and Washingtonians filled the park. And when the Yankees came to town, season-ticket holders sold enough high-priced seats to transform the place into Yankee Stadium South.

GREGG OLSON: "Once we moved, it just seemed like a different organization than the one at Memorial Stadium. How? I don't know. The fans were always out front by our gate at Memorial Stadium. Always the same people.

You waved at everybody, recognized all the faces. It just seemed like the organization changed, not so much the first year of the move, but after that. It was like a family at Memorial Stadium. Then it changed at Camden Yards—became more of a business. Maybe it was me. It was still fun, but there was a regular influx of free agents every year, and that changed the atmosphere. We weren't homegrown anymore."

Moving to Camden Yards changed the nature of the Orioles themselves, perhaps more than anyone envisioned. Since Paul Richards's days the club had relied primarily on pitching and defense, a sound blueprint for winning baseball and the basis for the 'Oriole Way' philosophy. But Camden Yards quickly proved to be a hitter's haven, making it harder to dominate with pitching and leading to speculation that the 'Oriole Way' could never rise again.

MIKE FLANAGAN: "I hate to think the Oriole Way only applied to Memorial Stadium, but in a certain way it may be true. The philosophy of pitching was always 'pitch to the large part of the ballpark, slant your defense that way.' I don't know if that would have worked in Camden Yards. [Back then] we had a team and a philosophy molded around that ballpark. And maybe that has yet to take place at Camden Yards."

GREGG OLSON: "I enjoyed pitching in Camden Yards. Only when I wound up leaving did I realize what a bad place it is to pitch. I couldn't figure out how some of these balls got out. I'd go, 'That was a pretty good pitch; I don't know how that got out.' Only when I left did I realize I was playing in the proverbial bandbox. And once the summer started heating up, the balls really flew. So you were in, I think, about the worst place to pitch in the big leagues.

"It's 350 in the power alleys, and the ball flies to left-center. I don't know why the ball didn't carry as well in Memorial Stadium, but Camden Yards isn't a big ballpark. You have to have pitchers like Mike Mussina and Scott Erickson who can keep the ball on the ground. I don't know if a power pitcher can survive there, because he's going to give up some fly balls, and fly balls go out there."

MIKE MUSSINA: "Pitching there is hard. It's not the same as Memorial Stadium—no question. But you still have to have pitching and defense to win. That's proven. Very, very rarely do you have a team that can just pound out enough runs to win consistently."

JIM PALMER: "I tend to look at it the other way: How many runs would those '69 to '71 teams have scored at Camden Yards? With the strike zone the way it is? And pitching the way it is? A lot of runs. Now, would our pitching be as good? No. But it would be relative to our hitting. Would I have a 2.86 lifetime ERA? Of course not. But I like to think I'd be able to figure it out and change my style and win. We had great teams and players then. That had something to do with it."

The Orioles opened Camden Yards in style in '92, with their first winning season since '89 and just their second in seven years. The club was close to front-running Toronto in the American League East all season and still within a half-game in early September before fading and finishing third with 89 wins. Toronto went on to win the World Series.

A new cast of players, some destined to become standard-bearing Orioles of the '90s, made their first major marks in '92. It was almost as if the franchise was trying to wipe out the memory of the dismal final years at Memorial Stadium with a new generation of players, and the change was clearly for the better.

Brady Anderson, a disappointment since being traded for Mike Boddicker in '88, suddenly blossomed as a leadoff hitter and outfielder, producing 21 homers, 53 steals, and 80 RBI and making the All-Star team. Also emerging was Mike Devereaux, who had 24 home runs and 107 RBI batting second and playing center field. Catcher Chris Hoiles hit 20 home runs, and third baseman Leo Gomez had 17 homers and 64 RBI.

BRADY ANDERSON: "I like to discount Memorial Stadium as part of my baseball life, because I struggled there, and then in '92, with the new park, I started playing every day. There was a transformation in my mind of what type of player I wanted to be or what type of life I wanted to have. I literally asked myself, would I rather be somebody who has a solid, nice, ten-year career, like Joe Orsulak, or struggle like I had for four years and then come out and do something maybe a little spectacular and have a few All-Star seasons.

"I really had this conversation in my mind. And if given that choice at that time, I would have taken the struggle with the chance to excel later. And that's what happened. Those struggles were actually the foundation for me as a ballplayer becoming even more determined, with the feeling that it's unacceptable to sit on the bench and watch other players play.

"I remember fielding baseballs in the outfield with my uncle in the off-season [after '91] when I came up with the theory that I'm not going to watch any more major league games from the bench. You know, 'I don't care what they do with me; I will be playing somewhere in '92.' And I was actually trying to get out of my contract with the Orioles to go play in Japan. I was close. Very close. I had a two-year deal with the Lotte Orions in Japan. They wanted me to play there.

"Roland had told my agent I was a sixth outfielder. Now, even in my first four years, I was a role player, but I was always at least a fifth outfielder and usually the fourth outfielder. I was insulted. I talked to Roland personally. I said, 'If you really view me as a sixth outfielder, I'm completely expendable. Get rid of me; I don't want to play here anymore. I hear Japan wants me.' The Orioles had initially asked for a six-hundred-thousand dollar or five-hundred-thousand dollar buyout, and Lotte agreed, and then the Orioles upped the ante to like nine hundred thousand dollars, I think.

"Then Johnny Oates said, 'No, I want to give him a shot as my leadoff hitter.' Because in September of '91 I'd played so well, hit almost .400 after coming back from the minors again. And that was another turning point, the '91 stint in Rochester when I got sent down. I went down there to try to improve and get back up. I told [manager Greg] Biagini, 'I just want one favor. I want to hit fourth. Because I'm sick of bunting; I'm sick of slapping the ball to the left. I'm going to stand up straight, swing the bat hard, and let the ball go where it goes. Nobody's going to tell me how to hit again.' I hit fourth for a few days. Roland saw that and switched me back to first, but I never changed my swing again, and I never went back to letting people alter my destiny as a player.

"They weren't trying to hinder me, and it wasn't intentional, but they just didn't see what I was. I didn't blame anybody. I blamed myself for not taking responsibility for my own career. And it's interesting being called 'uncoachable' when you're actually doing everything you can and that the coaches tell you. When I truly became 'uncoachable' is when I had my best years. And that's just about taking responsibility. When I go in the batter's box now, I marvel that nobody's going to help me and I don't want anybody to.

"In the spring of '92 Johnny Oates gave me the chance to win the job in spring training. There were three leadoff candidates that year: Luis Mercedes, who had won a couple of batting titles in the minors; a guy named Darrell Sherman, a little acrobat who played with the Padres; and me. Johnny came to me one day when we were playing the Twins, and I was already having a pretty good spring, and he said, 'How would you like to play left field and lead off every day?' I said, 'I'd love it. I'd love that challenge.' And he said, 'That's what I'm leaning toward doing. But would you do me a favor? I'm not going to ask you to bunt every time up or move the ball or advance the runners. I want you to play how you can play. Swing the bat how you want.'

"My first time up that day I popped up, and I go, 'Aw, shit,' but the wind took it, and it blew off the wall for a double. Little, tiny turning points in your life and your career like that make all the difference. And then I struggled to start the season, and people went, 'Johnny, how long are you going with Brady?' And he said, 'Don't judge him over two or three weeks; judge him over six months.' The whole season. And nobody had ever said that. That made me relax, and I had three hits the next day and just started hitting well. I wound up going to the All-Star Game and became the first player in history with 20 homers, 50 steals, and 75 RBI in a season. And I went from there."

JOHNNY OATES: "It was a no-brainer for me. In the spring of '92 we had a lot of guys we were looking at to hit leadoff, and I sat there for like two weeks, three weeks into the [spring] games, and finally I said, 'I've only got one choice.' He went oh for eight in the first two games and grounded out six times trying to pull the ball. I said, 'I don't want you looking over your shoulder, but you have to get a hit once in a while.' Then he took off, and he and Devereaux did just a super job for us batting one and two."

Rick Sutcliffe, a veteran pitcher signed as a free agent, threw a shutout in the first game at Camden Yards and went on to go 16–15. Perhaps most important, he helped take the pressure off Mike Mussina and Ben McDonald, the future of the rotation. McDonald went 13–13 and threw 227 innings, and Mussina, in his first full season in the majors, went 18–5 with a 2.54 ERA and made the All-Star team.

MIKE MUSSINA: "Sutcliffe took away most of the pressure that would have been put on me. I mean, I had a 2.87 ERA in '91, and he came in as the Opening Day starter. He took the pressure away from myself and Ben. I think I started the year as the fourth starter. And then I got to the All-Star Game, and the pressure could have been there if I was expected to be the 'next whoever.' And it just wasn't there. Sutcliffe had it. And that was in '92 and '93, too.

"I think I got lucky all the way through the early part of my career. After I signed I started [in '90] at Double A and then went to Triple A pretty fast. I was throwing well. But I also had to have the opportunity. The Orioles weren't having a good year, and guys were getting called up, so there was room at Triple A. I wound up pitching in the [Triple-A] Governor's Cup series in '90. I went from the College World Series to the Governor's Cup in three months.

"You need the opportunity, and you need the performance, and I had both going for me in '90, and that got me to the big-league [spring training] camp in '91. They kept me there longer than I expected. I didn't give up a hit in my first six or seven innings. I finally gave up a run, and they sent me to Triple A."

ELROD HENDRICKS: "Basically, we had to run Mussina out of spring training [in '91] because he was looking too good. He was ready. We had to send him out because he was embarrassing everybody else. We said, 'We'd better get this kid outta here quick.' All he needed was a little experience. He got it, came back, and started to dominate."

MIKE MUSSINA: "I thought I would get called up in September [of '91], but I went up on the last day of July. My first game, I lost 1–0 at Comiskey Park. Frank Thomas hit a solo home run off me. I was probably 30 starts removed from college. I certainly didn't sign thinking I needed 30 starts to be ready. I had no idea what to expect. I had no experience. I just started pitching, and I threw well."

JOHNNY OATES: "In our winter meetings our scouts were saying, 'Guys like this don't come along every day.' He was a good fielder, used all his pitches, threw 'em in the strike zone. There's always a learning curve, but Mike was always at the end of the learning curve. And I think it helped him that not too many people knew about him until he got to the major leagues. He wasn't like Ben [McDonald], where everyone knew him. Not everybody knew Mike. He just worked his way through the system and became a star."

43

Sold! (to the Lawyer from Baltimore)

It had to be the strangest day in the Orioles' long history: just weeks after hosting the All-Star Game at Camden Yards—a glittering baseball celebration—the club was put up for sale to the highest bidder at a bankruptcy hearing in New York City on August 2, 1993. How did such circumstances arise? They were the result of a sharp downturn in the finances of owner Eli Jacobs, who had bought the Orioles from Edward Bennett Williams's estate in 1988. When attempts to negotiate an out-of-court settlement with creditors failed, seven banks filed to have Jacobs placed in involuntary bankruptcy in New York, where he lived. As one of Jacobs's assets, the Orioles would be auctioned off in court as if they were an expensive piece of real estate or a fine dining room table.

Jacobs had conceded his financial problems in '92 and located a potential buyer for the club, a group led by Bill DeWitt Jr., a Cincinnati investment banker and minority owner of the Texas Rangers. DeWitt's father had owned the St. Louis Browns, and his group included other Ohio businessmen and Orioles president Larry Lucchino.

Peter Angelos, a Baltimore attorney who had become wealthy representing workers in lawsuits against corporations, had tried to intercede and negotiate with Jacobs, fearful that the Orioles would be sold again to out-of-state interests. Angelos put together a starry group of Baltimore-based investors including novelist Tom Clancy, tennis star Pam Shriver, movie director Barry Levinson, and sportscaster Jim McKay.

Jacobs refused to negotiate with Angelos and reached a tentative agreement with DeWitt on a $141 million deal, but when they were unable to close the deal before Jacobs was forced into bankruptcy, the club was thrown open for sale to anyone. Three potential buyers assembled in Judge Cornelius Blackshear's bankruptcy court on that hot August day. Jeffrey Loria was a New York art dealer who owned a minor league team in Oklahoma. Jean Fugett was a Baltimore native, former pro football player, and chairman of TLC Beatrice International Holdings, Inc., the world's largest black-owned business. The third suitor was an alliance of the Angelos and DeWitt groups, arranged hastily, just before the auction, with Angelos serving as the managing general partner.

The auction was a stunning drama that unfolded in a packed, stifling courtroom. Angelos and Loria quickly emerged as the only serious bidders. Every time Angelos made a bid, Loria topped it. The price went past one hundred fifty million, one hundred sixty million, and one hundred seventy million, more than twice the seventy million dollars Jacobs had paid just five years earlier. With the crowd gasping, the bidders sweating, and tension building, Loria finally capitulated in the sixteenth round of bidding, after Angelos offered one hundred seventy-three million dollars, easily the most ever paid for an American pro sports team, bettering the one hundred forty million paid for pro football's Dallas Cowboys four years earlier.

After fourteen tumultuous years of out-of-town ownership, the Orioles were coming home.

PETER ANGELOS: "DeWitt and I met that morning at his hotel, and I explained that I felt the team should be owned in the majority by local people, and I was prepared to bid whatever it took to accomplish that. I said to him without any bravado, just matter-of-factly, that I was going to make sure the majority ownership was in Baltimore. Then we sort of got together where he would get a percentage and our group would be in the majority, and when we revealed that to the judge before the hearing, Loria's lawyer got up and said, 'We don't care what they agreed to. We're going to buy this ball club.' When his lawyer got up and said that, he had no more chance of buying this team than he did of buying the planet Mars. That plays to my warped disposition of not letting someone tell me things like that. It was a challenge, a throw down. And he wasn't walking out of there as the owner of the team. We had figured one hundred sixty million was the number, and it went to one hundred seventy-three million as a consequence of that challenge. But we got it."

Who was this man who had bought the Orioles? Many baseball fans didn't know, even though Angelos, sixty-four, had lived and worked in Baltimore since his youth, run for mayor in the '60s, and become a towering homegrown success story as his law practice expanded. One of the country's most effective and successful lawyers, he was a brilliant orator and advocate—a feisty, dapper, and diminutive scion of Highlandtown, one of Baltimore's working-class neighborhoods.

His parents had emigrated from the Greek island of Karpathos and settled in western Pennsylvania before moving to Baltimore when Angelos's father, a one-time steelworker, impulsively bought a tavern. Angelos was eleven when he went to Baltimore. Growing up, he tended bar for his father, spoke Greek at home, attended Greek school, and belonged to the Greek Orthodox church.

Smart and ambitious, he turned to politics and won a seat on the Baltimore City Council at age twenty-nine, before he was finished at the Mount Vernon School of Law. But his lack of political connections and his confrontational nature undermined his career in public service. He ran for the council presidency in '63 and lost to Thomas D'Alesandro III, the son of Baltimore's legendary mayor. Then he lost again to D'Alesandro in the '67 mayoral election.

Turning his attention to his law practice, he soon earned a reputation as an advocate for union employees. He represented the United Steelworkers' locals and the Building Trades Council, and he also handled cases involving policemen charged with corruption and jockeys accused of fixing races at Pimlico Race Course. Business was good enough to enable him to buy a restaurant and some thoroughbreds, but his life changed forever when an asbestos-related disease was diagnosed in some workers at Bethlehem Steel. He went on to represent hundreds in a lengthy, complicated case with evidence going back decades, and when he won, his firm's fee was a reported three hundred million dollars. As the firm's sole partner, Angelos had made his fortune.

He was originally interested less in buying the Orioles than in bringing pro football back to Baltimore; when the city was vying for an NFL expansion franchise in the early '90s, Angelos considered joining a group Clancy was putting together. The two then decided to go after the Orioles after Jacobs put them up for sale in '92. When bankruptcy was forced on Jacobs and he lost control of the sale, Angelos saw the opening and attacked, just as he had attacked some of America's biggest corporations in courtrooms across the country. And just as he did in court, he didn't stop attacking until he'd won.

The baseball owners quickly approved the sale of the club to Angelos, who assumed control after the '93 World Series. The front office was shuffled at the top, with president Larry Lucchino resigning and former banker Joe Foss taking over the business side. On the baseball side, Roland Hemond remained the general manager (with a two-year contract extension), with Frank Robinson and Doug Melvin as his assistants.

LARRY LUCCHINO: "I left exactly three weeks after Peter bought the club. We went to lunches and dinners and talked about me coming on board with him. I kind of liked him. He has a charm about him. And we had the same [law] career and some common traits. But it was clear he did not need a copilot."

PETER ANGELOS: "I offered Larry the baseball side of the operation. I knew nothing about it. I said, 'Here, take it off my back.' He had learned a lot about baseball—a very bright guy and an excellent lawyer. I said Joe [Foss] will do business, and you will do baseball. He wouldn't accept that. He felt he'd been in charge of the entire operation [as president] and would be lessened in importance."

Although he originally said he planned to remain in the background and let his baseball operatives handle personnel decisions, Angelos jumped right in and orchestrated a high-profile free-agent signing. Balking at giving a large contract to injury-prone first baseman Will Clark, he signed Rafael Palmeiro, one of the game's top hitters, to a five-year, $30.5 million deal—a clear signal to the fans that the days of Jacobs pocketing the club's Camden Yards–generated profits were over.

Angelos said he would "do whatever it takes to field the winner this city deserves," and in the end, he authorized forty-three million dollars of free-agent expenditures before the first pitch of the '94 season, signing pitcher Sid Fernandez and third baseman Chris Sabo. Had he chosen to run for mayor then, instead of twenty-seven years earlier, the outcome might have been different.

But after the promise and euphoria of the early days of his ownership, a cloud of uneasiness moved in. Coming off a second straight third-place finish (with 85 wins) in '93, the Orioles struggled early in '94, spending the early season in second or third place. Angelos was displeased with Oates, whom he had signed to a two-year contract extension after the '93 season. Speculation mounted that Oates might get fired, especially after Angelos told a *Washington Post* reporter in June that Oates was "not a very good manager." Angelos sent an apology to Oates, but the manager was palpably tense for the rest of the season.

JOHNNY OATES: "There was a personality conflict between Peter and myself. Peter just didn't care for me. You can just tell with certain people. There's something where he just doesn't care for you. You're not his type person. And as that season unfolded I became very defensive and very withdrawn. I emotionally abandoned my family. I was dying inside. I was struggling desperately. I remember going back to my condo after a game, and my wife asked if I was coming to bed, and I said, 'Well, you go ahead.' I just wanted to sit there and feel sorry for myself.

"When the article came out with the quote [about being not a very good manager], I had gone home on Thursday for my son's high school graduation, and I came back, and everybody wanted to know what I thought. I hadn't even looked at the paper. And then there was an apologetic note on my desk from Peter's secretary that [the article] wasn't even supposed to be in print. I didn't mind that, but the problem was [Angelos] had misspelled my name on the envelope with the note in it. That hurt. Not only my last name, but my first name. On the envelope it said 'Johnnie Oats.' That probably hurt more than the [quote] in the paper, that they didn't care enough to know my name. Whether it was the secretary or Peter, I don't care. But that hurt worse. And to this day I still carry a copy of the letter. That's when I hit rock bottom."

PETER ANGELOS: "I said he wasn't a leader. I didn't expect the comment to be printed. I had spoken very offhandedly to the reporter. I didn't think it was going to be written. Pretty soon it was in the paper. What the hell was I going to do? I apologized publicly. And regarding the letter, I didn't type the letter. He can figure that out, can't he? I don't know how to type."

Later in the season, Angelos met with Oates to suggest that Leo Gomez, one of Angelos's favorites, play third base instead of Sabo, who had lost the job to Gomez after experiencing back trouble earlier in the season. Gomez was slumping, but Oates put him in the lineup and told reporters he agreed with

Angelos, even though the owner was telling him who to play, a no-no for any self-respecting manager.

PETER ANGELOS: "It was simple: I sent word to him to play Gomez. Sabo had a bad back. I got so mad one day, I said, 'If he puts Sabo out there again, there's going to be trouble.' And he played Gomez. But he had something very negative with regards to Gomez—didn't want to play him. I thought he was being ridiculous, because Sabo was hurt. I wasn't opposed to Sabo. I was the one who got him. I called Cal, and Cal said, 'Get him.' But he couldn't bend over."

With Palmeiro (.319, 23 homers), Cal Ripken (.315, 75 RBI), and catcher Chris Hoiles (19 homers, 53 RBI) carrying the offensive load, the Orioles heated up in July and pulled within a half-game of first place. But a slump ensued, and the club fell 10 games back as the deadline for a players' strike approached in August. The owners and players were at odds over how to handle the growing gap between the wealthier clubs and those with limited revenues, and when they couldn't agree on a labor contract, a work stoppage halted the season—for good, it turned out. The Orioles were in second place, seven games out, with a 63–49 record. Their .563 winning percentage was the best for any Orioles team since '83.

Before the last game of the season, a rainout on August 11 at Camden Yards, Oates met with Angelos and later told reporters he was confident he would return to manage in '95 if the strike ended the season. Angelos said, "[Oates] is still the manager, and there are no plans to make any changes." Six weeks later, Oates was fired.

JOHNNY OATES: "There were times Peter called and threatened to fire me and asked me to meet him at certain times, and he wasn't there, but some of his people were there. Then finally we met, the morning of August 11. I said, 'Peter, you've got to back me or fire me. I can't fight the press making headlines saying Oates will be fired, with a higher source saying it. You're the one guy that can stop 'em because I'm losing the team; I'm losing everything. And you're the one guy that can put an end to all this.' He said, 'I'm not going to fire you.' I said, 'Well, I'll continue to give you everything I've got, but I need backup.' I don't know how long we met, fifteen or twenty minutes. Then we went on strike the next day. I knew at the end of the year it was over. I didn't have to have him tell me that I was fired. Roland called and said, 'You're not going to be back.' And that was fine."

JOE FOSS: "The feeling was that Johnny wasn't evoking the confidence and respect that Peter wanted in his field manager. At least from our side, Johnny didn't exude that, either in terms of his own self-confidence or the confidence of the players. There was just a lack of confidence [in Oates] that quickly developed, and there was no relationship that ever really developed between Peter and Johnny to save the situation. So Johnny's contract wasn't renewed."

JOHNNY OATES: "I look back, and I think in every phase of my life the experience helped me. There's no doubt in my mind it was the best thing that ever happened to me. It helped me deal with the press but, more important, to see my family as how important they were and where the game of baseball fits in my life. I had become obsessed with being a big-league manager and doing well, pleasing people, to the point of losing my wife and children. And that's sad. And thankfully I've got them back, and I've got baseball, too, but baseball doesn't have a grip on me where it's life and death. And I thank Peter Angelos for that, because he taught me that it wasn't that important."

PETER ANGELOS: "He went on TV recently and said I told him he didn't know how to do his job. I never said that."

ROLAND HEMOND: "When the strike came about it looked like we were possibly on our way to a 90-win season. We'd just played a good series in New York, won two of three. I thought we had a chance to make a move. The [strike] was a real disappointment. The club seemed to be playing like the Orioles teams under Weaver—didn't start well but came on late in August and September. We seemed to be hitting our stride. But then the season ended so abruptly, and Johnny wasn't retained. I felt that if he wasn't getting the recognition he deserved, he was better off marching on elsewhere. You can help your manager only so much. There's no use seeing him being criticized and not appreciated for his contributions. So he moved on [to Texas], and his record [three division titles] speaks for itself."

With the players on strike and no World Series to slow the process, teams began making changes sooner than usual after the '94 season. The Orioles took an immediate hit when Doug Melvin, the heir apparent to Hemond, went to the Texas Rangers as their general manager (and immediately hired Oates). Melvin, a nine-year veteran of the Orioles' front office, was considered one of the industry's most promising young executives. The Orioles didn't replace him, leaving Hemond as the general manager and Robinson as Hemond's assistant.

Angelos appointed a four-man search committee to hire a new manager for the '95 season. The committee consisted of Foss; Russell Smouse, a senior attorney in Angelos's law firm; Hemond; and Robinson. Nine candidates were interviewed, including Davey Johnson, the former Orioles second baseman, who had won the '86 World Series and two division titles managing the Mets and had just led the Reds to a first-place finish in '94. The search committee picked a long shot—Phil Regan, the pitching coach of the Cleveland Indians.

Regan, fifty-seven, had pitched in the major leagues for thirteen years and coached in college for a decade before getting back into the pro game and rising through the ranks as a scout, minor league pitching instructor, winter-ball manager, and, finally, major league coach. Although he was a solid baseball man, he had never managed in the major or minor leagues, and picking him over Johnson was a gamble. Johnson, set to manage in Cincinnati for one more year before turning the job over to Ray Knight, said, "I heard they wanted an experienced manager and a proven winner; that's why I interviewed for the job. But I guess that's not what they wanted." The club also hired veteran executive Syd Thrift as director of player development, in charge of the minor league system.

When the labor dispute finally was settled in April of '95—after Angelos, the union lawyer, had refused to go along with the owners' threat to use replacement players—teams had three weeks to prepare for a belated Opening Day. The Orioles hurriedly signed three free-agent pitchers (starter Kevin Brown and relievers Doug Jones and Jesse Orosco), but with a new manager and a short spring, they started slowly and fell nine games out of first by June. With Palmeiro on his way to a 39-homer, 104-RBI season, and pitcher Mike Mussina on his way to 19 wins, the club rallied and pulled to within four and a half games shortly after the All-Star break. But then things really fell apart, and the club spent the last six weeks of the season at least 15 games out, finishing with a 71–73 record.

MIKE MUSSINA: "Changing Oates for Regan was the first serious change in personnel that I had to experience. That was a tough way [for Regan] to come in—to a situation where we had a lot of new personnel and my first experience in changing the manager. That was tough. We had a pretty decent club. Ben [McDonald] had won 14 games the year before. Kevin Brown. Myself. I remember the front of this Orioles magazine with the manager and the five of us, Sid [Fernandez], Arthur [Rhodes], Ben, Brownie, and me lined up, with the headline like 'Five Aces.' But a whole bunch of stuff just wasn't working for us that year."

RAFAEL PALMEIRO: "We should have been better. I thought we had a good team. It was a playoff team. But we just didn't play. Regan was put in a tough situation. He handled it all right. I know a lot of it gets put on the manager, but it comes down to the players, how we execute. And we just didn't play that year."

ROLAND HEMOND: "I never felt Phil stood a chance. It was an impossible situation for him. It's tough enough taking over a club. But we had a horrendous schedule because it looked like the league was upset with us [because of Angelos's stance during the lockout]. And spring training was awful. We'd play one day in Fort Myers, the next day in Orlando, the day after that in Clearwater. We had to train on one little field [in St. Petersburg] and hardly had any home games. We were a bus club. There was almost no chance of the club getting off to a good start. And the season just never got going."

PETER ANGELOS: "What happened with Regan, the poor guy had his authority literally taken away from him in spring training. He put in his systems and plays, and all of a sudden certain people in uniform overruled those systems, and the old systems were back. Regan was met with a very quiet but strong rebellion. I don't know why. Davey Johnson, who came later, didn't have it easy, either. But Davey is a different kind of guy. He's the kind of guy who'd say, 'Up yours,' and walk away. Regan was different and didn't have a track record, and he really was manhandled."

44

Chasing Gehrig

In their first forty years, the Orioles brought pennants, playoff games, World Series, Hall of Famers, and All-Star Games to Baltimore. The only element missing from their litany of touchstones was a single moment of history, a lasting accomplishment written in indelible ink, significant even within the chronicle of the game itself. That finally came at Camden Yards on September 6, 1995, when Cal Ripken Jr. played in his 2,131st straight game, breaking Yankee legend Lou Gehrig's seemingly invincible record for consecutive games played.

The moment was more than thirteen years in the making and realized with all the emotion and splendor of a coronation. The entire sports world stopped and saluted as a sellout crowd and a national cable television audience watched Ripken complete his dogged pursuit of a venerated record. Treasured locally as a native son's defining glory, the occasion also had more sweeping ramifications. Coming just eleven months after one of baseball's darkest passages— the cancellation of the '94 World Series due to a bitter labor dispute—it helped rekindle a nation's flickering faith in the game's ability to thrill.

Ripken had last missed a game on May 29, 1982, when Floyd Rayford played third base for the Orioles in the second game of a doubleheader at Memorial Stadium. Ripken started the next game and every other for a month at third, then moved to shortstop and settled in there as an everyday player. He didn't miss an inning for more than five years, until his father, then managing the Orioles, removed him late in a loss in Toronto in 1987, ending what historians believe is the longest consecutive-innings streak in major league history—8,243. The consecutive-games streak continued, and by the early '90s a countdown to Gehrig's record was underway.

It almost ended prematurely in '93, when Ripken twisted a knee during a brawl between the Orioles and Seattle at Camden Yards. He awoke the next morning with his knee so sore he feared he couldn't play. But when he went to the ballpark, received treatment from trainers, and limbered up, the pain subsided, and he played. The streak continued.

His pursuit was not always framed in a positive light. Ripken played on when he was slumping at the plate and dealing with various nagging injuries, leading some to accuse him of putting his interests ahead of the team's, a charge that galled and frustrated him. He also insisted the streak was never his primary motivation, a claim some found dubious as Ripken drew within sight of Gehrig.

But by '95, in the aftermath of the most devastating labor dispute in sports history, the negative connotations dissipated as Ripken neared the record. In an era when big money and guaranteed contracts motivated many players, the streak was considered one of baseball's few admirable elements, a feat fans could relate to, owed not to a particular skill or prowess, but to that simplest of habits: going to work every day. That and Gehrig's chilling legend helped expand the recognition of Ripken's accomplishment beyond the boundaries of the game itself.

With the Orioles under .500 for most of the '95 season and out of playoff contention by early August, Ripken's chase dominated the headlines and served as the season's focus. The Orioles placed giant banners featuring the streak number on the warehouse wall behind right field and, with inspirational music playing, dropped a new final digit each time a game became official. The streak reached 2,129 in a 5–3 loss to California on Labor Day at Camden Yards, the first of a three-game series that would make history. The next night, Ripken tied the record and hit a home run in an 8–0 win over the Angels.

Finally, the long-awaited moment was at hand. Camden Yards filled for the final game of the series on a clear, warm night, with an unmistakable charge of electricity in the air. Cheered at every turn, Ripken hit his second homer in two games in the bottom of the fourth, just as President Bill Clinton was voicing his admiration on WBAL radio. When the game became official after the last out of the top of the fifth, the banner on the warehouse dropped, and the celebration began.

Ripken, now baseball's all-time Iron Man, emerged from the dugout, waved to the cheering fans, shared hugs and kisses with his family, and pointed to his father, his mentor, who was watching in a luxury suite. His father, a hard man driven to tears, pointed back. Ripken finally returned to the dugout, but when the fans wouldn't stop cheering, he came back out, waved, and went back to the dugout again. With the cheering continuing, teammates Rafael Palmeiro and Bobby Bonilla finally pushed him back onto the field, and he took a "victory lap," a slow, jogging tour around Camden Yards during which he shook hands and exchanged high fives with fans.

The game finally resumed after a twenty-two-minute break, and the Orioles, with Mike Mussina pitching, went on to a 4–2 win that put a perfect final touch on the event. After the game, there were speeches and presentations from teammates and numerous local and national figures, including baseball legend Joe DiMaggio, who was there to honor Gehrig, a former teammate. Ripken finally spoke after midnight, giving special thanks to his father, who helped instill his sense of purpose and mental discipline, and to Eddie Murray, his mentor as a major leaguer. Thousands of fans stayed long after midnight, unwilling to put an end to the unforgettable night of history.

Ripken went on to play in every game for the rest of that season and two more after that as well, never missing a start despite moving back to his original position, third base, in '97. Finally, with speculation mounting that he was ready to draw the line, he sat out the Orioles' last home game in '98. Ryan Minor, a September call-up, replaced him at third on a Sunday night against the Yankees. The streak was over at 2,632 consecutive games, more than 500 beyond Gehrig's record.

Ripken would go on to achieve other significant milestones in the final years of his career, becoming just the seventh player in major league history to collect 3,000 hits and 400 home runs. He was a Hall of Fame player with or without the streak. But the streak was his triumph, an achievement certain to rank him among the most legendary players of any era.

CAL RIPKEN JR.: "I don't think most people understand. Well, maybe some do, but even people that are fairly close to me don't understand that the motivation was never the streak itself. Never, ever was the streak the thing. The motivation was to play. There's a need to play that you feel. When I was first drafted, the choice was between being a pitcher and a regular player, and I felt it down to my soul that I wanted to play every day. It just wasn't going to be enough for me to pitch once every five days. I want to play. And that [feeling] went on through my whole career.

"I don't think anyone really believes me. I didn't set out to play every inning for five years, or 2,600 games in a row. No one believes me. But I just kept doing what I always did. I honestly believe that when you're a pro baseball player, your job is to play. That's it. Then I just got lucky and stayed away from injuries. Any real injury could have ended it and almost did several times. But otherwise, you're expected to play. That's your goal as a player. And it's the manager's call in the end. Why did Earl play me every game? Why did Joe Altobelli play me every game? I don't know. Joe came to me after we won the Series in '83 and said, 'You had a great year, but I'm not doing that again—not playing you every day. I can't believe I did that.' But then he did. The purpose was to win."

BROOKS ROBINSON: "For a period of fifteen years [from 1960 to 1975] I played in just about every game. Like 97 percent. I didn't get hurt. Over in Washington one night they just said, 'We want you to take a night off.' I wasn't hitting. The old saying was, 'Sit out a game and watch.' But the fact is you came to the park, put on the uniform, took infield, and then you didn't play. Big deal. I mean, I sat out three or four games and came back, and I'd be just as horrible as I was before. Other times you'd sit out a game or two and come back totally refreshed. So I don't know if anyone has an answer for that.

"As Cal's streak unfolded, I thought it was unbelievable. I think he played a lot of times when he probably shouldn't have, and probably played a lot of times when it was detrimental to the club, but Cal's got that thing that clicks on and says, 'Hey, if there's a game, I have to be there.' I had it. In spring training my wife had a baby, my last son, in Miami Beach. We had a game the next day in Tampa, and I went, 'There's a game; I've gotta play.' That just shows you how stupid I was. I see guys now, their wife has a baby and they take off for a week. And mine was just a spring training game. But it was a game, and Brooks had to be there. That's the kind of mentality you've got to have. It comes from your love of the game, but it also came to Cal from his father, that mentality.

"When I started playing, the two records everyone looked at as unbreakable were Gehrig's and Ruth's. I would say, 'How are you going to hit more than 714 homers? And how are you going to play more games in a row than Gehrig?' That was just incredible. And Cal made it. It's just amazing that he played in that many games in a row. That's one record you'd have to say, 'Well, no one is going to break that.' I mean, no one's going to.

"There probably were times he should have sat out for a game or two. He went through some periods playing when he was really hurting. I think he probably shouldn't have played a few times when he was hurting, and that probably hurt the club some. But I understand the mentality. And it's a wonderful asset, a wonderful trait. It really is, because with all the money and the multiyear contracts today, I've seen so many guys just say, 'Well, I'm not feeling too good today; I won't play.' It happens all the time. But Cal still went out there.

"He didn't set out to do it. No question about that. It was just the way it happened. When you start getting close or see that you've got a chance, well, you play no matter how you're feeling. Maybe he should have taken a few days off in there when he was hurting, but you get that close to Lou Gehrig's record, you gotta go for it. You'd better. Because it's unbelievable, it really is."

CAL RIPKEN JR.: "The innings streak [from 1982 to 1987] wasn't really examined for several years. Then someone noticed that not only had I played in every game, but every inning, and it started to attract attention. It was a little bit of a [media] obligation. Nothing else to write about, I guess. My dad, from afar, saw that it was becoming a strain and I was struggling, and he took it into his own hands [to end it]. He was managing, but that was an occasion when he reacted like a father to relieve some of the pressure.

"An opportunity presented itself in a blowout. I think we lost 18–3 in Toronto. He called me over and said, 'What do you think about coming out?' I said, 'What do you think?' He said, 'I think it's a good idea.' I know if I'd said, 'I don't think it's a good idea,' I would have gone back out there. It was the top of the eighth. I batted and was on first when the inning ended. Billy [Ripken] brought my glove out. I was walking toward the dugout, and he gave me the glove, and I said, 'That's all right; I'm outta here.' There was a look of total disbelief on his face. Total shock. It was almost like time stopped. Very similar to what happened the night the [consecutive-games] streak stopped. That was also very surreal. Ryan Minor thought it was a practical joke right up to the end.

"When I came out in Toronto, I sat down on the bench, and Larry Sheets said, 'Come here; sit down; I can tell you about the bench.' It was the strangest feeling. I didn't feel bad so much as numb. I just sat there and didn't know what to do. I couldn't sleep that night, so I took out a legal pad and wrote down eleven pages. I'm not a diary guy, but at that moment I had some things to get out of my system. Was I happy or sad or angry? Did I give up on a certain principle or approach? Was it weakness? Strength? The right thing? The wrong thing? I wasn't angry or sad. But when you play every inning every day, you don't know any other feeling, so when you take a little of that away, there's a certain emptiness. I tried to figure it out. What your emotions were. I don't think I missed another [inning] for the rest of the year."

ROLAND HEMOND: "When I came aboard [in '88] it was admirable, what he had done, but to envision that he'd break the record, that was difficult to comprehend, that it was even humanly possible. I remember a game in '88 when Rick Schu was playing third base for us, and he and Cal were chasing a ball down the left-field line and had a pretty bad collision. They sprawled out. I said, 'Oh, my gosh. Both of them could be hurt.' Schu told me later that he didn't care if he was hurt; he just wanted to see Cal get up.

"Then we had that brawl with the Mariners [in '93], and Cal got tackled from behind. The next day [Johnny] Oates called my office from the clubhouse and said, 'Roland, Cal might not make it tonight. His knee is real stiff. He told [his wife] Kelly he doesn't think he can make it.' I felt so bad. Then I looked out of my office window and saw Cal walk out of the dugout and take some steps toward the right-field line and start jogging. Then I saw him taking ground balls in batting practice. And then he played. It just worked itself out.

"When I came aboard some people said we should move him to third. We tried it once in a morning exhibition game, no one around. But Weaver was right. He belonged at shortstop at that point in his career. He was so intuitive and played the hitters so well and still had good enough range and an accurate arm. There was that year he made only three errors in a season. It seems almost impossible, but he did it. He was the catalyst for the team most of the time I was there. We didn't get into the postseason, but he took us as far as we could go."

RAFAEL PALMEIRO: "He's the most professional player I've ever played with. He's very serious about his game. He knows how to prepare. Knows how to play. Gives himself up for the team. I know people try to find a lot of negatives, but there aren't any. The important thing is, he knows how to separate Cal Ripken the baseball player from Cal Ripken the person. When he comes through that [clubhouse] door, he leaves the other behind. He's got a lot to live up to, and he has. To come through as often as he has under the pressure and stress he has from trying to live up to who he is, it says a lot about his ability.

"When you play against him and don't know him that well, you have a lot of respect for him and look at him in a different way. It's almost like he's an untouchable. Then you come here, and he's so much a kid at heart. He's a prankster. Keeps guys loose. Makes you feel comfortable. That's the side not too many guys experience."

MIKE MUSSINA: "I never did really understand the criticism. People believe if you take a day off here or there it's going to make you that much better. I don't know. The mental rest is all you really need. You get enough days off during the season to give you enough physical rest. It's the mental aspect that's going to get you. And Junior is so tough mentally that he could handle it.

"He played sixteen straight years without a day off, and a regular person would probably take 10 games off a year. So let's say Junior had taken 10 games off a year for sixteen years. That's 160 games. That's a whole season. If he took off a whole season over sixteen years, he would not have 3,000 hits. He would not have 400 home runs. So the streak has done more than just stick him out there for that many consecutive games. I mean, 3,000 hits and 400 homers are pretty huge milestones. And the streak has actually allowed him to get them."

JOHNNY OATES: "We were on the field [in Texas] when he did it [on September 6], and they stopped the game and put it on this big screen for everyone to watch. I got very emotional because of what his family has meant to me, because I wouldn't be sitting here if it wasn't for his dad. There's no doubt in my mind. I probably wouldn't have made it to the big leagues as a player. I might have, but I doubt it. And I had played catch with Junior when he was six years old with a runny nose and his dad was my instructional-league manager. He'd be at the ballpark filthy dirty at nine o'clock in the morning, and Junior and I would play catch.

"When I was managing him [from 1991 to 1994], I made sure I didn't have anybody better at shortstop. I was going to make sure Cal played. And I don't think it ever hurt us a single time. When Cal was going good, everybody said, 'Yeah, yeah, yeah.' When he had a couple of bad ball games it was, 'He needs a rest.' A week later he was right back going great again, and those people who said he needed a rest never came back out. Cal, no doubt in my mind, was the toughest, strongest mental person that I've ever been associated with in the game. Nobody else is even close."

Roland Hemond: "The day before he tied the streak [Troy] Percival was pitching for California. I was sitting next to Frank Robinson, and I said, 'Wouldn't it be terrible if he got hit and couldn't play tomorrow?' The next pitch he got knocked in the dirt. It was his last at-bat in game [number] 2,129. He got right up and hit a screaming line drive. Showed his courage. He had a flair for the dramatic, which he showed with those home runs in [the next] two games. The day he was going to tie the streak, I kept calling the clubhouse and asking, 'Has Cal arrived?' I thought we should send a limo."

Bill Ripken: "There was so much electricity [on September 6] in the ballpark. You knew when you walked in that something special was happening. You just knew before the game had even started. It was so big that I think it hit Junior real hard, harder than he or anybody else probably thought. Because it was so cool. I had goose bumps for so long standing there, and then I just got tired of standing. I actually said, 'OK, enough Junior; go over into the dugout and do something because I'm starting to get a little tired.' I don't normally get goose bumps when it comes to things like that. That's how big that was."

Rafael Palmeiro: "Pushing Cal out [of the dugout on September 6] wasn't planned. We didn't talk about it. The fans were so incredibly into the situation. They just weren't stopping. It was a nonstop ovation. Cal wanted to get the game going again. It was fine for a few minutes, but his whole thing was, 'Let's get this over with and get the game back on.' And as long as he sat in that dugout, we might still be sitting there today. So we said, 'Go out there and do something, anything; just wave to them.' So he would, and that'd get them going even louder. Finally we said, 'Go run around the field or something and see if they stop.' He wouldn't do it, so we just pushed him out and got him going. And once he got going, he couldn't come back in the dugout. He had to do it. Now I think he's glad it happened that way. It was his way of saying thank you to the fans. What a way to do it, man. When people remember that night, they remember that victory lap."

Cal Ripken Jr.: "I'm probably the worst one to ask about the importance of the streak. Sometimes I couldn't believe the attention. When you're going through it, it doesn't seem so phenomenal. When people talk about it and say five years without missing an inning and sixteen years without missing a game, that sounds pretty remarkable. But you're just showing up and playing. Nine innings is nine innings. There's a certain grueling nature, but it's not like the ninth inning is the fourth quarter of a football game, where you say, 'I'm totally drained.' In that sense it never seemed that grueling. The most grueling part was the seven days a week.

"When I was twenty-one, I had great desire. Your life is your career. I lived, ate, and slept baseball. No kids, no family. Who wouldn't want to play every day? The streak was formed because the managers sat in the office and tried to figure how to win, and wrote my name in the lineup. All I brought to the table every single day was to say, 'I'm here, and I want to play, and if you want to put me in the lineup, you can.'

"But then time goes on, and the road gets rocky, and things happen, and fingers can get pointed, and suddenly you've got to defend your willingness to play. I've been with a million people that jake it, that don't want to play. Or have to be coaxed to play. Or you have to check with them to see if they're really OK for a day game after a night game. But I was the one getting that [criticism], which I couldn't comprehend. But I just said, 'OK, people are going to have their opinions; they're going to talk about this and that.' I mean I had to weather the storm when I had slow periods, which you know going in that you're going to have, but the streak complicated them, and the slow period was never just about itself, but about the streak.

"Then it all turned positive. People really got behind the number 2,000 and the possibility that something's going to happen. And that was a great celebration. I mean, that was a fun time. The best part about it was that the negative side wasn't examined all the time when you weren't doing things or the team wasn't doing good. All of a sudden, you got away from the negative and you accentuated the positive. It was a great celebration, a great period. There were a lot of great, special moments. It was just great all the way around.

"After that you keep playing, and a fog kind of sets in, and I kept thinking that too much focus was on [the streak]. I just remember thinking early in the ['98] season, I said, 'My job is to try to help us get in the playoffs, and we're going to make a run, and I'm going to continue to approach it the same way I always do. But if we fall out of it, then I'm going to put it to bed. Because it's starting to become draining in a way that I don't want to deal with it.' It was sad that it got to that point, but that's what I thought.

"Part of me said, 'You know what? I'll play 161 and take the last day of the season off. And the statement that'll make is that I could have played 162 if

I wanted to, but let's just put it all to rest, and now, when the manager sits in his office there won't be any streak-related issues. There won't be anything else. He'll have the freedom and the flexibility, which he always had anyway, to sit down and put out the lineup he wanted. That's what I did.

"I wound up doing it at home because we ended the season on the road and my wife said I should do it at home. She said, 'Everyone in Baltimore has followed you; do it in Baltimore.' Good advice. And it was a good moment. [Manager] Ray Miller thought it was a joke when I told him. He didn't believe it. There was a certain sadness, like you were compromising your principles. But then there was a great show of respect from [manager Joe] Torre and the Yankees, stepping up on the top of the dugout and applauding. That makes you believe that what you believe is right. But it was funny. People asked me later, 'Do you feel free now? Do you feel different?' And the answer was no. I felt the same. Whatever the circumstances were, I still wanted to come to the park and play."

45

Robbie, Raffy, and the Roller Coaster

Despite fielding a team that included Bobby Bonilla, Kevin Brown, Cal Ripken, Mike Mussina, Rafael Palmeiro, and Brady Anderson, the Orioles had finished below .500 in '95, failing to make the playoffs for the twelfth straight season. Shortly after the season, manager Phil Regan was fired and general manager Roland Hemond resigned under pressure, effectively leaving the club without a front office.

PETER ANGELOS: "I liked Roland a lot, but he was kind of paralyzed after the Glenn Davis trade didn't work out. I think he was kind of afraid to make the big deal after that. He was really intransigent for the two years I owned the club. As far as Regan, I brought him in, and I said, 'Look, you're going to get paid for your second [contract] year. Why don't you just go? The players really put you through the wringer.' He said, 'I really want to try again.' I said, 'No, why don't you just go home to Grand Rapids [Michigan]? You're going to be OK; you're a hell of a good guy; you don't have to put up with this.'"

ROLAND HEMOND: "I was OK with Peter. I admired the fact that he competed well and provided and wanted to win. I wish I could have had more direct contact with him. He was a very busy man. I had to go through other people sometimes to pass on my thoughts. That was my only difficulty. I respected the fact that he gave me the opportunity to remain after he bought the club and tried very hard to put a championship club on the field. I can't criticize that. I just wish we'd had more day-to-day contact."

Out of that disarray, the Orioles abruptly and improbably burst back into prominence, embarking on a dramatic, unpredictable, and exhilarating ride. The low ebb of '95 quickly rose to a high tide of passion and madness played out before sellout crowds at Camden Yards over the next two years.

It all started with a stunning stretch of additions and signings that started after the '95 World Series. Owner Peter Angelos ignored convention and hired a manager before a general manager, but his choice, Davey Johnson, was a popular selection tantamount to an admission that hiring Regan had been a mistake. Johnson, the former Orioles second baseman, now one of the game's top managers, had interviewed for the job a year earlier and lost out to Regan.

Hiring him was a coup, but Johnson then went to the general managers' meetings in November and pulled a bigger coup, luring Pat Gillick out of retirement to replace Hemond. A former Orioles minor leaguer, Gillick was one of the game's most esteemed architects and had retired after a long career in Toronto in which he built teams that won World Series in '92 and '93. Former Montreal GM Kevin Malone was named Gillick's assistant. Frank Robinson, the assistant GM under Hemond, was fired.

DAVEY JOHNSON: "The second time around I didn't know what to expect. But I met with Angelos, and I was hired. It was kind of a weird scenario. They hired me, but they were still looking for a GM even though they had Frank [Robinson] there [as assistant GM]. But then I went to the GM meetings and ran into Pat and started working on him. I felt he would be great. I'd known him for a long time, and I knew how good his skills were. I just felt it would be perfect for two Orioles to go back home. I mean, we were on the same team in Elmira in '63, with Weaver as the manager. Pat was a left-handed pitcher with a great curveball and a great pickoff move. And even then he was known for his photographic memory of *The Sporting News*."

PAT GILLICK: "I wouldn't have come if it wasn't for Davey. We'd played together and always kept a relationship. He was the reason I came, pure and simple. I was reluctant to come. I was consulting for the Blue Jays and very happy. But he just encouraged me. He very much wanted to come back. He grew up in the Orioles system, and he was excited about that. He convinced me."

FRANK ROBINSON: "As assistant GM I was out of the loop. I would go in the office and sit at my desk from eight-thirty to five. I sat, read, ate lunch, kind of educated myself on the rules and things. Not one call from another organization's person came across my desk. Not one decision-making call. Even when Roland was out of town, I didn't get calls. The setup supposedly was I had the National League and Roland had the American. But they never called me. I guess they called Roland. The only guy he let through to talk to me was [the Yankees'] Bob Watson. That was the only guy I would talk to.

"Finally they let me work on low-end contracts. But even then, when Larry [Lucchino] was there we had a scale to get them in between, and I had some room to move. When Angelos took over, there was no scale. It was just, 'There's the number; that's what we're giving.' I couldn't move one dollar without going back and asking. I told Roland, 'We're not negotiating; we're just messengers.' Do you know how ridiculous that is? You're talking to an agent, and he's within a thousand dollars of what you want, and you have to go back and ask?

"It wasn't my choice to go. When Roland left, I went to Peter and said, 'I'm capable of being the GM here. I'm healthy; I know the organization; I know the rules; I'm ready.' He said, 'How old are you?' He said, 'You're a little too old to be chasing agents and stuff. I have another job for you.' Some vice president of baseball job. I asked if that meant I was involved with the baseball people. No. Owner's side? No. 'What do I do?' I asked. He said, 'Sit in on meetings and report to me.' I said, 'That'll never work. I'm just in limbo.' He said, 'Well, that's the job. You're just too old for the other job.' A week later he hires Gillick, who is two years younger than me.

"When Gillick got hired, he poked his head in the door and said, 'I'm going away for the weekend, and I'll be back Monday for a meeting, and I want you in on it.' I thought, 'Great, I'm finally going to be involved.' We wound up having a conference call with a bunch of guys [in the organization] in a conference room. Pat was on the phone. He opened up saying, 'I want you to know I'm not a hatchet man. I'm not going to come in and take people's jobs. Your jobs are all safe for a year. At the end of the year we'll evaluate and make decisions.' We all kind of exhaled, you know, because we were in limbo. We went on to talk about some players and that was it.

"When Pat got in, Joe Foss stuck his head in the door and said, 'Pat and I would like to talk to you in my office.' I said OK. Now, I'm usually pretty sharp and can smell guys out, but I didn't think anything of this. I just thought they were going to talk to me about my role or something. But Pat says, 'Frank, when your contract is up at the end of the month, we're not going to renew you.' I said, 'Why? Peter said there was some kind of job.' And Joe Foss said, 'There is no job for you.'

"I went back to my office, and I sat down, and I got to thinking about that conference call about where they said we'd keep our jobs for a year. So I went back downstairs, and they were still in the office, and I sat down and said, 'Pat, I don't know you very well, but I've always heard good things about you. But you said our jobs were safe for a year and now this.' He said, 'That wasn't meant for you.' And that was it. I was gone. Never heard anything from Peter. I was at an owner's meeting in Chicago two years later, and I saw him, and he said, 'Hey, Frank, how you doing?' I started to say, 'How the hell you think I'm doing? I'm unemployed.' Nineteen years in the organization as a player, coach, manager, front-office guy, and I was pushed right out the door."

Joe Foss: "Frank's accomplishments as a player and manager go without saying. But Frank was not contributing much as a front-office individual. That predated our ownership and tied into the working relationship Frank had with his superiors on the baseball side. What Frank was asked to contribute alongside Roland and Doug Melvin, I can't speak to that. But Frank was focused exclusively on talent assessment at the major league level. Frank was not involved in contract negotiations. Frank was not involved in minor league assessments. To take on a bigger role as the GM, I don't think he had the breadth of experiences that would be necessary.

"When Gillick was hired, one of the requests Pat had, and it was a normal request, was to build his baseball staff with people he wanted. And he didn't see a role for Frank. Given the limited role Frank had been asked to play, Peter concurred that if Frank was not someone Pat wanted to use, it was OK to terminate him. I was at the meeting with Pat when Frank was told his services were no longer required. It was devastating for all three of us in the room. I had a great personal relationship with Frank, which I still have, and I didn't like being there, nor did Pat. But it had to be done."

Gillick embarked on a free-agent signing spree that instantly transformed the Orioles into a playoff contender. In a matter of weeks they signed second baseman Roberto Alomar, one of the game's most electric players, as well as outfielder B. J. Surhoff, closer Randy Myers, and reliever Roger McDowell—all veterans with track records—and obtained left-handed pitcher David Wells in a trade. Added to Palmeiro, Anderson, Ripken, Bonilla, and Mussina, the newcomers gave the Orioles as much talent as any American League club.

PAT GILLICK: "We got fortunate. Hit the right people at the right times. [Farm director] Syd Thrift had a relationship with Randy Myers through the Cubs. Syd was very instrumental in getting Randy. I had a relationship with Alomar from Toronto. I had a relationship with a player who was close to Surhoff and encouraged him to come. Davey had McDowell with the Mets. Then we made a deal with the Reds to get Wells. Everything just fell into place."

The early months of the '96 season were a disappointment, marked more by controversy than the expected success. Bonilla balked at serving as the designated hitter as opposed to playing right field, sparking a feud with Johnson. And Johnson, attempting to establish control of the team, pulled Ripken from a game for a pinch runner and made noise about moving him to third base—shocking developments coming just months after Ripken's 2,131 celebration.

The club spent most of the first half of the season in second place, close to the Yankees, but New York swept a four-game series at Camden Yards after the All-Star break, and the Orioles went into a dive. They didn't stop falling until they bottomed out at 12 games behind the Yankees and one game under .500 in late July. Trying to shake things up, Johnson experimented with putting Ripken at third and Manny Alexander at shortstop for a week, then he pulled the plug on the experiment when Alexander, terrified, didn't hit.

DAVEY JOHNSON: "You know how hard-headed Cal is. He didn't ever want to come out [of a game], and I did some things to take some of the burden off of him, moving him to third or pinch running or whatever. They were important things. He's the strongest human being in the world, but to have to bear a burden so big, that was tough. Plus, whenever there were any problems on the club, people ran to Cal. I mean, nobody's that strong. I think the one thing that came out of that summer, the things Cal and I went through, was his mind was freed up just to play baseball. I mean, Manny Alexander wasn't the answer. We all kind of knew that. And Cal knew that. But by him knowing the manager has to look at it differently, maybe you get better."

Pat Gillick: "The most difficult thing for someone who has been an icon is to accept anything less. We all thought we needed to bring some other people along, and that was the way to do it. We weren't going to cut Cal out of the picture entirely, but we needed to develop some other people. That went well, all things considered. Davey did a good job. Davey and Cal Sr. had a strong relationship, and that was instrumental in pulling that off."

Cal Ripken Jr.: "There was a lot of stuff that went on. Who knows why? A lot of controversial stuff that went on that, I thought, was pretty unnecessary. Not necessarily with me, just overall. The Bonilla situation. There just seemed to be a lot of little fires. Some people's theories are that [the front office] made the fires for motivational purposes, establishing control. Who knows? To me they just seemed to be counterproductive."

Disappointed in the season, Gillick was ready to make major changes by the end of July. He lined up a couple of trades, sending Bonilla to Cleveland and Wells to Seattle and receiving a handful of prospects in return. Among the prospects on the table at various times were pitcher Alan Embree; outfielder Jeromy Burnitz, a future All-Star; Chris Widger, a future starting catcher; and shortstop Desi Relaford. But Angelos stepped in and blocked the deals, saying he wasn't ready to break up a team with such promise.

Pat Gillick: "I liked the deals, really liked them. No one in the game is as patient anymore, but you still have to have somewhat of a program of integrating younger people to your team, because if you don't, everyone gets old and collapses at the same time. That's all we were trying to do, get the Orioles a mix of players in the system. Cleveland was looking for someone to play first because Eddie Murray had gotten hurt, and they were interested in Bonilla, so we were talking about Bonilla for Burnitz. We felt Burnitz was about ready to pop. We thought he'd hit 50 home runs in Camden Yards. Wells was going to Seattle. Widger was part of that deal, a catcher who was going to be here. We were going to get Widger, Relaford, and a third guy.

"I'd been [overruled] a couple of times in Toronto, but not very often, probably twice in twenty years—and never when I felt they were logical moves to make. I mean, Wells went on and did well, but to me he was a time bomb. To be frank with you, he's gone a lot longer than I thought he would. And regardless of what he did, I knew we weren't going to offer him a three-year contract after that season, and he would get that from someone, so he was gone. And rather than get nothing for him, we could get a catcher. You get pissed off [when you get overruled], but you find a way to work through it."

PETER ANGELOS: "After the fact, Pat now groups together all of the players who were mentioned at one time or another in the course of his efforts to trade Wells and Bonilla, as if he could have gotten the whole collection for those two. But that wasn't the case. Burnitz came into the picture all the way at the end when Cleveland really wanted Bonilla, and it was already in the papers that I wasn't going to let him do this.

"I said to Pat, 'You have to understand that this is not a baseball decision. I don't want you to be offended.' I used exactly that terminology. I said, 'I will not let you trade Bonilla and Wells when we're only five out in the wild-card race. I think we ought to continue because the team is still contending. What you're saying we could get in return is unimportant.' "

JOE FOSS: "I was in the meeting with Peter, myself, [team legal counsel] Russ Smouse, Pat, and Kevin [Malone]. As we approached the deadline, the team had been lackluster on the field, and Kevin and Pat made a very logical, detailed explanation as to why they wanted to break up the team, and the benefits of trading Wells and Bonilla and getting younger players back. Peter listened very carefully to these arguments, which were quite compelling, and Peter's conclusion was that he wasn't disagreeing with the baseball recommendations, but that there was a bigger issue, the support of the Orioles fans.

"You have to put it in context. The strike had affected part of the '94 and '95 seasons, and the Orioles were one of the few teams who in '96 had not lost much fan attendance. We were sitting in that July period of time with 3.4 or 3.5 million tickets sold for the season. And the team was four, five, six games out. And Peter said, 'I just can't send a message to the fans that we're going to quit on them. They invested in our team and bought the tickets believing we'd put the best possible team on the field, so I'm going to give the fans what they bought tickets for.'

"It was a defining moment for the Angelos ownership group. [When he blocked the trades] he made what turned out to be the right decision, but he wasn't making the decision focused on disagreeing with the baseball recommendation; it just happened that the players jelled, the team turned around, and we got into postseason play. The problem was our baseball front office went public that Peter had disagreed with their recommendation [to break up the team]. I personally was dumbfounded to read about that meeting the next day in the paper. I'd been in the business world for twenty-five years, and it's a normal occurrence to sit down in a conference room, shape a key decision, and then, once the boss makes the decision, you jump on it and make it work. But we read the next day about how Peter had overruled the baseball office, and I think they were somewhat embarrassed when the team turned around and won, not only in '96 but also in '97. I think the baseball people were embarrassed, and things were never quite the same."

After the deadline deals were blocked, the veteran club gathered itself and started to win, taking eight of ten games and then putting together two five-game winning streaks. Instead of breaking up the team, Gillick traded for veterans to bolster a run at the AL wild-card berth. Eddie Murray had returned from Cleveland as a DH almost eight years after his controversial departure. Then third baseman Todd Zeile came from Philadelphia, and reliever Terry Mathews also was added. The Yankees were too far ahead to catch, but with 37 wins in their last 59 games, the Orioles overtook Seattle and reached the playoffs for the first time in thirteen years, winning the wild-card race.

RAFAEL PALMEIRO: "The '96 club was the best team I'd ever played on up to that point. We had a lot of talent, and we were supposed to win. We didn't play very well in the first half, but we were a veteran team, so we didn't panic, and we were able to turn it around."

DAVEY JOHNSON: "We had a good club, but our right-handed side in the bullpen was really short. [Alan] Mills got hurt, and [Armando] Benitez got hurt. But we traded for [Terry] Mathews in August, and then Benitez got healthy, and Mills got healthy again to go with [Jesse] Orosco and Randy [Myers], and we were pretty good out there."

CAL RIPKEN JR.: "We really slugged our way into the playoffs. Hit just a million homers. But the only reason we were able to make a run was Davey went with a four-man rotation, and Wells and [Scott] Erickson and Mussina came through. Mussina isn't really suited to a four-man rotation, but he gave it all he had. We all had to give everything just to get in position to get to the playoffs.

"Davey certainly had influence from Earl in the way he managed. Who knows about all those little controversies, whether that was Davey's tricks or not? But Davey had a handle on a 162-game schedule. There were a lot of similarities between Earl and Davey in how he saw the long race. We got better as the season went on."

There was nothing subtle about the Orioles in '96. Unlike the glory-day Orioles, who won with pitching and defense, the '96 Orioles just clubbed their way to the playoffs—not that their pitching and defense were inadequate. Mussina won 19 games, Erickson won 13, and Myers saved 31. The defense committed only 99 errors, one of the league's lowest totals. But their bats carried them to the playoffs. They set a major league record by combining to hit 257 homers, 17 more than the '61 Yankees, one of baseball's legendary offensive teams. Seven players had at least 20 homers, and for the first time in franchise history, four had at least 100 RBI.

Among the many outstanding performances, two stood out. Palmeiro hit 39 homers and drove in 142 runs, breaking Jim Gentile's thirty-five-year-old club record for RBI in a season. (The old record was 141.) Even more remarkable, after having never hit more than 21 homers in a season, Brady Anderson put 50 over the fence to break Frank Robinson's thirty-year-old club record of 49. He set a major league record with 12 homers leading off games, set a club record with 92 extra-base hits, and tied a major league record with 11 homers in April. Needing one more for the club record, he hit number 50 leading off the last game of the season.

BRADY ANDERSON: "I hit seven home runs in spring training. And then I had a pretty bad quad strain and an appendicitis, and they wanted to operate, but I just plowed through everything and kept hitting homers. I had 30 at the All-Star break, and everybody was talking about 60. Even my mom said, 'Brady, are you going to hit 60?' I said, 'Come on, Mom, you too?' It's weird how people started projecting home runs like it was a sure thing.

"As it happened, I had 46 with five games to play. It didn't look like I was going to sniff 50. I mean, four home runs in six days. But then I got two in Boston, and I tied the club record on Friday night in [the season-ending series in] Toronto. I had to hit a home run off [Toronto pitcher] Pat Hentgen on the last day to hit 50. We had clinched the playoff spot the day before. All I told myself was, 'You're going to give yourself one shot to hit 50 and then go back to your thing.'

"Hentgen threw the first pitch of the game, a high fastball, and I took a great swing, hit a really high foul ball, and thought, 'All right, you gave yourself a chance, got a good pitch to hit, took a great swing; it just didn't work out.' Then he blew a fastball by me, and all of a sudden I'm oh and two. I thought, 'Forget the home run, go into survival mode.' Then I worked back to two and two and got another inside fastball and hit it. And it was so weird, kind of surreal, because the roof was open, and I thought the wind was going to push it foul, but it stayed perfectly straight and went in the upper deck.

"I couldn't get too excited because we had the playoffs coming up, and I'm not very demonstrative on the field, anyway. It was a very internal moment for me. Frank [Robinson] was happy for me. He really was. It was an accomplishment. McGwire and Sosa have distorted the perception. When I hit 50, only fourteen players in the history of the game had done it. Ted Williams didn't. Joe DiMaggio didn't. Hank Aaron never did. Eddie Murray never hit 40. When people ask why I never did it again, the question is why haven't any of those guys done it at all? It doesn't usually happen twice in a career. It just doesn't. It's too hard. And I did it."

Although the Orioles came away from Toronto with the one win they needed to lock up a trip to the playoffs, they also got caught in a controversy that almost overshadowed their long-awaited return to the postseason. In the first inning Friday night, Alomar was called out on strikes and started arguing with home-plate umpire John Hirschbeck. Emotions ran high, words were exchanged, and Alomar, normally cool, did the unthinkable: he spit in Hirschbeck's face; then he doubled his trouble later, telling reporters he felt Hirschbeck's work as an umpire had declined since the death of his son from a rare disease.

The next day, American League president Gene Budig suspended Alomar for the first five games of the '97 season—a light sentence for such a blatant act of disrespect, many observers thought. But Alomar paid for his mistake in other ways. Columnists and commentators across North America painted him as a poster child for a generation of wealthy, spoiled athletes and used his act as a symbol for the perceived loss of respect for authority in society. Fans across the country booed Alomar for the next two years. He was baseball's biggest villain.

Alomar performed brilliantly under the microscope in '96. The day after the incident, he hit a tenth-inning homer to give the Orioles a 3–2 win that clinched the wild-card berth in the next-to-last game of the season. He later had another key homer in the playoffs. He and Hirschbeck ultimately shook hands the next season, became friends, and tried to use their moment of infamy as a positive, raising money to fight the disease that cost Hirschbeck a child. But Alomar was booed for several more years and remained unpopular with many umpires.

MIKE MUSSINA: "He was going through some of the stuff John Rocker went through later. It was tough. Because I knew him and I'd played with him, I kind of assumed something went on at the plate that nobody else knew about. Either words were exchanged or something happened that nobody else knows about. I made that assumption because I never knew Robbie to be like that whatsoever. And that's just the way I looked at it. Something happened out there that we don't know about, and it'll probably never come out, but that's what I think. It was a bad thing, no question. A horrible thing. But that's the way I look at it."

RAFAEL PALMEIRO: "He wasn't that way at all. You talk about a class person, it's Roberto. What happened, in the heat of the moment, when you're in a fight like that, you might lose your mind for a second or two. You might do something you regret for the rest of your life. I know a few things were said, a few words were said, that Robbie might have misunderstood. He took them the wrong way, maybe. And he reacted like anyone would react to the heat of that moment. I'm not saying what he did was right. But it happened."

PETER ANGELOS: "I really didn't understand how [Alomar] could go off the deep end and do what he did. He was spoiled and a little bit narcissistic and self-indulgent, but that's part of youth and being part of who he is, but I was absolutely thunderstruck with what he did. I assumed, and I assumed correctly, that the curse word *MF* was used by the umpire. And it was used, along with some other words. I remember many years ago when I was a kid, if that word was used in East Baltimore in the manner the umpire used it, them was fighting words. Today, unfortunately, that word is used very frequently. It's just a profane word, not taken literally. But [Alomar] comes from a different culture. Those families in Puerto Rico are a little like the old-time families of fifty years ago. And he was very, very close with his mother. So that word *MF* precipitated the conduct.

"It got to the point where we went to Yankee Stadium and the whole park was calling him asshole and throwing batteries at him. I called Davey into the law office. He was present when the umpire used the language that precipitated an improper reaction from Robbie. That portion was publicized throughout the world, the player's inappropriate conduct. The umpire's inappropriate conduct was not publicized. I called Davey into the law office and said, 'You should tell the public that it was unfortunate that the umpire used such language that precipitated the improper reaction from the player.' I didn't want Davey to use the word, but I wanted him to bring it up to temper what was happening. And he refused to do it. He said the umpires would get on him. Well, so what? Truth is truth, and you got to stand up and be counted.

"I said to Davey, 'Come on, man, set the record straight. You're not going to condone what he did, but you can point out that some language was used that caused Robbie to go off the deep end.' Davey said, 'Not me; I'm not doing that.' I didn't like that. If I was the manager, I'd say it. I don't give a damn if the umpires were upset. That's just me. Maybe it's impolitic or unrealistic or call it what you like, but when the player is getting all of it, you do something."

RAFAEL PALMEIRO: "He went through a really tough time. I wouldn't want to be in that position. Everywhere we went the fans were on him so hard. It was so sad to see a player of that caliber going through something like that. Hirschbeck, who I also have a lot of respect for, didn't have to go through what Robbie went through. And both of them were at fault. But they both made it right and put it behind them."

PAT GILLICK: "I don't think Robbie ever got over it while he was in Baltimore. He got booed wherever he was. He is a very sensitive, emotional individual, and I don't think he ever got over it. I think it's behind him now."

As wild-card qualifiers, the Orioles faced a tough test in the first round of the playoffs—a best-of-five series with the Cleveland Indians, runaway winners of the American League Central. They were the defending AL champs and winners of 99 games, 11 more than the Orioles. Although the Orioles had played as well as any team down the stretch, the Indians were the class of the league.

What happened was as swift as it was shocking. Taking advantage of a format that gave the team with the poorer record the first two games at home, the Orioles battered Cleveland pitching and rolled to a pair of wins at Camden Yards, hitting six homers and scoring 17 runs. A grand slam by Bonilla broke open Game 1, and an eighth-inning rally in Game 2 left the Indians in trouble, needing to sweep three games at Jacobs Field to avoid elimination.

Cleveland's Albert Belle hit a seventh-inning grand slam to put away Game 3, but the Orioles won a wild, classic Game 4 to lock up the upset. The final game was one of the strangest in postseason history. Orioles batters struck out 23 times, setting a major league record for a postseason game. Booed throughout the game, Alomar responded with a home run to right-center in the 12th inning.

BRADY ANDERSON: "We line up for Game 1, and they introduce the Indians first, and then us. Brady Anderson batting first, 50 home runs. Robbie Alomar playing second. Rafael Palmeiro at first. Then Cal marches out there, and B.J. comes out, and then Eddie Murray hitting seventh, Todd Zeile hitting eighth, and Chris Hoiles ninth. And I'm looking at our lineup, and I looked over at their lineup, and I go, 'I don't know how in the world people think we're the underdogs.'

"I mean, their pitchers had to get through our lineup, and we had Mussina and some other pitchers. I remember feeling, not that we should be favored, but that there was no disparity in these two teams. They were both teams that just go out and mash. And offensively I thought we had the edge against them. Maybe because we had a little bit of struggle during the season, we weren't viewed as quite as good as they were. But we were great. And we played a great series."

MIKE MUSSINA: "They had really dominated us all year. We didn't win many games in their place that year, I don't think. Jacobs Field was new, and every time we went in, we just got whopped. And the aspect of the series that mattered was we had the first two games at home. So we came out and surprised them. They didn't play very well, and we won two at home. Put ourselves in a great position before their alleged home-field advantage kicked in.

And then Robbie won Game 4. He was getting booed constantly, and he drove in a run off Jose Mesa to tie the game and then hit the homer to win it—getting booed the whole way."

Returning to the AL Championship Series for the first time since '83, the Orioles faced the New York Yankees, the team they had chased all year in the AL East. The Yankees had beaten the Texas Rangers in their first-round play-off series and also were returning to the ALCS after a long absence, fifteen years in their case. The prospect of the two teams renewing their rivalry in the playoffs for the first time had fans in an uproar.

Not even the most implausible Hollywood screenplay could have matched what happened in the bottom of the eighth inning of Game 1 at Yankee Stadium. The Orioles were ahead 4–3, with Benitez in his second inning of relief. Leading off, the Yankees' Derek Jeter hit a high, deep fly to right. The Orioles' Tony Tarasco, a defensive replacement, retreated and settled under the ball with his back against the wall. But as the ball reached Tarasco, a twelve-year-old Yankees fan, Jeffrey Maier, reached out and tried to grab it as a souvenir. The ball bounced off Maier's glove and into the stands. Right-field umpire Richie Garcia signaled a home run, and Jeter quickly circled the bases. The Orioles argued bitterly that fan interference should be called, but the umpires were adamant. The Yankees went on to win on Bernie Williams's homer in the 11th.

Rafael Palmeiro: "I knew what had happened, but I didn't realize it was that bad until I saw a replay later. I think Tarasco would have caught the ball. He was a great defensive outfielder, and he was under it. That ball wasn't going to hit two feet above him on the wall. Even a bad major league outfielder wouldn't misjudge it by that much, and Tarasco was an excellent outfielder. It was going to go right into his glove. I don't know if we would have won the series, but things would have been a lot more interesting."

Pat Gillick: "The kid made a difference. We would have been in a hell of a lot better position. I've never quite understood officiating from the standpoint that if you know something isn't right, get it right. They should do what they could to get it right. I was sitting by third base, and I could tell the kid reached over [the fence and interfered] from where I was. It was hard to believe the umpires didn't see that."

The Orioles came back to win Game 2 the next day, with Palmeiro hitting a key homer, and they took a 2–1 lead into the bottom of the eighth of Game 3 with Mussina pitching at Camden Yards. But the Yankees turned the series their way with a two-out rally against Mussina, scoring four runs. They won that game and the next two at Camden Yards to close out the series. A season of many highs ended with a low for Orioles fans—the galling sight of the Yankees celebrating their first AL pennant in fifteen years on the field at Camden Yards.

RAFAEL PALMEIRO: "We weren't very far from winning it all. A couple of breaks and we could have been in the World Series. Things just didn't go our way. The thing with the kid, that made a difference. The momentum switched a bit. I mean, we were ahead. You never know what's going to happen, but that was Game 1, and we ended up winning Game 2, and we had Game 3 in hand at home going into the eighth. That's not much of a margin. A couple of breaks here and there, and we could be up 3–0. We were so close. But we didn't get the breaks, and it just slipped away."

Bonilla, Wells, and Zeile departed as free agents after the season, and Gillick signed a new batch of free agents as replacements. Bonilla, who went to Florida, was replaced by veteran outfielder Eric Davis. Wells signed with the Yankees, and, oddly, the Orioles signed the Yankees' Jimmy Key as a replacement. But the most newsworthy addition, by far, was Mike Bordick, who had started for Oakland at shortstop for the prior four years. His arrival ended Ripken's tenure as the Orioles' shortstop after fourteen and a half years. Ripken would move to third, the position at which he had broken in as an everyday player in '82.

JIM PALMER: "After Davey took the job, I walked into his office in Fort Lauderdale [in the spring of '96], and he said, 'How are we going to get Cal to sit down?' I said, 'Davey, you're making the money; that's your job.' He didn't sit him down, but he did move him over. You needed someone like Davey who was headstrong and not always rational in some of his thinking, but he understood what needed to be done. He had to make some real tough choices. He had to spar with an icon. But it was time for Cal to move from short to third, just like it was time for him to move from third to short in '82."

PAT GILLICK: "We had to get someone Cal respected. And Bordick is the same kind of guy as Cal, same makeup type, 'work hard, come to the park, Baseball Joe.' They're kind of two peas in a pod. Cal had a hell of a lot more ability when he was younger, but it's the same makeup. We did that by design. And Bordick came in and played great."

PETER ANGELOS: "Davey got me to take Cal to lunch one day in Little Italy. We talked three or four hours. Cal mentioned Bordick. He said he would step aside for someone like that. So they got on the phone and called Bordick. And Bordick got on the phone and called Cal. And Cal gave it his blessing. Bordick was a great addition, a great guy, and a great player. It was a ticklish situation, but it worked out."

There was also a key change in Johnson's coaching staff, orchestrated by Angelos. Pat Dobson, a 20-game winner for the Orioles in '71, had served as Johnson's pitching coach in '96, but he didn't win the confidence of many on the staff. Angelos stepped in and fired him, replacing him with Ray Miller, who had made a name as one of Earl Weaver's pitching coaches in the late '70s and early '80s, managed briefly in Minnesota, and more recently served as the pitching coach on division-winning teams in Pittsburgh.

PETER ANGELOS: "[Dobson] was having trouble with the pitchers. There was a bad exchange on the mound at Yankee Stadium with Mussina where they almost got into a scuffle. You can't have that, and I felt [Dobson] had to go. Davey didn't want Dobson to go, and I took the initiative and went out and got Miller. Davey said he was going to resign, told me that on the phone. He said, 'I want Dobson as the pitching coach.' I said, 'Dobson is finished. You had your turn; now it's my turn.' And that was the end of it. That didn't set well with Davey, as you might imagine."

From the first pitch of the '97 season, the reconfigured Orioles were even better than in '96. Two years of sharp free-agent signings had given them a powerful, high-priced nucleus and their best chance in years to get back to the World Series for the first time since '83.

They won on Opening Day at Camden Yards, reeled off three more wins, lost twice, then won five in a row. Eleven games into the season, they were in first place in the AL East with a three-game lead. They never looked back. A sweep of the Atlanta Braves in an interleague series in June pushed their record to 45–19 and their lead over the Yankees to nine games. The Yankees rallied, but in the end, the Orioles won 98 games, two more than the Yankees, and became only the third team in AL history to win a title going "wire-to-wire"—leading from the first day of the season to the last.

MIKE MUSSINA: "Davey was an even better manager the second year than he was the first. I think it took him a year to get used to the guys, and American League ball is a little different than National League ball. He just knew what was important, what was a big deal, and what wasn't such a big deal. He just sat down at the end of the dugout and made a decision here and there and let the guys go play. When you have a veteran club, that's a pretty good way of handling things. I think the players respected him. I think we knew we had a good club, a better club than '96. We thought we had a real good chance."

BRADY ANDERSON: "Davey was the perfect manager for those teams. In every way. I mean, he was a player who had had success with the Orioles. He had already had success as a manager and didn't feel the need to prove himself. He had a team that, basically, he could fill out a lineup and watch us play, make subtle moves when you needed to. And he could deal with all the garbage."

The difference between '96 and '97 was improved pitching. With Key, Mussina, and Erickson each winning at least 15 games, Benitez dominating as a setup man, and Myers experiencing a career year with 45 saves in 46 chances, the staff ERA dropped from 5.14 in '96 to 3.91 in '97. The bullpen led the majors in saves and fewest blown saves, and the overall staff allowed the fewest hits in the league. Ray Miller had made a difference.

The pitching was so strong that it didn't matter that the offense scored 137 fewer runs than the year before, the home-run total dropped from 257 to 196, and the .268 team batting average was just the ninth-best in the league. Palmeiro was still a solid run producer with 38 homers and 110 RBI, and although Anderson dropped to 18 homers, 32 fewer than in '96, he still had a strong season with 39 doubles and 97 runs scored. There was enough offense.

As upbeat as the season was, it wasn't without controversy. Alomar, again, was in the middle of it. Suffering from a sore shoulder that limited his ability to bat right-handed, he missed 60 games and seemed to stew in the clubhouse. When he missed an in-season exhibition without an excused absence and was fined ten thousand dollars, Johnson steered the fine amount to a charity for which Johnson's wife worked. The move would have enormous repercussions after the season.

A more emotional off-field saga involved Eric Davis, who left a game in Cleveland in May, suffering from severe stomach cramps, and later was diagnosed with colon cancer. Facing surgery and chemotherapy, Davis was thought to be through for the season. But he rejoined the team in July, worked himself back into playing shape while undergoing treatment, and was reactivated in September, in time for the playoffs. Although in just his first year with the club, Davis emerged as an inspiring figure and an emotional centerpiece.

In the first round of the playoffs, the Orioles found themselves on the other side of the dubious format from which they had benefited in '96. Even though they had the AL's best record, they were matched with the division winner with the second-best record, the Seattle Mariners. And not only did they have to play the first two games of the best-of-five series in Seattle, they also likely would have to face Seattle ace Randy Johnson twice—hardly a just reward for working all year to have the league's best record.

But unlike the Indians, who buckled in the same position in '96, the Orioles handled the adversity. Davey Johnson gambled in Game 1, pulling his left-handed bats from the lineup except for Anderson. The "B team"—reserves Jeff Reboulet, Jerome Walton, and others—came through, beating Randy Johnson 9–3 with Mussina getting the win. With another win by the same score in Game 2, the Orioles came home with a 2–0 lead and three chances to wrap up the series at Camden Yards. Seattle's Jeff Fassero beat them in Game 3, but Mussina, pitching brilliantly, beat Randy Johnson again in Game 4 to wrap up the series.

MIKE MUSSINA: "We had faced Randy [Johnson] twice that year and actually won both times, so before Game 1 [of the playoffs] I'm thinking, 'Well, why not? Nobody expects us to win this game. We're in their park with him pitching; we've already beaten him twice; who expects us to win? There's no way it can happen again, so let's just have some fun out there, enjoy the game, and maybe we'll get a couple of breaks.'

"I wasn't all fired up about it. I wasn't psyched up. I wasn't at all like that. It was just, 'Let's go play; let's see what happens.' And we sent our F Troop out there, Reboulet and Walton. We had a bench full of stars, Palmeiro and Baines and everyone. And what happened? Randy was wild, and we scored a lot of runs all over the place and won. I pitched pretty well.

"That was great, because it was the same situation Cleveland was in the year before, and they couldn't win one [game] in our park. After we won Game 1 [in Seattle], it was like, 'Can you believe this? We have a chance to win two here.' And we did. Then I'm thinking, 'We're going home, but we need to win Game 3, because we'll have to beat Randy again in Game 4, and then it's up for grabs in Game 5.' So it was like, 'We're going to blow it; we have to win Game 3.' But we don't. We lose. So I have to pitch against Randy again, this time on three days' rest, which I've never been a big fan of. I went out there thinking, 'Just keep us in the game, give us a chance, because Randy isn't feeling too good either, because he's also on three days.'

"Well, I'm throwing pretty good; he's throwing pretty good. We're going back and forth, and hardly anything is happening. Then Reboulet hits a home run. We get a 3–1 lead. I pitch seven innings and only gave up a hit or two, and then Benitez comes in, and Myers comes in after that and closes the door to top off his season, and we had beaten Randy Johnson four times in one season."

When the Indians upset the Yankees in the other first-round series, the Orioles were denied a chance at gaining revenge for their ALCS loss in '96. That was frustrating for the fans, but regardless, it still seemed the Orioles were headed back to the World Series at last. The Indians were more beatable than the Yankees on paper, with 86 wins during the season, 12 fewer than the Orioles.

For 16 innings, the best-of-seven ALCS unfolded exactly as the Orioles had planned. Erickson and Myers combined for a shutout in Game 1 at Camden Yards, and the Orioles took a 4–2 lead into the eighth inning of Game 2 with Benitez and Myers up and ready to nail down the win. But the Indians put two runners on against Benitez, and centerfielder Marquis Grissom hit a two-out homer to give the Indians a 5–4 lead, which held up for the win, evening the series.

The third game was bizarre. Mussina struck out 15, a League Championship Series record, but the Indians took a 1–0 lead into the top of the ninth. The Orioles tied it when Grissom lost track of a fly ball in center, allowing a run to score. But the Indians won in the bottom of the 12th when, of all things, shortstop Omar Vizquel missed a squeeze bunt attempt. Thinking the ball was fouled off, Orioles catcher Lenny Webster took his time retrieving it. But the umpire said the ball wasn't fouled off, and Grissom scored from third.

The Orioles had a 5–2 lead after three innings of Game 4, but they committed two errors and allowed two runners to score on a wild pitch as Webster scrambled for the ball and hit a runner with his throw to the plate. The Orioles fell behind 7–5 before rallying to tie in the top of the ninth for the second straight game, but the Indians' Sandy Alomar singled in the winning run off Benitez in the bottom of the ninth, and the Indians had an 8–7 win and a 3–1 series lead.

With no margin for error left, the Orioles won Game 5 with Scott Kamieniecki and Jimmy Key combining to throw eight shutout innings. They returned home needing to sweep two games, a possibility. Mussina was brilliant again in Game 6, retiring 20 of the first 21 batters he faced and striking out 10. But the Orioles stranded 14 runners and went hitless in 12 at-bats with runners in scoring position. With the game scoreless in the top of the 11th, Indians second baseman Tony Fernandez, a late replacement for ailing starter Bip Roberts, hit a two-and-oh pitch from Benitez over the fence for a homer—his first postseason homer in 133 at-bats. When the Orioles went down in the bottom of the 11th, the upset was complete. The Orioles were the first team in history to go wire-to-wire and not reach the World Series.

Cal Ripken: "That was a very intense series, a lot of close games. We very well could have been in the World Series that year. Honestly, I think we were better than the Indians. That was a year to make it to the World Series."

Brady Anderson: "I know how we lost. One home run. Grissom's [Game 2] home run. That game was in the bank and still would be in the bank to this day had Armando thrown a fastball instead of a slider [on a two-and-two count]. And Armando's great. I'm not faulting him at all. But there's a time for his slider. During the season, that's good, let 'em know that he has it. But at that point [in the playoffs], take the best shot [and throw a fastball]."

Mike Mussina: "I didn't know if I could pitch any better than the two Seattle games [14 innings, 16 strikeouts, 1.93 ERA]. But the two Cleveland games, quite possibly, were better. Quite probably were better. That was the best four games I've ever thrown, no question. It was the best four games I've ever thrown in a row professionally. I have no idea why. It just happened.

"We should have won that series. Offensively, we underachieved. I think we overachieved pitching-wise. We were as good as we'd been all year for the playoffs, for both series—for the four games against Seattle and the six against Cleveland. We threw ten of the best games we'd thrown over a consistent stretch, give or take a couple of innings. I thought we pitched more than well enough to win. We just didn't get a big hit when we needed it.

"You look back, the home run in Game 2, that hurt. That changed the whole aspect of the series. And the game I pitched in Cleveland, Game 3, when we just couldn't score and we should have been able to. But even when we got down 3–1 [in the series] Kamieniecki pitched great in Game 5, and Key was great in relief, and we came back thinking, 'OK, we have a chance at our place. We're within striking distance.' And we played great [in Game 6]. We had 10 hits and no runs. We had baserunners all over the place and couldn't get anybody in, and they had nothing going, and they get a solo homer in the 11th to win.

"That was our best chance to get to the World Series since I've been here, not that we didn't have some nice teams in other years. I thought we had a nice team in '92. I thought we had a good team in '94 and '95. But '97 was our best chance, and we played like it was our best chance. We played well the first two-thirds of the season. I think we won every close game. Randy saved everything. We had talent, and everybody stayed healthy for the most part. We pitched as well as anyone. We just didn't win."

DAVEY JOHNSON: "Yeah, that was the year to go to the Series. We had all the pieces. We beat Seattle, and I thought Cleveland should get clipped, too. And then [Benitez] hangs a slider [to Grissom]. But he was the guy that did it for me all year. I mean, I could have brought in Orosco in the eighth inning before I went to Myers. But Benitez was the guy that did the job for me all year, and he ends up just hanging a slider. And then later on [in Game 6] hanging a forkball to Fernandez [for the series-winning homer]. I mean, you look back, that's tough. We should have been there that year."

PAT GILLICK: "If we'd won the game where Grissom hit the home run, we would have gone to the World Series."

Within weeks of the loss to the Indians, there was a stunning turn of events: after back-to-back trips to the ALCS, Davey Johnson resigned with one year left on his contract. The announcement was made on the day he was named '97 AL Manager of the Year.

On the surface, it made no sense. Why would the Orioles tamper with a successful combination after struggling for so long to find one? With the '97 team coming back almost intact after winning 98 games and a division title, why not take another shot in '98?

But it wasn't that simple. Beneath the surface there was a problem—Johnson and Angelos didn't get along. Angelos was privately critical of the manager's work habits, and he was furious that Johnson had taken the money from Alomar's midseason fine and directed it to Johnson's wife's charity—a blatant conflict of interest, the owner felt. Johnson, for his part, felt keenly unappreciated.

Their conflict rose to the surface after the '97 season. Johnson asked for a contract extension. Angelos said no. Johnson finally resigned, faxing a signed letter to Angelos.

BRADY ANDERSON: "That was silly, what happened to Davey. That should have been avoided and rectified. You go to the ALCS two years in a row, you gotta come back. Absolutely. It's not a criticism of anybody, but when you have a unit that goes to the ALCS two years in a row, you let 'em continue their run. We deserved that. You go wire-to-wire in 1997 and lose it, you should come back again. I was disappointed.

"As it turned out, he wasn't fired. People can take their shots at Angelos for firing him, but in fact, [Angelos] didn't fire him. What [Angelos] did was not offer an extension, and Davey knew he could probably get a job elsewhere. Angelos told me, 'I wasn't going to fire him; I had no intention of firing him.' Maybe they had a contentious relationship, but he was going to manage at least in '98 if he wanted to, with or without Angelos's blessing. I was disappointed in him that he didn't come back. I thought he owed it to us to manage us one more year. He was under contract. And we'd rallied behind him on many occasions.

"If [Angelos and Johnson] didn't get along, that's the way it goes. They couldn't argue with the results. Davey had to appreciate that he played for a great owner who loves having a competitive team and was more than willing to put the players on the field that you needed. And whether Angelos agreed with Davey's decisions, you had to appreciate that we were in the ALCS two years in a row."

DAVEY JOHNSON: "I love the city, love everything about it. There were so many things that happened in the course of the two years that I don't want to go into and rehash. But suffice to say, even the first year, when it was the first time we'd been in the playoffs, there were some things that happened during the year that were uncomfortable. And at the end of the year I couldn't win Mr. Angelos's favor—in a lot of different ways. I couldn't make him happy. I failed in that regard and in hindsight probably needed to try to do more to please him. I thought maybe winning and getting the team back on solid footing was going to be enough, but I guess I came up short. I came up short both years.

"And that second year, with the fine, I mean, I was just in disfavor. It's that simple. And it was uncomfortable, so I talked with Pat [Gillick] about it. We'd come in this together. I just told Pat, 'I'm an obstacle. I don't think we can all be on the same page. I mean, for whatever reason, and it hurts me, but I think you're going to have a better chance without me.' I just said, 'I'm sorry; it pains me; I have a lot of love for the town and organization, and I don't want to be a problem.' I didn't have a choice. Well, it wasn't that I didn't have a choice. But things went wrong. It's too bad. We could have been good again in '98."

JIM PALMER: "Davey had to make a lot of tough decisions in his tenure, and you need to have an owner who understands that and trusts the guy. And Peter didn't trust him."

PAT GILLICK: "For me, the Alomar [fine] situation was the straw that broke the camel's back. The organization was looking for an excuse to get rid of Davey, and that excuse was used, and I thought it was absolutely ridiculous. I've been in baseball a long time, and managers tell players to write checks to charity. The only thing Davey did wrong was have [Alomar] write a check to his wife's charity. But it was still a charity. It wasn't like Alomar was giving ten thousand dollars to Davey's wife.

"I didn't like that they were using this excuse to make Davey look bad in public. I called the [owners'] player relations committee and said, 'What's an appropriate fine?' And they said a day's pay. Well, this wasn't even a day's pay. So we fined him ten thousand dollars, and then all hell broke loose.

"I was trying to get [Johnson] to stay, telling him, 'We had a great year and led wire-to-wire; let's keep it together.' I was trying to be like a Henry Kissinger and get the two back together. It didn't work. For me that was the straw that broke the camel's back. Davey recruited me to come over for three years. I said fine, and then two years into the deal, he's gone."

JOE FOSS: "During Davey's tenure, tensions developed on both sides. Peter and I took major exception to how Davey handled the Alomar incident, both in terms of the amount of the fine and having set it without review by higher executives. That was the tinder that fueled the fire. After the major controversy surrounding that had passed, I had a conversation with Peter, and he said he would bring Davey back for the third year of his contract. Notwithstanding the tensions that had developed or that he strongly disagreed with Davey's handling of the fine, he thought the best interests of the team would be served by bringing Davey back.

"Then the next day Peter gets a fax from Davey's agent demanding that they renegotiate and extend his contract. And that just was putting it over the top as far as Peter was concerned. He was willing to go the last year, but when the manager demanded that the contract be reopened, that was appalling to Peter. Peter responded that he would not extend the contract, and Davey resigned. Peter was intending to bring Davey back. But Davey had overplayed his cards. I don't know what was going on in Davey's mind, but I guess having his demand for an extension denied, to save face he resigned. Without question it was a setback for the club. He had the respect of the club, and he had an excellent record."

PETER ANGELOS: "Davey and I had had some differences over his handling of the Alomar [spitting] incident and the pitching coach change. And he also came to work every day at five o'clock. The game preliminaries were left to [coach] Andy Etchebarren and others. But other than that, we got along fine and were always cordial, and I thought he was very adept at handling a bullpen and running a game.

"But when you're going to impose a substantial sum as a fine, you need to consult with management. That wasn't done. And of course, no manager has a right to direct a fine anywhere. That's a front-office matter. Now, if Davey had suggested it, I would have said, 'Sounds OK; do it.' But it didn't play out that way. I thought it was grossly inappropriate that a fine be directed to a charity where the person assessing the fine had a relative.

"The other thing with Davey was, he began saying in July of that year that if he didn't go to the World Series, I was going to fire him. He kept saying it. I said to him, 'Why are you saying that?' He wouldn't answer me. I believe he thought it was a way to ensure he would get a renewal of his contract. All he had to do to ensure a renewal was ask for one. He was winning. I didn't have another candidate in mind. But then the press started coming to me and asking what I was going to do with Davey, and I was offended by that because I felt Davey was using a technique to put pressure on me and get me to give him an extension.

"Gillick had brokered a deal where Davey would issue an apology saying he would never handle a fine like that again and it was a mistake and all that, and he was going to come back. And in the middle of all that comes an ultimatum from his agent, which really scorched me. He sent me a fax saying he wanted a three-year extension and he wanted my answer by three o'clock or he would resign. Now, you don't do that with me. Maybe that's because I have the wrong disposition when you approach me that way. Generally I'm a cantankerous person. If I feel you're trying to bully me or pressure me, you're going to get the opposite. That's not a good trait, necessarily.

"He sent me the fax when he knew he was going to be named Manager of the Year, hoping I would concede to that. Well, I wasn't going to concede to that. That makes him the boss, not me. I'm not going to let someone who works for me be in charge of what I'm doing. I sent him a fax back saying he wasn't getting an extension; he had another year on his contract; if he wanted to resign, fine. And he did.

"I didn't take the ball club into consideration, and I understand probably more clearly now that that was a traumatic happening as far as the club was concerned. You look back and say, 'Well, maybe I should have. . . .' Baseball is different from business in general. But employees don't give public ultimatums to the people who are in charge, and that's exactly what he was doing, and he deserved to be terminated. Although he wasn't terminated; he terminated himself."

Angelos made Ray Miller the new manager and gave him a two-year contract, and Gillick, seeking to tweak a club that had won a division title in '97, signed four veteran free agents—starting pitcher Doug Drabek, outfielder Joe Carter, reliever Norm Charlton, and shortstop Ozzie Guillen. The Orioles were a consensus pick to return to the playoffs again in '98, but they fell hard from the highs of '96 and '97. The four free agents were busts, Miller struggled to maintain control of a brooding veteran club, and the Orioles sank all the way to fourth in the AL East.

After the season, Gillick, his contract expiring, opted to end his tenure as general manager. Rather than wait to see if he was promoted, assistant GM Kevin Malone, the heir apparent, went to the Los Angeles Dodgers as their general manager. Almost as quickly as the Johnson-Gillick era had begun in the fall of '95, it was over.

PETER ANGELOS: "I tell you what my assessment of Gillick's performance was. He wouldn't consider re-signing Jamie Moyer. He insisted on getting rid of David Wells. And he did not consider re-signing Kevin Brown. Those were three we don't need, he said. He got Drabek, Kent Mercker, Charlton, you want me to go on? What did he do for the three years he was here with an open checkbook? He didn't get Robbie Alomar. Robbie won't even talk to him. I got Robbie. I interviewed Robbie. I dealt with the agent. At Pat's request. And it wasn't me, either. It wasn't Pat. It was the Orioles' checkbook.

"Gillick is a great PR guy with the press. He instills confidence with the press. He's newsworthy. And he's a wonderful assessor of young talent. He's really, really good at that. But after he was gone I learned that we were not giving medical exams to prospective free agents when he was here. His statement to me was, 'If they tell me they're all right, they're all right.' Well, it's just a normal business practice to give such exams. The Yankees wouldn't sign Jimmy Key for more than one year, but Pat signed him for two years without an examination, and Jimmy pitched for six months, and he was done.

"After the [blocked trades] incident in '96, I don't think he really tried. The reasoning that was advanced for the refusal to permit the trades, he didn't accept. He was told it wasn't a baseball decision, it was a business decision. I think you would have seen a different Gillick if that incident hadn't arisen. He liked it here; his treatment was excellent; he had carte blanche. But after we missed the World Series by one pitch in '97, I told him 'Checkbook's open; who we gonna get?' He brought us Carter, Charlton, Guillen, Drabek. Now, you know that is not a Gillick effort, especially with an open checkbook. You draw your own conclusions. I've drawn mine."

PAT GILLICK: "After Davey left I had a year to go [on a contract], and I worked as hard as ever, but I knew I wasn't coming back."

DAVEY JOHNSON: "I think a bigger loss than me was Gillick. He put the farm system back together, he created harmony in the office, and he really was just a wonderful human being and executive. To me that is a tremendous loss. The bottom line is you knew what Pat was trying to do; he knew what we needed to do to be a really championship club, not just a good club. And Mr. Angelos didn't really use that knowledge, didn't let him be the architect he could be. There were several things that, if he'd been allowed to do them, would have the club in a stronger position now. But he was not allowed to do any of it."

46

The Drought

From the moment Jerry Hoffberger sold the Orioles to Edward Bennett Williams in 1979, the low-budget stability that had marked Hoffberger's ownership began to erode. Changes in the front office and on the field became more frequent in the '80s and early '90s, and that steady drip of change became a waterfall in the late '90s, as owner Peter Angelos orchestrated annual overhauls that left the organization struggling to maintain continuity, with predictably negative repercussions on the field.

The club was taken apart and put back together after the disappointment of '98, with a new general manager, Frank Wren, making the personnel calls and spending Angelos's money. Twelve Orioles were free agents after the '98 season, and many left. Rafael Palmeiro signed with Texas after negotiating with Angelos for months, knocking a huge hole in the heart of the batting order. Roberto Alomar left for Cleveland after brooding through '98, seemingly uninterested. Eric Davis, the inspirational cancer survivor, signed with St. Louis. Armando Benitez, whose stock had dropped after he precipitated a brawl with the Yankees with a dangerous beaning, was traded to the New York Mets in a three-way deal that brought Gold Glove catcher Charles Johnson to the Orioles.

RAFAEL PALMEIRO: "It was such a struggle for me. I had an agent who was helping me, but for some reason Peter wanted to talk to me, which was fine. I felt like we were close enough. But it was such a struggle to talk to him on the phone and get him up to where I wanted to be. He had offered fifty million dollars [over five years], but it was with twelve million dollars deferred, and I told Peter, 'There's no way I'm going to do that.' He gave me reasons, you know, that they were losing money. That's fine. But I said, 'I deferred eight million dollars in the first contract, and now you want me to defer twelve million dollars. I don't think that's fair. I'm not going to do that.'

"At no time did we have an agreement. It's been written about, that we had an agreement. I think Frank Wren said it. But I never spoke to Frank. I spoke to Peter, like three or four straight nights. One time I picked up the phone and called Peter and said, 'Come on; let's get this done. Let's stop playing games. You know I want to stay here. I'm not asking for Mo Vaughn money [eighty million dollars]. Let's get it done.' He said, 'Well, I can't do this tonight because I'm taking care of other business,' which I believe was the tobacco lawsuit. The very next night he called me back and told me he had gotten it done, and we started talking, and he brought up this deferred money thing.

"He said, 'Well, let's sleep on it and talk about it tomorrow.' And I said, 'Well, I'm meeting with the Rangers tomorrow.' And that was it. Once I sat down with Texas and gave them all the facts, things happened quickly. I said, 'Can you meet these numbers?' and they came back and said yes. I had said to Peter, 'If you want me to stay, don't give me the opportunity to go back home.' I'm not sure if I was the right player [for the Orioles]. I know they were looking at Mo Vaughn and [minor leaguer] Calvin Pickering. Our team was in turmoil, and they weren't sure which way they were going to go. We had nine months to lock it up, and it hadn't happened."

PETER ANGELOS: "There was a verbal agreement between Rafael and myself. We reached it at the Prime Rib [restaurant in Baltimore]. We shook hands and everything. [Jim] Bronner, his agent, was there. But he left and decided to go to Texas, and I think he did the right thing for a lot of reasons collateral to baseball. I think he decided he had to be with his family [which lived in Texas], and I think he made the right decision, and I would never say he betrayed us or anything like that. I think he did what he needed to do, and it was a wise decision, albeit we were sorry he left. But I have to confess, I had agreed to five years at ten million dollars a year, and I thought it was exorbitant because he was thirty-five years old. I thought three years was plenty. But I agreed to five primarily on the insistence of the fans. Then he went to Texas to be with his family, and it didn't matter."

The holes in the club were filled with veteran free agents signed to multiyear deals, including first baseman Will Clark (signed for two years), closer Mike Timlin (four years), second baseman Delino DeShields (three years), and controversial outfielder Albert Belle, one of the game's most productive power hitters and least popular players. Coming off a season in which he hit .328 with 49 homers and 152 RBI in Chicago, the uncommunicative slugger signed the largest contract in Orioles history, a five-year, sixty-five-million-dollar deal.

Rafael Palmeiro: "The whole time we were talking, Peter was saying, 'We're not going to pay anyone ten million dollars a year. We're just not going to do that. We're losing too much money.' I respected that. But then he turned around and gave Albert thirteen million dollars a year. I said, 'Peter, I thought your word was strong.' That bothered me. I don't know that he was being dishonest with me. Sometimes things happen in the free-agent market, and he had a chance to get a great player, and he had to pay. But he paid more than he said he would pay to keep me."

When right-handed reliever Alan Mills signed with the Dodgers, Wren attempted to replace him with Xavier Hernandez, a free agent from Houston. The Orioles announced the signing and then attempted to pull out of the deal when Hernandez failed a physical examination. It was too late to renege, however, and the Orioles ultimately had to pay Hernandez $1.75 million even though he never pitched for them.

The Hernandez fiasco was a portent of what was to come in '99. With Belle and the new players blending with veterans Cal Ripken, B. J. Surhoff, Brady Anderson, and Mike Mussina, the Orioles had one of the oldest, slowest clubs in the major leagues, and an unproven manager, Ray Miller. The result was a season even more disastrous than '98. The Orioles lost 17 of their first 23 games and never recovered, finishing fourth in the division with 78 wins.

Wren's free-agent signings struggled, to say the least. Timlin blew eight save chances before the All-Star break, while Benitez reemerged as a star closer for the Mets. Clark and DeShields battled injuries all season and produced below expectations. Belle became embroiled in several controversies, including one in which he almost came to blows with Miller in the dugout during a game. Belle finished the season hitting 31 points lower than in '98, with 12 fewer homers and 35 fewer RBI.

Peter Angelos: "Signing Timlin was a horrendous decision. When Frank told me he signed him for four years, I said, 'What? Four years?' That was a disaster for us. He's a nice young man, but he demoralized the club [with blown saves]. And Albert? Well, I had a lot to do with that. Wren said it was a no-brainer, and I was all for it. I'll take my full share of the blame and maybe more than I would assess to Frank. I don't know why he's not hitting as he did. Coming off the year he had [in '98], he should knock the fences down at Camden Yards.

"I regret signing [Belle] in the sense that I was the one saying you couldn't sign people for that kind of money, and then we signed him. If I had known that this would be the production level, I would have spoken in opposition. I thought he'd hit 45, 50 homers in this park. I thought he would do that, but he hasn't. As far as his conduct, it isn't perfect, and I don't like the idea that he won't talk to the press, but he doesn't bother anyone. He keeps to himself."

FRANK WREN: "Peter urged me to sign Timlin to a fourth year. I was leaving the general managers' meetings, literally leaving the parking lot of the hotel, when I got a call from Timlin's agent saying he was close to a deal with another club. I called Peter to give him the update and told him the agent had told us it was going to take four years to get him. He said, 'Let's just get it done. This will get us rolling.' That was his exact quote, 'This will get us rolling.'

"I thought we were getting a guy on the come. His stuff was still outstanding. And he was the best of what was on the market. Obviously, it's easy to sit back and say it hasn't worked out, but everyone in the organization told me that we couldn't go forward with Benitez because he was unreliable and going to break down any minute. Everyone told me that coming in, all the staffs, that we couldn't live with him.

"As far as Albert, I was in a meeting with my staff when Peter called about Albert. Called out of the blue. We hadn't even talked about Albert. He said, 'What do you think about Albert? The Yankees are about to get him.' When he says 'no-brainer,' I did use that statement. But only from an offensive standpoint. I also said we had to take into consideration other areas such as his defense and his conduct off the field. Peter said, 'Well, we can't let the Yankees get him. We have to get him.' That's the crux of it."

The most positive addition to the club in '99, arguably, was Wren, forty, a former assistant general manager with the Florida Marlins. Although his moves on the major league level failed for the most part, he was a strong believer in using the minor league system to develop major league talent—

an art the Orioles had mastered for years, then lost. Wren reorganized the front office, overhauled and modernized the scouting department, and enhanced the flow of communication throughout the organization with computers and E-mail. He also oversaw a landmark draft in June of '99, in which the club had seven of the first fifty overall picks and selected a new generation of young talent.

Many in the B&O warehouse building behind right field at Camden Yards—the site of the Orioles' front offices—felt Wren's youth, instincts, and priorities were a good fit for an organization that needed to get back to basics. Yet, after the losing season in '99, Angelos fired Wren, who had two years left on his contract. Angelos also didn't pick up Ray Miller's contract, forcing yet another managerial change. Wren was immediately hired by the Atlanta Braves, one of the game's top organizations, as the assistant GM and heir apparent to GM John Schuerholz.

PETER ANGELOS: "Do I really have to talk about Wren? You're not aware of his performance? Intellectually, he had a great knowledge of baseball. And yes, he spoke supportively of the minor league system, although that was nothing new. Gillick, had done that. But in practice, Wren simply didn't work out. Maybe it was because it was his first job [as a major league GM]. I think that was probably a major factor.

"He looked up to Gillick and talked to him repeatedly. And I'm sure it wasn't positive. I'm sure Gillick told Wren he'd better beware because he had had a 'meddling' owner. That was a problem. Wren was talking to Gillick, and it wasn't going to work. It was almost as if Wren was programmed to resist whatever was coming from the front office, for fear that if he collaborated or cooperated that he would be termed subordinate to the front office.

"After the experience with Gillick [not examining players before signing them] I said specifically, 'We sign no players until we examine them fully and get their medical records.' Wren certainly knew that going in. Then he signs seven players, none of them examined, one who couldn't pitch at all. Why that wasn't complied with, I don't know, because Wren is a very efficient, bright guy who, it seems, would follow company policy. But I think he was being talked to. I think he came to feel that if he followed our procedures he would somehow be less of a general manager. Wren has certain qualities that commend him, yet he made numerous bad moves. He should have been fired."

FRANK WREN: "I would say Peter is right that it can be difficult being a first-time GM in a market such as Baltimore. It wasn't a small-market club where you could get your feet wet in relative obscurity, without so much focus. That was not the case in Baltimore, and furthermore, the organization was in total disarray when I arrived. There was no assistant GM, no scouting director. A lot of pieces were missing. And there were ten or twelve free agents from the club on the market, none appearing ready to sign with us. It was a daunting task, to say the least. I inherited that.

"As far as me and Pat, I probably didn't have four conversations with him the whole time I was there. I know Peter feels otherwise, but it's just not true. Pat and I have never had much of a relationship, although I do respect him. But Peter felt all along that we were talking, for some reason. He didn't hide this from me. He repeatedly said to me in meetings, 'You must have got that from Gillick.' And that was just wrong, totally inaccurate. But the result of it all was I always felt I was fighting an uphill battle.

"As far as the players getting physicals, every club gets physicals for players, and every player we signed had a physical. It's a standard practice, regardless of what Peter says. He did say he wanted physicals, but we did it with everyone, Belle, Rich Amaral, everyone. We got caught in the Hernandez situation because we wanted to announce it, and he simply wasn't available at the time for a physical. The Anaheim Angels did the same thing with Mo Vaughn a week later—announced the contract terms before giving him a physical."

As the 2000 season opened, Angelos was on his fifth manager and fourth general manager since taking over in '93, giving the impression that he was ultimately unsatisfied with almost anyone who worked for him in baseball. The new manager was Mike Hargrove, fired in Cleveland after winning five straight division titles. The GM, with the new title of vice president of baseball operations, was Syd Thrift, who had run the minor league system under Gillick and Wren. Angelos's son John, a law school graduate, also joined the brain trust as an executive vice president, with increasing influence in many areas. Angelos's other son, Lou, also was sitting in on decisions.

The club struggled again in 2000, falling 10 games below .500 by the All-Star break in July, with the worst road record in the major leagues. With a third straight losing season looming, the club's decision-making apparatus under fire, Thrift on the hot seat, and former Orioles executives such as

Gillick, Wren, Larry Lucchino, and Doug Melvin having thrived elsewhere, it was hard not to conclude that Angelos, though clearly committed to winning and willing to spend whatever was necessary, was damaging the club's prospects with his involved, impatient management style.

With the Yankees in the midst of a dynasty that originated only when owner George Steinbrenner finally stepped back from his high-profile meddling with the day-to-day baseball operation, it was fair to wonder if the Orioles wouldn't be in better shape with a seasoned, successful baseball operative making the decisions—without significant input from the owner.

FRANK ROBINSON: "I remember [Angelos's] press conference when he took over. It was on the flag court [at Camden Yards], which was right under my [warehouse office] window. I had my window open, and I remember his words, 'I'm not going to make any changes. This has been a good organization for a lot of years, and I'd be stupid to come in and start making changes.' Those were his words. I sat up there and listened to him. And now it's getting worse. Four general managers?"

PETER ANGELOS: "There's no question that stability is desired. But stability is having a manager who is able to deal with the ball club as Hargrove is doing, as opposed to Miller, who is a good guy, but who was berating the players and making all sorts of statements. What do you do? Do you keep him on for stability? I have fired one general manager whom I hired, and that was Wren. Gillick left when his contract was up, and Thrift is still in office. That's one you can charge me with. Managers? I inherited Oates, so you can't charge me with [firing] him. Regan had to go, and Miller had to go. Davey resigned. Now we have Hargrove, and things are fine."

FRANK WREN: "Maybe he has only fired one GM, but he has made them all so miserable that they leave. That's his MO, to make you so miserable that you have to leave. I resigned two weeks after I took the job. I had seen more than enough. I couldn't deal with that level of involvement from Peter and his boys. You needed approval for things, and the approval process just dragged on forever, so long that you couldn't hardly get anything done. I had all these vacancies to fill when I took over, and I was having trouble even getting people in for interviews. And there were always these 'suggestions' being made. The level of involvement was very high. I walked in and quit after two weeks. He talked me out of it. Lasting eleven months was a chore."

Joe Foss: "Frankly, I don't think you have owners delegating or abdicating all responsibility anymore. I think that's a dated model. It's just different now than when Hoffberger was running the team. The financial stakes are much higher. And there isn't a company in America where the CEO isn't involved in twenty-five-million-dollar to fifty-million-dollar decisions, which is what's at stake today with contracts for superstars. The CEO has to be involved in those decisions.

"Baseball executives often don't have the background in business to understand the ramifications of a signing on cash flow and other financial areas. Not to say they aren't intelligent men, because they are. But they're only seeing one side of it. I talk to the presidents of the Indians and Dodgers and other large-market teams on a monthly basis, and I believe what the Orioles do under Peter's ownership is no different from what other large-market teams do with their CEOs on major contracts and decisions."

Peter Angelos: "Edward Bennett Williams was a super lawyer and a great intellect, and yet, when it came to baseball, he didn't perform at that level. I guess some people might say that while I'm not a super intellect or super lawyer, I should have performed better than I have as the head of this ball club. Maybe the game does it to us. We don't measure up to our usual performance. I think I've made mistakes. I probably should have forgotten about the ethical problems Davey Johnson presented with the Alomar fine. And I should have disregarded the fact that he wouldn't take up for his ballplayer, because that's the way it is in baseball. I should have gotten past that.

"But consider our record. We have been to the [League Championship Series] two times out of six years, which is a .333 average, which is better than any other team over that period other than the Yankees, Cleveland, and Atlanta. So out of 30 teams, we're number four. Am I satisfied? No. And from a standpoint of winning two out of six legal cases, I'd be pretty disappointed. But from a baseball standpoint, that's pretty good. [Six other teams have been to the playoffs three or more times in Angelos's six-year tenure. The Orioles have gone twice.]

"I think if I'm to be faulted, I have not been patient enough with the press. I have been too sensitive with criticisms that I feel are often inaccurate. But I'm not discouraged at all. I think the record is essentially good. I think we started with very little. I have spent a lot of money trying to give the city a winner. Our minor league system has improved considerably. It's not where it has to be yet, but I think we're on the way to getting where we want to go."

As the Orioles count down to their fiftieth anniversary in the major leagues in 2004, they and their sprawling constituency can look back on a history as rich as any franchise's in any sport. Along a continuum stretching from Paul Richards to Cal Ripken, from Brooks Robinson to Albert Belle, the Orioles have experienced the pinnacle of World Series triumphs, the nadir of 0–21, and every emotion in between. They have employed Hall of Famers and court jesters, cultivated fans as loyal as any in the game, and become a secular religion in Maryland and throughout the Mid-Atlantic region—a journey hard to imagine when Tommy D'Alesandro and Clarence Miles sealed the deal that brought the franchise to town in September of '53.

From '56 to '85 they had the best record in baseball with a .563 winning percentage. They also failed to attract a sizable following for much of that time, hastening Hoffberger's sale to Williams in '79. Two decades later, their attendance is as staggering as their revenues—they were number one in the American League in total attendance every year from '95 to '98 and number one in per-game attendance in '99—but they're still searching for the winning touch on the field. Through '99, seventeen other teams had gone to the World Series since the Orioles' last appearance in '83, and you could see the outline of a cruel joke: as much as Hoffberger's Orioles were winners on the field more than at the gate, Angelos's Orioles were now the exact opposite.

Quite clearly, the fall from the glory days was rooted in the collapse of the farm system, which finally ran dry after stocking the major league roster with talent for so many years. As of Opening Day 2000, the most recent everyday player the Orioles had drafted, signed, developed, and employed for long was, incredibly, Cal Ripken Jr., a member of the draft class of '78. In the ensuing two decades the club had promoted dozens of prospects who had either failed in the majors or failed to sustain long careers in Baltimore.

What happened to the farm system? There's no easy answer to that question. You can blame the scouts who obviously stopped selecting as many of the right players as they once had. You can blame the minor league system for failing to prepare enough players for the majors. You can blame the change in philosophy at the top of the organization, from a dependence on the minor league pipeline to a dependence on free agents, a shift that blunted the careers of numerous prospects.

True, free agency and skyrocketing salaries have changed the nature of the game, separating the major leagues into "haves" and "have nots" and lessening the importance of the minor league system. In that sense, the Orioles' slump is in some ways a by-product of the game's new economic realities, which have changed priorities and lowered the level of patience throughout the industry. But with other teams such as the Yankees, Expos, and Braves still excelling at player development, it's clear something has gone wrong in Baltimore.

JOE HAMPER: "Our success [in the '60s and '70s] was probably inevitable with the people we had working, the way they worked, and their dedication. We put it together from the standpoint of building a team and making a few dollars, and it was just a bunch of us working in the office. Nobody worried about who was what or who was going to get this or that, and we just did whatever we could to help each other. And you couldn't have had nicer people or a better situation. And ownership's emphasis was always on the team on the field. That was the case through [the] Hoffberger [years]. With ownerships after that, the emphasis has been on money."

JOE FOSS: "I think it's simplistic and a bit idealistic to think you can sustain dynasties. Look at the Green Bay Packers, the Montreal Canadiens, the Boston Celtics, the Dallas Cowboys, the Yankees. There are periods of history when you have a dominant team, and then you don't. The Orioles had that dominant period of time. And now we're trying to achieve that again. But it's hard to put the right combination together and keep it together."

CAL RIPKEN JR.: "I can't imagine any organization, past or present, that ran better in the period when my dad was in the minor league system. The Orioles and Dodgers were the models. I listened to Dad talk to farm directors, watched him fill out reports, listened to the philosophies about prospects and where they fit into the scheme of things. How they played 'em and how they helped 'em and how they protected 'em and how they grew 'em. All those things.

"For years it was good, professional people putting in their sweat and time and figuring out what worked and what didn't work. Kept the stuff that worked and threw out the stuff that didn't, and molded a pretty good plan. So through retirements, trades, and everything else at the major league level, they were over .500 for eighteen straight years because the talent kept flowing. The level was maintained. The Orioles made strong decisions and timely decisions. The goal was to develop players. If you made it through the Orioles' system, you were going to play in the major leagues somewhere.

"And then philosophically and developmentally and everything else, those principles eroded and changed. The talent pool started to dry up. Whether it was indicative of the minor league system, or a philosophical decision at the top, or just bad judgments at the top, I don't know. It could be a combination of the three. And when it actually occurred can be argued and debated, as can whether the people that were there should be held accountable or responsible. I don't know. But I do know there was a change—a change in everything. And once that started, it went all the way through. The front-office people, any of the old Orioles, were just slowly weeded out.

"Then once the talent at the big-league level started to go, there was no way to replace it. So now you're subject to the talent pool at the very top, like any other team. You're no longer pulling in from the minor leagues and giving yourself options. You just have to pay to get people in, like anyone else.

"When we signed those free agents in '85, that was an indication of a change. You know, 'We've got to go get talent from the outside as opposed to talent from the inside.' Then we had ownership changes, front-office changes, managerial changes, personnel changes, player changes. Just changes. And the team reflected that, because you no longer had the substance that you fell back on, the reason you had success for all those years. The talent just wasn't there anymore."

PAT GILLICK: "I wasn't here, but from '83 on there was like an expectation level, a mind-set, that you could duplicate '83. There was too much emphasis placed on the major league team and not enough on the minor league system. I think they thought they could plow little or no money into the minor league system and still get the results at the major league level. Unfortunately, Mr. Williams and Mr. Jacobs, I think, skinnied on the minor league system, and the proof is in the pudding. They haven't produced any players."

HANK PETERS: "I think there was a certain amount of deterioration over the years. The drafts weren't as good. We eventually gave up a lot of top draft choices because of signing free agents. We also had reached a point where we weren't really giving the young talent that we did feel had major league possibilities the opportunity to play, because of the philosophy that came down from ownership. Williams didn't believe that strongly, I don't think, in the farm system. He put financial restraints on us as far as what we could spend. I'm not being critical, because he had other [health] concerns, which were valid. But on the other hand, it certainly set this organization back a lot. But Williams died in '88, and if a mistake was made, there's been time to rectify it. That hasn't been done.

"But I think by and large there was a deterioration in the production out of the farm system. We lost some scouts, but we replaced them with others. As a matter of fact, some of these scouts are still with the Orioles, and they're good scouts, and some went with other clubs and did well. Sometimes there are many reasons why things happen and don't happen in the development of players. Part of the blame you have to put on my shoulders, but I've been gone now for twelve or thirteen years, and they're still struggling to really become productive. And they certainly now have the financial resources with Camden Yards."

EDDIE MURRAY: "The old way was over when Cal Ripken Sr. was promoted to the major leagues [in '76]. I don't think you'll ever see another person come down and do the things he did for us. People would laugh at him because they'd see him in a uniform at ten-thirty at night, but the man was just getting off the field so we could play on it the next day. That man was dedicated. He was the link. He was special."

PAT GILLICK: "The last couple of years have been better. They have had some good drafts. But there has to be continuity there, a continuing program of spending money on the minor leagues all the time. You can't spend ten million dollars this year and seven million dollars next year. You have to do it all the time. I don't think [Angelos] believes that. I don't think he does. He's seventy, and he has a large investment, and he wants it now."

JOE FOSS: "I disagree that we're not committed to the farm system. Every team wants to win now and wants to win in the future. If you have the resources to try to accomplish both, you try to do it. Because we have large revenues, we can dedicate a lot of dollars to free agents, but where I think Pat is mistaken, we've invested tens of millions of dollars in the farm system. We're investing four or five million a year just in signing bonuses and another eight to ten million a year in operating the farm system. How can you see that and say we're not interested in the farm system? Why would we just throw away twelve to fifteen million a year if we're not interested in doing it? Now, our success [at developing players] pales in comparison to, say, the Expos and Yankees over the last couple of years. But it's not that a team doesn't try. Sometimes you don't have good luck, and it just doesn't happen."

PETER ANGELOS: "I don't disagree that the fundamental change has to be with the minor league system, but I would say we have been doing that. We have always allocated the money to sign draft picks. We sign 'em all unless the kid goes to college. We have made the expenditures. It's just taken quite a while for the system to produce, but that's because the system was barren. There was nothing in it when we took over. And that's because our predecessors weren't really spending the money that had to be spent. In fairness to EBW, the team never drew at the 3.5 million attendance level when he owned the team, so he didn't have the revenues. And Eli only had the club for a few years, so you can't really fault him either. But in the interim, between Jerry Hoffberger and us, nothing was happening minor league–wise."

FRANK WREN: "In my case, he made a big commitment to signing those seven draft choices. He wanted 'em signed. I think this draft we had in '99 is the future of the club. There's a wave of good young players coming in two or three years. From that standpoint Peter did show a commitment. But as far as showing any interest in player development, he didn't. He didn't really care about it, didn't want to see it. I couldn't get him or the boys to go to a game twenty miles down the road [at Bowie]. I tried to get him to come see some good-looking kids. He said, 'Yeah, sounds good.' But he never went. Financially, no quibbles, he gave us what we needed. But he wasn't interested."

HANK PETERS: "After I left Baltimore I went to Cleveland [as general manager] in '89. When I got there it was a disaster. We had no big-league talent, nothing in the minor leagues, no scouts. When I took the job I told [owner] Dick Jacobs I would stay three or four years and that I didn't expect to win during this period, but I said, 'What I'll try to do is to lay the foundation so that you will someday become a winner.' So he gave me a free hand, and I mean a free hand. He provided the money. A very wealthy guy. And off we went.

"We started with rebuilding the organization and the scouting staff, and we changed the minor league personnel around. I had to get rid of people unfortunately, but those things happen. And we went into Latin America, and we did a lot of the things that hadn't been done. They didn't even have an instructional-league team. They had nothing. Well, it's worked there. It's worked great. Now the Indians have one of the best farm systems in all of baseball. I mean, the talent that has been produced is just phenomenal. Cleveland put the right front-office people in place and got Albert Belle, Manny Ramirez, Jim Thome, Brian Giles, Sean Casey. The list goes on and on. They all came out of Cleveland's farm system. Then you look at the Orioles and you say, 'OK, who?' "

Blaming the Orioles' shortcomings on Angelos has become popular, but with the club in a World Series drought dating to Ronald Reagan's first term in the White House, the blame obviously belongs on more than one pair of shoulders. At the same time, the job of getting the club back to the top does trace back to a single set of shoulders. It's up to Angelos now. It's his money to spend, his team to run, his front office to orchestrate, his mood to set. Can the Orioles really make it back to the top with a busy, practicing lawyer and his sons making major decisions? Against a backdrop of seemingly constant turmoil, what does the future hold for one of baseball's signature franchises?

HANK PETERS: "When you look at the Orioles, the farm system is where it's got to begin. I don't know enough about the organization to comment on it. It would be unfair for me to be critical of Angelos or anybody else, because I don't know what they're doing. I don't know what restraints, if any, they've placed on how they do things. I don't know what freedom they've given their baseball people to make decisions without being interfered with by his sons, himself, whatever. I don't know the extent of that. All I know is they might be able to speak the language of baseball, but they don't understand baseball. And until they are willing to commit to doing what Dick Jacobs was willing to do in Cleveland, just step aside, they're not going to be successful."

FRANK ROBINSON: "The only hope is something happens like what happened in San Francisco in the '80s. When [owner] Bob Lurie came in, he was real involved in the organization, and when [GM] Al Rosen and [manager] Roger Craig took over, Rosen said he'd come only if Lurie stepped aside and wasn't involved. That's the only way to turn the thing around in Baltimore. If someone comes in with that kind of agreement, that kind of say. And frankly, with [Angelos's] sons getting involved, I don't see it happening."

PETER ANGELOS: "Frank doesn't know what he's talking about. I am not involved. I practice law twelve hours a day. I make the fundamental decisions that every owner has to make. But I have an office there that I haven't visited for two years. If you ask the support staff over there how often I'm there or call, you will be surprised. If I run through that roster now and we look at those players, I'm not the person who signed any of them, good or bad. True, I signed Alomar, and I negotiated with David Cone when we didn't get him, because Gillick asked me. But all of the players we have are essentially the products of the various people who do that. All of the people in the minor leagues are the selection of the baseball professionals. There isn't one player on this ball club that I have instructed anyone to hire. So the impression being given to the public is false."

JOE FOSS: "I feel we're at the beginning of a transitional time for the Orioles—for probably the next five or six years. We have a number of kids in our [minor league] system that we think will be everyday players at the major league level. Unbiased assessments see our talent as the best we've had in years. I think we will see the transition away from an old, veteran team that was an assemblage of free agents to a team where you have a combination of free agents and our own draft choices. The transition is going to be painful and controversial, but it has to happen, and I believe it will.

"We're blessed in this community because we have the best ballpark in America, the support of the community, and ownership that considers ourselves caretakers of a community asset. That's not to say we don't make decisions that don't work out or aren't controversial, but the intention is always to win. This business, the Baltimore Orioles, isn't focused on how much money we make. This isn't a criticism of Eli Jacobs, but he ran the Orioles as a business generating millions of dollars in profit every year. The Angelos group has never set that as an objective. What Eli did was a normal business move, 'I'm going to spend less money than I take in.' He made millions of dollars. Our revenues are great, but we're not bottom-line driven. We're committed to trying to achieve one goal, and that's to win."

FRANK WREN: "I can't see it happening with Angelos owning the team. And it goes deeper than just him. It goes to all the people he listens to and is most comfortable listening to. His boys. Certain media people. There's no leadership in the [front-office] warehouse. None. The warehouse is completely void of leadership. Nobody can make a decision. Nobody can go forward with anything that's going to be productive without an OK from Peter, and he doesn't understand most of the issues. I just don't see how it can work.

"I think what happened when they had success in those early years and made the playoffs, he was just getting his feet wet. He knew what he didn't know then. He was more apt to listen to his baseball people. The longer he's in it, the less apt he is. His favorite phrase with me was 'the so-called baseball professionals.' He doesn't respect them, no matter who it is. He doesn't respect them at all."

KEN SINGLETON: "I see the Orioles turning more into something like the Red Sox, where they can't get over the top for whatever reason. The ballpark, in a way, works against them. It's too small. You're not going to win unless you pitch well, and it's hard to do that when a dinky fly ball is going to beat you. It's a beautiful park. The atmosphere is totally different from Memorial Stadium. More corporate. More about marketing. America is marketing and selling. That's what teams do. And the Orioles do it as well as anybody. People have disposable income, and the team is usually pretty good with a lot of veterans, so they're going to sell a lot of tickets. But on the field, I see them gravitating to be more like the Red Sox than the Orioles I remember."

JIM PALMER: "Earl didn't have a lot of rules. We didn't have guys worrying about being out there to stretch at the right time. You didn't have to have that. You had internal police. That's the way it should be. It's not about you. I was taught that early on. To make a good living and be able to support your family back then, you had to win. You really did. The World Series and playoff money was so significant. The economics of the game back then dictated that you play together, because that was the only way you'd make significantly more money. Now, the economics don't have anything to do with it. It's about pride. It's a different era. Different values. The money is a given. And the guys who understand the responsibility that goes with that, helping others and being for the them, those are the winners.

"When I was playing I saw Al Bumbry, who was not a very good outfielder, work every day. And then [in '95] I saw Curtis Goodwin come up [from Rochester] and watched Al [as a coach] try to hit balls to him and tell him about the angles at different parks, and Curtis didn't care. And Phil Regan put up with that. If I'm managing, I'd say, 'Either you do it or you go back to Rochester.' That stuff would never happen in our era because the players would never let it happen. The Orioles were able to understand that back then, as opposed to other teams that were playing for themselves.

"Mike Flanagan said it best. You can always tell the difference between a second-division player and a first-division player, because the second-division player plays for the name on the back of his uniform, and the first division player plays for the name on the front. And after Singleton, Bumbry, and I left in '84, the Orioles went out and got players who were more mercenary than substance. They tried to plug in the gaps. They didn't know anything about the character of the players coming in. You still had Eddie and Cal, but you lost the core players—the old, veteran guys who could carry on the tradition and the mentoring process. The replacements couldn't do that. And it all went away. For years the Orioles didn't have many phonies. But when you go into the free-agent market you don't know if you're getting the real deal or facsimiles. That's what happened to the Orioles. They started going for quick fixes, and there are no quick fixes in this game."

RAFAEL PALMEIRO: "Baltimore is the best town of all to play baseball in. The fans deserve a winner. They come out and support the team, win or lose. But change hurts. I think when you have a lot of change, that's tough. You need some stability. You have that when you have one general manager and one manager over a period of time. Here, they've had a lot of changes. Peter wants to win, I think, more than anyone. He wants the perfect guy. He means well. He wants to do it more than anything. But you have to have some stability."

INDEX